A HISTORY OF PREACHING

A HISTORY OF PREACHING
Volume III

From the Close of the Nineteenth Century
to the Middle of the Twentieth Century

(Continuing the work of the Volumes I and II
by Edwin C. Dargan)

and

American Preaching
(not covered by Dargan)
During the Seventeenth,
Eighteenth, and
Nineteenth Centuries

Ralph G. Turnbull

BAKER BOOK HOUSE
Grand Rapids, Michigan

DEDICATED

to

the unimportant and the unnamed
as well as the unpublicized
lay preachers and pastors of churches
whose faithful ministries
have sustained the preaching ideal
throughout our history

Preface

To link up with the preceding volumes written by Dargan is no simple task. Since his day the world has passed through times of change and revolution. Two world wars have disrupted the lives of millions of people. The pulpit in every land has been affected by the convulsions of world history.

Volume I—*From the Apostolic Fathers to the Great Reformers* (A.D. 70-1572)—has a discussion in its Introduction proposing the development of the following topics:

1. The Need of a History of Preaching
2. The Place of Preaching in History
3. The Historic Origins of Preaching
4. Outline of the History of Preaching

This set the standard in its field for comprehensiveness.

Volume II—*From the Close of the Reformation Period to the End of the Nineteenth Century* (1572-1900)—refers in its Introduction to the four periods of preaching into which, for convenience, it is divided. Two additional periods were deferred for later treatment: the *Dogmatic,* from the death of John Knox to the beginning of the Wesleyan Revival, about the middle of the eighteenth century; and the *Evangelistic,* or *Missionary* period, extending from the time of John Wesley to nearly the end of the nineteenth century.

Dargan did not continue the method of Volume I in Volume II but modified that plan because of the changing conditions and the diversity of preaching in several countries under review. Thus the content of Volume II is devoted to preaching in the seventeenth, eighteenth, and nineteenth centuries in various European countries.

Dargan, in a Preface to the second volume issued in 1911, wrote: "I still cherish the wish and purpose to write the third of the

5

proposed volumes—on Preaching in the United States—if life and opportunity be granted." Thus he hoped to complete his scheme by discussing a seventh period—beginning near the nineteenth century and including the age in which he lived—which might have been called the *Humanitarian,* or *Social* period; but he did not live to accomplish this.

Because American preaching was not included in the two volumes, this omission deserves special treatment in Volume III. The emphasis upon European preaching allied with British preaching found in the previous volumes was, however, inevitable because of the growth of the Christian church and its paramount influence in those areas at that time. Volume III, therefore, will maintain that emphasis and correct the previous omission by dealing with the following areas and periods of preaching:

1. American preaching during the seventeenth, eighteenth, nineteenth, and twentieth centuries;

2. European, Canadian, Oriental, and British preaching during the twentieth century.

The period 1900-1950 is used to conclude the survey and study.

In the Table of Contents in this new volume the schemata adopted by Dargan is continued. It seemed simplest and best to follow the divisions by centuries and to deal with each phase within that structure.

Edwin Charles Dargan (1852-1930), Professor of Homiletics in the Southern Baptist Theological Seminary, Louisville, Kentucky, gave us a monumental work of an encyclopaedic sweep. Since his day other volumes have been issued: *A History of Preaching in Britain and America,* 3 vols., by F. R. Webber (1952-1957); *The Christian Preacher,* by A. E. Garvie (1920); *Worship and Theology in England,* 5 vols., by H. Davies (1961-1974); *Varieties of English Preaching, 1900-1960,* by H. Davies (1963); and *A Brief History of Preaching,* by Y. Brilioth (1945). The strong biographical nature of these volumes provides an excellent approach to the subject and thus they supplement Dargan's work. Nevertheless, they have not been a continuation of his work as he outlined it. Our task in Volume III in following Dargan is to discuss preaching and the preacher in the historical setting.

The shaping of our age is seen in the many ways of life now current among us. Since the days of the Pilgrims and the Puritans, the American scene has changed dynamically. The jump from the seventeenth to the twentieth centuries takes us from the agricultural period of hamlets and small towns to the age of technology and space exploration. Each generation has its own emphasis, but the eternal gospel continues to be proclaimed in this most revolutionary period of history.

With Dargan's two earlier volumes in hand, we now proceed to enter that vast expanse of preaching whose development has reached its fullness in a time when many would denigrate it. It is my conviction that preaching has always been God's method of communication—above all other methods—and that the future is still bright for a revival of Biblical preaching in the apostolic and evangelical tradition. As we relate to our heritage of the past through these volumes, we will equip ourselves for the destiny of tomorrow.

Ralph G. Turnbull
Seattle, Washington
1973

Table of Contents

Introduction

Since Dargan issued his two volumes on the history of preaching, vast movements of the spirit of man have changed the outlook and habits of millions. Although a study of the history of preaching gains in historical perspective from our present vantage point, preaching itself can be evaluated only in the context of the culture of the first half of this century. Now, in the last half, we can trace the social, scientific, philosophical, and theological trends which have challenged traditional patterns of thought.

Social changes are seen in the redistribution of groups of people and the resulting polarization of former culture groups. People are linked together now by color, language, culture, or religious ideas. The United States of America has been reputed to be the melting-pot of the world. The various nations of Europe as well as other continents have sent their peoples to American shores to find a new life and opportunity for development. Within the nation itself redistribution is seen in the added factor of mobility. Because of economic unrest, and the search for employment and better living conditions, millions of our fellow Americans have moved from one place to another. In addition, the movement of population from the country to urban centers brings new perils to metropolitan areas with their already manifold problems of dense living.

Social change can be attributed also to the profound effects of the rise of permissive morality, the desire to be free to do what one wishes, and the hedonism which makes pleasure the thrust of all desire. Lawlessness and anarchy disrupt any sound basis for community and family life. Authority and justice are words no longer respected by many who seek license to live without discipline or restraint.

Contemporaneous with social change has come the advance of science. The word itself conjures up a large terrain with landmarks of grandeur. In contrast to the state of knowledge in earlier centuries, no educated man today could begin to master the principles now known to govern physics, chemistry, and biology. The mechanical world, the biological sciences, the theory of relativity, the quantum theory, the principle of complementarity, technological advances, and the Space Age—all these bring the student at school and man in his daily toil face-to-face with a world profoundly different from the relatively simple life of the past.

Preaching has to do with these scientific changes in that man lives his life in this context and not in the earlier environment once taken for granted. The ecology of our day with its threat of pollution, the population explosion, accelerated knowledge, scientific inventions for travel, communication, and one-world-now-realized—these factors face us as we bring the Christian message through preaching to all men. One of the most important facts of modern life is the fact of the world church—in that the Christian church is now, as never before in history, worldwide in its scope.

Philosophical change is another factor, as can be seen in the rise of Communism with its control of one-third of the world's population, and in the development of a material dialectic and a naturalistic philosophy. Add to these the sensate culture which sees man as dehumanized, two World Wars, and the spirit of revolt. How does the preacher communicate in this vortex of change and need?

Beyond these factors lies theological change which affects theological students and pastors and the church at large. No longer can we take for granted that those who graduate from theological seminary affirm the traditional and historic creeds or confessions of faith, or have even an avowed belief in the Bible as the supreme authority for the Christian. There have been many shifts in emphasis during the past sixty years.

From the atonement to incarnation, from the transcendence of God to immanence, from objectivity in theology to subjectivity in experience—so the pendulum has swung. Schools of thought were labelled; battle cries were loud and strident. Liberal theology was surrendering the idea of divine revelation for reason; philosophy of religion was taking the place of Christian and Biblical Theology. Albert Schweitzer trumpeted his views of eschatology as the key to New Testament scholarship; Karl Barth arose with a contrasting view of crisis and neo-orthodoxy: the Bible was now spoken of as a witness to the Word of God and any idea of propositional revelation was discarded. Existentialism in philosophy influenced theology; and Rudolf Bultmann taught that demythologizing was needed to articulate truth to this new age. Meanwhile, evangelical scholarship emphasized Biblical theology and the authority of the Bible as the Word of God. Without this, so it claimed, the truth of God and the eternal gospel would not penetrate the mind of man. One of the crucial conflicts of truth has been in this sphere. What is authority for the Christian and the preacher is basic for preaching.

Changes can also be noted in the new emphases in preaching, and in the modes of communication now available to the pulpiteer. Influenced by the ecumenical movement, churchmen have been conscious that while theological convictions play a vital role in what is preached, the one world and the one church ideas have likewise influenced the pulpit. Seminaries and colleges for the education of the preacher have broadened considerably in the books read and texts used. A wide theological spectrum has been discerned in broader areas offered for study.

The past half century has also seen a change in preaching styles. The use of the radio and television has tended to demand a shorter sermon and a more journalistic or staccato way of speech. Listeners were no longer a "captive audience"; the unseen people had to be attracted and held by the voice and manner of the preacher.

Life-situation preaching, the involvement of churches in social and political change, the challenge of a new generation which thought in terms of a new morality and a situation ethic have also affected preaching styles. The tragic view of life, a philosophy of nihilism, a generation without knowledge of the Bible and the Hebrew-Christian heritage have challenged the pulpit in new confrontation.

The ferment of the past sixty years cannot be treated lightly. Just as progress in science has come by new ventures and hypotheses, so in theology the church has been engaged in research and restatement of the truth. Reverent criticism, archaeological discovery, the Qumran "finds" of the Dead Sea Scrolls, fuller knowledge of the Bible text, and the resultant new translations and versions of the Bible have produced a renewed interest in Biblical truth. Religious publishing houses and booksellers have progressively improved in supplying the demand of the public for books to guide in Bible study and in the general search for religious knowledge of all kinds. The *kerygma* and the *didache* of the church's ministry and mission have been scrutinized critically.

In spite of the ferment and the new forms of ministry devised by the church, the heart of the ministry of the past half century was, as it ever has been, the proclamation of the good news, the gospel, and its claim upon the whole of life as taught by our Lord. While some voices demanded a moratorium on preaching because of its seeming impotency, the fact remains that this period was outstanding in preaching. With the ebb and flow of the tides of the Spirit, preaching remains as God's chosen way of confronting man with saving truth and a personal Savior, who is the Lord of all life.

PART ONE
The Seventeenth Century

Any estimate of this period must include an assessment of the Puritan heritage. Puritanism has always had its critics and many have tried to dismiss its influence on the history and life of these United States. The achievements of American life are sometimes ascribed to the secular spirit generated by the revolutionary doctrine of the rights of man and the age of reason. But we have learned that the foundation of our liberties is set in those religious ideals for which the Puritans lived and died.

Cotton Mather in his *Magnalia Christi Americana,* or *The Ecclesiastical History of New England* from its first planting in the year 1620, unto the year of our Lord, 1698 (First American Edition, 1820; first published in London, 1702), has testified: "One of the great and wonderful works of God in this age, that the Lord stirred up the spirits of so many thousands of his servants, to leave the pleasant land of England . . . to transport themselves . . . over the ocean sea, into a desert land in America, and this merely on the account of pure and undefiled religion. . . . And that the Lord was pleased to grant such a gracious presence of his with them, and such a blessing upon their undertakings, that within a few years a wilderness was subdued before them . . . " (p. 7).

Puritanism began with that concept of "pure and undefiled religion." It was this belief and conviction which spurred on the people to sacrifice their past possessions and homes to venture into the "wilderness." The "errand into the wilderness" was a phrase recurring again and again in the testimony of the Puritan. Never had a promised land looked more unpromising. Governor William Bradford, in his work *Of Plymouth Plantation,* 1650, wrote of that early history of the Puritan and Pilgrim settlement. The vision was that of an open door to a new life of incredible achievement, but the reality at the first was harsh and full of disappointment, though suffered with patience.

The Pilgrim Fathers brought with them the experience of struggle and strife on behalf of religion and freedom. The idea of Puritanism arose during the period of 1559-1567 when desperate men tried to purify the church of that day. The controversy which necessitated their separation from the church and the land of their birth had its grim and stern aspects. On the other hand, they also brought a new spirit and genius to the whole of life. The darker side of their uncompromising creed was balanced by their religious strength, their culture, and their contribution in founding a new world order. William Haller in *The Rise of Puritanism* (1938), documents the saga of this vision and reality in which men ventured by faith and courage to achieve a seemingly impossible task.

In the intellectual background of English Puritanism was the facility to discuss and debate crucial issues of life and destiny. The publication of their literature advanced their social and political ideals. Through the sermon as well as commentaries and tracts they influenced a generation learning to appreciate the benefits of the printing press. A free press was a product of this turbulent time— John Milton in his *Areopagitica* (1644) proclaimed the necessity of this dynamic concept for modern man. Out of this experience and background, the early settlers in New England brought an incredible optimism of faith in God and freedom for men. Thus old England contributed to the New England in a marked way. The Puritan was not a man of grim visage but a down-to-earth person with the usual strength and weakness of his time.

A reassessment of the Puritan tradition has now taken place and preaching can be set in a realistic historical context. Alan Simpson, Professor of History, University of Chicago, in his *Puritanism in Old and New England* (1961), testifies to the strenuous but sincere character of the Puritan whose faith in God and in freedom chartered a new way of life for us. Righteousness and moral character are firmly entrenched as the basis of this way of living. In *Literature and Theology in Colonial New England* (1949), Kenneth B. Murdock, Professor of English Literature, Harvard University, does not endorse the Puritan creed for his own life; nevertheless, as a man of letters he recognizes the wealth and grandeur of the Puritans' writings. Says Murdock: "Their religious system was the intellectual pattern of their universe; for the scholars among them every detail of it was fascinating; but the writings that impressed most readers, and probably seemed to their authors their most useful labors for God, treated not scholarly minutiae but a body of truth essential to every man who looked to God for life. The typical Puritan divine wrote more often for plain men than for pundits" (p. ix).

Samuel Eliot Morrison, Professor of History, Harvard University, has confirmed this point of view in *The Puritan Pronaos* (1935; now reissued as *The Intellectual Life of Colonial New England*, 1960), where he interprets the life of the mind in that day as "no glacial period." His conclusion is that "interest in literature and scholarship grew rather than diminished during the course of the seventeenth century; that the dominant Puritan clergy, far from being indifferent to culture and hostile to science, as the Adams' school briskly asserted, did everything possible under the circumstances in which they lived to stimulate, promote, and even produce intellectual activity. Moreover, it was largely the clergy who persuaded a poor and struggling people to set up schools and a college which continued to serve the community in later centuries" (cf. Preface).

Much of what is now accepted as distinctively American in thought, culture, and tradition is essentially the product of the founding fathers and their contribution as Pilgrims and Puritans. Any study of preaching must allow for that unusual investment of people from the old world to the new with the beginnings in New England. It is true that others came to these shores and made their contribution, including people of Jewish life and those of Romanist faith. Other labels are noted in followers of Luther and those with Episcopal tradition. But the predominant thrust was that of the Puritan.

The Protestant Reformation of 1516 rifted the old world, and out of this came many streams of theological and practical beliefs which cut enduring channels. Biblical Christianity gave moral and spiritual authority to multitudes who were newly-awakened to their standing before God as individuals based on the justification which is provided by the imputing of divine righteousness to the repentant. Even as the English-speaking people were later spoken of as "the people of the book," (i.e., the Bible; cf. John Richard Green, historian), so the people who came to America at the first followed in that tradition and practice. Here was the foundation for worship and preaching.

Among those who settled in America were the Episcopally-minded in Virginia, the Quakers in Pennsylvania, and the Presbyterian Scots in the Carolinas and other parts of the East. Each of these groups continued the special emphasis given by its leaders. George Fox, Robert Barclay, and William Penn were revered among Quakers; John Knox and John Calvin were certainly not forgotten by the Reformed groups and Presbyterians. Followers of Dutch and German as well as Scandinavian religious leaders settled at intervals in the new colonies and each brought a distinctive emphasis linked with Luther and the Reformation.

The Pilgrim was passionately devoted to the Bible as the one Book for study, guidance, and moral strength. In a new world of uncertainty, with frontiers whose horizons had not yet been explored, the Puritan sensed his "errand into the wilderness." In this he was not alone; the sovereign God was his guide and mentor. The Bible was basically his food and guide for spiritual understanding. Out of this background emerged the Puritan preacher with his power of appeal to the community. He was the parson, the chief and usually best educated person. He was therefore listened to with respect and usually obedience.

The Bible was the source of unchallenged authority in the New England of that period, and society was organized around the concept of "the chosen people." As Israel of the Old Testament was God's chosen people, so the Puritans sought to see life wholly within that same framework of divine election. Thus Church and State, law and justice, medicine and morals—all were within the matrix of this unique and powerful ethic. America's roots are here. Our understanding then of preaching must begin at this juncture. When, later, in 1776 this nation of the United States of America declared its independence from the old world, the people showed that they were the product of the Reformation and the Puritan revolution. The estimate that 95 percent of the population was Protestant may be high, but the influence of the founding beliefs was still potent. Changes would come quickly thereafter, but at that time the Reformed tradition through Puritanism was the hallmark of preaching.

Perry Miller, Professor of American Literature at Harvard University (1946-1963), has summed up this reassessment of the Puritan era in American life. To him more than any other we are indebted for historical research and reawakened interest in this period of history.

In him the downgrading and sneering attitude of others against the Puritanism of America has been arrested. He maintained in his books that the Puritans gave us the best foundation as a nation. He rejected the idea of "bluenosed hypocrites" and argued that the reconciliation of religious convictions with separation of Church and State became a model for the subsequent development in the United States of free education, religious tolerance, and economic liberalism.

In *The New England Mind: The Seventeenth Century, The New England Mind: From Colony to Province,* and *The Life of the Mind in America: From the Revolution to the Civil War,* Miller has documented and interpreted the sources for his thesis. The third volume was published incomplete since the author's death prohibited his writing the remaining six sections he had intended to add to the three in the volume. He had left, however, a schemata or working script, and in this he had altered nothing from his earlier exposition of his historical position concerning the foundations of America's life and spirit.

Here then is the setting that the seventeenth century gave to America's preaching—a background of belief in the Bible, strong doctrine, and the idea of a covenant people "under God." And, keeping in mind their concept of an "errand into the wilderness," a revised judgment of the early Puritans and Pilgrims can be made. We may proceed to a new evaluation of what this meant for preaching. We begin by distinguishing between those Puritans who came from England and the continent of Europe and those who were trained and nurtured in New England.

Chapter I

Preaching in the United States by Pilgrims and Puritans from Europe (1607-1650)

The preaching of this age was characterized by an intensity of spirit and a passion stimulated by strong doctrinal convictions. If heaven and hell were realities of destiny and states of eternal duration, then the preacher faced his people with beliefs which were incandescent. Dynamic, penetrating thoughts and words freighted with eternal consequences stabbed the hearer. The supernatural powers of the unseen held sway and nothing had yet intruded intellectually or socially to question this conception. The fiery tongue, the flaming speech, the burning heart—these are descriptions fittingly given to some of the Puritans. Certainly they claimed to be intoxicated with the love of God, but they also knew the dread fear of a fire within a fire by means of which souls were either purified or consumed.

The Idea of the Covenant

Only a few of the more notable preachers need to be mentioned to describe the preaching of this era. But we must not infer that Puritan preaching should be judged solely by the later men whose prominence and publicity prejudices many in their favor. According to Cotton Mather, the men who came from England at the first— before 1640—included "no fewer than seventy-seven ministers who had been preaching in England" (cf. *Magnalia Christi Americana* ... III, 2-3). In this he does not include some Baptists, Episcopalians, and Congregationalists who did not join with their brethren; the seventy-seven were settled pastors of the towns of Massachusetts and Connecticut.

Of the notable preachers we first note **John Cotton (1584-1652)**.

He came from Boston, Lincolnshire, England, where he had been pastor of a church. Most of his student days were spent at Trinity College, Cambridge; the rest at Emmanuel College, Cambridge. His Puritan convictions developed while at Cambridge, then the center of Puritanism. When he came to Boston, New England, he was called to be the pastor of the then First Church. But he was not only a preacher-pastor; he was also a teacher. According to B. M. Levy, *Preaching in the First Half Century of New England History* (1945), "At first each New England church had a pastor and a teacher. As John Cotton explained, 'the Office of a Pastor, is to attend by Exhortation, and therein to Dispense a word of Wisdom. The teacher is to attend unto Doctrine, and therein to attend to a word of knowledge. Eph. 4:11. Rom. 12:7, 8. Ez. 3:18, 19. Heb. 13:15.' The teacher usually preached one of the two Sunday sermons and sometimes alternated with the pastor in giving weekly lectures. The difference between pastor and teacher soon broke down, and the colonists discovered they could manage more economically with only one minister in each town" (p. 6).

Cotton's learning and preaching were allied in a strong and forceful style. He spoke with passion, his personality impressive in its sincerity. His preaching was also noted for incisive speech and clear exposition of doctrine. At the same time, his sermons followed the plain style of the Puritan. "Swelling words of humane wisdome," he said in 1642, "makes men's preaching seeme to Christ (as it were) a blubberlip Ministry." Christ, rather than giving men "a kind of intimation, afar off," had actually spoken "their own in English as we say. . . . He let fly poynt blanck." The Puritan minister should not quote in foreign languages: "So much Latine is so much flesh in a Sermon." In contrast to the classical style of preaching then current in England by such masters of prose as John Donne and Jeremy Taylor, Cotton and his associates cultivated the plain style. It was a style that Cotton had learned from the redoubtable William Perkins who taught men how to study and interpret the Bible and then preach from it (cf. *The Art of Prophesying,* 1592). According to Perkins, sermons were to be couched "in simplicity, which meant plainly and clearly, so that the simplest man may understand what is taught, as if he did hear his name." John Brown, *Puritan Preaching in England* (1900), has traced this Puritan standard of preaching. Plainness and persuasion with practical application, then, characterized this type of sermon.

John Cotton, however, moved away from earlier Reformed emphases. Luther and Calvin might stress the justifying grace of God on behalf of the sinner, but Cotton was concerned to direct the new Christian into a life of growth and development. Thus sanctification or holiness became his theme in preaching. In the context of that day the Puritan preachers generally legalistically followed a well-defined outline of sermon preparation as befitted their heirship to the Reformation. Their messages set forth the way of salvation, the steps to be followed, and the order of procedure that led to faith, and later to the duties and obligations of the Christian life. This last phase interested Cotton most.

Cotton was one of the first leaders of the holy experiment in New England, but inconsistently he did not believe in religious toleration. Neither Plymouth nor Massachusetts led the fight for religious tolerance. This honor belongs later to Roger Williams in Rhode Island. The freedom sought by the Pilgrims was often for themselves. Their blind spot lay not so much in the political realm as in the religious phase of life. Naturally, religious rigidity issued in political and social obstinacy and unbending laws. The laws which sought to compel people to attend public worship on pain of a fine and possible punishment did not seem to upset Cotton even when he preached the maturity and perfection of Christian living.

There is ample evidence of the relevancy of Cotton's preaching for his time. Religious ideals bred social and political convictions of strong application. The context of Puritan thought and life was the State, or society, and the preachers sought to dominate their age with religious motivation. Church polity loomed in the sermons as a means to move people to accept a political and social order based upon Biblical models. Cotton, though Congregationalist in church order and theology, was almost monarchical in political persuasion—as long as the monarch was not a king of England! The saints must rule, for they were the elect of God. His sermons, saturated with theology, were the model for New England orthodoxy.

Cotton defended the practice that no one should be admitted to citizenship until he had become a church member. This was the foundation of the Bible Commonwealth envisaged. At the same time citizens were limited in government. Cotton knew the natural depravity and innate selfishness of man. Power would corrupt; thus checks and balances had to be set up in government for the sake of the governed. This also applied to church power. "So let there be due bounds set, and I may apply it to Families; it is good for the wife to acknowledge all power and authority to the Husband, and for the Husband to acknowledge honour to the Wife, but still give them that which God hath given them, and not more nor lesse: Give them the full latitude that God hath given, else you will finde you dig pits, and lay snares, and comber their spirits, if you give them lesse: there is never peace where full liberty is not given. . . ." (Cf. Cotton's sermon on "Limitation of Government.")

Cotton was also noted for his paradoxes of Puritan orthodoxy. For example, "how could a Christian be separated from the world and yet engage in its business and affairs?" The sermon "Christian Calling" is a noteworthy sampling of this:

> We are now to speak of living by faith in our outward and temporal life. Now our outward and temporal life is twofold, which we live in the flesh: it is either a civil or a natural life; for both these lives we live, and they are different the one from the other. Civil life is that whereby we live as members of this or that city or town or commonwealth, in this or that particular vocation or calling. Natural life I call that by which we do live this bodily life. I mean, by which we live a life of sense, by which we eat or drink, and by which we go through all conditions, from our birth to our grave, by which we live and love and have our being. And now both these a justified person lives by faith.

The Puritan engagement in preaching led into what others perhaps regard as a contradiction in terms. This other-worldliness which Cotton preached was mixed with a worldly involvement. The so-called Protestant ethic is the logical outcome of this preaching. Here the preaching called upon the believer not to leave the world for a monastic life, but to engage in all social-political concerns. "No activity," proclaimed Cotton, "is outside the holy purpose of the overarching covenant."

We may say of such preaching that it bred a generation of strong-willed people who out of their religious beliefs were prepared to enjoy the ongoing life of their day and immerse themselves in the totality of human experience: eating, drinking, sex, marriage, education, social mores, politics, even the bearing of arms and fighting in battle if need be for survival. All these were part and parcel of the Puritan preaching as demonstrated by Cotton.

His persecution of Roger Williams and his judgment against Anne Hutchinson were justified in his mind by reason of the divine right of an elect people to govern the State and to impose such laws as a theocratic view of life allowed. This has been documented fully in *The Antinomian Controversy, 1636-1638,* by David D. Hall (1968). Here is the record of the debate between Cotton and Shepard, Winthrop, Bulkeley, Wheelwright, the report of the trial of Anne Hutchinson, and other relevant extracts. New England was affected by these proceedings, for a government was defeated in an election and Puritanism took on a new shape in its institutions and history.

Social Implications

The preaching of John Cotton illustrates the beneficent stress placed by the Puritan and Pilgrim on the Covenant idea of an elect people as part of God's plan and sovereign purpose in the new world. Here was an "absolute" which both William Perkins and John Preston in England had taught their followers, including Cotton. Only by this conviction and belief could such men subdue the wilderness and lay the foundation for an enduring civilization. Preaching which embodied the conviction of a covenant with God was bound to affect both church and social life.

During the crossing of the Atlantic, the appointed governor, **John Winthrop (1605-1676)**, although not a theologian, ministered by sermon and exhortation. In "A Model of Christian Charity" he explained to his people the nature of the covenant in its social implications. Having forsaken the old world with its religious and political tyranny, he naturally placed emphasis upon the new world and the new commonwealth as seen in the light of the divine government. As Winthrop put it:

> Thus stands the cause between God and us, we are entered into Covenant with him for this work, we have taken out a Commission, the Lord hath given us leave to draw our own Articles, we have professed to enterprise these Actions upon these and these ends, we have hereupon besought him of favour and blessing: Now if the Lord shall please to hear us, and bring us in peace to the place we desire, then hath he ratified this Covenant and sealed our Commission, and will expect a strict performance of the Articles which are the ends we have propounded, and dissembling with our God, shall fall to embrace this present world and prosecute our carnal intentions seeking great things for ourselves and our posterity, the Lord will surely break out in wrath against us, be revenged of such a perjured people and make us know the price of the breach of such a Covenant.

Although Winthrop preached (as a layman) about the ideals of the "city upon the hill," it was the preaching of Cotton which gradually crystallized into a rigid stress upon limiting membership to those who were of the elect and thus eligible for the political and social benefits. While it is true that Cotton's influence was unwavering, the rise of other emphases through Peter Bulkeley and later preachers brought revision and new interpretation of a more liberal type. The absolutism of Cotton was to give way to the more rational and man-centered view of theology which affected the newer preaching. Tradition gave way to experiment, and the systematized sermon to a program of doing good and a more tolerant application of the Covenant.

No one can discount the paramount influence of those early years in preaching. Worship was a means of grace. The lengthy sermons and the exhortations to godliness, the application of the Bible text to special situations dealing with any civil or political crisis of the day, and the accepted and assumed authority of the preacher—plus the applied authority of the Bible as the Word of God—this was the focus during the first half of the seventeenth century in New England.

Changing Emphases

Among other able men in this period was **Peter Bulkeley (1583-1659)**, of English background and from a good family. He finally broke with the established church, moved to New England, and became pastor at Concord, Massachusetts. As a preacher he was noted for his clear and capable style. In preparation no one was more conscientious. His diligence enabled him to argue his points without rancor, making plain and clear his thesis in a balanced fashion. If his preaching lacked adornment, the result was not negligible. His fame in preaching lies in his opposition to John Cotton who was then at the height of his power. Cotton stood for the unbending truth of the Covenant of God with his people. Bulkeley was forced by his study and reflection to modify this and found himself in opposition to the absolutism of Cotton's preaching. The severity of Cotton was countered by the mercy of Bulkeley.

The stress and strain of Puritan Covenant preaching was bound to give way as men learned to live with the new conditions of the new world. Gone was the absolutism of the divine right of kings in Europe, and no political or religious statute was threatening them with a conformity without choice. Modifying the majesty of the theology which came across the ocean, men like Bulkeley began to preach a less rigid and less demanding gospel for man. Thus the demands set for church membership were also softened and moral standards were seen as part of the grace of God.

In his sermon "The Gospel Covenant" (1651) based on Zechariah 9:11, "By the blood of thy covenant . . . ," Bulkeley argued that people could not assume that they were God's people based upon the Covenant unless their behavior gave evidence of it. Such moral conduct testified to their justification by the grace of God. "In the covenant of works, God's highest end is the glorifying of his justice . . . rewarding good, and punishing evil, condemning sin; but in the covenant of grace, he shows himself a God gracious and merciful, forgiving iniquity." Such preaching was indicative of the swing of the pendulum away from the emphasis on the severity of God and the absolute necessity of man's reliance on the grace of God without any personal choice. Now in Bulkeley the emphasis shifts to the goodness and mercy of God available to man, and man's freedom of choice in the light of the conditions set forth in the Covenant.

In his preaching Bulkeley also chose to expound the crucial question of divine authority for the elect and for the State. The Puritan theory of government first by God and then by the State consisted in this: when men have made a covenant with God, they have promised him to "compact among themselves in order to form a holy state in which His discipline will be practiced." Thus Bulkeley preached: "Where the Lord sets himself over a people, he frames them unto a willing and voluntary subjection unto him, that they desire nothing more than to be under his government . . . . When the Lord is in Covenant with a people, they follow him not forcedly, but as far as they are sanctified by grace, they submit willingly to his regiment." The Puritan state was ideally a "theocracy." God was the sovereign; his law was supreme for the whole of life. Magistrates and ministers were God's viceroys. But from another point of view the State was built upon reason and the law of nature. The ministers and magistrates, therefore, were also the servants of the people. This theory was ideal, but it did not allow for the unregenerate and the fact that the elect were a minority.

Bulkeley and his friends found delight not only in contending for the modified view of the Covenant, but they proclaimed with ardor the basic Christological doctrines of the gospel. According to Cotton Mather's account: "At Concord he preached over the illustrious truths about the Person, the Natures, the Offices of Christ. (What would he have said, if he had lived unto this evil day, when 'tis counted good advice for a minister of the Gospel, not to preach much on the Person of Christ?) . . . ." The dual nature of Christ was "strong meat" for the congregation and Christ was revered as the "God-Man" and as the perfect intermediary between God and man. For man, out of great and unmerited love, Christ performs three offices: prophetical, priestly, and kingly; that is, he interprets God's wishes, redeems man, and rules the church of the redeemed or elect.

The sermon and treatise on "The Gospel Covenant" illustrates his distinctive preaching method. Using the power of analysis, he juxtaposed fifteen dissimilar points. Under the old Covenant, dependence was on man; under the new, it is on God. Man formerly lost his hope of salvation by one sin; now his sins are forgiven. In other words, the possible has been substituted for the impossible (for fallen man could not hope to be sinless), peace for suspense. This work became a classic as a discussion of Pauline doctrine concerning the distinction between the law and the gospel.

This style owes much to the fact that, after much study, the preacher often spoke from notes; these notes he then worked over again before submitting the final result to the printer. For example, the book *The Gospel-Covenant* is the result of sermons based on Zechariah 9:11, "As for thee also, by the blood of thy covenant I have sent forth thy prisoners out of the pit wherein is no water."

Political Reconstruction

On the same ship with John Cotton came **Thomas Hooker (1586-1647)**. He also was a student at Emmanuel College, Cambridge, and he had acquired a reputation as a preacher in England before his removal to New England. Forced out of the State church, he joined the congregational order of Puritanism. Hooker was later to expound his church polity in *Survey of the Summe of Church Discipline*. This congregational ideal carried over from religion into politics and touched nature and reason.

Coming to Hartford, Connecticut, he rose to be the leader of the church in that state. He was a powerful and commanding figure. Cotton Mather said of him that he could put a king in his pocket. Known for his oratory and eloquence, he was, in style and manner, quite unlike Cotton. Cotton's logical, systematic manner with its scholastic spirit was not for Hooker. He preferred a more popular style and yet one well illustrated with similes and figures. In dialectic and argument he was outstanding, having been well served by his earlier training in the logic of Ramus. Ramus had followed an earlier Aristotelian dialectic, which put much value upon the individual's ability to think for himself. He saw the world as a dichotomy, composed of opposites; deeds were either good or bad.

Among the sermons of Hooker is the well-known Hartford Election Sermon, May 31, 1638, based on Deuteronomy 1:13: "Take you wise men, and understanding, and known among your tribes, and I will make them rulers over you." The doctrine set forth was that the choice of public magistrates belongs to the people by God's own allowance. This privilege of election which belongs to the people must not, therefore, be exercised according to their humors, but according to the blessed will and law of God. They who have the power to appoint officers and magistrates, have it in their power also to set the bounds and limitations of official power and place.

Only the notes of this sermon have survived. However, these clearly indicate Hooker's form of reasoning and logical development. The sermon itself may not seem unusual, but it led to *the first written constitution in America,* on January 14, 1639, which created government by the consent of the governed. While Hooker was not alone in this opinion, his sermon should not be dismissed as of little account. In a day when Church and State were threshing out their differences and areas of responsibility, the Puritan preacher gave leadership in thought for the people to ponder the implication of political responsibility. The sermon in 1638 spurred the ideal of democratic citizenship. If this was too worldly for some believers, Hooker proclaimed it from his other-worldly view of the people of God, elect of God, claiming the right to set up the standards for the life of the community.

Another type of sermon by Hooker is found in the terrible denunciation of sin and its consequences in life. "A True Sight of Sin" is typical, "wherein this true sight, and apprehension of sin properly discovers itself." While expounding the theme in the usual orderly manner of the Puritan, Hooker has recourse to many

illustrations and allusions outside of the Bible, and in this differs
from his illustrious contemporary, John Cotton. Reference is made
to things in nature (wind, corn); crafts (dross, gold, goldsmith,
metal, hammer, fire); travel (coasts, countries, cold, heat, beauty,
barrenness, traveler); war (ruin, desolation); reason and morality
(map, story, book—the Bible—bosom, pardon, authors, history).
These serve Hooker well in interpreting the nature and power of sin.
He says:

> How shall we see clearlye the Nature of sin in his naked hue? This
> will be discovered, and may be conceived in the Particulars follow-
> ing. Look we at it: First, As it respects God. Secondly, As it
> concerns ourselves. As it had reference to God, the vileness of the
> nature of sin may thus appear. It would dispossess God of that
> absolute Supremacy which is indeed his Prerogative Royal, and
> doth in a peculiar manner appertayn to him, as the Diamond of his
> Crown, and Diadem of his Deity, so the Apostle, He is God over all
> blessed for ever, Rom. 9:5 .... Now herein lyes the unconceavable
> hainousness of the hellish nature of sin, it would justle the Al-
> mighty out of the Throne of his Glorious Sovereignty, and indeed
> be above him.

A sense of vigorous prose is not wanting in Hooker. The hearers
no doubt were held in a spell as the preacher showed them their
sinfulness in the sight of God. If this was overwhelming, it carried
with it neither a fatalism nor a feeling of unrelieved doom; for there
was also the appeal to be "awakened sinners," and always the way
of repentance was pointed out. This is illustrated in another sermon, "Awakened Sinners and Their Ministers," wherein the doctrine is spoken of: "They whose hearts are pierced by the ministry
of the word, they are carried with love and respect to the ministers
of it." The goodness and the severity of God are intertwined. The
sinner is instructed clearly and persuasively to enter the kingdom
and live. Every device of rhetoric and illustration was used to this
final goal.

Hooker is remembered for his outstanding rhetoric and intellectual strength. His sermons are models of excellence. He left the best
interpretation of his own preaching in his *Survey of the Summe of
Church-Discipline* (1648) when he said: "That the discourse comes
forth in such a homely dresse and coarse habit, the Reader must be
desired to consider, it comes out of the wildernesse, where curiosity
is not studied. ... I have ever thought writings that come abroad,
they are not to dazzle, but direct the apprehension of the meanest,

and I have accounted it the chiefest part of Judicious learning, to make a hard point easy and familiar in explication." It "comes out of the wildernesse"—there is the secret of Puritan preaching as manifested by Hooker, who made no parade of his learning.

In *The Soules Exaltation* (1638), Hooker's insight into Biblical truth is displayed as he treats of the holiness of Christian living in union with Christ. With familiar allusions to the family and home, nature and pastimes, he brings the human touch in rich effect. Felicitous in poetic speech, he commands respect.

Democratic Freedom for All

Among the influential preachers of this period **Roger Williams (1603-1683)** stands out. His prestige today stands very high in the light of his struggle for liberty and the attendant results in American life. Although known more for his apologetic and disputation in times of crisis and debate, he was also a warmhearted preacher. His writings convey the impression of a well-stored mind and his personality shines through in his eloquence and strength of speech. There is a vitality about him which marks him off as a significant person in history. In a period when the Puritan preacher was in danger of settling down into fixed modes of address and habit, Williams broke through that crust in daring to be true to his convictions concerning democratic freedom for all people. Never aloof from life, his sociable and outgoing manner won many to his then novel ideas both in content and form.

Although Roger Williams began in the Church of England, he was moved to surrender the tenets of that august body and exchange them for a wider and freer fellowship of the spirit. He became an uncompromising Separatist. At the time of the Westminster Assembly of Divines in London (1643), grave issues were decided. Williams was cognizant of these, but he did not shirk the intellectual and spiritual struggle to make up his own mind. He certainly did not wish a national church in New England after the pattern of old England. He argued that such was not agreeable to conscience or to the Word of God. Christianity must be free of all State control if it is to be effective in the new world—this was the apologia of this large-hearted man. Because of this, he was marked off as a man with heretical views who had no further part to play in the old world thereafter.

John Milton was to issue, at that time, his epoch-making book, *Areopagitica,* with its majestic plea for freedom and liberty for the common man. The day of freedom was about to break for the English-speaking world and Williams found that his writings could aid this, at least in the new world of the American experiment and dream. The title of his book, *The Bloudy Tenet of Persecution for Cause of Conscience* (1644), is striking and provocative. No one could dismiss lightly the thesis set forth in his passionate and forceful argument. His principal points include: the nature of persecution, the limits of the power of the civil sword, and the tolerance already granted by Parliament. Here is no limpid brook meandering along, but a river in full torrent. All his rhetoric pours out in a prose which includes invective, sarcasm, and irony, uttered with imagination, humor, pathos, and abounding logic.

Perry Miller, author of *Roger Williams* (1962), has made a notable plea for understanding this man who looms so large in the American tradition then being formulated. Williams' concern for the poor and needy in England and later his identification with the Indians in America demonstrate his spirit of loving concern for the underprivileged. When he fled the civil authorities in Massachusetts Bay Colony, he went into exile in the wilderness to the south, where he lived for a time with the Indians. The puzzle then was why he did not try to convert the Indians to the Christian faith. He was respectful of their culture, language, and customs, and defended them against abuses by settlers. As the first well-educated Englishman among them, he might have brought many into the Christian experience. But he received only those in whose hearts "the Lord had wrought repentance."

If Williams is not known as a preacher who has a place in the roster of honorable mention in this period, let it be stated that his importance lies then not in sermonic work but rather in his influence on others who preached in those stirring times of controversy and change. His significance for preaching lay in the fact that his basic thesis of liberty for all paved the way for a democracy within which the church and its preachers were to work. The decision that men should be free to worship according to their conscience has had a profound impact upon American life. The increase of denominations was possible when neither state or civic power nor religious tyranny could impose rules and regulations to bind the conscience. Within this cultural context religious life has ever since found expression. All preaching from then onwards was indebted to

Williams for freedom of expression. As he was a prophet based upon a Calvinistic view of Scripture, so he respected and asked for the same liberty for others in their interpretations. A tolerant religious and theological climate for the new world was being prepared as the background for preaching.

Part of the preaching of this strong man lay in his "anti-Roman" bias. The "popishness" which he saw in the conflicts of Europe led him to speak out against the "badges of superstition" then in vogue. Even the cross on a flag was subject to his censure. We may discern an imbalance here, but in that day feeling ran deep and the challenge to the religious and civil leaders who were lax in this matter was effective.

As Williams had taken issue with the Church of England before coming to New England, so now in the new world he could not compromise with any power which threatened liberty. He was a preacher of church reform. He preached against excess of ritual and ceremony. The overtones of these views have continued in American church life ever since. The influence of this kind of preaching persists throughout the nation and is most alive at times of crisis or controversy, and at elections. When John F. Kennedy became a candidate for the Presidency he was the subject of many allusions in sermons and had to face a special gathering of ministers in Texas to be interrogated concerning these same issues raised by Roger Williams. As a Roman Catholic, Kennedy was under suspicion that if he became President he would be under the direction of the church to which he belonged.

Thus the preaching of Williams is to be noted for its acute influence upon the political scene; its dynamic thrust for political and religious freedom; and for the resultant American idea of the separation of Church and State, still an issue in subsequent centuries.

The well-known sermon, "The Bloudy Tenet of Persecution," is a sample of the pithy, direct, forthright style of this preacher. He stabs and probes as with a sharp instrument—the rapier thrust and the scalpel cut deeply. "Truth" and "Peace" are used in antithesis and in dialog as he argues against John Cotton and for his thesis:

> Peace: To end this chapter, Master Cotton affirmes, that civil peace (to speak properly) is not only a peace in civil things for the object, but the peace of all the persons in the city. . . . And if it be civil justice to protect one, then the other also.
> Truth: Civil peace will never be proved to be the peace of all the

subjects or citizens of a city in spiritual things: The civil state may bring into order, make orders, preserve in civil order all her members: But who ordained, that either the spiritual state should bring in and force the civil state to keep civil order, or that the civil state should sit, judge, and force any of her subjects to keep spiritual order?

The true and living God, is the God of order, spiritual, civil and natural: Natural is the same ever and perpetual: civil alters according to the constitutions of peoples and nations: spiritual he hath changed from the national in one figurative land of Canaan, to particular and congregational churches all the world over; which order spiritual, natural or civil, to confound and abrogate, is to exalt man's folly against the most holy and incomprehensible wisdom of God. . . .

For preaching, who shall say this is not pointed, pithy, practical? An age of controversy produced preaching of this kind.

Apart from controversy, Williams is also known for his choice spiritual classic of the Christian life, *Experiments of Spiritual Life and Health* (1652). In this he sought to provide a manual of self-analysis—a Puritan chronicle of the inner life under discipline through introspection. It takes its place alongside other and perhaps better known books of that kind, such as Richard Baxter's *The Reformed Pastor* and John Bunyan's *Pilgrim's Progress*. If not as highly acclaimed as these two, Williams' treatise nevertheless was a contribution to the theology and life of the leaders of the churches. Many preachers were indebted to its probing spirit to spur them on to greater endeavor in their proclamation of the truth.

Puritan Piety

Thomas Shepard (1604-1649) was one of the earliest divines to grace the New England scene. A graduate of Emmanuel College, Cambridge, England, he came to America in 1635 and became the pastor and leader of the group settled in Cambridge, Massachusetts. His teaching and preaching were shot through with attacks on antinomianism; but his chief contribution lay in the piety which he espoused and which was conveyed in his writings, especially in *The Sincere Convert,* which went into twenty editions. Another of Shepard's works was *The Parable of the Ten Virgins* in which the parable is expounded in minute detail and exegesis. His *Spiritual Experiences* and *The Sound Convert* were also books of strong influence. As a preacher he followed the traditional Puritan pattern of sermonizing. However, his insights supplied new ideas and ideals for the church.

Jonathan Edwards said that Shepard was "one of the greatest of the sons of men"—high praise, indeed; and Alexander Whyte extolled him by comparing him to Edwards! Edwards quoted profusely from Shepard in his *Religious Affections*. He was also indebted to Shepard's exposition on *The Parable of the Ten Virgins* which he used as the basis for some of his own preaching. The preaching of this Pilgrim Father is noted for incisive penetration into experimental religion. Here is a kinship with the apostle Paul, for Shepard never strayed from that outstanding interpreter of Christ.

Stylistically, Shepard does not stand in the grand tradition of his contemporaries. His education was as good as the others' and he was steeped in the classical and theological background of the Puritan, but the surprise is that his English is faulty in style. While John Bunyan wrote clear, simple, matchless prose, Shepard wrote almost unrecognizable English. "Atrocious English," said Alexander Whyte in speaking of him. Then why is Shepard one to study as a preacher? Is not good style the ideal, and the Puritan ideal the "plain style"? All this is true, but the fact remains that here is a preacher with poor English style who was used nevertheless in proclaiming the message of God.

Strange as it may seem, though his style is against him, yet his thoughts pursue and catch the hearer and reader. The mental quality of this preacher is perceptive and nimble. He does reach people. According to David Brainerd, there was in Shepard that which "passed for soul-saving religion." Some of the quotations and sayings from his preaching are memorable: "The more I do, the worse I am." "My idle words in my preaching, in my praise, and in my prayer." "The sins of one day I forget the next day." "I keep a private fast for the conquest of my pride." "My sins are sometimes crucified, but they are never mortified." "Surely I have always laid my pipe far short of the Fountain."

Shepard's preaching had a pungency about it. Sincere and devout, he always saw himself in the light of a standard to which he did not approximate. Sensitive about the failure of his family life, his introspection imparted pathos to his preaching. Poignant and tearful at times, it touched the conscience. Shepard was one with Paul in the sense of being "the chief of sinners" and in his evangelical mysticism. These became the overtones of his preaching. He would imply that his people should not imitate him for he believed he was a poor example. He was at home in the language of the psalmist who said: "The sacrifices of God are a broken spirit: a broken and a contrite heart, O God, thou wilt not despise."

In preaching, Shepard, like other Pilgrims and Puritans, joined Biblical exposition to relevant current events and practical exhortations. Speaking of the trials and persecutions before coming to New England, he has this to say:

> It is true, we might have suffered, we might easily have found the way to have filled the prisons, and some had their share therein. But whether we were called thereunto, when a wide door was set open of liberty otherwise; and our witness to the truth (through the malignant policy of those times) could not be open before the world, but rather smothered up in close prisons or some such ways, together with our selves, we leave to be considered. We cannot but see the rule of Christ to his Apostles and Saints, and the practise of God's Saints in all ages, may allow us this liberty as well as others, *to fly into the Wilderness* from the face of the Dragon. But if it had been so, that the Godly Ministers and Christians that *fled* to New England.

It is of more than passing interest that the words about "the wilderness," used later by Samuel Danforth in 1670 and which became the talisman or watchword for the Puritan experiment, were used by Shepard in regular and repeated emphases much earlier.

Certainly Shepard's contribution to preaching is worthwhile when we recall that in spite of his execrable style he was used to reach a generation with barbed truth. Men need to know the laws of God in order to act rightly. But they need more than that knowledge. They need a power to keep the laws and only grace can do that. Thus Shepard: "There is a sort of knowledge which some men have from the book of creation, some by power of education, some by the light of the law . . . some by the letter of the gospel, and so men may know much and speak well. . . ." But over against this there is quite another kind of knowledge which only the elect can acquire, whereby they "see things in another manner; to tell you how, they can not; it is the beginning of light in heaven."

Summary

In this period the preachers of New England were largely those who had come from the old world and with them a number of young men who did not complete their education until they later attended Harvard College. Of this number, Samuel Arnold, James Fitch, John Higginson, and Thomas Thatcher had their sermons published.

Only a short time elapsed until the men from England were replaced in the next generation by graduates of Harvard. In establishing Harvard College, the first settlers had planned that the early graduates would replace the pioneer minister. The men preaching in the 1650s and 1660s and having their sermons published in Cambridge or Boston instead of faraway London, included Samuel Danforth, Samuel Hooker, William Hubbard, Uriah Oakes, and Thomas Shepard Jr., as well as others.

These men willingly acknowledged the valuable contribution their predecessors had made to the pulpit, but the eulogistic nature of that tribute was based largely on the tradition which had been handed down orally. Only when there were sermons published and then studied could a fair and reasonable estimate be made of the earlier preachers. Of John Cotton, Thomas Shepard, and Thomas Hooker, the record is clear for they left much published material by which to judge. But many men are lesser known only because we have no basis of judgment. Even such a prominent man as Roger Williams has left little in print. Our appraisal of him would be better if more of his sermons were available. And how can we evaluate John Eliot, missionary to the Indians, who for sixty years preached to one congregation, none of whose sermons are available?

Within the context of the same general style of preaching, marked differences are to be noted. Anglican love of ritual and ceremony is sometimes reflected in the suavity of diction which the Puritans employed. In this particular, Hooker's style stands out above others. There is a grandeur of style and a wealth of vocabulary. Drawing freely from classical sources and wide reading, they used a logical and an intellectual approach in order to reason through the subject preached. Rhetoric loomed strongly in their words and delivery. Prose was enriched by metaphors and illustrations.

The Puritans who became the Congregationalists of that period followed more closely the strict rules of composition laid down by their teachers in England. Theology was strong and most marked, but they did not parade their knowledge of the classics or their strength of education. True, they had the finest classical education—no less than Hooker and others like him—but they kept to the injunctions of Richard Sibbes and William Perkins who taught that preaching should be "plain" and unadorned. Figure and illustration were utilized, but were limited. Prose was not enriched to give color and beauty. The aim was to stab the conscience in blunt speech and to give force and feeling to an appeal for action. Roger Williams, for example, apologized to Lady Vane the Younger for "the forme and stile (which) I know will seem to this refined age, too rude and barbarous."

Chapter II

Preaching in the United States by Puritans Educated in New England (1650-1700)

During the initial settlement of the Pilgrim Fathers and their associates, sermons and volumes of sermons were printed. The trend begun in England continued in New England, so that men prominent in England had a tendency to keep their position of leadership in the new world. This could be accounted for by the fact that the churches were in the larger towns. Human nature, then as now, was characterized by the instinct to magnify those who received publicity and praise, and at the same time overlook less famous men. Perhaps the publication of the sermons of the more publicized tended to minimize the excellence and devotion of the lesser known men whose preaching and writing were given minimal circulation.

Following the settlement of the pioneers, social structures and intellectual life were molded and formulated in the matrix of Puritanism. The traditions from the Reformation and the historic implications of renouncing the old world had far-reaching effects. The Covenant people of God through their leaders were prepared to build a new order and structure of society based upon their religious convictions and piety.

Puritan Education

In the transition from that preliminary period to what follows lies the founding of Harvard College in 1636. Schools were established in Boston in 1635 and the General Court of Massachusetts twelve years later ordered that towns within its jurisdiction should set up schools for the education of children. The public school system of America thus had its beginning. The college, later to become Harvard University, had as its inception the thought and gift of one John Harvard, a London-bred man whose library and sermons with certain theological treatises became the nucleus of the college and its library.

Puritanism believed in an educated ministry. To train young men for the ministry was a supreme object of these early settlers. They were quick to see that without trained men their ongoing cause would fail and die out. They themselves had received a college and university education in England; therefore they were ambitious to have their sons share in something similar. Harvard at the first was intended to train "Christian men, Christian citizens, and Christian ministers." The English-born and English-trained preachers were replaced eventually by a generation of Harvard men, and only to a smaller degree by later settlers from England after the Restoration.

Those who were the graduates of this new college were given a theological and cultural training suited to the temper and spirit of that period. If later generations were to have a broader and more secular education at Harvard, the ministers who came forth in the seventeenth century were noted for their piety and devotion. While later generations of students are known for their breadth and permissive ways, the early ones are appreciated for their depth and religious culture. The Harvard graduate become minister then replaced the pioneer pastor. While other religious groups on the Atlantic seaboard could tolerate the enthusiast and the preacher with very little education, the Puritan demanded an educated ministry.

"Errand into the Wilderness"

Samuel Danforth (1626-1674) stands out as prominent in this transition period. Educated at Harvard he served the church at Roxbury for twenty-four years as assistant minister to John Eliot. Cotton Mather has dealt with this amazing man in his major work, *Magnalia IV*. In sermon work he was an exemplary Puritan and spent long hours in preparation. Many were content to use notes in preaching and some memorized the script which they had carefully written beforehand. Danforth is said to have written his sermons twice—in an attempt to improve the rhetoric and style, not simply to depend upon the detailed outline with its lengthy notes. Cotton Mather testifies that Danforth had some fame as a "notable text-man" and usually used in his sermons from forty to fifty Scripture passages, each one of which was quoted.

In the sermon, "A Brief Recognition of New England's Errand," reference is made to various practical affairs then of interest to the community. In that day church people might seek to be stylish with long hair and loose locks as well as fashionable clothes. Some of these modes of dress were tilted at by some of the Puritan preachers who were afraid their parishioners might become "worldly." Danforth in this message in 1670 speaks of "gorgeous attire" and "pomp in Wilderness." To him these were signs of the degenerating times and he was fearful some of his people might lose their spiritual strength thereby. He knew, of course, that the soul's welfare in salvation depended upon grace and faith alone; nevertheless, these outward habits might be a sign of the jeopardy of these people!

A significant feature of Danforth's preaching lay in his interest in and knowledge of scientific matters. Natural history and botany filled a few Puritans with questions. Astronomy was one of Danforth's special concerns. He published "An Astronomical Description of the Late Comet or Blazing Star" in 1665. In this he interprets comets to be divine portents of disaster. They are not "Exhalations," but stellar phenomena, subject to natural law. The preacher owed something here to his student days when he studied astronomy and prepared a yearly almanac from 1645-1649.

Even as Danforth urged New Englanders to repent when he used his knowledge of astronomy, so he was not behind in the use of comminatory language in the sermon, "The Cry of Sodom Enquired Into," in 1674. The descriptions of hell-fire, the bottomless pit, the torments of the damned in an almost hysterical note weigh down the rhetoric and style of the sermon: "Hasten you after your lecherous Kindred into the stinking Lake; sit down with your Brethren and Sisters in the depths of Hell. . . . Hell from beneath is moved to meet thee, and is ready to entertain thee." Apart from this there was always the wooing invitation—for the elect could die joyfully and future bliss awaited the believer.

This particular sermon is a demonstration of Danforth's method. Occasionally the Puritan would by-pass the context of the chapter from which the text was taken. Here in Genesis 18:20, 21 the fate of Sodom and Gomorrah hangs in the balance. But Abraham's intervention and God's pledged mercy if any righteous men were to be found are both ignored. The congregation doubtless knew that whole story very well. The pastor-preacher surely could not imply that he had no righteous men in his congregation! Nevertheless, by so selecting these words out of a line or two he was able to frighten and awaken the staid and solid Puritans. At worship they must have been astounded at their pastor's tirade; yet they knew this was in keeping with the need to call them to repentance.

Danforth's sermon, "Errand into the Wilderness," delivered in 1670, became the catchword for much of the preaching which followed. The Puritans truly were in the wilderness, and had yet to ensue a long pilgrimage before they settled in the promised land. The frontier was real. The epic struggle and venture became the seedbed of our democracy and commonwealth of later years. Danforth's preaching was colored in thought and language by the cultural and sociological factors then impinging upon the Puritan. In the sermons of that period the emphasis was more on the "errand" than on the "wilderness." Such a metaphor enlarged the vision of preaching and gave direction to theological development. It was the genius and insight of Danforth to give to the world this concept in one sermon preached as an Election Day sermon, a phenomenon then common in New England.

That Danforth preached this special sermon in the presence of the General Assembly of the Massachusetts Colony at Boston on the Day of Election, informs us that the Puritan preacher was not averse to appearing before any kind of audience and to speaking at any time and place other than at the regular Lord's Day services. Certainly there was regular and systematic preaching from the pulpit of the meeting house or church, but there were those other occasions when the preacher found a gathered audience to listen. He could assume for the most part that those who were together in the General Assembly of the State were also members of the elect people of God and within the true church. While that opportunity is rarely if ever given to preachers in our day, the Puritan used it to good advantage both for the State and the Church.

Puritan Logic

During the seventeenth century there were not many graduates of Harvard to fill the ranks of newly opened churches and settlements. Pastors still came from England, but the few who began the historic succession included some whose ministries are not to be overlooked by the historian.

James Fitch (1628-1702) was in the finest tradition of the scholastic. In Europe the teaching of Peter Ramus in his *Dialecticae* had profoundly influenced the early Reformers and their followers. Much of the strong Puritan element leaned to the Covenant idea. They set forth their teaching of this idea in logical fashion. By grouping ideas, sensations, causes, and perceptions of the world, they developed a general schemata or pattern. This became the basis of study and later of the sermonic work of the preacher. Here in the sermon are the divisions and subdivisions, the blueprint of truth set out with care and design. Thus Puritan preachers were logicians and their sermons were markedly logical in structure. Fitch was an able exponent of this type of preaching. In "The First Principles of the Doctrine of Christ" (1679), a message of importance for him and his people, truth was revealed in a teaching method of arranging everything in sequential pairs: man with woman, sun with moon, cause with effect, subject with adjunct. The general came before the specific, the genus before the species, the important before the subsidiary.

Such preaching tended to assimilate the humanism of the Renaissance and blend it with the Christian theological system. Culture had its place in the preaching of the Puritan. Although Puritanism broke with many religious structures, it still retained an awareness of its age and background. The major departure from the humanism of the Renaissance came in the acceptance of the authority of the Bible which was to be believed as a foundation and premise.

William Hubbard (1621-1704), minister of Ipswich, preached with a historical sense of destiny. On one occasion he stood before the Governor and Council of the Massachusetts Colony on Election Day at Boston, 1676, and there proclaimed his thesis of how God acts in history on behalf of his people.

Uriah Oakes (1631-1681) graduated from Harvard to become a pastor and teacher, and later President of Harvard for four years. His strong mental ability and his nimble wit shone through his public utterances. His preaching is judged to be among the best of that period. Care and polish mark his preparation.

A theme Oakes set forth is that God concurs in the operation of natural causes to work out good for man. In a sermon based on

Ecclesiastes 9:11 (1677), given at an Election time, titled, "The Sovereign Efficacy of Divine Providence," this doctrine is stated and then developed with marked logical acumen. The text states, "I returned, and saw under the sun, that the race is not to the swift, nor the battle to the strong, neither yet bread to the wise, nor yet riches to men of understanding, nor yet favor to men of skill; but time and chance happeneth to them all."

From this striking text Oakes gave the exhortation based upon the following. (1) Second causes may have a sufficiency in their kind, to produce this and that. (2) The Successes, and Events of Affairs and Undertakings do ordinarily depend in some respects upon the sufficiency of second causes. (3) Second causes, though of greatest sufficiency in their kind, have not the certain Determination of successes and events in their own hands; but may be frustrated and disappointed. (4) The Defeat and disappointment of Agents of great sufficiency in their kind, is from the Happening of Time and Chance unto them. (5) Time and Chance which happens to men in the way of their undertakings, is effectually ordered and governed by the Lord. (6) The great God has in His own power the absolute and infallible Determination of the successes and events of all the operations and undertakings of created agents and second causes. The Application or Instruction of this sermon climactically delineated several principles to be followed in practical ways. Thus God is seen as the first and the all-sufficient cause. All secondary causes may appear to be of chance and accident, but in the sovereignty of God there is plan and purpose.

Preaching then was not according to the mood or the spirit of the hour. Scripture was interpreted as an art in the hermeneutics of a logical system based upon a well-defined pattern. Thus theological terms were necessary and so used in preaching. It was Oakes who said that if any interpreted Scripture otherwise, they were guilty of "parologizing themselves." That is, to reason amiss, and to conclude that which is not in the premise of the text. This kind of preaching was rich and strong in the hands of Oakes and others like him. It developed strong believers and men of theological stature.

Preaching in this fashion gave the preacher an opportunity to work his way through books of the Bible or to spend many sermons in the interpretation of a given text. The duty of the preacher was to clarify the text in all possible ways. In using Deuteronomy 32:29, Oakes went on to develop and analyze the whole Song of

Moses. His listeners learned that it started with a "Rhetorical and pathetical Apostrophe" which is the "Exordium, Proem or Preface, wherein he labors to procure Benevolence, Attention and Docility"; then came the Narrative; then a prediction of "the Apostacy, Idolatry, and horrible Ingratitude of Israel"; then a "severe Commination of the deserved Chastisements and Punishments"; and last a word of Consolation with a concluding line.

Cotton Mather's critique of Oakes is worth noting. Says he, "Consider'd as a Preacher, he was an Orpheus that would have drawn the very stones to discipline; had Austin been here, he might have seen Paul in the pulpit: indeed, he was, as one said, An uncomfortable Preacher. Why? he drove us to Despair, namely, Of seeing such another." This quotation indicates that Mather was eulogistic and not always realistic concerning the object of his writing. To be among "the best of preachers" did not require comparison with the Apostle Paul. When talking about **John Davenport (1597-1690)**, he cites that he was "a man of more than ordinary accomplishments; a Prince of Preachers; . . . he had been acquainted with great men, and great things, and was Great himself, and had a great fame abroad in the world; yea, now he was grown old, like Moses his force was not abated." However we may revise the euolgistic estimates concerning these men, their supposed public glory and image lasted for a few generations. Not all stand the test of time, and the peril of such unrestricted praise is obvious. On the other side, the enemies of the Puritans endeavored to discredit them.

Puritan Principles

The influence of **Cotton Mather (1663-1728)** was marked in the new world if only in his writings. His preaching was characterized by the same tradition as that of John Cotton (his grandfather on his mother's side). His father was Increase Mather, the son of Richard Mather, both ministers, and his grandfather was also President of Harvard College. Thus Cotton Mather was born within the theological and religious framework of cultured Puritanism. A leader of orthodoxy, he is best remembered for works apart from his sermons. These, however, reflect his preaching and his theological insights. His zeal and work are revealed in his literary output—some five hundred books, tracts, and pamphlets.

His outstanding work is *Magnalia Christi Americana: the Ecclesi-astical History of New England* (London, 1702). Here is the first regular history of the new world. Dealing largely with the church and preachers, it opens a window into the life and behavior of the period. The most important book dealing with preaching is his handbook for theological students, *Manductio ad Ministerium* (1726), in which he outlines the basic studies for a would-be pastor and preacher. The manuals and textbooks brought from the old world included William Perkins' *The Art of Prophesying* (1592), which was standard as long as the Pilgrim preachers were dependent upon their past. However, Mather's book was the first produced in the new world and as such became a useful tool for the young men rising up to prepare themselves for the ministry. The goal for a minister was to be both an educated man and the leading man in the community. All realms of knowledge therefore were to be explored as well as Divinity, the queen of the sciences. Included with theology are science, experimental philosophy, the classics, modern languages, and polite letters—a remarkable breadth by any judgment.

The tradition of Puritanism lay in a well-informed ministry. Sermons and preaching were to be part of the fruit of a lifetime of study, so that each week the regular diet of ministry came forth from a well-stored mind and a warm heart. The ministry was believed to be God's agency for the advance of the gospel and the Kingdom of God. With Mather's manual the task of training was encouraged by making Piety—which is "Christ formed in you; and Christ living in you"—the primary requisite. Then followed the plan to cultivate "that Learning and those Ingenuous and Mollifying Arts, which may distinguish you from the more Uncultivated Part of Mankind." As preparation for preaching and the delivery of the sermon, a broad general education was encouraged, with the addi-tion of the special areas of Theology. The preaching and sermons still extant from that period reflect the wisdom and learning of such preparation.

The reiteration of the necessity of quality and preparation served to emphasize that in the education for the Christian ministry the Pilgrims and the Puritans saw that everything depended upon the grace of God, and that a man should work diligently at his studies alongside of all others engaged in other areas of the world order. Thus Harvard College from its founding provided a liberal arts education as deemed necessary for the theological student. Both breadth and depth were conjoined for the future pastor.

Of the Mathers, Richard, Increase, and Cotton emerge as leaders in their day. **Richard Mather (1596-1669)** claimed to be the usual Puritan in preaching with the plain style. As his son, Increase, reported: "His way of preaching was plain, aiming to shoot his Arrows not over his peoples heads, but into their Hearts and Consciences." This ideal on his part and the part of his contemporaries was in contrast to their successors in New England. The grandson, Cotton Mather, was known to use frequent citation and quotation from the learned tongues. By the 1660s the Puritan style was in process of change. It became obvious in the mannerisms of **Increase Mather (1639-1723)**. His exceptional learning and scholarship in languages led him to use such knowledge in flashes of erudite quotation. By pointed phrases and contrasting statements, he enlivened many a sermon for those who could benefit thereby.

Among others in this period was **Samuel Willard (1640-1707)**, whose preaching was characterized by stressing the sovereignty of God and Covenant theology. His writings defended the alliance of Church and State in New England. The work *Compleat Body of Divinity* (1726) embodied an interpretation of the *Shorter Catechism* based upon a Calvinistic view. The Colonial period was one of rapid change. Willard's preaching was that of a second generation Puritan defending the faith against the erosion of the Reformed belief.

Summary

Like their predecessors who came from England and the continent of Europe, the later Puritans who were the products of Harvard and Yale continued the tradition of "the plain style." For men on the frontier whose errand into the wilderness necessitated the building of settlements and the building up of congregations and communities by further immigration, it was deemed the right thing to keep to the plain speech. The Puritans in their education were exposed to all the niceties of classical and rhetorical excellence. In their private lives and in their study they did not shrink from admiring these standards. They also pursued in their own way the study and mastery of these traditions of literature and rhetoric. But in preaching this was laid aside with the laudable aim to speak

plainly to all who heard the swiftly running words of grace from
Biblical exposition. Based upon the King James Version of the
Bible, sermons had already a tradition of the finest prose, the
beauty of phrase, memorable sayings, and acceptance of the authority of God's Word. Thus the preacher capitalized upon a ready
response resulting from a willing belief in the efficacy of that Word
of God, and in the sermon as the means of grace and the one
outstanding way in which God spoke to his people.

This kind of preaching brought no offense to people. The preacher did not call attention to himself or parade his learning by
quotation or allusion to the general works he knew or had read. In
this way he countered pride and strove to be the servant of all men
whose speech was ordinary and plain.

In Jonathan Edwards we see the brilliant mind, the learned
educator, the genius and philosopher stooping to the level of
ordinary people to share with them the deep things of the divine
revelation. His speech and prose are filled with rich ideas and images
to make clear the truth, but he was the faithful Puritan in conceal-
ing his fuller knowledge of the vast hinterland of truth beyond their
ken. Only at a funeral sermon or at an ordination sermon was there
a slight departure from the norm. Then for the occasion references
might be made concerning the great gifts and background of the
departed, or there would be stress upon learning and preparation
for the ministry, but this was laid at the foot of the cross. Like
others, Edwards could write the finest prose, and in his more
theological and philosophical works there are flashes of that more
academic style glimmering through. But the regular preaching of
these Puritans was limited to the plain style to which they faithfully
adhered. Unconsciously, they also shaped the speech and ideals of a
generation in the best English based upon the background of both
Renaissance and Reformation. Directness and decisiveness marked
the speech of the oncoming generation.

PART TWO

The
Eighteenth
Century

The godly experiment of the "errand into the wilderness" in the seventeenth century opened the door for many groups to enter the promised land of the new world, establish a common life and follow various religious patterns. New forms of service and structure in church life resulted. While the new groups transplanted replicas of the old customs, manners, and mores of family life in the newly settled towns and hamlets, they refused to endow any one church body with supreme powers. All religious groups became "free." This had not been so at the first.

Others besides the Puritans arrived on these shores. Those preferring Anglican and Episcopalian ways of worship settled along the Eastern seaboard, though not in New England at the beginning. Others came from the lowlands of Europe, adapting their own national tongues of Dutch and German to the more commonly accepted English language. Some settled in Virginia and Maryland, gathering in improvised places for worship, and following *The Book of Common Prayer* and observing Communion with preaching.

Political attitudes and prejudices played an important part in how men chose to worship and how they wished their pastors to preach. Not all came to these shores for the same reason. The American religious tradition, nonetheless, has been that which magnified the pulpit and gave a listening ear to the preacher. Exhortation and moral appeal loomed large in those days of new beginnings. William Warren Sweet, in his *Religion in the Development of American Culture* (1963), has shown how preaching and religious life in general have molded the life and culture of our history.

While the early Roman Church leaders laid the foundation of an authoritative body and a clerical priesthood, the people of that order were not motivated in the tenets of democracy and the priesthood of believers as were the Puritans. In religious, social, and political affairs this affected vast numbers of people who depended upon their leaders, whereas the Puritan preacher sought to encourage his people to use responsibly their freedom of judgment in these areas. The rise of denominations was a stimulant to the healthy dialog and discussion that took place as part of the common life in the town meetings. Thus moral and spiritual values also played their part in the developing life. The new century was noted for its eminent preachers who enthusiastically ministered the Word of God and were part of the revivals and awakenings characteristic of the period.

Perry Miller, in "The Puritan State and Puritan Society," has pointed out that the end of the seventeenth century and the beginning of the eighteenth century marked the first real break with the Middle Ages in the history of European thought. After the Renaissance and the Reformation came the scientific era, beginning with the time of Isaac Newton. The world of nature as well as the world of the spiritual began to have relevancy. Politics and religion could now be separated and the plurality of denominations or churches became a possibility in American life. The former European tyrannies and enslavements of mind and body gave way to freedom of spirit and liberty of conscience. Gradually the spiritual awakening of the new century was destined to give to men an experience of God which would allow them to look at life politically and socially, as well as religiously—not in one fixed way of expression, but in the diversity of common life and conviction. While the first Puritans retained the unity of State and Church through a membership in both bodies, the new movements on the frontier were breaking this down. Thus the preaching of this epoch took on newer dimensions of speech and spirit.

Chapter III

Preaching in the United States by Puritans (1700-1750)

That the Puritan strain did not die out in the passing years is a significant fact of American preaching. What was begun by the first settlers had, it is true, its period of decline, its ebb and flow. But while changes were taking place in New England, the influence of the preacher continued largely to be that of the Puritan. This was inevitable since the places of ministerial training and the textbooks studied were those produced by the Puritan.

After attending Harvard College, whose first students were trained for various aspects of common life, a large percentage of graduates inevitably entered the Christian ministry. The library had in it more theological books than books in any other category. The teachers were committed to assist the holy experiment by sending into the churches a steady stream of godly and learned men. The relationship with Reformed Theology and the idea of the Covenant of God caused a Calvinist interpretation of truth to be stressed. This particular shaping of American religion forwarded the ideas then current so that the next generation would not lightly lay aside the basic teaching. There was *a marrow of Puritan divinity* so strong and rich that the newer pastors then engaging in their work were not divorced from those sterling convictions.

The founding of Yale College at New Haven was an added achievement in theological education and a new inspiration for general education. 1701 is, therefore, an important date to set aside that of 1636, and thus began the rivalry between Yale and Harvard. Southern New England was now to balance the rest of New England as Congregationalists in particular gave of their substance and life to propagate "the blessed reformed Protestant religion in this wilderness." The college was founded in part to buttress against the coming defection from faith on the part of a new generation. The structure of society based upon a Biblical and theocratic principle was now giving way, weakened by the erosion of new ideas.

The curriculum at Yale was not unlike that at Harvard. Harvard may have begun with a few hundred books, but Yale began with some forty tomes as the genesis of its library. These books were valued for their rarity and for their heritage of being brought from Europe by Puritans. Later, as the college enlarged its vision to teach men in other fields than theology, the library was increased by further gifts of books from England. Thus the other branches of learning provided an appropriate balance.

Cotton Mather is given credit for the idea of naming the new college Yale, although John Davenport had earlier proposed that there should be another school "for the better trayning upp of youth in this towne, that, through God's blessing they may be fitted for publique service hereafter, in church or commonweale." Good literature, the arts and the sciences were to be studied as well as theology. The school was not to train men solely for the ministry but also for the magistracy. The college from its inception was intended to be independent so that it depended upon donations from its constituency of interested people and not from the state.

The graduates of Yale were to have a strong influence upon the churches and the religious life of the community. The training and education was that of the highest then possible. It was assumed (and generally could be) that entrants had already received a good grounding in the English Bible. In any godly home of that period, the young man was under the influence of a tradition where the good Book was read and partially memorized. Daily familiarity with Scripture molded the thought and speech of the young. At school in the community a place was given to Bible reading and some explanation or comment.

The foundation stone of all theology and rhetoric for the Puritan preacher was the English Bible of the King James Version, as is obvious in the sermon. Even apart from its religious and theological implications, here is the greatest English classic. Men of letters are quick to testify to the inspiration of this book in forming the best tastes for our notable national writers. In rhetorical style and in use of vivid imagery, the Puritan preacher owed a debt to Biblical prose and poetry. The young theological student coming from homes and schools where the English Bible was revered and read was profited in his early studies in divinity.

After the Bible came study of the ancient languages for the Yale divinity student. The curriculum then offered at Harvard became the standard at Yale. Mathematics, geography, natural science, logic, and theology were wedded together. In an early catalog is found the following admonition to the student: "And I would advise you, my Pupils, to pursue a Regular Course of Academical Studies in some Measure according to the Order of this Catalogue. And in the First Year to Study principally the Tongues, Arithmatic and Algebra; the Second, Logic, Rhetoric and Geometry; the Third, Mathematics and Natural Philosophy; and the Fourth, Ethics and Divinity. Other less principal Studies may be occasionally intermix't with these. Above all have an Eye to the great End of all your Studies, which is to obtain the Clearest Conceptions of Divine Things and to lead you to a Saving Knowledge of GOD in his Son JESUS CHRIST" (Clap, A Catalogue of the Library of Yale College in New Haven, New London, 1743, preface).

For the preacher of that period the trend was to become increasingly Calvinistic. Whatever Lutheran influence came to New England, such as found in the Augsburg Confession and in the sermons of Lutheran ministers in other parts, the fact remains that the Reformed faith was mediated chiefly through the Puritans and John Calvin. Luther, Erasmus, and others were found in the Yale Library, but the works of the Puritans predominated with Calvin increasingly represented. Because of this we can expect a strong Reformed note in the preaching of this period. The new settlements and communities throughout the area were served by young men coming out of Yale as well as Harvard.

Edwardian Preaching

This era was noted for the rise of America's outstanding mind and spirit in the person of **Jonathan Edwards (1703-1758)**. His life is now well documented in the biographies by Ola Winslow (*Jonathan Edwards, 1703-1758*) and Perry Miller (*American Puritans, Their Prose and Poetry*), whose researches above all others enable us to see the preacher as he was. Until further study can be made and the Edwards *Miscellanies* at Yale University Library is published, we shall not have any more notes to add to that interpretation. Naturally, differences of view have been set forth. Some see in this Puritan preacher the stern, harsh, unbending parson of that day whose word and will were law for the people of the parish. This caricature is drawn by those who have no sympathy with the strong creed and convincing faith of the one whose life had far-reaching influences on American religion and culture. Others have come to recognize the whole man as a blend of strength and beauty, of strong will and gracious love and kindness.

The mind of Edwards was fashioned by good books, a Christian home, a sound education, and a tradition of godliness. His inborn genius and creative insights gradually unfolded as he matured in his chosen vocation and calling. He saw the world around as created by God and the mind of man as the battleground for ideas seeking mastery. The will of man held in its awesome power of choice the balances of good and evil, life and destiny. Over-arching all was the theological and practical belief that God was sovereign over reasoning man. Although at first he opposed this idea, he later came to see in it the foundation of all that was best for belief in God.

For twenty-four years Edwards was pastor at Northampton, Massachusetts, where he preached to his people the memorable sermons now printed for us to ponder and probe. What kind of preacher was he? How was he influenced by his age? What results came from that kind of Puritan preaching?

The preaching of Edwards was noted for its logical order and its simple and plain style. This was in the best Puritan tradition. The training of the Puritan preacher depended heavily upon those textbooks which laid down the principles of true preaching. As stated previously, the English Bible in the King James Version was a supreme influence on style and ideas. William Perkins' *The Art of Prophesying* was typical of the best texts then used in the schools of theology, in which the principle was laid down that the preacher should saturate himself in Bible knowledge and from that become an expository preacher. Only by giving people the words of the living God would they be able to hear the thunders of Sinai and see the darkened sun of Golgotha.

Like all Puritans, Edwards followed a basic pattern of sermon construction from which he hardly ever varied. The outline was precise and the main points were repeated. Divisions and subdivisions were there as useful tags for later catechizing. Logic structured the whole. Little is used by way of illustration and nothing personal intruded to parade his profound and rich learning. The simple, plain style prevailed. Vision, poetry, symbols, and metaphors were real to Edwards, and he made them alive to his listeners by vivid imagination and a realism transcending the ordinary.

Edwards believed in certain doctrines and preached accordingly. At the same time that John Wesley in England was stressing other doctrines and was engaged in the Evangelical Revival, Edwards in New England preached with zeal and enthusiasm and yet with soberness and passion. He believed profoundly that "the sermon was an agency of conversion" and that he was "a voice from God." The preaching of this practical mystic has not been surpassed as he "sought out acceptable words" by which he prevailed upon people to accept Christ as their Savior and Lord.

Edwards' preaching was affected by his view of the will of man. In his *magnum opus, The Freedom of the Will* (1754), he ponders man's illusion that his will is free. The will of man is governed by the heart, which the Scripture denotes as the seat of man's affections and personality. Because man's heart is depraved, his will is in spiritual bondage. Though the will is otherwise free, it is not free towards God. In this respect it must be made free, and only God can make it free. Yet in this Edwards does not belittle man, rather he exalts the glorious power and splendor of Almighty God. Edwards' sermons reiterate the truth of the depravity of human nature and man's need to cast himself upon the mercy of God.

In his preaching Edwards would distinguish between the natural light of conscience and reason in man and—what is one of his best sermons, printed in 1734—"A Divine and Supernatural Light." The age of the Puritan in New England had known man's attempt to live his life within his own little circle of knowing and doing. This became a world within the world. Self-enclosed and self-defined, it was in danger of shutting out a larger and vaster world. The result was a self-centered existence. Out of that existence came judgment upon everything without, including those who did not share the Puritan concepts of life and faith. Edwards preached a relationship of life within the Covenant of God. In this God has related himself to his people whom he has chosen. They now think with the mind of Christ which has a transforming power over their minds. The natural is superseded by the supernatural. It is enough that man has a nature enabling him to think; it is even more to God's glory that man can think contrary to God's divine ordinances. Thus by his thought man is humbled in order that he may rise again by the power of the gospel.

Another factor in Edwards' preaching is his knowledge of "cases" or the study of spiritual experience. Long before William James of Harvard gave us *The Varieties of Religious Experience* (1902), this

New England pastor had studied and separated the claims of those who professed conversion during the Great Awakening and similar religious revivals. His pinpointing of the genuine and the counterfeit enabled him to publish his fascinating volume titled *A Faithful Narrative of the Surprising Works of God in the Conversion of Many Hundred Souls* (1737), two years after the Great Awakening. This was followed by another book, *Some Thoughts concerning the Present Revival of Religion in New England* (1742). He was interested in searching out the secrets of the mind in the light which the Holy Spirit shed upon the intricacies of the human heart.

The basic aim in his preaching is revealed in these burning words—"I conclude with a use of exhortation to come to Christ." He believed that the passions were the prime movers in life, and, therefore, was not afraid to appeal to those elementary instincts of self-interest and fear. "Take away all love and hatred, all hope and fear, all anger, zeal, and affectionate desire, and the world would be in a great measure motionless and dead; there would be no such thing as activity amongst mankind or any earnest pursuit whatsoever" (*Works III*, pp. 19, 20, on "Religious Affections").

Another of his preaching aims is revealed in his stress on a threefold argument and appeal. Like a refrain we find them repeated in various sermons, though not always in the same words: "The unconverted are in a condition of infinite sinfulness—and therefore deserve infinite punishment which awaits them and from which only the goodness of God has kept them free up to this time." "This punishment is utterly beyond imagination—universal, eternal, intolerable—the most extreme that an infinite God infinitely enraged can invent." "The only hope of escape is by the free gift of salvation from God. This cannot be won by man's efforts, but if one is violent in seeking salvation and diligent in fulfilling all the duties God has prescribed, there is the probability that God will give him saving grace—although, of course, He is not bound to do so. Therefore, be violent for the Kingdom" (*Works III*, p. 245).

Edwards also aimed to awaken the conscience for a verdict. He believed profoundly that the sermon was the agency of conversion. It was not enough to be brought up in the church environment or to be linked with the preceding generation of Puritans. No one in his congregation was to know assurance and peace of mind based on someone else's experience. Edwards' grandfather, **Solomon Stoddard (1643-1729)**, had taught the view that a second generation could attend the communion of the Lord's Supper without professing conversion. He and others allowed that this service could lead to conversion, hence the term of the Half-Way Covenant. Edwards' became Stoddard's associate and successor. This Half-Way Covenant, so common in that day, was finally rejected by him. After much study and reflection he preached the necessity of individual conversion. He stressed that the sinner should "press into the kingdom of God." Since the gospel is related to man's moral nature, Edwards appealed to man's ability to distinguish between right and wrong. He tried to foster a warm and emotional religious experience, a sense of personal and immediate communion with God. This experimentalism was an antidote to the formalism and empty profession then common in the church. In "The Farewell Sermon" Edwards said, "I have not only endeavoured to awaken you, that you might be moved with fear, but I have used my utmost endeavour to win you" (*Works I,* p. 75). Here spoke the heart of the man of God as the under-shepherd of Christ and the flock.

Known as the outstanding sermon of Edwards is "Sinners in the Hands of an Angry God," delivered at Enfield, Connecticut, July 8, 1741. The Great Awakening was at its height, and a revival of some years' duration continued. Although not generally known, this was the second time this sermon was preached. As pastor at Northampton, Edwards had given this sermon to his own congregation but without any marked result in his pastoral ministry. Called upon to take the place of an absent pastor at Enfield, he decided to retouch and rewrite parts of the text. In so doing he stressed the imagery of the insect dangling over fire and so brought home to his hearers the note of fearful judgment in the hands of God. Was this preaching aimed to terrify people? Certainly their understanding of the truth that day caused them to cry out and seek mercy at the hands of God.

The background of the sermon is significant. There was corruption in Boston business and politics. People were members of churches in profession only, without any genuine heart experience of the grace of God. Many concluded they were "Christian" because of the Half-Way Covenant and their traditional heritage through family ties. Edwards had the task of breaking through this crust of indifference and lethargy of spirit. He stabbed the conscience and probed the hidden things of life. Imaginative reason was aflame in the preaching of that sermon, "Their foot shall slide in due time" (Deut. 32:35). Looking into the terrors of hell, people were moved and sought God.

We should know that in the midst of this awesome presentation Edwards stressed the mercy and grace of God as well as the terrors of the law. Since Edwards believed that people were moved by their emotions, the element of fear was used as a prime agent in moving the will of his hearers. In the context of the sovereignty of Almighty God, he lifted men to heights of vision and truth beyond the earthy dimensions of their common life. In that light they saw light. When religion in that era was befouled and morality had slumped, he was the instrument of God to revive the church in New England. While the sinner was portrayed as hanging over the pit of hell, that was not all. The sinner was *in the hands of God,* the hands which also offered mercy and forgiveness, hands wounded on the Cross of Christ.

Judgment of this mighty preacher must weigh the evidence of all his sermons extant in full and in notes. Examination of them shows that while Edwards was the Puritan preacher in the historic tradition, he was effective because the unity of his spirit and work was complete. He was the pastor-preacher and should be so judged. But he was also philosopher, intellectual genius, man of letters, and these encomiums should be seen alongside of his primary vocation. As most Puritans, he engaged in pastoral preaching. From the 1,185 sermon notes and manuscripts found in the special collection at Yale and Andover-Newton, and especially the actual sermons in print, one conclusion is obtained. The sermons of judgment and destiny, the imprecatory, are found to comprise approximately only *10 percent* of the total. Edwards should not be judged, therefore, on the basis of one sermon with this emphasis. Such a judgment is unwarranted and unfair. As theologian he grappled with the great themes, including that of human destiny. As revivalist he offered more than judgment and the nemesis of sin. As pastor-preacher he sought to shepherd his people and provide for them the faithful words of God by preaching (Further details may be found in *Jonathan Edwards the Preacher,* R. G. Turnbull, 1954.).

Modification and Reinterpretation

Charles Chauncy (1705-1787) was an able preacher whose chief distinction lay in his reinterpretation of accepted doctrines. At first

Chauncy followed the main lines of preaching. He wrote to a young man about to begin his career: "Preach much about the misery of the state of nature; the preparatives to conversion; the nature of conversion, or effectual calling; the necessity of union and communion with Christ; the nature of saving and justifying faith, and the fruits thereof—love and good works, and sanctification." He changed his ideas somewhat, however, in the light of the revival movements then emerging.

Though Chauncy originally supported the general idea of revival, he gradually began to be critical of much of the emphasis in revivalist preaching. His main critical attack was against the "enthusiasm" or the sensate basis of religious experience then being claimed. He attacked the revivalists' claims to be neo-prophets and apostles; their erroneous doctrines, emotional outbursts, and censoriousness; their claims of immediate inspiration; and their itinerant preaching. These dangerous tendencies were, in his judgment, the way of disaster for the church.

While Jonathan Edwards recognized the aberrations of the revival, he did not condemn everything in the movement. Chauncy, on the other hand, seeing these aberrations, was ready to condemn the movement. To Edwards the will and emotions were one in action. To Chauncy religious experience had to be based on the intellect to be valid. The preaching of Chauncy and those who were likeminded stressed the primacy of the intellect. Having followed the traditional educational preparation of the New England pastor, he would not give up that worthy foundation for preaching. Certainly the Great Awakening disrupted the normal life of the preacher and his congregation. The style of preaching, even the plain style of the Puritan with its homiletical exactness and its logical steps of close reasoning, no longer was the criterion of judgment and effectiveness. Preaching was now to be judged by the emotional effect it had upon the experience of the hearers.

That Chauncy criticized the ecstatic and emotional preaching now emerging was not surprising. Even Edwards was not wholeheartedly in favor of it at the expense of the intellectual. At that point he was one with Chauncy, but Chauncy was not with him in admitting any emotional element at the expense of the intellect. Chauncy preached, in effect, "Follow your intellect." Edwards said, "Combine intellect with emotion."

Typical of Chauncy's preaching is the sermon "A Caveat against

Enthusiasm" (1742) based on I Corinthians 14:37—"If any man think himself to be a prophet, or spiritual, let him acknowledge that the things that I write unto you are the commandments of the Lord." The style is that of the traditional Puritan—close reasoning, logical acumen, practical application. The outline is clear: (1) Some account of Enthusiasm, in its nature and influence; (2) A rule by which you may judge of persons, whether they are under the influence of Enthusiasm; (3) What may be proper to guard against this unhappy turn of mind. In the usual method Chauncy begins by defining and explaining the meaning of Enthusiasm. Etymology is cited—as signifying *inspiration from God.* Next he points out the bad sense, in which there is "an imaginary or unreal enthusiasm, into which the person mistakes the workings of his own passions for divine communications, when all the while he is under no other influence than that of an over-heated imagination."

Significantly, he sent a copy of this sermon with a cover letter to James Davenport (1717-57) who also was engaged in the controversy about revivalism. Davenport had gone to such an extreme that he was caught up in the movement and could see nothing else. Wild displays of enthusiasm as manifested in imagination-run-riot were in need of correction, according to Chauncy. Unfortunately, Chauncy attacked the whole movement and also Edwards in particular, when he should have distinguished between a man like Davenport, the extremist, and Edwards, the balanced preacher, with his genuine gifts of utterance on the subject. Chauncy and Davenport represented the extremes; Edwards, the moderate intermediary. Chauncy's sermons attacked the excessive emotionalism of Davenport with its derision of education and formal worship in the church. He also was not ready to accept Davenport's use of the lay person in testifying and preaching. (The preaching of Davenport was unlike that of his eminent grandfather, John Davenport, who ministered at New Haven.) James Davenport was influenced in part by George Whitefield and held a pastorate at Southold, Long Island, in 1738. Trumbull's *History of Connecticut* (1818) cites examples of his unbalanced nature in the conduct of services. He seemed to be able to induce people to cry out in hysterics, swoon, or alternately groan or laugh, so that the passions were easily aroused.

Chauncy kept to the well-traveled pathway of Puritan preaching. Learned, intellectual, logical, and systematic, he was unwavering in his exposition of the truth as he knew it. His ability to explain and illustrate the profound truths with simplicity stood in his favor as an acceptable preacher. His sense of the dramatic was noted in the way in which he preached, using statements for effect and for balancing contrast: "God therefore stabs the wicked, as an enemy, with his sword, but lances the godly, as a surgeon his patient, with the lancet."

The same period brought to prominence **Samuel Hopkins (1721-1803)** as a preacher who stood for the "Calvinism" of his teacher and mentor Jonathan Edwards. He proclaimed a "Consistent Calvinism" in a time of controversy with Arminianism. Hopkins and **Joseph Bellamy (1719-1790)** were responsible for the ongoing of Edwards' theology for half a century. In addition to sermons given to defend their theological position, these men preached against slavery. They attempted in their preaching to reconcile sin with the Calvinist view of predestination. With this they sought to blend the new spirit of revivalism, resulting in the development of what is known as "Hopkinsianism," a modified form of Calvinism. Hopkins moved many by his earnest pleas in combining a covenant-pledge membership in the church with the revival plea for conversion and decisive committal on the part of the individual.

Other preachers of this period included **Jonathan Edwards, Jr. (1754-1801)** and **Nathanael Emmons (1745-1840)** who spread transitional theology in a changing age. Such preaching was apologetic, doctrinal, and given with didactic skill and thoroughness.

Chapter IV

Preaching in the United States by Evangelicals (1750-1800)

The watershed in ministerial education is the enlightenment period, or, in America, the Revolutionary time (roughly 1775-1800)—so judge H. Richard Niebuhr and Daniel D. Williams in *The Ministry in Historical Perspectives* (1956). Before that epoch the teaching and training of pastors was left in the hands of individual pastors who took into their homes would-be students for the ministry. Bed and breakfast—in fact complete living accommodations—were provided, usually by the pastor's wife and family, for the youthful aspirant. The daily study and instruction followed according to the experience and accumulated store of the pastor's wisdom. His own example of piety and preaching, his pastoral concern for the people of the parish, and his home life were also part of the training absorbed by the young man.

Log Cabin Education

Because the mainstream of population was still in the East, the preachers and pastors now trained and called settled for the most part in established communities. But the expanding frontier gave to the churches of that day an opportunity to send out missionaries and evangelists who took the Bible and the Christian message to an increasing number of people, both Indian and settler, now finding an America farther west than the eastern seaboard. Each denominational group was forced to begin a college or training center as time went on. Special religious convictions and tenaciously held tenets as befitted the times brought distinct emphases in theology and in the education of the minister.

Yale College had held sway since 1701 and had given to the

church-at-large a steady stream of men for the ministry while not omitting training for other walks of life. Within the period under review another college was to emerge with far-reaching results. This was known as the Log College situated at Neshaminy, north of Philadelphia, Pennsylvania. There in a hamlet with a Presbyterian church began a most significant development in Christian education. Out of this was to grow what was later called Princeton College, Princeton, New Jersey. The Great Awakening in the 1740s brought a stimulus to learning and education. When the emotions were touched by the persuasive preaching of the evangelist, people were also moved to seek further knowledge of the faith which was now the new way of life for them. Young men heard and felt a call to minister to the needs of others. Instead of the earlier training by an individual pastor in his home, the need was now met by training men in colleges.

In this evangelical thrust the Log College emerged as a center of theological learning. Originally, a log cabin adjoining the church was used for ministerial study. This was the humble beginning of a seat of learning! When the first Presbyterian ministers came to this country, they were mostly men of liberal education. They had studied in the universities of Scotland and Ireland. A few later studied in New England centers. And although ministers were scarce in those days, no one thought of anything except an educated ministry in that denomination. George Whitefield records in his *Journal* that he knew of "The College" but it was spoken of in terms of contempt because it was simply a log cabin about twenty feet long and nearly as wide. What was spoken of in derision was the seed-bed of good theological education and a long lasting institution. And in those pioneer days it served as a training center from which men were sent forth into evangelical ministries.

One man responsible for the Log College was **William Tennent** **(1673-1746)**, a Scot brought up in Ireland who, after settling in America, was attracted to the Presbyterian system of government and doctrine. Separating from the Episcopal Church, he was examined and received into the Synod of Philadelphia in 1718. In 1726 he became the pastor at Neshaminy and there was instrumental in the founding of the college. The low state of religion then existing in the colonies was one of the factors which influenced him to seek the help of George Whitefield in preaching and also to assist him in his dream of a college to train others for the Christian ministry. Not much is known concerning the full life and labors of William Tennent, but the tradition has been related that he was a devout man of God who labored zealously for his Lord in the little parish twenty miles north of Philadelphia. He is not known from his sermons or any extant writings. His claim to any distinction lies in his vision of the college.

In Quaker preaching, all that is modern has roots in **John Woolman** (1720-1772), the significant name among the Society of Friends after William Penn. In the latter part of the eighteenth century he traveled throughout the American colonies proclaiming with simplicity and feeling the message of life transformed through the Spirit of God. He was a preacher of spiritual sensitivity who was socially concerned for people. For some thirty years he supported himself by tailoring. Deeply mystical, his *Journal,* (published from 1770 to 1772), and his *Essays* portray the spirit of a man seeking social justice for the poor. Purity of style is characteristic of his teaching and preaching.

The American scene would have been limited without the Episcopal Bishop **Samuel Seabury** (1729-1796). His status as the first Bishop of the Protestant Episcopal Church in America was received when the Scottish bishops at Aberdeen ordained him in 1784. The Church of England at the time of the Revolution in the colonies refused ordination to the American leaders who sought independence from the English body. Seabury was given ordination by the Nonjurer Scots Bishops. A Constitution was drafted and the first General Convention held at Philadelphia (1785). Seabury as leader stood for churchly preaching and orderly worship. His influence set the standards for the newly-organized body.

Great Awakening Preaching

Gilbert Tennent (1703-1764), William Tennent's son, is widely known by his exciting life and labors. As the eldest son he had the advantages of the manse as well as the Log College, though no doubt he had finished his regular education before the college was established. Gilbert was also born in North Ireland and was a boy of about fourteen when his father landed in America. Taught in the manse, he early engaged in the same work as his father. Converted in youth, he soon decided to become a minister of the gospel. The Presbytery of Philadelphia licensed him in 1726, the same year as the founding of the college. He assisted his father in the college and later became pastor in New Brunswick, New Jersey.

With respect to the preaching of Gilbert Tennent, many testimonies have been given concerning its virility and vitality of spirit as well as its intellectual qualities. A clear and persuasive style characterized his delivery. Out of much reading and study he knew the heart of man and was able to expound Biblical truth in a penetrating manner. He was known for awakening the sinful who listened to him. Law and gospel were intertwined so as to produce conviction and a sense of need which would lead to conversion. Whitefield testified to the "searching sermon" he heard by Gilbert Tennent, and how he seemed to preach out of a deep experience of the grace of God in his own life. These two evangelistic preachers joined forces on more than one occasion. Like Paul with Silas and young Timothy, so Whitefield liked Gilbert Tennent as a companion and as a fellow preacher.

Revival was the order of the day and through the Great Awakening thousands of people were brought into the kingdom of God. At the same time church members in their low state of spiritual life were stimulated and revived. The preaching of Gilbert Tennent was used of God to bring this to pass wherever he ministered in the East. But here also emerges one of the many crises in the history of the church.

Within the Presbyterian body Gilbert Tennent found occasion to criticize his fellow clergymen for what he considered to be their barrenness and hypocrisy. History might condemn Tennent for what he said and preached in "the Nottingham sermon." That he claimed to judge his brethren by reading their hearts and motives is a serious claim. But it was in this context that the "new-light" idea of Tennent and his followers was stressed over against the "old-light" of his brethren. The Presbyterian Synod made a judgment contrary to this aspect of Tennent's theology. But the New Brunswick Presbytery, of which Tennent was a member, objected to this judgment of the Synod. A schism followed when the Synod expelled Tennent and his fellow Presbyters.

Looking back across the centuries, we can see how Gilbert Tennent criticized the then "liberal" brethren when he was strongly "evangelical" in theology and preaching. "Liberals" tended to a literary style which depended on manuscript reading, and would criticize the "awakeners" such as Tennent and his school. The evangelical, on the other hand, spoke to congregations in meeting houses or in the open air in the free style of extemporaneous speech. Such men as Whitefield and Tennent touched the emotions and moved the affections. Both spoke out of their own warm spiritual experience. This led Tennent to criticize the cold and impervious utterances of the liberal who, in his mind, was ofttimes unconverted. No doubt because he had had a particular kind of spiritual experience, he felt it was a necessity for all others, especially for those who would preach.

Hence we have the well-known sermon "The Danger of an Unconverted Ministry," based on Mark 6:34—"And Jesus, when he came out, saw much people, and was moved with compassion toward them, because they were as sheep not having a shepherd." Delivered in 1740, Tennent's burning, scorching words and ideas aroused much opposition on the part of the hearers as well as those to whom it was directed. This sermon has been spoken of as "one of the most severely abusive sermons that was ever penned." Printed and published by Benjamin Franklin, it was one of the most widely publicized sermons of the century.

Reading this sermon we are introduced to the kind of evangelical thrust of the period. Tennent's proposition was that "as a faithful ministry is a blessing to the church; so, on the contrary, an ungodly ministry is a curse and judgment: these caterpillars labor to devour every green thing." The printed edition carried on its title page a text from Jeremiah 5:30, 31—"A wonderful and horrible thing is committed in the land; the prophets prophesy falsely, and the priests bear rule by their means; and my people love to have it so: and what will ye do in the end thereof?" When this text is put alongside of the other, the stage is set for a trumpet blast of denunciation in prophetic strain. Some excerpts give a clear idea of what was intended:

> Is a blind man fit to be a guide in a very dangerous way? Is a dead man fit to bring others to life? A mad man fit to give counsel in matter of life and death? . . . Isn't an unconverted minister like a man who would learn others to swim, before he has learned it himself, and so is drowned in the act, and dies like a fool? . . . Now, what savour have Pharisee ministers? In truth, a very stinking one, both in the nostrils of God and good men.

At the very end of the sermon come these words of Paul, "And no marvel; for Satan himself is transformed into an angel of light.

Therefore it is no great thing if his ministers also be transformed as the ministers of righteousness; whose end shall be according to their works" (II Cor. 11:14, 16).

Tennent warned his hearers against the choice of a minister who might be a liar and a hypocrite. His invective and irony were intermingled with a feeling of scorn as he became judge and executioner of all who did not measure up to his interpretation and to his standards for the ministry. His eloquence and influence carried far and the schism which came to the Synod of Philadelphia was caused largely by his words. Reasons for his diatribe included the charge that the preaching of "carnal ministers" was unsuccessful and "with the appearance of uncontentedness under it." When men did not desperately seek decisions they were showing their unconcern, and therefore must be lacking in the essentials.

Like many sermons of that period, there is a prolix choice of words. The torrent which came from his extemporaneous utterances caught the congregation with tremendous force. His strong personality and exuberant spirit made an impact not to be forgotten. Tennent's scathing words made a lasting impression, but the price was the schism among his brethren. He believed he was a prophet of God in his denunciation and exposure of sin. He forgot that he was not the judge of men's hearts in his ignorance of the secrets of the heart. His zeal for a pure and converted ministry lies at the heart of this sermon and much of his preaching. Revival preaching deals with plain and unvarnished issues which are obvious. Theological doctrines were stressed and practical issues debated. When Tennent passed from his more itinerant ministry to become pastor in Philadelphia, he wrote and read his sermons. This altered his preaching style and cramped his vigorous, incisive speech and animated personality.

Samuel Davies (1724-1761) is one of the key figures of colonial America, spending his greatest years in Hanover County, Virginia. During the years 1753-1755, he traveled in Scotland and England on a fund-raising mission in behalf of the trustees of the College of New Jersey (now Princeton University). He also used this trip to ease the pressures on religious nonconformists in Virginia, to raise funds for Indian missions, and to secure books for his work. When Davies was in England, King George II listened to him and in spite of the king's indolent manner he was forced and compelled to give attention by the sheer eloquence and message of the preacher. In

1759 Davies was chosen to succeed Jonathan Edwards as president of Princeton College.

As a preacher he wrote his sermons with care, but in delivering them he was free and eloquent. He said about his own preaching: "Perhaps once in three or four months I preach in some measure as I could wish, that is, I preach as in the sight of God and as if I were to step from the pulpit to the supreme tribunal. I feel my subject. I melt into tears or shudder with horror when I denounce the terrors of the Lord. I glow, I soar in sacred ecstacies when the love of Jesus is my theme. . . ." He would quote Richard Baxter's word: "I preach as if I ne'er should preach again; And as a dying man to dying men."

The sermon "The General Judgment" is from John 5:28, 29—"The hour is coming, in the which all that are in the grave shall hear his voice, and shall come forth; they that have done good, unto the resurrection of life; and they that have done evil, unto the resurrection of damnation." The title of this sermon reminds us that many of the preachers of those days used similar themes. A striking part is the description of the reluctant soul of the wicked, joined "to its body in the day of resurrection, denouncing the body as the cause of its failure in time and its misery in eternity." To read the passage aloud is to sense the tremendous emotional over-tones and the feeling of the "numinous" or the awed spirit of the preacher as he traffics in the theme of divine judgment. He is weighed down by the solemnity of the occasion. His language is that of the rhetorician and yet it is not declaiming for the approval of an audience, but pleading for an eternal response from souls weighed in the balances.

"Ever since sin entered into the world, and death by sin, this earth has been a vast grave-yard, or burying-place, for her children. In every age, and in every country, that sentence has been execut-ing, 'Dust thou art, and unto dust thou shalt return.' The earth has been arched with graves. How numerous are the sons of Adam! . . . Let imagination call up this vast army: children that just light upon our globe, and wing their flight into an unknown world; the gray-headed that have had a long journey through life; the blooming youth, and the middle-aged, let them pass in review before us from all countries and from all ages; and how vast and astonishing the multitude!" In this vein Davies' powerful sermon began. Not an anecdote, not an engaging story to catch attention, but the serious demeanor of a man engaged in a task fraught with destiny. The preacher then could command interest and attention because of the climate of thought and theology, and the realization of the brevity of human life. Mortality accompanied people daily and man's short life span brought home to them the necessity of making their election and calling sure. Famine, pestilence, war and unsettled conditions of life contributed to this state of affairs.

The sermon is logically outlined in four major divisions. The climax is a peroration by an orator whose aim is to arouse the hearers to action and decision. He warns them of impending judgment and pleads with them: "I intreat, I charge, I adjure you to awake out of your security, and improve the precious moments of life. The world is dying all around you. And can you rest easy in such a world, while unprepared for eternity. Awake to righteousness now, at the gentle call of the Gospel, before the last trumpet give you an alarm of another kind."

In Davies was the blend of preacher, poet, and patriot. He became in his day the most eloquent and popular preacher in the American Colonies. Logic and imagination went hand in hand for Davies. His sermons came straight out of the text and were expressed in beauty and grace. He preached in the time when preachers were expected to appeal to men by dwelling upon the great themes of repentance, judgment, and forgiveness. Never physically strong, he battled with ill health. He thus expressed himself: "Finding my self on the borders of the grave and without any hopes of a recovery, I am determined to spend the little remains of an almost exhausted life in endeavoring to advance my Master's story in the good of souls." This is the vibrating power of his sermonic work.

As the poet-preacher, Davies penned the following:

> Almighty Grace, my soul inspire,
> And touch my lips with heav'nly fire!
> Let faith, and love, and zeal arise!
> O teach me that divinest art,
> To reach the conscience, gain the heart,
> And train immortals for the skies!

Before the end of the eighteenth century, nine editions of his sermons had been published. This was remarkable when it is recalled that they were published after his death. His patriotic spirit is well expressed in sermons during the struggle for liberty by the

Colonies. He called for men to stand for freedom, civic and religious. In so doing he did not divorce this from the gospel, but pleaded with men as an ambassador for Christ. If men were free in Christ then they should stand for freedom for all men and in every area of life and in the nation.

In the masterpieces of preaching a high place must be given to Davies. The reports may be exaggerated at times, but the testimony of the records indicates a man whose spirit was irenic, whose voice was pliant, whose imagination painted pictures of truth, whose tones were tender and pleading, and whose appeal was made in the light of eternal realities believed in profoundly. The most moving passages in print are those which deal with the termination of life and all it implies. This is in keeping with the greatest of writers, dramatists, and preachers.

After the Great Awakening with its strong Calvinistic overtones came the Second Awakening with its more democratic stress and Arminian theology. The religion of the "head" was now replaced by that of the "heart." These are general terms of reference as obviously head and heart were intermingled in all the preaching of the times. **Timothy Dwight (1752-1817)** is a luminous example of the changing times and his leadership and preaching guided a new generation. He was born at Northampton, Massachusetts, where Jonathan Edwards had ministered, and it is noteworthy that his mother was a daughter of the famous preacher. Dwight had the advantages of piety and education. In his early studies at Yale he moved from Law to Theology, which act led him later to become a pastor and eventually President of Yale University.

As a preacher he had a fine physical presence which gave him a strong, resonant voice. His sermons were delivered with vigor and his speaking was enriched by a remarkable memory. Some said that he could recall a sufficient portion of any subject studied so that he could speak at a moment's notice with interest and fluency. His delivery was clear and distinct, free of any mannerisms or idiosyncrasy. He had a musical voice, but at times his preaching became monotonous, a reminder that even one with his outstanding gifts can have times of failure. Generally in preaching he rose to heights of eloquence with a steady stream of ideas and words matched in majestic harmony. He was famed for his ability to command attention as he preached extemporaneously.

Dwight appealed especially to the well-educated, attacking the infidelity and skepticism prevalent in intellectual circles. In the leading colleges Deism was an accepted belief and the European philosophy with its man-centered emphasis had encouraged a lack of ethical integrity. Spiritual fervor characteristic of the Great Awakening had declined. The transcendentalism of the new era denied the deity of the Christ, disbelieved the total veracity of the Bible, discounted miracle and prayer, and stimulated a naturalistic religion. By 1800 Yale had only one church member among its graduates. The "age of reason" dismissed divine revelation and the mood then was against any idea of the supernatural.

In this context came the preaching of the President of Yale. Dwight thundered against the naturalism of that day and stood for the orthodox beliefs in a God omnipotent and incarnate. The Second Awakening moved in to change the atmosphere. Here the heart of man was stirred by strong emotion as preachers like Dwight stressed again the need of spiritual and moral renewal. The revival movement touched many colleges and students gathered for prayer and Bible study. Many so moved later became leaders of orthodox Christianity in college and seminary. Archibald Alexander, for example, was converted at Washington and Lee College (Presbyterian) and later became the theologian of Princeton. At Yale Timothy Dwight's preaching and lectures influenced the students to an unusual degree as many were converted and revived in their faith. Among those so moved was young Lyman Beecher, then a student. Later he studied theology under Dwight and so laid the foundation of his enduring ministry. Another outstanding student who had a similar experience was Nathanael Taylor who went on to become a preacher and then Professor of Theology at Yale.

Theodorus Jacobus Frelinghuysen (1691-1747) was born and trained in Holland where he was also ordained to the ministry of the gospel. Coming to New Jersey, he early showed promise as a pioneer among people of his own background who were then settling in that area around New York. His work lay with the Reformed Church, a branch of the Reformation movement which had roots in the Dutch language and culture. The origin of this group lay in the work of Peter Stuyvesant who kept Fort Amsterdam from 1647 onwards as the special preserve of the Dutch in their life and religion.

1720 was the year when Frelinghuysen came to America and

thus was involved like others in the Great Awakening. He, too, was an exhorter, seeking to revive the religiously hardened settlers. Vigorous preaching disturbed the spiritual deadness of conventional church life. In his preaching his piety and warmth of spirit were revealed as he stressed a deepening of spiritual life pleasing to God. He believed that he had found the crux of the matter by insisting upon conversion. This stress of Pietism his critics did not like, but he preached it faithfully with assured results eventually. The fruit of faith must accompany the profession made by the church member, otherwise he questioned the reality of that supposed faith. Members might recite the Catechism or quote from the Bible but holding to the confessional standard of the church was not sufficient. Indeed, this Dutch preacher believed in the confessional church linked with the Synod of Dort, but he also insisted that believers should show spiritual fervor and zeal.

Heinrich Melchior Muhlenberg (1711-1787) was a contemporary of the well-known preachers of the Great Awakening. However, his contribution in preaching has been somewhat overshadowed. A German by birth, he had come to the United States to transplant the Lutheranism of his native land to the new world. Known as a Pietist, he brought from Halle to the Atlantic seaboard a breath of spiritual life in danger of being lost by the early settlers. Others such as Berkenmeyer and Falckner had laid the foundation of the Lutheran work in America and possibly they were noted for preaching superior to that of Muhlenberg. But the latter not only preached; he knew how to organize and how to work with other Christians.

One of the impressions gleaned from this period is the marked impact made upon people by preachers. However, such preachers were generally those who held to strong beliefs and refused to compromise their convictions of faith and duty. Preaching then was not always successful and some preachers failed when this was not the case. While other Lutheran preachers were influential, Muhlenberg, seemingly limited by his preaching, was strong in organizational gifts. He formed the first Lutheran Synod, Philadelphia (1748), and prepared the polity for congregations as well as for ministers in the Synod. His lessened influence through preaching may have been due to the "ecumenical" nature of his fraternizing with those of other denominations. Instead of concentrating upon his own tradition, he spent time preaching and teaching with those of other traditions. In such association he made compromises in doctrine, and thus instead of increasing his power he lessened his influence at large. The lack of the positive teaching of Luther's Catechism and the decline of sermon emphasis on those truths he believed in led to doctrinal indifference.

In **George Whitefield (1714-1770)** there is manifested an unusual type of preacher whose influence has not ceased over the ensuing centuries. Dargan in Volume II of *A History of Preaching* has given him high praise for his gifts and abilities. His work in England has been covered, but only briefly does he find a niche in American preaching. Further studies in his life and labors have brought to light the enormous contribution he made to American culture and social needs. He came to the United States on seven different occasions and in his tours of preaching made an impact few others have made. His itinerary covered largely the Eastern seaboard and notice must be given to his part in the New England revivals and the Great Awakening. That he died in New England in the midst of preaching is a token of the zeal and enthusiasm with which he lived his life:

The preaching of Whitefield in America was characterized by earnestness and sincerity. His voice was large and ample in strength and power. He was heard by Benjamin Franklin, politician; Lord Chesterfield, worldling; David Hume, philosopher and skeptic; David Garrick, actor—all these agreed that the evangelist was the outstanding orator of that period. The printed sermons do not convey the force and magnetism of the spoken word. His preparation and any writing he did were swallowed up in the actual extemporaneous speech of the occasion. Many of his sermons were reported by others and then reproduced. However, such reporting cannot bring back the lightning and the thunder of his speech or the tremendous impact made by a personality caught up in the proclamation of the message.

In estimating the worth of the sermons there is value in rereading them aloud, for in this we catch something of the clarity, the simplicity, the sympathy, and the passionate concern of the evangelist appealing for a decision. In the sermon "The Burning Bush" (Exod. 3:2, 3), the introduction is typical of the times by its allusion to common ideas and its connection with the text of Scripture itself. "It is a common saying, and common sayings are generally founded on matter of fact, that it is always *darkest just before break of day;* and I am persuaded, that if we do justice to our own experience, as well as consider God's dealings with his people in preceding ages, we shall find that *man's extremity has been usually made God's opportunity. . . .*" Here are two common-place sayings which have been handed down orally from one genera-tion to another (and are still being quoted!). Whitefield used them as he was about to quote from the text of the Bible: "The chapter in which is our text, is an instance of this. . . ."

As he moves into the context, there is a graphic description of the life and call of Moses. He tells this as if the people listening knew little or nothing about Moses. He takes nothing for granted. The Biblical background is good and as Whitefield preached to crowds in the open-air this method could be used most effectively. The good-will and feeling he has for his congregation is heightened by a touch of humor when he refers to Moses as a methodical man, and thus while the "name of a Methodist is despised . . . the devo-tion and business of a Methodist go hand in hand: I will assure you Moses was a Methodist, a very fine one, a very strong one too. . . ." The Methodism of Whitefield shines through in playful allusion.

The sermon is well illustrated by allusions to his own experience in his earlier life when he was attacked by those who rejected his message in England, the stoning he underwent, and the strong feeling he knew was there but which was controlled by the grace of God. The subject of the sermon is developed passionately and persuasively to show that like Moses a man can be in a dangerous situation but then it is that God sends deliverance. The Burning Bush becomes the symbol of life's hardships but also the occasion of the glory of God in the midst of enduring faith. "I know," he said, "I had more comfort in Moorfields and especially when the rotten eggs, the cats and dogs were thrown upon me, and my gown was filled with clods of dirt that I could scarce move it: I have had more comfort in this burning bush than when I have been at ease. . . ."

In the 18,000 times of preaching (so estimated) over thirty-four years of ministry, reaching large assemblies of people chiefly out of doors, Whitefield's contribution was most effective. His sonorous and clear voice could be heard about a mile while his extemporane-ous speech caught the minds of the multitude. Evangelical experi-ence of divine grace resulted from this ministry and later there flowed into the social structure the benefits resulting from changed lives. Orphanage, academy, school, college, university—all these benefitted. Preaching in this tradition brought to America stimulus and strength for the cause of evangelism. Whitefield stood out with his histrionic gifts and his voice, which was "like an organ, a flute, a harp, all in one." Lecky, the historian, testified that the preacher moved people by "a large command of vivid, homely, and picturesque English, and an extraordinary measure of the tact which enables a practiced orator to adapt to the character and disposition of his audience."

While Whitefield is reckoned to be one of the greatest of English preachers, ranking with John Wesley in the eighteenth century, his place and prominence in American preaching needs further amplification. Because of the Great Awakening and the revivals of the colonial period, the thrust of the preacher lay in his skill to "awaken" those who hitherto had shown no interest in religion. Following the first settlements and the Puritan instruction in settled congregations, another generation was given to casual contact with the Christian faith. Morale and morals were lowered. With the advent of waves of immigrants the frontier again became the place of evangelism and missionary service. Notable preachers are found in this era and most of these were extemporaneous in speech, not using the formal address or the manuscript of the pastor.

Whitefield was associated with Jonathan Edwards in a close alliance during this time. His visit to Northampton has already been duly noted. The enthusiasm created by the preaching of Whitefield was like a triumphal tour as he moved from place to place. However, this was also a time of bitter controversy with those who opposed extreme forms of evangelism. Charles Chauncy has been mentioned as one who differed in his method and message, and he with others such as Jonathan Mayhew, Timothy Cutler, and Devereaux Jarratt condemned such emotional preaching and those "protracted meetings."

During three decades Whitefield held sway and was supported in this type of preaching by others of varied traditions and backgrounds. The Tennents, Theodorus Jacobus Frelinghuysen, Samuel Blair, and Samuel Davies were among those who were sympathetic to and who shared in this kind of preaching.

New Voices and Ministries

John Witherspoon (1722-1794) was one of the many Scots who came to the new world for religious freedom and also for the opportunity it afforded for the ministry. His life is an example of that American "success" which came to many in the days of the settlement of the new land. His rise to become President of the then Princeton College, New Jersey (1786), and his vigorous leadership of the emerging Presbyterian denomination, as Moderator of the General Assembly of the Presbyterian Church (1789), marked him out as a leader of renown.

His own training in Scotland included the study of rhetoric and letters then counted necessary for the preacher. At Princeton he stressed the rhetorical exercises in dialogues and held prize contests in reading English, reading and speaking Latin, and "pronouncing English orations." He himself taught the art of public speaking in the college. His own custom in preaching was to memorize the sermon before delivery. His voice as reported was not clear and strong, so he could be heard only with difficulty in church or lecture hall.

Although he was known as a Presbyterian pastor and then as an educator, Witherspoon may best be remembered for his political involvement. There have always been those who have kept out of politics. Pastors of congregations have often been warned to stick to their own last! The time of Witherspoon brought an opportunity to the Christian preacher to speak out when political controversy had strains of moral urgency in it. He became a delegate to the Continental Congress (1776), and having participated in debate he finally signed *The Declaration of Independence,* the only clergyman's signature upon that historic document.

If little is known of Witherspoon's regular sermons, we may deduce from his political presentations in the legislature that he was capable of emotional appeal, fiery invective, or even elegant delivery. When agitation against British policies was at its height, the preacher-educator did not trail Patrick Henry in being carried away with warmth and fiery utterance, but he also spewed out "a copious stream of irony and sarcasm, bitter name calling, and abuse, hotly denounced Tory officials and raised the cry that liberty was endangered by tyranny." One report has it that in the Congress much speaking was off-the-cuff and extemporaneous, but Witherspoon was one who ordinarily wrote out and read his speech.

All of this throws light upon the preaching of Witherspoon. From his involvement in the Congress and his teaching at Princeton College, we gain knowledge of the method and scope of his preaching. Witherspoon taught elocution or public speaking and his lectures were given during the period of 1758-1794. They were gathered after his death and published. He maintained that the orator—the preacher—was made, not born, and that the best method of training was wise study coupled with intimate knowledge of great models. His teaching of rhetoric was in the classical tradition. Witherspoon's teaching is a surprising thing—for at a time when the preacher was considered to be a man "born" to the task and not "made," Witherspoon went against all tradition in teaching the opposite! Certainly a man should have been "called of God" if he were to be "made" or trained by the discipline of the schools.

Preaching in the day of the ordeal of revolution and independence called forth strong reactions and much heart-searching. Protestant pastors especially were involved in the destiny of the nation and were vocal about the issues then emerging. During the latter part of the eighteenth century, the leading preachers could not escape some mention of moral issues then impinging upon the decisions and policies of the leaders of the nation. The Declaration of Independence, the Constitution of the United States, and the Bill of Rights were documents not far removed from the one book which guided the religious life of church people and citizens—the Bible.

The Founding Fathers were not motivated solely by economic, political, or military necessities in their stand for freedom and the formation of a new nation. They also respected the tradition of religious freedom, and liberty for all was conceived from the matrix of that Puritan and Pilgrim "errand into the wilderness." The clergyman-preacher instructed his congregation in moral standards that shape the whole of life. Education, college, school—these were words which spoke of a heritage of religious convictions with various strands and traditions. Even though many leaders of the emerging nation were not committed to the Christian way of life, they were quick to recognize the influence upon their heritage which was represented by those religious men who also were patriots and leaders of a new nation. Protestant Christian and Enlightenment ideals merged in shaping the new ideas for government. A new nation might conceivably be likened to the old nation of Israel, and the Bible was never far away in influencing these men of destiny. A covenant idea was pervasive.

The preaching then of this period stressed the nation's place of privilege and responsibility in history. Since that hour the ideal has never been forgotten, although the nation may have failed to implement the idea from time to time. The dream of a new nation to expand from ocean to ocean was redolent with light and meaning as pulpits reminded people that God had made his covenant for a destiny yet to be worked out in honor and in peace. "The clergy saw God as the active agent of history and America as God's eighteenth century Israel, an empire-servant to bless all mankind" (James H. Smylie, *The Princeton Seminary Bulletin,* April, 1962).

From the sermons and publications of Jonathan Edwards to the teaching and politicking of John Witherspoon, an eschatological foundation of hope had been laid for the future. Providence had placed the new nation in a strategic place, and the ministry of the church should proclaim the new day and the new order for all who cared to avail themselves of the privileged life. The subjects of "freedom," "voting," "rights," "authority," "destiny," and others were constantly emerging in the Biblical contexts of sermons. In the light of the national and political crises through which men were passing, what should be more natural than that the preacher should relate themes with national-political overtones to a religious calling? The citizen was reminded in many a sermon that if he had any religious conviction he should also be part of the nation's destiny by his sharing in the convulsions of that hour. Thus the authority of God was accepted as being over all other authorities.

If in preaching the pastor believed and taught that "righteousness exalted a nation while sin was a reproach to any people," then it was inevitable that politics would become a moral obligation and religion have political overtones. If the centuries since have shown an imbalance from time to time in the self-righteous confidence which so easily besets a nation, we must also remember that the influence upon the nation through preaching has been for a moral sensitivity in government and for an awareness that there are checks and balances provided within the nation when professing Christian and non-Christian intermingle in the social and political scene. What has been established over the centuries is the fact that the pulpit in America has been one of the most important channels of influence for good upon American culture.

Francis Asbury (1745-1816) has a unique place in Methodism and in the development of the Christian Church in America. An Englishman sent by John Wesley to continue and advance the evangelistic cause begun by Wesley, he was appointed Superintendent by Wesley in 1772, a year after his arrival. His ministry was a saga of travel and itineration. By horseback he traveled 300,000 miles, preached some 16,500 sermons, organized churches, appointed hundreds of preachers, and saw the Methodist Church increase to become one of the strongest churches in America.

As a man, Asbury knew the early rigors of the frontier and gave himself to the self-discipline of daily prayer and ministry. He was the itinerant Methodist and, like his distinguished friend John Wesley, kept a *Journal* with a daily entry of his labors. Wherever people met he would preach and that several times a day. In the home, in the schoolhouse, in an open air gathering, and also in the meeting houses gradually being erected across the country—no opportunity was lost to spread the good news.

It is interesting that amid the seeming success of those pioneer days, Asbury confessed that he had his moments of despair and defeat: "Losing some of my ideas in preaching," he wrote in the *Journal,* "I was ashamed of myself, and pained to see the people waiting to hear what the blunderer had to say. May these things humble me, and show me where my strength lieth!" He was known for his simple and clear presentation of the sermon. Certainly the simple outline preserved on the subject "Lord, are there few that be saved?" is a sampling: (1) What we are saved from; (2) How we are saved; (3) Why there are few saved.

The early Methodism which spread the gospel to every succeeding frontier of America owed much to **Thomas Coke (1747-1814)**, a contemporary of Francis Asbury. Coke also ministered in the West Indies, but his association with Asbury is significant in that together they formulated the Doctrines and Discipline of the Methodist Church in America. As a preacher he was known as an attractive speaker. Small of stature like John Wesley, he had, unlike Wesley, a high-pitched, almost boyish, voice. His Welsh background gave him eloquence of utterance while his rapid speech led him into torrents of words which often overdid what he sought to communicate. The people of the expanding frontier were not well-versed in his peculiar idioms; nevertheless, he had constant effectiveness in preaching to the new Americans. His zeal in evangelism and in preaching could not be denied.

Coke's preaching should be estimated alongside of the social and moral conditions then prevalent. The moral state of the Revolutionary period (1776-1800) was one that concerned even the Continental Congress. Among the laws enacted by the Congress was one on morality. In the original and revised Articles of War adopted then, the mention of punishment for swearing or blasphemy in the use of the name of God is recorded. The twenty years following the Declaration of Independence were years in which morals were at a low ebb. In biographies, newspapers, and records of church bodies, reference is made to "the lamentable decay of vital piety," "the gross immoralities," "the degeneracy of manners," and "the prevalence of vice." A cause of such lowered morals would be the War itself with the breakup of homes and the scattering of families, even as the loss of parental discipline, loose morals and manners, and an excess of drinking, had broken down earlier Puritan discipline. As Asbury, so Coke in preaching touched on these aspects of life, and did not hesitate to preach against indulgence in liquor. Intemperance, infidelity, indulgence—these were associated with drunkenness, gambling, lotteries, horse racing, profaneness, luxury, injustice, lewdness, and debauchery. The Sunday laws also were broken, and business and amusements flourished in spite of the "blue laws" of the period.

Since these practices became increasingly commonplace, every church group was affected. However, in Methodism, thanks to Asbury and especially Coke the church took its stand against certain evils. For example, slavery was not acceptable according to the teaching and discipline of the church. If a person had slaves when he became a member or inherited them later, he had to arrange within a certain time to free them. If he sold the slave within a specified time, he had to specify the future date at which the slave had to be set free. The strong *Discipline* which was developed by Coke and others indicated how seriously they took their task of leadership in the light of John Wesley's concept of how Christians and church members should "walk" in life. Trials within congregations were not unusual, and many members were disciplined for their disorderly conduct.

The preaching then of the Methodist missionary and evangelist was colorful in its denunciation of the sins and low morals of the times. A note of judgment entered into the sermons but always with the appeal to repent and turn back again to the disciplined standards of John Wesley, the interpreter of the New Testament concept of how Christians *ought to walk in newness of life,* even a life of holiness. Coke's preaching spread this doctrine and inculcated these ideals.

PART THREE

The
Nineteenth
Century

This period is marked by trends away from the older, established heritage of preaching and belief. The erosion of belief did not make its full impact in the first half of the century. The carry-over from the eighteenth century with its Puritan and Evangelical emphases continued for about fifty years. Strong pulpit voices were still heard, the clear trumpet call of the apostolic message was still heard throughout these United States, but other sounds began to be heard which muted and subdued the earlier music and harmony of the gospel.

Among the disturbing elements of change are those following in the aftermath of the Great Awakening. Every movement has its rise and progress followed by periods of decline. There is an ebb and flow which must be recognized. The benefits of the movement under consideration were many. One was the stress on gospel preaching. Everywhere this was characteristic of the men of that day. The tradition of the Puritan and the stimulus of the evangelical movements in revival were still felt across the fast-growing nation. From the Eastern seaboard missionaries and evangelists moved ever westward in the wake of the new settlers and the immigrants now seeking a new home. "Errand in the wilderness" was taking on a new format and the sound of the coming millions tramping across the plains inspired the Christian church to meet the spiritual and moral needs of people. Those who responded to this service were preachers who, with zeal and passion, carried out the Great Commission to proclaim the gospel to every creature (Matt. 28:19, 20).

The advance to the frontier caused the increase of denominations. Each church group took with it the emphasis for which it had been raised up. Personalities led in this movement. Those with the gifts of leadership were not lacking in followers. Revival meetings and camp meetings met social as well as religious needs. People were thrown together in the trek to the frontier, and thus new communities sprang up and the demand for pastors and preachers increased.

The dream of an America coexistent with the Biblical ideas of millennium and kingdom was not alien to those early pioneers of faith. By faith they labored and lived and died in the hope of widespread advance of the truth in the new nation. Evangelicalism also taught an ethical and moral standard in keeping with the doctrine proclaimed. Regeneration implied a new way of life thereafter. The vision of communities governed by the ideals of the kingdom of God was never obliterated. A solidarity of life and environment was expected out of the evangelism then practiced. While this was achieved in part, there was the other disappointing side of feuding and division when leaders did not agree. The proliferation of denominations and differences in belief was inevitable. The seeming competition gave to each group the right of freedom and the liberty of conscience. Out of this dream and thrust came the vision of a nation "under God" and a people set apart for a better life.

The aftermath of religious revival brought changes both in the congregations and in the cities. Church statistics point to increased memberships and large congregations. In the post-Awakening period vast changes began to take place. The earlier enthusiasm waned and the idea of liberty and freedom was wrought out in deeds which advocated a unity in the midst of diversity of operation. While it appears to the historian that there seemed to be competition, among the religious leaders there was an understanding that while each group went its own way, they were united in the faith.

Chapter V

Preaching in the United States by Evangelicals (1800-1900)

This period marked the rise of prominent men who received nationwide publicity in their ministries. The growth and development of associations of Christians for united effort brought distinction to otherwise unknown men. Ecumenicity became a reality among evangelical people whose convictions were based upon a belief in the veracity of the Bible and whose thrust in evangelism brought them together for united service. Movements of union and unity were commonplace. The founding of the YMCA under George Williams in England led to its counterpart in America. One of the sponsors and leaders was the evangelist Dwight L. Moody. His untiring efforts to secure money were crowned with success as he with other laymen inspired the movement in our larger cities. The YMCA at that time was known for its evangelical witness and as an instrument to win young men for the kingdom of God. Christians of all denominations supported it and worked in and through its facilities.

The American Sunday School Union, the American Tract Society, the American Bible Society are other examples of the cooperation then achieved among Christians. These and many other agencies became the means of influencing the nation morally and spiritually. The missionary agencies for work overseas, such as the American Board of Commissioners for Foreign Missions (1810), and church denominational missionary societies, gave impetus to this united thrust and involvement. City missions as well as "foreign missions" became the hall mark of evangelical witness wherever poverty and need existed.

Charles I. Foster, in *An Errand of Mercy, The Evangelical Front, 1790-1837* (published in 1960), has documented this period of expansion. He lists 158 agencies and societies actively involved in evangelism and the moral and social redemption of society. These agencies were free from denominational control but were operated by Christians of all denominations working unitedly. Slavery was eventually seen to be wrong in the sight of God and the way was opened for dynamic change. However, this was not accomplished without Civil War and the disruption of the nation in its political affiliations and also in its religious prejudices. Denominations were divided as North and South engaged in the struggle. Only a chastened nation could look back and reflect upon what might have been.

Another aspect of this period was a decline in the fervor for spiritual life. During 1845-1855 the passions and actions of multitudes were engaged in controversy and strife, both political and religious. A climbing population and a measure of prosperity brought attendant evils. Across the land there was a wistful yearning for better days in religion. Suddenly the movement of the divine Spirit became obvious. About 1857 the Second Awakening in American life had begun, based not on preaching but on prayer. Prayer meetings and groups sprang up everywhere. Prominent among these were the daily theatre gatherings in New York and later in the well-known Fulton Street prayer meeting. As thousands gathered to pray and to seek God, tens of thousands were turned to God and united with the churches. Anywhere up to one million people is the estimate made of the ingathering.

All of this was to affect preaching. In the intellectual life of the expanding nation it has been estimated that out of one hundred eighty denominational colleges in existence in 1860, four-fifths were founded and maintained by those churches which gloried in evangelical conviction (cf. K. S. Latourette, *A History of the Expansion of Christianity*, vol. IV, p. 221).

Revival Preaching

A lawyer by profession, **Charles Grandison Finney (1792-1875)** was outstanding as a preacher. After his conversion he soon sought to persuade others to the Christian faith. His earlier studies in law became the practical preparation for his eventual ministry. Unlike others who were trained in a theological seminary, Finney built upon his legal training and his natural ability as he pleaded with men. Through the study of law he became interested in the Bible (with its revelation of divine law) and was led to seek a deeper knowledge of the Scriptures.

Whenever he engaged in study of the Bible, his legalistic mind would not take for granted anything said by the preachers he heard. After he became accepted as a preacher, he spent time as pastor of a Presbyterian Church and then associated himself with the Broadway Congregational Church, New York. This latter gave him more freedom for ministry. Later he was invited to assume the Chair of Theology at Oberlin College, Ohio, and finally became the President of that institution. All this for a man who had no formal theological training! However, during the years of his early ministry he acquired some knowledge of Latin, Greek, and Hebrew, although he confessed he was not a classical scholar.

His theological stand was that of a Calvinist at first, but he modified this to preach a gospel of "free and full salvation." He fell into the inconsistency of clinging to Calvinist terminology while at the same time discarding the meaning of certain terms. He preached a general atonement but still held to the doctrine of election. Finney taught that foreknowledge and election are not inconsistent with free agency, but are founded upon it—"The elect were chosen to eternal life, because God foresaw that in the perfect exercise of their freedom they could be induced to repent and embrace the gospel." Thus in his view the elect were not elect because they were better by nature than others, or because Christ paid their ransom solely. The elect were those who would be converted with God's foreknowledge in order to bring about the wisest administration of his moral government. Brushing aside certain apparent inconsistencies, Finney preached to sinners that their salvation was suspended on their choice. This was the mind of the evangelist over against the theologian. No doubt he felt more at home in the pulpit than in the classroom. He had a power in preaching which was somewhat diminished in the study when he came to work over his *Lectures on Systematic Theology*. But even these had been hammered out on the anvil of revival preaching.

Although he did the work of an evangelist, he is best known as a revivalist. Evangelism is the appeal to people outside the formal life of the church, while revival is the appeal to people within the church. There is some overlapping no doubt, but generally the thrust of Finney's ministry stirred up the professing Christian who had become lax and lukewarm in faith and practice. His belief was that once a Christian was revived by the Spirit of God, a concern for the outsider would follow.

Once a client came to Finney soon after he had begun his new vocation and asked if he was ready with the case. Finney replied: "I have a retainer from the Lord Jesus Christ to plead his cause and I cannot plead yours." Thus he left the law for the gospel, but he did not leave behind his legal acumen and skill. This was used for the work of preaching. His language was brief and simple so that people would understand easily. His legal mind led him to believe that results would follow his presentation of the claims of Christ. He pleaded and persuaded as a lawyer expecting a verdict from his hearers. He said, "More or less convictions occurred under every sermon that I preached." "The sword of the Lord slew them on the right hand and on the left."

The people of that period were not accustomed to hearing a preacher like Finney. The lawyer-preacher-evangelist presented the truth in such a manner that people were not left unmoved. Careful reasoning, discussing the case as in a legal brief, was the foundation of his appeal. He believed that no one should be moved in spirit until the mind had accepted the truth as reasonable and convincing. His argument respected principles and facts. They were the basis of exposition. He was not abstract but concrete, specific in dealing with sin. In one sermon preached late in his ministry and then at Oberlin he referred to the gardening and farming tools he wished to use, but went on to point out that "brother Morgan and brother Mahan had borrowed his plow and harrow and another had taken his hoe and spade." He went on to apply this in public. "How can society exist when such a simple duty as that of returning borrowed tools ceases to rest as a burden on the conscience?" "It is in such delinquencies as these that the real state of our hearts is brought to the light of day."

A sermon like the above which pricks the conscience is likely to bring home to many the sinfulness of sin. Finney preached to the conscience. Motive and attitude, action and deed were unveiled. In a day when men liked to discuss the finer points of doctrine and weave the tapestry of subtle threads of argument, Finney cut through the pretense and facade behind which men hid from God. He penetrated the inner life and spoke to the conscience. Because he believed that the gospel has a direct relationship to the moral nature of man, he appealed directly to the moral nature of his hearers. Doctrine and duty were intertwined.

Finney wrote much and what he said was reported so that several volumes bear evidence of his beliefs. "If sinners are to be regenerated by the influence of truth, argument, and persuasion, then ministers can see what they have to do, and how it is they are to be workers together with God. So also sinners may see that they are not to wait for a physical regeneration or influence, but must submit to and embrace the truth, if they ever expect to be saved. Ministers should aim at and expect the regeneration of sinners on the spot, and before they leave the house of God."

In his preaching we have statements which are direct and penetrating: "The Holy Spirit was upon me, and I felt confident that when the time came for action *I should know what to preach.* . . . The Spirit of God came upon me with such power, that it was like opening a battery upon them. For more than an hour, the Word of God came through me to them in a manner that I could see was carrying all before it." In saying this he is revealing that when he did preach he was incisive and earnest. Nothing cold or casual was found in Finney's sermons. Even to read them now, aloud, is to feel the surge of deep emotion.

In the sermon on "Prevailing Prayer" from the text, "The effectual fervent prayer of a righteous man availeth much" (James 5:16), Finney spoke of the two means requisite to promote a revival: one is to influence men, the other to influence God. "The truth is employed to influence men, and prayer to move God." In sequence of exposition we have these words: "Effectual, prevailing prayer does not consist in benevolent desires merely. . . . Effectual prayer is that prayer which obtains the blessing it seeks. . . . One must pray for a definite object. . . . It must be in accordance with the revealed will of God. You must pray with submission to the will of God. . . . It must be by the intercession of the Spirit. . . . It must be persevering prayer. . . . It must be offered in the name of Christ. . . . You cannot prevail in prayer without renouncing all your sins. . . . You must pray in faith." Prayer was much spoken of by Finney, and when he visited Glasgow, Scotland, in 1859, this was his theme as he related the revival experience through which he had passed.

Another sermon, on "Stewardship," illustrates the same logical procedure of outline and development. "Give an account of thy stewardship" (Luke 16:2) was the text. His thesis was that all men are God's stewards and must give account. This then refers to (1) Time; (2) Talents; (3) the Influence he exerts; (4) the Property in his possession; (5) your Soul; (6) the Souls of Others; (7) the Sentiments you entertain and propagate; (8) your Opportunities of doing good. This comprised half of the sermon; then came the "Remarks" for the rest of the sermon with some ten points which were emphasized before the final exhortation and appeal for a verdict.

It is not to be thought that Finney dwelt only on themes of revival and prayer. His preaching struck a blow against slavery and intemperance. His voice was raised decisively against vested interests and the social results of wrong-doing.

In his published works the spirit of the preacher comes through. His *Autobiography* is self-revealing in its honesty and singleness of purpose. His *Lectures on Revivals of Religion* are a separate volume from his *Revival Lectures*, and his *Lectures to Professing Christians* are to be distinguished from his *Sermons on Gospel Themes*. While there is some overlapping of subject and exposition, the books reflect the keen analytical mind of the lawyer turned evangelist, the advocate become preacher. Finney cannot be dismissed as a "ranter" or a "fanatic." His ministry illustrates how God takes the mighty intellect, the nimble mind, and the disciplined will to make an instrument efficient to move multitudes in the valley of decision.

Archibald Alexander (1772-1851) was a noted preacher of this time. In 1821 a new seminary was established at Princeton, New Jersey, under the aegis of the Presbyterian Church. As Professor in Theology and as President of this institution he made a lasting contribution to preaching.

Alexander had his idiosyncrasies of dress, deportment, and manner. Although not an attractive man to others in public, when he preached he became a man gripped with a message which needed proclamation. Back of his preaching strength lay the fact that he had memorized large portions of the Bible and from time to time he would quote and recite from the text of Scripture. This had a telling effect upon people. Also true of his classroom teaching was that he used Scripture and would expound a passage in the midst of the theology lecture.

His preaching style was not that of the rhetorician and rarely was he eloquent. He was himself in the pulpit, without any airs, and endeavored to be as natural as possible. Exposition of the text or passage was given priority in his preaching, believing as he did that the actual Word of Scripture had in it profound power and meaning which could stab the conscience and appeal to the minds of the hearers. Solemn warning and vivid compassionate appeal varied his approach and application of truth. He used notes in the pulpit, and his conversational tone added much to the warmth of response. His preaching was didactic and illuminating rather than hortatory. Throughout he was the evangelical.

Frontier and Camp Meeting

The first half of this century was characterized for the most part by evangelical preaching. The liberal strain had begun but had not yet received publicity and widespread influence. Naturally, every period is not always well defined and there is considerable overlapping in personalities and dates. Nevertheless, there is a well-defined pattern which is suggestive to follow.

Prominent in this transition from the eighteenth to the nineteenth century were Peter Cartwright and Matthew Simpson.

Peter Cartwright (1785-1872) is the one prominent Methodist whose evangelistic zeal carried him to the frontier as a missionary-preacher in revival camp meetings. An exhorter in the Methodist Episcopal Church, he was ordained a traveling preacher by Bishop Asbury. Cartwright, a man in the Wesley tradition, had dramatic gifts of oratory. It is estimated that he preached some 15,000 sermons in the course of his itinerant ministry! Surely another John Wesley. Like his illustrious predecessor in England, he traveled thousands of miles on foot and on horseback. In addition to his ministry, he served the Legislature of the State of Illinois, and was a candidate for the United States Congress in 1846. He was defeated at that time by no less than Abraham Lincoln.

Of Cartwright's preaching many stories have been told as he was probably the best known of the circuit riders. Throughout the heartland of America he made his way with the fiery message of repentance and revival. And the need was there. Religious life was at a low ebb, and rationalism was rampant. The legislature of the State of Kentucky had abolished prayer to Almighty God. Ministers were content with a show of things but lacked the power and passion needed for the challenge of the hour.

Itinerant, revival preaching was steeped in Biblical allusion and story. Pungent wit and arousing words were poured out in vehement oratory. The nightly meetings of the camps drew people from a wide area. Cartwright stayed in a community as long as there was a response. Large gatherings of people for protracted meetings were commonplace in that period.

His first sermon was from the text, "Trust ye in the Lord for ever: for in the Lord Jehovah is everlasting strength" (Isa. 26:4).

Much stress was placed on the evils of slavery as his preaching pointed out:

> Slavery is certainly a domestic, political, and moral evil. Go into a slave community, and you not only see the dreadful evils growing out of the system in the almost universal licentiousness which prevails among the slaves themselves, but their young masters are often tempted and seduced from the paths of virtue. . . . Let any one travel through slave states and see the thousands of mixed blood, and then say that I have misrepresented the dreadful causes of domestic disquietude that often falls with mountain weight on honorable wives and mothers.

Cartwright was against slavery but he was not in favor of the Abolitionists. He was a convinced believer in moral persuasion as a method of solution and saw plainly the tragedy of the Civil War and the disruption of the Union.

Some of his sermons denounce the evils of liquor. In a message delivered in the open, near a spring, the evangelist was able to point to the gushing water and use this in illustration:

> There, . . . there is the liquor which God the Eternal brews for all His children. Not in the simmering still over the smoky fires choked with poisonous gases, surrounded with stench of sickening odors and corruptions, does your Father in heaven prepare the precious essence of life—pure cold water; but in the green glade and grassy dell, where the red deer wanders and the child loves to play, there God brews it. . . .
>
> And everywhere it is a thing of life and beauty—gleaming in the dewdrop; singing in the summer rain; shining in the ice-gem. . . .
>
> Still it is beautiful, that blessed life-water!

This is the thought-form and the plenteous speech of the frontier preacher as he talked of the liquor God promised as opposed to the demon's drink, alcohol.

Cartwright's preaching was that of the enthused exhorter who lacked much education but who made the most of a limited schooling. That he did well with his endowment is obvious. He had a poor view of education for ministers and so stated his convictions in a time when Methodism was seeking to advance and improve the men who felt called to the ministry. Later on Bishop Matthew Simpson extended the requirements for ministerial preparation, but in this day he had to allow for men of Cartwright's caliber. People then were not educated except on an elementary level of knowledge. Cartwright thought that this gave him the opportunity to reach them where they were, since his own level of knowledge matched theirs. However, it is evident that even then the Methodist evangelist learned much from experience and self-help if not from book learning. Nature without and human nature within were twin teachers of Cartwright, who with the Bible as guide and text was able to proclaim the word of the Lord effectively and with passion.

Social-Political Preaching

Matthew Simpson (1811-1884) stands out as a strong advocate of the application of the gospel to the whole of life. He is remembered as a key leader in Methodism and as an outstanding orator. His glowing rhetoric moved multitudes. His mighty declamations against slavery were successful in changing the mind of his generation. His personal friendship with President Abraham Lincoln and other members of the Cabinet opened doors of service in the cause of the emancipation of the slaves. He pastored various congregations, taught in a college, edited the *Western Christian Advocate,* and as a Methodist Bishop exercised his position of leadership for high moral ends. He was a preaching bishop. Nothing gave him greater pleasure than this recognition.

Simpson knew his power as a preacher and sensed the responsibility. The opportunity to preach he always accepted with joy and eagerness. In contrast to Peter Cartwright, Simpson was not the eccentric or the enthusiast-exhorter. He was the educated, polished, and influential personality of his church. Trained in medicine, he gave this up in favor of the religious life of the preacher. He was steeped in the classics, in science, in the Bible and John Wesley. He believed in an educated ministry. Eloquence was his secret and strength, seen not merely in his speeches but in his overall confidence and enthusiasm for the ends in view. His early preaching dealt with texts which were imperatives. He sought and expected conversion. "He that is not with me is against me: and he that gathereth not with me scattereth."

At the beginning Simpson moved around the midwest as any other saddle-bag preacher. He learned the art of extemporaneous speech in facing all kinds of groups and congregations in diversified places. He preached much the same sermons over and over again, but he enlarged and polished as he progressed. "It is very seldom that a sermon can be very ably wrought out by the first effort of either speaker or writer." Thus he told the students in the *Yale Lectures* which he gave under the general title of *Lectures on Preaching* (1879). In these he dealt with the general field of the pastor's life and work, referring to his own ideals, methods, and practices as a preacher. He was never a systematic sermonizer, so he said. "No one told me how to make a sermon. I had listened to good preachers, but the only sermons I had ever read were those of Mr. Wesley."

Although Simpson shared his inner struggle with the students, it is not to be inferred that he told them to copy him. He warned them against adopting his methods, except that they should read and study all they could to *prepare themselves*. This, to Simpson, was most important—the preparation of the preacher by prayer, meditation, study, and above all, a desire to reach people with the love of God in Christ. With that a man could stand up and let himself go in his utterance as he sought to persuade others for the kingdom's sake. "I would not advise any young man to do as I have done. I would breathe into you, if I could, the earnestness and love of souls and the devotion of my earlier ministry; but I would urge you to make a better preparation, and to become workmen more approved both of God and man."

The sermons of Simpson were no closet sermons. Although most of his messages were never written out, they were published later as recorded by listeners. A wise reporter of the Methodist journal has preserved samplings for us. They show the extemporaneous style and the ready thought of the one preaching. Fresh and vigorous, they are natural yet intense. The themes of the sermons extant revolve around the chief doctrines of Christ's gospel. Eternity and time, God and man, sin and holiness, heaven and hell—these are the regular notes sounded. The content is Biblical, yet its appeal is to the emotion of people. He sought to move the hearer to action through his affections as the primary avenue of response.

The sermon "Living for Christ" is based on Philippians 1:21,

"For to me to live is Christ, and to die is gain." No anecdote or contemporary story introduces the theme. He begins by assuming that his listeners will respond to the Pauline life and experience implied in the text. The proposition is that the Christian life is simply the same as Paul outlined it—living for Christ. This is the maxim and standard. Illustrations are few, as the whole of the preacher's mind is saturated with the subject. He iterates and reiterates the subject as in a refrain. A final appeal is made for decision and commitment. Although the sermon is organized after a fashion, there is little of homiletical clarity. The points made show no relatedness except that each point undergirds the theme.

The well-known gospel text of Romans 1:16 deals with "The Gospel the Power of God." Again, Simpson plunges in without introduction. He is at Rome as Paul was and we are being confronted with the demands of the gospel at once. In contrast to the power of Rome, divine power is superior. "Possibly the inquiry may arise in some minds, if the gospel be a system of power, the power of God, wherein does this power reside? I answer, in the first place, the power of the gospel resides partly in the thoughts of the gospel." Examples of power are given—in nature, in battle, in the clash of minds—and then divine power is explained as more effective. "All power resides in thought. . . ." The thought of the gospel embraces the most potent dynamic in the world. His closing appeal is to "avail yourselves of this mighty power of the gospel." Thus the preacher concludes at the height of oratory with passionate appeal.

These are not written messages, but are the outpouring of a well-stored mind, suffused with divine enthusiasm and passion. The language is born of conviction, without any reservation, as personal faith bears witness to the mighty acts of God in Christ.

The complement to these gospel sermons is found in the full-orbed preaching and lecturing of Simpson when he dealt with social and political problems. The gospel provided him with insights to interpret the will of God for his time. Nationally he became known through his friendship with President Lincoln as a strong supporter of all that made for human improvement and social stability. The slavery issue was crucial. Americanism, or patriotism as a way of life, was part of his message for he saw this nation under God as a favored people, not unlike Israel in the Old Testament. Chosen of God, Americans were a people of destiny. Sometimes, however, the American way of life seemed to be equated with Christianity.

As a lecturer, Matthew Simpson gave utterance to deep-seated convictions which came out of Biblical belief and constant preaching. His lectures were an extension of his sermons in another context. "Instead of serving, obeying, and honoring God, and holding the world as a gift from God, man looked to other powers." Because of the sin and fall of man, man was no longer able or fit to rule the earth, and chaos came. Nevertheless, God had a plan to renew this world by the coming of Christ; and eventually something of that renewal would be achieved through this nation. The optimism of Simpson can be seen in his view of a nation becoming more Christian, and a people more obedient to divine laws. Economic advance, national weal, government betterment, prosperity—these proclaimed the blessing of God upon this chosen nation. As a missionary medium, America could fulfill the divine plan.

Simpson advocated the mission of America in no uncertain terms. The message of Christianity through Methodism's brightest mind and speaker identified itself with the destiny of America. Certainly the fiery orator had the ear of a willing people! America could become the example of what God would do with a nation obedient to his will. Preaching has ever reckoned with this emphasis from time to time in the annals of the United States.

Pastoral-Scholarly Preaching

Charles Hodge (1797-1878) was an eminent figure in the Princeton tradition of theology and of preaching. Like Archibald Alexander before him and Benjamin Warfield after him, his influence was widespread. Devotional spirit of a deep and mature kind was wedded to the Biblical themes of theology for which he was noted. He combined intelligent piety with practical concern. Theology threshed out in study and class came alive again in the sermons of Hodge.

His massive learning is expressed in three volumes of *Systematic Theology;* his *Commentary on Romans* expressed doctrinal truths by a catechetical method of exposition. For almost fifty years he wrote articles and reviews for *The Biblical Repertory and Princeton Review* indicating the versatility and fertility of his mind. In *Princeton Sermons* we find him as preacher in the seminary chapel to students, as well as in many pulpits. Although he was excelled by others at Princeton as an exegete, he stood high as the theologian.

Before preaching, he thought out his topic with pen in hand—an analysis of the subject came before the writing of the sermon. Thus the preached message in the pulpit was delivered with warm heart and a clear outline. Although a teacher of theology, he never lost the desire to proclaim the gospel and reach people for Christ. He believed and so practiced that "the preaching of the Gospel was a privilege superior to any other entrusted to men."

In the period of transition and change during the Second Great Awakening from 1800-1835 outstanding personalities included Nathanael W. Taylor, Lyman Beecher, Albert Barnes, and Charles Finney. Of these **Albert Barnes (1798-1870)** is often passed by as having been less influential than the others who received such publicity and prominence. However, Barnes was a leading pastor and preacher of the period. He was a modifier of the theology of hyper-Calvinism and the interpreter of the neo-Edwardian views still prevalent.

In Barnes' Presbyterian Church of the time there were many who spurned any change in the age-long doctrinal position formulated in the Confession of Faith and in the Creeds. Any suggested revision was heresy. A rift developed in the church coming to its height in 1837, involving two groups in schism, spoken of as "Evangelical" and "Unevangelical." These represented evangelical Calvinists and evangelical Arminians. However, Barnes preferred to divide them into "hierarchical" and "evangelical" denominations, noting that the gospel must not be made to depend for its success upon the nonessentials of church liturgy or polity, "but on solemn appeals to the reason, the conscience, the immortal hopes and fears of men attended by the holy influence of the Spirit of God."

In the controversy Barnes followed the evangelical view expressed by Lyman Beecher in a sermon, "The Faith Once Delivered to the Saints" delivered in 1823. In that sermon Beecher stated what became the essence of the evangelical view and creed: Belief on faith alone in "the great Christian fundamentals" of the miraculous birth, death, and resurrection of Jesus to save men from damnation as being the only essential element in Evangelical theology. During the thirty-five year pastorate at First Presbyterian Church of Philadelphia, Barnes had a pulpit from which to preach and teach these views.

In preaching Barnes is remembered for his sermon in 1829 on the "Way of Salvation" in which he denied that Adam's descendants inherited his guilt. This became an issue of heresy before both the local Presbytery and the General Assembly of the church. But he was able to stand against the opposition and remained in his pastorate. Lyman Beecher, then President of Lane Seminary, Cincinnati, was also charged for his views on original sin. Though the assembly was torn by controversy, Beecher also was acquitted. Following this the more liberal forces founded the independent Union Seminary of New York.

Barnes was not as liberal as some men when he advocated the evangelical application of the gospel preached. His endeavor to find a new interpretation of the essential truths held in common by his church was expressed in his sermons. His new approach is seen in his words: "This is an age of freedom, and man will be free. The religion of forms is the stereotyped wisdom or folly of the past, and does not adapt itself to free movement, the enriched views, the varying plans of this age. The spirit of this age demands that there shall be freedom in Religion; that it shall not be fettered or suppressed, that it shall go forth to the conquest of the world. . . ."

In the new wave of evangelical revivalism, men were caught up in the pragmatic appeal of that which gave to the individual a sense of importance in the choice he made and the decision he willed. Here was a new hope and a confidence in man's worth and value. The surge of activity which followed cannot be denied. This became one of the most encouraging signs of social renewal and reformation for American life. The movements for improvement and the humanitarian benefits influenced all missionary and education work as well as social redemption efforts (cf. Timothy L. Smith, *Revivalism and Social Reform*, 1957).

During the time of his ministry, Barnes also sent out volumes of essays, sermons, and notes for Bible study. His Bible commentaries cover most of the Bible, now published in twenty-seven volumes. These notes and expositions made a contribution to the needed clarification of doctrine. His revision of certain theories of interpretation brought him into contact with the leading minds involved in the acute controversy of the day. His beliefs were orthodox in his confidence that the Bible was the Word of God. In order to send out such a large amount of material, he would rise early, between four and five o'clock, and write until nine o'clock in the morning.

Albert Barnes was a leading Biblical preacher in his denomination. He stands out in his ability to express himself, though his gifts were in writing not in speaking. He was a conversational preacher with a voice never loud, and in no way an orator like some of his famous contemporaries. Oratory was not for Barnes as the pastor of a regular congregation. Nevertheless, he gained in influence during the course of his long pastorate, and those who waited upon his ministry were satisfied with his teaching. He stands out as an example of the pastoral preaching ministry then emerging after a time of controversy.

Alexander Campbell (1788-1866) was the leader of a religious movement that developed during the period between the Revolutionary and Civil Wars in America. Under his preaching a new denomination, known as the Disciples of Christ, arose. The setting of this group and its leadership is not unconnected with its social and cultural background. Europe was the background of those people who followed Campbell. Refugees from many lands settled in America and brought with them much of their ways and outlook on religion and life. Among these were Protestants whose rich heritage of freedom demanded liberty for all. Campbell, in a sermon "The Remission of Sins," speaks of the Lutheran doctrine of justification as the test of a rising or diminishing church. This group had much in common with the Protestant movement in Europe in that it believed in the power of preaching. The Word of God was accepted in its entirety, and the basic doctrines of Christianity were followed. Through the changes of a century and more, there was an unbroken witness to truths tenaciously held.

Part of the influence of Campbell lay in a particular view of Covenant Theology mediated to him through some Scottish theologians while he attended Glasgow University. According to this view, the plan of salvation was that man believes, repents, and is baptized. Then God forgives sin, gives the Holy Spirit and life eternal. This view rejected the rigid view of predestination, election, and prevenient grace. Coming to America in 1809, he led his own movement according to his view of the plan of salvation, and laid the foundation of the new denomination.

The early thrust of the Disciples of Christ under Campbell was in frontier camp meetings, revival gatherings and a free type of service instead of more formal gatherings. Theologically the appeal to the will and the Arminian doctrine of decisive commitment to Christ enabled the evangelist and missionaries of those early days to reap harvests of souls. Days of colonization and settlement made the opportunity ripe for this type of preaching. Associated with these truths was a strong millennial view of history and Scripture. The freedom of the frontier opened the way for expansion and growth in numbers and in spirit. Spectacular was the advance of this denomination. From 1860 to 1900 over one million people were joined in this fellowship, a phenomenal development by any test.

In the preaching of those years the prophetical interpretation of the coming kingdom of God was most marked. William Miller and Robert Milligan preached and published books which stressed this impending event: *The Signs of the Times, The Midnight Cry, The Faithful Watchman, The Second Advent of Christ* were among the titles of magazines which were circulated. Setting himself apart from the aberrations in judgment on the part of these men concerning chronology, Campbell with a wiser and sounder judgment spoke of the foundational facts of the advent view in prophecy. If millennium meant one thousand years, then Christ would return at the end of that time. Before that could happen, changes in society must occur, such as the conversion of the Jews, the downfall of the papacy, the overthrow of Mohammedanism, the downfall of paganism, and the triumph of Christianity. Campbell's preaching was a wise correction against the others who expected the end of history in 1843-44!

Campbell and his followers also turned away from the stilted ways of European preaching, including the essay sermon. They preached simply and movingly with a direct appeal to the Bible where they found the simple gospel and the view of the church as a gathered people. Campbell was conscious of the fact that the eisegesis of many preachers did violence to the text of Scripture. He urged the study of whole books of the Bible as background for preaching. The earlier exhortatory method was laid aside for a better teaching model.

The simplicity of the method in Campbell's preaching lay in its insistence that the Word of God must be taken in its plain sense and meaning. Thus "Christ died for our sins. He was buried. He rose from the dead for our justification. He is ascended to the skies to prepare mansions for his disciples. . . . " Out of this came a distinct emphasis on the *kerygma* and an objective basis for faith. What God had done in Christ was a matter of record in the Bible. "The record of the testimony is the object of faith. Hence faith requires testimony, testimony requires facts, and facts require a witness. The historian records facts." Preaching was the work of the evangelist and also the pastor in the measure that this was a message to those outside the church. Teaching was distinguished as the exhortation of truth to those within the church. Lay witness was involved and was the basis of church expansion.

Alexander Campbell has a striking sermon "On the Justification and Coronation of the Messiah," dealing with the texts: "Without controversy great is the mystery of godliness: God was manifest in the flesh, justified in the Spirit, seen of angels, preached unto the Gentiles, believed on in the world, received up into glory" (I Tim. 3:16); and, "But we see Jesus, who for a little while was made less than the angels, that by the grace of God he might taste death for all, for the sufferings of death, crowned with glory and honor" (Heb. 2:9).

In the sermon he said, "The destiny of a man, a nation, an empire, a world is sometimes suspended on a single event. On one act of one man, God, in His infinite wisdom and benevolence, suspended the entire destinies of the world." The two texts are then treated exegetically as he takes each phrase apart and gives interpretation. The two major divisions of the sermon are shown in a complementary way. Each balances the other. In this two-part sermon (made a part of F. W. Robertson's ministry), echoes of controversy filter through even near the climax of the sermon when an appeal is made.

> We have carnalized and secularized rather than spiritualized the Gospel and its institutions. We seem to prefer the husks that envelop the Gospel fruit rather than eat and enjoy the ripe corn in the ear—the weak and beggarly elements of a hoary tradition, even in its dotage, than the bread and water of life of the new kingdom of grace. We have created our metaphysical and theological idols, and after them we will go. One will have his faith alone, that is, his opinion; another acts as though he believed in water alone; another in his works alone. One changes water into wine; another wine into water. One fights for the word alone; another for the Spirit alone. One converts his god into a wafer and eats him; another fattens upon new dreams and visions of some spirit which he mistakes for the Spirit of God. But the small remnant, the true elect of God, believe all that God says; hope for all that God promises; obey in aim and in heart all that God commands, and endeavor to keep themselves pure from all the idols of the world. As many as thus walk we will say and pray with the Apostles, "Peace be upon them, and mercy, and upon all the Israel of God."

The language is Biblical and clear, but the theology is obviously biased as Campbell interprets the New Testament. He tilts at certain doctrines held by those who in his judgment have departed from apostolic doctrine or who have encrusted over the pure gospel. Nevertheless, the sermon indicates no casual exhorter but a man who has taken pains to study and prepare well. Nothing is left undone in the body of the sermon, for there the preacher expounds diligently the entire two texts in their relation one to another. As a doctrinal sermon this is one that would stand up in any period for its quality and spirit.

From the time of Campbell, an intrepid Irishman whose work blazed the trail of a new denomination, to the present time America has witnessed a remarkable development in church life. Campbell's influence continues, and the Disciples are noted for their warm-hearted, Biblically based, and evangelistic preaching. The Disciples of Christ have since united with the Christian Church, another group destined to play an important part in American Protestantism.

The colorful personality **Thomas DeWitt Talmage (1832-1902)** ministered in a period when many other preachers competed for the limelight of public approval. The crowds and the press found Henry Ward Beecher and Dwight Lyman Moody, for example, as the kind of men to run after and hear. As personalities they provided a stimulus to imagination and faith in a time when people were beset with acute social and economic problems. However, in the perspective of American preaching the pastoral-preaching of Talmage has a unique place.

From a background in the Dutch Reformed Church he became the pastor of Central Presbyterian Church, Brooklyn, where for twenty-five years he attracted audiences which numbered from 3,000 to 5,000. His church building was at that time spoken of as the church having the largest seating capacity in America. The appeal of Talmage lay in his flowery speech, his surprising phrases, and his sense of the dramatic. A flamboyancy and a strain of sensationalism added to his public appeal.

Talmage's preaching had a quality of emotion and the art of the storyteller in it so that people were touched in an unusual way. The fact that the daily press carried his sermons in the thousands of papers published throughout America and the English-speaking world, contributed largely to his fame. His sermons were easy to read. In a day when the sermon had a prominent place, the effect of its message was multiplied by printing. In Great Britain alone one weekly magazine carried a sermon of Talmage alongside of one by Spurgeon for fifty years so that a generation which had not heard

Talmage but was still being attracted was reached through his printed message. Talmage as a preacher was "good copy" and it is estimated that millions of readers knew his sermons as published.

The message of Talmage, the same as other evangelists and revivalists of that era, was that of personal salvation. It was his style and florid delivery which gave him a new angle of appeal. Reports affirm that if Talmage traveled on a train to a western city he could gather a group to hear him with an announcement by his friends that he would be at a railway junction for some time. There a meeting place would be found and taxed to its capacity, so well known had he become through the press. His sermons were read more than those of any other preacher of that period, and people sought to see and hear the preacher who could be read with ease. He had also become the "greatest one-man attraction in America" for his appearances on the lecture platform.

In preaching Talmage would give a vivid description of an event or incident, such as the return of the victorious Northern armies, which would move the congregation with deep emotion. His sense of audience response made him realize that the emotions of his hearers could be stirred when he touched on the Civil War or a personality like Abraham Lincoln or a patriotic chord. Talmage used a studied approach in telling of the desolation of the land as well as of the victory won. The words were quarried in the depths of his study and of his mind before being sent out in the oratory of the moment. His well-planned rhetorical order could be discerned in his preaching and lecturing. The seeming extemporized speech or sermon had behind it careful thought to catch that moment when the public, being swayed by powerful emotion, would respond to his ideas and thought.

Talmage, as a pastor preparing sermons, did not always confine himself to strictly orthodox ways of preparation. Sometimes he would go to the underworld of the metropolitan area and there at night see for himself the people who were involved in the life of that lower element of society. There the vices and sins of men and women were seen firsthand. Thus he took to the pulpit a knowledge of what was underground, and with his flair for the sensational he was able to capitalize on his experience and knowledge to a remarkable degree. No other preacher could relate firsthand the sins and shame, the foibles and fury of that group sunk in the mire of self-destruction of body and mind. He breathed the atmosphere of the fetid and foul breath of those who indulged in drunkenness and debauchery. And since he usually visited haunts of sin in company with a church officer or a policeman, he had witnesses with him. The press, therefore, knew that what he reported in the sermon had validity and did not come out of some vain imagination. Here was fact.

This was the preaching of Talmage. Its appeal was unconventional for the pulpit and did not receive approbation from fellow clergymen. His speech was sensational by conventional tests, and occasionally he made assertions which seemed to be beyond proof in the argument of persuasion. His florid rhetoric would paint scenes with vivid word pictures, but this was not always with the finesse of the true artist. A sermon on the "Handwriting on the Wall," based on Belshazzar's feast in Babylon (Dan. 5), portrays most vividly the scene, the banqueting hall, the principals, the guests, the servants and slaves, the orgies and debauchery, the drunkenness and vice ensuing, but this is also matched by the stories of the underworld in which he has seen similar groups in more sordid surroundings. His sermons were Biblical and yet worldly-wise; they were faithful accounts of what the Word of God revealed and yet were also modern and up-to-date with social relevance.

William Mackergo Taylor (1829-1895) was a Scot whose ministry had already been honored in his homeland before he came to New York and the Broadway Tabernacle for twenty years. There he introduced a new way of sermonizing and preaching. His logical acumen and his clear writing style were qualities used in developing sermons which were built up step by step to their conclusion. He also had a historical and biographical approach to preaching, which he later incorporated in the Yale Lectures, *The Scottish Pulpit* (1886). He was honored in giving the Yale Lectures twice, the other volume being *The Ministry of the Word* (1876). The latter deals with the preacher's preparation, doctrinal and expository preaching, and the conduct of public worship.

Taylor was a strong man and a strong preacher. His lectures demonstrate some of the traits which characterized his own life and work. His many published sermons, and his volumes on Bible characters and on the miracles and the parables, are samplings of the fertility of his mind and the scope of his teaching. Evangelical in spirit, Taylor was abreast of theology and literature so that his background equipped him for readiness in preaching. To unfold the text of Scripture was for him the highest of ministries. This meant ceaseless toil and strict self-discipline in writing. He knew that writing made for clear thinking, and he made use of this method. He contended that the communication of truth demands this writing of a script, pruning, and often the rewriting of it before its oral delivery. The method of delivery will vary according to individuals, admitted Taylor, but the basis should be writing.

To Taylor the Bible was an inspired book, given by God through selected men whose minds were set aflame with the message which they recorded in their own personal fashion. This was a foundation of confidence for preaching. His own utterances became inspiring and heart warming by the illumination of the same Holy Spirit who at the first had given the revelation of God. In this spirit he set forth the mind of God for human life.

John Hall (1829-1898) served The Fifth Avenue Presbyterian Church, New York, in the period when a galaxy of notable preachers ministered in New York and Brooklyn. That was the day of Beecher, Storrs, Behrends, Crosby, Parkhurst, Henry van Dyke, and William M. Taylor. All of these men commanded large congregations, but this Irish pulpiteer stood high in that company. Hall was a contrast to Henry Ward Beecher. Beecher was dramatic, liberal, and exuberant; Hall was reserved, conservative, and quiet. His evangelical Calvinism was given out in plain, simple, and dynamic exposition of the Scriptures. He spoke without notes and with a strong voice touched with the accent of North Ireland.

Hall gave the fourth of the Yale Lectures on Preaching, the first to follow Beecher. He did not, however, seek to compete with his predecessor. The title indicates the cast of his mind, *God's Word through Preaching* (1875). In these lectures we find the emphasis of the man: "to get then, the mind of Christ, and to declare it, is the primary end of the teaching officers of the church. The living body of sympathetic men, *saturated with the truth and feeling of the Book*, must bring it into contact with other men, through that marvellous organ, the human voice, and with such aid as comes from the subtle sympathy that pervades assemblies of human beings. . . ." "The work of speaking the truth is the justification, the 'reason to be,' of the Christian ministry."

With his preaching he combined intensive visitation of his parish (brought as a custom from Ireland), which involved much climbing

·

of stairways in the apartments then being erected. The physical strain eventually told upon him, but he demonstrated that a pastor who visited also had people coming to hear his preaching. Hall's preaching stressed the grand particularities of the orthodox faith then being questioned by new schools of thought. He maintained his convictions with strength, and expressed them with gifted utterances of speech.

No discussion of preaching by evangelicals in the United States of America would be complete without the inclusion of the scholar and professor **John Albert Broadus (1827-1895)**. From several points of view he is a giant and an olympian. His friends and colleagues in the Southern Baptist Church were naturally prejudiced in his favor and no one could blame them for that. Those who recall him have written and testified to his outstanding abilities and gifts.

From the time when he yielded his life to Jesus Christ, he began to study, to serve, and to witness, learning to preach as well as teach. He early committed his mental gifts and potential attainments to the service of God, and soon found opportunity to grow in knowledge and in grace as he prepared himself for his life work. After the early years of experience, he became Professor of New Testament and of Homiletics at Southern Baptist Theological Seminary, Louisville, Kentucky. From that center he became well known as a preacher and teacher of preachers.

The Lyman Beecher Lectures on Preaching at Yale were delivered by Broadus in 1889, but his Notes from which he lectured were never published. *A Treatise on the Preparation and Delivery of Sermons*, comprising his lectures, notes, and exposition of the subject, was published in 1870 so that it would seem that Broadus drew from his class lectures and this volume as the foundation for the Yale Lectures on Preaching. In the Lectures he discussed the preacher's life and work in general terms of preaching, reading, use of hymns and the Bible, his freedom and outfit, and his private life. The basics of the materials for preaching, the arrangement of a sermon, style, delivery, and the conduct of public worship had been dealt with in the book which came out of the teaching routine.

No sermons of Broadus were published during his lifetime. Since his death, however, several volumes have been published, including *Sermons and Addresses*, and *Favorite Sermons of John A. Broadus*. Other published writings partially related to his preaching are: *Commentary on Matthew, Harmony on the Gospels*, and *Lectures on the History of Preaching.* These books give glimpses of his own style and embody the principles he had taught to others as he stimulated hundreds of men for the ministry. Ideals and standards were set high. Generations owe him much in this regard.

Broadus pleaded for a sense of sympathy on the part of the preacher as the principal quality for effective presentation of truth. Without that there would be coldness and brittleness of feeling; with it came rapport and understanding of heart. Extemporaneous preaching was one way of looking directly at people and feeling their response. This made for effective delivery. Hence, Broadus preferred to leave his manuscript or notes behind and to preach without them.

Simplicity was characteristic of his messages, though his preparation was thorough. A simple outline would be used for the sake of his hearers. In the sermon "In Jesus's Name" based on "Verily, verily, I say unto you, Whatsoever ye shall ask the Father in my name, he will give it you. Hitherto have ye asked nothing in my name: ask, and ye shall receive, that your joy may be full" (John 16:23-24), four points are noted: (1) Up to this time men had not asked in Christ's name; (2) What is implied in asking in Christ's name?; (3) Encouragement to ask in Christ's name; and (4) The result of asking in Christ's name. Each unit is expounded clearly and simply. Progress to an effective climax is unmistakable. The sermon ends on the note of joy, a gift which is the high privilege of the Christian who asks in the name of Christ.

Broadus endeavored to be a true interpreter of the whole Bible, shunning nothing difficult or obscure. He believed in preaching the great texts of the Scriptures, including those which others may have been afraid to develop because of their finality and majesty. With care in statement, balance in observation, and vigilance in scholarly interpretation, he was no charlatan claiming too much, but he stated his case in irenic tones. Homiletics was not used or taught to be a crutch to assist the lazy and unbalanced doctrinal propagandist. Those qualities which shone through his lectures are found in his own sermons.

To Broadus the Bible was the one Book supreme. His study of Greek and Hebrew caused him to dig into the textual riches of the Bible before preaching. He would commend the Book of books in asides in preaching, such as: "We can learn about such a subject as this only from the Bible"; "The greatest privilege of earthly life is to give some fellow creature the blessed word of God, and then try by loving speech and example, to bring home to the heart and conscience . . . the truths it contains." He would endeavor to draw from a text as well as from a passage the main theme and to set it forth in the light of the rest of Scripture. His aim was to let Scripture speak for itself. Thus he was heard with profit by both the well-educated and the least educated in the community or church.

In the main he was an expository preacher, basing his preaching on sound exegesis. Preparing for a sermon as an exegete of the text, he did not aim for a cleverness which could obscure the subject, but rather for a simple elucidation of the passage. The sermon on "Jesus: Saviour" based on "And thou shalt call his name Jesus: for he shall save his people from their sins" (Matt. 1:21), illustrates how he used exegesis as the basis for preaching.

The introduction of this sermon embodies the fact that Hebrew names were commonly significant—a natural and pleasing custom. Some names are great and can be copied for inspiration. Other names are sullied and we tend not to repeat them. "But the name here directed to be given was not in vain. The word *Jesus* means Saviour. And truly did he become a Saviour. He is Jesus Christ, the Saviour anointed—he ever lives to save. In the reasons assigned for giving him this name, there are taught great and glorious truths. Let us attend to them." Then follows the outline in three major divisions with sub-points of exposition. Notice how the sermon is built upon his exegesis in this comparison with his *Commentary on Matthew:*

Commentary:

v. 21—*"Jesus"* is the same name as Joshua, signifying in Hebrew "Jehovah is helper," or "Help of Jehovah." The Greek form "Joshua" is found in the Septuagint, and so in Acts 7:45; Heb. 4:8.

"For he shall save." In Revised Version, "it is he that shall save." The word "he" is here pretty clearly emphatic in the Greek, "he himself," he and no other, though Revised Version rather exaggerates the emphasis. The word "save"

Sermon:

The word *"Jesus"* means *Saviour.* And truly did he become a Saviour. He is Jesus Christ, the Saviour anointed—he ever lives to save. In the reasons assigned for giving him this name, there are taught great and glorious truths.

I. *He shall save.* Emphatic in the original. (1) He, and not we ourselves, saves us. We could not have accomplished the work. And it is not a joint affair, by the union of his merit and ours. He alone saves. (2) He is the Saviour, and not our signifies primarily to "preserve," secondarily to "deliver," and it often conveys both ideas at the same time.

"His people," would to Joseph naturally mean Israel. May have meant to denote the spiritual Israel, including some of the nation. Or it may have meant simply the people of Israel, i.e., the truly pious among them, not intending to exclude the Gentiles from being saved by Jesus, but confining the view at present to the salvation of the Jews. So the angel announces to the shepherds "great joy . . . to all people."

"From their sins," from both the *consequences* and the *dominion,* both the *penalty* and the *power* of their sins. Messiah did not come, as the Jews commonly supposed he would, simply to save his people from the dominion of foreigners; it was something deeper and higher, to save them from their sins. And not to save them *in* their sins, but *from* their sins.

faith in him. (3) He is to be seen, not as exalted, but as humbled— not as living a life of splendor, but as dying a death of shame. . . . He shall save.

II. *He shall save his people.* No longer in a national sense, as the Jews would have supposed. . . . All that receive him, that believe on his name become his people— "power to become the sons of God." What an honor, what a happiness to be the people of Jesus! . . . So angels as they come on their missions of love, with what interest may we suppose them to gaze on those here whom they know to be heirs of salvation. Who of you would not be of his people?

III. *From their sins.*

(1) From the penalty of their sins. It is well to reflect upon and seek to realize the awful truth that we deserve to die, to suffer eternal damnation.

(2) From the dominion of sin. Ye shall die in your sins, a most terrible doom. It were a very inadequate salvation to be delivered from positive punishment, and be left sinful. And this Jesus came to accomplish: (a) If we love him, we have new motives to resist our sinful tendencies. (b) Jesus has procured for them that believe on him the special indwelling of the Holy Spirit the Sanctifier.

In a day of widespread acceptance of the Bible as the inspired Word of God, Broadus had no difficulty in finding hearers who rejoiced in this type of ministry. As a visitor to Baptist church pulpits, he was eagerly welcomed. His preaching had thrust and appeal. The text was given its proper place as the authoritative Word of God, as he stated in his lectures *Preparation and Delivery of Sermons* in which he laid down the principle: "To interpret and apply his text in accordance with its real meaning, is one of the preacher's most sacred duties. He stands before the people for the very purpose of teaching and exhorting them out of the Word of God. He announces a particular passage of God's Word as his text with the distinctly implied understanding that from this his sermon will be drawn—if not always its various thoughts, yet certainly its general subject."

Broadus embodied what he taught and gave excellent examples in his sermons of the art and discipline of the interpreter in expository preaching. Nowhere do we find the censorious spirit of critical judgment when speaking of the limitations in preaching by others. He was eminently a wise and kind person and knew only how to be gracious. In his *Lectures on the History of Preaching* there is a clue to the practical mind of Broadus in a changing age which he saw approaching. He suggested then that science and religion should not be in tension; that skepticism would arise; that humanitarian tendencies should be utilized for the gospel message; and that greater freedom in composition would come instead of his more classic and rhetorical methods of sermonizing. He was pleased in all this to "preach the definite doctrines of the Bible, and an abundant exposition of the Bible text." In this he was a shining example for his age in American preaching.

"Truth Through Personality"

The changing climate for preaching brought to light the gracious and beneficent ministry of **Phillips Brooks (1835-1893)**, a contemporary of Beecher, but with a difference in personality and public utterance. Whereas Beecher was the popular preacher attracting crowds, Brooks was the discriminating preacher bringing help and healing to special congregations who valued his type of preaching. His background in education and teaching gave him unusual preparation for the study of theology and the entrance upon a pastoral and preaching ministry. Episcopalian in belief, he exemplified the finest tradition of his church, and his ministry had powerful repercussions throughout the whole church and the English-speaking world.

In his now famous *Lectures on Preaching* given at Yale in 1877, he gave the church the imperishable idea about preaching: "Preaching is the communication of truth by man to men." Usually this is quoted as "preaching is truth through personality," an adaptation of the fuller reference. The context of the lecture states: "The truest truth, the most authoritative statement of God's will, communicated in any other way than through the personality of brother man to men is not preached truth." Thus the shortened, revised form of the quotation. Brooks was the demonstration of his definition.

The two essential elements in preaching, then, are truth and personality. "Suppose it written on the sky, suppose it embodied in a book which has been so long held in reverence as the direct utterance of God that the vivid personality of the men who wrote its pages has well-nigh faded out of it; in neither of these cases is there any preaching. And on the other hand, if men speak to other men that which they do not claim for truth, if they use their powers of persuasion or of entertainment to make other men listen to their speculations, or do their will, or applaud their cleverness, that is not preaching either. The *first lacks personality*. The *second lacks truth*. It must have both elements."

Brooks was known as "a prince of preachers" and the pulpit was his "throne." In his first major pastorate in Philadelphia, Pennsylvania (1859-69), and in his second at Boston, Massachusetts (1869-91), he had different emphases as he sought to meet various needs of the times. In Philadelphia his ministry stressed social and national problems, but while his sermons received a good hearing, he did not reach the zenith of his influence until he went to Boston. There he aimed more at the individual and as a result his friends thought that he achieved even greater influence in meeting the social and national needs of the day.

The sermons of Brooks exemplify the message of the statue and memorial erected to his memory in Boston. There is the figure of the living Christ overshadowing Brooks who stands with an open Bible in hand. The concept is that of one who preached the Word of God and loved people in the spirit of his Master. He was the Christian humanist, and with culture and rich gifts of person and preaching he exerted a power for righteousness.

The ferment of the times found Brooks ready to minister out of a well-stored mind, a disciplined spiritual life, and an urbanity which could take its place unmoved in any situation. His beliefs were broad in the sense that as an Episcopalian he was not tied to any particular school of thought, but moved freely from an evangelical spirit to a more liberal expression. In a time of transition he stood for the eternal verities of the traditional Christian faith but with a liberal outlook and a humanitarian grasp of needs. Thus he ministered in two metropolitan areas to generations of people. Brooks gave himself unstintingly to the calls for civic, social, and national service when he took part as the representative of the church and her Lord, but he never forsook the major thrust of his vocation, that of the preacher-pastor.

No finer example could be found than Brooks, who studied and wrote constantly in preparation for the chief end of preaching. His full manuscript was used usually in the morning diet of worship, but he also preached extemporaneously in the evening and on other occasions. His preparation was meticulous in study and in writing. If "truth is communicated through personality," then Brooks was the finest example of his own dictum and theory of preaching. With or without a manuscript, the preacher excelled in communicating the truth as he felt it and experienced it. The text is elaborated, the topic is unfolded, the plan is outlined, and the exposition is forceful and pleasing. A mind attuned and a voice increasingly forceful as the theme progressed—such was Brooks at his best. His words came rapidly and with feeling. The effect of the sermon is felt by the people as a voice for God has spoken to them.

"Dedicated to the love of God and the service of man" would be a fitting description of Brooks' preaching at its best. To him the religious life was beautiful and necessary for the fullness of life. Simplicity and sincerity marked his preaching. The sermon was a divine instrument for the "persuading and moving of men's souls." Thus "preaching is truth through personality" in that a sermon is an instrument of power designed for the "persuading and moving of men's souls." It will be so only when the essential truth that has entered the preacher energizes every faculty and emerges with the unique stamp of his own personality. Brooks believed, as in his own life, that the cultivation of the whole man was necessary in training a preacher. Then would come effectiveness and grace in expression as the would-be preacher is lifted to a more generous and exalted life, the basis of a truly noble style.

In delivery, Brooks demonstrated that whatever training in elocution or public speaking might contribute, "the real power of oratory must be your own intelligent delight in what you are doing. Let your pulpit be to you what his studio is to the artist, or his court room, to the lawyer . . . only far more sacredly let the pulpit be this to you, and you have the power which is to all rules what the soul is to the body. You have enthusiasm which is the breath of life." Brooks was not like Beecher who was almost the actor and dramatist in preaching. He preferred to be the pastoral preacher to a congregation with whom he sustained a close relationship as shepherd to flock. Brooks worked at homiletics, the art and science of preparation and delivery of the sermon. He practiced planning sermons and carefully outlined them so that the progress of thought moved with fluidity and grace. Writing gave them precise and fresh expression. His sermons are not easily classified as expository, topical, practical, or hortatory. He simply took a text and found its theme, then developed it as the flow of thought moved on, not with argument but with a persuasive spirit. He was poetic, using images freely and speaking in pictorial language. His gift of imagination was strong.

In the broad influence of the Anglican order, Brooks preached a comforting gospel. His stress lay more on the Incarnation than on the Atonement. This was in keeping with the trends of his time. Reactions against the earlier Puritan dogma resulted in more modifying emphases of doctrine. The conception of the nature and character of God was seen in a new relationship to what was termed the brotherhood of man. Preaching then had breadth rather than depth. Theology was modified and the practical demands made more important. Here also "brands were not being plucked from the fire" as in the days of Edwards, Wesley, and Whitefield. Now was sweet reasonableness appealing to the best and most noble in human nature as part of God's creation. As Christ is the highest pinnacle of human life under God, so man can be redeemed to live in that light and approach that standard. Brooks stood in his day as the leader and the guide for this preaching emphasis which has held sway largely within Episcopacy.

Nevertheless, we discern in Brooks' sermons and writings the personal sense of belonging to Jesus Christ. In his life and ministry his preaching never departed from the Christ-conscious center of faith and experience. Theological variations there were, but at the center he remained a devout disciple and, as such, ministered to souls in need.

His sermon titles are indicative of the spiritual and imaginative strain of his mind: "Going Up to Jerusalem"; "The Candle of the Lord"; "In the Light of God"; "The Fire and the Calf" are samples. In the last of these the persuasive art of the preacher is at its height. He pleads with people to face up to their accountability for all actions and at the same time reminds them of the new birth which is possible in the "newly-awakened selfhood." "So the only hope for any of us is in a perfectly honest manliness to claim our sins. 'I did it! I did it!' let me say of all my wickedness. Let me refuse to listen for one monent to any voice which would make my sins less mine. It is the only honest and the only hopeful way, the only way to know and be ourselves. When we have done that, then we are ready for the Gospel, ready for all that Christ wants to show us that we may become, and for all the powerful grace by which he wants to make us be it perfectly."

His volumes of sermons are still available to give light and wisdom on the art of sermon composition. The principles are not out of date; the essentials remain unchanged. In his Lectures he has said all that needs to be said on this subject. The quintessence of a well-stored mind, prepared from years of reading and reflection, poured into all his preaching. Succeeding generations may well learn the value of his Christian humanism. Christ, to Brooks, has taken his stand over and above culture, yet relates to culture. This gives the preacher the best opportunity to relate to his own culture. Thus Brooks was the living example of his own ideals and counsel regarding preaching. Character is the principal thing in making a preacher; personality is that rare indefinable essence and spirit which distills the message preached; and truth is that final reality without which no message of God is proclaimed.

Brooks never wavered in his adherence to the doctrines which he held as his faith. In an age when the Unitarian and Emersonian doctrines were strong in New England, Brooks stood firmly on the Trinitarian affirmation as disclosed in the Bible and formulated in The Apostles Creed as well as in The Thirty-Nine Articles of his church. Strong churchman that he was, his preaching was the stimulus for that body in a day of shifting standards and his voice was heard throughout the English-speaking world. Preaching to him could not afford to be uncertain at this point, and the sermon he prepared and delivered was full of this doctrinal quality and strength.

The influence of Brooks was far-reaching in his own day and has been ever since. The Christmas carol he wrote, "O Little Town of Bethlehem," is an enduring monument to his poetic vision of the truth of the Incarnation. He would be known and remembered for this if for nothing else, but in addition there is the strong doctrinal emphasis of his preaching and his *Lectures on Preaching*—these three constitute a strong cord unbroken even now. His preaching spirit can be summed up in his well-known exhortation in the *Lectures:* "Preach doctrine, preach all the doctrine that you know, and learn forever more and more; but preach it always, not that men may believe it, but that men may be saved by believing it."

Adoniram Judson Gordon (1836-1895) stood out in his day as a preacher-pastor with missionary passion and vision whose teaching affected the lives of a generation. The aftermath of the Civil War found many American leaders, such as Theodore Munger, George A. Gordon, Newman Smyth, and Washington Gladden—all in New England—restating the Biblical message in terms of the then evolutionary views and the so-called scientific methodology imported from Germany. The new theology became popular. Fresh and startling interpretations of the Bible in particular were common. As a result, the Higher Criticism of the era led to a widespread instability among church people as to the authority of the Bible. Each major denomination passed through this period of transition with much the same results.

Over against this changing situation stood men who were known as conservative and often spoken of as fundamentalist. In the midst of the New England upheaval in theology, Gordon continued his ministry unaffected and unchanged. His pastorate at the Clarendon Street Baptist Church, Boston (1869-1895), was in the midst of the new teaching all around him. He did not accept the new views and his exposition of the premillennial movement coupled with missions and evangelism must always be reckoned with as a major contribution to evangelical Christianity. Out of his ministry came steadfast teaching to others and later the development of what is now Gordon College at Wenham, Massachusetts, and also Gordon-Conwell Theological Seminary at South Hamilton, Massachusetts, near Boston.

Gordon's preaching, characteristic of a particular school, was based upon a confident belief in the absolute integrity of the Bible and the hermeneutics of a dispensational scheme. These were coupled with dogmatic conviction and fearless exposition of the truths.

Such preaching was largely expository in character, the emphasis emerging out of the hermeneutical principles laid down. "The value of the premillennial scheme of interpretation," he wrote, "lies in this—that it gives attention to 'dispensational truth,' as it is called. It finds a map of the ages in the Scripture, and studies to locate doctrine, as well as to comprehend it, and to determine its relation to the great whole."

Gordon's views did not follow strictly the Scofield notes found later in the edition of the Bible to which Scofield's name was attached. He saw the Papacy as the Antichrist and did not see the pretribulation rapture of the church, concepts which gained acceptance by those who followed Scofield. He did take part in the Bible conference movement and was a leader in prophetic interpretation. Biblical criticism did not find lodgment in his system of Bible study. He saw in it a threat to the truth of the verbal inspiration and inerrancy of Scripture. Nevertheless, he was no controversialist, for he believed that the best apologetic lay in letting the Bible speak for itself. Allied to his beliefs was a desire for personal holiness of life, a piety which was nurtured in private and shone out publicly in his preaching.

In one of the sermons, "The Christian's Footprints," which appeared in *The Beacon,* a Boston newspaper (March 8, 1884), he stressed the proper way to spiritual illumination: "I believe the Scripture is the guide, and the infallible guide, of the Christian; but I know that if a Christian has some private prejudice or personal prepossession, he may so deflect the compass of Holy Scripture as to make it lead him entirely out of the way. . . . You must seek the aid of God's Spirit to interpret God's Word for you." Thus Gordon's preaching was subjective in that he felt its power as a talisman for his own inner life. Objective truth was balanced by subjective obedience to that supreme authority.

Samuel Porter Jones (1847-1900) was one of the unusual preachers of an age which was accustomed to hearing the "great" preacher, the "genius" preacher, as well as the "unique" preacher. A colorful Methodist preacher of the South, he could command large congregations. Also on the Chautauqua platform he could attract as many listeners as the best-known orators of the day. He had a reputation as a master of assemblies. A description of him reads: "What strange paradoxes were wrapped up in this masterful man and his brilliant career! He was a genius without eccentricity, a great personality without peculiarities, unique without being erratic, a wonderful orator, a marvelous preacher with little concern for homiletics."

As a preacher he loved people whether black or white, saint or sinner, Protestant or Catholic. His sincerity was obvious. His denunciation of sin and his colorful language pointed up the issues and the personalities involved. Homely wit relieved the severity of tone, and an appealing tone of voice moderated the zeal of this preacher. Often his torrential utterances had in them a hint of almost irreverence as if the truth had become too familiar to the people who listened. Hypocrisy was unmasked, religious sins were shown for what they were, and congregations were startled again and again by the surprise element in his preaching. The earthiness of his language shocked the mind.

In calling people to repent and believe the gospel, Sam Jones had unusual sayings: "What is culture worth if it is but whitewash on a rascal? I would rather be in heaven learning my ABC's than sitting in hell reading Greek." "Many a man imagines he has religion when he only has a liver complaint." "It is considered vulgar now, really vulgar, for a man to get up and preach hell to sinners. . . . It is not polite to believe that way, and many a little fellow has scratched that out of his creed; but he won't be in hell more than fifteen minutes before he will revise his creed and have nothing in it but hell." "Look here, friends, if we wake tonight, let us stand up like men and flee from the wrath to come." Such was the tenor of his preaching appeal.

Carl Ferdinand Wilhelm Walther (1811-1887) stands in the succession of those men of Lutheran conviction who gave to the church in America direction and guidance for preaching. Born in Germany in a pastor's family, he was educated at Leipzig University where he prepared for the Lutheran ministry. A group of students kept alive the spirit and faith of the Pietists and through this body he was led eventually to emigrate to the United States with the prospect of an enlarged ministry. Unlike others who had gone to New York and the Eastern seaboard, this group went to New Orleans and by river to St. Louis in the heartland of America.

After spending several years as a pastor, Walther was led to develop the Evangelical Lutheran Synod of Missouri and became its presiding officer. His early church paper became the precursor of publications by the group. Christian day schools and colleges for advanced study were established. The emerging of Concordia Theological Seminary to become the largest of its kind in America established Walther as a president as well as an editor and a preacher to would-be preachers. The period was one of argument and debate in religion, but in controversial issues Walther stood fast for the orthodox position of Lutheranism. By his lectures, publications, and preaching he kept alive a purity of belief which has stood for a century and more in his denomination. His preaching was based upon the belief that the Bible was God's inspired Word which revealed the truth and was therefore superior to human reason. His defense of the historic faith did not allow him to compromise.

Walther's preaching is known for its distinction between law and gospel. His view on this is found in a book, *The Proper Distinction between Law and Gospel,* published after his death, and consisting of shorthand notes made by others listening to his lectures. It is a worthwhile contribution to homiletical literature, revealing wide reading, careful thought, and practical principles of sermon preparation. The distinction between law and gospel is a basic truth for preaching, says Walther. "The Word of God is not rightly divided when a person's salvation is made to depend upon his association with the visible orthodox Church, and when salvation is denied to every person who errs in any article of faith." From passages like Matthew 16:18 and Ephesians 2:19-22, Walther showed that the church is not a visible institution. Rather it is, as Scripture teaches, "a field in which both wheat and tares are growing, a net cast into the sea which encloses both good and bad fishes, a marriage feast to which both wise and foolish virgins come, and a feast to which some come who are not dressed in a wedding garment." "Thus does the visible form of the Church contain both righteous and unrighteous people, both true believers and sham Christians. . . . Only God can see the heart of man. Since the Church is composed of true believers, hence the true Church is invisible." Walther also distinguished between law and gospel in proclaiming sin and salvation. He proclaimed the law in all its severity and the gospel in all its sweetness. He directed the sinner aroused and alarmed by law to find his way by faith to the promises of the gospel—not to wrestle and pray and seek to win his own way into a state of grace.

Walther's preaching was also summarized in his lectures, *The Voice of Our Church on the Question Concerning the Church and the Ministry.* This topic, with proofs from Scripture, was developed in sixty-six theses in which he showed the rights and duties of the local church and how these should be exercised. Having enunciated that the ministry or the pastoral office is distinct from the priestly office, which belongs to all believers, he goes on to say:

> That the holy ministry, or the ministry of the New Testament, is not a human ordinance, not an institution established by the Church, but a word of *divine wisdom*, an establishment of God Himself, appears from the Old Testament prophecies; the call of the Apostles to the ministry of teaching by the Son of God; and finally, the divine origin of the ministry appears from those passages in which also those who have been mediately called are represented as having been called to God: "And God hath set some in the Church, first apostles, prophets, teachers . . . " (I Cor. 12:28, 29). "And Christ gave some, apostles; some prophets; and some evangelists; and some pastors and teachers . . . " (Eph. 4:11). Thus the Apostles coordinate themselves with the ministers of the Church who were called *mediately* as with their colleagues in office.

Walther's preaching and teaching exalted the office of the pastoral preacher and teacher. It was not an arbitrary office, not a peculiar order set over and against the common state of Christians and higher than the latter like the priesthood of the Levites; but it is an office of service. It thus has authority to preach the gospel and to administer the sacraments and the authority of a spiritual tribunal. The ministry of preaching is conferred by God through the congregation, as holder of all church power, or of the keys, and by its call, as prescribed by God. Reverence and unconditional obedience are due to the ministry of preaching when the preacher is ministering the Word of God. According to divine right, the function of passing judgment on doctrine belongs to the ministry of preaching. However, the laymen also have this right, and for this reason they also have a seat and vote with the preachers in church courts and councils.

Because of these convictions, Walther promoted respect for the congregation as "the priesthood of believers" and he would have them trained in school and confirmation for church life: "I speak as to wise men; judge ye what I say" (I Cor. 10:15). One of his sayings was: "Rob the congregation of the right to judge doctrine, and you give them over into slavery." Another was: "I bow to the humblest member coming with Scripture." He said it; he did it. As he respected the congregation of intelligent believers, so he preached out of the Word of God truth for them to respect and by which they grew in grace and in knowledge. Walther maintained that "every sermon must be a work of art"—and he suited the action to the word. He polished his sermons till the very minute he had to go into the pulpit; he was the finished homiletic artist. His words were fitly spoken, like apples of gold in a network of silver (Prov. 25:11).

Walther's contribution to preaching was that of a leader who knew the perils and dangers of an untried people in a new world. He laid foundations of doctrine and shaped moral standards and conduct. The denomination which was later to give the modern world a preacher like Walter Maier and a Lutheran Hour reaching around the world through radio and television was the same which listened earlier to Walther. It was Walther's preaching and teaching which gave rock-like stability to a young and new denomination which has grown in strength and influence to take its place in the space age unperturbed at changing ways of doctrine. What were held by Walther to be the historic beliefs are still held. How well and how penetrating was the preaching of Walther alongside of many wider-publicized giants of the pulpit! He left the legacy of Bible preaching which held to the authority of the Word of God.

National Issues—Slavery, War, Vested Interests, Heritage, and Destiny

Preaching by men of various faiths has contributed to the special emphases found in the several denominations. However, neither the preachers nor the churches lived in isolation from one another. Instead there was a crossing over of theological, cultural, and ethnic influence. In this way we see unity of doctrine among men of various backgrounds and denominations. And yet, there is a distinct quality about much of what was done in the South of America. In the South a greater degree of division has been noted regarding the Civil War and the questions of race. These have not left the churches in the South unaffected, and preaching has had to deal with crucial and grave issues from time to time.

The question of *slavery* raised its problems for the nation but especially for the church. This was in itself a revolution. The election of Abraham Lincoln as President brought many ideas to climax and confrontation, and in the Civil War the nation and the churches were involved in divisions and tragedy. Unanimity of judgment and oneness of interpretation for the preacher was not possible. Honest convictions regarding truth and its application divided and caused a rift in the churches. Some pulpiteers adhered to past habits and attitudes; their consciences pleaded for religious convictions without change. For these men, slavery had become an accepted way of life and had sanctions even from the Bible! Whether this could stand up to the exegesis of a passage in the Book of Genesis concerning Ham is questionable for many today, but then it was questioned by only a few. Thus political upheaval and religious ferment shook the nation. Men were forced into decisions and stands were taken pro and con.

The preaching of that period reflects the crucial issues which disrupted the nation and the church. As North and South took issue, voices were raised on either side. Wendell Phillips of Boston is reported as saying: "Calling a slave-holding nation a Christian nation—that is the fatal error: encouraged by the pulpit, which forms the mind on which your statesmen are to act." The moralism of the Christian teaching was the result of the earlier Puritan tradition which was now being tested in the crucible of new experience. The stern necessity to judge issues as either right or wrong was typical, and theological relevance and moral judgment became dominant notes of preaching.

Modifications there would be, but the main issues were clear. Theological interpretation and relevant preaching came with the issues of slavery and civil war. Sectional viewpoints confused and confounded man. Some Christians were convinced that slavery was an absolute wrong which should be abolished at once. The consequences of this for the Union were not weighed. Some felt that it was natural, and a valuable arrangement if the will of God were invoked! Again, if the evil of slavery were recognized, could there be some other way to resolve it and let the institution die slowly? The Civil War seemed to be the final method of resolving a deep-seated problem. The preaching reflected this; and in the end the nation emerged, as under a judgment of God, chastened and purified, having suffered the agonies of division and death. All had shared in the burden of contrition, and a new sense of nationhood slowly emerged from the baptism of blood.

The divisions of denominations into North and South sections has remained a feature of American church life. Trends and attempts towards reunion have not been successful, but hope of ultimate regathering is still bright in many minds. Preaching over the years has followed more conventional themes, but in the ferment of the years of struggle the pulpit was not afraid to express personal and congregational convictions. In this the Southern Baptists were exceptions. The preachers who stand out in this denomination are men who were noted more for their evangelistic passion than their attempts to resolve the slavery issue by political preaching.

Among those who tried to justify the continuance of slavery was the Presbyterian **James Henley Thornwell (1812-1862),** who became Professor at Columbia Theological Seminary in South Carolina. He was a leader in the organization of the Presbyterian Church in the South. A Biblical defense of slavery was the key to much of the argument against their brethren in the North. In Thornwell's *The Rights and Duties of Masters,* the argument was made that slavery was the fulfillment of God's providential plan. In Thornwell's words: "It is not repugnant to the spirit of the Gospel, in its present relations to our race. It is one of the conditions in which God is conducting the moral probation of man—a condition not incompatible with the highest moral freedom, the true glory of the race, and, therefore, not unfit for the moral and spiritual discipline which Christianity has instituted. It is one of the schools in which immortal spirits are trained for their final destiny" (A Sermon Preached at the Dedication of a Church, erected in Charleston, South Carolina, for the Benefit and Instruction of the Coloured Population, 1850).

Thornwell's preaching was logical, balanced, argumentative, but more a reasoned discourse than an exposition of any Biblical passage. The redeeming feature in the argument lay in the avowed aim of the preacher to encourage his brethren to "Go on in this noble enterprise, until every slave in our borders shall know of Jesus and the resurrection; and the blessing of God will attend you—and turn back the tide of indignation which the public opinion of the world is endeavoring to roll upon you. Go on in this career, and afford another illustration of what all experience has demonstrated, that Christianity is the cheap defense of every institution which contributes to the progress of man."

In contrast to Thornwell's stance, the Synod of Kentucky (1835) had modified its position from the then current practice by stating that "the New Testament does condemn slaveholding, as practiced among us, in the most explicit terms furnished by the language in which the inspired pen men wrote."

The preaching of this period reflected the Christian church's *doctrine of MAN*. The doctrine of God was not in doubt, but "man created in the image and after the likeness of God" was. With the slavery conflict and the Darwinian evolutionary ideas emerging, the church faced a day of the application of interpreted truth. How should man be treated in the light of revelation, history, and redemption? Should man be free entirely? Could he remain free spiritually and yet be free socially, economically, and politically? The Unitarian **William Ellery Channing (1780-1842)** endorsed the anti-slavery movement whereas many orthodox people stood by the opposite view. Unitarianism seemed to be at odds with Calvinism more over the nature of man than over the nature of God. "A doctrine of total depravity," Channing said, "undermines moral responsibility and human freedom. Man's nature is essentially good, his rational and moral faculties essentially unimpaired. Man therefore has rights—not granted by an indulgent society, but rights inherent in his very nature. Man's rights belong to him as a moral being, as capable of perceiving moral distinctions, as a subject of moral obligations." Channing expressed the deep-seated convictions of many that the primary question to be proposed by a rational being is, not what is profitable, but what is right. No judgment can be just or wise but that which is built on the conviction of the paramount worth and importance of duty.

Channing took the Scriptural texts which were used to buttress slavery, and one by one sought to answer them by an interpretation which recognized their historical context and then their principles of universal action. In this he built a case that the New Testament in the light of the teaching of Christ did not condone what was slavery in America. In the general tenor and spirit of Christianity and of Christian social duty he urged men to rally against slavery.

Both Channing and Thornwell are to be respected as outstanding exponents of different points of view in a day of tragedy and tension. Each endeavored to act as Christian men professing Christian standards of conduct. The result of the conflict did not bring a cessation to the dynamic differences of interpretation. The cleavage continued in the pulpit and pew for generations. A glance at the preaching emphases in that time is salutary and enlightening. Not all sermons were preached directly on the subject from Sunday to Sunday. The themes found discussion as they emerged on special days such as Thanksgiving, the Fourth of July, a Fast Day, or occasions when groups or gatherings met for church business. It is true that Theodore Parker drew thousands in Boston and Henry Ward Beecher ministered to large crowds in Brooklyn, but for the most part the pastors who plunged into the inferno of argument in preaching did so only occasionally and when some need or crisis arose.

The preaching, then, was noteworthy for its appeal to Scripture, its rational demands on life and duty, its political benefits, and its debate on the sinfulness of slavery. In this confused and mixed up era, both sides claimed divine support and prayed for God's blessing. To be in the pew then demanded a nimble mind and "a conscience void of offense toward God and man."

Mercersburg Theology

The early Colonial expansion brought many diverse groups from the old world. The main lines are fairly well known, but some of the lesser known need to be given place. Among the latter arose preaching which assisted the immigrants to settle in the new world and find their security among people of their own national culture and faith. Among the denominations thus formed were The Reformed Church in the United States, The Evangelical Synod of North America, and The Evangelical and Reformed Church. These groups gradually merged into one larger body and in later years finally united with The Congregational Christian Churches to form The United Church of Christ.

The eighteenth century brought people of the Reformed faith from Europe, part of whom were from Germany and part from Holland. Others came from Switzerland. Yet again another group came from the Scandinavian countries. Many of these associations of believers have maintained their identity in America. On the frontier of America old world customs were retained at the same time that new advances were made in self-perpetuation of church and gospel. From the German people who began in the seventeenth century and on, came Mennonites, German Baptists, Brethren, Dunkers, Amish, and Moravian groups belonging to the fringes of German Protestantism. They held to tenets which were modifications of the reform movement under Luther and others. Some practiced baptism for adults instead of baptism of children; some kept the Lord's Supper as a memorial act only. Church government was congregational, not presbyterial or episcopal.

Those of the Reformed groups held to The Helvetic Confession (1566), The Heidelberg Catechism (1563), The Palatinate Liturgy (1563). Others refused to be bound by these confessional statements, preferring to be free in what they believed as long as they found Biblical bases for their faith and practice.

The Mercersburg Movement in the 1840's had a profound effect upon the fortunes and future of the Reformed groups thus severed from Lutheranism. After the pioneer days and settlements, various colleges and theological centers were founded. Allegheny in Pittsburgh, Lancaster, and especially Mercersburg in Pennsylvania were noted in those days. Some of the trends and currents in American religious life at that period had included revivalism and sectarianism. Puritanism and Methodism stressed the "gathered church" and personal piety. An anti-Romanism was expressed in political and religious circles. A reaction had set in against things European in theology. The leaders of these Reformed churches did not altogether object to revivalism, but were against some of its methods. They desired a true revivalism within their congregations, guided through their own teaching and catechetical system. They saw their church as apostolic, and although Rome had distorted the church earlier, they believed in the on-going nature of the church as a divine organism. For thirty years the people of these groups were in tension. Some continued in the status quo and retained customs held dear; others stood against the old Reformed in an attempt to conjoin the best of the old with new expressions.

The Mercersburg group claimed the ancient as well as the Reformation creeds. They called themselves Christocentric, not Bibliocentric. They claimed that the whole person of Christ was basic, not just his teaching, his work, or his death. **John Williamson Nevin (1803-1886)** was the President and Theologian of the group; **Philip Schaff (1819-1893)** was the Professor of Historical Theology and the Historian and Liturgist of the movement. Nevin had preached and published *The Anxious Bench* (1843), an appeal for true revival within the congregation. Schaff spoke of "The Principle of Protestantism" (1844), a proclamation of the nature of the church as one, holy, and catholic.

Nevin was foremost in preaching and in advocating the Mercersburg position. In *The Mystical Presence* he interpreted John Calvin's doctrine of the spiritual real presence of Christ in the Eucharist in a way that was countered by his former teacher at Princeton, Calvinist Charles Hodge. In *The History and Genius of the Heidelberg*

Catechism he reinterpreted that symbol to support his previous thesis and also spoke against the extreme individualism then creeping into sectarianism. Schaff also expressed his convictions in *What Is Church History?*, stressing the objective factor in man's salvation as represented by the church with the Word and the sacraments.

The next era's wave of immigration brought people of the same background from Europe, but not all free from Lutheranism. The new denomination struggled to be free and eventually merged with the body first on the field. German-trained pastors were not sufficient to meet the needs of the growing churches, so colleges were established. Eden Theological Seminary, Lancaster Theological Seminary, and Mission House Theological Seminary trained the young German-American men. English gradually superseded German, and the new generation accepted this for church life and ministry. In the inevitable merger of the two Synods of German Reformed peoples, the new denomination became The Evangelical and Reformed Church (1934). This was to be a fellowship of believers in Christ. The Evangelical Synod held to the Augsburg Confession and the Lutheran and Heidelberg Catechisms; The Reformed Synod held only to the Heidelberg Catechism. "The Scriptures of the Old and New Testaments were recognized as the Word of God and as the ultimate rule of Christian faith and practice. The doctrinal standards were accepted as interpretative statements of the essential truth of evangelical (Protestant) Christianity as taught in the Holy Scriptures. In these statements of faith, ministers and members are allowed liberty of conscience whose final norm is the Word of God." Here was the basis of unity.

The next union of this one body with the Congregational Christian Church provided an added dimension of growth. In preaching the noted emphasis by the leaders was, as it has always been, the fellowship of believers in the universal church. They took The Apostles' Creed and John 17 seriously as pointing to a oneness of life and fellowship; hence the idea of the church as one, holy, and catholic. Another emphasis has been that of a cultivated piety within the life of the religious community. Sermons stressed this, even expecting recurrences of revival as in the past, but for some like the Mercersburg group it was welcomed within and not as a divisive and separating movement.

Outstanding in preaching has been the didactic spirit. As pioneers in a new land, the leaders sought to indoctrinate their families and youth in the historic faith which was theirs. Thus catechetical instruction was given, and in preaching there was the solid exposition and exegesis of The Heidelberg Catechism in particular. The theology and the Biblical basis of this outstanding work gave sufficient material for many series of sermons. The distinctiveness of Reformation doctrine and faith is brought out within this framework. Any preacher following this systematically would cover the major doctrines year after year to his own profit and that of the congregation.

Preaching, then, tended not to be oratorical or topical in a popular sense. It was Biblically based and systematically expounded, and exhortation was wedded to a practical demand for living out what was believed. After the earlier names of Michael Schlatter, Philip Schaff, John W. Nevin, Lewis Mayer, and others must be added the later names of John Zimmerman, George W. Richards, James E. Wagner, and Louis W. Goebel. These men were typical of the best in preaching to their times and to their people.

Evangelistic Preaching

America's most important evangelist was **Dwight Lyman Moody** (1837-1899), a layman whose ministry was worldwide and whose message dramatically awakened men from the lethargic church life of Great Britain and the United States. After Finney no name is better known than Moody's. His beginnings were modest and humble in that he knew little of culture or of the gospel, but after conversion he earnestly sought to work for his newly found faith. This led him into youth work and into the Sunday school movement.

Moody began adult life as a shoe salesman; his zeal in business was eventually transferred to evangelism. Having been successful in business and having saved money, he decided to devote himself full time to Christian service. Later, he served the soldiers in the Civil War, ministering to them as an unofficial chaplain and as a volunteer missionary. The Sunday school he organized grew into a church which later bore his own name in memorial and which still continues to serve the city of Chicago. He also advocated the work of the YMCA as an outlet for evangelism.

The major step in his life was his first visit to Great Britain where he went to conduct services. With Ira D. Sankey, the singer, he went on a third visit and then it was that Moody was given openings and publicity never afforded any preacher of like stature. The romance of preaching surely is demonstrated in that throughout this and subsequent visits as well as his ministry in America, the people thronged to hear him. No one can explain this except that God's hand was upon him for special service. An anointing of the Holy Spirit marked his preaching. Wherever this new ministry penetrated, the days of Wesley and Whitefield were recalled as the only comparable wave of preaching and revival. Evangelistic preaching became the focal point of the church, and people outside the churches gave attention and showed interest.

Moody as a preacher was not the product of the schools. He went to the day school with its limited education. He was a business man with vigorous speech and persuasive style. Now his gifts found enlargement of opportunity in preaching. His stocky figure and bearded face matched the absence of cultured speech and a style which had no literary polish. His Americanisms, mistakes in grammar, colloquialisms, and rough voice, which normally would have hindered acceptance (especially in Great Britain), were no longer hindrances as God used him. Holding the Bible in hand, he told the Bible stories as if they had come alive and the characters were men and women walking the streets of any city. He had the rare gift of seeing human nature as it was, and with stories out of life he touched the chords of memory and of conscience.

The period in which Moody preached was a time of social reform and industrialization in America, while in Great Britain the industrial revolution was also vibrant. The era saw the rise of the industrialist and the corporations with enlarged profits and a widened gulf between them and the people who were the workers and the poor of society. Some preachers accepted the status quo and advocated patient endurance in the providence of God. Others proclaimed the need to change radically the social order to help people. Moody stood as an evangelical to offer Christ to the individual and the encouragement that the converted man would then change his lot. The new creation would have new strength to meet life's burdens and resolve life's problems.

In the sermon "What must I do to be saved?" (Acts 16:30), Moody deals with the question by playing upon the idea of "What must I do" and then urging the addition of "to be saved?" "A man of business gets up in the morning and asks, "What must I do today? What shall I do to make the most money? It is hard times, and it is hard to make both ends meet. It is hard to meet the notes that are coming due. But there is a good deal more important question than that, when a man is sick and asks what he must do to save his life; and even that is not so important a question as we have before us tonight. A man had better lose the life of the body than the life of the soul; and it is better to go into bankruptcy, and lose all through failure in business than to fail to save your soul."

Moody's beliefs were the usual orthodox tenets of theology then held. He believed the Bible to be God's Word to man and the death of Christ on the cross to be the means of redemption, so that his messages were always Christ-centered. It was the vicarious nature of Christ's death which caused him to say: "because He died for me, I love Him. Because He died for me, I will serve Him. I will work for Him, I will give Him my very life." When Moody heard Henry Varley say that "the world has yet to see what God can do with and for and through a man who is fully and wholly consecrated to Him," Moody said, "A man! He meant any man. He didn't say he had to be educated, or brilliant, or anything else. Just a man. Well, by the Holy Spirit in me, I'll be that man."

The motives which moved him to preach were those he also used in his appeal to the heart. Four general areas of motives are seen: (1) relief from life's miseries and sorrows; (2) the effect of love, friendship, and loyalty to parents and friends on us; (3) fear of death and the grave; and (4) the security faith gives for holding to a way of life.

One of his methods of preparation for the sermon was to take a theme in the Bible and use the concordance references to trace the subject. In this way he became well informed on that subject and also saw it in Biblical relationship. He would gather further material by placing in an envelope any cuttings or references to a given subject or text. He was not ashamed to say that he was helped by others. Hearing another speaker or reading other sermons or addresses led him to take notes which he would put through the sieve of his own mind when the time came to use it in a sermon of his own.

For preaching Moody used an outline of notes on sheets of paper 8½ by 11 inches. Biblical quotations used were cut out of a Bible and pasted in the proper place in his notes. There was no attempt to present his material according to the traditional practice of introduction, exposition, and conclusion. He brooded over his subject, then with a mind filled with its spirit and meaning, he poured out his message in sincerity. Everything was aimed at the goal of application as he asked for a response at the end. No rhetorical devices were used in the seeming artlessness of the sermon. The majority of Moody's words were of one syllable. Not many were found to be beyond three syllables. His was simple and graphic speech—the speech of the rugged Anglo-Saxon English Bible understood by the common man.

His style was simple and clear with a surge of feeling which persuaded people hearing him to respond. Strong emotional content was part of his message. Homiletics was not Moody's strong point, but the message in its thematic form got through in the sincerity of its tones and the urgent appeal it made. The illustrations he used were from everyday life and common to his time. Moody was a man of one Book, and his saturation in the Bible enabled him to counteract any early deficiency in education.

The simplicity of Moody's preaching appealed to the crowds which thronged to hear him. An example of that appealing simplicity is found in a sermon "Heaven: Its Hope," based on Colossians 1:3, 5. In it he said:

> A great many persons imagine that anything said about heaven is only a matter of speculation. They talk about heaven much as they would about the air. Now there would not have been so much in Scripture on this subject if God had wanted to leave the human race in darkness about it. What the Bible says about heaven is just as true as what it says about everything else. The Bible is inspired. What we are taught about heaven could not have come to us in any other way than by inspiration. No one knew anything about it but God, and so if we want to find out anything about it we have to turn to his Word. . . .We believe it is inspired because there is nothing in it that could not have come from God. God is wise, and God is good. There is nothing in the Bible that is not wise, and there is nothing in it that is not good. If the Bible had anything in it that was opposed to reason, or to our sense of right, then, perhaps, we might think that it was like all the books in the world that are written merely by men. . . . Like all the other wonderful works of God, this Book bears the sure stamp of its Author. It is like Him. . . .

Here is the blend of rugged speech, clear style, forceful utterance, persuasive appeal, and the conviction that people can trust God concerning the future destiny of life because it is reasonable and dovetails with the Biblical revelation which reflects the nature of God. It was this kind of preaching which reached the ordinary man. Like those who thronged to hear his Master, the common people heard Moody gladly. But the cultured heard him as well. Millions of people heard him even in a day without the buildings and the technological help now available for mass meetings. For Moody appealed to the hearer and discovered the springs of human need.

It is not without significance that this lay evangelist with limited education was instrumental in founding institutions of learning. The Moody Bible Institute of Chicago, the Mount Hermon School for Boys, and the Northfield School for Girls at Mount Hermon, Massachusetts, still continue their work. The Moody Memorial Church in Chicago, the major missions in Glasgow and Edinburgh, and the Bible Training Institute in Glasgow, Scotland, are monuments to his influence and ministry. The YMCA, the American Sunday School Union, the American Tract Society, and the American Bible Society are examples of his wider interest and show how he worked with other Christians in united efforts for the whole church.

The preaching and missions of Moody served to unite Christians of differing theologies and backgrounds. The press gave him publicity as his sermons were copied and extracts circulated widely. Many books were published with selections of sermons. His keen mind saw in the printed page an outlet for wider evangelism. Henry Drummond said of him: "He was the biggest human I ever met." In Moody's character was "tenderness, humor, common sense, insight, immediateness, passion, breadth, and modesty," according to G. Campbell Morgan who knew him well. He stands as the one, single great evangelist of the American nation.

Chapter VI

Preaching in the United States by Liberals (1800-1900)

This period is marked by the rise of dynamic movements which threatened to change the traditional beliefs and mores of the nation. People who assumed that Christianity was their heritage and took for granted the regular practices of public worship soon found that disruption was upon them. The theory of Charles Darwin that in evolution nature had constancy and progress from lower forms of life to the highest became a decisive factor. Taught first as a theory in biology and with references only to nature, it then was taken up by educators who saw in it another approach of teaching. Theological studies were also affected and in seminaries the evolutionary concept was applied to the history and literature of the Bible with far-reaching effects.

In the earlier periods of the seventeenth and eighteenth centuries there was coming to birth a new way of looking at things. This was based on observation and induction rather than authority and tradition. The older pre-Aristotelian concept of the universe was passing. Not that previous views of science were held to be non-factual in basis, but that the old facts were now seen in a new perspective. The new way of looking at the universe was the product of Christian men, and a new beginning was made in the understanding of the vastness of the universe. Natural science began with this Christian view of God and the world. Not nature alone, but history also must be reckoned with if an adequate interpretation was to be made.

Isaac Newton's contribution in the seventeenth century freed the science of nature from the bonds of philosophy. It had become an independent discipline. However, with the dawn of the nineteenth century, scientific method was for the first time seriously applied to the study of man. Man was seen now not merely as a biological organism but as a social creature related to history, civilization, and social organization.

Preaching in this era was forced to take note of the challenge of these revolutionary changes of a new world-view of history and mankind and the effect on the attitudes of men. The break with tradition is seen in the work of Hegel (1770-1831), Professor of Philosophy at Berlin in 1818. He dominated Continental thought and also that of the English-speaking world in expressing an evolutionary view of the universe. This was taught through the dialectical process of thesis, antithesis, and synthesis. All of life was then viewed in the light of this new concept of evolution. Herbert Spencer and T. H. Huxley also were linked with this view. Later, Karl Marx (1818-1883) applied this concept to history and economic determinism, with a view to bringing about the classless society. All men of that school of thought looked for the perfection of man in the progress to be made.

Charles Darwin (1809-1882) is thought of as the originator of this theory of evolution, but it is obvious others had been before him. The publication of *On the Origin of Species* (1859) caused debate and much conflict in theological and religious circles. Biological research was not alone the issue as now the theory was applied to history and life. Out of this historical application came new books on history and finally new religious research as the theologians applied this to the Bible and Christian beginnings. Thus the stage was set for the new theological upheaval in the nineteenth century as the result of this change in historical thought.

Religious leaders were also caught up in the romanticism of the Continental movement. The way was open for critical studies of the Bible with the attendant surrender of many cherished beliefs and defection from historic standards of faith and authority usually vested in the Bible as the supreme literature for the Christian. A struggle ensued among the churches as teachers and pastors found themselves in the ferment of controversy over the newer critical historical methods. The conservative element held on to their cherished beliefs and interpretations; the more liberal theologians gave up much in their attempt to impose the newer ideas of interpretation. The period was thus characterized by the struggle wherein the Bible was interpreted on the one hand as the actual Word of God, fully inspired because it was divine revelation, and on the other hand as a work of human derivation from man's experience and inspiration, a gradual work of evolution of man's ideas about God.

Diverse groups with varying shades of emphasis came into existence, each with labels and battlecries. The church in the United States of America was sharply divided and sub-divided. The concept of the essential unity of the Bible in its diversity of literature and its ancient authority as from God were lost as preaching began to expound its diversity. The changing culture of America and the slavery issue resulting in the Civil War were at the back of the proliferation of church groups, and within these groups eventual breakdown into the various factions with their distinctions in theology and emphases. This was also the time when each church group built and founded colleges and seminaries for the training of their young people. The end of the frontier and the passing of the camp meeting necessitated a more permanent form of religious life. This resulted in enlarged building movements and the increase of churches, institutions, and charities. A growing social consciousness and the rise of material standards challenged the church to proclaim a message to meet the changing times.

Theological Tensions and Change

Preaching then was by outstanding personalities whose ministries are recalled for their public acclaim and the strong proclamation of the message of God as they conceived it to be. In that liberalizing movement stands **Nathaniel William Taylor (1786-1858)** who espoused but modified the Edwardian ideals. In the doctrine of the Atonement the stress was now on the "governmental" and not the "satisfaction" theory. Taylor had an apologetical purpose in his preaching. His experience of the Second Great Awakening had motivated him to preach that man in his sinful state needed to use his freedom and moral agency to find salvation. Lyman Beecher, who was Taylor's friend, carried the revival spirit into the heartland of New England Unitarianism. It was Beecher who transmitted the Taylor emphasis to one Charles G. Finney (1792-1875) whose ministry was to electrify church life for a period. Finney, like Beecher and Taylor, strongly advocated the work of the will in the individual redemptive experience.

Finney has his place in the evangelical stream, but Taylor's place lies in this transitional movement away from the strong Calvinism of Edwards to the newer school which modified much of Calvin's dogma. Taylor's sermon "Concio ad Clerum" (1828) is noted for its discussion of human nature, sin, and freedom. These are not new topics and they are never out of date. Taylor was that rare combination of the intellectual and the revivalist. (He later became Professor of Didactic Theology at Yale.) He opposed Unitarianism, but found himself differing from orthodoxy in his emphasis on human nature. Scottish Common-Sense Realism was his philosophical view.

The text "and were by nature the children of wrath, even as others" (Eph. 2:3) is the basis of a sermon in which Taylor stresses God's moral government rather than his absolute sovereignty as the key concept. In this sermon is the evangelical thrust of a probing spirit confronting man's conscience. The finely spun argument and eloquence of the day come through in this message delivered in the chapel of Yale College. Strong in doctrine, the preacher begins with the truth of moral depravity as a characteristic of human nature. "By this I intend generally, the entire sinfulness of their moral character—that state of mind or heart to which guilt and the desert of wrath pertain." The startling thing about this sermon—"Advice to the Clergy"—is the evangelistic note for them. His proposition as given at the start was in the Puritan tradition. Discussing the truth both negatively and positively, Taylor clears God of any responsibility in creating man in this state. "It is man's own act, consisting in a free choice of some object rather than God, as his chief good—or a free preference of the world and of worldly good, to the will and glory of God." He summons the testimony of apostles, of the ablest divines, and of common sense. John Calvin and the Westminister Divines are quoted, as well as Jonathan Edwards. His hearers would understand his allusions and the familiar names.

The second division of the sermon stresses that if man is depraved by nature, then we understand that "such is their nature, that they will sin, and only sin in all the appropriate circumstances of their being." "To bring this distinctly before the mind, it may be well to remark, that the question between the Calvinists and the Arminians on the point is this—whether the depravity or sinfulness of mankind is truly and properly ascribed to their nature or to their circumstances of temptation?" He proceeds to argue from the text and other related passages that the facts are as he claims.

Finally, the third section is given to Remarks or the summing up with its application. He claimed that in the light of this doctrine "infants should be saved through the redemption of Christ." Everyone sins as soon as he can, not "must" or "will necessarily" but "will" sin. "The universal depravity of mankind is not inconsistent with the moral perfection of God." God's provision of redemption is given as the answer to human nature's sin. Thus the providential government of God is exhibited as the basis of submission, confidence, and joy, under all the evils that befall his dependent creatures. "It also presents, as no other theory in the view of Taylor does present, the Moral Government of God in its unimpaired perfection and glory, to deter from sin and allure to holiness his accountable subjects." Closely reasoned and presented with fine argument, this sermon would not be "popular" for the ordinary congregation. It presupposes people with an adequate theological background, hence its counsel to clergy.

In **Lyman Beecher (1775-1863)** the revival strain was intermingled with his teaching ability as a theologian and as president of Lane Theological Seminary. In the new emphasis of a modified Calvinism and a partial Arminianism, his preaching showed a belief that the supernatural harvest of souls was partly the result of stirring up men. Beecher was an exhorter in preaching and his persuasive powers of personality can not be easily dismissed. An emotional quality was dominant. As the new nation advanced and felt the stirring of progress, so the work of God kept pace with similar stirrings of the soul. "Let me then call attention of my readers to our only remaining sources of hope—God—and the interposition of his Holy Spirit, in great and general Revivals of Religion, to reform the hearts of this people, and make the nation good and happy" (*The Spirit of the Pilgrims,* iv, Boston, 1831). Calvinist as he was, Lyman Beecher believed profoundly in conversion and anyone not converted had no hope of salvation. This was part of his theological emphasis in preaching.

In New England his ministry moved from Litchfield, Connecticut, to Boston, Massachusetts. As an exponent of evangelical Christianity he stood without apology against the Unitarianism then prevalent. He was a staunch believer in the orthodox position, and so preached. However, as time went on he mellowed somewhat as he moved away from a more rigid adherence to certain theological tenets. His polemic was lessened, and a more conciliatory note was heard. Gradually he favored a more modified Calvinism.

In 1832 Beecher went to Lane Seminary, Cincinnati, Ohio, a

Presbyterian school of some eminence in that time of turbulence. There he was involved in the theological debates of the day, such as the question of man's freedom in relation to an innate depravity. Because of his views on original sin, he was accused of heresy before the Presbytery of Cincinnati during the controversy between the Old and New School schism in the Presbyterian Church. But he was acquitted of the charge. The slavery issue also brought tension and division to the Presbyterians. When the slavery issue arose in Beecher's seminary and some students formed an anti-slavery society to divide the seminary, Beecher was caught in the controversy and stood against slavery. Some abolitionists left Lane Seminary for Oberlin. However, Beecher remained at his post in Lane until he retired. His daughter, Harriet Beecher Stowe, was also caught in the slavery storm of controversy when she wrote *Uncle Tom's Cabin.* During the conflict between the Old School and New School groups, Beecher stood with the New School group, but was unavowedly evangelical and conservative in theology. He still adhered to the Westminster Confession of Faith, although like many of his contemporaries he did not give it a place superior to the Bible, but only as it claimed to be—a subordinate standard.

Lyman Beecher is remembered for his sermons against the liquor traffic. His sermons against intemperance included one from Proverbs 23:29, 30—"Who hath woe? who hath sorrow? who hath contentions? who hath babbling? who hath wounds without cause? who hath redness of eyes? They that tarry long at the wine; they that go to seek mixed wine." He sought an enlightened expression of public opinion. Arguments against the evils of drink, social and national, religious and civil, physical, mental, and moral, were set forth with a power of logic and a sweep of eloquence sometimes overwhelming in effect. In describing the effects of drinking upon the body he said, "If all diseases which terminate in death could speak out of the grave or tell their origin upon the coffin lid, we should witness the most appalling and unexpected disclosures."

The advocates of moderate use of alcohol heard him argue: "We might as well speak of the moderate use of the plague; of fire handled prudently among powder; of poison taken prudently every day; or vipers and serpents introduced prudently into our dwellings to glide about as a matter of courtesy to visitors and of amusement to our children." The remedy was suggested also as he commented upon the blight in national life. His first principle was "to extend universal information on the subject of intemperance, its nature, causes, evils and remedy may be universally made known. Every pulpit and every newspaper in the land may be put in requisition to give line upon line on this subject until it is done." Also advocated was the formation of associations to deal with the social and civil remedies needed. Out of this preaching came the formation of the American Society for the Promotion of Temperance and later its successor the Anti-Saloon League. Although Beecher advocated general prohibition, he made clear that legislation is not sufficient until matched by public conviction.

The purpose of such preaching was to stir the conscience and call for action. Church people responded and the new associations of reform and renewal began. Beecher likened the drink traffic to "a Molech" where children were kept in torment and where the voices and tears of victims could be heard. He pictured the dark caverns of iniquity associated with blood-money, vested interests, and the ghastly and revolting scenes of the drunkard. This was a slavery just an iniquitous as the slave trade of America. The fire of his eloquence blazed, and he drew thousands to the banner of temperance and reform.

The importance given to Lyman Beecher in preaching is well justified, for when he preached on the prevailing issues, controversies, or sins of his generation people listened and acted. Doctrinal content was allied to practical demands for action. The ethical import of the sermon was never in doubt. He attacked dueling, and laws were passed to make this illegal. He attacked intemperance, and men gave up their indulgence. He preached against the liberalism of many pulpits, and people returned to orthodox faith. In one sense Lyman Beecher was a bridge-builder between people and issues, ever holding to dogma yet seeing new applications. Not only were the throngs who listened to him gladly influenced by his preaching, but his own distinguished son, Henry Ward Beecher, was profoundly motivated by such preaching to follow the steps of his father. Another was Wendell Phillips, the orator and reformer, who came under the spell of Lyman Beecher's preaching as a young man and the spiritual awakening of the times left a lasting impression on him. As an apostle of social justice, he became the enemy of the oppressor and the friend of the weak and the exploited.

Beecher also opposed the inroads and teaching of the Roman Church. He was able to unite with him men of different schools who saw in the Roman body a threat to freedom. With others he identified the Papacy with Antichrist.

He believed that the "Moral government of God" was the basis of enduring worth for the American nation, and so preached in many a sermon. The moral reforms of the nation, the movements of the Holy Spirit in revival, and the advance of the church he saw as precursors of the coming millennium and kingdom.

Liberal Convictions

The illustrious son of Lyman Beecher is known as one of the outstanding preachers of all time in America. In **Henry Ward Beecher (1813-1887)** American preaching reached a high pinnacle of worth and influence. By inheritance he was destined to be a national figure and by endowment and training he was prepared for a ministry almost worldwide. He was an impressive personality with lion-like appearance. With a finely controlled voice of organ proportions, he was a gifted orator. In temperament he was impulsive and not given to reflection. His preaching had spontaneity and a wide appeal for all kinds of people. Although he was criticized for an indiscretion in conduct, the charges did not mar his ministry or diminish his influence.

The modifications and changes begun by his father, Lyman Beecher, led Henry Ward Beecher to continue and advance the gains made. His preaching was conspicuous for its evangelical spirit which was allied to a practical ethic. This was proclaimed in a sermon where the thought is well defined, clear, and persuasive for action. The style was forceful, racy, and pungent, with a popular way of illustration. He saw the practical bearings of religious truth. To tremendous force of will—so essential in the art of persuasion— intensity of emotion, and vivid imagination, there were added the presence, the voice, and the occasion which he used to the fullest advantage. Some would say that Beecher was a genius and no less a judge than Dr. R. W. Dale, Birmingham, England said that he was "the greatest preacher of the Christian Church."

The ministry of this striking preacher can be divided into three parts: (a) before the Civil War, 1847-61 (14 years), with evangelistic stress on the love of God; (b) during the Civil War, 1861-65 (4 years), with ethical emphasis on the will of God; (c) after the War, 1865-87 (22 years), with emotional appeal on the grace of God.

From Indianapolis to Brooklyn he moved not only geographically but also in church affiliation. A liberal Presbyterian in the tradition of his father, he later became a Congregationalist of the independent type. The Plymouth Church built for him by popular request suited his temperament and gave him freedom and scope for his work.

In a period of social and economic unrest due to the Civil War, he knew how to capitalize on the popular themes of the times. Colorful in preaching, he attacked the evils of that period, such as intemperance, prostitution, gambling, and slavery. The press gave him publicity by copying his sermons and reporting his judgments. A large public thronged his church, especially in Brooklyn, to hear and see what would catch their interest. On one occasion he placed a slave girl before the congregation and asked that she be freed. To do this his people gave an offering that day of money and jewelry to free the girl.

The unconventional was prominent in Beecher's preaching. No one knew when or whether he would follow the usual conventional homiletical pattern of a sermon. One of the limitations of his preaching lay in his overuse of humor. His family was noted for their hilarity and joyful times together. However, the tone of the Puritan pulpit had been serious and only on rare occasion allowed for humor. Beecher shattered that tradition with his constant wit and subtle remarks which caused much laughter in the service of worship. Another limitation was thought to be his adoption of the theory of evolution at a time when this issue was causing serious division among Christian theologians. Hitherto, the Bible had been accepted without question but now the newer views concerning science and the world impinged upon the Bible's view. His broadening views led many to estimate that he held loose convictions concerning the Person of Christ and the question of miracles, and that his preaching tended to stress "religion" rather than "the Christian faith."

Theology to Beecher was not the important thing to preach. He sought a life pattern tinged with Christian ethics. Hence, his sermons were not theological in the Puritan sense, but only incidentally, so that belief was not paramount if action was called for. Instead of argument, he used illustration. He had reacted against the earlier controversies of the New and Old Schools of Presbyterianism, having witnessed how his father had suffered an eclipse thereby. He was against sectarianism and avoided heresy. In his evaluation of Jonathan Edwards' sermons on judgment, it is evident that he missed the implications of that Puritan mind wherein justice and mercy commingled.

Beecher was an adapter in preaching. He trimmed his subjects for the occasion and gave the people what they desired. Adaptation can be dangerous, for people desire more and more what is pleasing to them. Beecher lacked in the preaching they needed most, not in what they wanted. Thus his popularity.

Nevertheless, the preaching of Beecher was effective—thousands were drawn to him and his influence was great. "Henry Ward Beecher did more than any other preacher to break up and abolish the Calvinistic Moloch. He pleaded for the infinite Father of Mankind when all the seminaries of the land, with their prestige, their learning, their opportunity and power, were putting first God, the Sovereign, God, the Moral Governor of the world. It was an immense battle. . . . Contrary to all expectations the professional failed. Greater influence upon the religious belief of the people of the United States has been exerted by none than by William Ellery Channing and Henry Ward Beecher" (George A. Gordon, *Ultimate Conceptions of Faith*, Yale Lectures, 1903, p. 341).

Beecher's mind was ever open to new ideas. His acceptance of the theory of evolution caused him to revise earlier views of life and revelation. Herbert Spencer, philosopher and evolutionist, had a profound influence upon Beecher. The nineteenth century included this broadening base for religion as mediated by Beecher more than by any one else. His concept of his mission lay not in the future life but in the present order of living. Thus, we note the great importance of man in his preaching. "The thing the preacher aims at all the while is *reconstructed manhood,* a nobler idea in his congregation of how people ought to live and what they ought to be." In the sermon Beecher was able to convey a friendship to men as he discussed their problems and their needs. He expressed their inner yearnings, indicated their ideals for betterment, and warned them of the dangers to be shunned. His manly approach and his straightforward speech convinced many. He said, "If I know my business— and the presumption is I do—it is to hunt men and to study them. Do you suppose I study old, musty books when I want to preach? I study you! When I want to deliver a discourse on theology, I study you! When I want to know more about the doctrine of depravity, I study you! When I want to know what is right and what is wrong, I see how *you* do; and I have abundant illustrations on every side" (Anecdotes of H.W.B.).

Blessed with robust health and exuding a magnetic feeling of well-being, Beecher was sensitive to the feelings of his people before him. Thus sympathy and not judgment swayed him. He owed more to variety than to profundity. In preparation for the sermon he read and thought around the subject but did not like to write out the sermon in case it could not be reproduced again at the time demanded. He preferred to make notes and before the actual delivery spend time in an outline so that he could think through the major points and react informally to the mood of the congregation. A surprise element in his preaching brought inspiration to his listeners. It was not only *what* Beecher said but *how* he said it that his hearers found most enjoyable.

Beecher is also known for instituting the now famous Lyman Beecher *Lectures on Preaching* given at Yale annually since 1871. When he delivered the first three series in 1871, '72, and '73, he laid the foundation of the Yale Lectures and set the standard for them. One of his church members, Henry W. Sage, contributed the money for investment and encouraged Beecher to give the lectures to show others how they could preach extemporaneously. For more than a century now the lectures have been given and are esteemed as the one single monumental contribution to this field of study.

Beecher's views on preaching are given in the three opening years of lectures, and from these we glean that some of his convictions created a new approach to the art of homiletics and practical theology. These emphases include the increased use of *humor.* Hitherto the Puritan and Calvinistic preacher was sparing with this ingredient in public speech. The decorum and order of the sermon was such that the seriousness of the message predominated. As stated before, Beecher came from a family accustomed to mirth and it was a natural outcome of his personality to bring humor into the pulpit increasingly. This has always been a marked trait of successful public speakers and orators—the right use of humor to bring relief, change of pace, and a subtle barb of truth to the listener.

Another factor was the lessening of content and the increased use of *illustration.* In its heritage, American preaching had been heavy on doctrinal content as was fitting to those who were the heirs of the Puritans. The frontier movements and the Great Awakening had

opened the door for a more elastic style of preaching. The evangelist could extemporize and adapt as he reacted to the mood of the
people gathered around him. Some of this came to Beecher as
principles of public speech. His development of stories and anecdotes, especially out of life and human experience, became a
marked feature of his preaching.

A third change in preaching taught by Beecher was his insistence
that the doctrine of God in his majesty and might was not so
important now and should be replaced by the new stress upon *man*.
Thus preaching tended gradually to be the study of man in his life,
sin, and goals. The reconstruction of manhood was spoken of as a
new gospel and Beecher's words were soon reported, prompting
others to talk in similar fashion. Thus the new trend in preaching
was humanitarian.

Such was the influence of Beecher in preaching that he set new
standards and methods for the generation to follow. Never an
expository preacher, he is best known as the popular and topical
preacher. A good example is in the sermon "The God of Comfort,"
based on "Blessed be God, the Father of our Lord Jesus Christ, the
Father of mercies, and the God of all comfort; who comforteth us
in all our tribulation, that we may be able to comfort them which
are in any trouble, by the comfort wherewith we ourselves are
comforted of God" (II Cor. 1:3-4). The expository preacher with
his careful exegesis would treat this unit and theme step by step to
unfold its meaning and give its application. Beecher discusses the
truth and subject of the text as the first major point; then his
second point is the application. A long, ten-paragraph introduction
brings one to the text itself, as if the preacher has to feel his way
slowly into the vestibule of truth.

As Beecher develops the subject, he gradually unfolds a structure
which takes up several points to support the text as he discusses the
nature of Fatherhood, human and divine, and shows how we need
not fear God but take from him what we need in the hour of
trouble and tragedy. In this sermon there are ample references to
indicate his doctrinal belief in the goodness and benevolence of God
(nothing here of any judgment of God), the central place of human
nature in need of help, and finally, the call that when we are helped
we should help others. Humor and allusions to studying man rather
than bothering with books also come through. Read aloud, there is
the pulse of a great heart, and one senses a little of what this must

have been when preached with all the intensity and force of that giant personality.

One of the giants of the nineteenth century is **Horace Bushnell** (1802-1876), whose name is contemporary with Beecher and Brooks. He is known chiefly for his sermons and theological works. His book *Christian Nurture* (1847) was an epoch-making treatise and pioneered a new way for Christian education in a day when the stress was largely upon conversion. He brought a balanced view to the training and teaching of the young within the family and the church. At Yale he studied the arts, law, and theology. As a Congregationalist he held only one pastorate at North Church, Hartford, Connecticut (1833-59). He was an original thinker, an impressive speaker, a strong writer, and a man involved in many civic and social projects.

Bushnell was part of the new liberalism which had reacted against the earlier Calvinism and Puritanism in New England. His father was Arminian in theology. The new-found idealism in philosophy and literature found him moving away from his earlier views. Especially was this so when he could not accept the dogma that a child should experience the torture of guilt and conviction before conversion. He taught that a child in a Christian home should be trained and instructed in the Christian faith so that as a child of the Covenant he would never depart from that belief. Thus his idea of growth clashed with the traditional idea of conversion. Now, a century later, Christian education is accepted alongside of conversion as complementary one to the other, but then the idea was revolutionary and disruptive.

In preaching Bushnell incorporated many of these ideas in his works *The New Life* and *Sermons on Living Subjects*. The titles of the sermons carried similar implications: "Every Man's Life a Plan of God," "The Dignity of Human Nature Shown by Its Ruins," "The Hunger of the Soul," "Living to God in Small Things," "Duty Not Measured by Our Own Ability," "Respectable Sin," "Enduring Discipline," and "How to Be Christian in Trade." These are samples of topics he introduced in a time when the major emphasis in preaching was on theological doctrines.

The subjects of Bushnell are religious, interesting, short, and clear. His homiletic method can be discerned in its Introduction followed by the Proposition. A key sentence usually gives the intended substance of the plan to be followed. He stressed the value of a strong topic, a strong proposition, and strong structure. This last is most important to Bushnell. One of the outstanding sermons ever preached was "Every Man's Life a Plan of God" based upon "I am the Lord, and there is none else, there is no God beside me: I girded thee, though thou hast not known me" (Isa. 45:5). The heathen king Cyrus is seen in the hands of God. From this text and truth, Bushnell states his Proposition: *"God has an exact life plan for each one, girding him visibly and invisibly for some exact thing which it will be the true significance and glory of his life to have accomplished."*

The development of the major points of the sermon reveals the strong structure: (1) the Scriptures, wherein individuals are shown to be part of God's plan for life; (2) the works of God, in which we trace design and not chance. In this part of the sermon, Bushnell expounds these truths with fitting illustrations. He also allows the possibility of the individual missing God's plan when he says, "God has, then, a definite life-plan set for every man; one that, being accepted and followed, will conduct him to the best and noblest end possible. No qualification of this doctrine is needed, save the fearful one just named; that we, by our perversity, so often refuse to take the place and do the work he gives us."

In the second part of the sermon, Bushnell raises the question: "How can we ever get hold of this life plan God has made for us, or find our way into it?" He then gives practical answers to this question, some negative, and some positive: (1) you will never come into God's plan if you study singularity; (2) as little will you seek to copy the life of another; (3) you are never to complain of your birth, your training, your employments, your hardships; never to fancy that you could be something if only you had a different lot and sphere assigned you; (4) you also give up the hope or expectation that God will set you in any scheme of life, where the whole course of it will be known, or set down beforehand.

Following the negatives, the positive note is sounded with the question: "How, then, can a man, who really desires to do it, come into the plan God lay for him, so as to live it and rationally believe that he does? You are on the point of choosing, it may be, this or that calling, wanting to know where duty lies and what course God himself would have you take. Beginning at a point most remote, and where the generality of truth is widest: (1) Consider the character of God, and you will draw a larger deduction from that, for, all

that God designs for you will be in harmony with his character;
(2) consider relation to him as a creature; (3) you have a conscience; (4) God's law and his written Word are guides to present
duty; (5) be an observer of God's Providence; (6) consult your
friends, and especially those who are in the teaching of God; (7) go
to God himself, and ask for the calling of God; for, as certainly as
he has a plan or calling for you, he will somehow guide you into it.
And this is the proper office and work of his Spirit."

In the third and final section of the sermon, Bushnell discusses
the objections and problems raised by his thesis, and in ten paragraphs (not unlike the Puritan structure) he makes the Application
pertinent and personal without dubiety. Prosperity and adversity,
knowledge and ignorance, success and failure, young and old—all
are brought under review. His Conclusion and Appeal sounds the
conviction that it is never too late to seek and find God's plan. A
condition is that "there must be a complete renunciation of self-
will. God and religion must be practically first. . . ." "Take your
duty, and be strong in it, as God will make you strong. . . . Understand, also, that the great question here is, *not what you will get,*
but *what you will become.* Take your burdens, and troubles, and
losses, and wrongs, if come they must and will, as your opportunities, *knowing that God has girded you* for greater things than
these. O, to live out such a life as God appoints, how great a thing it
is!—to do the duties, make the sacrifices, bear the adversities, finish
the plan, and then to say, with Christ (who of us will be able?)—'It
is finished!' "

The magnificence of this sermon is found in its simple theme
which comes naturally out of the text and context of Scripture and
history. The profound conviction of a divine life-plan catches the
imagination, fires the mind, and challenges the will. Bushnell has
outlined and elucidated in this sermon the deep things of God in
planning and providentially caring for those who seek his mind and
will. In this sense the insight of the sermon becomes timeless in its
application and influence.

Bushnell may not be given the preeminence of Brooks or Beecher
but his sermons have a tectonic quality about them deserving
greater appreciation. His theological ideas also merit consideration
and study. Believing as he did in the moral influence of the
Atonement, he reinterpreted this doctrine as Brooks the Trinitarian
stressed the Incarnation of our Lord rather than the Atonement.

Bushnell used texts but was mostly a topical preacher, using themes in a grand manner and seeking to reinterpret the doctrines then in dispute. He did not give up belief in conversion when he taught Christian nurture; he did not abandon faith in the atoning work of Christ when he reiterated a new facet of truth concerning the moral influence of Christ's death; and he did not surrender his faith in the sinless humanity of the Son of God when he discussed, as in his work, *Nature and the Supernatural.* However, in an era of changing theological views, his liberal mind and his ready pen did prepare the way for others to abandon many of the traditional orthodox interpretations. While this may be regretted, the fact of his preaching ability should not be dismissed. He stands as one of the superlative examples and ideals of how a sermon ought to be viewed and written. His method and mastery complement each other in sermons of enduring worth with strong structure and force of appeal.

In the controversy about the nature of the Kingdom of God and entrance into it by the new birth as over against what he termed Christian nurture, Bushnell was ready with his teaching. Looking back, we can make a reassessment in which these two points of view can be maintained without contradiction. The text, "Bring them up in the nurture and admonition of the Lord" (Eph. 6:4) gave Bushnell a foundation for his thesis. Again, as in his sermon structure, he states his proposition: "That the child is to grow up a Christian, and never know himself as being otherwise." In other words, "the aim, effort, and expectation should be, not, as is commonly assumed, that the child is to grow up in sin, to be converted after he comes to a mature age; but that he is to open on the world as one that is spiritually renewed, not remembering the time when he went through a technical experience, but seeming rather to have loved what is good from his earliest years. I do not affirm that every child may, in fact and without exception, be so trained that he certainly will grow up a Christian. . . ."

Bushnell carefully expounded the alternatives with balanced judgment and maturity of thought. In clear and irenic language he tried to bring a new insight into the religious life of the family and the church. The revivalism with its insistence that every individual should have an experience of change and regeneration was reacted to, and it was in this light that Bushnell endeavored to bring a complementary and not contradictory point of view. Overemphasis on the means of grace, whether in evangelism or in worship, outside the church or inside the church, tended to an imbalance of truth and doctrine. Individual and social responsibility were thus scrutinized in his preaching. Bushnell's sermons and public utterances have become timeless in truth and command a hearing at all times. His sermons belong to "the literature of power" in which the divine speaks to the human, the eternal to the temporal.

Social Gospel and Awakening

The latter part of the nineteenth century found the American scene rifted by competing views resulting from social and economic conditions then prevailing. Rapid growth in immigration, acceleration in industry, development of urban life, and the upheavals of war led on the one hand to the amassing of large fortunes by prominent leaders of industry and finance, and on the other hand to a deepening and spreading of poverty and to social disintegration throughout the country. Tensions were created and unrest was everywhere, especially in centers of population. The exploitation of immigrants in the labor force added to the sores of humanity.

During this time the increase in church life was stayed by a wave of defection from the church due to the inference that the church was not concerned and not involved in the total life of people. The revivalist, the evangelist, the orthodox pastor preached for the conversion of people as a personal experience. Although this was excellent, there was a growing concern that the pulpit had little or nothing to say about the conditions in which people had to live. Environment, economic opportunity, social improvement, educational facilities—the growing emphasis on these and other factors tended to offset the former concerns. In answer to the cry for reform, various movements spread across the land in an attempt to rectify abuses and bring in a better day.

As the church began to speak against the evils in society, it was forced to play the role of mediator between groups and classes, and to guide people away from revolt toward working out solutions to the acute problems. The established groups of major denominations tended not to be too active in this, though there were some fine exceptions. Differences of interpretation abounded as to the gospel and its proclamation. Many saw the need to be the spiritual and moral transformation of the individual, who could then make an impact upon society and the environment. On the other hand, some intrepid pulpiteers believed that it was vital for the pulpit to deal with these social and economic issues as part of preaching the gospel. Men like Finney and Moody took the first road of preaching, and men like Gladden and Rauschenbusch were among many who saw the wisdom of adding to the personal gospel a social dimension. **Francis G. Peabody (1847-1936)** wrote *Jesus Christ and the Social Question* in an attempt to reinterpret the Christian faith in a new environment. He was one of many voices for the changing emphases in preaching.

Washington Gladden (1836-1918) is sometimes known as the forerunner of what has been called "the social gospel." Pastor of a Congregational Church, Columbus, Ohio, he preached and wrote with evangelical conviction about the new dimensions of need and the remedy. He gave the Yale Lectures on Preaching, *Social Salvation* (1902), in which he stressed the communal aspect of Christian influence rather than the more personal application. He dealt with religion and the social question, the care of the poor, the state of the unemployed, our brothers in bonds (criminals), social vices, public education, and the redemption of the city. Some argued that these had nothing to do with the gospel, but it is plain that the gospel affects each and all of these areas of human need. The fault of the liberal preacher lay in making these things the content and nub of the message while neglecting the New Testament basis. The evangelical saw that the gospel was to be applied to these social issues by the involvement of Christian citizens in meeting people's needs.

Gladden stated his belief: "I am therefore unable to understand how Christianity, whether as a law or as a gospel, can be intelligently or adequately preached or lived in these days without a constant reference to social questions. No individual is soundly converted until he comprehends his social relations and strives to fulfill them. . . . It would seem, therefore, that the minister's work, in these days, must lie, very largely, along the lines of social amelioration." This may well be questioned by the evangelical if Gladden had substituted these items for the call to repentance and faith in Christ and the dynamic gospel as the inspiration of transformed lives and societies.

The socially involved preaching and teaching of Gladden was spelled out in the Yale Lectures as well as from the pulpit. He had been the editor of the *Independent,* a paper without sectarian bias devoted to discussion of major issues of the times. Competition was now viewed as a betrayal of Christianity, and his pen advocated cooperation between capital and labor. One of the revolutionary ideas promoted was that the worker should have a stake in the industry through profit-sharing. In *The Christian Pastor and the Working Church,* Gladden spelled out many sermonic ideas, advocating the equality of man to man in sharing the benefits of an ever prosperous society. Material prosperity should be a benefit of the spiritual ideals held by faith. The new creature or creation should be matched by a new environment and a new order of a new society in which to live the abundant life. "You have the Gospel message to give, and nothing can supersede that," was one of his sayings.

Gladden mirrored the changing emphases of the American pulpit in its impact upon life and culture in a theological light. The strain of liberalism in theology found in Bushnell and the reaction against the older Calvinism seen in Beecher brought through Gladden preparation for the preaching and teaching of Rauschenbusch. Gladden's preaching was based on the new critical approach in Bible studies, and this enabled him to take Biblical statements and apply them to his new view of man and his environment. The swing away from divine sovereignty to divine immanence affected the whole theological point of view and altered the basis of religious authority. Thus Gladden developed the new "social gospel" in the expression of "the fatherhood of God and the brotherhood of man." The kingdom of God became now the total life of man in the promised new social order. He looked for *a warless world* in 1909. One wonders what he would have said if he had lived through the two World Wars just about to begin and the other wars and revolutions still with us!

Any summation of Gladden's preaching—which had incalculable influence upon a generation of preachers and congregations—should not omit his best legacy in the enduring hymn he composed:

> O Master, let me walk with Thee
> In lowly paths of service free;
> Tell me Thy secret; help me bear
> The strain of toil, the fret of care.

> Help me the slow of heart to move
> By some clear, winning word of love;
> Teach me the wayward feet to stay,
> And guide them in the homeward way.

Teach me Thy patience; still with Thee
In closer, dearer company,
In work that keeps faith sweet and strong,
In trust that triumphs over wrong.

In hope that sends a shining ray
Far down the future's broadening way;
In peace that only Thou canst give,
With Thee, O Master, let me live.

The social changes of this period bring us to Walter Rauschenbusch (1861-1918) who in the steps of Washington Gladden and Francis G. Peabody expounded the social gospel out of a social theology. As a teacher and preacher, Rauschenbusch was one of the leading exponents of the newer trends in preaching. Using the Gospels' report that Jesus came not only to preach, but, as he taught, to bring release to the captives, Rauschenbusch interpreted this to apply to social conditions as well as moral and spiritual deliverance from sin. The social gospel implied that this was now the most important emphasis to be made from the pulpit.

The rise of higher criticism in seminaries, the teaching of evolution in schools, the study of comparative religions, and the changing ideas about the Bible produced the climate in which the new gospel flourished. As professor at Rochester (N.Y.) Baptist Theological Seminary, Rauschenbusch undertook to indoctrinate many with his radical views. He has been described as "the most creative spirit in the American theological world." He believed that "the religion that lived in the heart of Jesus and spoke in his words not only had a social faith; it was a social faith." "Where the Kingdom of God has taken the existing order for granted and has devoted itself to saving souls, it has become a conservative force, bent on maintaining the great institution of the church and preserving the treasure of doctrine and supernatural grace committed to it. When we accept the faith of the Kingdom of God, we take the same attitude toward our own social order which the missionaries take toward the social life of heathenism" (*Christianizing the Social Order*, pp. 96-102).

In this context of teaching and preaching he taught that the Kingdom of God idea implied these views: (1) a social hope with society remade; (2) the end of war and strife; (3) growth, the means without divine intervention and crisis; (4) a universal and not Jewish kingdom; and (5) a present reality and not merely a future hope. All these were part of the eschatological interpretation of the teaching of Jesus. Just as the eighteenth century witnessed the Great Awakening in spiritual revival, so the emerging twentieth century saw the Social Awakening in America.

The key to understanding Rauschenbusch lies in the background of his father's Lutheranism and his own conversion in a personal experience which led him into the Baptist Church to become pastor of the Second German Baptist Church in New York's "Hell's Kitchen." There he saw the inhumanity of man and the dereliction of people who were the victims of the then oppressive social order. While he is assumed to be one of the liberals of that generation, it is significant that he did not abandon his earlier evangelical experience but was motivated by it to espouse social concerns.

In the classroom he was a teacher of Christianity and the social crisis seen in the perspective of church history. As a preacher outside the classroom, he found his interest in seeking solutions to the problems and this gave him a prophetic utterance on social questions. His limitation at this point would seem to be that he divorced his earlier doctrinal ideas of sin and salvation from his social theories. Each became increasingly separate. He thus moved from personal to institutional responsibility and sought to see sin as something which could be reformed in the social structure.

His chief doctrine was The Kingdom of God, which to him meant Christianizing American social life. This was an inference from his accepted premises of what the social gospel was and not a principle based upon any definite exegesis or hermeneutics of the Gospels and the New Testament. Rauschenbusch said: "The Kingdom of God is humanity organized according to the will of God. . . . It is organic union between religion and morality, between theology and ethics. . . . It contains the teleology of the Christian religion. It translates theology from the static to the dynamic. . . . By laboring for it we enter into the joy and peace of the Kingdom as our divine fatherland and habitation." His book, *The Social Principles of Jesus,* points again to this emphasis. War made the goal more uncertain. In fairness to him we must acknowledge that he did not substitute social activities for religion. He said: "If the church comes to lean on social preachings and doings as a crutch because its religion has become paralytic, may the Lord have mercy on us all! We do not want less religion; we want more; but it must be a religion that gets its orientation from the Kingdom of God" (*Christianizing the Social Order,* p. 378).

Theologically, Rauschenbusch had moved away from the Lutheran view of justification by faith and the Reformed view of the sovereignty of God. He made the Kingdom of God central and foundational for his hermeneutic and message. His concept of the Kingdom as humanity organized according to the will of God was idealistic in a world rifted by social disorder and World War I. He failed to see that our Lord's teaching always presupposed a reborn man as disciple in an elect group, the church—not every man without distinction. Rauschenbusch gave to the church a volume of prayers, *Prayers of the Social Awakening,* which distills the best of his ideals and brings a salutary reminder for social change.

The preaching of Rauschenbusch influenced a generation, and ministerial students as well as pastors everywhere followed his guidance. Later benefits came in society—shorter working hours, increased welfare help, facilities of popular education, voting rights, improved housing, rights and privileges given to minority groups—all these were part of the gains made in the movement.

The implications of this teaching-preaching by Rauschenbusch permeated the American theological atmosphere, bringing a new message to many a pulpit. Congregations at first were shocked at the inference of their failure, then began to do what was possible to rectify wrongs. Preaching especially expected a utopia to come, equating the message of the Kingdom of God with the social benefits accruing in America. Disillusionment, however, came with the knowledge that beyond World War I was World War II. Only at first was there the optimism that all was well with human nature and the good in man would overcome the bad, that peace was coming soon and man would learn to live justly and lovingly. How false all this was in the light of subsequent events! At the time, however, this was the mood of sermons and the expectancy of the liberal school of theology. Professor H. Richard Niebuhr, Yale, wrote *The Kingdom of God in America* (1937) in an attempt to show the perils of the overemphasis by Rauschenbusch, and at the same time to attempt a new synthesis of interpretation by avoiding the extremes of either the liberal or the conservative.

In the aftermath of Rauschenbusch's preaching and teaching, professors at the University of Chicago furthered this emphasis in theology and philosophy. The emerging National Council of Churches had its origins in what was then the Federal Council which was strongly motivated by the social gospel. Neo-orthodoxy and its criticism of the earlier Liberal Theology sought, however, to correct much of the limitations of the social gospel regarding the nature of man.

Unitarian-Universalist Trends

Following Edwards' era, changes in theology and in preaching were inevitable. The broader and more liberal elements in New England were determined to modify and reinterpret the Calvinism of their forebears. Enlightenment was the order of the day and the reaction against the rigidity of earlier Puritanism had begun. During the preaching of Chauncey earlier, there had been intimations of change concerning the doctrine of man. The Arminian view instead of the Calvinistic saw man as the center of the universe and as a being who could respond to God in his own way. The idea of both good and evil in man indicated that man might after all be able to rise to higher levels of life by his own efforts. The questions of divine sovereignty and man's free will were now debatable.

The sermons preached over a long period indicated that much was at stake. In fact, the ongoing life of the churches in America was to be influenced profoundly for generations thereafter. Conrad Wright in *Three Prophets of Religious Liberalism* (1961), has given the judgment that William E. Channing's Baltimore sermon, Ralph Waldo Emerson's Divinity School Address, and Theodore Parker's South Boston Sermon were the three major expositions given in this connection.

Significantly, the break with orthodoxy had not taken place regarding the trinity, for most of the earlier liberals believed in the divine nature of Jesus, though many saw him as preexistent and yet created by God and thus subordinate to him. The break was found rather in a shift in authority. The primacy of reason was held to be crucial in a period when Biblical revelation held sway. The "reasonableness of faith" was to become a constant word on the lips of the preacher.

To the Unitarians, however, the doctrine of the trinity was irrational as it limited a view of God whose unfolding was mystical, and the doctrine could not be clearly found in the Scriptures according to their interpretation. The title of Unitarian gradually became an accepted term by those who espoused this break away from the older views. Thus the person of Jesus Christ was reinterpreted in such a way that deity no longer was affirmed in the sense of Godhead and stress was given to the human nature of the Son of Man.

The preaching of the Unitarian at first used few metaphors or literary allusions. There was a freedom not found in the Puritan structure. Out of the rationalism came a use of language that was argumentative, pointed, and interpretative in presenting the new claims of truth. At first there was a marked use of Scripture as befitted tradition, but gradually this declined in favor of the essay-sermon with a more literary bent. Naturally, the different men in this newer mode of preaching followed no conventional pattern. Among the representative minds, Channing stands out above all the others.

William Ellery Channing (1780-1842) was a Harvard graduate and a minister in Boston. He stands as the best and most influential example of the Unitarian preacher. In his own background he believed in the pre-existence of Christ, in his miracles, and in his resurrection. In Christology he stressed the subordination of the Son to the Father. The major emphasis on man's nature and man's ability to achieve new life was the trend in Unitarian preaching, but Channing is best recalled for his Christological emphasis. When he interpreted the doctrine of man, it was in the light of Christ's teaching. To Channing more than to any other single influence we are indebted for the revival of the New Testament interpretation of human nature.

In the sermon "The Character of Christ" based upon "This is my beloved Son, in whom I am well pleased" (Matt. 17:5) we have a sampling of Channing at his best. Here is an almost evangelical spirit which could persuade many that the preacher, while reaching for the new, had not relinquished the old. The sermon illustrates the strong structure and the literary affusion of a rich mind and heart. The preacher said:

> The character of Christ may be studied for various purposes. It is singularly fitted to call forth the heart, to awaken love, admiration, and moral delight. As an example, it has no rival. As an evidence of his religion, perhaps it yields to no other proof; perhaps no other has so often conquered unbelief. It is chiefly to this last view of it, that I now ask your attention. The character of Christ is a strong affirmation of the truth of his religion. As such, I would now place it before you. I shall not, however, think only of confirming your

faith; the very illustrations, which I shall adduce for this purpose will show the claims of Jesus to our reverence, obedience, imitation, and fervent love.

The conventional introduction opens the way to major points to be dealt with in sequence:

(1) to show that the character of Christ, taken as a whole, is one which could not have entered the thoughts of man, could not have been imagined or feigned; that it bears every mark of genuineness and truth; that it ought therefore to be acknowledged as real and of divine origin; (2) that the sublimity of the character claimed by Christ forbids us to trace it to imposture; (3) you have seen the consciousness of greatness which Jesus possessed; I now ask you to consider how with this consciousness, he lived among men; (4) we have not yet reached the depth of Christ's character. We have not yet touched the great principle on which his wonderful sympathy was founded, and which endeared to him his office of universal Saviour. Do you ask what this deep principle was? I answer, it was his conviction of the greatness of the human soul. He saw in man the impress and image of the divinity, and therefore thirsted for his redemption, and took the tenderest interest in him, whatever might be the rank, character, or condition in which he was found. This spiritual view of man pervades and distinguishes the teaching of Christ.

Channing's preaching was characteristic of the best thought, expressed in a period of transition. He kept some of the traditional doctrines and in seeking to reinterpret and redefine he did not go as far as others of like mind. A man like **Aaron Bancroft (1755-1839)** was an apologist in preaching, arguing for the newer views of the Unitarian theology. Controversy was proclaimed with verve and force and the religion of man was seen as rational and voluntary (cf. sermon: "Religion in Man a Rational and Voluntary Service"). **Nathanael Emmons (1745-1840)** was another who participated in controversial preaching. He could attack the Unitarian as well as the Arminian, as he moved away from earlier orthodoxy. "On the Doctrine of the Trinity" was a sermon in which he forcefully argued in lavish language for his position in accepting the newer, liberal views of theology. He was more orthodox than Bancroft and was associated with Lyman Beecher, who also tended to defend the orthodoxy of tradition while revising some of the truths therein expressed.

Throughout this period the intellectual side of preaching took on greater overtones. Channing stood out as a beacon light with radiance in New England. His preaching brought "sweet reasonableness" in a time of controversy. Bancroft became the exponent of an "orthodox" Unitarian view, but even this was modified for the leaders of the movement as time went on. In the structure and homiletics of that time the arguments were not as precise as that found in the Puritan logical acumen. There was a lack of strict exegesis and gradually the major points or divisions no longer stood out. Scripture was now used in a new way—not to be the basis of truth and proof text, but used rather in general terms for illustration and reference. The older exegesis was given up in favor of a rhetoric which flowed freely and had greater practical application.

By the time of **Ralph Waldo Emerson (1803-1882)**, the preacher-essayist, we have moved into a new era of Unitarian thought. In his "Divinity School Address" of 1838, new directions are suggested to the students at Harvard Divinity School. Still Unitarian in idea, Emerson now surrenders anything of the supernatural in Christianity. At the same time he affirms strongly the ability of man in his human nature to achieve what he wills. The word and idea of "miracle" is given up as related to Christ's ministry. In man there is intuition and this ought to be sufficient for faith without a Bible basis. Transcendentalism thus came into the thought of New England with its attendant transformation of idea and theology.

The Emersonian influence was felt chiefly in New England when as preacher he followed the conventional way of the pulpit. He was the scholar endeavoring to share new insights with people and yet abide within the straightened area of his church life. He said the correct things at first. Then he promised to use "new forms of address, new modes of illustration, and varied allusions." These included "the printing press, the loom, the phenomena of steam and of gas, the magnificence of towns, free constitutions, and a petulant and vain nation." Emerson tried to change in topics as well as in style—to be practical and down to earth as well as given to dogma.

In this sampling of preaching, the selections reveal more interest in the individual, his virtues, his conduct, and his attitudes than doctrinal and social themes. "Man the Reformer" is a sermon title indicative of this emphasis. Here trade is seen as selfish, wealth as tainted, scholars and intellectuals as faithless and compromising.

Out of sermonizing came his later *Essays* which dealt with "History," "Self-reliance," "Compensation," "Spiritual Laws," and "The Over-Soul." They were also part of his subject matter when lecturing. To this latter task he gave many years after leaving the regular pulpit. The "Courage" and the "Enthusiasm" he spoke about to bring self-help to everyman were part of his Unitarian and humanitarian ideals. "The secret of culture is to learn that a few great points steadily reappear . . . the escape from all false ties; courage to be what we are, and love of what is simple and beautiful; independence and cheerful relation, these are the essentials—these, and the wish to serve, to add somewhat to the well-being of men." This is his style and message.

Theodore Parker (1810-1860), whose preaching followed in the Emersonian heritage, also added to the dialog of the period. He sought to clarify what was permanent and transient in Christianity. The rise of Biblical criticism and Continental rationalism helped him to express his views. Doctrine could be that of the permanent, but matters of the Bible could be subjected to the transient as the text was criticized and revised. In preaching, his style was polemical and argumentative. Emerson and Parker set the tone of the newer day of preaching which was to engage the ensuing century. Nature, history, philosophy—these are more frequent themes now than Scripture and Christ. Eloquence and flights of imagination are there, but no longer is it necessary to use a Biblical text for exegesis in a sermon. Here then is the basis of that more intuitive approach to man's faith, now divorced in part from orthodox Biblical bases. While these later Unitarians stressed the apologetic to win a case, Channing in his transitional days had said: "I have spoken doctrines which you will probably preach; but I do not mean, that you are to give yourself to controversy. You will remember, that good practice is the end of preaching, and will labor to make your people holy livers, rather than skillful disputants."

A sampling of Theodore Parker's life and ministry reveals that during his twenty-two years in the pastorate he wrote 925 sermons and preached approximately 1,500 times. During the last fifteen years of his ministry he addressed weekly congregations of 3,000. While Parker did not write anything in the nature of either rhetoric or homiletics, he had a conscious bent for the subject. His library of 20,000 books gave him ample opportunity to read and study the best published and known. Included in that were books on rhetoric.

His belief that he could best *feel* rather than *see* when discussing doctrine influenced his speech and delivery. He saw his mission as a preacher to break down false conceptions of theology and to build from the emotions or feelings an alliance with thought to influence the whole of life. Gifted with a phenomenal memory, he could recall and recite poetry and prose to enrich his public utterances. He believed that to be an impressive speaker of lasting influence he must traffic in "superior ideas."

If "the style is the man," then this sampling of Parker's materials indicates that he favored the classical orators as a model for his study. Writing was a discipline; and delivery was forceful as he felt keenly his belief in the subject under discussion. He had moved away from the "plain style" of the Puritan, favoring the more colorful idiom of his day. Nevertheless, he strove to make clear and simple the truth in the sermon. He used the manuscript largely, but in preaching gave the impression that he was so moved by the subject that he brought the manuscript to life by the force of his personal feeling and emotion. His *Diary-Notebook* and his *Letters* as well as his sermons indicate how hard he worked to model himself after the classical masters of speech. "I have on my side the example of the great masters of speech. . . . It is with customary tools that we work the best, especially when use has made the handles smooth. . . ." Thus the period of preaching moved on from Puritan to Unitarian and beyond.

In estimating the rhetoric and preaching style of the period, we should keep in mind the fact that after the Colonial Period the learned Unitarian preacher was noted for his cadenced prose and careful wording. His style was different from the passionate exhortation of the Puritan, and certainly far removed from the frontier missionary-evangelist such as the Methodist Peter Cartwright. Unitarian preaching lacked the homely touch. Wisdom and education were commonplace ideas and religious intellectualism dominated the church life. It was found chiefly in New England where the intellectual ferment of the nation was also based. This was the home of Lowell, Whittier, Holmes, Adams, Quincy, Hawthorne, Longfellow, Bryant, and other giants whose names were nationally known. In religion Channing ranked as an orator alongside of Everett and Phillips; and Theodore Parker was like a prophet, while Emerson had found a special niche in essay writing.

As men everywhere enjoyed listening to orators and politicians who debated the issues of slavery and abolition, so in religion people attended diets of public worship for varied reasons. The devout and pious went to worship God, but many went for an additional reason—to hear the sound of running words and thrusting prose speech which could stir them to thought and often action. The public speaker was held in high esteem and this was an advantage for any preacher who could give a clear exposition of what he believed. The sermon was still held as one of the highest forms of public address. Rhetoric and speech were taught in the emerging colleges as a required subject. Debates were common in class and in public. Political studies required public speech and studies in Law and the Government demanded some form of public address. During this classical period of education in the United States, the preacher was one to benefit by these trends. Literary societies and college and university theses indicate the widespread nature of this profound interest in the speaking man.

Harold Munhall (1866-1932) stands as a representative of a movement which stemmed from Unitarian theology and found expression in a day of liberal thought and search for a new basis of truth. A Bostonian by education and pastor of the Universalist Church beginning in 1891, he also became the head of their publishing house in 1917. In his preaching he sought better relations between various church leaders and industry. His was the religion of "brotherhood and its application." As a preacher he was epigrammatic in style and rich in the note of practical mysticism, with interpretation of truth according to his theology.

"The great discovery of the age is not the universe with the atom, but the universe within the soul. This has enabled us to rediscover the religion of Jesus, and we find it was neither a church nor a creed, but a way of life by which we possess ourselves. The first and most dazzling result of this discovery has been to give us back our long-lost spiritual freedom." He thought that Paul, Augustine, and Calvin laid upon lesser men "The Great Fear" and distorted Jesus' way of life. Because there is one God and Father of us all, no one can be outside the pale of human brotherhood.

The appeal of the position taken theologically—liberal and humanistic, coupled with the emphasis upon the brotherhood of man and the Fatherhood of God, prevailed for a period in American preaching. However, two World Wars have dissipated the idea of man's inherent goodness without admitting his latent depravity, so that much of the kind of preaching of that period has diminished.

PART FOUR

The
Twentieth
Century

The momentum of new ideas in the fast growing nation served to stimulate the religious and social life of the American people. The ferment caused by the evolutionary theories in science now applied to social studies and history could not be dismissed lightly by the theologian and the preacher. Here again a division is obvious. The conservative remained true to his convictions in the integrity of the Bible and refused to be sidetracked by these changing fashions. The more liberally-minded preacher was influenced by the changing theology and his sermons were affected accordingly. A new school of preaching developed based on what soon became labelled as "the social gospel."

In philosophy the teaching of Josiah Royce (1855-1916) at Harvard was noted for its emphasis on idealism, and his writings interpreted the religious insights of man in this light. Following him was William James (1842-1910) whose work was that of the pragmatism of applied psychology in religion and life. The other outstanding name is that of Walter Rauschenbusch (1861-1918) whose preaching and later teaching at Rochester Seminary, New York, won a hearing for the social implication of the gospel. Religious experience was stressed as the prelude to action in the social crisis of the times, and the social aims of the gospel were transmitted in sermon and organization.

From this background, the American way of life was profoundly motivated in the direction of idealism. The influence of Harvard with Royce, James, and others (including Santayana) gave a spurt to the philosophy of religion in the academic world and in the theological schools. Hitherto, systematic theology and dogmatics had held the primary place in ministerial training, but now a shift was discernible, especially in the more liberally-oriented seminaries. In Royce's *The World and the Individual* (1900-01), Gifford Lectures, the idea of community and the development of selfhood were stressed as a divine goal. Human goodness and happiness came as the society was purified. Royce was not taking the teaching of Jesus as the fountain head of his views. He was more Pauline in seeing the church as the divine instrument of social change. To him loyalty was the goal and heart and highest duty among the virtues of moral life.

Of William James it can be said that he stood out as an eminent psychologist and teacher whose writings influenced a generation and more. His practical and earthy way of teaching, as he set out his "case-studies" of the individual, are noted particularly in *The Varieties of Religious Experience* (also Gifford Lectures). A classic in its field, it gave to our era a concept of religious experience which marked a modern study and critique since Jonathan Edwards' pioneering in that field. James is linked to the romantic tradition, but the key to his thought may well be in his *The Will to Believe* where choice is the foundation of every good. He believed in the reality of the unseen and in the necessity for the preacher to begin where man lived with his problems and human situation.

The Changing Age

Preaching has to be seen against the background of the age in order to estimate its worth and contribution. Rapid and kaleidoscopic changes took place in the United States of America during the 1918-44 period. The post-World War I era saturated the mind with disturbing ideas, and unsettled millions of people in their social and religious outlook. The preacher found that those formerly eager to hear were turning to other voices. The preacher, hence, had competition. The word *crisis* was on everyone's lips. A new day was being born. A depression struck the world, and multitudes were living in the grip of penury and needs unmet by work or benevolence. Students who had graduated from college could not find work. Men who manned the major industrial plants were found walking the streets or sitting at home discouraged and beaten.

In this failing democracy and with the rise of dictatorship in Europe in view, American people were subjected to a variety of preaching emphases. The watchwords of optimism were quoted and repeated, but the harsh realities of living on a pittance did not make for faith and easy response. It was a time for the presentation of "isms"—one contending for socialism as the panacea for trouble, another advocating communism as the solvent for the new age. Capital and labor relations were acute, and tensions burst into flaming opposition. Christianity was challenged by the emerging forces of a world in upheaval. Social privileges and civil rights were also in question and people of diverse color and creed cried out for justice and equality. Samplings of the sermons indicate that in the United States the more liberal preachers were wrestling with these manifold problems as they endeavored to bring hope to their people.

The social crisis united many voices in the pulpits of the land, but there was variety in the needs faced and the solutions offered. The preacher of the divine message found that he had much to relate to human need and life situation.

One such voice was **Kirby Page (1890-1957)**, editor of *The World of To-morrow*. He saw the millions of unemployed and the hunger and desolation of many more. He said that "socialism was closer akin to the Christian gospel than capitalism." His point was that where there are resources in the hands of some, those resources should be made available to the needy. He contended that some form of planned economy and social adjustment was necessary as an expression of the Christian message. He felt that the Christian church was too much enmeshed in capitalism and was not sufficiently concerned with human need. His emphasis then on "sin" was that of the sin of complacency in a world of need. "Sin," he said, "is any attitude or practice which debases personality, embitters human relations, and separates man from God." This is inadequate as a definition, but it could be qualified in the light of that context. "Corporate sins are those in which men are involved as members of a group, class, nation, or race." In the economic realm, this lay-preacher saw the largest number and widest variety of collective sins—self-interest and covetousness, greed, and materialism were the basic ingredients. Much of this kind of preaching called for repentance on the part of the affluent who should give cooperative service to the poor and needy.

Communism was another ugly word which was given birth because of the Russian Revolution earlier and the post war upheaval in social relations everywhere. Was this an answer to the clamorous need? At least preachers recognized the challenge. Communism presented a front which called people to commitment of time, money, strength, and even death. It was intolerant, dictatorial, and hostile toward Christianity. Nevertheless, preachers then saw in it not only its antipathy to the Christian faith, but its sensitivity to need, its willingness to identify with others. Certainly the people of Russia were exploited and revolution seemed inevitable, although at first it was not expected to become bloody and violent. Championing the poor and needy, the revolutionaries were undaunted by the difficulties confronting them. Out of this came the doom of the existing order. The preachers of that age who saw this were men who in their liberal theology had a sense of social justice and concern. They also saw the similarity of Christianity as a revolutionary force at work in the matrix of society. This point of view was well expressed: "We must prove that Christianity has a greater dynamic power, a greater capacity to sacrifice, a greater ability to reconstruct the economic order for the benefit of all the people than Communism. It is only thus that we can meet its challenge."

Another phase of needed change lay in the industrial order with its inequalities and injustices. Here was another situation which brought preachers to speak and act against wrongs. They saw the economic order as part of the responsibility of the spiritual order. Some saw in the American system of free enterprise a distortion of what they considered right for all men. "Our first function is to bring to judgment this order which is now bringing such misery to the lives of human beings as it has long brought such corruption to their hearts and souls." The General Conference of the Methodist Episcopal Church declared: "The present industrial order is unchristian, unethical and anti-social, because it largely depends upon the profit motive, which is an appeal to selfishness." However, differences of judgment were apparent, even then, but this was the new emphasis in many a sermon.

The race problem also arose as a major controversy in this period. What had been achieved in the Civil War and written into the warp and woof of American life was freedom for all. The former slaves were now free. However, it was obvious that this did not bring social equality or job opportunities for all. A mounting cry of discontent was heard throughout the nation, and the pulpit was not silent about this. At first some thought that it was not the function of preaching to deal with this sore spot, but in the light of Christian morality and standards, it was inevitable that men should preach against injustice. While the fundamental purpose of gospel preaching is the reformation of sinful individuals and sinful society, the latter is usually achieved through the former. However, there was the false assumption held by many that one race was superior to others; so that in industry and education inequality and prejudice held sway. Work and social freedom come by acceptance and opportunity. The message of the pulpit would break down ancient prejudice, false views about the nature and destiny of man, and inadequate interpretations of Biblical theology. Only in this way would the Black as well as other groups (Indian, Oriental) find political freedom and responsibility. In preaching much was made of Peter's vision at Joppa (cf. Acts 10) where Peter saw that God was making clear the duty of the Jew to share the gospel with the Gentile. No one race, and no Christian, was to have a monopoly of the good news. The vision also implied the unity of the human family. In Acts 17 Paul taught the "one blood" of all men in their kinship in the race.

There were prophetic ministries in major cities as preachers saw the opportunity to deal with these manifold issues. In addition to the social and economic issues plaguing the nation, the preacher began to have people ask him about their moral and marital problems. Families needed help in their home life. Disease and divorce, moral and mental breakdowns, and the false lure of success broke up many lives. The preacher found that he was becoming a consultant or adviser as well as pastor in the ordinary sense. Also he began to deal with these moral issues from the pulpit. The language of *Macbeth* by William Shakespeare,

> Canst thou not minister to a mind diseased,
> Pluck from the memory a rooted sorrow,
> Raze out the written troubles of the brain,
> And with some sweet oblivious antidote
> Cleanse the stuffed bosom of that perilous stuff
> Which weighs upon the heart?

could well be applied to many preachers as they felt their way along untraversed pathways and over stormy seas which often would swamp them in the vastness of the depths of human need. Certainly preaching had more spice and color to it!

One other crucial issue arose when prohibition was repealed and the barriers were let down to open the way to further indulgence and drunkenness. There were the abuses and corruption attendant upon prohibition, but when multitudes violate or disobey the law there is bound to be trouble. Crime and the underworld were never far away. New police and government enforcement problems were obvious.

It was Bishop Edwin Holt Hughes, of the Methodist Church, who called attention to the fact that some preachers had ceased to be ministers and had become prohibitionists! It was easy to be sidetracked and fail to declare the whole counsel of God. The temptation to ride a hobby and attack one element of evil intoxicated some preachers. But Hughes wisely counseled that in preaching the preacher should have a sense of proportion and weigh up the Biblical teaching as well as social and political motives. Drunkenness was condemned and abstinence counseled. The ideal life was that of temperance and self-control. However, the emerging abuses and easy obtainment of hard liquor posed new problems and temptations. In this the preacher learned anew that preaching should deal with issues in different ways. Social welfare, the idea of being a brother's keeper, the example of the Christian man, the moral consequences of use and abuse of intoxicants, and the spirit of Christ above all were being preached as the application of the eternal gospel in a new context of human need. The rise of the technological age with machines and automobiles brought sterner standards for a man's self-control, so that the preacher did well who knew how to handle these matters.

The social crisis after World War I found a group of preachers, liberally oriented, dealing with these issues. Among them were Francis John McConnell, Merton S. Rice, William L. Stidger, Edwin H. Hughes, and G. Bromley Oxnam. S. Parkes Cadman was outstanding in this era in skillful innovations involving a radio ministry, and a question and answer type of sermon, handled journalistically through the medium of the newspaper. Contemporary preaching was shifting and changing as fast as new demands were made upon it.

Conciliar Ideals

During 1919-20 the American people burst from their singleminded military drive into a confusion of new interests in a new era. War was behind and a new optimism pervaded their outlook.

Disillusionment and retreat soon followed to be climaxed in the great depression of the thirties. During this period church forces became involved in the social and economic structure of American life. There were those who felt that the church should speak to the conditions of that period.

The steel strike stood out as a phenomenon of gravest import for the economy. In this many saw a test for the democracy they espoused as the American way of life. Because of the success of idealism in winning the war against tyranny, many felt that in America there should be the application of those ideals in the realm of industry. How could the church share in overcoming disorder and bringing in a new order? The Interchurch World Movement linked with Protestant leaders of American denominations to make this effective. Methodist Bishop Francis J. McConnell, a long-time social gospel leader and a spokesman for others of like mind, sought "to point out the moral principles involved in all industrial relations and to suggest some methods applicable to the present situation . . . to indicate the Christian bases upon which these problems can be solved" (cf. Report of the Findings Committee, National Industrial Conference of Christian Representatives, printed in *Interchurch Newsletter,* Oct. 2, 1919).

In review, this statement was similar to the Federal Council of Churches document "The Church and Social Reconstruction" formulated a few months earlier, and the American Catholic "Bishops Program of Social Reconstruction" adopted in 1919, calling for the application of Christian love to industrial relations, supporting the right of collective bargaining, and advocating equal opportunity for women, Blacks, and foreign-born in industry. Again, related to this was the preaching of a social gospel.

The social gospel opposed social radicalism while defending the rights of organized labor against big-business oppression. But in that day the public saw the dangers of organized labor. Here was one of the turning points in social relations wherein the laboring people were gradually alienated from much of church life. At the time of the steel strike, churchmen took a side on the issue and played a part in the controversy. Peace came but the wounds remained. The social gospel moved along into other fields of interest, but a decline had set in. Whatever weaknesses were there before, the steel strike marked a point of change.

All this points up the preaching of that time. From major pulpits of liberal persuasion particularly came the social message of Jesus, the Sermon on the Mount, and the teaching of the prophets of the Old Testament in new dress. Much of this was food for thought and probed the conscience, but again much of it diverted attention from the heart of the gospel of redemption.

Chapter VII
Preaching in the United States (1900-1950)

Among the many preachers heard at this time was **Russell Herman Conwell** (1842-1925), whose life was one of America's success stories. For forty years he was pastor of Grace Baptist Church which met in the Baptist Temple in Philadelphia, Pennsylvania. He was a public speaker for nearly fifty years. During the mature years of his ministry, he was billed as "Dean of the American Platform—the Greatest Lecturer in the World." Perhaps his greatest claim to fame lies in the founding of Temple College in 1886, later to become Temple University.

As a young man Conwell worked his way through college. His occupation for a time was that of lawyer and newspaper man, serving also as an officer in the Union Army during the Civil War. Out of this background he became a preacher of the Christian faith.

He preached thousands of sermons in his lifetime. These gave evidence of his oratory and ability. His genius in communicating to others lay in his mastery of language and the use of symbols. Ability in description and narration, persuasion and argumentation had been acquired in his legal studies and were put to effective use in preaching. He put to good use his ready wit, strong voice, vigorous speech, and persuasive spirit. He was an orator-preacher.

In his own lectures on Oratory given to students at Temple College, he defined oratory as the science of effective speech. Oratory must seek to achieve a definite goal in producing results. It must move the heart and stimulate to action. This was not elocution though that was included as well as rhetoric, logic, and grammar. He taught that a preacher by a combination of these could write and speak so as to impress some good on the hearts and minds of others. Conwell was a student of human nature and claimed that love, hate, and fear were the prime motives inducing men to act for good or evil. The voice, gestures, illustrations, ideas, and delivery by extemporaneous speech were all that were needed. Language ought to be simple, and thus the preacher would be ready for action.

An example of these principles is found in his famous oration "Acres of Diamonds," which can be seen as a sermon as well as a lecture. In it are all the qualities laid down by this master speaker. If results are the measure of what a sermon can do, then this one is remarkable. It is estimated that he was able to raise eight million dollars for Temple College through this lecture delivered more than six thousand times and heard by some thirteen million people.

Conwell founded Temple College to give opportunity for higher education to the many who could not afford to attend the prestigious colleges and universities. Underprivileged young people found it almost impossible to secure an education. In his concern to meet this social need crying out for attention, Conwell founded an institution of higher learning, and then went out to raise the money to finance it. Though he proclaimed the gospel chiefly in the tradition of Moody and Finney, he applied the gospel to the social need of bringing education to as many young people as possible.

Conwell did not wish the church to enter the political arena, but he preached and taught that his purpose was to "teach men to be good and the government will be right." His preaching was also touched with the idea that worldly success would come to every man who will strive for it and grasp the opportunity that lies at his feet. In that famous lecture "Acres of Diamonds" the thesis was stressed that "when you seek for the highest and best in life, you do not need to go to the ends of the earth to find the treasure. It lies at your feet and if you use the God-given opportunity that is before you you can achieve your goal."

Conwell also conducted evening school classes for the working man. This enabled him to contact thousands for the church. This inspiring story is only one of many such achievements in America coming out of the influence of the social and reform movements of the nineteenth century. Preaching was motivated by this involvement in the structure of society. The many social organizations which were created in this period testify to the influence of the preaching and teaching then given.

Evangelistic Preaching

The era of D. L. Moody saw the introduction of the type of evangelism which commanded the interest and support of church people in a new wave of appreciation. Leading citizens and public men backed this method of evangelism as they saw the accrued benefits in community and state.

Following Moody came evangelists who copied his new methods and sought to duplicate what he had begun. Not all were successful. Among the best were Reuben A. Torrey, J. Wilbur Chapman, Gipsy Rodney Smith, and "Billy" Sunday. These men had a nationwide hearing as they went from city to city. Torrey and Chapman also visited Great Britain and there witnessed results not unlike those of Moody's day although on a more limited scale. Australia also was virgin territory for this kind of evangelism and the response there was overwhelming.

Reuben Archer Torrey (1856-1928) was a contrast to Moody. Unlike Moody, Torrey was well educated and a graduate of Yale University. His theological training was taken at the Yale Divinity School. During graduate studies in Germany, he was exposed to the higher critical position concerning the Bible. His questioning mind at first was shaken by the newer views then emerging, but after study and reflection he became a decided advocate of the more fundamental interpretation of the Scriptures.

Out of this experience Torrey was influenced by Moody who was quick to see in him the man to head up the Bible Institute of Chicago and to be the pastor of nearby Moody Church. Thus Torrey found his life work as an educator and preacher. In 1912 he was to undertake similar duties for twelve years as Dean of the Los Angeles Bible Institute. However, in between he was led to assist Moody in one of the campaigns and then in 1902 he began with song leader Charles M. Alexander a work not unlike that of Moody and Sankey.

Torrey's preaching was of a Bible-teaching nature, even as he was evangelistic. He sensed the decay of faith and a creeping unbelief. His sermons became a means of instruction for those who had doubts or who had little or no knowledge of the Scriptures. Blunt and forthright in speech, he was different from Moody. Moody had an experience of the Spirit of God which mellowed him, and in his preaching the emphasis on the love of God was most marked. Torrey, while proclaiming the same gospel of grace, gave more attention to the judgments of God in his denunciation of sin. His logic and plain speech attacked the conscience with terrific force. He saw the depravity of sinful man and so had cause to speak of judgment upon unrepentant man.

His pulpit style was strong and powerful. The major doctrines of the Bible, and especially of the Christian faith, were expounded, and later volumes were published with a selection of these Bible studies and sermons.

Following Torrey came **J. Wilbur Chapman (1859-1918)** who with the same song leader, Charles M. Alexander, led many evangelistic campaigns throughout America and overseas in Australia and in Great Britain. He had begun his ministry as a Reformed Church pastor. Later he went to the Bethany Presbyterian Church, Philadelphia, where he was associated with John Wanamaker, the merchant prince, who had led in the building of the largest Sunday school in the nation. In 1903 Chapman was invited to be the leader of the Presbyterian Church's Committee on Evangelism and as such had leave of absence from the pastorate to engage in evangelistic campaigns. This led to his wider ministry.

As a preacher, Chapman had no tricks of speech, no rhetoric beyond the normal use in a regular pulpit of a church, and he could not be compared with either Moody or Torrey. He was nurtured in a Christian family and did not have Moody's background. He was trained in Lane Seminary but did not have the intellectual ability or scholarly habits of Torrey. He was the pastor doing the work of an evangelist. What was blessed of God in the congregation was now taken to city-wide campaigns with increasing honor from God.

Chapman would, for example, preach on "What Think Ye of Christ?" The one-thousand-voice choir would sing the spiritual, "Were you there when they crucified my Lord?" Out of this combination it seemed that the message of Chapman went home to all classes of people. Portraying the reality of a living Christ who had come to be with the individual, the preacher then traced how he was accepted by some and rejected by others. The climax came in the testimony of those who found no fault in Christ and believed on him. Here he would plead for a commitment of life.

Standing almost without gesture or motion, with a quiet and pleasing voice, a sympathetic manner, and a direct appeal, Chapman was given the seal of God upon his manner of evangelism. His themes centered on the redemptive work of Christ, and his confidence in the Bible supported him in convincing preaching. His chief work lay in reactivating church people who had a nominal faith but who needed to make a decisive personal commitment. Thus the evangelism began with the "religious" who supported his crusades and reached at the same time the unchurched who were attracted.

William Ashley Sunday (1862-1935) was in the tradition of the Moody era of evangelists. Others were Gipsy Rodney Smith and Samuel P. Jones. "Billy" Sunday had a dramatic conversion which led him from professional baseball and drunken debauchery into the YMCA and later into evangelism. Unlike other preachers who had pulpits in churches, Sunday reached a community or a city with the help of groups of Christians, using either a tent or a wooden tabernacle. There with hard benches and a sawdust floor he proclaimed the gospel and appealed for decisions.

To Sunday preaching meant a close application to the sins of society. He was especially firm in denouncing the liquor traffic. While others appealed for temperance, he tried to convince a generation that prohibition was needed. Many think his preaching and influence was a major factor in swaying public opinion before election time. He was a crusader for civic righteousness who did not merely hint at public and private sins, but boldly bared them to the congregation. Gross sins were attacked and the Ten Commandments found prominence in his preaching.

Freed from the convention of a special sanctuary, Sunday used the tabernacle together with unconventional preaching. No pulpit imprisoned him: he used the entire platform for his movements as he preached. He dramatized his themes with language not geared to propriety. His forceful speech sizzled with a vocabulary of slang and stinging epithet. Believing that people could be reached through everyday language, he turned aside from the more conventional and literary speech of the better educated. For example, in speaking of an obnoxious odor he would startle the people by using the word "stink." Thus he epitomized the colloquial preacher of the early part of the century, dramatizing when necessary, acting out a part or an event, taking off his coat, standing on a chair, shaking his fist, but always as part of the preaching of a particular message. He was "Billy" Sunday to the crowds and the common people heard him gladly.

Life-Situation Preaching

No other name compares to that of **Harry Emerson Fosdick** (**1878-1969**) whose meteoric rise to prominence took place in that liberalizing period of American preaching. A volume of sermons entitled *The Living of These Days* (1956) indicates the thrust of his time. With the advent of radio, Fosdick reached a generation ready to hear by this new channel of communication and made eager to listen by the ferment of social change. No one else commanded such large numbers of people as a congregation week by week. Fosdick took the social gospel of Gladden and Rauschenbusch and with a critical interpretation of Scripture made his sermons man-centered and problem-conscious. He did not begin with the Bible but began with a problem or with a question to be discussed and answered.

His preaching was based on the views expressed in the Yale Lectures, 1924, *The Modern Use of the Bible*. Believing the primitive origins and man's quest, he viewed the Bible as depicting the progress from concepts of a changing God in the past up to the concept of Jesus in the present. Historic doctrines of the Church were discarded and the Bible to him was no longer an infallible guide for faith and practice. Fosdick declared that his position had its perils as "irreverence, sentimentality, and ethical disloyalty of Jesus." While he gave his hearers a feeling of importance and urged them to strive for higher things, he did not bring to them the dynamic gospel of the New Testament. The human emphasis too often blurred the divine majesty.

His sermon "Forgiveness of Sins" begins with the words, "The only persons to whom this message is addressed are those conscious of moral wrongdoing." The introduction has no reference to the Scriptures and no text is announced, though later in the discourse reference is made to one. No doubt he used this style to catch the attention of radio listeners. He then takes up the question of forgiveness and what we mean by sin. This is a topical approach aimed at the casual listener. Gross sins are mentioned and then the more refined but just as damning sins of the spirit. The sins of social attitude are pointed out as well as the sins of neglect.

> Sins of the flesh, sins of temper, sins of social attitude, sins of neglect—I suppose there must be others, but this ought to take in

most of us and make us wonder whether, after all, we may not have a share in the need of the gospel of forgiveness.
This morning in particular I stress the difficulty of forgiving sin.

Fosdick decries any easy forgiveness or gospel and then the sermon is developed in three major emphases. Dealing with the question, Why, then, was it hard for Jesus to forgive? he says, "In the first place, because he took sin seriously. In the second place, Jesus found it hard to forgive because he loved people. In the third place, Jesus found it hard to forgive because forgiveness is such a terrific experience for the man who is forgiven." It is here that he introduces an association with the cross of Christ. "Is not that what Christians have always meant when they associated forgiveness with the cross of Christ? I do not know what theory of the atonement you may hold, and I might almost say I do not care whether you have any theory at all, but recognize this fact: behind all the explanations of atonement that have arisen and taken form and faded away in the history of Christian thought, this conviction has lain deep—the cross means that it was not easy even for God to forgive. It cost. And that is true to life."

Throughout the sermon there is deep concern for this truth. Illustrations are drawn from classical writers and from modern psychiatrists. He stresses the universal idea, not necessarily the Biblical revelation. He wishes men to forgive one another. He is not so much concerned that men seek and find divine forgiveness first of all. Only a passing reference here and there to Christ and the gospel tie this message in with the historic truth. Nevertheless, this sermon serves to illustrate the gracious spirit of the preacher, the intellectual strength of his writing, the wealth of his illustrative power, and the thrust of his words to the conscience of his hearers. The last paragraph is climactic and appealing, almost like the evangelist:

> We know that most clearly when we are at our best. We have gross, brutal hours, when we forget our unforgiven sins, lock them in the hold, let the roar of the world fill our ears until conscience cannot be heard, but ever and again the finer hours return, when we know that unforgiven sin still is here because unforgiven. Any minister who takes preaching in earnest cannot look out over congregations like this, Sunday after Sunday, without thinking of all the un-advertised needs that must exist beneath our respectable exteriors. Who can sum them up in their infinite variety? But deepest of all,

the unforgiven sins! There must be many here this morning. Go
down into that secret place. Unlock that hidden door. Take out
that unforgiven sin. For your soul's sake, get rid of it! But there is
only one way. Whatever theology you hold, it is the way of the
cross—penitence, confession, restitution, pardon.

Fosdick's many volumes of sermons have a strain of evangelical
liberalism. Perhaps this is what made him appeal so richly to his
listeners. His written work in manuscript and in sermon was carefully accomplished after a week's work as he toiled daily to express
truth and polish vocabulary. His strength lay in the strong homiletical build-up of each sermon, climaxing in an appeal to action.
According to Fosdick, preaching was never easy, but he believed in
it as the effective communication of truth.

During his long ministry, especially at Riverside Church, New
York (1931-1951), Fosdick discovered that to preach well he had
to write well. He confessed that he did not see how a man could
preach without writing. He always thought with his pen in hand.
His preaching naturally began to turn into books. While he did not
cherish any ambition to be an author, he did wish to teach and
preach. His shorter books on *The Manhood of the Master, The
Meaning of Prayer,* and *The Meaning of Service* were developed out
of addresses and sermons.

His method of dealing with life-situations and human problems
pioneered a new way in preaching. Many have done it since without
the Biblical strength of Fosdick, for Fosdick had been nurtured in
the Bible and he saw it in the light of man's experience of life and
of God. It can be said that he helped to make the Christian position
intellectually respected, socially responsible, and generally appealing to a generation influenced by liberalism in theology. The radio
gave him national coverage and publicity, and his published sermons
carried his message everywhere.

Neo-Orthodox Preaching

Edwin Lewis (1881-1959), Professor of Systematic Theology at
Drew Seminary (Methodist), published his essay, "The Fatal Apos-
tasy of the Modern Church" in 1933. Here he attacked the fantasies
of the liberal school and reaffirmed his faith in a Christological
theology. He preached and wrote about the need to be "saved" and
brought back terminology which had been thrown aside for many

decades. To Lewis the church of that time in America had drifted away from its moorings and needed to return to its historic position. Religious humanitarianism was not enough in a world of need. The motivation of the Christian gospel was required for the task. Liberalism had failed to produce anything like the gospel which had been the thrust of an earlier time. The economic troubles of the Great Depression and the coming of war in Europe deeply dented the optimism of the liberals and the social humanitarians.

During the thirties neo-orthodox theology also arose to challenge the older liberal theology. Its influence on the American theological scene caused the pendulum to swing once more in the direction of a more conservative view of the Bible and of life. Karl Barth of Switzerland was the strongest voice recalling the preacher back to the Book of God. Barth stressed the necessity of divine revelation, for it is God who seeks man, not man who seeks the truth. Biblical revelation was to be the beginning again for the theologian and preacher.

The new movement was a healthy reaction against some of the emphases of modernism, such as the immanence of God and reliance upon reason. This going back to the historic origin of the Christian faith was salutary, and the stress on the mighty acts of God in history as well as a reassertion of Christ's redemptive life and work was helpful. However, the crux of this new Barthian theology lay in its doctrine of the Word of God. It declared that the Bible is an authoritative witness to the divine disclosure. This differed seriously from the preaching of the historic evangelical view which held that the Bible itself is the Word of God. Neo-orthodoxy also believed in the sinfulness of man, and that divine revelation came apart from any natural revelation.

Reinhold Niebuhr (1892-1971) is a prime representative of the neo-orthodox movement. His early ministry was a pastorate in Detroit where he became involved in crucial industrial, economic, social, and political issues. Sensitive to the needs of his people, he assumed a position of identity with them, and from that perspective interpreted the Word of God for them. In *Leaves from the Notebooks of a Tamed Cynic* (1956), he expounded his ideas as a preacher in the midst of human need. Here the relevance of theology to human situations found deep expression. His record of acute human suffering and the Christian answer give "some indications of the uneasiness about the general presuppositions which informed a youthful ministry. . . . What we think of man and God, of sin and salvation, is partly prompted by the comparative comforts or dis-comforts in which we live. It is a very sobering reflection on the lack of transcendence of the human spirit over the flux of historical change."

Niebuhr was a long-term Professor of Christian Ethics at Union Theological Seminary in New York City. There he lectured, wrote, and preached according to the changes of theological perspective that he experienced. He modified his earlier liberalism for an emphasis on the sinfulness and depravity of human nature, seen in the context of modern industrial society. His *Moral Man and Immoral Society* (1932) was an application of theology to the social order. His Gifford Lectures, *The Nature and Destiny of Man* (1941) embody the sweep of his massive mind in wrestling with the glory and the tragedy of man. What Niebuhr calls the Biblical view of man and which he counterposes to the classical and modern view of man is his own view, won by reflection on his political and social experience. His Detroit pastorate gave him a grim perspective.

Man, to Niebuhr, was a finite, limited being whose judgment is infected by an ineradicable bias from which he can only partly liberate himself. His criticism of "liberal Christianity" was couched in strong terms and ever since he has had his followers in the pulpits of the land. The limitation of his influence and preaching has been that he was strong on diagnosis but weak on remedy. One would have liked to hear the triumphant notes of the gospel with its power to redeem and remake human nature. His neo-orthodoxy brought insight and balance to preaching, but it still lacked the wisdom and power of evangelicalism. Although he gave more years to teaching than to preaching, Niebuhr claimed that he was more preacher than scholar (cf. "Ten Years That Shook My World," *The Christian Century*, April, 1939). There in autobiographical vein he sums up his ideas. "Whatever measure of Christian faith I hold today is due to the gradual exclusion of alternative beliefs through world history. As did Peter, I would preface my confession, 'Thou hast the words of eternal life,' with the question, 'Lord, to whom shall we go?' Even while imagining myself to be preaching the gospel, I had really experimented with many modern alternatives to Christian faith, until one by one they proved unavailing." What was true of Niebuhr was characteristic of hundreds of others who tried to follow him in their newly awakened awareness of social and theological change.

The older liberal theology was inadequate and now a new liberal position was established which affected the preaching of the times.

The Niebuhr of the pulpit was really the teacher of the classroom. His utterances in many pulpits were not in any wise models of homiletical structure or in the traditional mold. As a man wrestles with his doubts and endeavors to clarify his thought at the moment, so was Niebuhr in his sermons. The titles of some of his books indicate the range of his mind and the expression of his apologetic. In *The Irony of American History* (1952), *Beyond Tragedy* (1937), and *The Children of Light and the Children of Darkness* (1944) he explores the demonic elements which torment our common life and society. Moral standards and moral issues are brought under a searchlight in which satire and irony also play their part. Niebuhr saw the Christian faith and the Christian as always under judgment. The Incarnation of Christ our Lord postulated the involvement of the church in the warp and woof of human struggle.

Like many another well-known personality who stirred up the contemporary scene, Reinhold Niebuhr delivered the Yale Lectures on Preaching in 1945 and also the Warrack Lectures on Preaching in Scotland in 1947. These were subsequently joined and revised to be published in one volume, *Faith and History*, a comparison of Christian and modern views of history, in 1949. As a clue to his preaching this is the closest we can get. In his introduction he says that "since I had no special competence in the art of homiletics I thought it wise to devote the lectures to a definition of the apologetic task of the Christian pulpit in the unique spiritual climate of our day. Since several of the Beecher lectures in the past half-century sought to accommodate the Christian message to the prevailing evolutionary optimism of the nineteenth and early twentieth centuries, I thought it might be particularly appropriate to consider the spiritual situation in a period in which this evolutionary optimism is in the process of decay."

Niebuhr's penetrating analysis of the period in which he ministered is invaluable for the acute and perceptive way in which he endeavors to relate the gospel in preaching. He stated his belief in the ageless gospel and then tried to see the task of the pulpit to relate that gospel to the special problems of each age. In doing so, however, he admits that there is temptation to capitulate to the prejudices of an age. He does not ask for rational validation of the gospel as the first thing needed by modern man. He sees and proclaims that modern man must first be apprehended by repentance and faith. This leads to the thesis that it is important for the preacher to understand, and come to terms with, the characteristic credos of his age. It is important in our age to understand how the spiritual complacency of a culture which believed in redemption through history (a counterfeit way) was now on the edge of despair.

Niebuhr's style was not simple and easy flowing. Nevertheless, to those who listened with effort and attention, there were rewards in understanding. Niebuhr was heard as much in college and in university chapels as in church pulpits for obvious reasons. Nevertheless, the unfolding of some doctrine which impinged upon life's needs and problems was not unwelcome when Niebuhr thought through the subject in the pulpit. His "homiletical" stance lay in taking a text or phrase from the Bible and then dealing with the theme inductively and directly. This thematic approach did not lack for hearers. Often Niebuhr would stop without necessarily having concluded his discussion. No formal conclusion was given. Perhaps he imagined the application could be made by any intelligent listener!

The preaching of neo-orthodox men like Niebuhr was given publicity and encouragement in this period when people reacted against the extremes of liberalism and fundamentalism. The swinging of the pendulum finally rested here. Barth's idea of the Word of God pervaded the teaching of preaching and homiletics. Thus Barth taught: "Preaching follows from the command given to the Church to serve the Word of God by means of a man called to this task. It is this man's duty to proclaim to his fellow men what God himself has to say to them, by explaining, in his own words, a passage from Scripture which concerns them personally." Thus the end of preaching should be expository and not topical. In Barth's works there is stress on the Word of God. That Word comes first in the Incarnation and then it makes contact with the spirit of man through the Holy Spirit and brings itself home to faith. Preaching, then, rests on the given Word, which it cannot supersede; it is an act demanded and controlled by the Biblical witness.

Barth taught that there are three forms of the Word of God: (1) Something *proclaimed* in the church, and proclaimed as that which has its source beyond the church itself. Preaching is the event in which God is speaking through the speech of men. (2) The Word of God is *written*. The message of the church is spoken in the expectation that God will reveal himself to those addressed, but also in recollection that already God has spoken once for all in Jesus Christ in the great event of the Incarnation, which is in history, but not of it. As witness to the revelation in Jesus Christ, the Bible is the written Word of God, declared by prophets and apostles. (3) God's Word is *revealed*. The Bible is the one means through which the church is given the revelation. The Bible gives authoritative witness inasmuch as it lets something else be the authority, viz., God's revelation. *It must never be identified with the revelation itself.*

In this light Barth brings to the neo-orthodox idea of preaching the concept that the Bible as now written is not actually the Word of God but only the vehicle through which that Word comes to us. Exegesis then is to be used in order that the Bible should be free to tell us what the Word of God really is. The Bible is the canon or rule of preaching for the definite reason that it imposes itself as such, in virtue of its content. The Bible then is God's Word insofar as he speaks through it; and this he does when a portion of it lays hold of us in God's name and by the working of his Spirit. In that event it becomes God's Word to us, and he makes it so to men. The Bible *becomes* God's Word in this event, and it is to its *being* in this *becoming* that the tiny word "is" relates, in the statement that the Bible is God's Word. It does not become God's Word because we accord it faith, but because by the act of God the Bible has reached out to us and *become revelation for us,* here and now.

Here is the crux of neo-orthodox preaching. The older idea of the evangelical and conservative scholar and preacher was to accept the Bible as it is as the Word of God. To do this is to affirm that what is recorded is already the divine revelation—whether we realize it or not. In the evangelical stance the Bible *is* the divine revelation—it does not *become* such existentially. God has already, according to Hebrews 1:1-4, unveiled himself in different ways and through human channels until finally he speaks through his only begotten Son. Revelation is divine disclosure in *speech* as well as in act. That revelation has been made in life and is now fixed in the literature of the Scriptures. The Bible then is not only a *witness* to revelation: it is the revelation. Nevertheless, the influence of neo-orthodox preaching has been significant. It brought many "liberals" back to the Bible for the basis of their preaching. Instead of the topical sermon, new forms of expository sermons were given to congregations in an attempt to find out what the Bible had to say to this generation. A new hermeneutic was developed in which the aids of archaeology, comparative religions, Israel's place in history, and the life and work of the church in the world were harnessed to give light and insight in exegesis. The interpretation in this way stressed essentially the mighty acts of God—the exodus of Israel and the exodus of Jesus Christ—two foci of history by means of which new light was shed on the meaning of revelation.

Two things have emerged from neo-orthodox theology. One is that preaching was stimulated and brought many men back to a more Biblical ministry. This was a decided gain. On the other hand, there was the surrender of the Westminster Confession of Faith (and other confessions, e.g., Heidelberg, Thirty-Nine Articles) which held the point of view that the Scriptures as written are the Word of God and complete and final as revelation. In neo-orthodoxy the Bible is to be viewed only as human and fallible as a witness to the Word of God. Only when God uses it, does it become the Word of God. Along with this came a defective view of the Confessions of the church. They are no longer binding in the older sense of acceptance as the subordinate standards next to the Bible; they have become museum or monumental pieces of a symbolic nature in the history of the church as it changes doctrine to suit new eras of expression.

Psychological Preaching

Closely akin to life-situation preaching is the preaching of those who bring understanding and sympathy to their congregations through the word which is therapeutic and healing. Such men use their God-given endowments and insights from psychology and psychotherapy. Of this group **Norman Vincent Peale (1898-)** is most prominent. He has had a long and enduring ministry in New York.

Peale would not like to be put into a special category and labeled; but where else put him? His life has been one of constant sharing with others the wealth of the good news in Christ. He believes thoroughly that in the gospel there is the dynamic for renewal of mind and heart. Although preaching is his paramount thrust, he is associated with other ministries to help people. The American Foundation of Religion and Psychiatry has honored him in testimonial. This organization, it should be known, was conceived in the mind of Peale when he became concerned over mental and emotional distress caused by the Depression of the thirties.

The Foundation maintains an outpatient clinic where trained clergymen, psychologists, psychiatrists, and social workers provide counseling for the hundreds of people on its rolls. It also trains clergymen to deal with emotional problems of people in their congregations. "Americans are so tense that it is impossible to put them to sleep with a sermon," says Dr. Peale. To help them relax he goes strongly for popular psychology in his sermons, talking in a chatty style. His radio talks have several million listeners and his television programs receive a like hearing. His books which are the result of his sermons and talks have sold in similar quantities.

In his background, Peale, the pastor of the Marble Collegiate Church in New York (Reformed Church in North America) is the product of an orthodox upbringing and belief. He has not deviated from that and is never ashamed to be linked with the historic faith of the Christian. In the theological spectrum he claims: "I'm a conservative, and I will tell you exactly what I mean by that. I mean I have accepted the Lord Jesus Christ as my personal Saviour. I mean that I believe the way of salvation is set down clearly in the Scriptures. I mean that I believe my sins are forgiven by the atoning work of grace on the cross. I personally love and understand this way of stating the Christian Gospel. But I am absolutely and thoroughly convinced that it is my mission never to use this language in trying to communicate with the audience that has been given me."

Peale does not hesitate to give an invitation at the end of his sermon at the church. Sometimes he comes down from the pulpit (or platform) to encourage the people to surrender their lives to Christ. Standing intimately before the congregation, he asks men and women to come forward and to acknowledge publicly their desire to begin again in Christ. Typically he asks people in the congregation to silently commit their lives to Jesus Christ, and to fill out a card which is in the hymnal rack and mail it to him. At times he invites people to come to an after-meeting.

Wherever possible, Peale presents his message in the language of the marketplace. He views his mission as one of reaching people who are not being reached by the church, to talk to them about the vital, real, new life in Christ in terms different from the language which means so much to some groups of people within the church.

Peale's preaching is psychological in that it is designed to meet the needs of people by talking in everyday businessmen's language and by sharing what he knows and has experienced. He is a friendly man, relaxed in talk, and filled with good fun and humor. As he preaches, he is facing hundreds of people and addressing thousands by radio, but his thought is on the individual. He had learned from college days, when he served as a reporter for a newspaper, that people are interested in human events and so he dealt with individuals. As he wrote and reported, he was unconsciously laying the foundation for the later writing of sermons and their delivery. He also left his Methodist heritage of home and church to engage in the ministry of the Reformed Church. This church had its Dutch and European tradition but it also had an opportunity for a committed man who believed in his message in a positive way. There also began the seeds of what later became his best seller, *The Power of Positive Thinking.* New York has been known as the graveyard of ministers, but since 1932 he has continued his ministry in the one pulpit with continuing encouragement and ever-widening congregations ready to listen to him.

His preaching is "out of his yesterdays" which is to say he draws from experience and weds that to the Bible text or theme to be shared with people. He has discarded notes, and he has not memorized his sermons. For some weeks ahead he chooses the topics and then begins to add what he gathers by way of illustration and quotation. Thereafter, an outline is prepared with main headings and subheadings. He then studies the outline and sequence of ideas, "picturizing" himself actually in the pulpit delivering the sermon. He does this over and over again until the main structure of the sermon is fixed in mind. With prayer he believes he will be guided in speech to say that which will be of special help to people seeking some word from God. Peale is no actor but learned from an old actor who urged him always to "practice loving your audience." He aims in speech to be clear and definite, to vary voice inflection, and to relieve the emotional tension with a touch of humor at the appropriate time.

Some of his best remembered sermons have been preached on Easter on the themes of immortality and the deathlessness of the human spirit. "We do not try to prove immortality," he would say, "so that we can believe it. We try to prove it because we can't help believing it. It is instinctive with us, and a true instinct. Every

person here will pass through the act known as physical death. But
God makes none of his natural processes terrible. He is a God of
love, and everything He does is done with love." In the climax of
this sermon he raises the question:

> Isn't that logical? Isn't that the way God has made the world? Is
> He going to change and do it differently over there? He doesn't
> change! That is why Socrates said, "No evil can happen to a good
> man, either in life or after death." That is why you read in the
> Book of Revelation these words spoken by a man who was terrified
> of death: "And He laid his right hand upon me, saying unto me,
> Fear Not." Some people may say, "You can't prove this." Well,
> you can't prove it isn't so either, can you? On our side we have the
> weight of the deepest instincts of man and twenty centuries of the
> Gospel of the Resurrection of Jesus Christ and all the logic and
> common sense in a world in which nothing, so the scientists tell us,
> is ever destroyed. Oh, yes, you can hold this faith. It isn't false. It
> is sound. Get it into your mind. Hold it and believe it, and you will
> find that it is true!

In other books with the titles, *The Art of Living* and *You Can
Win*, the same message of the sermon has been sent on to wider
missions. At first this was not so, but as he has mastered the art of
direct speech and the shorter sentence his printed messages have
become more used. He learned also by being willing to speak to
men in their clubs and associations. This opened doors for him so
that he learned the speech of the business man and was able to
communicate the Christian faith in terms understood outside of the
pulpit and in nontheological language. Peale has had his critics who
have objected to the simplicity of his message and method. The
formula sounds too much like an appeal to follow certain prescribed rules and then success will follow. Too often this has been
translated into material terms and has been geared to the more
pleasant things of our common life. Prayer becomes a means of
tuning in to God and sharing with God his plans for you so that
eventually all will be well.

If Peale's preaching has sounded superficial to the critics, he has
had something more durable in mind. In his gospel of good cheer
and well-being is the insight that when a man is in accord with
divine laws and obeys the directives of the New Testament for the
Christian life, there is renewal and re-creation of personality. But
this is no mechanical experience. He recognizes man's failure, frustration, and foibles. Sin is a reality and forgiveness by God is shown

to be a necessity. Peale's experience has taught him—and for this he preaches—the abiding life which becomes abounding in Christ who is Savior and Master of the whole of life.

The psychological preaching in which Peale excells was learned out of hard experience. He admits that in his earlier ministries he did not get through to his people. He then took time to analyze his own weaker methods and studied those who seemed to have influence in their preaching. Listening to others, he saw that effective preaching lay in telling something arresting, something logical, something of personality in enthusiasm and sincerity, something simple and clear, and in projecting the sense of being used of God. Thus he has specialized in the age when psychology and its jargon has become familiar in college and in business.

In an aside to a friend he discussed this problem of preaching to people, and said: "Why should there be a difference? I'll bet Jesus never sounded like that. He was a storyteller, the greatest that ever lived. He kept things short and simple. He knew how to reach people. He drew crowds to Him. These men, good men though they are, actually drive people away from Him and from His church!"

Philosophical Preaching

The modern era with its ferment in theology and in philosophy has brought out numerous cadences of thought to stimulate the church of God. The interaction of orthodoxy, liberalism, neo-orthodoxy, and others produced a man who could look at life in new dimensions and categories of thought.

Paul Tillich (1886-1965) came to America out of the holocaust of Germany, and the new world opened to him an opportunity of development and ministry closed to him in Europe. As a pastor in Germany and an active member of the Christian Socialist party, he came into conflict with Hitler. Coming to the U.S.A., he became a Professor at Union Theological Seminary, New York. There in the field of Philosophical Theology his influence increased and he made an impact upon American religious thought. He is best known as a teacher and professor. His writings take a high place in the history of doctrine and the ongoing discussion of religious values and meaning.

As a preacher Tillich moved within the realm of existential thought. Grappling, wrestling with ideas, he saw man in the encounter and endeavored to lead him to truth and final knowledge before God. Truth is no mere academic question, but is the truth of man's being, the meaning of life. When Tillich preached, he did not follow accepted rules of homiletics—yet people listened, carried away by the compelling force of his thought. This was no oratorical trick but simply a preacher who was one with his theme standing as a man among men. In this concentration Tillich was able to move into the minds of others. In his preaching was diagnosis of human frustration and trial, analysis of truth in order to liberate men from bondage and error.

The ultimate in God is the foundation for Tillich from which he views the superstructure of analysis by which he leads thought to action. Theology, then, is the interpretation of the symbols of man's ultimate concern. Not the creation but the interpretation of symbols is the task of theology. Symbols in this way become the avenue of revelation, which is the self-manifestation of the ultimate. Ultimate reality is expressed through symbols of ecstatic experiences. The principle of the interpretation of the symbol is the Logos; the New Being is the universal Logos of creation.

Tillich published many works, including his major theological works—*Systematic Theology* (3 vols., 1967), *The Interpretation of History* (1936), *The Protestant Era* (1948)—and sermons—*The Courage to Be* (1952), *The Shaking of the Foundations* (1948), *The New Being* (1955). From these we can discern the pattern of his thought and the message he proclaimed. Man, knowing his predicament, reaches out for meaning and then finds, as Tillich claimed, that the Ultimate breaks through into man's existence. At one point he condemned "traditional supernaturalism" as objectifying God, as making the Ultimate a being among other beings, and therefore no longer witnessing to its ultimacy. Faith in the ultimate is either the expression of "ultimate concern" or it is not faith in God as the power of being.

Tillich affirmed that our freedom is never infinite. If man forgets his finitude and aspires to infinite freedom, he will end in tragic self-destruction. In history he saw the demonic expressed as in World Wars. He distinguished between religion and ethics, the latter dependent upon the former. Religion is the root of culture, and his book *The Theology of Culture* (1919; 1964) probed this idea. He rejected the nineteenth-century liberalism and tried to keep within his Lutheran tradition. As a mystical theologian, he saw love as the nature of being, the nature of God himself. The Trinity is fulfilled through the Spirit, the dynamic unity of logos within that love. While these restless thoughts permeate his theology, it is in preaching that he came through in simpler terms and so we begin to understand him.

His sermons clarify much of his theology. The practical interpretation and application are couched in terms which are not Biblical or theological, but are words for today's man. The sermon was developed apologetically. Jeremiah 4:23-30, "I look out on earth . . . lo, all is chaos; I look at heaven . . . its light is gone . . . ," is the text for the sermon "The Shaking of the Foundations." Here is the preacher speaking in a cataclysmic time. Ranging across the pages of the Bible and across history, he weaves in the illustrations of man's failures and the upheavals of society which plague man.

> In the language of the prophets, it is the Lord who shakes the mountains and melts the rocks. This is the language that modern man can now understand. And so God, who is not bound to any special language, not even to that of the prophets, spoke to the men of today through the mouths of our greatest scientists, and this is what He said: You yourselves can bring about the end upon yourselves. I give the power to shake the foundations of your earth into your hands. You can use the power for creation or destruction. How will you use it? This is what God said to mankind through the work of the scientists and through their discovery of the key to the foundations of life. But through them He did even more. He forced His Word upon them, as He had forced it upon the prophets. . . . Not only do they feel the shaking of the foundations, but also that they themselves are largely responsible for it. They tell us that they despise what they have done, because they know that we are left with only a slight chance of escape. Wavering between little hope and much despair, they urge us to use this chance.

This is apologetic preaching! It also savors of apocalyptic preaching in the manner of the prophets. The *eschaton* is in mind. The application to the social and moral problems of the age are stressed again and again. Here is no "moralism" but *kerygma*.

In his book *The New Being* Tillich develops the thesis that the New Being as Love and the New Being as Freedom lead to the New Being as fulfillment. Based upon Paul's word "A new creation" (Gal. 6:15), the theme is expounded in a variety of sermons. This, to Tillich, sums up the Christian message. He uses "the new being, the new reality" as terms to interpret the familiar "the new creation." He sounds like an expositor who has done his exegesis. He discusses what Paul thought of as the negative aspect—what this new being is *not*, then proceeds to the positive—what he *is*. "Christianity is more than a religion; it is the message of a New Creation. Christianity as a religion is not important—it is like circumcision or like uncircumcision: no more, no less! Christianity in the present world encounters several forms of circumcision and uncircumcision. Circumcision can stand today for everything called *religion,* uncircumcision for everything called *secular,* but making half-religious claims." Comparative religions and also secular movements are reviewed as part of this complex. "How shall Christianity face them? Shall Christianity tell them: Come to us, we are a better religion, our kind of circumcision or uncircumcision is higher than yours? Shall we make of the Christian message a success story, and tell them, like advertizers: try it with us, and you will see how important Christianity is for everybody?"

In discussing this rhetorical question in his reasoned discourse, Tillich gives answers and is able to show convincing evidence why Christianity is something different and unique. It is not in a comparison of "religions" where the answer is found, but "I want to tell you that something has happened that matters, something that judges you and me, your religion and my religion. A New Creation has occurred, a New Being has appeared; and we are asked to participate in it. . . ." In a thematic word and strain there is reiterated this truth: "Salvation does not destroy creation; but it transforms the Old Creation into a New one. Therefore we can speak of the New in terms of a re-newal: The threefold 're,' namely, reconciliation, re-union, re-surrection." This tripartite fusion of words and combination of truths is his interpretation of the underlying truth of the Christian faith. This was necessary for preaching. Tillich could reason with philosophical acumen concerning the theological views in ferment, and endeavor to convince students and others in the world of intelligent enquiry and debate. However, in the pulpit he laid aside his tools in order to present in simple proclamation what he believed as a man of faith. His summation before a congregation indicates that here is the New Reality. "A New state of things has appeared, it still appears; it is hidden and visible, it is there and it is here. Accept it, enter into it, let it grasp you."

Such preaching was philosophical yet evangelistic; deep yet simple; rooted in theology; transcendental yet down to earth; based on ancient thought forms yet given in modern everyday speech for the ordinary man to understand. Its substance came with sufficient dynamism to touch the hearers with a deeply moving and at times crushing force activated by love and empathy. Although few could understand him in the study and in the classroom as he wrestled with language and thought, he was able in grasping the ideas of our common culture to synthesize all of life's values to give meaning to the presentation of the truth as he knew it: and the truth sets free.

The Professor as Preacher

Edwin Charles Dargan (1852-1930) came to the Southern Baptist Theological Seminary, Louisville, Kentucky, in 1892 when John A. Broadus was President. He was an instant success and soon took his place with the choice teachers of that seminary. His background, his widely recognized ability as a preacher, and his church standing commended him to students and to the public alike. Teacher of Homiletics and Biblical Theology, he taught until 1907 when he returned to the pastorate. During those later years he brought out his *magnum opus,* the two-volume *A History of Preaching* (1912). Its enduring quality is attested to by the fact that it is still in circulation and use. Another work, *The Art of Preaching in the Light of History,* was based upon lectures given at the Southwestern Theological Seminary, Fort Worth, Texas (1921).

Dargan's literary work continued throughout his ministry, and what he had done in the seminary courses came to final fruition in the books which abide as a significant contribution on the subjects of homiletics and preaching. As a preacher, he was given to fresh research in sermon preparation, and his teaching gifts found scope in effective proclamation of the truth. His sermons grappled with themes dealing with society, the kingdom, and the church. These sermons revealed historical perspective, keen judgment, and a fine style.

Lutherans in America had many preachers whose distinction lay in their faithful pastoral ministry, following the liturgy of their church. In **Richard Charles Henry Lenski (1864-1936)** they had a teacher of preachers. From 1887-1911 he was pastor and theological teacher, then from 1916-1921 Professor of Languages and Theology at Capital University, Columbus, Ohio. From 1921-1936 he was Professor of Dogmatics, New Testament Exegesis, and Homiletics. With this broad experience Lenski influenced more than a generation of Lutheran preachers. Using the Pericope of the church, he stressed a literary and exegetical sermon in the finest tradition. His own preaching is reflected in *Preaching from Paul* (1916), and *The Sermon: Its Homiletical Construction* (1927). In addition, he published *Commentary of the New Testament* (11 vols). In all of his work he exemplified an acute mind and skill in the interpretation of Scripture which led to Biblical preaching.

The ministry of **Henry Van Dyke** (1852-1933) was varied. He held pastorates, especially at the Brick Presbyterian Church, New York; he served as Professor of English Literature, Princeton University; then as Ambassador to the Netherlands and Luxemburg. He served a second period at Princeton University and also gave the Yale Lectures on Preaching, *The Gospel for an Age of Doubt* (1896). If Conwell was a cautious conservative, Van Dyke was a cautious liberal. Certainly he espoused the chief doctrines of orthodoxy but held to a modified Calvinism. Preaching on the sins and failures of human life, he endeavored to identify Christ as the Master of all good life to be lived.

His Lectures on Preaching indicate the bent of his mind in a time of social and economic ferment, and his questioning of the veracity and authenticity of the Scriptures. Van Dyke sought to be a mediator between extremes, seeking to conserve the best from the old and yet be open with a liberal mind to new aspects of the new age. His sermons point to the practical application of eternal truths. In construction of the sermon, Van Dyke was an artist. His choice of language and his knowledge of English and literature enabled him to use the beautiful for appeal to the cultured hearers who attended his ministry. Felicity of diction and direct and engaging moral appeal enriched his sermonic presentation. He was the Christian gentleman of culture and understanding reaching the people who had to make decisions in government, education, economics, and religion. While Conwell appealed to more of the working men of that era, Van Dyke touched the conscience of well-educated leaders of American life.

The essential nature of his ministry is best summed up in the ideals which guided and prompted him throughout his life. He was a convinced believer, but at the same time his Christian faith had to be part of the culture of the world in which he lived. With his flowing prose and choice English, Van Dyke held a unique place. Around him were those who gave more attention to the thrust of the message in the variety of appeals of the evangelist, revivalist, social reformer, and pastor wrestling with the needs of a congregation. In his broad experience he was able to minister to a select group of the people in two pastorates, then as professor, and most of all in his writings and books. He never shifted his position but remained the same, steadfast preacher of the eternal message in an age of uncertainty. His story *The Other Wise Man* delighted millions with its message of the Christmas story told in a unique way.

Henry Van Dyke is given a place as one of the best types of preachers in a long tradition—scholarly, gifted, cultured. Such a man fills a niche in history, and his unusual qualities of character and devotion are redolent with accomplishments not given to the ordinary preacher. Of Van Dyke it might be written that he was one of the few ten-talented men in the history of preaching. He preached and gave lavishly from a well-equipped and well-stored heart and mind.

Archibald Thomas Robertson (1863-1934) was known particularly for his scholarly life, his output of books, and especially for the monumental and voluminous work, *A Grammar of the Greek New Testament in the Light of Historical Research* (1914; 1931), an indispensable tool for the serious student. At the Southern Baptist Seminary, Louisville, he served as Professor of New Testament Interpretation (1888-1934). Not only in the classroom, but in pulpits and at conferences, Robertson preached in his own inimitable way. Most of his books are samplings of his hermeneutics as he took the original text and exegeted the Scriptures for the edification of congregations. *The Glory of the Ministry* (1911) is an example of this. Here is "Paul's Exultation in Preaching," an exegetical and expository treatise of II Corinthians 2:12—6:10. If every pastor could do this with Robertson's skill, what preaching would result! Geared to human needs, the interpretation and application came from a professor whose heart was warm and whose aim was to let the truth speak for itself. Thus the scholar and professor proclaimed the whole counsel of God with acceptance. Robertson points the way to become an expository preacher of the New Testament order, and demonstrates it with simplicity and sincerity.

Lynn Harold Hough (1877-1971) held a few pastorates but his chief ministry lay in training young men as Professor of Homiletics,

Drew Seminary, New Jersey. His uncluttered mind, scintillating with brilliance, was lively and spacious. His knowledge of literature, theology, and philosophy gave him an unrivaled influence in his denomination and beyond. He had a nervous style and his delivery was swift and terse with interesting facts and sentences. He was a Christian internationalist and humanist. His books and lectures as well as sermons have a quality of choice quotation, rich allusion, and an appeal to the culture of the day. Intellectual fervor adorned this preacher as he found in Scripture and human life the answer to man's needs.

John Gresham Machen (1881-1937) carried on the struggle for the supernatural view of Scripture and Christianity. He was Professor of New Testament at Princeton Seminary, New Jersey. After that seminary had compromised its historic position theologically, Machen with others withdrew and founded Westminster Seminary, Philadelphia, Pennsylvania. At this new center men have been trained for the ministry according to the Westminster Confession of Faith and a belief in the Bible as the inspired Word of God.

Machen was not only a teacher but a preacher of strong conviction. The sermons of Machen were characterized by the faithful exposition of vital doctrines in series. He also could use the polemical style and was strong in apologetic as he defended the Christian faith. In his volume *What Is Faith?* we are led along by sheer logic into the conviction that the divine and the human are met in a spiritual encounter of trust and committal. Reason as the handmaid of faith is stressed to point up the reasonableness of the Christian faith. This emphasis was much needed when men were struggling to find certitude.

Machen was the author of many scholarly works, including *The Origin of Paul's Religion* (a discerning study and interpretation of the New Testament and its background), *The Virgin Birth of Christ* (a monumental work which stands as the latest definitive exposition on this subject), and *Christian Faith in the Modern World* (in which he defends his theological position).

The sermons are published in *The Christian View of Man, What is Christianity?*, and *God Transcendent*. He reiterated in his sermons that men cannot give lip service to a creed or recite the Apostles' Creed and then deny that they are bound to commit themselves to its statements as truth. This to Machen was hypocrisy and blatant unbelief. In his preaching he was the scholarly exegete of a text or passage. Nothing was left to chance. His careful and detailed study gave him strength and superiority as an expositor. He must be accorded tribute for his investigation of the Greek text and the spiritual insight that permeated his writings. Some of those who opposed him in the issues of churchmanship could not but respect his sound scholarship and unchallenged stature as an expositor of the Bible.

Machen's preaching is reflected in his own comments about preachers he heard in his day. He preferred to use a full manuscript, although he developed a freedom of utterance as time went on. Naturally his sermons were related to the issues of doctrinal controversy then acute in his day. His book *Christianity and Liberalism* reflects much of his preaching. Although he treated profound theological themes, he was able to present them in simple terms. Thus in talking about faith in Christ, he said: "It is natural for a child of the covenant to learn first to trust Christ as Saviour almost as soon as conscious life begins, and then having become God's child through Him, to follow His blessed example. There is a child's hymn—a child's hymn that I think the Christian can never outgrow which puts the matter right:

> O dearly, dearly has He loved,
> And we must love Him too,
> And trust in His redeeming blood,
> And try His works to do.

That is the true order of Christian pedagogy—'trust in His redeeming blood' first, and then 'try His works to do.' Disaster will always follow when that order is reversed."

Dr. John A. Hutton, the editor of *The British Weekly* of Great Britain, Presbyterian minister, and outstanding literary critic, heard Machen and said of him that he felt no one could be indifferent to the message Machen spoke—whether he agreed or not! "In one passage," said Hutton, "there was a grandeur and vastness in its truth as Machen described our place here in the unfathomable depths of space." He paid Machen the high tribute that this utterance seemed to be on the level of the closing passages of John Henry Newman's *Apologia*—high praise indeed! If some of Machen's American colleagues criticized his position theologically, the British theological leaders acclaimed him in no uncertain terms as they reviewed his books. Machen can be described as the scholar as preacher. His message was that of faith in the eternal message of the Biblical revelation of God's grace in Christ.

Halford Edward Luccock (1885-1960) is a luminous example of a preacher whose best work was not done in a single church and pulpit, but who ministered to all through his books and articles as well as his lectures to students. Thereafter, these men were always in his debt as they went about their own ministries. Luccock was a man of faith and experience in the deep things. He was destined to preach, yet accepted the role of a teacher of preachers, an expositor, and an interpreter of literature in the service of preaching.

As Professor of Preaching at Yale, he gave the Lyman Beecher Lectures entitled *Communicating the Gospel* (1954), in which he proclaimed his convictions about preaching. "The aim of preaching," he said, "is not the elucidation of a subject, but the transformation of a person. . . . The purpose of the preacher is not to explain something, but to persuade people to think, and to act, in a certain way. . . . The Gospel was not merely an idea, a message, but an idea in process of communication." Also *In the Minister's Workshop* (1944) brings stimulation and encouragement to the lethargic pastor so that he can achieve results. Says he, "A sermon is like a wrestling match, or rather two wrestling matches, first with an idea and then with an audience, with the absorbed tenseness of those first moments which will determine whether one can get an effective hold on idea or on people."

These extracts indicate the strength of his simple yet clear style. Ideas move; his writing scintillates; his thoughts cover a wide area of study and research. He saw the need of life-centered preaching, allied to social preaching, and the use of literature as a means of communication. With a "springboard" for a sermon, he taught, any pastor could at least start something worthwhile. That the form of the sermon should follow function was one of his ideals. Everything was grist to the mill of his homiletical mind. By word and example Luccock influenced thousands of preachers to learn their craft.

Andrew Watterson Blackwood (1882-1966) will be remembered by all Princeton men and beyond in the wider ministries of men of all denominations. For twenty years he taught homiletics and by his many books on practical theology continues to be a teacher of preachers. In the pulpit he was at home as pastor for seventeen years before assuming the role of professor. Nevertheless, he continued throughout his active life to preach as often as opportunity came. Especially did he find joy in visiting the pulpits of former students.

Like Luccock of Yale, Blackwood led a full life of teaching and writing. Among his books were *Preaching from the Bible* (1941), *Planning a Year's Pulpit Work* (1942), *The Fine Art of Preaching* (1937), *The Fine Art of Public Worship* (1939), *The Preparation of Sermons* (1948). *The Protestant Pulpit* (1947; a selection of sermons, past and present) was the actual text of outstanding preachers to study. Thus a student and preacher could use the laboratory method of finding out how a sermon was built up and then delivered.

A comparison of Blackwood with Luccock indicates that the latter scintillated with a brilliance and a sparkle which was not always found in the former. However, if Blackwood was more pedestrian than Luccock, that was accounted for as a difference in personality and temperament, as well as religious background. Blackwood stood in the tradition of his forebears, made of sterner stuff and more sober mien. There is a solidity and strength in Blackwood's writings which make them wear well in a timeless manner.

In the sermon volume, *The Year of Our Lord* (1943), we discern the heart of the pastoral preacher once more reaching out of the classroom into the pulpit. The sermons are related to the outstanding days of the year—Christmas, Easter, Pentecost, Labor Day, Stewardship, Thanksgiving—and serve to illustrate the professor's way of putting into practice what he taught to others. Always Biblical and always at the heart of the gospel, Blackwood's Christian faith pervades the pages. Every sermon is well organized and adequately expounded. The purpose was to show the will of God for people in days of war and of reconstruction.

Open-air Preaching

James Wallace Hamilton (1900-1968) has been hailed as "one of the greatest preachers in our country." His niche among the great is a puzzle to some and a settled conviction for others. In an age which saw vast technological developments come to pass in America, this man seemed to retain an unchanging spirit of simplicity and humanness. He will be remembered not only for the books of sermons published but also for the winsomeness of his ministry in a church where for forty years he lived and labored. That in itself is unusual in modern days—usually ministries are much shorter and only the unusual can be found for so long a time in one pastorate—and that in a Methodist church!

The preaching of Hamilton was based on solid, hard work, day in and day out. Nothing else mattered to him. This Canadian farm boy who never attended college or seminary preached to thousands of people every week. However, it should not be overlooked that he owed much to the three years he spent at The Moody Bible Institute, Chicago. There he studied in detail the English Bible and learned in practical ways how to speak to people and reach the ordinary man with his message. The Institute was not only a place of preparation but also a proving ground for him. The mastery of the English Bible, even without the knowledge of the original languages, is in itself no mean achievement. Most of our colleges and seminaries (with a few exceptions now) do not give priority to this study. Yet here is the secret of Bible knowledge—mastery of content and familiarity with its doctrines.

In the light of the above, Hamilton was not an uneducated man. An idea would grip him and he would then gather scribblings, clippings, and anything germane to the subject for his brooding hours. His writing came only after he "listened"; then when the flow began he wrote for the occasion and finally put it on a tape recorder for his own playback. After writing the sermon in its final form he was ready to deliver it without notes in the pulpit. His own formula lay in his words: "Tell the Good News well, clearly, and vitally. If in any part of the sermon you have a word that doesn't sing, then find one that does. . . . It is a frightening thing to see how dull and tame we have made the words of Christ. . . . We must make them live. . . ."

The unique presentation of his sermons was made not in a building like the conventional church, but out and beyond the building in the parking lot where people sat in their automobiles. The advent of the automobile changed the habits of millions of people. This opened the door for one church to invite people on wheels to drive into the church parking lot and listen in while they sat in their cars. This gave Hamilton an unprecedented opportunity to reach thousands who could not be contacted otherwise. Of course, the location of the Pasadena Community Church, St. Petersburg, Florida, was an ideal situation, for the climate was warm and sunny and inviting to the traveler. In the eighteenth century, John Wesley in England and George Whitefield in America stood in the open air and preached to the crowds with marked results. Hamilton was in their succession in the modern age and with microphone and loud speakers he stood in his pulpit and proclaimed the gospel to the larger congregations who came to hear him.

Like other well-known personalities who have had the ear of crowds, he dealt with the whole range of human need and desire. In a sermon which showed the cutting edge of his thrust, he said, "I hope you'll forgive what may seem a flippant title, 'Sit-ins among the Shut-Ins.' I couldn't resist it because it exactly describes the situation. There they were: exiles, a shut-out people; and a man knowing he must sit in with them to learn the language of their tears. And don't write off Ezekiel's story as just a bit of ancient history. It's more. It's a story of a need—a need which grows larger in a world which grows smaller every year." He was relating how Ezekiel said in the text (3:15) "I sat where they sat." He then developed the ideas of (1) Imagination; (2) Appreciation; (3) Compassion. Thus he moved along in the message with valid and up-to-date illustrations of how people find themselves in situations of need—and how the servant of God must sit there with them to help them—through the avenues of identification and approach.

Sometimes the sermons seem loaded with illustrations while more Biblical exposition might have been included. But here we recall that Hamilton's preparation was not that of the schools but was based upon a mastery of the English Bible. We would not wish to change him. His thrust and success lay in the fact that he remained himself and in that natural endowment he was able to express the deep things of God. Nothing clever is paraded but there is a clarity and conciseness, a crispness of speech which comes through in the printed page. Hamilton had one aim and one mission—to reach the ordinary man of his day with the eternal message. Using the incarnational approach, his language was down to earth and seasoned with the commonplace ideas and references of his day and people. He spoke their language but in good, sound, Anglo-Saxon speech. Like his Master, "the common people heard him gladly"—and they did increasingly over the years for they understood what he said! The living Word of God was spoken in lively words by this preacher.

Many other churches now have their open air parking spaces

filled with automobiles—especially in warmer climes—and thousands gather weekly to hear some preacher proclaim the eternal message. Hamilton stands as the best example of this type of ministry. His classification was not liberal or neo-orthodox; he was simply a man who believed the Book and shared its message directly and simply. The hymn "Tell Me the Old, Old Story, Of Jesus and His Love" would summarize the heart of his ministry in content and in delivery. The evangelical nature of Hamilton's message gave him acceptance with people of every background and opened doors of ministry which were nationwide. There was no muting of the sound of the trumpet when he preached. The positive note was there. Human nature was seen clearly for what it was, but in the gospel preached there was the redemption of human nature. In a world of confusion Hamilton pointed to the sanity and security of the eternal message of Christ.

Black Preaching

A new age and a cataclysmic time introduced to the American scene a new phase of preaching. The unrest and tensions of American society in the twentieth century has led to a new publicity and ministry for our Negro or Black preachers. The colored (as sometimes preferred in speech) have had a minimal place in preaching in the past, partly because of the history of slavery and the consequent absorption of the church within its closed walls of separation—both white and colored. This has changed, and we welcome the opportunity to estimate the worth of the preaching of these brethren.

During the days of slavery, preaching was limited to small groups on Southern plantations and gradually extended to the churches where these servants of others had a place to attend and listen. For their own gatherings, colored preachers rose up to lead them. At first these men were not well educated, but they had a feeling for the truth and a knowledge of the Bible which brought them vivid identification with people and events recorded in the Bible. The struggle of the Israelites in Egypt and their march to freedom was reenacted in many a pulpit by the preacher retelling the story and finding the parallel in his own congregation and among his own race. The Bible came alive in this way. Thus preaching was forceful and emotional; and, reinforced by the singing of the people, especially the "Negro Spiritual," who would not be moved by the message of a suffering people praying and working for liberty? Standing out among the more recent leaders as preachers are Martin Luther King, Jr., James H. Robinson, C. A. Tindley, Adam Clayton Powell, and Jesse Jackson.

The movement in 1940-1960 in America which brought the Negro people into prominence through certain leaders was one of far-reaching influence. Christian preachers were in the vanguard of this stride toward freedom. We have been persuaded by our brethren to call them Blacks when addressing them. Thus the term Black Preaching has emerged in this generation. Following the days of slavery and the Civil War, the Blacks at first worshiped alongside of their masters, but gradually this was changed as God raised up pastors and preachers from among their own people.

Among the earlier preachers was **Richard Allen (1769-1831)**, father of the African Methodist Episcopal Church. He was pastor and then bishop after much haggling with white men who did not assist him in a democratic way. It was inevitable that the Blacks should have their own church buildings and their own structure in the church. At first education was limited for these share-croppers and small farmers. But they gave time for reading and studying whenever a young man showed promise. Another leader was **Jacob Benjamin Boddie** whose leadership in the Baptist communion was noteworthy. He preached in a fiery manner, using a pictorial manner of presentation wedded to a vivid imagination. His words were simple and poetic, yet not flowery.

The best known Black preacher of earlier days is reputed to be **Harry Hoosier,** or "Black Harry" as he was known. From 1784 until his death in 1810 he preached as an orator. Crowds in both the North and South waited to hear him, and both white and black followed his ministry with eagerness.

The preaching of these men of earlier days was grounded in their knowledge of the Bible. This Bible knowledge was what they had learned in their homes and in their association with the congregations in which they were nurtured. For some favored few who struggled to achieve it, there was college and some theological training, but usually of a limited kind. For the most part, their equipment lay in their native gifts of utterance and persuasive emotional appeals. The characters of the Bible came alive as they stepped into their places, transcending history and bringing them up-to-date. The trials and tests, the victories and influence of Bible men and women were reenacted by the preacher before the people who came to listen. Delivery was without notes, and the black idiom and the Negro spirituals aroused the congregation to a high degree of receptivity and response.

As the preacher of the twentieth century came into his own, he was in the leadership of millions of Black people who now belonged to more denominational churches. It is true that many "storefront" gatherings continued in the cities, but in the South new congregations with excellent buildings were a feature for almost a century. In the North the same has been true. The new day of liberty and progressive equal rights in society and in education were punctuated by the struggles of black groups endeavoring to achieve what they claimed as their birthright. Federal legislation and civic reform might be passed by political majorities at Washington, D.C., and in the States, but what was given as a right took many years and much heartache to realize on a large scale. Only through the religious ideals and the strong convictions of outstanding preachers were the Blacks able to receive better social, economic, political, and educational opportunities.

Martin Luther King, Jr. (1929-1968), is noteworthy as the man fully involved in the social struggle of his people. He proclaimed a nonviolent attitude and his movement was thus marked. The Southern Christian Leadership Conference was noted for its insistence upon the rights of the Blacks, but always with a sense of Christian idealism. Modeled often upon the fact of the exodus of the Israelites from Egypt, so King and his followers tried to lead their people into the fullness of freedom as promised under the Constitution of the United States. The demonstrations, the march to Selma, the various operations of protest, and the appeals to the nation's conscience and government had their origins in the sermons which he preached. The vast rally at the Lincoln Monument, Washington, D.C., was in essence a religious service in which he proclaimed his well-known slogan and message "I have a dream."

King was a pastor in Montgomery, Alabama, and also in Atlanta, Georgia. In these Baptist churches he found freedom to preach his message. "Love in Action"; "Loving your Enemies"; and "Shattered Dreams"; were sermons prepared while in Atlanta jails where he was imprisoned on charges of disturbance. His sermons brought to bear the Christian message on the social evils which clouded his day. He himself said that the sermon should be directed to the listening ear rather than to the reading eye. King was a man of imaginative insight. He stressed the "Tough Mind and the Tender Heart" in the text: "Be ye therefore wise as serpents, and harmless as doves" (Matt. 10:16), where Jesus blended these opposites for disciples facing a hostile world. The sermon "Transformed Nonconformist," based upon "Be not conformed to this world . . ." (Rom. 12:2), used the old expression to toughen his followers for their struggle and also to expound the proposition of standing for what one believes to be right. "On Being a Good Neighbor" was based on "and who is my neighbor" (Luke 10:29), a reminder that regardless of the color or race of people we need to be helpful to all without distinction or exception if we are to carry out the law of love.

His sermon, "Paul's Letter to American Christians," is an imaginative attempt to stab the conscience of the American churches about the race question. In this sermon much of the essence of the struggle can be discerned. After the usual salutation in Pauline language, he speaks of a longing to see them, and reflects upon what he has heard about them. He then reminds them of their responsibilities as Christians with respect to the ethical and moral sense of the gospel. He refers to the affluence of our society and then quickly points afresh to the needs of multitudes who still await help and succor from us. "Another thing that disturbs me about the American church is that you have a white church and a Negro church. How can segregation exist in the true Body of Christ? I am told that there is more integration within the entertaining world and other secular agencies than there is in the Christian church. How appalling this is!" "I understand that there are Christians among you who try to find Biblical bases to justify segregation and argue that the Negro is inferior by nature. Oh, my friends, this is blasphemy and against everything that the Christian religion stands for. I must repeat what I have said to many Christians before, that in Christ 'there is neither Jew nor Greek, there is neither bond nor free, there is neither male nor female: for ye are all one in Christ Jesus.' . . . So, Americans, I must urge you to be rid of every aspect of segregation. Segregation is a blatant denial of the unity which we have in Christ."

King led the dramatic "walk for freedom" in Montgomery which resulted in bus desegregation. His "I have a dream" message given at Washington, D.C., is remembered for its moving passages and tremendous oratorical climax. Here is Black preaching from an educated, well-read, theologically-oriented pastor whose timeless sermons abide as a contribution to preaching. The times were evil and explosive; hence his powerful illustrations lay all around him in the deeds and social unrest of his time. The untimely death of Martin Luther King by the assassin's bullet did not still the fiery message once sent forth. His spirit and message continue as men refer back to his witness and dedication in preaching.

Others who have made an impact include the **Rev. Jesse L. Jackson** of Chicago. Unlike King he has not crusaded throughout the country, but has centered most of his work in Chicago. He leads a large congregation and is President of millions of Blacks in their Baptist order. He and his people have launched a campaign for the placement of Blacks in the Chicago job market. This is called "Operation Breadbasket." Here is a demonstration of preaching and practicing; of revival and relevancy; of faith and action. The Blacks are thus mobilized to seek and demand and secure employment.

James Herman Robinson (1907-1972) of New York, a Presbyterian, also an educated Black, was noted as the first Black pastor to give the Yale Lectures on Preaching, published later as *Adventurous Preaching* (1955). In these lectures we see his mind and ministry at work. His autobiography, entitled *Road Without Turning* (1950), gives a revealing life-story of a poor boy out of a poverty situation in the South making his way gradually by work and toil to secure an education until he reaches the goal. During his ministry in one church in New York City Robinson combined the preaching of the gospel with every kind of service to his hardpressed people. He led in social services; he helped to found an interracial hospital; he engaged in politics; and he enlarged his outlook by involvement in world missions. His visits and work for the church in Africa especially led to an acute awareness of the needs of mankind.

In preaching to the same congregation over many years, Robinson shared his concerns for the social relevance of the gospel without obscuring the heart of the evangelical message. To him the preacher was under judgment and so was his preaching. The minister was unique but not apart from people, rather among them as one who had something to say from God. Theology and terminology were important for the art of communication. As he expressed it, "God does not need parrots, he needs prophets and priests. Purity of heart is more important than intellectual capacity." He believed that the deepening of the inner life of the minister was most important. Here was the place to share with others life's longings and confessions of need.

As pastor of a city church, he was conscious of the flux and movement of people around. Thus he favored multiple ministries by a staff as the source of extra strength and power. He was acutely aware of the peril of the false and evil prophet even as he sought to be the true prophet. One thing he learned by bitter experience—it was not his place to be a politician but to stick to his ministry. He was defeated for election to the City Council and accepted this to concentrate henceforth upon his major work. Adam Clayton Powell was one in similar circumstances who did carry a pastorate and yet maintained a political position in the Congress of the United States. To Robinson, dynamic preaching was incarnational, and in the inner city he found ample open doors of service for his preaching and action. He called for adventurous faith and a willingness to be expendable.

In the Negro spirituals and in the New Testament he saw how the Black preacher could proclaim a message of hope rising out of despair and loneliness. "In the agony of solitude when all temporary foundations give way, he found in the deeper introspection of religion that 'trouble doesn't always last.' He marched out to meet the promises of God." His words reflected his spirit and beliefs when he said: "Christianity is not an illusion. It is real, and its faith and methods have been proved in fire and famine, by persecution and prison, by the sword and the stake, by heroism and humility, by slave and by king, by the rich and the poor, through the most excruciating agony. It has survived the time and change of every human institution in which men have found themselves. It rose above the ruins of Imperial Rome; it survived the dark ages and ushered in the enlightenment. It can steady our shaking foundations and build stronger and more enduring ones when those that ought to die have crumbled into dust." This eloquent peroration is a sampling of the emotive quality of the speech of James Robinson whose Pauline convictions were expressed in II Corinthians 4:8, "We are troubled on every side, yet not distressed; we are perplexed, but not in despair. . . ."

Another Black leader has been **Howard Thurman (1899-)** whose creative mind has brought new standards to Black worship and theology. After his years of pastoral work and graduate study, he became the Dean of the Chapel and Professor of Spiritual Discipline and Resources at Boston University. He has maintained his connection with the Church for the Fellowship of All Peoples in San Francisco, which he helped to found. As an author he has engaged in a wider ministry through his books, including *Meditations of the Heart* (1953), *Deep Is the Hunger* (1950), *The Creative Encounter*, and *The Negro Spiritual Speaks of Life and Death* (1947; 1969). Some of these have been given as lectures under foundations, but most have been gathered from sermons preached to many congregations throughout the nation.

In preaching Thurman conveys the deepest quality of persuasion in the feeling engendered by his words. Though men live in a world of little sentiment, there is yet room for feeling in religion and the preacher enters into that area of man's need. Thurman especially touches the chords of sympathy and emotion. A rich voice charged with feeling, a penetrating mind, a strong appeal through the sermon—these are his qualities. Here religious experience is interpreted by a preacher who dwells in the secret place and comes forth with power. The inwardness of Christian experience is stressed as he sees God and man in close encounter. Out of this comes the bearing of truth upon daily life and conduct. The motive of piety produces practical ends. Life's responsibilities are then unfolded in the disciple's quest for and devotion to the will of God.

Thurman speaks with personal testimony and shares the richness of his own inner spirit. "This is the testimony of a personal quest with many indications of seeking and perhaps little evidence of finding. No claim is made other than that of one who, despite fumblings, errors, and grave shortcomings, senses that

> ... to KNOW
> Rather consists in opening out a way
> Whence the imprisoned splendour may escape,
> Than in effecting entry for a light
> Supposed to be without.

In this spirit Thurman speaks to his generation.

The sermonic pattern is that of a thematic message. No elaborate or strong outline is thrust upon people. He begins almost gently and proceeds with increasing momentum until the climax is reached. The illustrations are generally taken from life and indicate a pastor who has not forgotten how his people suffer and struggle in their world around them. His use of words demonstrates a poetic feel.

The philosophic mind is disclosed as it wrestles with profound questions, not expecting easy answers. Closely woven thought and rich expression are wedded to a burning heart. The perceptive spirit of the preacher comes through in devotional meditations which speak to the heart.

Unlike some of his contemporary Black preachers, Thurman does not participate in politics or march to demand social justice. Not that he is insensitive to these aspects of our common life. He is the pastoral shepherd seeking the lost and caring for the flock at their most intimate depths of need. He sees the need of piety and the motive of love to bring people into a personal encounter with God in Christ. This is to him the foundation of all other activities. Without this, there is no more than a humanitarian outreach common to all. The Christian heart must dwell in the deeps before its reaches for the heights.

In "A Sense of Presence" we sample Thurman at his maturest in thought and writing. "Whenever the mind of man has been uplifted; whenever I have frustrated the temptation to deny the truth within me, or to betray a value which to me is significant; whenever I have found the despair of my own heart and life groundless; whenever my resolutions to be a better man have stiffened in a real resistance against some form of disintegration; whenever I have been able to bring my life under some high and holy purpose that gives to it a greater wholeness and a greater unity; whenever I have stood in the presence of innocence, purity, love, and beauty and found my own mind chastened and my whole self somehow challenged and cleansed; whenever for one swirling moment I have glimpsed the distinction between good and evil courses of conduct, caught sight of something better as I turned to embrace something worse; whenever these experiences or others like them have been mine, I have seen God, and felt His presence winging near."

In this sampling Thurman lays bare his secret. When the roster of the saints is complete and men look back to creative thought to bring them closer to God, the modern Thurman may well find his niche and be given notice as a man of true piety within that august company. Here is preaching in the grand tradition of the saintly souls of the ages.

Black preaching has been a proclamation of the Christian faith in the finest tradition. Simplicity of language, relevant illustration, strong emotion and persuasion, and a thrust to meet current human social and moral problems is the heart throb of Black preaching. As our Lord in the Gospels was at the place to meet human need, so the Black preacher envisages himself in similar situations reliving that event in the here and now as he preaches the sermon for people in the throes of poverty, discrimination, and struggle. It is this identity with his own people that gives him an intimacy with and impact upon those who come under his spell.

"The black experience in America is not the Jewish-Christian experience in ancient Palestine. But as the tale of sorrows of a people awaiting deliverance, the black narrative has a message consistent with the Biblical witness though not to be found in that witness. It is a testimony of its own, distinct from Scripture even as it would proclaim its word to us in Biblical images and in the categories of Scriptural revelation. . . . Though not of canonical status, the story of the black man in America is a self-validating account of faith which when heard and heeded, helps black and white respond more creatively to the divine word for our present situation" (Robert A. Bennett, Episcopal Theological School, Cambridge, Mass., *Theology Today,* Jan., 1971). There is nothing here like the back-to-Israel movement for the Zionist or the earlier Jewish return from exile to the Promised Land. Blacks have no return-to-Africa movement. America is their homeland and here they have been part of the national life. The revolt against segregation continues and the preacher in that movement sees Jesus as the symbol of protest against all vested interests which threaten the promised freedoms for the Black. Thus God speaks, according to the Black preacher, through the given Word of God and the history of yesterday for today.

Dispensational Preaching

The rise of the dispensational school of theological interpretation brought especially to the American scene a new concept in hermeneutics and consequently a new thrust in preaching. The movement known as "Dispensationalism" had its origins in England but its progress and seeming success has been most apparent in the United States.

The belief in and promotion of this theory of Biblical interpretation is connected with the early centuries in some of the writings of Irenaeus, Origin, Tertullian, and Montanus, and even the eminent

Augustine. The idea of the "Millennium"—the one thousand years of Revelation 20—and the concept that throughout Scripture God deals in epochs of history fashioned after this analogy was spoken of as "Chiliasm."

From this beginning, the church in every age had those who thought in these terms, and gradually the Scriptures and history were seen in the light of divisions marked by time periods such as a thousand years. In Bradford, England, lies a deposit of papers written by J. N. Darby who is known as the father of the modern movement. He left the Church of England to become an independent and formed groups of those who wished to engage in Bible study. His views were set forth in sermons, studies, and notes for publication. He was a remarkable man and an avid student of the Bible. It was from this source that the teaching took root in America and for this we turn to the work of **Cyrus Ingerson Scofield (1843-1921)**.

Here was a man who trained for the legal profession and who became a U.S. Attorney for Kansas. His conversion to the Christian faith prompted him to engage in religious work and theological study which in turn led him to become a Congregational pastor at Dallas. His association in the Bible Conference movement brought him into friendship with D. L. Moody, and he then served at Northfield, Massachusetts, as pastor of Mr. Moody's home church. However, he is best known as the editor of the reference Bible published by the Oxford University Press and now popularly known as the *Scofield Bible.* For seven years he gave all his time to preparing notes to interpret the Scriptures. He was aided by several other well-known ministers and scholars, but he decided the final notations to be published. Over the years millions of copies have been sold and Bible study has been stimulated especially among the conservative people of the churches.

The preaching of Scofield—for it was basically preaching at first—was based upon the dispensational view of Scripture. Where earlier students of this schemata saw history divided into three or four eras, Scofield claimed seven dispensations as follows: (1) Innocency; (2) Conscience; (3) Human Government; (4) Promise; (5) The Law; (6) Grace; and (7) The Fulness of the Times or The Kingdom.

During these epochs of history God revealed Himself in a special way and men were also judged or tested in that light. At the climax of history would be the return of Christ, preceding the one thousand years of the millennium. With this was the proviso that the church would escape the period of great tribulation which is to come upon the earth. At this point came controversy. Some arose to say that Christ's return would be postmillennial; others who were amillennial said that this was to be spiritualized. Scofield, however, maintained the premillennial position. His adherents numbered millions. Not that these became a denomination or sect. They are to be found throughout all denominations and stand on common ground in conferences and organizations based upon this simple belief in the "dispensations" of history.

Because this was in the area of eschatology, there were Christians who accepted the belief without much difficulty since it was theory for the future which did not impinge upon their salvation and Christian service. However, the claim was made by exponents of the doctrine according to Scofield that this belief was the one conviction to motivate people to act in missions and evangelism before the coming of the Lord at the Second Advent. The signs of the times were studied and history was viewed as moving to its climax. The Jewish people were expected to return to their land and become a nation again (which is taking place in this century). Those who did not accept Scofield's views entirely saw a peril in making dispensations speak of differing ways of salvation for different epochs, whereas the death of Christ was sufficient for all ages. The legalism and often also antinomianism which crept in startled some to review the earlier notes of Scofield. However, millions of copies of the Bible have been sold. The Dallas Theological Seminary, Texas, promotes the Dispensational hermeneutic.

The preaching of this interpretation of Scripture is seen in Scofield himself as a pastor. He was expository and Biblical in detail. Word study played a large part in his exegesis, a habit he had cultivated in his days of legal training. What did this word say or mean? Study of the word became the foundation of the interpretation of Scripture.

Scofield's preaching was not glamorous or exciting. He was the lawyer with logical acumen. He used words carefully and expounded meanings with clarity. His *Addresses on Prophecy* (1900) exemplifies this principle. *Rightly Dividing the Word of Truth* (1885) demonstrates his principles of hermeneutics. *The Doctrine of the Holy Spirit* (1906) is suggestive of the devout and faithful disciple rather than the skilled debater of truth for a conviction. In this work we find exposition and simple, clear enunciation of the Biblical truth regarding the person and work of the Spirit of God as unveiled to the Church.

Harry (Henry) Allan Ironside (1876-1951) was a preacher somewhat different from Scofield but in the same tradition of thought and belief. Scofield was the lawyer-like expositor of a more rigid cast of mind and one who engaged in a specialized ministry. The embodiment of his convictions are not to be found in books of sermons so much as in the notes added to the English Bible which bears his name. In the case of Ironside we have the pastoral preacher who was also the expositor-evangelist. Characteristic of him were the human touch and the dynamic utterance. He was a genial person with a smile and a lively look suggesting humor behind that bright countenance.

Ironside was born in Eastern Canada of Scottish parents whose background was deeply pious and evangelical. He was nurtured in the Brethren fellowship and never ceased to be linked with that body, even though he became the pastor of one of America's outstanding churches—the Moody Memorial Church, Chicago. Among the Plymouth Brethren Ironside found maturity, after being linked for a short time with the Salvation Army. There he had learned evangelism while with the Brethren he learned the value of Bible study and exposition.

Although lacking formal theological education, he was steeped in the English Bible (which he read through once a year) and Bunyan's *Pilgrim's Progress* (which he read more than twenty times in those early years). The Brethren were divided into "Open" and "Closed" groups. Ironside began with the former but moved into the latter and for thirty years he had fellowship with this exclusive group. Among the beliefs then accepted was the imminent return of Christ, the headship of Christ, the unity of the Spirit and the oneness of the Body of Christ. No salary was offered and no special ordination of preachers was necessary. By faith the preacher accepted what God sent in to meet needs, and the God-given (not man-imposed) ordination was the recognition of a preacher's gifts by a congregation.

When Ironside became pastor of Moody Memorial Church, he relaxed somewhat his earlier "Brethren" practices, but there was not much difficulty in fitting into the new situation. At Moody expository preaching of a Biblical nature was expected. Here he excelled. Usually several verses or a paragraph would be selected for study; verse by verse and word by word in some cases would then be dealt with in sequence. The overall exposition was a carefully worked out exegetical study of the passage. Constantly using this method, he demonstrated his intimate knowledge of the text.

Out of his saturation with Scripture, Ironside, blessed with a retentive memory, could quote freely. His powers of illustration were also marked by those who sat under his ministry. With his resonant voice he was able to proclaim his message often without the benefit of electronic amplifiers. No hearer was in any doubt as to the forcefulness of his speech and the pointed nature of his words. He was an extemporaneous speaker, but behind his presentation was careful preparation. Thousands of sermons were delivered in his ministry and the titles indicate their Biblical nature: "The Imminence of Christ's Coming"; "Inside the Veil, Outside the Camp"; "Paul's Charge to Timothy"; "Prayer and the Unseen Foe"; "The God of the Valleys"; "The Finished Work of Christ"; "The Chains of our Sins."

In addition to regular sermons of a topical type, books of the Bible would be unfolded for a series of messages. Those on "Expository Messages on the Epistle to the Galatians" illustrate his method. After an Introductory sermon in which he outlines the Epistle and discusses its historical background and authorship, its place in the New Testament and the intent in writing it, Ironside proceeds, by paragraphs, through the rest of the book to expound its leading ideas.

A sampling of his style as a preacher is noted in the sermon "No Other Gospel" (Gal. 1:6-9) in which the last verse reads—"If any man preach any other gospel unto you than that ye have received, let him be accursed."

> These are very strong words, and I can quite understand that some people may have difficulty in reconciling them with the grace that is in Christ Jesus. Twice the apostle pronounces a curse upon those who preach any other gospel than that which he himself had proclaimed to these Galatians when they were poor sinners, and which had been used of God to lead them to the Lord Jesus Christ. Some might ask, Is this the attitude of the Christian minister, to go about cursing people who do not agree with him? No, and it certainly was not Paul's attitude. Why, then, does he use such strong language? It is not that he himself is invoking a curse upon

anyone, but he is declaring, by the inspiration of the Holy Spirit of God, that divine judgment must fall upon any one who seeks to pervert the gospel of Christ or to turn people away from that gospel. In other words, the apostle Paul realizes the fact that the gospel is God's only message to lost man, and that to pervert that gospel, to offer people something else in place of it, for a man to attempt to foist upon them an imitation gospel is to put in jeopardy the souls of those who listen to him. Our Lord Jesus Christ emphasized this when He pointed out that those men who taught people to trust in their own efforts for salvation were blind leaders of the blind, and that eventually both leader and led would fall into the ditch. It is a very serious thing to mislead men along spiritual lines; it is a terrible thing to give wrong direction when souls are seeking the way to heaven.

Followed by a telling illustration from life in which someone does not heed the counsel of the true but follows the advice of the false, Ironside drove home the distinction involved in the Pauline teaching.

In another sermon "Honor to Whom Honor Is Due," based on Matthew 23:8, "Be not ye called Rabbi" and Romans 12:10, "In honor preferring one another," Ironside makes his point with a story: "On one occasion when in London, I was walking home from a meeting; part of the way I was accompanied by the Marquis of Aberdeen (who had presided) and the Lord Bishop of Norwich (who had been one of the speakers). Being an American, and unaccustomed to titles, I felt embarrassed as to how I should address men of their position. I expressed my perplexity, and the Marquis replied, 'My dear brother, just address us as your brethren in Christ. We could have no higher honor than that.' We are told to give honor to whom honor is due. On the other hand, the servant of Christ is to seek the honor that cometh from God only. The first passage delivers from rudeness and that pride which apes humility, as it refuses to recognize the gifts which Christ has given to His Church. The other is a rebuke to all self-seeking and fleshly ostentation on the part of those to whom the Lord has entrusted any special ministry for the edification of His Church." Well-spoken words by the preacher!

Ironside's style was clear, simple, even conversational with that touch of human concern and love. Illustrations abound through his writings and sermons. For them, he culled from literature, the Bible, and human experience.

Dr. Ironside was known throughout the English-speaking world as an expositor of fundamentalist convictions. In 1937 he was awarded a prize by the American Tract Society, New York, in their competition for a manuscript of relevance to the times and written in an evangelical vein. This book entitled *Except Ye Repent* is another expression of that fertile mind and nimble word study which characterized the preacher. The subject of repentance was one of the neglected themes in that period. Here it is considered in a practical and Biblical manner. Needs are set forth as the times demanded, the state of the church in its inner weaknesses was demonstrated, and the preaching needed for the age was encouraged. His own exposition in this book illustrates how the nature and importance of repentance must be considered; then systematically he expounds the subject through the books of the New Testament. Then comes a discussion of problems connected with the lack of repentance; difficulties when men think it impossible to repent; the desirability of repentance; and finally, the preaching that produces repentance.

His views of preaching as given here are the result of his own convictions and experience. He points out the use of the terms involved and agrees that it is not always necessary to use the same words for the actual fact. Using the sermons of the New Testament, he traces the unifying method of diagnosis and prescription—always calling for repentance and action on the part of the hearers. He gives a historical perspective by referring to Augustine, Luther, Socrates, Whitefield, Wesley, Edwards, Finney, Moody, Spurgeon, and Chapman—stalwarts of evangelicalism and orthodox belief.

> Back to the Gospel, brethren, if like the men of God throughout the centuries who have turned many to righteousness, you would bring men to repentance and lead them to heaven. This will never result from substituting a social gospel, which is really no gospel at all, but an attempt to make the cross of Christ of none effect. By saying this I do not mean for one moment to cast a slur upon well-meant efforts to ameliorate conditions under which millions of our fellow men are struggling. Everywhere that the pure evangel had found lodgment in human hearts it has bettered the social environment into which it has found its way. Even unsaved men profit by the love and grace set forth in the teaching of our Lord Jesus Christ. Men are ashamed to do in the light what they will do in the dark unblushingly, and so the gospel has curbed many social evils and bettered living conditions, wherever it has been received.

Here is the fundamentalist preacher; here is the Biblical expositor of his generation. Harry Ironside will be remembered for his genial expression and his salutory word in preaching.

James Hall Brookes (1830-1897), Presbyterian pastor at Saint Louis, Missouri, was a Biblical scholar, writer, and Bible conference speaker. He stressed the premillennial view of Scripture. In addition to preaching, he was an editor and writer for over twenty-three years. In the Fundamentalist movement he was most influential, reaching especially other pastors and teachers.

Arno Clemens Gaebelein (1861-1945) was a German-born pastor in the Methodist Episcopal Church. He became editor of *Our Hope*, a magazine given to exposition, prophecy, and Jewish evangelism. His preaching was noted for its incisive manner, wealth of Biblical detail, and strong sense of Zionist orthodoxy in the area of prophecy.

These men are representative of preachers whose influence continues in churches where prophecy is a major emphasis in teaching.

Southern Preaching

The Southern pulpit has had an honored history. In the time of the Civil War voices were heard declaiming against the issues and some for them. No easy way was found for the preacher who stood to plead with his congregation. The issues were clear and yet much confusion remained regarding social ideas and practices which had been part of normal life. Following this period came the aftermath of readjustment and rebuilding. During this time fresh voices were heard as a new generation arose to look to the future for the church at large. This was true of the Southern Baptist Church, a denomination destined to become one of the two largest in the nation. Its remarkable advance and increase in millions of members was due in part to the dynamic preaching of its leaders. These men were primarily preachers and evangelists in the tradition of the pioneer missionaries.

George Washington Truett (1867-1944) has been spoken of by his fellow Baptists as "the greatest spiritual giant and the most effective preacher." Evidently he had the ability to hold a congregation spellbound by his preaching. In his lifetime Truett became a world citizen in his association with the Baptists of the world through the Baptist World Congress. His contacts with millions of his fellow believers gave him an opportunity to minister widely. His meteoric rise to fame and prominence did not prevent him from remaining as the pastor of the First Baptist Church, Dallas, Texas, where he served for forty-seven years.

The life of Truett followed an American pattern of the boy from the little farmhouse advancing to the highest denominational pulpit and having influence among millions. His one distinction was that he lived to preach. The Evangel was the heart of his message and was delivered with passion and power to both large and small congregations. He was a "plain" speaker, using ordinary language—the language of the people—and not the specialized talk of the intellectual. Sheer physical strength and moral conviction shone through his sermons. He belonged to that class of preacher who believe in the supremacy of preaching as a means of reaching men. Preaching to Truett was the embodying of a message, and he communicated freely and forcefully from the heart. He can be described as one possessing the shepherd heart in his zenith as pastor and preacher.

The sermon "We Would See Jesus" (John 12:21) is an illustration of his strength and clarity in preaching. He feels the age-long needs of the human race; he voices the cries of representative men in their search for God; and he portrays the coming of people to the Christ who is the Way. The sermon indicates a strong Christology of faith:

> Why would we see Jesus? We may well wish to see Him, because of what He was and is in His own personality. He was both God and man, the God-Man, in one person. Never did hyphen elsewhere mean so much as here, the God-man. It both joins and divides. It marks distinction and yet unity. Jesus was as really God as though He were never man, and as really man as though He were never God. . . . The most stupendous truth ever submitted to human thought is that stated in John's five simple words: "The Word was made flesh." . . . In the study of Jesus we need always to begin with His humanity. That is where the early disciples began, and that is the rational order. A proper conception of His humanity must be the basis for a proper understanding of His divine nature and work.

The development of the sermon proceeds along logical lines and from one proposition to another. "Behold Him, not 'A Son of Man,' but 'The Son of Man,' for all humanity was summed up in Him. He was the one perfect, ideal, complete man. 'Which of you convinceth ME of sin?' was and is His fearless challenge. 'I find no fault in Him' was and is the universal testimony of His friends and foes. In Himself Jesus combines all those gracious qualities that abode severally in His people." Illustrations are drawn from Biblical characters such as Moses—meekness; Job—patience; Solomon—wisdom; Jeremiah—pity; Paul—zeal: and these are then shown to be found completely in Jesus. "All other men have but a fragmentary goodness and greatness; that of Jesus is complete, perfect, wanting nothing."

Thus Truett comes to the final proposition in his question and answer: "Jesus is the preeminent miracle of all the ages. Who was that one and only perfect man? Was He not more than a man? The only rational solution of the humanity of Jesus is the acknowledgment of His Deity. For men to laud Jesus as a great and good man while they repudiate His deity, is to involve themselves in logical contradictions and moral inconsistencies which it is impossible either to reconcile or understand."

In the practical summation of this sermon, there is the weaving together of many relations in life—to see Jesus is to make much of His Book, to know much of secret prayer, to watch against sin, to magnify Christian fellowship, to be busy for Him, to give ourselves to His guidance. He concludes with a well-known poem of George MacDonald:

> I said, "Let me walk in the fields";
> He said, "Nay, walk in the town."
> . . . Then into His hand went mine,
> And into my heart came He,
> And I walk in a light divine,
> The path I had feared to see.

Whether preaching on revival, the gospel, prayer, temptation, faith, or a Bible character, Truett was always the pastor-evangelist, yearning for and reaching out in compassion and pleading voice. The shepherd-heart is obvious in all his messages. Evangelism was the heartbeat of this preacher. Homiletically, there is structure, balance, progression, and down-to-earth illustrations from a wide experience of life and men.

As an illustration of Truett's human touch, the sermon on "The Conquest of Fear" is typical. Revelation 1:17-18, "Fear not . . ." is made the basis of all New Testament references to overcoming one of man's mortal ills. The theme is stated, a proposition is given, illustrations are presented, and many Biblical allusions are shared.

There are three divisions to the sermon: (1) Jesus bids us be unafraid of life; (2) He bids us be unafraid of death; and (3) He bids us be unafraid of life and of death, but He also bids us to be unafraid of eternity. The structure is simple and clear. It is the mark of the evangelist. Illustrations from life abound—perhaps too many—and poetry is often quoted. The end is the appeal of the pastor-evangelist in calling people to come forward to confess Christ and follow him, given as a well-known hymn is sung. This is Baptist preaching in the South at its best.

When we reflect upon the changes in our modern age, especially in the United States, we can trace the swift rise of a liberal spirit in preaching. Many of the prominent pulpiteers in the North were men of this persuasion. However, in the South, there were those who remained faithful to their early convictions in theology and Scripture. And to the end of their day, they could count upon thousands of faithful listeners in their own churches and throughout the South. Men of this caliber were men alive with the instinct to preach and uncompromising in their understanding of the historic gospel. Among these are **Clovis Gillham Chappell (1882-1972)** and **Robert Greene Lee (1886-)**. Primarily, these men were pastors and gloried in their pastoral preaching ministries.

Chappell had notable pastorates in the Methodist Church in Washington, D.C.; Dallas and Houston, Texas; Memphis, Tennessee; and Birmingham, Alabama. Wherever he served, he preached to full churches as people waited upon his word with eagerness. He stood in the mainstream of the Methodist tradition and while loyal to that background he proclaimed the gospel to hungry people with the zest of his heritage.

In addition to giving sermons, he published about thirty volumes of sermons and addresses. Biblical characters claimed his interest in preaching. His insight into character and his strong imagination gave him ways of expressing the moods of the soul. Biblical characters walked again in the downtown sections of the cities where he ministered as he threw them upon the screen of imagination through Biblical reference and modern illustration. In *The Christian Century* poll he was voted as one of the ten most effective preachers in America at that time. He served his churches in downtown pastorates in outstanding cities longer than any other minister in Methodism. This in itself testifies to the effectiveness of his method and message.

The sermon "Growing Power" is a sample of the easy-flowing style for which he was known. Chappell begins by referring to a Biblical text such as Mark 4:26-29 in which the kingdom of God is viewed as soil into which seed is cast and the resultant harvest is sure in the blade, the ear, the full corn, and the ripened fruit. He reconstructs the scene and the occasion when Jesus preached, speaking of the things that really matter, the fundamental things, and yet with authority and simplicity.

Easily, almost casually, he proceeds to outline and build the sermon from stage to stage. First, "Look at this power of growth, it is all but infinite. It is seen in the vegetable kingdom. It is experienced in relation to ourselves as individuals." Second, "Growth is neutral. It may be our angel. It may also be our devil. It is akin to certain other powers that we know. Money is a tremendous power. Gravity is an essential power. Power we may have as our friend and ally. But if we refuse to have it as our friend and ally, it will become our deadliest foe." Third, "Growth is spontaneous. True whether we grow good or bad seed." He uses the story of the farm and his early work there to illustrate this. He tells of David's sin of adultery to supplement the concept of bad sowing. Fourth, " . . . growth is . . . gradual." Generally speaking, the seed we sow does not come to harvest within the hour. Here we can engage in evil by playing with temptation or we can sow to the Spirit of God for goodness. Fifth, "What, then, is the choice before us?" It is not ours to choose what seed will germinate and what lie dormant. No more is it ours, having sown the seed, to decide on the harvest. We must reap as we sow. The one choice that we have is the choice of our sowing. Having made that choice, the harvest is inevitable.

The illustrations are simple, from familiar backgrounds of life, and the final appeal for decision is clear cut. The same is true of his preaching in general. In "The Forks of the Road—Moses" he has a similar treatment from Hebrews 11:24-26. There the man of God is seen as a familiar person on life's pathway. He is no dim, shadowy form of the past, but the man today. Historical narrative is employed to describe the nature of Moses' life and task. Supreme is his choice in a revealing hour. Again he develops a simple outline of several divisions, dealing with the fact of that choice, the two elements in that decision (one negative; the other positive), and the fact that the decision was costly, requiring the giving up of much in Egypt's life—its pleasures and its treasures. Then the cost of a choice of suffering. Chappell discusses how Moses came to that choice in that he saw the difference between right and wrong, that sin brought only temporary gain, and he saw the value of eternal things. Finally, the sermon moves swiftly and surely to note the outcome of that decision. Moses received the reward of a Christlike character; he rendered a great service to the world. Chappell concludes that this was "the best day's work that Moses ever did." Faith was the hallmark of that decisive hour.

This and other sermons make an appeal to ordinary people by their simplicity and saturation with Biblical story. Human interest and Chappell's love for people shine through. Books such as *Living Zestfully, Faces about the Cross,* and *The Road to Certainty* combined with studies in Biblical personalities to render effective service to congregations located in the heart of major cities.

In Robert G. Lee the South has another well-known preacher whose span is long and satisfying. Like Chappell, Lee has also ministered in leading pulpits but for the Baptist Church. His best known pastorate is that at the First Baptist Church, Memphis, Tennessee. He has been honored by his denomination as President on three occasions. His fame has been nationwide and his ministry acceptable to people of all religious backgrounds. One of his sermons, "Pay-Day Someday," has been preached four hundred times and filmed in technicolor. Lee has been a contributor to religious journals and the secular press, as well as author of some twenty books.

Part of the secret of Lee's effectiveness lies in his oratory. He is one of the few men left in this era who has a link with past oratorical preaching. He takes a theme and works it thematically. Putting several texts together as in a string of pearls (I Cor. 15:3; I Peter 3:18; Rom. 5:6; 5:8; II Cor. 5:15; I Peter 2:21-24), he connects them by the central theme that "Christ has died for our sins, for the unjust, for the ungodly, for us, for all"; and then he plays upon this majestic motif as in music repeated again and again. The refrain comes through with meaning and persuasion. Here is the theme of "Deity, Death and Disposition"—indicative that it is Christ and not an ordinary man who has died, that it is the fact that Christ died which is all-important, and that the disposition of this means that we must do something with Christ.

In setting forth the message the orator-preacher uses the rhetorical device of repetition. "Christ, Creator of all worlds. . . . Christ, who is God. . . . Christ, Lamb of God slain. . . . Christ, solution of

all your questions. . . . Christ, whose character is all of God. . . .
Christ, solving the mysteries of redemption. . . . Christ, literature's
loftiest ideal, Philosophy's highest personality, Criticism's supreme
problem, Theology's fundamental doctrine, Christianity's cardinal
necessity is Hell's dread, Heaven's wonder, the only hope of this
head-dizzy, body-weary, mind-tortured, soul-famished, sin-smitten,
heart-broken, blood-soaked, tear-drenched, war-scarred, bomb-
scarred earth." Another sampling of repetition is "The Supernatural
hovered over Christ in His cradle. . . . Supernaturally great was
He. . . . Supernaturally wise was He. . . . Supernaturally marvellous
was He. . . . Supernaturally helpful was He. . . . Supernaturally glorious was He. . . ." In the second section of this sermon, dealing with
Christ's Death, he articulates with the rhetorical question—"A
King? Then a crown He should have! A King? Then a regal robe He
should wear. A King? Then a scepter He should have! A King? Then
He ought to have a throne!" Then there is added: "Christ died—
preferring humanity to divinity. Christ died—putting away sin by
the sacrifice of Himself. Christ died—willingly in love." At its close
Lee makes a strong appeal to respond to the claims of Christ. Here
the repeated words are "Christ yearns for all to come through Him
to God. . . . Christ yearns for regenerate followers who will dare
anything for Him. . . ." One can hear the symphonic appeal in the
motif of redemption and the arias of invitation to receive the
gospel.

This type of preaching is passing and only a few men are left who
declaim in this fashion. Nevertheless, Robert G. Lee stands as a man
who knew how to use words with effect and appeal. In the last
quarter of the nineteenth-century America witnessed the beginning
of the Chautauqua movement. People gathered in vacation time at
centers (such as Chautauqua, N.Y.) where they could hear orators,
preachers, entertainers, singers, lecturers, and great music. This met
a need and was much in vogue until the first quarter of the
twentieth century. Among the well-known speakers were William J.
Bryan, the statesman-layman-preacher and Russell H. Conwell, the
Baptist preacher with his famous lecture on "Acres of Diamonds."
These men and others like them were much in demand because of
their prowess in speaking. Robert G. Lee stands in that succession
for his excellence in speech and his wizardry with words. Lee was
not out of class with the eminent men named. His ministry as
pastor is noteworthy. His preaching marks the end of a type of

declamation and rhetoric now almost unknown. With the advent of radio and television the new day requires shorter, less ornate forms of speech, to be given within a limited time span. The splendor and glory of Lee's effusive speech was for a more leisurely day.

The South had others in the tradition of faithful, Biblical preaching. **Gerald Ray Jordan (1896-1964)** was a pastor, and since 1945 Professor of Preaching at Candler School of Theology, Atlanta, Georgia. Of sound Methodist background, he exhibited vitality in preaching. Lively utterance is also characteristic of his books, among which is *You Can Preach.*

Edgar Young Mullins (1860-1928) was a scholarly pastor. This served as preparation for a professorship and finally presidency of Southern Baptist Seminary, Louisville, Kentucky. His lectures on systematic theology, and his conservative, Biblical, and evangelical spirit brought inspiration to hundreds of pastors and students.

Quaker Preaching

A luminous example of lay preaching is manifested in the life and career of **Rufus Matthew Jones (1863-1948)**, known as the representative Quaker of his generation. He was a true intellectual and was erudite in his field of philosophy, a subject which he taught at Haverford College, near Philadelphia. His other major interest, which he also taught, was mysticism. Throughout his influential life he gave himself to the discipline and cultivation of the spiritual life. As a Quaker he was closely identified with the Society of Friends— perhaps a more descriptive designation—and took his share of ministering in the Meeting House which was for him the local "church" and fellowship.

During the fifty years in which he spoke and wrote, he issued some fifty-four books, all of them concerned with "what is vital" in religion. His heritage of home and school sharpened and enriched his native gifts of mind and heart. His spirit yearned to share with others the endowments of the spiritual life which for him made life steady and whole. In one of his last books, *A Call to What Is Vital,* there is the summary of all he believed and taught.

In the preaching of this layman and spiritual leader there is a simplicity and directness of speech. Sincerity shines through all his utterances, whether in the quiet of the Meeting House on a Sunday morning, in a lecture in the classroom, or in the more public gatherings to which he went to speak or lecture throughout America and often in other countries. His name was as well known abroad as at home. As a college preacher he was heard gladly for the radiance of his religious experience, mediated through a rich culture. He sought to share with others the light of his knowledge as practical mystic, one who was in touch with God.

To youth seeking reality and not sham, Jones was a man for the hour. His book, *The Reality of God,* brings a title and contents immediately relative to the needs of those who are searching for God. Rufus Jones testified in the delivery of his message that God was real and God was present with him at all times.

This closeness of God in human experience is one truth which Jones stressed in his preaching. He breathed this atmosphere and was able to penetrate the minds and hearts of those who might be dull and apathetic in faith and awareness. He described the Spirit of God as being as close about us as the air we breathe. Said Jones, "We have never been separated from the Spirit of God. Even though we have not been aware of God's Spirit which is 'closer than breathing, nearer than hands and feet,' God's Spirit has nevertheless been around us, keeping watch over us all the time. The purpose of religion is to make us aware of God's presence."

Jones proclaimed that God is a God of goodness, beauty, and truth. These can be experienced in man's life. Prayer leads to the heights of spiritual stature. Through music, poetry, drama, reflection, friendships, merciful deeds toward others—as well as through prayer—the presence of God can be practiced. In his sermons and talks he furnishes illustrations of this truth. He reminds us that a girl coming from a symphony of music is a little taller than when she went; an American theologian came into his first great awareness of God as he saw John Drinkwater's *Abraham Lincoln* enacted in a New York theater; Emily Dickinson regarded the appreciation of literature, especially poetry, as an experience which takes us "up" the mountain trail.

Any beautiful and creative experience may be the occasion of the divine presence. Scientists are regarded as men in search of the unknown who again and again find the presence of God in the midst of life. Both the tiny cell and the vast and mysterious universe are the hinterland of spiritual experience according to Jones. Kindly deeds of mercy, acts of healing, prayer itself—these are pathways of reality by which God will come to the waiting spirit. As a Christian mystic, he knew full well this pathway like a mountaineer climbing Mount Everest. The mystic has been to the shining heights! This is the vitality of which he spoke in sermon and address.

His many books contain extracts and copies of his meditations and sermons. In the Quaker manner and spirit there is little that is declamatory. However, any appraisal of his preaching must recognize its difference from what is known as Biblical preaching. Jones said in his "Striking a Vein of Reality":

> I am more and more impressed with the feeling that Biblical-text preaching is antiquated and out-grown. Too much time is spent with words and phrases and too often the preacher is capriciously at the mercy of an ancient situation and setting that does not fit our modern life and present-day problems. Only by a *tour de force* does the preacher get from his starting point to the vital task with which he is confronted. *It is my aim* always in preaching to strike a vein of reality from the very take-off of the sermon. I want the whole message to be born and to spring out of life and experience. I usually have some such aspect or problem of life come freshly before me during the week, springing out of intercourse and conversation with my students or others, or frequently I am impressed by some central issue that breaks upon me in my reading. Sometimes the next vital topic for consideration is vividly presented to me as I sit in quiet meditation or it may be as I am taking a meditative walk in the fields.

Thus Jones spelled out his philosophy of preaching, and it is well illustrated in his printed messages where the absence of a Biblical text is noted. As Jones did not write out his message, his few notes constituted the basis for what he would say. The message had to come thereafter fresh from his mind, so that wording and phrasing were born on the spot. Said he,

> If I use a Bible text, I use it as illustration rather than as point of departure. I use passages from the poets with frequency but they come to me spontaneously, for my memory is well stocked with important quotations from a large line of poets, ancient and modern. My speaking has extraordinary simplicity to it. I always have children in mind, though I never talk down to them. Nevertheless, they tell me again and again that they understand every word of my sermon. It is usually the sermons that the children understand that older people like best. I preach in summer to farmers and rural dwellers. But I speak to them precisely as I do to the college and university audiences. My prayers are spontaneous, unpremeditated, very brief, voicing the profoundest longings and aspirations of my soul and the corporate needs of the group.

Thus Rufus Jones lays bare his heart and we can detect his sincerity and spirituality of mind. If he is not in the line of the historic Biblical preachers, there is a reason. He was the Quaker with the "inner light" of reason, illumined by the Holy Spirit seeking to express the divine message. In this he has become the mentor of many who are challenged by the testimony of spiritual experience and witness. Jones articulated his experience of God in a quiet, fruitful ministry. A scholar with scholarly habits, he was at the same time an indefatigable worker and toiler in brooding and meditating upon the deep things of God. He laid tribute to the arts and poets, the mystics and philosophers, the seers and writers of the Bible, and all with the vision of a voice for God in his day.

There are serious limitations to preparing to preach by the discursive method without writing and follow-up. In the hands of the novice and lesser men, discursiveness is a bad habit and often reveals the lazy man. However, that was not true of Rufus Jones. He toiled assiduously and thought creatively. He had to be free from a manuscript in order to reach his hearers. He was always at the heart of things. "The Progress of the Soul in Religion"; "The Way of Dedication and the Entrance into the Kingdom of God"; "The Spell of Immortality"—these and many other sermon titles indicate the sweep of an extraordinary mind. *The World Within* volume deals with living issues of the soul and points the way to the radiant life lived in the plenitude of the Spirit of God.

Any estimate of Jones' preaching must see in his spoken word how he treats life's problems. There we see the layman, professor, scholar, mystic, writer, Quaker, at work.

> The struggle for a conquering inner faith has in these strenuous days been laid upon us all. The easy, inherited, second-hand faith will not do for any of us now. We cannot stand the stern issues of life and death with any feeble, formal creed. We demand something real enough and deep enough to answer the human cry of our soul today. We need to be assured that we do not in the last resort fall back on the play of molecules but that underneath us are everlasting arms. We want to know not only that there is law and order but that a genuine Heart of Love touches our heart and brings us calm and confidence.

Since Quaker preaching by the leaders of that society is done by laymen and the meeting house message is the sermon, there is no accumulation of volumes of sermons to study modern trends. However, the sermon has found its way into the books and publications of men like Jones. Permeating all he spoke and wrote is the fact of mysticism—the encounter and meeting of the soul with God. Appreciating the beautiful, sounding the depths of love, expressing concern for the forgotten and the needy—these are marks of Quaker preaching. The right use of spiritual literature and the fellowship of "spiritually contagious persons" Jones counted among the important aids to the deepening of the mystical capacity.

Rufus M. Jones could talk of John Woolman as the best example of this ideal of mysticism. "Here was a mysticism and it was the type to which I dedicated my life—which sought no ecstasies, no miracles of levitation, no startling phenomena, no private raptures, but whose over-mastering passion was to turn all he possessed including his own life, 'into the channel of universal love.' " Jones proclaimed that salvation "is an actual change in a man's life"; and of Christ he said: "We find at length one single Personality, who was sinless, who lived entirely open to God, who had a sole purpose—to do His will, and from it this truth emerges that this Personality is a complete expression of Divinity and Humanity." How blessed indeed were those services of the Society of Friends where Jones attended worship—for then not many would be led to break the silence and speak—and how fortunate that he was usually guided and led to speak!

Since the worldwide renown of Rufus Jones, the Friends have had no greater preacher-teacher than **David Elton Trueblood (1900-)**. He represents the Quaker ministry in its excellence and devotion. Professor of Philosophy and Religion at Earlham College, Richmond, Indiana (1946-66) his teaching has influenced many, but outside of the classroom he has maintained an itinerant ministry from pulpit and platform. From the writing of *The Predicament of Modern Man* to *A Place to Stand,* over thirty books have come from his pen. Through the circulation of these volumes he has become one of the most widely quoted interpreters of the Christian faith in this era.

In preaching, there is the distillation of much writing and the discipline of study and meditation. With a well-stored mind, a conversational approach, occasional use of humor, and abundance of illustrations, he engages the hearts and minds of congregations, whether they be a congregation in church or a group of students in college or university. Retired from active teaching in academic circles, he continues as Professor-at-large with his base at Earlham

College, where he uses his library as a seminar room in which to continue his teaching and writing.

Trueblood will be remembered as the pioneer of the lay movement which has restored the primacy of the ministry of all men who are Christians, laity not clergy. In the Fellowship of the Yoke thousands now find *koinonia* under the symbol of the yoke for committed life in discipleship. Dr. Trueblood's preaching is alive and incarnate with this primary idea. Urbane and yet down to earth, mystic yet full of mischief and fun, he brings to the modern age a touch of that eminence and greatness associated with the saints of the ages.

In Elton Trueblood we hear again the accents of William Penn, John Woolman, and Robert Barclay. He stands for a reasonable faith, one that is spelled out by the mind as well as the emotions. Pithy and eloquent, his preaching style quietly catches the listener on all levels of interest. Christ-centered and compassionate for the lost and the least, his message is not hindered by any generation gap. His is the pen of a ready writer, and an inward spiritual well which overflows in kindly speech and glowing mind. Here is excellence in preaching.

Scandinavian-American Preaching

During the nineteenth century wave of immigration, hundreds of thousands of Scandinavian people came to the United States of America. Among them were those who had been quickened into newness of life during the revivals in their native land during the 1800s. The new world beckoned as a place of opportunity and a door of escape from limitations and restrictions. These were partly economic and partly religious. The State Church with its Lutheran theology and clergy-dominated control had stifled the lay expression of Christian faith. A generation was connected with the church in form and ritual but lacked the dynamic of spiritual power. This was the ground which received the seed of revival that brought forth a harvest of awakened people.

The church in that day owed much to the Reformation under Luther; it had kept faithful to that tradition and teaching. Other forces, however, had entered, including those who are generally listed as "Pietists" or independent groups which sprang up across Europe in the wake of the Reformation. **Phillip Jacob Spener (1635-1705)** at Frankfurt; **August Hermann Francke (1663-1727)** at Halle; and **Nikolaus Ludwig, Count von Zinzendorf (1700-1760)** at Herrnhut; and others contributed to this stimulus of spiritual life and power. Spener's *Pia Desideria* (Pious Wishes) embodied the plea for a reawakening of those things which bring renewal. **George Scott (1804-1874)** came to Sweden from England in 1830, and in the Wesley spirit challenged the barrenness of religious life. He continued what Pietists and Moravians had started in the previous century. Others were **John Paterson** and **Ebenezer Henderson** from Scotland. These brethren had been associated with **Robert** and **James Haldane** of Scotland, two leaders in the changing life of that nation.

The orthodoxy and ritual of the Lutheran Church was now challenged, and the establishment of Church and State was seen in a new light. The wave of new ideas included the belief that spiritual life was received in a conscious act of conversion and new birth. In practice people gathered together in homes and in groups known as conventicles, which in essence seemed to decry the regular diets of worship within the church buildings in every parish. Another development was that of *läsare* (readers) who not only read the Scriptures to the people gathered, but began to interpret the same.

The teaching of **Paul Peter Waldenstroëm (1838-1917)** brought a new insight into the theology of the period. In his theory of the Atonement he claimed that the death of Christ on the cross did not appease the wrath of God (then commonly held) but that God himself in Christ died to satisfy justice and moral law. Out of this came God's love to sinful man in full measure. Here he stressed—not God's reconciliation to man, but man's reconciliation to God. In essence this broke with the traditional Lutheran view.

Another practice arose in the Communion held in these groups in defiance of the regular altar in the church. If, as Waldenstroëm claimed, the Scriptures were to be followed and not the Augsburg Confession, then every Christian had the same rights and privileges within the church fellowship. Clergy were not above others in the priesthood of believers. Attendance at Communion had been a matter of State law; now the breaking away indicated a movement of men's minds to choose for themselves. One objection made by these was that an unconverted priest should not serve at the altar and that only believers or converted people should receive the Lord's Supper. Here was a stress on the purifying of the church through the new spirit.

These groups were considered irregular according to the official church government, but later they were given sufficient freedom to act as they chose yet always within the framework of the church which alone was recognized. However, the day came when even this was broken and then these groups became "societies" and eventually a new body with a new format of life and religious expression. The rise of the readers (*läsare*) and the spread of colporteurs, lay preachers who traveled throughout the country, led to further developments. These men (*predikanters*) spread the message of new life and thus revival ensued. With this was the discovering of preachers gifted by nature and spiritual life. These were the first of a long line of preachers who laid aside the read manuscript and spoke extempore and with fervor.

When the tides of immigration touched America, it was inevitable that these Swedish-Americans should continue the religious ways just begun. Bringing the zeal and stimulus of the new life in Christ, many entered the various settlements from East to Midwest. Chicago became an early center, with Minneapolis-St. Paul following. Those who remained in the East clustered around Boston, New York, and Philadelphia. Scattered yet gathered, these clung to their new-found faith. Among the preachers, the names of Carl August Bjork, Fredrik Franson, Erik August Skogsbergh, Johan Gustav Princell, and Gustaf Frederick Johnson were prominent.

The second half of the nineteenth century then witnessed the formation not only of the Augustana Lutheran Church with its continued tradition, but the establishment of three new groups, offshoots from the old world. They found abundant opportunity to spread in the new world and their preaching made this possible. After the early use of the preacher who had studied and developed himself came the trained pastor who was needed in the new settlements. Among the leaders it should be noted that several inclined toward a strong central organization which brought into being The Evangelical Covenant Church of America. Others preferred a fellowship less rigid and so united several independent groups of Danish, Norwegian, and Swedish backgrounds into The Evangelical Free Church of America.

What of the preaching? Covenant Church preaching was best exemplified in Peter Waldenstroëm's service in America where he continued his doctrine of the Atonement. No less an evangelist than Dwight L. Moody was influenced by this and preached in a similar vein. Because of their appeal to the new Americans coming into the

Midwest, Moody and others of the Covenant persuasion reaped harvests in spiritual life and renewal. The mood was there and receptivity was heightened by the times. Since the preaching was in Swedish, there was no language problem at first, but later this was to change in the passing of one generation to another. The new culture and environment, with American education, tended to shape up a new kind of religious life and preaching.

David Nyvall (1863-1953) brought intellectual stimulus to preaching-teaching as a leader in educational matters, such as the rise of North Park College and Seminary, Chicago, and the development of teaching materials and other publications. Nor were the sick, the poor, the widowed, the needy forgotten. Out of preaching and teaching came the stimulus for the erection of homes, institutions, hospitals, orphanages, and other agencies of relief. A strong social consciousness was there from the beginning and, although the church as a body was not affluent, the giving of life and money as well as service increased.

In church government the preaching tended to retain the emphasis which had been garnered in the old world—freedom with a little centralization and membership in the church for believers only. However, when it came to the Sacraments, the Covenant people generally practiced infant baptism (as the Lutherans did). They were not against immersion and would do this when requested. The Free Church people tended to practice immersion rather than the other mode although there is nothing in their doctrinal statements to make this a test of membership. In fact, both denominations now accept membership based upon personal faith in the Lord Jesus Christ and baptism of either kind or even in some cases without baptism. The Lord's Supper again was only for believers. Some of the tenets preached by the pastor and the evangelist were the necessity of the New Birth, repentance and faith, a separation from the world, and an awareness that judgment was coming when Christ returned in the Second Advent.

Ernest August Skogsbergh (1850-1939) began to preach as a young man in Sweden and was called to Chicago to take the then large Tabernacle. His gifts were those of the evangelist. He had known something of Moody and Sankey and when he settled in America he copied Moody's methods, using the invitation to decision. Gospel preaching with fervor and zeal characterized this man. Later in Minneapolis he built another tabernacle, and finally another in Seattle. He loved the crowds and responded to them in preaching. He had wit and humor combined with a strong emotional appeal. And the Swedish language he used touched the chords of memory and of hope. Skogsbergh said: "The secret of our success has been the simple preaching of the Gospel in the power of the Spirit. . . . We have been weak in education and parliamentary procedure, but we have been strong in the pulpit." He might have added "the Swedish pulpit."

Also in preaching, the trend was to emphasize prophecy, especially the premillennial view. **John Gustav Princell (1845-1916)** was the outstanding exponent of this position. He with Franson and others held conferences on the subject and their preaching profoundly influenced the mission groups then being founded. The millennium, the salvation of the Jews, the kingship of Christ over Israel, the interrelation of Jew, Gentile, and the church were themes discussed and interpreted in preaching. Other leaders in the Covenant denomination inclined more to the amillennial view while still believing in the triumph of Christ and his Kingdom. They also preferred a more ordered church life, a trained pastorate with suitable ordination, and other church forms which allowed for commitment and decision. Princell transferred to the Evangelical Free Church to become an influential leader.

Interestingly, **Gustaf Frederick Johnson (1873-1959)** was a pastor for a decade in the Free Church and then went on to become the pastor of the Tabernacle Covenant Church, Minneapolis. His meteoric rise in influence was due to his preaching ability and the almost magnetic psychological power he exercised upon a congregation. His gifts of utterance and appeal were such that thousands heard him gladly and were moved. He, like Skogsbergh, was a master of assemblies. Perhaps he lacked the balanced judgment of other leaders and caused the church anxious moments. Nevertheless, he ranks as one of the truly outstanding preachers of his generation.

It is significant that the Free Church at first, under Princell, taught Waldenstroëm's theory of the Atonement but gradually gave it up. The Covenant people somehow never proclaimed it, although some of the pastors and preachers held it as part of their theology. Today the doctrine seems not to have any advocates left. The preaching of the Free Church brought a congregational form of government which is maintained in autonomous congregations loosely knit in fellowship with a general conference. The Covenant Church had developed a more centralized form of government, while still giving each congregation its freedom of choice and order. They still maintain in their preaching the earlier emphases inculcated by Waldenstroëm and the influence of the Haldanes of Scotland. "What do you think on that subject?" would be asked. Then would come the answer but with the repeated demand that it had to be supported by Scripture. Whatever the Confessions said or any preacher and teacher taught in the light of the Creeds had to be shown to be strictly Biblically based.

Covenant preachers were influenced more by the Reformers and especially Luther, whereas the Free Church men were influenced more by the Pietists and the Independents. Each had experienced revival movements and each stressed that the new expressions of faith must be that of personal conversion and testimony to the rebirth of life based upon Biblical truth.

The third group, known as the Swedish Baptist Church and related to the Baptist General Conference of America, also experienced similar movements of revival and renewal. The present flowering of the Bethel Theological Seminary and College at St. Paul is the fruit of one hundred years of struggle and development from the days of immigration and pioneering. The chief influence here has been the Anabaptist groups of Europe and England and the same discovery of the *läsare* revival in Sweden during the 1840s wherein laymen initiated the new way of ministry. **Fredrik Olaus Nilsson (1809-1881)** was a pioneer who was exiled from his native land because of the judgment against him in preaching without permission of the clergy and of the State Church. **Gustaf Palmquist (1812-1867)** was another pioneer. His ministry in America especially laid the basis of the Swedish Baptist Church. The one conviction which gave power to their preaching was the necessity of immersion in baptism. Unlike the practice of other groups from Sweden, this was made a demand for church membership. This belief arose from private study of the Bible, and finding that others had shared it in Europe, they saw in it a return to apostolic life and practice. In any case this was a way of purifying the church as over against the State Church which baptized infants who often grew up without spiritual life.

George Scott, the Methodist who came to Sweden, influenced **Anders Wiberg (1816-1887)**, another leader in the early years. He was gifted as an author, producing books and tracts. He expounded chiefly the doctrines then endorsed by his group. Having left the Lutheran Church, he was zealous in promoting the layman's place in the congregation, the desire for a believing church, communion only for the converted, and baptism by immersion as a confirmation of personal faith. Thus the Methodist influence which came through John Wesley and his follower George Scott assisted the Baptist group even as it also stirred the other groups already mentioned.

In America the Swedish Baptist Church was a frontier group, and they scattered over the Midwest and far West. The demand for pastors necessitated a training center and this was the dream and work of **John Alexis Edgren (1839-1908)**. For some time it was convenient to use the Swedish department of the then Baptist Seminary, University of Chicago (as the Covenant Church used a similar avenue in the Chicago Congregational Seminary) before beginning their own schools.

Characteristically, the preaching of these men and their successors has always been evangelistic and revivalistic. Pastor **Frank Peterson (1847-1929)**, The First Swedish Baptist Church, Minneapolis, led his people in visitation evangelism as early as 1905, thus ensuring a continuous influx of new people into the congregation. As a result he preached expecting results from former nonchurch goers. His preaching had in it the spirit of revival and of apostolic church at work. These early preachers came from Sweden. They were usually strong in body, vigorous in mind, clear in faith, rich in devotion, and zealous in proclamation of the gospel. Their sermons would be known as "simple," but this did not mean they lacked content. They knew how to spell out the doctrines of the Christian faith, and their word came with power as they related how God had dealt with them individually. This "witness" within the sermon was noteworthy and appealing. **Eric Sandell (1856-1918)** was an example of the nimble mind and the acute thinker, one who concentrated through hard work on philosophical ideas. Out of this came rich and stirring preaching as the sermon was given logical presentation. He taught as he preached, a requirement then to meet the needs of a growing church.

Theologically, the preaching of these Swedish men stressed the major doctrines of sin and grace, the need of the new birth and a sanctified life, and the second coming of Christ. Calvinism and Arminianism did not divide them; they accepted modifications of each emphasis and endeavored to hold them in balance and in perspective. In church doctrine they have insisted that only the twice-born should be a member, baptized by immersion, living a dedicated life in moral strength. Once a controversy arose regarding the Waldenstroëm view of the atonement which threatened to become disruptive. However, wise counsels prevailed, and after study and discussion the leaders agreed that this would be too one-sided an interpretation of the death of Christ, and encouraged other views as well. Another possible disruptive idea arose when the subject of sanctification was emphasized. Here the work of the Holy Spirit was claimed by some to be Pentecostal in the healings and the speaking in tongues which broke out in certain congregations. Here, again, wisdom and good judgment prevailed. Conferences were held and after prayer and consultation this was recognized as a work of grace, but it was not to be sought for as a standard to divide or exclude others who did not have this experience. The work of the Holy Spirit was taught and preached, but always with a balance which did not let emotion override the mind. The new birth and other fillings of the Spirit were considered equally as valid evidence for faith and spiritual life as Pentecostal experiences.

Here also the preaching of that developing church was characterized by a humility willing to learn from others. **John Ongman (1845-1931)** is a luminous example of how a pioneer preacher from Sweden, with limited education, learned from the Bible and from others. His was a missionary-preaching life which was honored and blessed. Because he felt a coldness of heart, he sought help from outside. A. J. Gordon of Boston and A. B. Simpson of New York were then issuing their books and preaching on the work of the Holy Spirit and the deeper life hid with God in Christ. Ongman learned much from these two spiritual leaders, and mediated that teaching to his own people. His life is an incredible story of achievement—the one talent of opportunity grasped and used—and phenomenal results. He was typical of Swedish Baptist preaching, and its glory is still undimmed.

Liturgical Preaching

Joseph Fort Newton (1880-1950) stands out as a fitting medium for the communication of divine truth in modern days. He traveled far in his religious pilgrimage. Nurtured for a little in a Methodist church, he entered the ministry of the Southern Baptist Church, then served in the Congregational order before finding his final years in the Episcopal body. We are fortunate to have his autobiographical memoirs in *River of Years* (1946). In this volume Newton talks with those who will listen to him as he looks back over a strenuous life and recaptures some of the richness of the maturing process.

His early years in America were preparatory for the significant ministry he exercised at the City Temple, London. There in that citadel of nonconformity made famous by the work of Joseph Parker, Newton, although different to a marked degree, was able to sustain a full ministry of preaching in the heart of London. His gifts of utterance were marked early in life and he could recall the first sermon he ever delivered to a small country Baptist church in rural America. The text was taken from Romans 8 where in closing Paul sings: "I am persuaded . . . that nothing in all creation, shall be able to separate us from the love of God, which is in Christ Jesus our Lord." The details Newton could not recall. Later in life, when asked to contribute to a symposium, *If I Had But One Sermon to Preach*, he took the same text, pointing out that every preacher has only one sermon to preach, no matter how many texts or topics he may employ. It consists of the truth nearest to his own heart, "his truth," the truth central in his faith, although he may use many variations and improvisations of emphasis and appeal.

When it was thought that preaching was in decline because of World War I, Newton took the occasion to point out the variety and splendor of much that was then being proclaimed! In fact, Newton himself was one of those voices which was being heard by thousands who waited upon his prophetic ministry. When a master of the pulpit emerges, there are always people to listen. Within the scope of the gifts which were his, he wrote and spoke with moving force and appeal. The more personalized appeal for salvation was now being replaced by the "Gospel of the Kingdom." The new issues, new outlooks, and new enterprises caused by the cataclysm of war led many to proclaim a new emphasis, broader based and widely applied.

Dr. Newton was a writer of no mean ability and used the pen with as much power as the spoken word. The one was allied to the other. Post-war preaching was thus set forth by this master as few could match in the art of description. In his own inimitable way he tells of the art of preaching in the light of history. Every age discovers its new emphasis and new idiom. Each age has its needs, its problems, and its perplexities. He stresses the truth that "we must interpret the awful and mysterious word of God in accordance with both the novelty of the age and the eternal antiquity of the truth."

In the postwar era after 1918 the former days of stability in doctrine began to be questioned. In the past everything had been clearly defined and fixed. Now, though the eternal truth remained, it needed a fresh presentation to a weary and disillusioned generation. The best and the worst in human nature had been seen on the battlefield and also in the populations affected at home. Reaction set in amid dark and confused days of spiritual devastation, moral anarchy, sour cynicism and despair. The old evils still had to be met, but now the situation was further complicated for the preacher by the rise of a new morality and worldliness of life. Atheistic negation and a nonreligious humanism arose to plague the counsels of the church, and the secularism of society threatened to sweep away the Chrsitian tradition.

The period of unrest affected the churches, and the preacher was often unable to cope with the new situation. Spiritual values were no longer seen as just "personal"; there was now also a "social" dimension. To the age-long sins of the individual were to be added the newer sins of war, racism, bigotry, obsession with sex, and economic exploitation. The vested interests which had become bloated through war profits and labor shortage had to be faced by the preacher who would lead people to think in terms of the Kingdom of God. If God's will is to be done on the earth, preaching must spell out some of these concerns and suggest solutions when men feel they are losing their dignity and value in a material order.

The preaching before the War was stately and urbane. Its style was often ornate. Newton and others like him laid this aside for a simpler, more direct utterance. He was a man talking to his fellow men. It sounded a desperate note. Less romance and more realism pervaded the sermons. Someone described Dr. Newton as "a religious Wendell Willkie." That name recalls a fervent, liberally-minded politician and dynamic speaker. Newton the preacher does not suffer in comparison, but holds his own in the company of the truly great. As an orator and speaker he stood high. He could tilt a lance at many contemporaries who had the ear of the public—

George Bernard Shaw, Lloyd George, John Dewey, to mention a few whose words called out Newton's rejoinders. Whether touching on religious, theological, political, historical, literary, or Masonic matters, Newton had the pen of a ready writer and the voice of a fearless man. Wit and wisdom colored his productions and the lively prose writings are still worth reading.

In London, Joseph Fort Newton became as well known as certain outstanding political leaders, for his utterances were timely and yet eternal. The press found him good copy. Then, in later years in Philadelphia, as rector of St. Luke and the Epiphany Episcopal Church, he found time for many years to write a column for *The Churchman* (magazine) and a weekly sermon or religious essay and notes for the Philadelphia *Evening Bulletin*. This weekly column, "Everyday Religion," was eagerly anticipated by a large audience and manifested the sermonic master using the journalistic style to reach a wide group who sought solutions to the problems of daily living. Here he dealt with such practical matters as bad temper, the place of prayer, how to get rid of anxiety, how to love people, how to emerge from sorrow's crushing blow, and the healing power of silence. These, and many more, formed the nucleus of his essays. He had preached on these themes and now wrote the daily and weekly stint to offer common people "a faith to live by, a self fit to live with, a work fit to live for, somebody to love and be loved by—these make life." "If we learn how to give ourselves, to forgive others, and to live with thanksgiving, we need not seek happiness—it will seek us." The Saturday sermon written for the Philadelphia paper was the only feature of its kind in the American press for many years.

Newton's versatility of mind found expression not only in regular preaching but also in his books of sermons, essays, devotions, and literary interests. He also treated such subjects as Lincoln, and the Masonic order. His nimble mind was ever ready to speak and to write in order to reach others. His insight into and profound belief in the Christian gospel found expression in sermonic literature. In the sermon, "The Immortal Life," we catch the poetic strain and music of his faith:

> No one else has ever spoken such words to humanity; no one can do it. Never once does Jesus say, "I believe," as we must needs do, praying help for our unbelief. No. "I am the Resurrection and the Life"—it is not merely an anthem of affirmation; it is a revelation

of another order, rhythm and cadence of life. He does not argue; he unveils the truth. He does not promise immortality in some dim, far time beyond; he illumines it, bringing both "life and immortality to light." It is not only a prophecy but a possession—such a reversal of faith, such a transvaluation of values as baffles thought and bewilders imagination. God is here, Eternity is now, Death is nothing to the soul. . . .

As Dante said, Jesus taught us "how to make our lives eternal," and if we learn his secret we shall know neither fret nor fear. . . . By the wonder of his personality he released a new power in human life—"the power of an endless life"—power over sin, power over sorrow, over brute matter and black despair. Here lies the secret of social stability and nobility, no less than of triumphant character.

As one of the interpreters of the postwar generation to itself, both in Great Britain and in America, Joseph Fort Newton succeeded in proclaiming the truths of the Bible in contemporary language and idiom. The period has been characterized as one active and awake in its concern for the solution of social problems. Deadness in the pulpit has spoiled many ministries but not that of Newton. He was alert to human needs. Among his words were:

Some things are clear. Religion remains the most intimate and personal of all human concerns, but it is also corporate and communal. God calls men not *en masse*, not in crowds: He calls each man by his name, but each is called to a fellowship, not that he may render less social service, but vastly more. Social service is a result, not a cause.

In that quotation he summed up the needs of his age and the answers which he brought in his preaching.

The preaching of **Paul Ehrman Scherer (1892-1969)** was characterized by an intellectual quality and a strong presentation borne by a forceful personality. Standing with his shock of white hair and a commanding presence, he started to preach with something "extra." That well-equipped mind and spirit and that rich voice with its resonance touched many. His sermons were published in several volumes, such as, *When God Hides* (1934), *Facts that Undergird Life* (1938), *The Place Where Thou Standest* (1942), and *Event in Eternity* (1945).

He delivered the Yale Lectures on Preaching; his volume, *For We Have This Treasure* (1943), gathers up his ideals and standards for preaching. As a Lutheran he was disciplined by the pericope, the systematic exposition of selected passages of Scripture related to the Church Year. In this context he became a Biblical preacher. Thoughtful and reflective, he possessed a probing mind which employed the surprise element of the unexpected question.

In sermon preparation Scherer was known for his hard work. He was never an extemporaneous speaker. Instead, his practice was to write out his sermons completely, spending some twenty hours of labor on a sermon before being willing to preach it. His reading included a heavy diet of science, philosophy, and theology, knowledge of which was needed for relevant preaching in his changing times.

Isaiah and Paul find special mention in the thought and writing of Scherer. The sermons in *Event of Eternity* are based upon the prophet. The scope of these messages is seen in such topics as the glory and majesty of God, God in history, God's eternal purpose, the God who would be Man, and the divine vocation. There is a wrestling with profound truths in the context of preaching. Shining through these messages is the conviction that God will not only reveal his purpose in history, but that he will bring to pass his will in human life. The secularism of the age is discussed as Scherer deals with the manifold issues of our common life—selfishness, the escape into psychoanalysis, the desire to be human without God's help.

Scherer is always the bright and shining example of high-class preaching. As the sun shines in our eyes on a summer western journey, so we feel the blinding flash of his scintillating mind and thought. Not many can touch him there. His contribution to preaching was incisive and sparkling. The human situation was never more challenged as Scherer thundered forth with his majestic prose and resonant voice. "Life's imperatives spring out of God's indicatives." "There is something on this earth that never wears a uniform; yet it gets justice done." "To most of us, salvation is such a pious word; so tallow-faced, with the tips of its fingers together." "Religion is not the kind of sentimental first-aid kit we have made of it." "It is God's mercy that gives its justice its cutting edge." Scherer not only writes well; he paints pictures in preaching and so persuades.

Scherer was one of many distinguished Lutheran preachers. His longest pastorate lasted twenty-five years, at Holy Trinity Lutheran Church, New York; following that he was Professor of homiletics at Union Theological Seminary, New York, for fifteen years, and also for seven years at Princeton Theological Seminary. Thus as pastor, professor, and radio broadcaster, his varied ministries give him many hearers and a nationwide influence.

Pastoral Preaching

Mark Allison Matthews (1867-1940) was known for his work in the city of Seattle, Washington. There in the Northwest of America, where the people and the cities have had a history of slightly over one hundred years, this man stood fearlessly for the evangelical truths of the faith and proclaimed with unerring aim the gospel of God's grace. He was from Tennessee and trained at first as a lawyer, then engaged in pastoral work, reading and studying theology as he progressed in the art of preaching. He stood six feet six inches in height, had long hair, and with his top hat and morning coat he was known by all when he walked in the city. Growing up with the city, he exercised a profound influence on its political, civic, and moral structure.

For thirty-eight years he led The First Presbyterian Church of Seattle, then the mother-church of the area, founded by George Whitworth in 1869. Matthews assumed its leadership in 1902 and soon the congregation increased, requiring new buildings. The third was the largest, seating 3,000 (the largest of any kind in the city), and here he proclaimed with fervor and faith the eternal verities of divine revelation. During his ministry he founded twenty-four branch Sunday schools with the eventual establishment of twenty-two congregations, a truly remarkable record. Sunday nights found the youth from these outlying points crowding in to the main sanctuary downtown and listening to the preacher with his dynamic utterances.

Gifted as an orator, Matthews preached without notes. He had piercing eyes and seemed to select individuals out of the large congregation to whom he spoke with fervor. By evangelistic preaching and the use of many assistants doing pastoral follow-up work daily, the church reached eight thousand members. This was at one time the largest membership of any church in America. The lawyer-preacher lived for his work and was known throughout the country for his preaching and influence.

Mark Matthews was a remarkable man by any account. He would stand in court to plead for an unfortunate man and yet at the same time hesitated not to preach the word which condemned the man's sin. He organized a campaign against a mayor of the city who was in association with the underworld. Matthews even cashed an insurance policy to engage a Pinkerton detective to come and find the facts for him. With these facts he confronted the erring civic leader and was able to unseat him and assist in placing in office a man of unquestioned morals. Thus Matthews by preaching and action helped to clean up the politics of his city. He engaged in founding the Day Care movement and was behind many of the social and civic movements for reform and improvement in that turbulent era.

The criticism is often made that the evangelical preacher is interested only in "saving souls" and has nothing to do with social action. Matthews gives the lie to this imperfect judgment. He, as the evangelical preacher, had in his message the personal note of repentance and faith, but it was allied to the social and civic actions of social redemption for the city and community. The sermons of Matthews indicate how he thundered against the sins and blights of a growing metropolitan area with its seaport and underworld struggle. His sermons brought moral courage to civic leaders and men testified that they owed their souls to Matthews. Such preaching is in the Biblical tradition and the results abide in a city. Like Phillips Brooks of Boston who is remembered with a monument, so Matthews was remembered by a grateful city with a monument near the heart of that city in a public park. This was not given by church people but by the community.

His preaching was the oratory of that day—rich and colorful, forceful and pointed. He was the first there to use radio and established the first radio station in the church. His message was for all people without distinction or exception. He was the pastoral evangelist pleading with men.

In **Clarence Edward Noble Macartney (1879-1957)** America heard one of its best preachers in the twentieth century. Of Covenanter stock and persuasion, he is remembered for his three important ministries in Paterson, New Jersey; Philadelphia, Pennsylvania; and Pittsburgh, Pennsylvania. He was always worth hearing for the throb and pitch of his living proclamation of truth. All his preaching was centered in the Bible and delved into human life. His heart was steeped in Biblical thought and his grasp of literature and theology brought depth and meaning to his utterances.

Meticulous preparation meant hard work and diligent study. After roughing out the sermon with a logical outline and some notes, he would dictate a draft which was then to be edited and revised. His sermons were noted for their rich and memorable ideas wedded to relevant illustrations. In delivery it was the thrust of extemporaneous speech which captivated the thousands who waited on his ministry Sunday after Sunday. Whatever limitations he might have had it was not that of a limited influence. Men thronged to hear him regularly and in abundant numbers, far in excess of the usual congregation. In his weekly Tuesday men's luncheon meeting, he would speak to a thousand men in the heart of Pittsburgh. He sustained twenty-seven years of preaching in the First Presbyterian Church, Pittsburgh, morning and evening, with one of the largest evening attendances in the country.

Macartney was an omnivorous reader, specializing in history. A diligent student of Abraham Lincoln, he became one of the three most important interpreters of Lincoln in America. All he read was turned into sermonic material; history was a rich source of material for him. His familiarity also with biography brought to him a source of inspiration and fed an imaginative mind and spirit.

When Macartney stood up to preach, one could sense that here was a man about to speak for God. No humor burst forth, except in a subdued manner, for this was serious business and souls were in the balance. He was a pastoral preacher, ever visiting the people in all walks of life, and he stressed "the grand particularities of the faith," according to Thomas Chalmers' view. In preaching he had a warm rapport with his hearers. His gestures were few but fitting to the emotion and mood. His sturdy figure and sonorous voice were gifts of nature which added to his spiritual stature. Preaching was in his blood and this was his master passion. He lived to preach.

The sermons indicate the breadth of his interests. Biographical preaching was close to his heart and over the years he preached sermons and published books on Bible characters. Macartney knew human nature and with his insight into life and the Bible, his message did not lack for relevance to people's needs. He was the American Alexander Whyte, and the personalities of the Bible came alive in modern guise as he preached. Macartney felt honored to be in the Whyte tradition, for he was indebted to the Scottish preacher's writings with their strong pietistic and imaginative vein and emphasis on sin and salvation.

An examination of the sermons reveals that the greater number used a topical method. While he always rooted his sermons in the

Bible text and passage, he believed profoundly that the greatest preaching dealt with subjects. He could point to the outstanding preachers of the past as examples of this (cf. *Great Sermons of the World,* ed. by C. E. Macartney). In his Introduction he said: "We can print the written record of what the preacher said; but the light in his eye, the glow of his cheek, the sweep of his hand, the attitude of his body, the music of his voice, that we cannot print. . . . The thunder and the lightning are gone." In this volume, and in *Sons of Thunder,* and in lecturing to seminary students and ministers, Macartney would point out the advantage of preaching the topical sermon. He did not engage in the expository sermon, although there was careful exegesis and exposition of the theme under review. He did not spend time in going through paragraph after paragraph of the books of the Bible (as G. Campbell Morgan). He preferred his own method of finding in a text the theme and developing that.

Possibly his best known sermon is "Come Before Winter," preached for the first time on October 10, 1915. This was used of God to reach young men. Because of the response, he decided he would preach it again the next year. Thereafter, people asked for it and for almost forty years he repeated the sermon to appreciative congregations not only in Philadelphia but also in Pittsburgh. In thought and development the theme is not difficult. There is an immediacy about it. Here is what Macartney said:

> If a preacher has really worked and studied on some high biblical theme, he ought never to throw away his effort, for any conse-crated work of that kind will be useful to him a second, third, or even a fourth assault upon the citadel of truth. Nor should he hesitate to use the same text. Indeed, this is the honorable thing to do (*Preaching Without Notes*).

The evangelistic note was always present in his sermons. This is part of the secret of their appeal. While he could enter into controversy (and did) he was always the Christian gentleman in debate or argument. In the bitter period of Presbyterian history when Fosdick led the liberal wing of Protestantism for a while, Macartney took issue with him and those in the Presbyterian Church concerning the essential doctrines of the Christian faith as expressed in the Presbyterian Westminster Confession of Faith. When Fosdick preached his challenging sermon in the fundamental-ist-modernist controversy of 1922-1925, he entitled it "Shall the

Fundamentalists Win?" He tried to conciliate both groups by suggesting a synthesis of doctrine. However, Macartney in replying countered with the title "Shall Unbelief Win?" In this he denounced Fosdick's views as contrary to Presbyterian doctrine and a departure from the historic faith. Fosdick withdrew from the First Presbyterian Church, New York, where he had supplied the pulpit, and went on to Riverside Church. Macartney left Philadelphia for Pittsburgh and twenty-seven years of magnificent preaching at the height of his powers. Controversy gradually waned and each group continued its teaching ministries according to its belief and conviction.

Other issues also met with his attention in preaching and speaking. Ever sensitive to the pulse of the city and the nation, he had a concern for the forgotten sons and daughters caught in the mesh of evil habit and sin. His sermons dealing with moral and social conditions probed the conscience. He never sought to be popular, but stood firm by his convictions.

During his ministry, Macartney was pastor and preacher. However, he also found time to travel, lecture, and write. Some fifty-seven books came from his pen in the fields of history, biography, and religion. In the field of homiletics, he published books of *Illustrations* and *Preaching Without Notes*, in which he summarized much of his own method and the maxims according to which he ministered. His words in the latter volume reflect the serious purpose and the grandeur of his utterances: "Across many of our sermons, if the truth were told, would be the indictment that not one of them would have converted a titmouse! There are, it is true, sermons for comfort and instruction, for condemnation, for special occasions. Nevertheless, the great *aim and purpose of the sermon* is to convert the sinner to the will of God in Christ. Our commission is still that which was given by our Lord himself to Paul: 'To open their eyes.' "

Themes which were held firmly by Dr. Macartney included the truth of the incarnation, the historic fact of the virgin birth, the doctrine of immortality based upon the bodily resurrection of Jesus Christ, the death of Christ as the atonement for sin, the sovereignty of God, divine providence in personal life, and the awful message of the final judgment. In the Reformed tradition, there was no uncertain note to the proclamation of the gospel. In his autobiography published posthumously, *The Making of a Minister*, he concludes by telling of his preaching. He was thankful that the majesty and glory of the Christian faith had never faded from his eyes. He said:

> My favorite theme for preaching has always been the Penitent Thief, and I have often said that the greatest text of the Bible is that word of Jesus on the cross, "Today shalt thou be with me in Paradise." Now in bringing these memoirs to their close, I take, as the expression and the summing up of my own faith and hope, those words inscribed under the portrait of the great Polish astronomer, Copernicus, in St. John's Church in Torun, the city of his birth: "I do not ask the grace which thou didst give to St. Paul: nor can I dare to ask the grace which thou didst grant to St. Peter; but, the mercy which thou didst show to the Dying Robber, that mercy, show to me."

This personal testimony ran through his sermons like a motif in music. He was a messenger of grace.

Among those with long pastorates **Ernest Fremont Tittle (1885-1949)** stands out, for he served thirty-one years at The First Methodist Church, Evanston, Illinois. He was essentially a pastor-preacher who took his task seriously. As a parish minister he was most influential in society. His sermons relate to personal, social, national, and world-shaking events. Tittle's sense of the "prophetic" embodied the idea of being a man in the midst of every day events. The sermon interpreted the Bible for the modern era. The application had thrust and bite in it. To Tittle, God was the sovereign Lord of history, and all human needs and problems were to be placed under the searchlight of eternal truth. He sought to speak the truth in love and tried to be what he preached.

Preaching in this manner enabled Tittle to be direct and personal in speech. After writing and brooding over his sermon, he reduced it to brief notes with key sentences for reference. A definite aim was crystalized, a statement of the goal was decided, and then words were chosen honestly and quoted with discrimination. Tittle's conversational tone and naturalness enhanced his delivery. He owed much to a voice teacher and continued voice exercises all his life. He followed John Wesley's counsel, "Scream no more at the peril of your soul," believing, "No man can be bullied into heaven, and never was." For Tittle the sermon was an act of worship, and generations of worshipers were led into the depths and heights of spiritual worship through his ministry.

Expository Preaching

The dawn of the Space Age and the sixties brought into focus several preachers who stand as representatives in the evangelical tradition in America. These include Donald G. Barnhouse, Harold J. Ockenga, Paul S. Rees. Because of the national scope of their ministries, they convey in strong tones the faith "once for all delivered to the saints" and that in no uncertain sound.

Donald Grey Barnhouse (1895-1960) as Presbyterian pastor, especially at Tenth Street Church, Philadelphia, was famed for his Sunday ministrations followed by four and five weeknight services in other parts of the country. Travel, study, writing, lecturing occupied his days in an incredible amount of toil. He was gifted as a teacher, his strength lying in Bible exposition, and like several counterparts in Great Britain he maintained this form of preaching throughout. By means of radio broadcasts and the editorship of the monthly magazine known first as *Revelation* and then *Eternity*, his message was carried to Christians everywhere.

Given rich physical, mental, and spiritual endowment, Barnhouse would spend many months working through a book of the Bible, e.g., Romans or John. A text is taken and then the light of the entire Bible is focused on that text by way of commentary in any one sermon or lecture. His wide reading gave him a wealth of illustration and his translation of the original languages gave him fresh insights in his exegesis of the Scriptures.

Barnhouse preached in this manner because he believed that the submission of one's entire being to the truth of the Bible as it operates in the preacher's life was most important. This was a lifetime work. During his pastorate in Philadelphia, he took three and a half years to cover the Letter to the Romans, preaching from this every Sunday morning. The response of a regular congregation was remarkable in growth and spiritual strength.

Harold John Ockenga (1905-), a Presbyterian by background, gave his best years, over thirty, as pastor of the Park Street Congregational Church, Boston. There he majored in the expository art of preaching and linked this with an emphasis upon missions and missionary giving. His record is outstanding in its penetration of New England culture and in its outreach to the ends of the earth.

This preacher expected the sermon to be a message from God,

not an essay, or treatise, or Bible reading. Believing in the presence and work of the Holy Spirit to touch his mind and illumine his thought, he allowed the sermon to be born out of devotion, prayer, Bible study and reflection on life's experience. These were combined to give the expository message to be delivered. After writing and note-making he preached the sermon without notes.

The advantage of this method is that the preacher is not left to wonder what to preach. In the course of systematic work, week by week, topics unfold and call for treatment. When the Bible speaks of giving and tithing, the preacher does. When the text deals with immorality, social problems, political or national items, then the preacher will follow through accordingly. In this way the whole counsel of God is given. Step-by-step the major doctrines and the outstanding events of divine revelation are given study and exposition without forcing anything on a congregation.

Ockenga's strength in preaching lies in this background of preparation and study. The clear, strong outline is memorized so that the sermon flows steadily and unhindered to its application. The intellectual appeal is marked although the whole person is confronted with the claims of the preacher's Savior and Master. Having published many books, Ockenga has had a ministry from this historic church that has spread beyond the local scene to eager minds ready to benefit from this kind of preaching.

Paul Stromberg Rees (1900-), a disciplined man of God, matches the times in which he ministers. Nurtured in the Holiness groups, his major ministry centered as pastor of the First Evangelical Covenant Church, Minneapolis, for twenty years before he assumed a Bible-teaching ministry under World Vision, a missionary organization which allows him freedom to minister to pastors of national churches in all lands, especially to the young churches of Asia, India, Japan, and Africa.

In pastoral preaching to a regular congregation, he brings the Word of God to the heart by winsome emotion. Rees has a mind aflame. For him, reason must be the handmaid of faith or else the message fails. He recognizes that preaching is divine work, empowered by the Holy Spirit. The listener feels that this man is in tune with the eternal and senses the living encounter between himself and the preacher as he delivers his message.

Rees' many books reflect the genius of his homiletical skill and his power of illustration. They extend the pulpit ministry over a lifetime. He is ever writing so that material accumulates for publication in magazines as well as for sermonic use. This careful and diligent discipline has been rewarding as he expresses himself in a style at once swiftly flowing and fraught with deep feeling. Rees loves the beautiful. The world of nature, the world of people, and the world of poetry constantly fill his mind with awe. This is then transmitted in the message delivered.

Paul Rees is a spiritual giant and can stand in any company as one of Christ's witnesses. His academic standing, his intellectual strength, and his spiritual maturity set him apart from the ordinary preacher. The devout spirit and the willing, obedient heart of the preacher comes through in speech and personality. Gracious and winsome, radiant and down-to-earth, this preacher speaks to his day and generation.

Going back a few years, we will look at an expository preacher of the earlier part of this century. Few preachers had the strength and vitality of **James Martin Gray (1881-1935)** who began as a pastor of the Reformed Episcopal Church, Boston, and ministered there for fourteen years. Then he became President of The Moody Bible Institute, Chicago. Conservative in theology, he was irenic in spirit and positive in preaching. At the same time he was civic minded and socially alert to the needs of his day. He excelled in expository preaching, working his way through the Bible. His books include *Synthetic Bible Studies, The Christian Worker's Commentary,* and *How to Master the English Bible.* In this last is the essence of method and spirit for those who would learn the art!

Lay Preaching

The Fundamentalist-Modernist controversy was characterized by war cries and sometimes bitter words. Each side was stirred by the issues. Fundamentalists were dogmatic in preaching the doctrines of the Christian faith as given by God and declared in an inerrant Bible. Modernists were nebulous, insisting that one should search for truth and not accept necessarily what was written in the past. Five major doctrines were debated—the virgin birth of Christ; Christ's substitutionary atonement; Christ's resurrection; the second coming; and the infallibility of the Bible.

The claim has been made that the Fundamentalists were more vociferous and denunciatory in preaching, whereas the Modernists were more reasoned and theoretical. The mood of the times lent itself to these divergences. On the one hand, there was exposition of the Bible as authoritative; on the other hand, there was thinking aloud in a search for truth. **William Jennings Bryan (1860-1925)**, nationally known as a prominent layman, an American political leader in the Democratic Party and presidential candidate, was also engaged in the controversy. A master of oratory, he knew how to sway an audience. The introductions to his speeches and sermons reveal carefully planned approaches to the mind of the listener.

Possibly the outstanding Christian layman of his day, he was an eloquent preacher. Like William Ewart Gladstone in Great Britain, Bryan exercised a similar influence in politics and in Christian witness. Throughout his sermons he displayed his belief in the infallibility of the Bible and with this an opposition to the theory of evolution. He defended the Bible doctrine of creation and the reality of the supernatural in a day when these were being denied. The Sprunt Lectures at Richmond, Virginia, entitled *In His Image*, were a defense of his Biblical view of man.

The dramatic trial at Dayton, Tennessee, in which he debated with Clarence Darrow, the agnostic lawyer, concerning the subject of evolution, was marred by the untenable position in which Darrow placed Bryan, denying him the opportunity for self-vindication. After this disgrace, Bryan died suddenly a few days later and so ended an era of controversy. True, there were a few engagements thereafter, but the main battle had ended. Who won is not yet clear. The conservative trend which emerged from the rigid fundamentalist position continues unabated and increases in power in preaching. The modernist is now replaced by the so-called liberals who claim to lead the major denominations through pulpit proclamation of liberal theological emphases.

William Jennings Bryan was not the only eminent lay preacher in the United States. There were others who stand out for their caliber and strength. Of these the name of **Robert Elliott Speer (1867-1947)** is preeminent. Possessing fine attributes of character, no one was held in higher esteem for his works' sake.

Speer began his life of service as a student at Princeton University where in the midst of his studies he early showed promising qualities of leadership. A champion of all that was good and pure in student life, he became a confessing Christian and a churchman. In theological study at Princeton Seminary, Speer aimed to be provided with full equipment for his life work. This, however, was not to be, as he was interrupted by an invitation to become the Secretary of the Board of Foreign Missions of the Presbyterian Church in the U.S.A. He was then twenty-four years of age and already committed to serve his Lord in the field of world need as a missionary. Thus began a unique career for a young man. He did not finish his theological education. He did not go overseas as a missionary in a formal way. He did not become a pastor of any church in the homeland. Yet, in spite of these seeming limitations, he became the one layman of his generation to stand out as having fullest theological knowledge; he knew most of the fields of the world which received the message of the gospel; and he ministered in the major pulpits of the land, becoming a preacher's preacher.

In the preaching of Speer there is a strong emphasis on the historic doctrines of the Christian faith. Particularly was this true of Christology, as he stressed the centrality of Christ. The Biblical unveiling of Christ was ever on his heart and mind. Whether in the pulpit or in the less formal atmosphere of a conference, Speer stayed close to the eternal verities of his faith and experience. Out of his preaching and speaking came his books. They reflect his theological convictions. He wrote and edited sixty-seven books. The subjects included studies of the Bible, expositions of missionary policy, studies of the principles of the Christian faith, with the supreme emphasis on the meaning and finality of Christ; seven biographies, and five volumes containing biographical sketches.

As Speer was an incessant traveler and constantly in demand for speaking engagements, he had to think and write wherever he was. Sermons were also prepared in this way and did not seem to suffer because they did not come out of the quiet study. Perhaps it was this background which gave to his utterances a quality and force which stabbed and prodded his hearers. His speaking was usually extempore and only when he had to quote would he take out a little notebook and then read the quotation from his source book which he always was compiling from his wide reading.

Speer never tired of speaking about his Lord and Master and titles of several books reflect this. In *Studies of the Man Christ Jesus* Speer expounds the Biblical passages teaching the full humanity and full deity of Christ. The "righteous man" is also "the Son of God," and as he affirms the uniqueness of that God-Man Speer stands in the true apostolic succession. His own words testify:

"Christ is something more than an exalted ethical character. If he were only this, our faith were vain. Christ is the world's life. Passing centuries, however many their number, could not erect an exalted ethical character into Christ of today and forever, and the study of that Character is largely profitless save as it leads men and nations to hear the voice of Jesus."

In *The Man Christ Jesus* lies the seed of much to come. Later, in the L. P. Stone Lectures at Princeton Seminary, he gave *The Finality of Jesus Christ*. This remains as a permanent contribution to theological thought. Here is the substance of Speer's preaching and witness. Everything that made Speer was poured into this volume. Christianity to him was unique and final. Christ was the revelation of God and thus the work of Christ has eternal significance for man's salvation. Here in burning sentences he proclaimed the gospel: "If Christianity is not such a religion that every man needs it, no man needs it. If Christ cannot save every man, He cannot save any man. An atonement that is enough for one must be enough for all. And no man has found a Saviour in Christ or can find a Saviour there and not incur the obligation of sharing Him with all men. If the obligation is not there, neither is the salvation. If Christianity is not superior to the non-Christian religions, its days are numbered in the United States."

The preaching of Robert Speer was characterized by an intensity of expression. He was a man "under orders" and his speech was never trivial or careless. Nothing but the best for his Lord and Master dominated his mind. All reading and reflection were brought into subjection to the one end in view—to make Christ known. Thus the sermons were illustrated with telling incidents from his life experiences and missionary travels, and his wide reading and contacts with some of the best minds of the day.

In *Christian Realities* are gathered up some memorable sayings found in much preaching, showing what Christ meant to him: "He gives me a clearer moral vision and the courage to try to live by that vision. He gives me confidence in the truth and helps me to rest, no matter what happens in the world, because I know that truth must prevail. He gives me grace and strength to try, at least, things that I know are impossible, and to attempt, first of all, the things that are hardest to be done. He saves me from the fret and killing of pride and vanity, and helps me to cease to care for the things that make people sick. He helps me to keep the central things clear and not to be fogged and broken down by the accessories and secondary things."

The humility of Speer was most marked. His self-effacement was not artificial but deep and real. He did not seek the limelight although he was forced into the public gaze of his generation. His devotional life and the cultivation of the inner spirit laid the foundation for his public utterances. The messages of this layman had that radiant quality of personal conviction and were allied to experience. His hearers sensed that he was not preaching at them; he preached to them out of the fullness of his own heart. What he shared with them he felt himself. Pastors, missionaries, students, ministers in all phases of the church's life and work, were glad to sit at his feet. His sermons were solidly based on Biblical foundations; they were theologically balanced by deep reflection; they were clearly illustrated from life and literature as he quoted from his thesaurus and selection of a lifetime of reading and writing. His impressive presence and commanding voice and the sunlit touches of humor were used to proclaim the eternal message of the Son of God. Truly Speer was "a man sent from God" for his day as a layman preacher.

"Preaching Out of Life," a sermon-address given by Speer gives a summing up of his views on preaching. "Out of life" is a phrase which has two different meanings. It may mean "from within life," or it may mean "from outside of life," and it was both of these aspects which intrigued Speer. His preaching exhibited the tone and manner and language of life. It was just as natural and real as all the rest of life. Here is conversation lifted to a higher level than talking to a single individual. Then, too, Speer felt that "out of life" should be the source of much content. Out of the actual life experience of people came the imagery and illustrations. Parables of Jesus were like that, nothing academic but practical. Experience, then, counted for Speer so that preaching arose from all living, study, rumination, and writing.

His era was noteworthy as a time when the many radio personalities and psychological speakers were gaining the ear of the crowd. Speer was not like Peale, Cadman, or Sheen. He was more Biblical and theological. Nevertheless, his public messages to congregations and colleges laid hold of the principles that endure. He was not far apart from Rabbi Silver and the down-to-earth spirit. He aimed to lay hold of what does not change, to introduce men to what does not pass, to ally men with things unseen. The greatest preaching has always been like this.

Frank Ely Gaebelein (1899-), known chiefly as the Headmaster, Stony Brook School (boys), Long Island, 1922-1963, was nurtured in the Reformed Episcopal Church, served as Deacon and Presbyter, and has been preacher to colleges, schools, and universities. His knowledge of and insight into the Bible has given him the ready hearing of students and boys. Letting the Bible speak for itself, retelling the basic truths of the Bible, but with a human interest appeal, is part of the secret. Gaebelein is linked with other cultured lay preachers—Glover, Manning, Lewis in England; Speer and Lowry in America. Howard Foster Lowry (1901-1967) was President of Wooster (Presbyterian) College, Wooster, Ohio. Gaebelein published *Christian Education in a Democracy* (1951) which includes both ideals and practices. In preaching he was involved in the culture of his day and spoke to that effectively.

Missionary Preaching

Samuel Marinus Zwemer (1867-1952) gave his life to the Moslem world in a day when students believed the slogan: "the evangelization of the world in this generation." This young American of Dutch extraction had the persistency to tackle one of the most difficult situations as a missionary. Through the Reformed Church in America and also the Presbyterian Church he gave his whole life to missionary evangelism and the proclamation of the gospel. Years of service in the Arab world led him to found and edit *The Moslem World* quarterly. He also wrote some fifty books dealing with missions, religion, and Bible subjects.

Zwemer was an able preacher and developed his sermons and addresses with logic and clear outline. His compelling power of illustration was most effective. In delivery, wit and humor bubbled over from time to time as he was a rare teller of tales. All this was used to press home the truth. He had zeal, tact, charm, and courage. In a day of controversy he stood for the unpopular without rancor or dismay. No laziness was found in him and few equalled him for the strenuous life he lived. He was the close friend of John R. Mott and Robert E. Speer and the triumvirate were one all their lives. Together they made a mighty impact upon the student world and upon the church at large. Their witness to the Great Commission of

Christ stimulated thousands to think in terms of worldwide evangelization.

In preaching on the Christian message, Zwemer liked to follow a strong outline, stating what it is—personal and not social initially, central and not peripheral, fact and not fiction, history and not myth, glorious and yet hard; and what its motive is—not ecclesiastical, not success, not pity for the heathen, but the command of Christ and the love of God. His conviction in preaching was that the Holy Spirit took the Word of God and applied it to men. The cross was central and all-encompassing. Zwemer would "die for their life, be offered for them all."

Eli Stanley Jones (1884-1973) was one of the spiritual leaders of the twentieth century and his niche has been secured through his many books and missionary labors. Allied to these were the incessant preaching missions he conducted and the extent of his earlier ministries in India.

A Song of Ascents (1968) is his spiritual autobiography. At this juncture his books have been translated into eighteen languages, set in Braille, and have sold in excess of three-and-a-half million copies! Missionaries generally work within the sphere of their chosen field overseas and this Jones did, but he also was a preacher and an evangelist throughout the world.

As a preacher he never got over the sheer wonder and glory of his conversion to Christ and out of that the finding of his life-work. Thus he found that the Ashram movement in India could be transformed into an instrument of the Kingdom of God in all the world. He discovered that as an evangelist he could convey the Good News to America as a constant message for all times and seasons. His message brought hope and salvation in that Christ touches the total person and appeals to the mind, spirit, and body.

Jones spoke with ringing words, a spirit of enthusiasm in the Wesley tradition, and a personality aflame with love. In preaching there was the centrality of the cross of Christ. "As for me, my bed is made," he said. "I choose the power of the cross. I have seen a glimpse of what it can do if applied to a national situation. But that glimpse has led me more and more to the world-shaking and the world-redeeming power of 'the Lamb who is at the heart of the throne.' The ultimate power is the power of self-giving love." "So my contact as a Christian missionary with a non-Christian nation has led me more and more to the cross."

His preaching stressed the need of conversion, the abundant life, Christian maturity, victorious living, the Christ of the Indian Road, the Christ of Every Road, and the fact of transformation through Christ for everyman.

Frank Charles Laubach (1884-1970) was known as "Mr. Literacy" by multitudes around the world. Leading magazines have told his story and educators respect his genius and work. His major program as missionary-teacher-preacher was the "Each One Teach One," which has resulted in reaching millions of people in all lands.

As a missionary, his chief service was given in the Philippines and that included preaching as well as teaching. He is linked with those other missionary figures who have made an impact upon a people not his own. His sense of vocation came partly from the knowledge that half of the people of the world are illiterate. His teaching methods were made available in lessons for others in over three hundred languages.

Behind these commitments lay the inner life of Laubach as a man of prayer. His diary from day to day indicates how prayer was his "native breath." He spoke of prayer as "the mightiest force in the world." A sense of urgency was in all that he attempted. In public his preaching generated action as he himself became the incarnation of what he preached. His own example of reaching people and teaching them shone out in action.

Preaching, to him, was a message given by God as he brooded and prayed. He dedicated his powers to God for each occasion. He expected God to speak through him. A favorite phrase was "Christ lives in me," and thus the implication is that preaching is alive. A homiletical structure of logical development may have been absent, but the fire and passion of a man aflame with God's love was there in the sermon. He said, "All of us had the sense of being caught up in a purpose we only dimly understand. . . . God was using us to help prepare illiterate men to read His Word." In that last word is the Word which was the heart of the message of this missionary-preacher.

Radio-Television Broadcasters

Samuel Parkes Cadman (1864-1936) was known to a generation through his multiple ministry in the pulpit, in the press, and by radio. An Englishman, he soon became one of America's distinguished preachers. On radio he was the pioneer voice of the Question and Answer program. He liked the forum with the address and discussion and the informality of dialog, before the days when television became a commonplace medium of communication. In his day Cadman was the foremost radio preacher in America. Although well grounded in an intellectual background, he knew the vocabulary of the common man of America.

The preaching of Cadman was characterized by a spaciousness and largeness of thought. He was noted for his rich and fertile mind which issued in a wealth of illustration and references in speech. Closely-knit sentences and decisive speech made a dynamic impact upon his hearers. His sermons were planned as by an architect, all the pieces fitting together according to the blueprint. Here is energy, enthusiasm, and attractiveness. At the Central Church, Brooklyn, Cadman came to the zenith of his years and ministry. A reporter noted that the congregation usually was middle-aged and predominantly male. Here the business man and the professional man rubbed shoulders as they sat under their prophet and mentor.

In speaking about "Treasure in Christ" (Col. 2:3) Cadman related his faith as deep and enduring. He saw the Christian ideal as the center and synthesis of truth—a faith simple, universal, profound, satisfying.

> No wonder that Christian theology is hastening, under pressure, to restore central authority to the doctrine of the Incarnation. Christ himself, no book, no creed, no ecclesiastical form, has seized the life of this age, so vast, so complex and so baffling, and now, as never, history gives testimony and the ages chant: "Thou hast the words of eternal life." If you ask why this changeless power over society exists in Jesus, the only reply is, because He ever lives as a present authority. Other masters are an echo; He is a voice. They died and left their systems to the blemish of time; He controls the event by being with its happening. Hence, the adaptations of the religion He founded among different races. Christianity began in Rome, hidden in the catacombs, and upward it came to rear into Italy's pure and brilliant skies its monuments of faith.
>
> Much of the treasure is hidden, but since treasures are hidden in Christ, they are as safe as He is and as abiding as His eternity. The mighty strands of Brooklyn Bridge are gathered into one great heart of masonry at either end, and there buried out of sight, and we cross its stream in safety. So the complex web of life, its apparent antinomies, its grief, its pain, its ministries, its explanations, are gathered up into the mighty heart of Jesus, and whatever

> wonder awaits man, however fecund his discoveries and phenom-
> enal his advances, he will continue to cross the gulfs of time in
> safety, since life, knowledge and wisdom are hidden with Christ in
> God, to whom be glory forever and ever.

This extract from a sermon does not do justice to a great preacher when read in the press or in a volume of selections. Those who heard Cadman testified to the strength of his personality and the glowing radiance of his speech. He was a natural orator and according to Joseph Fort Newton he manifested grace, ease, fluency, fertility, and resource, with a copious vocabulary rich in content and quality. He was an omnivorous reader and student of all that was best. His mind readily assimilated and minted anew the wealth of knowledge accumulated and stored.

Homiletically, we do not find marked strength or an unusual method. The outline is not always clear and strong. His strength lies in the virility of thought and the incisive reasoning which leads one to think with him about the theme in hand. His sermons dealt with the great things of life: about God and man, about following Christ, about the crown of sanctity and the building of that city which has foundations. Cadman fortunately lectured on the subject of preaching and in his book, *Ambassadors of God*, we have the self-revelation of much of his thought in that direction. Nothing unusual is here that had not been said before in Broadus, Brooks, and Beecher. He tried to show the *function* of preaching, not its history nor its techniques.

No doubt the lectures would have been better if reported and taken down at the time of delivery. Cadman was less effective as a writer than as a speaker. He did have a sense of the fitness of the sermon as the divine means of communication. He saw it as the heart of the hour of worship and not a thing apart. In this way he was able to inspire and to interpret. Cadman's secret lay in his ability to prepare himself adequately and recall on his feet the background of his reading and reflection.

Cadman was at his best in answering questions—whether at a forum or in the press, and sometimes in preaching. Here is a sample: The question asked was—"What is the matter with the church? Where are the great preachers, such as we used to have?" His answer was:

> Internally, sectarian strife; externally, the prevalent indifference and the superficial character of much of the national mind. Preaching has killed the Christian church. We go to church to hear the star in the pulpit. We have become sermon tasters instead of Christian workers. You hear a fat old grocer boast that he has sat under the pulpit of Rev. "Blowhard" for twenty years, and all the time you know he has been skinning the public. We are a sorry lot and make a poor fist at religion.

This is not the best answer in the light of history! However, it shows that Cadman used the language of the time and could take liberties. It is inelegant and it lacks something. Nevertheless, his was the only popular voice which had the ear of the public as he talked religion and mediated a Christian message.

His answer to another question reflects his mind and method. The question was: "Has Christianity failed? After two thousand years of its influence, why are we in such a mess?" His answer was:

> No; Christianity has not failed; as Chesterton said, it has been found difficult and laid aside. I should like to see a demonstration of its efficiency in every sort of man, using the leading churches for the occasion. Get together the regenerated Pharisees, the converted nobodies, the saved who were once lost and far away from God. Let the preacher for once retire. What eloquence could equal the story of such transformed lives! The outcome would be that many of us would perceive that the same power that brought St. Paul to the feet of Jesus, that sent Henry Martyn to India and Father Damien to the lepers, that touched the tongues of St. Bernard and of Beecher, is an everlasting power and has signs and wonders attending it.

When dealing with the apathy and indifference about preaching which he saw in his day, Cadman tried to interpret the waning influence he discerned. He was sensitive to the criticism and antagonism expressed when the pulpit tried to adjust the message to the changing times and needs of that period. As to the cause of this waning influence, Cadman spoke of the intellectual and social movements of the nineteenth century, the evolutionary hypothesis, theological unrest, theories of social reform, ecclesiastical apathy, and resentment of the working man. Among these causes he saw the dogmatism of the high churchman, the liberalism of the broad churchman, and the rigidity of the more fundamental churchman. The claims of science disturbed multitudes and many lost faith in the integrity and authority of the Bible. The preacher was no longer the one voice to hear and his position was no longer accepted as the final word. The secular press was becoming more critical of the church. Popular fiction, sensational publications, and a sectarian spirit were also seen to be contributing factors.

Apart from the lectures given in seminaries and colleges, Cadman used the pulpit to meet the challenge of the new day. His preaching dealt not with theories but with things he knew. As a doctor in the sick room, he wanted to be sure of what he was doing. Certainty and knowledge were the watchwords of his discourses. He spelled these out in a hundred ways. Once he related his own experience of God:

> You can't wear such a wonderful experience as that on your sleeve, for everyone to see. It was an overwhelming experience. I was sixteen years old, my father was a Methodist preacher and I was raised in religious surroundings and I wanted to be converted; I had expected to be converted. When the experience came I found a new direction for my whole life. I have been headed in that direction ever since.

Cadman moved from the Methodist Church to the Congregational Church in America. He was twenty-two years at the Central Church, Brooklyn, and received thousands of people into membership.

Born and nurtured in England, where he trained at the Methodist Richmond College, London University, Cadman became one of the best exponents of American-English friendship and cooperation. The common spirit, the historical relationship, and the similar ideals of government and life were expounded by Dr. Cadman over a long ministry in America. He was indeed an ambassador of God and of good will.

While Cadman was a renowned preacher, his chief niche in history is in the radio field. As the pioneer radio preacher of America, he was the first to broadcast a religious address. Not wishing to disturb other churches and their pastors, he did not at first broadcast from his own pulpit, but from the YMCA where on Sunday afternoons he spoke to men. The ferment of discussion and dialog were in his blood. As in his press column of "Questions and Answers," he frequently used this method in broadcasting. His mind worked that way. For some thirty-five years he held sway and no one competed or took his place. He began in 1928 and continued throughout the rest of his ministry. One of the best-known clergymen in the United States, he was an institution. His capacity for work was prodigious. He lived to write and speak.

Charles Edward Fuller (1887-1968) was a layman who early discovered the value of witnessing to his faith in Bible class teaching and eventually by radio. Independent and without denominational support, he was dependent on the gifts of his listeners to pay for the time available on radio. In 1925 he launched the "Old Fashioned Revival Hour" (Long Beach, Calif.) and with gospel music and an informal service he centered his preaching on Bible texts and doctrines. This simple preaching appealed to the millions of people who listened over one thousand radio stations each week around the world.

Fuller was unlike Maier the Lutheran who was the scholarly Professor of the Old Testament. He was not to be compared with Sheen, the Roman Church orator whose magnetic and dramatic personality touched multitudes. He was far from the urbanity of Cadman whose churchliness and knowledge gave him an entry into many minds at the beginning of broadcasting. Neither Fosdick nor Peale with their life-situation and psychological peace-of-mind messages resembled Fuller in any respect. How then did Fuller succeed with his "one talent" and his simplistic message?

His secret lay in the wholehearted way in which he devoted his full time to steeping himself in the English Bible. He aimed to hear God's message and then with obedience sought to share that with his listeners. People in all walks of life tuned in week after week. Nothing profound, nothing extraordinary, nothing startling was ever said by Fuller. Yet the fact remains that his preaching touched the inner springs of life. Letters poured in weekly for forty-four years telling how this ministry had helped people, brought them to Christ as Savior, led them to a new awareness of the power of God's Word, and assisted them to new life.

Typically fundamental, Biblical, and spiritually motivated by prayer and a belief in the imminent second advent of Christ, his winsome ministry captivated millions of listeners.

Walter Arthur Maier (1893-1950) was another of the modern "scholar-preachers." His notable contribution to preaching was his use of the radio as a pulpit to reach millions of people. His name is for all time associated with The Lutheran Hour in America. At the beginning of his academic career as Professor of Old Testament

Studies at Concordia Theological Seminary, St. Louis, Missouri, he discovered the medium of radio. The thrust of his preaching was such that twenty million listeners is the estimate given as his weekly audience. The religious program each week was carried over 1,236 stations, in 55 countries, and in some 36 languages—possibly a record then unmatched by any other religious radio service.

Beginning when radio was in its infancy, Maier saw its potentiality to reach millions. He gave himself without reservation to this medium. Each week he prepared himself for this one single opportunity to proclaim the eternal message to an unseen congregation. American church life had entered a period of slumping numerically, and spiritual life was not vigorous. From 1930 to 1950 he reasserted the historic and classic exposition of the Christian faith and brought back reassurance of faith to multitudes in that period.

The aims of the broadcast were expressed by him in these terms: "The Lutheran Hour proposes—

> a faith built not upon the towering heights of skyscrapers, but upon the love of God;
> a faith founded not on hoarded wealth and gilt-edged bonds, but upon the Scriptures and the sacred promise of our heavenly Father;
> a faith that strengthens the mind and heart for every challenge life offers.

The opening sermon at Cleveland, supported by Bach's majestic music and a choir, was launched with the announcement of "The Lutheran Hour—Bringing Christ to the Nation from Coast to Coast!" The address on that occasion was "There Is a God!" and the text was Psalm 14:1, "The fool hath said in his heart, There is no God." In giving this opening message, Maier stated bluntly and forcefully:

> This evening we are to dedicate the message of our first broadcast to the fundamental conviction that there is a God; that the great and infinite Father of the entire human race who has revealed Himself in many and remarkable ways is no fantastic formation of superstition, no creature of childish tradition, no will-o'-the-wisp of religious delusion; but that atheism, materialism, agnosticism, and all the many other similar theories which deny or question the existence of God are not only irrational and disappointing, but also anti-Scriptural and therefore destructive from every point of consideration.

One of the outstanding themes through the years was the Reformation emphasis and on the 450th anniversary observance held at

Olympia Stadium, Detroit, he preached to the 16,000 present and the millions listening by radio. After the singing of "A Mighty Fortress," Luther's hymn of the Reformation, the sermon followed, titled "Back to Luther!" This was a plea for a twentieth-century reformation through correction of destructive tendencies in the churches. An extract from his message indicates the trend of thought:

> While Lincoln dealt with bodies in bondage and minds coerced by mental slavery, Luther threw off the shackles of . . . spiritual tyranny. . . . All Protestantism, yes, Roman Catholicism itself, as its eminent scholars have admitted, not only owes him an everlasting debt of gratitude but also needs the re-statement of many of his principles. . . . Picture the cancerous growth of modern infidelity as egocomplexed pulpiteers, disguising the breed of the wolf beneath silk cassocks . . . read from the Scriptures with crossed thumbs, tongues in cheek, and mental reservation, who place the Bible on the one level with heathen philosophies. . . . Think of the smooth, oily surrender of the deity of our Saviour. . . . I still repeat the cry, "Back to Luther."

As a preacher whose vocation was that of an Old Testament Professor, teaching Hebrew and leading students into Hebrew history and literature in the classroom, the surprise is greater that Maier was able to step from the classroom into the pulpit of a worldwide radio congregation. In doing this he was aided by a pious family background. His knowledge of the Bible, his strong conviction concerning the veracity of the Bible, his assured personal experience of the living Christ, and his dedication to proclaim the gospel fired him to an enthusiastic and passionate utterance on the occasion of broadcasting. No one could doubt the sincerity of this radio preacher. He preached what he believed and felt.

He could censure (as in the indictment against the false teachers in the pulpit); he could plead (as when he asked for commitment to Christ); and he could declaim as a prophet (as when he restated the Reformation credo and called for a similar experience in this day). His voice was strong, but not too melodious. His gestures were vigorous even though he could not be seen on radio. In the studio he would take off his jacket to be free as he put his whole being into the preaching of the sermon.

The preaching of Maier was Christocentric and Biblical. Characteristic of his many sermons is the theme—"not to know anything . . . save Jesus Christ, and him crucified" (I Cor. 2:2). "Addressing you from the campus of a divinity school that for almost a century has dedicated its resources to the Christ of the Scriptures, *I offer you* in the name of the Triune God not the Christ of present-day compromise and concession, not the Christ of twentieth-century indifference and indecision, not the Christ of modern doubt and denial, who has been exalted in His humanity only to be robbed of His deity, but the Christ of the Cross. *With my hand on the Bible, I dedicate this radio mission to the preaching of that Cross.*" Here is the heart of Maier's preaching. The gesture of the hand on the Bible came spontaneously, we can imagine, and was not studied as an actor. This was typical of him as he would take the Bible in hand as he preached.

Maier's preaching was based on meeting human need. Biblical in background, theological in content, it touched life at all points. Sermons which touched on love and marriage, the home, family, and youth are there. The problems of fear, pain, guilt, inner peace, immorality, meaninglessness, materialism, and death loomed large in the many sermons given. Generally, the sermons related to the Church Year, so that he was able to give emphasis to the great doctrines of the Christian faith: faith, love, prayer, salvation, sin, and correlated themes which stressed the authority of the Bible and the person and work of Christ. Annually, there would be sermons dealing with national and international issues. National repentance was called for and moral issues were dealt with as they impinged upon our national heritage and destiny.

Maier's preparation began with a scholarly study of the text of Scripture which had been chosen early in the week. Then on Fridays he referred to his files for illustrations or other special items already prepared from his past extensive reading. After writing an outline of the sermon, he would dictate to a secretary as he walked up and down in his study. The manuscript usually exceeded the length of an average sermon and this had to be cut in delivery. Maier's rapid delivery enabled him to use most of the manuscript, and what was not used was not discarded. The complete manuscript was available for publication later. In this way some twenty volumes of sermons were published over the years. The contents reveal Maier's orthodox theology in proclaiming the sinfulness of man and the remedy through the salvation offered in Christ the Savior. As a good Lutheran he did not fail to emphasize law and gospel. Reason, emotion, and will intertwined in his appeal to people. He used contemporary events and situations as a background to penetrate the minds of his generation. As he said, "I must keep pulse on human affairs."

Maier's rhetoric was natural and spontaneous. The sheer force of his personal utterance came through strongly. Concreteness, iteration, contrast and comparison, alliteration and imagery were marks of his style. The rapid speech, the intense voice, and the urgent tone characterized a boldness of appeal which was akin to a prophet. As a preacher the professor had that urgency which gave the impression that the time was short and here was possibly the last opportunity of hearing the message! Certainly this scholarly professor of Hebrew and Old Testament was an evangelist of the first order when he proclaimed the gospel through the use of radio to millions around the world. No doubt the extreme demands of time and strength for his ministry exacted its toll near the end. Yet in the fullness of the years he left a legacy of dynamic preaching via radio that touched his generation.

Contemporary with Dr. Maier was the representative preacher of the Roman Church in North America. Known to millions because of his television program each week for many years, **Fulton John Sheen (1895-)** has a niche to himself. While others were slowly struggling to use the medium of the radio, Sheen jumped instinctively to the other medium of television. He saw its potential and grasped the opportunity with enthusiasm and delight. Whoever saw him on the screen could hardly doubt he was equal to many actors in dramatic presentation and a master of speech and logical acumen in the buildup of his message. That message was not strictly a sermon (such as given from a church pulpit), but the balanced talk, the illustrations, the finely-spun tale, and the touch of humor would punch home the main line of truth to his listeners.

Bishop Sheen usually worked out of New York City, but he seemed to be at home everywhere and his message was to all people. There was little, if any, apologetic for the church he served unless it was the background of the books in the bookcases, the table, and the barely visible figure of the Virgin Mary. Apart from that his message was a God-centered message for all.

Sheen's television personality was striking—wearing the garments of the church and showing the eyes and voice of a prophet. His masculinity was never in doubt. His deep-set, gray eyes held his listeners as his voice moved from a soft whisper to a resonant roar.

Some have thought him "theatrical," but his style has stood the test of the years. For many years he was the head of his church's Society for the Propagation of the Faith and for over twenty years he maintained the Catholic Radio Hour (1930-52) and television program (1951-57). His association with the outreach and missionary arm of his church no doubt influenced his thrust and approach in preaching.

The sermonic work of this best-known of all Roman Catholic preachers was that which was built up from a reservoir of study and research. Sheen's method was to work on the subject with notes and ideas culled from reading and reflection. An outline would be made so that illustrations and relevant material might be fitted in. He then would give his mind to the mastery of the outline with its sub-points. Having done this, he was ready to preach. He would think his way through as the occasion demanded and generally recalled what he had set down beforehand. In extempore speech Sheen looked at his congregation and should any interruption come he was able to utilize the moment and use a word of humor or an aside to relieve the tension.

In the sermon "The Greatest Trial in History" the introduction is direct and historical in appeal.

> Some of the famous trials in history were those of Socrates, who was accused of blaspheming the Athenian gods; the trial of Aaron Burr, which lasted for eight months; and the most famous trial of France was probably that of Alfred Dreyfus, who was banished to Devil's Island; England's most famous trial was that of Mary Stuart and her execution by the consent of her cousin, Queen Elizabeth of England; Ireland's most famous trial was that of Robert Emmett.
>
> But all of these trials fade into insignificance compared with the great trial before Pontius Pilate when the Accused was not Man alone, but the Son of God in the form of Man. All the figures in this trial are representative figures; they stand for species, rather than individuals. The Cross is not something that *has* happened; the Crucifixion is something that *is* happening. It can be found at any place and at any hour in the human race, for it is the epic struggle of the forces of good and evil.
>
> The trial took place in Jerusalem, but it could just as well have taken place in Athens or Rome, for it involved every human soul in the world. The place of execution was Calvary, but it could just as well have been Peiping, Moscow, Broadway, Place de la Concorde, or the Chicago Loop. The three dominant forces in the trial were:

1. The political power of the State
2. The people or the masses—you and me
3. The divine in the human.

Here is a sampling of Sheen's approach. He begins in a conversational manner and talks with his hearers as he leads them step by step through a historical vestibule into the larger room of discussion. He may assume that the historical events are well-known, but also he may have in mind to inform some that out of history comes the background for his message at that hour. The body of the sermon is a straight-forward development and retelling with comment of the events reported in the gospels. Nothing unusual here, the story simply is retold in his own graphic way.

Sheen knew how to deal with the ills of modern society. He had sermons which grappled with the problems of drunkenness and alcoholism; a cure for selfishness; suffering; boring work; social problems; economics; freedom; the making of traitors; nurses and doctors; Moses and the Ten Commandments; and "The Hound of Heaven." From these subjects one can see how his mind was alert to meet modern needs and questions. Human passions fascinated this preacher in the sense that he was constantly scrutinizing man's inner life and needs. Here, like Peale the Protestant, he dealt with jealousy, fear, pride, greed, lust, and hatred, and the need for the divine love to flood man's being with new meaning and power. The sinful man's sense of guilt was dealt with and the remedy offered in the gospel. The conclusion of a sermon on "Freedom" indicates how Sheen could appeal in the manner of an evangelist:

> Man's misuse of freedom became for God the occasion of offering himself as a Holocaust of love, not to force men back to Him, for His hands and feet were nailed, but to entice them back by a revelation of greater love in which He laid down His life for His friends. Those who understand this victory of love over evil see that all the free choices of the world should be dedicated to the perfection of the soul in love. In seeing this, man comes to the understanding of what is the greatest freedom in all the world, namely, the freedom to be a saint.

In one unusual sermon, Sheen takes the poem by Francis Thompson, "The Hound of Heaven," and uses it as the message. In four major points he works through the theme of how God seeks man by the Holy Spirit. Using the era of psychology and its insights, he refers to the popularity of depth psychology as giving man a chance to live in another dimension than the purely horizontal one on the earth.

> In the days of faith, man lived in a three-dimensional *universe:* heaven was above, hell below, and the earth between the two was a mere anteroom in which he would say 'aye' or 'nay' to eternal destiny. As these three eternal verities slipped away, there was left the flat surface of the earth; and escape was sought by picturing three dimensions *inside the mind;* for heaven there was substituted 'super-ego'; for earth, there was the 'ego'; and for hell there was the 'id.' The most important part of the mind was now the cavernous depth of the unconscious which man could dig into, explore, and analyze, in the hope of unearthing new mysteries, or else of stirring up latent energies and powers which would bring peace. Thompson describes the serpentine ways of the mind, with its fears and glooms, in his opening words:

> I fled Him, down the nights and down the days;
>   I fled Him down the arches of the years;
> I fled Him down the labyrinthine ways
>   Of my own mind; and in the mist of tears
> I hid from Him, and under running laughter.
>   Up vistaed hopes I sped;
>   And shot, precipitated,
> Adown Titanic glooms of chasméd fears,
>   From those strong Feet that followed, followed after.

Using these insights of depth psychology and the poetic genius of the poem in its spiritual unveiling of man running away from God, yet never escaping him, Sheen draws lessons from—

1. The unconscious mind.
2. Illegitimate love or sex.
3. Children.
4. Science.

Sheen ends with the appeal that "those who think that religion is an escape should try the Cross. There are various cheap kinds of mysticism, expressing themselves in drama and poetry in which the soul is in perpetual search of God. There is seldom any depth to these, because they allow the heart to be complacent. Thompson takes the reverse step; it is not a soul searching for God, but, far more terrible, God searching for the soul. Very few people know what they are letting themselves in for when this happens. . . ." Thus the preacher is "relevant" and "up-to-date" in his contact with modern, sophisticated man, even as he is linked with the timeless and eternal truths of divine revelation. Sheen always confronted modern man with *The Choice: the Sacred or Profane Life* (a title of one of his many books).

As an ambassador of the Word, Sheen had widespread influence. He was a seeker of the lost, and opposed antitheistic philosophy, especially Communism. He never failed to attack Communism as a false faith for man. In sermon after sermon he utilized his findings from his study of the subject of Communism. Perhaps this was overdone, but the point of view of his church and his own feeling could not be otherwise in a postwar era of uncertainty and confusion. His sermons have both the warning note and the wooing note. And he could be epigrammatic as when he said that "one must either live as one thinks or think as one lives." He was confident that preachers of the Word need never fear the outcome in the struggle against the forces of paganism. In the sermon "Ambassador of the Word" he said that "Popularity may not always come their way, but when the smoke of battle is cleared, the most precious thing in the world will be their heritage, and that will be victory. For if truth wins, we win; but if truth—ah, but truth can never lose."

With the national media available, denominations were able to appoint representative preachers to broadcast each week to a wider constituency than just their own members. Several excellent preachers exercised a fruitful ministry.

Peter H. Eldersveld (1911-1965) was the minister of The Back to God Hour, the radio and television voice of the Christian Reformed Church. For nineteen years he was heard over more than three hundred radio stations, speaking for Biblical Christianity as it was interpreted in the historic confessions of that body. Over two million copies of his sermons were distributed annually. It is estimated he spoke to over three million people every Sunday.

His message was based upon the belief that the Bible is the authoritative Word of God. That millions of regular listeners heard him indicates that lay people in large numbers liked his interpretation which brought confidence and committal. In a period of doubt and questioning, Eldersveld's Reformation emphasis concerning "The Divine Initiative" (Eph. 1:4, 11), dealing with the doctrine of Election, found wide acceptance and linked both hearers and preacher with the Reformers of the sixteenth century.

Henry Bast (1906-) was pastor, Professor of Bible and Practical

Theology, and the speaker for the Temple Time broadcast for fourteen years. In this worldwide ministry he was a spokesman for the Reformed Church in America and was heard on over 100 stations in America and 170 outlets overseas, translations being carried in five languages.

As President of the General Synod of the Reformed Church for a year, Bast's leadership was not diminished but maintained as the preacher at heart. There was nothing semisecular, nothing entertaining here. The spirit of this pastoral preacher revealed a loving concern for others in need. In "The Secret of Contentment" (Phil. 4:11 RSV), we sense the yearning note of a man who thinks that this sermon might be his last to preach! Speaking extemporaneously, he then wrote out the sermon for publication in the week after its delivery. Like the practice of other broadcasters, the message was made ready to be sent to inquirers.

These two church bodies may be thought to be small in numbers, but their influence is far beyond some major denominations. American preaching has been enriched by the rise of church groups which have broken away from the major denominations or have followed leadership which brought a more vital Christian experience and fellowship in periods of routine and casual church life. Drawing from their roots in the Reformation and caught up in the revival spirit of the nineteenth century, smaller church groups have developed and cultivated earnest preaching. Among these are the Assemblies of God, the Nazarene, the Free Methodist, the Wesleyan Methodist, and some of the Pentecostal churches.

Typical is the Church of God which arose from this background and was influenced by the teaching of John Wesley in England, Alexander Campbell (1788-1866) of Scotland, and John Winebrenner (1797-1860) of the German Reformed Church. The spiritual awakening of Daniel Sidney Warner (1842-1895) in 1865 marks the watershed of the advance of the Church of God. In a free and informal association of people, preaching has been based Biblically upon the spirit of testimony and witness. Following John Wesley, this group has stressed Arminian theology, the New Birth, the fellowship of all believers without sectarian labels, simplicity of worship, and the emphasis on conversion and holiness of life, themes which have filled their preaching.

In **William Dale Oldham (1903-)** we have a representative whose preaching has been recognized in the Church of God and beyond.

Oldham maintained a dynamic ministry for sixteen years as leader of the church at Anderson, Indiana, the location also of the denomination's college and seminary. For more than twenty years he has been the radio preacher of the Christian Brotherhood Hour, a special network program broadcast weekly over 330 radio stations. Pastoral preacher, he has published messages and books, traveled worldwide for mission-evangelism, and majored in the use of radio to proclaim the eternal message. His preaching has the spirit of the shepherd heart, a compassionate note, a rich voice, the evangelist's appeal, and the free dynamic utterance of a man inspired by the Spirit of God and ever a man among the people.

In **Charles Morse Ward (1909-)** the Assemblies of God has contributed an international broadcaster of the gospel. During the first part of the 1900s the church had become a potent force in evangelistic preaching. An informal manner of talking and preaching has been an effective way of reaching those who are not reached by the more formal and traditional sermons. By means of their radio program over hundreds of stations, this preacher, like the prophet Ezekiel (3:15), sits where the people sit. The secret of appeal and simplicity lies in Ward's graphic, down-to-earth, timely message. His speech is seasoned with grace and salted to rub in certain truths. In the style of the evangelist of the gospel message, his sermons are not unlike Old Testament prophetical barbs which stab and disturb the listener. Today's problems and current events are recreated to shatter complacency and cause the conscience to feel twinges of guilt and judgment. He uses the direct form of address in preaching—interjecting "mister," "neighbor," "friend," and other words and terms which recur as in a vocabulary specially minted for that elusive "man in the street" or "the ordinary man." At the same time, the note of judgment is sounded for the casual and careless church member who has settled down and "lost his first love."

Such preaching is the kind which reaches "outsiders" and "prodigals" who understand the concern and language of "Brother Ward," who prefers not to be called by any formal religious or church title. Over the ABC network and other independent radio stations the radio sermons of Revivaltime (by which the program is known) tell us something in a history of preaching! The response is heartening, and John the Baptist, George Whitefield, and Billy Sunday in other days would have found in C. M. Ward a kinship.

Among distinctive broadcasters has been **Barrett Batsell Baxter**

(1916-) who has served The Church of Christ in this nation and among other lands. After pastorates in California and Nashville, Tennessee, he became Professor of Speech and Homiletics at the David Lipscomb College, Nashville. His radio and television work has been a service to his denomination and a means of outreach to those who have found in this church an evangelizing agency.

Baxter has also published several books which, like his preaching, advocate the gospel and are thoroughly Biblical. Among these are *Speaking for the Master* (1954), and his penetrating study of the best in preaching found in the Yale Lectures entitled *The Heart of the Yale Lectures* (1947; 1971). Here Baxter discusses the preacher, the sermon, and the congregation, covering both content and technique. The Herald of Truth nationwide radio and television programs confirm the ideals which he exemplifies in enthusiasm, interest appeal, and a convincing spirit that not only presents the truth of God but invites people to respond.

William Franklin Graham (1918-), known by the vast multitude of people throughout the world as "Billy" Graham and given a hearing more than any other preacher, stands in the forefront of those who have made their contribution in history. Not as a pastor but as the itinerant evangelist Graham comes to the bar of history. Linked with the Southern Baptist Church, he has ministered largely to people of all denominations and to all levels of life. No final figures can be given, but the estimate already is that in preaching he has reached more millions of people in his lifetime than any other man in all history.

Such a verdict is only possible when we recall that Graham emerged in the period when radio and television had become available on a total scale. He also had the benefit of a press coverage which took his name and picture to millions. The Billy Graham Association, Minneapolis, Minnesota, has been a strength in planning and preparing his campaigns and crusades throughout the world, thus leaving him free to concentrate upon his own preparation of the message to be delivered. No financially embarrassing questions have plagued Graham, whose campaigns are usually underwritten by local support. Then, too, the monthly magazine *Decision,* edited by Sherwood E. Wirt, reaches over four million subscribers, the largest subscription list of any religious periodical. With this advance publicity, Billy Graham has held evangelistic crusades in the largest exhibition halls and baseball and football stadiums throughout the world. In the open air he has repeated the miracle of George Whitefield, this time with the benefits of electronics, large choirs and efficient organization.

What of the method and message of Billy Graham? He stands in the space age as the outstanding representative of evangelism in the evangelical tradition and in the succession of Dwight L. Moody. Using practically the same methods of follow-up, Graham proclaims the same gospel with more polish and more relevance of illustration and language. There is a simple message, fervor, exposition of the gospel, and a final appeal for people to commit themselves to Christ. Thousands do at every service.

In preaching, Graham usually begins at a high pitch of emphasis and then sustains the intensity of utterance. His voice is clear and reaches out without impediment. A sermon on "The Grace of God" (Titus 2:11-13) is spelled out by taking the letters of the word "grace" and using them as "Grace-Righteously-Appearing-Christ-Exhort"—nothing profound and yet simply applied for people who may not have a background of Biblical knowledge. Graham would be the first to admit he is not a "great" preacher, but he makes the most of his gifts in building a sermon. His power of illustration has been enhanced over the years, and he has included more of the events of his own day as background material.

Another example of this is the sermon "Made, Marred, Mended" from "the vessel made of clay was marred: so the potter made it again, as seemed good to the potter to make it" (Jer. 18:3-4), wherein he reiterates the truth of the divine creation of man, man's fall into sin, then God's re-creation by Jesus Christ. Typical of his message is the Biblical picture and the Christian doctrine of sin and forgiveness, faith and repentance, the cross and salvation.

Critics on the right and on the left have attacked him either for his religious association with those who are not wholly known as traditionally orthodox or for his lack of social action within the gospel proclaimed. However, if at first his message was the simple, evangelistic, and personal call for committal to Christ and one that seemed to ignore the social claims of the gospel, his later growth and maturity would indicate that he has stressed more and more the need for the newly-committed man to involve himself in the social, political, and racial aspects of modern living. This is not the time to estimate the influence of Billy Graham's style and type of preaching. That verdict must await another era.

The period of the 1930s and following witnessed the rise of many independent preachers who either dropped their association with the major denominations or initiated a new group under their own leadership. Among the representative men are **Billy James Hargis** and **Carl MacIntyre**. The former was an exponent of right-wing extremes in all aspects of the Christian life and theology. His Christian Crusade from Tulsa, Oklahoma, was carried by means of radio stations and city-wide rallies across the nation. He found supporters who gave liberally for his cause. His special emphasis was opposition to Communism as the foe of Christianity and the one major threat to America. He was thus able to combine a religious and patriotic spirit by his fearless preaching against the enemy within and without our gates.

MacIntyre had been a Presbyterian pastor and formed his own church after leaving the one he deemed to have become apostate. During the Machen controversy within the Presbyterian Church, MacIntyre stood with Machen and later separated from him to pursue his own way. He also formed the American Council of Christian Churches as he drew together several independent groups who were opposed to the National Council of Churches on theological and social grounds. Again, by means of the radio with hundreds of stations carrying his daily messages, MacIntyre propagated the Twentieth Century Reformation Hour as a means of rallying orthodox Christians within all churches to see in him a champion for those truths now in jeopardy. He, like Hargis, had a strong patriotic spirit and attacked anything savoring of Communism. Fearless, his words carried weight and influence in many quarters.

While these two representative men had much in common, they were diverse in that MacIntyre had the benefit of theological education and continued as the pastor of his own congregation in Collingswood, New Jersey. Both preached with vigor, with reactionary rhetoric, and sometimes a vitriolic touch.

Holiness-Pietistic Preaching

Albert Benjamin Simpson (1844-1919), known across the church as "A. B." Simpson, brought from his Canadian birth and background a rich heritage of Scottish and Convenanter devotion. The classics of the soul were his reading materials, and the marrow of classic divinity envigorated his interest. He was nurtured at home and at Knox College, Toronto, with the finest theological teaching of that time, and was subjected to rigorous tests before ordination. After a pastorate in Hamilton, Canada, he was called to Louisville, Kentucky, and then to New York City. After a year there, he was so touched by the social and economic distress that he decided to engage in mission work when the more established church would not act. He founded the Gospel Tabernacle and this eventually became a church of strength.

The missionary aspect of the church's work had begun in Simpson's mind in Canada, but did not come to fruition until he settled in America. The young preacher saw the need and desired to arouse his people to attend to what he thought was primary for the church. When little response was given, he was led to America where his evangelical preaching attracted many of like mind so that he became the leader of a new church group bent upon evangelism and missions. His own labors in missionary work in New York prepared him and his people for overseas missions.

As Simpson preached the obligation of the church to send out missionaries to the whole world, the response was such that it was necessary for him to lead in building a Missionary Training College adjoining the church. This was later removed to Nyack on the Hudson and is now named Nyack College; others have been established at St. Paul, Minnesota, San Francisco, California, and Regina, Saskatchewan. Thousands of young people have been trained and sent out from these schools into service at home and abroad.

The preaching of Simpson was noted for its strong doctrinal emphasis. The cross of Christ and the second advent of Christ were central. Another strong truth was that the Holy Spirit could fill or baptize the Christian in power. Witnessing as a result would be without difficulty. This doctrine was linked with the teaching that the Christian's body should be kept in health and strength. The healing of the body was a tenet of belief and, in the perspective of Simpson, a large part of the life of the believer. Thus the doctrine of holiness or sanctification was promoted with these ideas in mind.

Simpson, knowing that the church was not too enthusiastic about missions, founded the Christian and Missionary Alliance in 1887 to encourage Christians to band together in their common objective. Over the years this organization has become a church in itself. With its training centers and its magazine, *The Alliance Witness* (formerly *The Alliance Weekly*), it also owns a publishing house, Christian Publications, Inc., Harrisburg, Pennsylvania. All this came from the dream and dedication of one man. His own writings include many books as well as articles and editorials. Thus his preaching ministry was enlarged and widened for the church universal. His influence has permeated many groups and denominations. The preaching emphasis upon giving and giving by tithing has built up a church which has one of the largest ratios of people engaged in missionary work overseas to members working at home. They are close to the Moravian Church in this respect. Their monetary giving and their giving of life stands near the highest in American church life.

Simpson taught and preached that Jesus Christ is Savior, Sanctifier, Healer, and Coming King. On this fourfold structure he built a ministry which continues to have meaning and purpose from one generation to another. His best books include *The Holy Spirit or, Power from on High* (2 vols., 1899); *Christ in the Bible* (a 24-vol. commentary, 1902-1907); and *Discovery of Divine Healing* (1902).

Henry Clay Morrison (1857-1942) in American Methodism is linked with Francis Asbury as one of the pioneer preachers who laid foundations of lasting worth for the church. His ministry emphasized the doctrine of sanctification, and he claimed that since John Wesley this was *the* doctrine which gave Methodism its birth and worth.

In preaching and teaching the fact of *entire* sanctification, or the perfection which holiness of experience brings, was at the heart of this man's ministry. He testified to a Holy Spirit experience in 1888 which transformed his life. Evangelism and revivalism characterized his years. One of these ministries took place at Wilmore, Kentucky, and out of that time of harvest came the founding of Asbury College and Seminary.

Part of the fruit of earlier ministries lay in the institution of *The Herald*, the magazine which spelled out the meaning of holiness in the Wesleyan tradition. Like Wesley, Morrison preached and taught that "there is no holiness without social holiness." Thus his preaching castigated the liquor interests, the use of tobacco which hurt the body, the need to act concerning the racial issue, and in politics the need to find out the causes of the depression in the 1930's.

Morrison's preaching stimulated the whole church. It influenced a generation of young men who were given a vision of the need of an education for the ministry. Evangelism, missions, revivalism, social action, and personal piety have ever been the concerns of those who followed this preacher and advocate of the Christ-centered life.

Julian C. McPheeters (1889-) also was President of Asbury Theological Seminary, and served as pastor of the Glide Memorial Methodist Church, San Francisco, for eighteen years. Out of this came many books and many magazine articles, as well as ministries of evangelism and missions. For some sixty years he has stood without compromise for the same doctrines as his forefathers. He claims to preach the unsearchable riches of Christ. Part of that ministry has been in the old-fashioned camp meeting, a link with frontier days in America but still carried on in certain parts by those of this persuasion. Always a student of the Scriptures, McPheeters is careful in preparation before abandoning himself to the Spirit of God who anoints and empowers for delivery of the message. Thus this modern Methodist expects divine unfoldings of power and persuasion through his preaching.

The school of pietism is one of long standing and constant experience. Of the moderns who have stood out in this respect is Aiden Wilson Tozer (1897-1963), familiarly known in his ministry as "A. W. Tozer." His unique and abiding distinction lay in his preaching and teaching which flowed from study and pulpit eventually to the printed page. His influence was worldwide, and he never left the small religious group known as the Christian and Missionary Alliance with which he identified himself throughout his life.

As a preacher Tozer was scholarly and precise. Limited in education as a youth, he became a scholarly preacher, with every day filled with some study, reading, writing, and thinking. The last became his watchword, for he could not imagine much being done for the Kingdom of God without thought. Associated as he was with a very conservative group with whom the more emotional appeal might have effect, Tozer stood out as the preacher who invoked the will and sought to capture the mind. His study of the Bible made him a Biblical preacher with a keen zest for the spiritual insights of truth. He became known as a Christian mystic, but even as he sought that experience of God, he felt it should be checked in the light of revelation. He was a seer in modern guise. Tozer was convinced that religious orthodoxy was decadent and dying of spiritual inbreeding. He was grieved by the outlook of religious books which were echoes of other books and lacked fresh, creative thought. It was in this light that he gave himself as a voice in the midst of the cries of modern city life (Chicago) to listen for the divine voice and then translate it to others by preaching and writing.

Alongside of the Bible the chief aid to Tozer's inner development lay in mystical literature. The spiritual classics of the soul appealed to him, and across the centuries he found spiritual teachers to help him. Any label on these people—such as Catholic, Protestant, Independent, or otherwise—made no difference. He sought and found the message of their creative writings and their deep awareness of God. He began to drink at those wells, and his own quest for the eternal was quickened and vivified. John of the Cross, Jan van Ruysbroeck, Henry Suso, Thomas Traherne, Molinos, Bernard, Frederick Faber, Lancelot Andrews, Tersteegen, Tauler, Eckhart, Boehme, Julian of Norwich, Thomas a Kempis, Isaac Watts and many others are there in their catholicity of interest and appeal.

As an evangelical he preached about "The New Birth." In this he pointed out that "this was a miracle and no psychologist could explain it. 'Create in me a clean heart, O God; and renew a right spirit within me' is a foreshadowing in the Old Testament. There was need of this miracle. Not the reasoning of yourself into a position, but something happened that could not be explained." Another of his maxims in preaching was that "no one rejects Christ on philosophical grounds, but the rejection of God's light brings the worst darkness." He said, "The darkness of the night before the sun comes up is one thing. The darkness of the hermit who hides in caves among the cobwebs and bats and will not come into the light is something else again. . . . Where does Christianity destroy itself in a given generation? It destroys itself by not living in the light, by professing a truth it does not obey. Jesus said: 'For everyone that doeth evil hateth the light, neither cometh to the light lest his deeds should be reproved.' Now if that means anything, it means that our Lord teaches that people who reject Him reject Him for moral reasons."

In discussing the theme "Do you give heed to the Inner Voice of God?" Tozer probed and dissected as he said: "I'm against the idea of putting the 'big' preachers on tape and playing them back to the congregations that feel they are being starved by listening to 'little' preachers. Fallacy, brethren! If we could have the Apostle Paul on tape recordings and let him stand here and preach, he could do no more for you than the Holy Spirit can do, with The Book and the human conscience."

During the sixties there was a renewal of interest in the charismatic and the doctrine of the Holy Spirit. Tozer preached regularly on this subject and sought to find a balanced view. His volume of ten sermons points up this theme in the title, *The Ministry of the Holy Spirit*. Evidently he did not believe in begging God for the Holy Spirit as the Holy Spirit had been given and was here! Expounding Acts 2 and Pentecost, he interpreted the characteristics of a Spirit-filled congregation. The kinds of people who will be at home in such a church are unfolded and directions given about their earthly habits. The main emphasis of interpretation is that when "Jesus is exalted then the Spirit came!" Thus no one needs to beg God for this.

In strong speech he pointed out that a Spirit-filled people will be useful to the race of men. "Now I am not worried about what the critics say. . . . I do believe that the Christian church ought to be useful to the whole community. We can help the neighborhood where we live. . . . No need to apologize. Actually, they owe us a great debt, for our kind of transformed people keep the crime rate down, and where we have more God-filled, Spirit-filled churches we are going to have less policemen on the street. Wherever there's more godliness, there's less crime. . . ."

Tozer taught that everyone filled with or by the Holy Spirit knew it. "Be sure to the point of conviction, that you can be filled. Be sure that this is your desire. Be sure you are willing to be possessed by the indwelling Spirit. The Spirit will expect obedience to the Word of God and He will not tolerate the self-sins if He is to abide. Be sure that you need to be filled. Times of anxiety and disturbance will come. You cannot 'earn' the Spirit—He is a gift. How to be filled with the Spirit is—present yourself; ask God; give willing obedience; have faith in God; and thus will come the experience." Several passages of Scripture are woven together for the sermon.

Tozer preached regularly in series, and in his *Ten Sermons from the Gospel of John* there is evidence of his clear insight into the devotional and practical aspects of that classic of the Christian life. His expositions were marked by lucidity and color. He was ever the individualist, passionate, and persuasive. He did not hesitate to disagree with so-called "authorities"—even those he knew were in the same theological school of thought. He moved through the gospel by selecting texts which stood out for him and then preached on them—not textually, but by the development of the theme found therein.

Dealing with the text "as many as received him" (John 1:12) he went on to show that this was an "aggressive act of the total personality." Thus the text to him is "explosive" in its teaching about the mysterious rebirth of a man. Tozer outlines clearly and logically. He moves from one major point to another, and his analysis of the context is always satisfying. He said, "It certainly cannot be handled without a warning that evangelical Christianity is on a dead-end street if it is going to continue to accept religious activity as a legitimate proof of spirituality." His "radicalness" was often questioned, but his courage in preaching was matched by his burning, piercing sentences as he thrust the rapier of truth into the conscience.

Tozer's preaching was permeated by the theology of *the sovereignty of God*. This led him to preach and write about this most engrossing of all subjects, in his book *Pursuit of God*. Considering the infinitude of God, the immutability of God, the attributes of God, and the atonement, led him to see that the divine omnipotence was the key to the message of God in this generation. He constantly stressed this in sermon and publication. In this he said: "It is the uniformity of God's activities, the trustworthiness of His behaviour, that forms the foundation of scientific truth. With this the scientist begins, and from there he goes on to achieve many great and useful things which are beneficial to mankind. However, God the self-existent creator is the master of all phenomena, the source of all power ('Power belongeth unto God'), and since He is infinite whatever He has is also limitless. He possesses what none of His creation can possess: absolute potency, plentitude of power. And while we know by revelation, it agrees with reason."

Thus Tozer in his preaching reiterated the truth that the Holy Spirit of God was the power behind all things. The church needed above all other needs the power of the Holy Spirit. As he saw the kaleidoscopic scene of modern life—living in the heartland of America—he discerned the recurring loss of power and spirit within the church and the lowered morale. He felt that his mission as preacher and as editor of *The Alliance Weekly* (now *Witness*) and as writer was to reiterate the need for old-fashioned piety. Men might laugh or deride this idea, but Tozer knew in his heart that only as a man comes into living touch with God in Christ would there be any change of spirit in the nation as well as in the church.

Tozer was not one to preach on current events or try to capitalize on the spectacular. He stuck to his one idea of preaching Biblically and letting the Bible speak its own word to the listener and the occasion. There was awareness of need and relevance, and as he preached through the Bible by using book studies, he covered life's needs and expounded Christian doctrine. His preaching was imbued with the spirit of true worship as he believed worship to be the highest act of the soul. As he said, "Worship is to feel in your heart and express in some appropriate manner a humbling and delightful sense of admiring awe and astonished wonder and overpowering love in the presence of that most ancient Mystery, that Majesty which philosophers call the First Cause but which we call Our Father Who Art in Heaven."

Though he had a full life of missionary-evangelistic preaching, Tozer yet found time to study and write. Imagine a small study on the second floor of a frame house next to a church on the complex of endless streets in south Chicago and (as the writer can testify) there was found this evangelical mystic and preacher. Scholar and student, reader and researcher, writer and toiler, praying man and practical individual—this was Tozer.

Myron S. Augsburger (1929-) is one of the younger men emerging in the 1900s as a preacher who now represents the smaller and the newer denominations which have arisen during recent years. The major churches of America have had a long tradition of eminent preachers whose names have been widely publicized through the various media of communication. The emergence of independent groups of churches has not always received notice. One such is the Mennonite Church which has links with Europe over a century and more.

Augsburger at present is President of the Eastern Mennonite College and Seminary, Harrisonburg, Virginia. He is a product of his denomination and has taken graduate studies, earning a doctor's degree. He is abreast of modern thought and theology, but does not thereby relinquish the theology and heritage of his fathers.

In his sermons "When Christ Becomes Real" and "Christ in the Midst of His Church" we have samplings of his evangelical spirit and the witness of his personal faith. The style of preaching is conversational and direct—a man speaking to another man—sharing what he knows and believes and inviting others to accept the same. In the former sermon it is declared that "man does not become a true man until Christ becomes real to him. Because man is estranged from God today, he has turned his back on God, has shut God out of his life and has set himself at the center, so he needs to get away from ego-centeredness and become a Christ-oriented person." In the latter sermon the lordship of Christ is stressed as the key to life's fulfillment. "What are the implications of a Christology that sees Jesus Christ standing at the center of the Church? First, His Lordship stands over against the idolatry of power. Second, His sword of division stands over against the syncretisms of faith. Third, His message of love stands over against the humanistic interest of universalism." Strong meat for traditional people.

The Mennonite Church has broadcast its message by radio using **David Augsburger (1938-)** and published its doctrinal position in preaching through **John H. Yoder (1927-)**, Professor of Theology and Ethics at Associated Mennonite Biblical Seminaries, Elkhart, Indiana. Their preaching restates their 'separatist' position concerning war, capital punishment, the State and politics.

Another group within our American culture is the Brethren in Christ Church, with its Messiah College, Grantham, Pennsylvania. Preaching over the past century has stressed the synthesis of revivalism and the church as total community. Their attitude to the "world" indicates a movement from separation to an increasing acceptance of American society. Like those in many other Reformation groups who escaped to the new world, their language and theology have tended to stress their particular tradition in order to survive and yet become part of the new. Any realistic assessment of their teaching-preaching awaits further data.

Jewish Preaching

Felix Adler (1851-1933) was German born, the son of a rabbi, and came to the United States in 1857. His studies were climaxed by graduate work at Columbia University, New York, as well as at Berlin and at Heidelberg in Germany. He was writer, lecturer, and preacher. He founded the Society for Ethical Culture and gathered around him many liberally minded people, both Jew and Gentile.

Unlike his more orthodox Jewish friends, he took his liberalism in theology into a way of life and thought which appealed to a wide audience in his day. Life and its meaning were the subject matter which engaged his mind. In "The Meaning of Life" we find him proclaiming his beliefs: "There are two kinds of light, the light on the hither side of the darkness and the light beyond the darkness. We must press on through the darkness and the terror of it if we would reach the holier light beyond. We are here—no matter who put us here, or how we came here—to fulfil a task. We cannot afford to go of our own volition until the last item of our duty is discharged. We are here to make the mind master of matter, soul of sense. We do so by overriding pain, not by weakly capitulating to it."

The style is clear and flows swiftly. The reasoning is logical and appealing. Nothing here necessarily has a Biblical basis or a use of Scripture, although he must have known the Torah and the Prophets. Nevertheless, preaching of this kind appealed to people outside the established communions through its humanism and man-centeredness.

Stephen Samuel Wise (1874-1949) ranks as one of the finest examples of preaching among the Hebrew synagogues and is known for his excellent ministries to his people in New York and in Portland, Oregon. Active in relief for persecuted Jews in Europe and supporter of Zionist affairs, he served as a President of the Jewish Congress at Paris. His preaching style has been noted for its oratorical qualities—his imposing presence, his impressive voice, and his rich imagination.

Whether in the synagogue pulpit or at a public gathering, Wise could be depended upon for some volcanic utterance and fluency of words. Something of the ancient Hebrew prophet's passion and persuasion was heard in his message, namely, that God is vitally concerned with human affairs. As a preacher Wise gathered material for several sermons or addresses and kept this in envelopes until he needed to use them. By reading and brooding he came to the moment of selection and was ready to write. Then he made a summary of what he was to say. He did not read a sermon, preferring to be free in thought and action as he thought through what he was preaching.

Wise viewed preaching as something of the ambassador's vocation, whether Jewish or Christian. "The business of the man in the ministry is to bring the vision of God the Father to men and the vision of men as brothers to men. The business of the minister is to do what my Fathers have always taught—that religion means, above all things, *holiness,* that Jewish term which long preceded the *Imitatio Dei*—holiness—which can not be without equity and righteousness in the relations between man and man."

Wise believed that ministers need not be scholars, but they must be creative in the sense of being helpful thinkers and teachers to assist others in the struggle of life.

One of the leading examples of Jewish preaching in modern days in America was Rabbi **Abba Hillel Silver (1893-1963)** of Cleveland, Ohio. The public, and especially the Christian, knows little about the ministries of rabbis. The contacts are limited and the opportunities to hear these men are not easily available. In recent years more has been done through Brotherhood Weeks and civic and social relations to share in the speech of our Jewish friends.

Rabbi Silver was once photographed standing beside a replica of Michelangelo's *Moses* in the Temple in Cleveland. He had the imposing look of an ancient Jewish leader. Tall and dark, he had a massive head and a shock of black, graying hair. When he preached, his words came out in organ tones. Born in Lithuania, he represented the fifth generation of rabbis in his family. Recalling that Moses was "slow of speech," and had to have his brother Aaron talk for him, the modern rabbi felt that he must somehow still speak for Moses!

When Silver was installed as the spiritual leader of Temple Tifereth Israel in Cleveland, he was given the opportunity to make clear his affinities with Zionism. His friend Rabbi Stephen S. Wise of New York had asked him to do so. Silver's position was that of supporting the spiritual and cultural forces of Zionism. Such a center in Jerusalem would meet with his sympathy and be a galvanizing force in Jewish life, while the political aspects of Zionism were of secondary importance to him.

He was able to do much for Zionism. In 1920, for example, he spoke at rallies in New York where he made addresses which led to the pledging of over one million dollars, and the giving of nearly two hundred thousand dollars. At that time Silver was acclaimed as the ablest rabbi in America by Stephen S. Wise, who said of him, "He is the ablest today, barring no one, a remarkable youth, only twenty-seven, who, if God gives him health and strength, will do great things for Israel. He is a most ardent Zionist and gives of his time and strength to the cause." As an ardent Zionist linked with the Jewish Reform division of Judaism, he also organized support for resolutions favoring the new State of Israel in the United States Congress and the United Nations Assembly. At the ceremony of inauguration for Dwight D. Eisenhower he offered a moving prayer which made a deep impression.

Silver tried to meet the religious apathy and indifference which he felt was creeping over American Jewry during his time. His preaching was geared accordingly. Much of his thought and outlook as a teacher and preacher is enshrined in his book *Religion in a Changing World.* Of religion Silver said: "I have always looked on religion as a quest for social justice and a quest for God. The one found greatest expression among the prophets, the other among the mystics. In preaching I try to synthesize the two."

Silver followed the Hebrew tradition of the readings and the homily which later became the sermon. However, the modern practice is not unlike much of the preaching of Protestant ministers—based on a Bible text—although many rabbis will speak on anything that is of contemporary concern to their congregations and to the community. It may be topical or textual. The format of the Jewish sermon follows the generally accepted format of most modern preaching. On the Holy Days a more Biblical or "legal" sermon is given: the Sabbath before Passover; the Sabbath of Repentance between Rosh Hashanah (New Year), and Yom Kippur (Day of Atonement). Sometimes on the eve of Atonement the preacher deals with the problem of sin, repentance, and atonement. The sermon today is part of worship, and the ethical stress is most marked.

Silver has declared that he began his ministry in the orthodox fashion of selecting a text and expounding it. He soon changed his method and worked from a theme rather than a text. Here he found that illustrative texts usually came in abundance. His sermon topic is stated in the form of a problem of moral import and relevance to people in the pews. Some problems may be worldwide, economic, political, or social; others are more intimate in relating to destiny and the present life. He has found that the most appealing are those which relate to parents and children, to marriage and the home, to human struggle and aspiration, to the meaning of human existence and how to face life.

Significantly, Silver did not discuss books or plays in the pulpit. To him they were not subject matter for legitimate discussion. He knew the temptation of using this approach but said that "all this is book reviewing, not preaching." He tried to bring a positive message. He knew he must not be a confused guide to his people. He tried, as he said, "not to exhort, but to interpret and to illumine. I present the judgment of religion, as I see it, on problems or phases of human experience. I present the accumulated wisdom of religion. I spend little time defending religion per se, I let the message speak for itself."

His method of preaching is revealed when he writes:

> I find that I do my best work when I have been deeply stirred by something which I witnessed, read or experienced. A prolonged uneventful period of quiet study and reflection will give to my sermons a refined academic air and perhaps the polish of an essay. They will read well in print, but as sermons they fail of their objective. They leave the listener unmoved and unillumined. They are not living trees—only lumber. When, however, I have been emotionally or intellectually stirred by something with which I contacted in my pastoral work—some flash of rare human courage, or sacrifice, or joy, some glint of human tragedy, something which plumbs the depths—then there is added the touch of the living coal to the spoken word. Wings soar. There is a lift and an inrush of the spirit. A mood is created. Something *happens!*

Silver said he would have preferred to preach only once a month but the weekly stint kept him busy. He did not speak without preparation, but always wrote out his sermons. Then, decrying any inspiration of the moment, he would memorize the script, thus avoiding any reading of a manuscript. He did not try to be "modern" and did not aim to impress his people with scientific jargon or current shibboleths. To him, "a new terminology does not necessarily imply a new truth." He did not preach to the "modern mind." To him that mind was a passing phenomenon. He sought to speak of and to the eternal spirit of man. Man's basic hunger and need remain the same.

In dealing with social issues or political crises (such as the War and Jewry's part in this as well as the European holocaust), Silver believed in using principles of truth and judgment which had stood the test of the ages—the unchanging and immovable values. He tried to recapture the enduring realities in the moral realm when preaching. His aim was to correlate the temporal with the eternal. He said:

"I try to recapture for men something of their lost spiritual equilibrium and perspective and to lead them into the quieter fields of thought where one may reflect not so much on what is timely as on what is timeless."

Of course, there were those who did not care to listen to this type of preaching in a busy, restless generation. Silver stood for preaching which touched life at all points. Preaching to him always had something of the volcanics of prophecy. His voice would woo and warn, convince and convert, counsel and show compassion. He was fearless in his convictions, yet never spoke as an agitator or propagandist; he was guide and teacher through preaching. He had the kindly touch, an absence of the whip. His own reactions would be his means of knowing when he preached well or otherwise. He did not need the reactions of the people in the pews. "When I have given utterance to something very close to me, emanating from my inner self, to something necessary and vital, which I feel to be, in substance and manner, in the main stream of the great religious tradition, I *know* that I have preached well." In that self-disclosure Rabbi Silver stands as one of the best out of Judaism in America.

In **Abraham Joshua Heschel (1907-1972)** American Judaism has a leader in teaching and preaching in an age of ferment. As Professor of Jewish Ethics and Mysticism at Jewish Theological Seminary, New York, he has influenced his generation as an interpreter of Judaism. Like others caught in the struggle with Hitler, he came in 1940 to assume his present position. The inner life of devotion has always captivated this preacher and teacher even as he was aware of the social, political, and legal demands on the Jewish people now scattered among the nations. In *Man's Quest for God* (1954), we have a sampling of his style and emphasis. Heschel stresses prayer and symbolism as part of common worship. Words are important and have dignity and meaning. Preaching, to this Jewish teacher, is that part of worship which should lead to the offering up of our desires to God in prayer, and this in the context of praise. This challenges the Christian idea that preaching is the climax of a service or the goal of worship. Jewish preaching from this foundation cannot but stimulate the sluggish minds of our age. What is the goal of the religious people of all faiths in America when in their houses of worship? Is life purified? Social effort and involvement in the nation and in the community are worthwhile—if the inner acts of worship produce strength and creative energy from God.

Jewish preaching still maintains its traditional ways in the teaching and nurture of congregational life. Many rabbis take note of the events of the passing moment and will exhort and speak out on the issues which confront the minds of this generation. Such preaching, with comment and interpretation in the light of modern Judaism, is what the Reformed and the Liberal congregations expect. The Orthodox still maintain the Scriptures and Torah as the basis of all liturgy and preaching. Judaism in America is set within a changing era and an erosion of traditional ways can be noted. Over all, both Orthodox and others still maintain observance of the Hebrew Year of Holy Days and Feasts and Festivals.

Nationally Known Preachers

The twentieth century for American preaching has been variously estimated and critically assessed. Comparison of American preaching with that of other countries would indicate that here there is less doctrinal and expository preaching. However, American preaching is livelier and more colorful in its richness and versatility. There have been those who have seen the decline of preaching, and there is warrant for this judgment when we compare some of the pulpit efforts with those of earlier centuries when the pulpit held a more commanding influence in the nation. However, there are others who maintain that the era of great preaching has not ended in spite of the critics.

An interesting experiment was attempted in the years 1924-25. *The Christian Century* editor Charles Clayton Morrison undertook to find the twenty-five most influential and representative living preachers at that time. The entire Protestant ministry of the United States was polled; ballots were put into the hands of about ninety thousand ministers in all parts of the country. These included ministers of all groups and schools of theological thought in all denominations. Each minister was invited to name ten preachers whom he regarded as the most influential—the men of deepest and most prophetic vision; the men of outstanding pulpit power; the men whose messages, in his estimation, most vitally interpreted the mind of Christ; the pulpiteers whose thinking most deeply influenced the thinking of the church and the course of events in the life of the nation. When the poll closed the number of ballots returned was about twenty-five thousand. A total of 1,162 names were voted for. Credit was given to every name on every ballot, and the twenty-five men receiving the largest number of votes was announced. No announcement was made as to the relative standing of the preachers in the list of twenty-five; the names were announced in alphabetical order. The word *greatest* was used only in terms of objective service.

Several outstanding preachers were given prominence in the poll. Their ministries have covered long periods in historic pulpits. These selected men represented a large number of contemporaries who in distinctive spheres of service have contributed much to the American scene. In their own communions they have been respected for their leadership and pulpit influence above their fellows. Perhaps they have received the publicity, but they would be the first to speak up for their lesser-known brethren who also have carried the load of preaching year after year without fanfare but with devotion and diligence.

Henry Sloane Coffin (1877-1954) was one of the Presbyterian group whose ministry in New York at the Madison Avenue Presbyterian Church demonstrated how a pastoral-visitation-preaching approach to people brings steady results in the building of the church. His later years as President of Union Theological Seminary, New York, and his Professorship in Homiletics there, widened his ministry as he educated young men in the historic art of preaching. A clear thinker and an able expositor, he exemplified scholarship and sincerity in his sermons. His social Christianity was poised and balanced as it sprang from doctrinal affirmations. His Yale Lectures, dealing with the theme *In a Day of Social Rebuilding* (1918), reveal the sensitivity of his heart of concern at a time when the nation was torn by war and when the demands made upon the church and its conscience were increased. To Coffin preaching included the work of a shepherd, a teacher, a friend. His Warrack Lectures in Scotland, *What to Preach,* reveal his continued interest in correlating doctrine with the practical, the spiritual with the natural.

John Timothy Stone (1868-1954) came to the flowering of his preaching at The Fourth Presbyterian Church of Chicago. Resourceful and dynamic in outreach, Stone led this congregation into manifold ministries which, however, were always inspired by his messages of courage and hope. His preaching was matched by his winning of men during the week as he contacted leaders in groups and in private. He believed in "the victorious life," knowing full well that the great battles of life are of the soul. A pastorate of twenty-one years is testing, but Stone measured up with preaching which came out of intensive preparation and a heart which recruited men for Christ.

William Pierson Merrill (1867-1954) sustained a strong ministry at the Brick Presbyterian Church, New York, for twenty-seven years. There he held people by wise preaching in which he endeavored to bridge the tensions of the controversial years of modernism and fundamentalism. His Yale Lectures had as title, *The Freedom of the Preacher* (1922), a theme in keeping with his experience. His moderate views and his original treatment in lecture and in sermon enabled him to carry out the Protestant principle of the liberty of testifying to his faith. His aim was ever to see Christ as "the way, the truth, and the life."

James Isaac Vance (1862-1939) had his ripest years of service as pastor at the First Presbyterian Church, Nashville, Tennessee. He served there for two terms of ministry. He was not an evangelist, yet did not hesitate to hire a theater near the church for his own evangelistic services on Sunday nights during the winter months. His Sprunt Lectures on *Being a Preacher* spell out his ideals. He was noted for his evangelical preaching. The sermon "The Old Rugged Cross" is a fitting sample of his type of preaching. The well-known hymn title is used to give point to the message which deals with the grim reality of that timeless event. His was effective preaching as seen by the responses in hundreds of lives.

George Arthur Buttrick (1892-) is known primarily for his ministry at Madison Avenue Presbyterian Church, New York, and as the successor to Henry Sloane Coffin. In delivery he had a quiet force, a dignity of utterance, a probing word, and the occasional thrust of the sword. His preaching had in it the quality of the artist who has woven the tapestry well. His knowledge of literature was freely incorporated. He used a fully written manuscript in preparation and then let it come alive for him in the pulpit. His Yale Lectures, *Jesus Came Preaching* (1932), embody his secrets of preparation and utterance. He had to toil vigorously to be a master of the art of preaching.

Chicago has had its share of notable preachers. At the heart of the city, in what is known as the "loop," there is a church with no regular church building. The Central Church meets at the Central Music Hall. Several distinguished men have served there, reaching the crowds at the heart of the city and drawing discriminating hearers from afar. Among them was **Newell Dwight Hillis (1858-1929)** who later succeeded Lyman Abbott at Plymouth Church, Brooklyn. As he had followed David Swing, Presbyterian controversialist, he was assured of public interest. His preaching was for the cultured, and he had a brilliant and distinctive style. His sermons were published in a Chicago paper on Monday mornings, an index of the influence he wielded. The sermons had a pictorial quality in them and in structure showed originality.

Frank Wakeley Gunsaulus (1856-1921) followed Hillis and maintained an almost exotic ministry of public appeal. The Congregationalist preacher had a strong voice which could be projected in the large auditorium he used. He had eloquence and a command of lavish language. When Robert G. Ingersoll attacked Christianity, Gunsaulus delivered a magnificent sermon based on I Corinthians 14:10 in which he made mention of famous men and incidents throughout history, showing the debt of mankind to the Bible and the Christian faith. He lacked the strong evangelical note, but his contribution is garnered in the Yale Lectures, *The Minister and the Spiritual Life* (1910). Poetic expression and felicity of phrase combined to make the Latin-endowed preacher rich in color and homiletical backbone.

Frederick Franklin Shannon (1877-1947) was selected for the Central Church of Chicago by Gunsaulus who found this young preacher whose sermons had already made their way into print. Homiletically, he instinctively brought everything under tribute to the making of a sermon. His genius was in line with some of the masters of the centuries. With the advent of radio his listeners multiplied. Nothing sensational or superficial is found in his sermons. Literary allusion is imbedded with Scripture. In comparison with Gunsaulus he lacked the large frame and seemed slight in stature. Nevertheless, in preaching he became eloquent in his bodily movements and gestures which were tuned to his voice. He never repeated a sermon to his regular congregation. He preached from an outline and then after delivery would write out the sermon. To Shannon the homilist was not a maker of sermons, but a preacher was the proclaimer of the life eternal.

Among the distinguished Methodist preachers was **Edwin Holt Hughes (1866-1950)**, who came from a background of circuit riders. His appointment as Bishop carried on that time-honored practice. Throughout the nation and the churches Hughes preached as an evangelist and under-shepherd. He was a master of assemblies and a teacher and leader of men, and with his Welsh tradition he stirred the souls of men. In him were wedded preaching and personality. The lilt of his words, the high moments of proclamation, and the warmth of the heart have characterized his preaching. He was more appreciated for his spoken than for his written word. The message was poured out with passion as he thought through the theme of the sermon on his feet and under the compulsion of the moment.

William Fraser McDowell (1858-1937) was another fine example of Methodist preaching and as a Bishop he exercised leadership in a transitional time of changing theologies. His chief distinction was that of a religious statesman. Churchmanship engaged his time on behalf of his church at large. Nevertheless, he found time to preach; and in his ministries to students, his lectures to colleges, and his missionary interests, he did not neglect the proclamation of the Word of God. The Yale Lectures, *Good Ministers of Jesus Christ* (1917), fittingly embodies his ambition of what a preacher should be—the shepherd of the people. His insights here are gathered around special texts of the New Testament: (1) The Ministry of Revelation—"Show us the Father"; (2) The Ministry of Redemption—"He shall save his people from their sins"; (3) The Ministry of Incarnation—"The Word was made flesh, and dwelt among us"; (4) The Ministry of Reconciliation—"We are ambassadors for Christ." And much besides. These excerpts demonstrate the spiritual illumination of a rich mind and heart. Wedded to unusual gifts of illustration, his preaching is worthy of emulation for the practical contribution it made.

Robert Guthrie Freeman (1878-1940), a Scot who came to America as a lad, was, like many others, motivated toward the ministry by a faithful Bible class teacher. His story has been repeated many times. His major ministry was at The First Presbyterian Church, Pasadena, California. There his preaching had in it the heart of the supernatural gospel. Personal spiritual cultivation and devotion was apparent in his work. He had a remarkably carrying voice, mellow and flexible. His elocution and diction approached perfection. The Scottish accent was not a handicap, rather the opposite! In one volume of sermons, *What of The Twelve?*, humor and sympathy shine through as he unfolds the characteristics of the apostles. He had the knack of using the best poetry without overdoing it. He wrote verses himself, and the soul of the poet shone through his preaching. A preacher is the total sum of his heredity, faith, training, and experience. Freeman stands out as that faithful minister of Jesus Christ.

The dawn of the twentieth century in America brought, in the judgment of Edgar De Witt Jones, one of the rich periods of preaching because of the able preachers then ministering from the pulpits of our churches. In 1933 he gave that appraisal out of long acquaintance with the outstanding active personalities. He commented on the general qualities of preaching which de-emphasized theology and stressed ethical and social notes with simplicity, directness, and restraint. Later, in 1951, he presented more mature conclusions of his long study in *The Royalty of the Pulpit.* Jones saw in the seventy-five years of the Beecher Lectures on Preaching at Yale the "close relation to the varying currents of thought and experience," historical trends being reflected in the character of preaching. Drawing sketches of the great personalities, he notes the shift from the formal, oratorical style to the direct and conversational.

One of the losses has been the decline in doctrinal, expository, and dialectic sermons found in other generations. While this is true generally, there is still a segment loyal to these age-long ideals, namely the evangelical preachers who adhere to the timeless gospel and the conviction that creeds and confessions do express what the apostolic teaching began. No one can deny the need of the ethical and social emphases in modern preaching, but some of it is done at the muting of the evangelistic trumpet note. The appeal to the conscience and to the will is also less potent and the role of the prophet has been in decline. The Billy Sunday type with his pulpit actions and gyrations has practically disappeared and a new type of evangelist, more restrained, has emerged. The advent of the radio has also affected the style of preaching. The conversational preacher has appeared with more topical sermons and less of Biblical exposition and themes except where the evangelical continues his witness.

Possibly 1930 is a watershed in American preaching. At the time of the Great Depression which affected the whole of life, there was a marked shift in the message of the pulpit. Gradual changes were on the way with the influence of the idea of progress (to be dissipated by a second World War and its aftermath), the evolutionary theory as applied to life and to the Scriptures, and the decline of revivalism. The controversy of the 1920s prepared the way for a confused pulpit in the 1930s, and the attempt to relate to human social and economic needs led the pulpit to be a sounding-board which projected more of current opinions and less of the eternal truth. Changing emphases in American preaching were most marked where theological controversy was current in colleges, universities, and in seminaries, and where the distillation of these new ideas penetrated the churches of the land. The so-called "modernism" or "liberalism" in theology was chiefly involved in this.

The social crisis of the 1930s raised up new voices in the pulpit dealing with Socialism, the Communist uprising, industrial problems, the threat of revolution, and the social gospel in relation to life situations. Many of the pulpiteers of the more liberal persuasion believed that the gospel of a better society, a new environment, a reconciliation of classes and of nations, support of the League of Nations and later of the United Nations should be part of preaching. Many held the conviction that a warless world was possible in their generation. But depression, secularism, and the breakdown of moral standards everywhere offset these unrealistic ideals. The religious press through magazines, journals, and church publications had promoted much of this idealism.

With the coming of radio and television American preaching has undergone changes in style and structure. Some have attempted to retain the old ways of preparing the manuscript and then reading it. Many are not good enough readers to make it "live" when delivered. Others have maintained their usual style of preaching from notes, keeping their congregations interested from week to week. The advent of the radio has altered the style of others who have been adaptable to the new method of reaching out to an unseen group of listeners. Here the idea has been to visualize an individual and speak to him through the script for radio preaching. The preacher sometimes has his regular service broadcast unchanged. On the other hand, the special service is one in which the preacher speaks only to the radio audience and therefore trims his words, shortens his format, and endeavors to speak simply and clearly without theological terms for the unknown listener who it is assumed knows little or nothing about the Christian faith.

In this period, whether by radio or in the regular course of public worship, many pastors stand out as the most influential throughout

America. Their names suggest that preaching was a force in the land and the pulpit respected in that generation.

Charles Reynolds Brown (1862-1950) made a rich contribution to preaching both as a pastor and as professor at Yale. He became the Dean of Yale Divinity School and also had the distinction of delivering the Yale Lectures on Preaching on two occasions, *The Social Message of the Modern Pulpit* (1906) and *The Art of Preaching* (1923). Embodied in these as well as in volumes of sermons are his ideas and ideals for preaching.

To Brown preaching sprang from deep sources of brooding and preparation. In the idea of Moses delivering the Israelites out of Egypt, he saw the analogy of modern man waiting to be set free from the many enslavements common to his age. If this was geared to the social issues of that day, this was what preaching had to deal with from time to time. The need was for moral leadership and there was a Biblical basis for freedom and for such leadership.

Preaching also was seen as an art. Brown, pastor in a Congregational church and then Dean of a theological school, stood for the rights of preaching when critics were beginning to downgrade its importance. No apology was needed for preaching. Length was no barrier if the preaching was interesting; humor was permissible when spontaneous. The speaking man stood always under the Great Taskmaster's eye. Sanity, common sense, and diligence in preparation gave him his appeal under God. He claimed that the King James Version of the Bible and Shakespeare's plays enabled him to cultivate his style in preaching. Hundreds of students were given ideals for preaching by a master whose Biblical messages were related to human needs.

Charles Edward Jefferson (1860-1937) was known as pastor of the Broadway Tabernacle Church, New York, in an area linked to the world of the theatre, movies, clubs, and other forms of entertainment. For forty years he ministered and also published many books of sermons and lectures. In an area of sophistication, he never succumbed to the cheap or the sensational. He steadfastly maintained a realistic ministry of Christian witness and his preaching was straightforward and never demeaning to the gospel.

Jefferson had a rich, trained voice. In a community of actors he could stand up with the best. He was a rhetorician but preferred to preach in simple language. He was a doctrinal preacher, the atonement being central. There was a precision and orderly manner in his utterances. Jefferson was also a preacher to preachers and his books, *The Minister as Shepherd* and *The Minister as Prophet,* demonstrate the orderly mind and the passionate heart of the preacher. His Yale Lectures, *The Building of the Church* (1910), illustrate his conviction that the best preaching is within the context of the church. While others think of the Bible or worship as avenues for preaching, here is a choice idea that the whole church engages in preaching. Because Christ is building the church, this is the context for the preacher's whole life and ministry. Jefferson spoke as a preacher "out of life to life."

In **William Leroy Stidger (1885-1949)** America and the Methodist Church in particular had a preacher of extraordinary gifts. Poet, journalist, publicist, traveler, litterateur, lecturer, advertising specialist, as well as preacher, Stidger has been appraised as a combination of Walt Whitman, Buffalo Bill and Theodore Roosevelt. If he did not make the front page of the newspaper once a week something was wrong! What Peter Cartwright was to another century, Stidger was to the twentieth. "Bill" Stidger was the type of man who exuded health, confidence, optimism, warmth, and genuine good will to all sorts of people, whether in private or in public. His preaching had that wholesome quality about it. He loved to read, to study, to preach. He read voraciously, wrote diligently, and filled the days with work. He was trained by an editor in a newspaper office to concentrate and so write accurately and correctly the first time. His secret is in the title of his lectures, *Preaching Out of the Overflow* (1929). In Boston he touched the public as few preachers since Brooks, and also coached many would-be preachers to work at their task of preaching.

Charles Clayton Morrison (1874-1966) had the unique distinction of serving a denomination and yet having another pulpit which reached out to the world. Brought up in the Disciples of Christ Church, now the United Church of Christ, he was soon marked for lecturing and writing beyond the pastorate. He became the editor of *The Christian Century* (1908) and in it, during his lifetime, found a sounding board for his theology and religious convictions. As a preacher of sermons he lacked spontaneity as he felt for the right word, even hesitating until it came forth. His was the kind of preaching which was the distillation of his study and reading, coming alive as he brooded in the pulpit. However, his chief ministry was through the printed page. His Yale Lectures, *What Is Christianity?,* implies that he was more concerned with content than with techniques of preaching. He was the reformer, the educator, the advocate, the statesman, the peacemaker, the uniter, combining all these in seeking to bring churches, denominations, theologies, and people into a unity for this new age.

The preaching-teaching ministries of Morrison and his church body have emphasized those doctrines which they held to be of supreme importance. For example, the doctrine of baptism has been taught in the mode of immersion only. In fact, where the word *baptize* occurs in the New Testament the word *immerse* has been substituted as the interpretation and the practice. This view has been surprising when it is remembered that Campbell sought to go back to New Testament times for the orders of the church and sought to include all Christians in a universal ideal. But here, at one point of practice, he excluded many other Christians! The government of the church was seen to be Congregational in the best democratic sense. Each congregation was autonomous; no denomination was called "the church" but only the local congregations were entitled to use the word *church* in that localized congregational sense.

Morrison, however, stood in a more modern day to relate these truths in his preaching and yet seek at the same time to broaden the fellowship to all who could find oneness with them. In his honest search for catholicity and the oneness of the whole church in an ecumenical ideal, Morrison saw the dangers and perils of fragmentation. He saw the passing of much of sectarianism and his own group making strides toward a closer working with other groups different in government and doctrine. He believed that "over all our private and group ideological convictions is the fellowship of Christ in his living community. This living community *is* Christianity, and nothing else is. To it we bring our beliefs for its judgment. And to it we bring our disagreements in belief. For it is in the communion of the faith, and preeminently at the one altar where the whole body of Christ meets in common worship, that our disagreements may find reconciliation in the unity of the Spirit and the bond of peace." He envisaged a catholicity of baptism, ordination, education, liturgy, Lord's Supper, and creed as the goal of this dream.

One other eminent example of Disciples of Christ Church preaching is **Edgar DeWitt Jones (1876-1956)**, who is best known for his book *The Royalty of the Pulpit* (1951). Dr. Jones had read all of the then seventy volumes in the Yale Lectureship series on Preaching, hence the title and scope of the book. This strenuous task he completed because he loved to preach himself and he was one of the few men who knew most of the living lecturers as well as having knowledge of others. His skillful pen is obvious and the attention given to the analysis of preachers, types, periods, and emphases is done in a masterful way. Other books of his include *American Preachers of Today, Lords of Speech,* and *Lincoln and the Preachers.* His own ministry was crowned by the long pastorate at the Central Woodward Christian Church, Detroit, where he maintained a high level of excellence in preaching.

The sermon "The Light on the Lord's Face," based on the text "For God, who commanded the light to shine out of darkness, hath shined in our hearts, to give the light of the knowledge of the glory of God in the face of Jesus Christ" (II Cor. 4:6), brings into focus a much needed truth. The Christian life is seen here not as rules and regulations but as something to be viewed with imagination and devotion, and approached with awe. As a painting is often spoken of by a title or reference, so the whole of Christianity is compressed in this one text. Here the vision of the Christ is replete with color and description. The "face" is the character, personality, being—not the countenance.

Merton Stacher Rice (1872-1943) supplied the regular pulpit of a Methodist church but with the foibles and fancies also seen in the ministries of Talmage, Bishop Quayle, and the evangelism of Billy Sunday. He was the storyteller, the weaver of tales, the folksy speaker, the born preacher not bound by rules. His sermons in print do not read like some of the masters, but the "punch" in them in delivery must have been something to hear. His major pastorate in Detroit for over twenty years is indicative of how a preacher becomes part of a city and stands to speak to its conscience.

Rice was a man's man, and his anecdotes and humor made him appealing to many outside the regular congregation. The torrent of words was not always given according to the rules, but he struck home with his rugged speech. In front of the Woodward Avenue Church there stands a statue depicting a man struggling with a serpent entwined around a leg. The man has grasped the reptile around the neck and is winning the struggle. The serpent is in the throes of death. The man's face is upturned and his look is one of victory. Here is epitomized the message of the preacher who had told a story of this nature and was asked by a sculptor who had heard him for permission to fashion such a statue. In one way, this embodies the truth which Rice stood to proclaim—that no one needs to despair in the struggle with sin: triumph is possible through divine strength given in Christ.

The preaching of Rice was informal but incisive. He preached with buoyancy and sincerity. Nothing of despair or gloom pervaded his ministry. He was the optimist who saw the victory of faith for everyman. The aim of his preaching was to win people over to the side of Christ. Theological study was left behind in the sermon delivery where he strove to be natural and down to earth, using common language understood by the people. Behind this were a personal faith and strong convictions in the foundation of the unchanging Christian gospel. Above all, Rice said, he feared the loss of passion in his task. To lose passion is to lose all.

Samuel Moor Shoemaker (1893-1963) brought to the Episcopal Church and to the worldwide community of faith a buoyancy and witness which made an effective impact upon his generation. In New York he saw a struggling parish come alive in Christ and in Pittsburgh he reaped the fruits of his ministry in countless lives. While this was partly due to his personal dealing with men, his preaching was the background of all he attempted. He also worked with Alcoholics Anonymous, the Moral Rearmament (Oxford Group Movement), and Faith at Work, but his major ministry lay among men in the local parish.

Shoemaker had the elements of a prophet, and his evangelism was couched in a modern approach yet with the Word of God at its heart. Twenty-eight books came from his pen, and with the radio broadcasting of his messages he reached thousands. His books include *Twice-Born Ministers; The Conversion of the Church; With the Holy Spirit and Fire; How to Become a Christian*, the titles indicating the depth and quality of his preaching beforehand. He saw himself as pastor, priest, and preacher.

As preacher he believed that people were moved by the sermon. The message then should have a strong element of teaching in it, for many are spiritually illiterate. He made his preaching evangelistic in intent and presented the Good News with conviction, clarity, passion, and compassion. He did not disdain emotion, saying that just as two young people finding each other in love would be impossible without emotion, so the Christian experience must have emotion in it. Thus he tried to reach the heart.

Upon the conversion of individuals, Shoemaker sought to enlist them into groups and through the group engage in fellowship, prayer, reading, and sharing, so that they in turn would reach out to others through the normal contacts of life. This was one of the effective avenues of missionary work. The sermons of this great heart stressed the "Church Year" for guidance in the choice of themes, reiterating the basic truths of Christianity. He knew that in preaching to many, he was always speaking to one. That was his secret—to reach one man at a time. His preaching brought renewal and revival within the Episcopal Church.

Ralph Washington Sockman (1889-1970), pastor of Christ Church, Methodist, New York, for forty-four years, also sustained an incredible ministry as the preacher each week on the National Radio Pulpit for thirty-four years. He gave the Yale Lectures on Preaching, *The Highway of God* (1941), based upon an arresting interpretation of the ministry of John the Baptist. Among his published sermons were books: *The Higher Happiness* (1950); *How to Believe* (1953); and *The Meaning of Suffering* (1961).

His style of preaching was molded by an awareness of the congregation and the listener. Transients and visitors attended the Methodist preacher's ministry, and thus he centered the sermon on "some life principle or life situation and then let the radiations reflect on the current problem." Always down to earth, wrestling with Biblical passages and incidents, he made the gospel relevant. In delivery he was conversational and talked as man to man, and was blessed with a rich and strong voice which was used effectively.

Peter Marshall (1902-1949) is remembered for his dynamic ministry at the New York Avenue Church, Washington, D.C. during a period of American life when the capital city of the nation gave an ear to what he said. His rise from a Scottish immigrant to pastor of one of the distinguished pulpits of America is a story oft repeated in many walks of life. Gaining a theological education, with limited means, he made the most of his time by industry and the exercise of certain gifts.

His native burr in speech was not played down, but utilized for an effect to which many were receptive. His burly, manly figure, and his man-to-man way of speaking had appeal. He cultivated a written manuscript and learned how to set forth the paragraphs and sentences in an unusual style to catch the eye and give emphasis. Thus as a reader of a sermon he was able to read well and put himself into the message.

He was evangelical in spirit and Biblical in background. Allied to his pulpit ministry was the opportunity to serve as Chaplain to the Senate. There each day he opened the proceedings with prayer. His prayers did not follow the conventional line, but usually were written with some relevant and pithy expression to catch the ear of those who shared in that act. These prayers were recorded as was the custom and later were copied. Out of this came a wider influence for Marshall and perhaps this was one of the ways in which he became so well known across the nation.

When at his early death sermons of his were published, there was an immediate response in enlarged circulation and distribution. *Mr. Jones, Meet the Master* is a volume which brings some of his best sermons into focus. Here the preacher talks to the ordinary man and seeks to introduce his Master to him. Cheerful in outlook, attractive as a personality, gifted in speech and eloquence, Peter Marshall became a popular preacher. How he became that is one of the elusive mysteries but his concentration to the task developed his gifts and thus he served.

American preaching in the first half of this century has seen the rise of many new personalities whose influence cannot yet be measured within their lifetime. However, a few stand in the succession of those who already have made their impact.

John Sutherland Bonnell (1893-) came from Winnipeg, Canada, to take the pulpit at Fifth Avenue Presbyterian Church, New York. There he sustained a remarkable standard of steady preaching and a counseling ministry. Overshadowed in publicity by his neighbor Norman Vincent Peale, he brought the insights of earlier training in hospital and mental institution to bear upon human needs. His psychologically oriented sermons brought therapeutic help to listeners and complemented the private cure of souls in the study.

Robert James McCracken (1904-1973) came from Glasgow, Scotland, and McMaster University Divinity School, Hamilton, Canada, to succeed Harry Emerson Fosdick at Riverside (Baptist) Church, New York. At the beginning of his many years in that pastorate he seemed to "copy" his distinguished predecessor in the life-situation sermon. However, he wisely left that type of sermon and turned to the more traditional method of Biblical exposition allied to practical needs. With vivid phrasing, arresting illustration and careful exposition, he sustained an exacting ministry with divine encouragement. With Scottish order and marshalled logic, he dealt with basic issues. His first volume published, *Questions People Ask,* is a sampling of that fine heritage of solid preaching.

Edward Lee Roy Elson (1907-) spent twenty-six years as pastor of The National Presbyterian Church, Washington, D.C. From other pastorates and service as chaplain in World War II he brought the fruits of tested years to the ministry at the heart of the nation's capital. There he has touched political leaders as well as presidents and outstanding people from all nations. He has addressed himself to the issues of the day with directness of speech and sound Biblical exposition touched with the evangelical spirit. With imagination and skill he has preached to the times but always with eternal values in view. Peace or war, plenty or poverty, multitude or individual, he has proclaimed the gospel without apology. Like Peter Marshall earlier, he was to serve as Chaplain to the Senate.

Gerald Hamilton Kennedy (1907-), a Methodist, stands as a gracious example of a pastoral preacher in the grand tradition of the spirit of Wesley. Pastor and professor, he is best known for his leadership at large as Bishop of Portland, Oregon, and then as Bishop of Los Angeles, California. He has always maintained a close pastoral relation to people and congregations, although his overseer work as a bishop has given him a wider constituency.

To Kennedy, preaching has always been a delight and a joy. In delivering many series of lectures in colleges and seminaries across the country, he has ever maintained the thesis that *With Singleness of Heart* (1951) the pastoral ministry enshrines the best for God's servants. In the care of souls lies the heartbeat of the true shepherd and preacher. His many published books carry out this mandate in numerous interpretations. Volumes of sermons also have come from his preaching and these stress the same view.

Kennedy saw the pastor as critic, leader, and repairer, but he must be saint, revealer, and evangelist if he is to fulfill his ministry. He saw the peril of the popular preacher in becoming a double-minded man. The plan he follows is to plan his preaching at least a year in advance. Subjects, texts, ideas, illustrations are pondered and filed. Outlines are made tentatively for months ahead, and then each week comes the discipline of writing, transcribing to notes, then rereading, until he is ready to preach without notes.

However, method is not all. In the pulpit Kennedy comes alive with saturation of the subject. He lives for that. Throughout the sermon there is discerned the personal faith of the preacher. In *Who*

Speaks for God?, a volume of sermon-essays, the idea is stressed that the pastor-preacher stands up to testify. In the sermon, "Why Am I a Christian?" based on Luke 4:18 and John 17:18, Kennedy's style and spirit are obvious. The language is simple and the thought is clear. Illustrations are like windows of light when needed. Well read in modern literature and noting the passing events, Kennedy stands as an interpreter of God's love to frustrated modern man.

Many are the names of men who have made their contribution in this field. Among those whose ministries in the art of preaching have been influential the following are worthy of note.

David James Burrell (1844-1926), Reformed Church in North America, is known for his preaching at Marble Collegiate Church, New York, and then his teaching of homiletics at Princeton Seminary. Conservative in theology, he also delivered the Sprunt Lectures on Homiletics at Union Seminary, Richmond, Virginia.

Another Reformed Church pastor is **Howard Garberich Hageman (1921-)**. He served at First Church, Newark, New Jersey, where his preaching was noted for its excellence in content, balance in structure, progression in thought, and a surprise element in the selection of texts. His preaching has been extended by articles in church magazines, theological journals, and the exposition of the Reformed doctrine in the art of worship found in his volume *Pulpit and Table* (1962).

In the Reformed tradition but with sharper distinction of orthodoxy was **Herman Hoeksema (1886-1965)**. This is noted clearly in his *An Exposition of the Heidelberg Catechism* (9 vols., 1955). From his Dutch background came *Door Strijd Tot Overwinning* (1930), a series of meditations in which are found strong dogmatic affirmations, characteristic also of his preaching. His major work was *Reformed Dogmatics* (1966), the fruit of a lifetime of study and teaching in the church of which he was pastor and also as Professor of Dogmatics in the Theological School of the Protestant Reformed Churches, Grand Rapids, Michigan.

From the Netherlands came **Samuel Volbeda (1881-1953)** to teach and preach that preaching is pastoral in its genius. Theology and history were the allies for his Biblically-based strength of conviction. During the Professorship of Practical Theology at Calvin Seminary in Grand Rapids, Michigan, he influenced many of the present day pastors of the Christian Reformed Church. His example and teaching have been effective in nourishing and building up the family of God in the Bible and Reformed faith, so necessary to the strength of the congregations.

Garfield Bromley Oxnam (1891-1963), a leader of Methodism, brought passion and verve to his preaching. He served as pastor at the Mount Vernon Methodist Church at Baltimore (1937-48), the First Church at Evanston (1950-62), and at Christ Church, New York. The many lectures on the subject of preaching and his interpretive spirit for the new days then in process of being born gave him a commanding leadership for a period. Among his lectures were *Contemporary Preaching* (1931); *Creative Preaching* (1930); *Effective Preaching* (1929); *Preaching and the Social Crisis* (1933); *Preaching in a Revolutionary Age* (1944); and *Varieties of Present Day Preaching* (1932). A strong ecumenical spirit dominated his preaching and teaching.

Harold Augustus Bosley (1907-) at Evanston, Illinois, and now at Christ Church, New York, follows in the train of Oxnam and of Sockman. Acutely sensitive to the spirit of the age, he endeavors to preach to catch the ear of the secular mind. *Preaching on Controversial Issues* (1953) carries samplings of this method. Form and function are wedded together in effective style.

Although Episcopal preaching in the 1900s had no Phillips Brooks, several men are worthy of note. Among representative preachers who had influence upon the training and education of their students and congregations was **Angus Dun (1892-1971),** who graced the Cathedral Church with solid doctrinal preaching. *The Saving Person* (1957) sums up the theological emphasis needed in this period. As Bishop of Washington, D.C. (1944-1962), Angus Dun gave strong leadership. Others of the Episcopal Church include **Henry Knox Sherrill (1890-),** Presiding Bishop of the Protestant Episcopal Church (1947-58), and a Yale Lecturer (1948). **Frank Dean Gifford (1891-1970)** was Dean of the Philadelphia Divinity School (1946-59). **Austin Pardue (1899-1968),** Bishop of Pittsburgh (1944-68); **Theodore Otto Wedel (1892-1970),** Warden of The College of Preachers, Washington, D.C. (1943-60); **John Heuss (1908-1966),** Rector, Trinity Church, New York (1951-66); and **Frederick Myers Morris (1906-),** Dean, St. Mark's Cathedral, Minneapolis (1948-54), were excellent leaders in their ministries.

In **Stephen Fielding Bayne, Jr. (1908-1974),** Bishop of Olympia, Seattle, Washington (1947-60) the Anglican Church found a nimble mind, clear thinker, and an interpreter of his church's theological ideas as applied to preaching, ecumenicity, and social, family, and national relationships. His call to be the first Executive Officer for the worldwide Anglican Communion at the Lambeth Conference, London, gave him outlet for his gifts and leadership.

Walter Russell Bowie (1882-1968) is well known as a prolific writer, and his deep feeling for people made him an outstanding preacher. He drew from the rich resources of extensive reading and reflection. For thirty-one years a pastor, he served at St. Paul's, Richmond, Virginia, and Grace Church, New York City. He was Professor of Practical Theology at Union Theological Seminary, New York City (1939-50), and thereafter Professor of Homiletics at the Virginia Protestant Episcopal Seminary (1950-1955).

The several groups of the Lutheran Church in America have had outstanding men as teachers and preachers. Usually the conservative emphasis has prevailed, but in the changing era new methods of communications have been used. While liturgical preaching has predominated and law and gospel has been central, there has come more and more a wider sweep of appeal.

Otto Albert Frederick Geiseman (1893-), Missouri Synod, has been a notable pastoral preacher, serving since 1922 at the Grace Church, River Forest, Illinois. Broadcasting regularly, he has also seen his sermons published. He speaks of marriage, peace, old truths for a new day, and comes to grips with modern issues.

Richard Rudolph Caemmerer (1904-), in similar fellowship as Geiseman, was pastor at Mt. Olivet Church, St. Louis (1928-40); since 1940 he has been Professor of Homiletics, Concordia Seminary. His strength as a preacher lies in doctrinal affirmation, in careful interpretation through exegesis, and in clear speech. He expounds the Christian faith which deals with the cross, the church, and man's redemption.

Reuben Kenneth Youngdahl (1911-1968) for thirty years led the Mt. Olivet Church, Minneapolis (1938-1968), to become the largest Lutheran congregation in the world, with ten thousand members and allied services of evangelism, education, and social services. Based upon the Scandinavian piety of Hauge of Norway and Resenius of Sweden, the contemporary church has a warmth and oneness of spirit. Youngdahl used the radio and his published books to share with people the vital faith, the ever-present Savior, and his shepherd concern for others. Here was Lutheran preaching with heart-care for people as people.

Among the Lutherans, **Otto Piper** and others published lectures in a symposium entitled *Reality in Preaching* (1942), an expression of what was then outstanding within the liturgical tradition of Lutheranism. Earlier **Miles H. Krumbine**, in *American Lutheran Preaching* (1928), presented the Lutheran contribution to preaching. Professor **H. F. Baughman**, *Preaching from the Propers* (1949); **R. Caemmerer**, *Preaching for the Church* (1959); and **Oswald C. J. Hoffmann**, *Reaching through Preaching* (1955) are representatives of strong Lutheran preaching who continue to set forth the message of the Reformation as seen in their published books.

Oswald Carl Julius Hoffmann (1913-) is the successor to Walter A. Maier on the Lutheran Hour heard each Sunday. During the 1900s the Lutheran Church reached out by modern techniques to the public and, since Maier's ministry, the pastor has taken over and continues to speak the same evangelical word around the world. Hoffmann has a deep sonorous voice, a strong sense of advocacy, and the note of conviction as he presents Christ to the nations.

Raymond Calkins was a man whose ministry as a Congregational pastor had durable results. His books incarnate much of his ideals and principles of preaching, as noted in *The Eloquence of Christian Experience* (Yale Lectures, 1927); *The Modern Message of the Prophets* (1947); and *The Romance of the Ministry* (1944). In each there is the sure step of a man who knows where he is going in his work. Each title indicates his awareness of the times in which he lived, the changing challenge and the new needs to be met, and his mental and spiritual adjustment in preaching without in any way surrendering the faith. His literary style and his forceful writing express the way he preached.

Harris Elliott Kirk (1872-1953) is noted for his fine, expository preaching from the Bible. At the Franklin Street Presbyterian Church, Baltimore, Maryland, his long ministry brought to light the hidden treasures of the Scriptures, especially in his series of character interpretations with the "saga" in mind, contemporary with John Galsworthy, the English novelist and *The Forsyth Saga.*

Bryant Mays Kirkland (1914-) has emerged as a diligent student, a conscientious pastor, and a strong preacher of ethical and moral helpfulness. An evangelical background prepared him for pastorates at Narberth, Pennsylvania, and then Haddonfield, New Jersey. The Presbyterian Church has used him in preaching missions, and service men have found his appeal one that is understood by men in difficult situations. Later, he succeeded J.S. Bonnell at Fifth Avenue Church, New York City. His preaching is direct, clear in outline, contemporary in illustration, Biblically based, and applied with psychological insight and healing concern.

David Haxton Carswell Read (1910-) came from Scotland where, after education and pastorate, he was Chaplain to the Armed Forces; a prisoner of war in Germany (1939-45); University of Edinburgh chaplain to students; and then subsequently successor to George A. Buttrick, Madison Avenue Church, New York City. The 1950s were ready for his longer and richer ministry as well as his writings. Scholarly and well-written sermons continue to reflect his flair in getting through to people in a modern society, but without sacrificing Christian truth. The Warrack Lectures, *The Communication of the Gospel* (1951), summarize his ideas of method and content for a post-war generation.

William Bell Riley (1861-1947), First Baptist Church, Minneapolis, stood against the tides of evolution and skepticism in his day and by systematic expository preaching left a rich deposit of material in print.

Lee Rutland Scarborough (1870-1945), a Southern Baptist, was Professor at Southwestern Baptist Seminary, Fort Worth, Texas, as well as a pastor and evangelist in many pulpits. His genial and well-illustrated Bible sermons effectively caught the ear of a generation brought up in the "Bible belt" of the South.

The poll of nationally known preachers carried out in 1924-25 brought twenty-five names of prominence. We can look at them as representative men of that period. In 1953 another survey was made—not by a poll, but by newsmen for *Life* magazine and others—who at the dawn of the '50s saw an increase in congregations and listeners. Representative men include those who had the benefit of radio and television as well as standards of excellence.

Louis Hadley Evans (1898-), senior pastor at the First Presbyterian Church in Hollywood, California, saw the congregation increase from 2300 to 6400 members, then the largest of his denomination. He is athletic in appearance and strong, a man among men. His sermons deal with the basic needs and fulfillments of life. At age fifty-five he left the pastorate to become minister-at-large, preaching and witnessing in colleges, service clubs, and educational and religious rallies to reach a wider public at all levels of life.

Theodore Parker Ferris (1909-1972) had the distinction of as-

suming the pastorate at Trinity Episcopal Church, Boston, with
Phillips Brooks still a household name around the religious world.
At thirty-three this young preacher soon established himself as
pastor, preacher, and author. His sermons were expository, and in
simple speech and illustration he caught the ear of students and
professional people in Boston. Believing that the parish pastor
touched people by regular ministry, he maintained this position
some thirty years as a committed believer in the efficacy of preaching. He lectured on preaching at the Episcopal Theological School,
Cambridge, during most of his tenure at the church and also
published a number of distinctive books, including one on preaching, *Go Tell the People* (1951). This book embodies his view that a
pastoral preaching ideal given with warmth and understanding of
people is the effective ministry.

Among the rising representative preachers of the second part of
the 1900s, the following have already shown their sense of fitness
and responsibility for larger ministries.

Baptists include **Wallie Amos Criswell (1909-)**, with various pastorates from 1937-1944. Since 1944 he has served at The First
Baptist Church, Dallas, Texas, with probably the largest membership in America—more than 12,000 people. Biblical preacher, he
uses the Greek language to quote and explain texts in sermons, in
simple and down-to-earth language of the people of the city. He
follows in the tradition of George W. Truett.

There is also **H. C. Brown, Jr.** (1921-73) whose rural and village
pastorates (1943-49) added to the enrichment of the shepherd heart
in preaching and complemented his academic and theological higher
learning. Thus the experience has made him an interpreter of what
is best in Southern Baptist preaching and education. Now Professor
of Preaching, Southwestern Seminary, Fort Worth, Texas, his teaching, preaching, and published textbooks have given many preachers
strong direction for pastoral ministry to their congregations.

Presbyterians include **William Marion Elliott, Jr.** (1903-), educated in the traditional Southern Presbyterian ideals. He held pastorates from 1930 to 1944; and has served at Highland Park
Church, Dallas, since 1944. Truly Biblical, expository, and pastoral,
Elliott uses his theological and academic skills in hermeneutics to
advantage. The sermon has been thoroughly digested and readied to
deliver in clarity, simplicity, and probity. Serving a long pastorate,
wearing well because he maintains standards of Christian living,
Elliott emerged as a leader and a voice for God. *Coming to Terms*

with Life (1944) is a volume of messages which in its title enshrines his goal in Christ.

The Reformed Church in America brought to the whole church gifts of immigrants. In **Joseph Richard Sizoo (1885-1966)** Holland prepared a sturdy and strong individual able to sustain many difficult pastorates for thirty-five years. New York heard his voice at the St. Nicholas Collegiate Reformed Church (1936-47) as well as Washington, D.C., where the New York Avenue Presbyterian Church (1924-36) was stirred by his sermons. His style was that of the forthright man who stands up to declare what God has said against sin and secularism. He affirmed positively that the future was not with Communism but with Christianity, with God at the center of the universe and sovereign over all of life. His lectures on preaching, *Preaching Unashamed* (1949), command respect from a preacher whose presence in the pulpit reflected a sensitive, shy man. His voice and delivery touched the depths. President of New Brunswick Theological Seminary in New Jersey, he also taught and ministered at George Washington University, Washington, D.C. Learning and the Christian faith were wedded in lyrical imagination and speech. A theology based upon the Reformed Church Catechism and the Bible was the key to his confident declarations of truth.

The Roman Catholic Church in America has had several outstanding men who appealed as preachers, although preaching has not been their strength as a body. A questionable popularity was given for a pliable period through the radio talks of **Charles Edward Coughlin (1891-)** whose message stabbed many a listener to pay attention to the social, political, and religious demands of the times. However, the depression of the 1930s and the New Deal philosophy of the period led the "radio priest" of Royal Oak, Michigan, to the conclusion of his work and influence.

Alongside of the national appeal of Fulton J. Sheen who has been the preacher for the Catholic Radio Hour and then television, mention should be made of **Robert Ignatius Gannon (1893-)**. A strong church administrator and for thirteen years President of Fordham University (1936-48), Gannon implies that he does not like to preach, preferring to be a leader in education. However, when he preaches he speaks well and in a natural, flowing style. In American preaching, he has been spoken of as the best Roman Catholic preacher. His gift of humor is an asset in public life and in addresses before various gatherings, but in the sermon he is serious.

He tries to inculcate reverence and not the laughs which tend to sidetrack. His sermons are not in the grand tradition of the Protestant and are therefore inordinately brief. As he said, "I go on the adage that no souls are saved after ten minutes." Having returned to the pastorate, Gannon now has opportunity to revise his theory in the more practical context of congregational life and work.

Among the more recent Christian movements have been those associated with offshoots of Methodism and others reemphasizing Wesleyan doctrines in danger of neglect. There are the various Assemblies of God, the Nazarene Church, the Wesleyan Methodist, the Free Methodist, and some who are listed under the Pentecostal banner. During the 1900s these groups have made progress faster than the older denominations.

James McGraw (1913-), Church of the Nazarene, held pastorates from 1936 to 1939 and 1949 to 1952, teaching in between, then became Professor of Preaching and Pastoral Ministry, 1953, at Nazarene Theological Seminary at Kansas City. By his use of Biblical, contemporary allusion and concrete illustration, the imagination of the pastoral heart comes through in his preaching. His clear insight into the heart of the Christian faith is demonstrated by the spoken word becoming dynamic even in print. The professor-preacher has steeped himself in the knowledge of others, as witness his book, *Great Evangelical Preachers of Yesterday* (1961), with a breadth of understanding and appreciation of chosen men of God. In **Ralph Earle (1907-)**, Professor of New Testament at the same seminary, scholarship and evangelism combine to express fitness for the decade ahead. Earle is a preacher of Biblical passion and, like his colleague McGraw, exemplifies in preaching what he teaches in the classroom. The warmth of holiness is expressed with the tools of learning: truly the continuance of the Wesley tradition.

Leslie Ray Marston (1894-) of the Free Methodist Church, is an educator, professor of psychology, and Bishop of his denomination since 1935. His evangelical zeal and radio ministry has influenced not only his own constituency, but reached out to others. Generally, his preaching deals with basic facts of the gospel, man's hunger of soul, his concern about self, and the unveiling of the Savior who alone can satisfy. Language and form blend in fitting speech to penetrate the modernity which needs the eternal spirit.

Others whose contribution to preaching had value are **James Henry Snowden (1852-1936)** Professor of Systematic Theology at Western Seminary (Presbyterian), Pittsburgh (1911-1928), who as both teacher and religious journalist gave his preaching a new emphasis in the light of what he published, *The Psychology of Religion and Its Application in Preaching and Teaching* (1916).

Charles Kemp (1912-) of the Reformed Evangelical Church kept in touch with the movements of change in America and published *Life Situation Preaching* (1956) as an adjunct to other stresses on Counseling Preaching.

Baptists include such men as **C. Oscar Johnson** (1886-1965), an exuberant preacher at First Church, Tacoma, Washington, and Third Church, St. Louis, Missouri, outstanding for oratory and power of illustration from life, abounding with humor, bringing "light in the valley" of life; **Carlyle Marney** (1916-), a cultured pastor at Myers Park Church, South Carolina, modern, yet conservative in preaching on the need of the New Birth in Christ; **Theodore F. Adams** (1907-), First Church, Richmond, Virginia, since 1936, also President of the Baptist World Alliance, for five years; and **Herschell H. Hobbs** (1907-), Pastor of the First Baptist Church, Oklahoma City, since 1949; past President of the Southern Baptist Convention, yet broadcasting also on the Baptist Radio International Weekly program. A keen student and a prolific writer, Hobbs' steady preaching is sustained as he plans for six months in advance. He uses the historical-grammatico method of study, seeking the exact meaning of the Scripture. Using only an outline after meditation, he finds this most effective in communicating to a congregation and over the radio.

The first fifty years of this century witnessed many changes in preaching. The art of "communication" dominated the thought. The rise of radio and television determined a more staccato style of script and speech. The unseen congregation influenced the preacher. Psychological insights into character and personality were related to Biblical insights. In the South especially the Bible preaching of the past continues so that the people of that area hear more Bible exposition than others. However, the changing scene continues as new voices are heard and new methods of preaching are tried. The dialog-sermon has arisen but it is too soon to estimate its worth and its lasting contribution.

Ecumenical Preaching

The twentieth century is the age when the ecumenical movement has had its greatest momentum. Not that Christian people were noncooperative before this. In Dwight L. Moody's time the result of much of the evangelism then was to bring Christians of all kinds of backgrounds and denominations together in support of the evangelist. This unity was expressed in their working together with Moody and in the witness to the populace of America. Out of that experience came further avenues of cooperation. Begun by the ecumenical movements of an evangelical nature were: The American Sunday School Union, The American Tract Society, The American Bible Society, the YMCA and the YWCA. Charles I. Foster, in *An Errand of Mercy, The Evangelical United Front, 1790-1837* (1960), documents what was done. He lists 158 agencies and societies founded to meet varied social needs, such as rescue missions in the cities, orphanages and homes for the aged, temperance societies, anti-slavery groups, and hospitals. Also, the major missionary thrust both in our nation and overseas found Christians working together. These united efforts were the result of evangelical movements and prepared the way for others.

What is commonly spoken of today as the ecumenical movement arose in the aftermath of the World Missionary Conference, Edinburgh (1910) out of the need of missionary groups to work in unison. **Charles Henry Brent (1862-1929)**, missionary bishop of the Philippine Islands, Anglican Church, regretted the differing denominational emphases which were imposed upon the nationals who became Christian. A rising interest in this led to the World Conferences of Churches—Lausanne (1927); Edinburgh (1937); Oxford (1937); Amsterdam (1948); Evanston (1954); and Delhi (1961). Each of these brought more denominations into alliance for consultation and, in the meantime, a few were united with one another (The United Church of Canada, 1925).

With this climate favoring "union" of church bodies as well as denominational cooperation overseas, the time had come for a sermon to be preached which would again accelerate the ecumenical movement. This was the occasion when **Eugene Carson Blake (1906-)**, Stated Clerk of The United Presbyterian Church in the U.S.A., stood in the pulpit of the Grace Cathedral, San Francisco, at the invitation of the Episcopal leaders. There on December 4, 1960, he preached on "A Proposal Toward the Reunion of Christ's Church" from the text—"Now the God of patience and consolation grant you to be likeminded one toward another according to Christ Jesus: that ye may with one mind and with one mouth glorify God, even the Father of our Lord Jesus Christ. Wherefore receive ye one another, as Christ also received us to the glory of God" (Rom. 15:5-7).

Blake proposed in the sermon that the Protestant Episcopal Church join with the United Presbyterian Church in inviting the Methodist Church and the United Church of Christ to form a plan of church union "both catholic and reformed." Through this came a representative body to engage in joint discussions called "The Consultation on Church Union" (COCU). The sermon outlined those major ideals upon which ultimately would rest any cooperation and unity:

(1) Christ wills that his Church be one.

(2) Divided churches cannot speak with one voice to the nation.

(3) Our need to put our traditions and systems under the judgment of Christ, seeking his correction.

The sermon also stressed that the church, to be reunited, must be *reformed and catholic.* Thus the principles of reunion that are important to all would include the following:

1. The reunited church must have visible and historical continuity with the church of all ages before and after the Reformation.

2. The reunited church must clearly confess the historic trinitarian faith received from the Apostles and set forth in the Apostles' and Nicene Creeds.

3. The reunited church must administer the two sacraments, instituted by Christ, the Lord's Supper (or Holy Communion, or Eucharist) and Baptism.

These were given as the basic points and suggested as a beginning for discussion and study. Only in joyful witness and in good conscience within the fellowship of the united church would this be seen.

The principles of reunion were then stressed—

(a) The reunited church must accept the principle of continuing reformation under the Word of God by the guidance of the Holy Spirit.

(b) The reunited church must be truly democratic in its government, recognizing that the whole people of God are Christ's Church, that all Christians are Christ's ministers even though some in the church are separated and ordained to the ministry of Word and sacrament.

(c) The reunited church must seek in a new way to recapture the brotherhood and sense of fellowship of all its members and ministers.

(d) Finally, the reunited church must find the way to include within its catholicity (and because of it) a wide diversity of theological formulation of the faith and a variety of worship and liturgy including worship that is non-liturgical.

The great confessions of the Reformation must also have their place in the confession, teaching, and history of the reunited church just as do the ecumenical agreements of the undivided church. In the conclusion of the sermon, Blake said: "Now I have not forgotten that this is a sermon and that it is an unconscionably long time since I announced my text. To you who have patiently listened to my longer than usual exposition, I ask one thing more: that you pray for the reunion of Christ's Church and that as you think about it and examine your own heart and mind, you do it in the spirit of the Apostle Paul when he addressed the saints and bishops and deacons of the church at Philippi: 'Complete my joy by being of the same mind, having the same love, being in full accord and of one mind.' " This was followed by other extracts from the Philippian Letter, and then the preacher concluded: "If you, dear friends, and all others who consider and discuss this proposal do so in the spirit and from this motive, I have no fear but that the eternally recreative God will find His way to renew and reunite His Church."

Since that historic occasion the churches aforementioned and several others, nine in all—The African Methodist Episcopal Church, The African Methodist Episcopal Zion Church, The Christian Church (Disciples of Christ), The Christian Methodist Episcopal Church, The Presbyterian Church in the U.S.—have had meetings for consultation. Various plans have been drafted, revised, and studied until finally a basis of union was sent out in 1970 for study among the churches. After some ten years the interest seems to have waned, and the hopes and ideals of the sponsors have not been realized. Changing times and new revolutionary forces in the world at large have set back the dream for the present. Most of the support for the COCU has come from the more liberally-oriented theologians and pastors. The evangelical-conservative theologians and people have not responded, chiefly in their reaction against some of the premises that accepts the bishopric and the equal place of tradition alongside of *sola scriptura*. What the future has we do not know. With the thrust of the ecumenical movement toward the reunion of churches, major bodies such as the Lutherans, the Southern Baptists, and the smaller bodies have not involved themselves in participation. Many fear a "super" church, monolithic like the Roman Church, and see freedom only in maintaining their own convictions as expressed within their distinctive groups.

Summary

The new age brought with it rapid change and much acceleration in science and technology. What was now spoken of in ecumenical circles as a worldwide church had come to pass in that the young churches of the so-called mission fields were now organizing and becoming articulate. This has been the one single outstanding fact of this age for the church. At the same time, methods of travel had changed drastically. Instead of the sailing vessel or the steamship transporting the missionary overseas on a long voyage, the airplane has become the outstanding means of transportation. Almost in one day or at the most two days, one could travel to any other part of the world.

The advent of radio and latterly of television has changed the habits of multitudes in their ideas of listening and looking. Here again, the media brought the message into the home and wherever the instrument was available there came the message. This worked. two ways. The messengers of evil and of corruption were not slow to use this means of propaganda, and this in itself changed the outlook of millions. The church cannot be sure any longer that its people would listen to the Christian message. The world was not Christian and vast areas still challenge the faithful. The Christian church was slow to use the newer media, but gradually this was done and across America churches, groups, individuals, by paying for time, could make use of the opportunity that was there to proclaim the Christian message.

The Space Age had come also, an age when men flew off into space, walked in space, and landed on the moon. The advent of this new knowledge enlarged the horizons of thought and brought a new awareness that this earthly life was limited and that the divine revelation with its speech of mystery, time, eternity, space, "heaven and earth," and man in the midst of this unfolding universe of the Father's House, had something to say after all.

The older conflict between science and religion had now been replaced by the awareness that science and religion were complementary and each had a ministry in the divine providence. Man was on the frontiers of new knowledge and miraculous discoveries. God the Creator was closer to man in man's thinking now than ever before. Man could learn that in the vastness of the mysterious universe he had a place as the creation of God and as one for whom Christ died. Space Age Christianity was the key to ecology, the theology of nature, the nature of man, and the interrelation of God's revelation in nature as well as in Scripture and finally in Christ.

The Nuclear Age introduced questions about the physical sciences, the biological sciences, and the social sciences; and this new age demanded a fresh look at preaching. No escape was possible from space, time, and matter in the light of life and of death within the orbit of the transcendent realities of divine revelation. Scientific truth and theological truth find meeting place. When a scientist obeys an exacting standard of honesty and humility in his search for truth, then the Christian preacher must also measure up to the same. Both scientist and theologian should be aware that at the heart of all reality is the cross.

As the era made way for the 1960s, the most striking feature in preaching was the phenomenal increase in what is known as *Pentecostal* preaching. At its inception in America, no one thought of it but as a passing phase. A rigorism of practices was allied to spiritual claims that the hallmark of the Baptism of the Holy Spirit lay in *glossolalia,* speaking in the ecstacy of tongues. The doctrine of the Holy Spirit is preeminent; and a second work of grace is claimed as a sign of divine approval. Acts 2 is the basis of belief that Pentecost is repeated in every age, and that unusual manifestations then will follow.

At first, the movement was sporadic and its leadership had a limited education. However, by the 1940-50 decade, conferences held in London, Stockholm, Toronto, Jerusalem, and Helsinki had representatives of a worldwide fellowship numbering millions of people. The preachers were C. M. Ward, evangelist of The Assemblies of God; George Jeffreys, England; Oral Roberts, Tulsa, Oklahoma; and David J. Plessis, South Africa. These preachers had in common a simplistic style of speech, profusely illustrated from experience, striking claims of healing and charismatic revival, a strong emotional stress, and an evangelistic appeal for decisions. Such preaching may lack something of the polish and skill of that found in the major church groups, but Pentecostal preaching would claim that only in strong emotional preaching do we reach the underprivileged, the poor, and the frustrated. The warmth of the fellowship is mediated in preaching which is in testimony as well as in text.

Later, Pentecostal preaching would not be confined to these newer groups but become a movement within the major church denominations, until Anglican, Lutheran, Baptist, Presbyterian, Methodist, and Roman Catholic pastors and people would begin to sense the same experience and claim similar signs of divine power.

At the end of the 1900-50s, the postwar generation was being readied for new ideas of preaching to meet the demands of those who had no background of a Christian heritage.

The sixties were days when the ministry at large became nebulous and uncertain in its search for meaning and in its diversities of message. The waning influence of neo-orthodoxy, the burial of the modernist-fundamentalist controversy, and the rise of the ecumenical movement brought other openings and emphases. The radical right arose to demand a hearing in the antinature of the sermon and address which then boomed largely through radio to multitudes. Race relations also threatened to disrupt communions, and many sermons were preached dealing with the social, political, educational, and economic issues created in that time. Arising also was the reaction against a patriotism which maintained that war was justifiable (e.g., Vietnam), a reaction which for America was to be most disruptive. In this era, Presidents Kennedy and Johnson particularly had committed the nation to this involvement and as it accelerated, the next President, Richard Nixon, had the unenviable task of delivering the nation from that involvement, with all the attendant economic, political, and ideological tensions created earlier.

This was the time when preaching, if estimates are correct, showed marked decline in influence. Not that individual pastors and preachers in certain congregations lacked influence among their people. There were still the centers of preaching where people went and listened eagerly. But across the nation there was the general impression that somehow preaching was no longer a strong influence. Radio and television commentators and performers had taken hold of the population. Allied to this was moral decline, the permissive age, situation ethics, the breakdown in morale through drugs, drink, and depravity. America was conscious of the increase in crime, the revolt against authority, the lawlessness which characterized society throughout.

The training of pastors in counseling, the increased attention given to psychotherapy, and the reduced teaching in the areas of preaching and homiletics in seminaries—all this fostered the mood that preaching for this new age was "out" and that other forms of ministry were more acceptable. The number of students for the ministry decreased and many who offered themselves had no thought of the regular pastoral ministry, but inclined to ministries in industrial, social, and political relations. Here was the denigration of preaching at the time when preaching was most needed.

Chapter VIII

Preaching
in Canada
(1850-1950)

For a century or more Canada was a nation in the process of growth. The population has never been large in relation to the territory. From the Atlantic to the Pacific and from the American border to the Arctic, it is a land mass that has challenged but few pioneers. This, of course, changes with every new discovery of the mineral wealth and as more and more people are realizing the potential of this nation.

The British tradition has persisted most of the time since the inception and founding of Canada. The Eastern part of Quebec, however, has remained loyal to its French origin, heritage, culture, and religion. Predominantly French in language and religion—Roman Catholic—periodically this section has thought in terms of seceding and establishing its own form of government. However, since the Confederation of the Provinces, and up to the present, this has not been achieved. Canada, although having two strains and languages, has remained together as one nation.

During the century several church groups have led the people of Canada. Anglican, Presbyterian, Methodist, Congregational, Baptist, and Roman Catholic have been in the ascendency. Other groups, such as the Mennonites from Europe, have brought their contribution, and across the vast land small ethnic and religious groups continue to worship in freedom and to play their part in the total life of the nation.

After the period of the missionary and the pioneer came the major denominations with their church building. In 1925 a union was achieved between the Methodists, Congregationalists, and some of the Presbyterians. This became The United Church of Canada. One-third of the Presbyterians continued separate on doctrinal grounds, and The Presbyterian Church in Canada continues alongside the others.

Because of the limited history of the church in Canada, there are not many outstanding names to consider in the history of preaching. At the beginning when new churches were formed and buildings erected, the major source of supply of pastors came from the old world, especially the British Isles. Good sound worship, the use of the same hymn books and psalters, the traditional way of ritual and order of services—this was the pattern to be followed. In the Protestant groups this was not questioned, and as immigrants arrived to swell the congregations, there was continuity between the old world and the new. This tended to give security and wholesome appreciation to the newcomers. Where ethnic groups carried their native language with them, this was used in the services until the passing of the first and second generations. Now it is a rare thing to have a service in any other language than the accepted English or the French.

Whereas Canada depended upon the old world for the major preachers to fill important pulpits, it is also significant that many Canadians (whether native born or naturalized) have been called to outstanding churches in the United States. A steady drain has been noted in this respect over the years, especially in the 1900-1950s. Some of these men have not only continued to be pastors and preachers, but a few of them have also been called to be professors in universities, colleges, and theological seminaries for the training of men. In the study of preaching in America, some of these names have been referred to in other connections.

James Robertson (1839-1902) was born in Scotland and came to Canada as a missionary. His itinerary reached its climax when he came to Winnipeg where he remained as pastor of Knox Church. His strength of character and skill of mind were recognized by his brethren and he became the Superintendent of Missions for the West. Endowed with extraordinary talents, he was entrusted by his church with the major task of spreading the gospel to the Pacific. During his lifetime he saw the church with four congregations give itself to missions and thus grow to 141 congregations. This, after 21 years, produced 226 missions, serving 1,130 places.

In this far-reaching ministry, Robertson was the preacher with the message and a man under orders from the missionary mandate. His preaching was noted for its vitality of spirit. He did not belong to the class of preachers who have the time or the inclination to embellish the sermon with literary and classical allusions. His thrust in preaching was otherwise. Robertson's ministry and preaching was graced by a sensitivity of feeling: an awareness of how men reacted in times of stress and strain. He ever had in mind the vast spaces of the prairies and the far West ever beckoning the missionary and the settler. As Canada opened up to the Coast, the Presbyterian Church of that day recognized the responsibility to follow and accompany the immigrants and minister to their needs.

After his pastorate at Knox Church, he is remembered for his work among lumbermen, miners, and railroad workers, and his care for the people of the manse in their needs. Public speaking and preaching gave him the opportunity to think of "others," and thus his sermons and words brought sympathy and healing. Truly he had the shepherd heart of the true missionary.

Charles William Gordon (1860-1937) was known far beyond Canada because of his pen name—"Ralph Connor," a name to be reckoned with in other days whenever Christian people sought for a book to lighten dull moments or to seek a measure of escape from their ordinary lives by the imaginative stories of this gifted preacher and writer. Some preachers do more with the pen than with the pulpit. Authorship is another way to proclaim those things surely believed.

His early years were spent in Western scenes and in preparation for ministry. Then came missionary pastorates, and later, a pastorate in Winnipeg, Manitoba, at St. Stephen's Church (Presbyterian). War days saw him as Senior Chaplain to the Canadian forces. His work overseas and his contacts with leading men led him to involvement in the search for the means of peace for mankind. Throughout these strenuous days Gordon knew no rest in a life packed with incident.

He is reported to have said on a return visit from the European war zone, in extolling those who had enlisted and were serving their country, that "every man who died for his country on the field of battle was actually offering himself as a sacrifice and would be saved." If this be true, was it the settled belief of the preacher? Perhaps he was carried away and said this in an unusual context? Prominent Canadian and famous though he was, Gordon did valuable work as an ambassador of goodwill between Canada and the United States and Great Britain. At the close of the War he sought to promote the ideals of the League of Nations in his speaking and preaching. This, to Gordon, was the one hope of the world for peace in our time. The idealism and the hopes of millions were wrapped up in this new attempt to bind men and nations together. Like an evangelist, Gordon carried the message across Canada. He did not live to see the end of his era. The birthpangs of another era, in which the depravity of human nature was unleashed in a more terrible way than he had known, followed.

Gordon as a preacher never lost the gaiety of youthful courage and faith. He never became old as there was still work to do. Churchman, missionary, pastor, writer, he is also remembered as a preacher. Perhaps the overtones of those stories he told assisted him to enter the hearts of thousands, and families waited upon his ministry with zest. It is significant that he reached the height of his power in the pulpit after he had retired from the active ministry in St. Stephen's. He then devoted himself to preaching and lecturing missions across Canada, the United States, New Zealand, and Australia. He knew the mission of the church in desperate times, and he sought to bring the message of the church to war-weary people.

Readers of Ralph Connor's novels—*Black Rock, The Sky Pilot, The Man from Glengarry,* and others—will know that he could touch the conscience and heart with tenderness and understanding. Five million of these books were bought in his lifetime! That in itself was noteworthy before the days of modern best sellers with all the publicity stunts accompanying them. Ralph Connor was a household name. He touched the springs of emotion, and the pathos of his story telling was remarkable. Gordon the missionary and preacher could "preach" best in his books and did so. As revealed in his *Postscript to Adventure: the Autobiography of Ralph Connor,* he was a deeply religious man. Out of that came, not so much theological convictions, but the homespun way of assisting people to have courage and faith in the struggle of life. Here was meat for his preaching and thus he ministered.

As a representative of Canadian preaching, Gordon is best recalled by his books which made him a universal name. Building upon that output of stories, he was welcomed as the pastor-preacher in Winnipeg and beyond. The homespun variety of his writing touched chords of memory and brought fresh light in dark places of human need. His preaching was imbued by the spirit of what he wrote:

The measure of a man's power to help his brother is the measure of the love in the heart of him and of the faith he has that at last the good will win. With this love that seeks not its own and this faith that grips the heart of things, he goes out to meet many fortunes, but not that of defeat (Preface, *The Sky Pilot*).

Frederick William Norwood (1875-1958) was one of the many who found their best years of ministry in Canada, although not a native son. The saga of this giant in the pulpit was one that began in Australia, a continent we little think of as producing many preachers of eminence and power. Nevertheless, in the divine providence, Norwood was nurtured in his homeland and early entered the Baptist Church ministry. He lacked much in early education. In a sense he was self-made. His wise use of time and his reading habits made up for much he had missed elsewhere. At seventeen he started to preach wherever he could find a congregation and learned to speak with that facility of ease and poise which men noted about him. Later he developed into a pulpit orator.

His early ministry in Melbourne, Australia, demanded that he work as anyone else in regular employment during the week and then minister on Sunday, which he did for ten years. During that time he attended Ormond College (Presbyterian) and Melbourne University and was able to take classes while he worked. Norwood believed that out of that experience he learned most for preaching. Preaching, as he said later, lies in dealing with the elemental facts of life, and religion is an eternal necessity. Not only in the treasures of the past, but on the anvil of experience does one learn to preach. "Preaching at its best is experience, and the communication of it to others. The preacher cannot know too much of the experience of other men in bygone days, but he must not bring with him the aura of the antiquarian. It should never seem to him that a poor fellow is out of reach because he lacks the traditional training but is up against the same elemental things which once shaped the creeds."

Norwood never doubted that he had natural gifts. He said, "My ear tasted words as the palate tastes food. I was born with a love of lucidity. But I was saved from the exploitation of my gifts, and largely from the curse of self-consciousness. . . . Under the inspiration of an almost selfless man, I was carried past many a pitfall of the youthful preacher. Eloquence is composed of true feeling, lucidity, sincerity, and naturalness, and gains its real strength from its matter rather than from its form."

During World War I, at the age of forty, Norwood entered the chaplaincy in association with the YMCA, so that he had freedom to move around among the Australian troops. Out of this came the visit to the City Temple, London, where, unknown and unheralded, he was at the end of the War called to be its minister. For twelve years he ministered at that citadel of nonconformity, made famous by the ministries of Thomas Goodwin and Joseph Parker in other generations. There he was the eloquent speaking man witnessing to eternal truth in an ever changing world.

In Canada, Norwood was pastor at St. Andrew's Wesley United Church, Vancouver, B.C. (1939-43) and later at St. James United Church, Montreal, Quebec, until his retirement. Any assessment of his contribution to preaching must keep in mind his natural ability as a lucid and free extemporaneous speaker. Whether on a platform or in the pulpit, he was the same. He brooded long over his theme following much reading and thought. Then he began slowly until he caught fire—the spirit became incandescent and he moved along at a rapid rate to his peroration. The sweep of his mind and spirit was inspiring. His first sermon in Vancouver was "And Jesus Came Preaching." In that utterance he pledged himself to follow his Master in proclaiming the gospel. He had the shepherd heart and was also aware of the needs of the community. He was a force for righteousness and fearlessly faced any challenge.

The contribution of Norwood is not easy to assess because of the wartime conditions and the postwar era of reconstruction. Nevertheless, he stood in the tradition of sound speech and notable preaching. The pulpit to him had no meaning except it had relation to the universal. "A pulpit," he said, "savours of impertinence, but the greatest of all irrelevancies is to regard the parish pump as its axis. Therefore one must think of the world at large, even at the risk of being indiscreet." Thus he was world related in preaching. There was an amplitude in his speech and thrust, and he liked to paint on a large canvas.

Norwood's contribution lay in the period of War and reconstruction. While not neglecting the individual, there was a sense of the fitness of things as he wrestled with the changing currents of the times and the appeal to a war-torn generation. In this he was specially fitted—he was a man's man. His sermons were rugged and strong. He was matched against the delusions of the age in which men raised questions about eternal values. "There is all the difference in the world between a religion and a gospel. Religions are as thick as autumn leaves. . . . But not every religion could be called a gospel. That title is reserved for Christianity. Christianity did not appear in the world as a new religion, but as 'glad tidings.' It brought hope of deliverance to all from sins and sorrows which are shared alike by all. That was the secret of its power."

Playing upon the word *atonement*, Norwood spelled this out as *at-one-ment* and reiterated this throughout sermons as the interpretation. Thus he sought to bring people into relationship with God. His was the surge of the orator as he turned this way and that in short sentences which stab and prod. He moved to the climax ever seeking the appropriate word in his extemporaneous utterance. As a man to man so he spoke with the masculinity which appealed to ex-service men and families disrupted by war and stress. He stood in the day of the ordeal as a mediator of truth.

George Campbell Pidgeon (1872-1971) has been a household name in Canada. Being the first Moderator of The United Church of Canada brought him many accolades and recognition as the organizer of church union. He is to be seen against the social and religious pressures of an age of change. Last of the Moderators of The Presbyterian Church in Canada (although that body continued), he passed from one communion to the other as leader and guide. After several ministries from East to West, he gave thirty-three years as pastor of the Bloor Street United Church, Toronto (1915-1948). There he came to the zenith of his powers as a preacher.

Estimates of George Pidgeon from those who were his friends and from those who sat under him acknowledge with one voice that he was the consistently greatest preacher of his time in Canada. From his first sermon at sixteen years of age in 1888, to the last known occasion in 1960 at the age of eighty-eight, his ministry of the Word spans seventy-two years! To him the pulpit demanded a high standard of scholarship, intellectual excellence, and literary erudition. He always spoke from the Bible, and as one put it, "His mind is simply saturated with the Scriptures."

In a volume of his messages, *The Indwelling Christ* (1948), he says: "I have been trying in these closing months of my active ministry to give the essence of the Gospel I have preached through the years. Its centre has been the living Christ. What I have asked young Christians to confess as they became members of the Church in full communion I have tried to set forth in these expositions—the experience of Christ as Saviour and obedience to Him as Lord." One testifies that the most sublime sermon he ever heard was preached during the church union controversy on the text, "By this shall all men know that ye are my disciples, if ye have love one to another." It was at a communion service. It was so moving that the elders, prounion and antiunion, exchanged handshakes with one another during the service in full view of the congregation.

Like many another, Pidgeon began his ministry by writing his sermons in full but taking into the pulpit only key words for each sentence. Then he tried preaching without notes, and this became a settled practice. He was a devout man and his inner life of prayer and meditation was background for preaching. He usually chose for exposition Biblical passages which figured in his own religious development. He was widely read in the classics, theology, and secular works. These fed his homiletically fertile mind. He was Professor of Practical Theology for six years at Westminster Hall, Vancouver (1903-1909) and while he taught students the art of preaching, he was glad to return to the regular pulpit of the church.

Pidgeon has shared in lecture and sermon some of his ideals and attitudes concerning the sermon to be preached. To him preaching came first in a pastor's life. He had to spend time in preparation, and while he spoke without notes it also had to be a finely shaped product in presentation. He was not an expositor as was G. Campbell Morgan, but he was, nevertheless, a Biblical preacher applying his message to human needs. He said: "First, find the central thought of the text; second, enforce it." This, to Pidgeon, was the rule by which he regulated himself. Loyalty to divine truth is the first qualification of the expositor. New light is constantly thrown upon the ancient texts by discoveries in scholarship and archaeology. To discern the bearing of the divine revelation on human need prevented the aimless message.

In his sermon, "The Peace of God" from Isaiah 57:19-21, Pidgeon quotes the text, " 'Peace, peace, to him that is afar off and to him that is near. . . . I will heal him. But the wicked are like the troubled sea . . . it cannot rest. These is no peace to the wicked.' The promise of peace is one of the most frequent in Scripture. It is spoken of as the peculiar privilege of a child of God. It is contrasted with a storm-tossed condition of the wicked. One can see this clearly in the words of Isaiah, in our text." This is the opening paragraph which in itself introduces the subject from the text. Thereafter, Pidgeon takes three paragraphs to develop this as a heritage from God in the light of world conditions. Then he says, characteristically, "Turn now to the Scriptures to see the characteristics of this peace and the conditions on which it is bestowed." Then follows the body of the sermon as outlined:

1. Peace with God is the door into the peace of God.
Supported by Romans 5:1.
2. Trust is essential to peace.
Supported by Isaiah 12:2.
3. This suggests that peace is the result of a personal relationship.
Supported by John 14:27.
4. This suggests another characteristic of Christ's peace.
Supported by Luke 24:36.
5. Another passage of profound significance in this connection.
Supported by Philippians 4:6-7.

In application, Pidgeon stresses the need to "pray through" "with thanksgiving" and ends with two verses of a poem by some unknown author. The sermon is given with illustrations and references to Winston Churchill, Charles G. Finney, Charles G. Trumbull, John H. Jowett, Sir Edwin Arnold, Goldwin Smith, Charles G. Raven, Abraham Lincoln, Stonewall Jackson, and "once a farmer. . . ." All these indicate the catholicity of taste and reading behind this preacher.

Although some would say this is "simple" preaching, it carried with it the profundity of truth and the spirit of a man who lived in the secret place and was a guide and mentor to troubled people. His aim was holiness of life as he related the gospel to practical affairs. Pidgeon had an evangelical background and a tradition of piety which, however, was joined to the roadway of life. His biographer has finely said of him, "He was a student rather than a scholar, a teacher and adviser who loved books but did not live for them." "He did not doubt which aspect of his ministry was primary: he was a reforming preacher, not a preaching reformer."

In a sermon "Fifty Years Trying" (1944), Pidgeon spoke of the arduous nature of his calling:

> There is no harder taskmaster than the ambition to excel in the pulpit. No slave-driver ever drove his victims as mercilessly as the art to which one's life is dedicated. She calls for thorough prepara-

tion every time you enter her sanctuary, but she requires more than preparation. There is a mystic way into her holy of holies which only the elect can find; she has meanings hidden in every text, or theme, which she discloses only to those who love her so that they cannot but follow her to the end.

Pidgeon found preaching a spiritual exercise of the highest order. He was a pastoral preacher and lived for his congregation. His message was graced by a literary quality, but his spirited discourses never failed to arrest and arouse the mind in seeking the spiritual good of his listeners. Thus he was evangelist and expositor, pastor and persuader. The hour of crisis or the important occasion never found him wanting either for text or sermon. Of him it can be said that he was a straightforward speaker of winsome personality. Clarity and simplicity were his attributes.

John Sutherland Bonnell (1893-), born and educated in his native land, had two early pastorates at Cavendish, P.E.I. (1921-23) and at Saint John, N.B. (1923-29). Then began his major ministry in Westminster Presbyterian (United) Church, Winnipeg (1929-35). His early experience in hospitals for the rehabilitation of the mentally ill served to unite theology and pastoral counseling in preaching and the cure of souls. His sermons indicate the care of preparation, the sympathy and empathy of the shepherd heart, the concern that the sermon become the agency of God to bring healing to the whole person. Thus is the salvation of God interpreted to a lost and anxious generation. From 1935 and for the next twenty-seven years, Fifth Avenue Presbyterian Church, New York, as well as an ever wider circle, benefited by such preaching.

From a Scottish background and Canadian education, **David Alexander MacLennan** (1903-), son of a Presbyterian pastor, has had service in Canada and the United States. Academic and theological training in Winnipeg and Montreal led later to two significant pastorates at Emmanuel Church (United), Montreal (1930-36); and at Timothy Eaton Memorial Church, Toronto (1936-49). From that vantage point he became Professor of Preaching and Pastoral Care at Yale University Divinity School (1949-55), before returning to the pastorate first at Rochester, New York, and then at Pompano Beach, Florida. Throughout his preaching ministry he gave to many the beaten oil of the sanctuary. *No Coward Soul: Sermons* (1949), distilled his own faith and courage in a day of adversity, his awareness of people's cry for something from God, and a willingness to lead as well as point the way. His speech style arouses the lethargic, lightens the load with humor, and shows a nimble mind which has been enriched from the thought and writing of our culture. From his many published articles, the eleven volumes he has edited, and the nineteen books of sermons and lectures on preaching, the church at large has known the dynamic utterance and enlarged ministry of this tireless worker. He is the only Canadian to give the Warrack Lectures on Preaching in Scotland.

Thomas Todhunter Shields (1873-1955) of the Jarvis Street Baptist Church, Toronto, has been acclaimed by many competent judges as "the Spurgeon of Canada." Like Spurgeon, he was born in England in a family which was Christian and was engaged in public ministry. Anglican and Methodist strains were in this lineage. A conversion experience led into a relationship with the Baptist Church and the beginnings of preaching. He learned early in life to write his sermons as a discipline for the effective use of words and clarity of thought. After several pastorates in Eastern Canada, he came to the outstanding pulpit of the denomination in 1910 where he exercised his major ministry. Self-made, he was never a student in college or seminary, but his early education served him well as he knew how to read and study for the pastorate.

During his life he was at the center of much controversy. Theological education for the denomination was in the throes of change, and Shields took a stand against the liberalism then seeping into Canadian religious life. He was also a staunch defender of Protestantism, and in this he stood to proclaim the evangelical message while refuting the claims of the Roman Church. These two challenges colored his lifework, and his addresses and sermons were related to these issues for many years. Not unlike Spurgeon in London, Shields was led to publish a paper, *The Gospel Witness,* which carried his message into print. He also founded a Bible Institute and Seminary to train young people for Christian service.

Although remembered for his controversial life, Shields was an excellent preacher with the pastor's heart and concern. A gifted speaker, a forceful personality, a decisive expositor, he preached sermons of substance. The Bible to him was the Word of God and this emphasis is discerned in the volume *Christ in the Old Testament.* His mastery of the English tongue gave him a skill and thrust above many in his day. So clear was his thought and expression that the sermons when stenographically reported needed little editing.

Because of his opposition to clericalism and the unwarranted claims of the Roman Church in Canada's political and religious life, Shields stressed the evangelical message—not only in opposition to the dogmas of Rome, but also to invite people to receive the Scriptural gospel of grace. Here is a summary of the sermon "One Sacrifice for Sins for Ever," on the text, "But this man, after he had offered one sacrifice for sins for ever, sat down on the right hand of God" (Heb. 10:11-13). The introduction is simply a statement in the "belief in the immortality of the soul as held by people but which is not distinctively a Christian doctrine. Belief in the resurrection of the body is distinctively Christian, and the truth is revealed in the Word of God exclusively." His argument is developed in each paragraph and then comes the text once more. "I shall speak to you therefore of the priests whose work is never done, and of the one Priest whose work is gloriously finished; and shall endeavour to show you how, through Him, and through Him alone, we may come into right relation with God."

The major points of this sermon are typical of Shield's method and development: (1) There are priests, then, whose work is never done: in this this principle is true of the Roman Catholic religion, and there are forms of Protestantism that, in principle, are not protestant. (2) This Man, after He had offered one sacrifice for sins for ever, Sat Down! Who is He? Jesus Christ is God! The meaning of the Death of Christ. (3) What is it to Believe? Here it means to accept God's estimate of His Son. Are you glad the work is done? Finally, he appeals for people to act in commitment.

Thoroughly Biblical, clearly theological, simply illustrated, and practically presented—this was Shields in his day of influence. No name was better known throughout all Canada by friend and foe alike. Men might disagree with his theology, but no one denied his natural and spiritual gifts as a powerful preacher. He stands as the exponent of evangelical truth in a period of theological and religious controversy.

Oswald Jeffrey Smith (1889-) is still in active work for the Kingdom of God. He is an unusual man, with a sense of mission, whose life has been given to the spread of the gospel throughout the world. As a preacher he has emphasized not only the gospel in its simplicity, but chiefly the interpretation of the Great Commission. In this light we assess his investment of time and strength.

Smith began his life as a pastor-preacher but soon decided that what his people needed was to see the world in need. Thus his whole ministry was oriented to appeal to people to give their money and time to this end. He has written hundreds of hymns, edited a magazine, made world preaching tours, published thirty-five books, and sustained a regular ministry in The People's Church, Toronto, for more than forty years (1915-58). His son, **Paul Brainerd Smith (1921-)** succeeded him (1959-). Several times a year he has gone to conduct missionary conventions in other churches throughout Canada and the United States. His church has sent out and sustained more than four hundred missionaries and the annual day of giving brings in sums exceeding $300,000. Over the years a total of more than seven million dollars has been given.

As a man, Smith looks frail, pale, thin, and not robust in speech or form. Once he begins preaching there is an evident change. He seems to have an inner fire burning. His speech comes rapidly and there is a torrent of words as he pleads and urges his listeners to action. The sermon "Only One Way" on the text, "Now is the accepted time; behold, now is the day of salvation" (II Cor. 6:2) is typical of his gospel preaching. In length it has nothing in common with the short twenty-minute sermon of his contemporaries. Here is a sermon an hour in length, or sixteen pages when taken down, and the homiletics not easy to follow. Yet, in this are a Biblical background, Biblical illustrations, certainly many stories from his own experience, and a personalized approach. Questions are asked and the answers given as he engages in a "conversation" with the people.

Emphasis on missions and the call to give life and/or money for this cause has been the paramount thrust in his preaching. The sermons thus delivered reveal one passion and one conviction—no one should hear the gospel twice until everyone has heard it once. There is an intensity about Smith as his whole mind and spirit catch fire with this conviction. Everything he does as a preacher is directed toward this one end. Men may disagree with his theology and with some of his methods, but no one can deny the sincerity of this message. He has taken the Great Commission realistically, and the response has been phenomenal. The missionary-minded church is honored in a unique way with Smith as the leader and sponsor of this principle.

As a preacher in this context, Smith has stressed that the work of God needs money! Without apology, he pleads for people to pledge in faith and to give according to their means. Thus his church is able to look back and see how this preaching has resulted in millions of dollars given to missionary work. Backed by prayer and missionary conferences, the preaching of Oswald Smith has seen "signs following." If great preaching is effective preaching, then this is a test or a proof of what God does through a man yielded to him and dedicated to this unfinished task of evangelizing the world.

Here is an emphasis in preaching which is different from that of most pastors. Everything in Smith's preaching is subservient to this one end in view—the proclamation of the Good News to the end of the earth. Smith has been used to send out hundreds of people as missionaries and his home base and church has given the money to support this overseas army. Thus preaching is the New Testament thrust of giving the Christian message under a mandate for missions. Oswald Smith is the incarnation of his message in his restlessness and desperate high-strung speech pleading with others to act.

John Robert Paterson Sclater (1876-1949) found in Canada a ministry at its flowering after earlier years in his native land of Scotland. At Old St. Andrew's United Church, Toronto, he shared the harvest of the years. His chief contribution to the preaching of Canada lay in the high standards he set for this ordinance within the context of Christian worship. Worship to Sclater was the atmosphere for the heights of preaching and the sermon was the message from God to man.

He was honored in giving the Warrack Lectures on Preaching in Scotland, and then the substance was revised and repeated in the Yale Lectures (1927). He was the preacher-scholar, a man of wide and deep reading. His preparation for the pulpit was thorough. His method was to make careful sermon outlines or full notes, photograph them in his memory, then preach freely after brooding over these. He was free in gesture and contact with his congregation.

Grounded in church history and theology, he also knew the best in literature. He had a special feeling for the conducting of public worship with reverence and devotion. Standing in the holy place, he preached in the grand tradition of his generation. In the lectures, *The Public Worship of God,* we sense the spirit of a man who loved the total hours of worship and gave attention to its many-sided details. His love of the beautiful is obvious. To him worship was the highest end of the soul. To lead people to the heights was his aim, and his words inspire those who read what he has to share.

As he preached, so he taught that preaching is the presentation of truth, the awakening of the emotions, and addressing the individual before the community. In worship preaching is to glorify God and to bring men to God in order to be good. The first is immediate and the second is final. In preaching Sclater always remembered that he and his people were still worshiping God. Thus the sermon is an act of great dignity and beauty. This was his contribution to Canada's church and worship.

Toronto has had many outstanding men in the pulpit and a few should be mentioned for their loyally sustained ministries.

Willard Brewing (1881-1951), nurtured within the Reformed Episcopal Church, served that group as a pastor for twenty-three years before transferring to The United Church of Canada in 1930. He ministered at St. Andrew's-Wesley Church, Vancouver, B.C. for eight years, and then from 1938 to 1951 was pastor at St. George's United Church, Toronto.

Brewing believed that there was something greater in preaching than any sermon ever given. His ideal was to magnify the office. The man before the sermon—this is where we begin.

To find a text from the Bible is first, although it often finds the preacher. To him the whole Bible is the center of his library. He sought the meaning of the text by Hebrew and Greek study, then would write out the implications and applications. He used a written manuscript in the pulpit. His wide reading provided the background of illustration and thought. His ideal was that the preparation of the sermon is in reality the preparation of the preacher.

He published *Faith for These Times* (1945), and in the sermon "God's Unspeakable Gift" (II Cor. 9:15), the near approach of Christmas gave it color, although he said this was not a Christmas text, written as it was fifty years after the Bethlehem event. The sermon is thematic rather than analytic and discusses the idea of "unspeakable" at length; then turns this way and that way by illustration and quotation to elucidate its inner meaning. Thus the theme and principle of the text find a modern relevancy and application. This sermon, like most of his sermons, is not long. He preached within limits and always gave people something practical to think about.

James Ralph Mutchmor (1892-) stands out preeminently as one of the architects of union and mission in The United Church of

Canada. Born of a pioneering family in Manitoba, he had a family tradition of Calvinist forebears and sturdy people of faith and work. Primitive and plain were the things of boyhood, and preaching was something to hear for stimulus and vision. After the struggle to get an education, he studied theology and during that period as he testifies, "I found God. Or, I was found of my Heavenly Father. Henceforth, I can truthfully report, I had only one desire and purpose. I was a fully committed Christian. In those student days, as after ordination, I gave everything I had to the one task. My hand was on the plough: I never turned back."

However, he was caught up in the World War of 1914-18 and served overseas as a soldier, returning to plunge into home mission work in Winnipeg, Manitoba. There he early found his niche as a church pastor and social worker. Every demand upon a church and an institute were made by the incoming immigrants. After twenty years of involvement in spiritual and social concerns, he was appointed as Associate Secretary of the Board of Evangelism and Social Service by The United Church. His work included welfare, homes for the aged, and other redemptive agencies of the church reaching out to work among the underprivileged.

Mutchmor saw the church as the conscience of the State, and in preaching he stressed the validity of the gospel as God's dynamic thrust into the lives and needs of people. He was happy that his work was evangelism *and* social action, not one *or* the other. He liked this unique combination and partnership. The whole person was thus in view for redemptive renewal and reformation. In preaching he said: "I believe there is a good New Testament authority for these functions of the church. I contend that the basic New Testament words are repent, believe, go and give, and in that order. 'Jesus came preaching, Repent and believe the Gospel. . . .' "

No one had a better right so to interpret the gospel for his day than this man. Canada was passing through the birthpangs of a postwar period, with its attendant unrest and problems of labor and capital, government and immigration, and inadequate housing and social conditions, which hindered people from living a full life. He saw that the dynamic of the gospel was needed to change people so that in their new state they would assist in changing the environment. The gospel was related to life and he believed that its first fruit was "goodness." "In my evangelistic work," he preached, "I first related the acceptance of Jesus Christ as Saviour and Lord to the witness of the believing Christian. Out of this comes the action." In his application of the gospel to the moral, social, political, economic, and international fronts of life, Mutchmor had a lifetime of opportunity to test out his beliefs. Later, in the Second World War he became Moderator of his denomination and gave leadership in a large way.

Temperance problems with liquor, gambling, and sexual promiscuity were hit hard by this preacher. Wherever he ministered, whether in the pulpit or from the platform, his clear voice and message let all know the implications of the good life in Christ. Behind many of the social problems of Canada lay moral issues. War and Communism also were brought under review. The exploitation of the young by vested interests also received his attention. In preaching he said: "It is essential for the church to pinpoint corporate sin and evil. We live in a power-mad world. . . . The new power in nuclear weapons makes it that there is no way to contract out of the new situation. Man stands in fear of a handful of dust. . . . This new and terrible power tends to corrupt every area of life. The Christian Church must witness in the face of corporate sin with corporate salvation. This way of salvation has been given by God in Jesus Christ. . . ."

What kind of preacher was Mutchmor? Certainly he was every inch a man—a man's man. He ministered to the poor and needy as well as to the statesman and the labor leader. He conceived the gospel to be something personal, yet having social implications. He was one of the rare and few men of Canada of whom it could be said that as an ambassador of his Lord, he was a fearless prophet of his day and generation. He was a crusader for righteousness and the persistent foe of evil. His rugged exterior was matched by a kindness of spirit for all. He knew how to use humor in his ministry and lightened many a sermon or address with a telling tale. His voice was soft-spoken with a deceptively mild manner, because in the torrent of words he could flail and attack sin and vested interests with blistering effect. Thus Mutchmor, not unlike John the Baptist in tradition, was a sincere Christian witness to a nation.

John Short (1896-) succeeded Willard Brewing at St. George's United Church, Toronto, in 1951. He was another of that earlier group of men who came from Great Britain. Short is a Scot whose ministries have included two in England. He followed first the well-known R. F. Horton in London and then J. D. Jones in

Bournemouth. He early came to maturity and responsibility for one so young. After fourteen years at Bournemouth, he came to Canada. Well endowed with a nimble mind and strong speech, he has sustained an outstanding pulpit over many years.

Short believes that self preparation is essential to steady preaching. Love for Christ, his church, his cause, and for people are also essential. The preacher must also be gripped and possessed by his theme.

To have something on hand from week to week is a help. Often this can be a series of themes from the Bible. Old words are finding a new relevance and need exposition. Says Short, "I am now wondering how in the years left to me I shall ever be able to tell all I want to tell about the glorious Gospel of the blessed Lord. The themes are inexhaustible." Having chosen the theme, there is then wide reading on what the Bible says, the textual study, and gathering anything that is grist to the mill. Selection and summary follow as the preacher makes a digest in notes for preaching.

Short published *All Things Are Yours* (1939), and many sermons in church publications and religious periodicals. The sermon, "The Peace that Passeth Understanding" (Phil. 4:7) illustrates his emphasis and method. He holds aloft these ideas of "peace" and "a balanced relationship" as the key to life's fullness. Balance, character and personality, God's purpose, resources—these are the predominant words as he marshals the facts and presents his case. Here is the philosopher-psychologist type of preacher using an awareness of what takes place in the mind to bring everyman under the spell of the mind of Christ. Well illustrated from contemporary life, his sermon speaks to people's condition.

Andrew Ian Burnett (1905-1972) was born in Nyasaland, Africa, where his father was a missionary of the Church of Scotland. After graduating from Edinburgh University, he was pastor successively at Newhaven, Edinburgh, and then Springburn Hill, Glasgow. In 1943 he became the pastor of St. Andrew's Presbyterian Church, Ottawa, until his ministry ended (1960). He became well-known, if not for his preaching alone, for the fact that prominent personalities attended that church. During the Second World War the then Princess Juliana of the Netherlands was a member of that church in her exile and one of her children was baptized there. Lord Tweedsmuir, Governor-General of Canada, attended frequently. Among his congregation was the late Rt. Hon. W. L. Mackenzie King, Prime Minister of Canada.

In recalling Burnett's preaching strength, we can see his appeal in the story of a farmer in Western Ontario who heard him give the funeral address and conduct the service for the Prime Minister. This service was broadcast across the nation. After hearing this, the farmer, touched by it, drove two hundred miles to watch the funeral procession and to see the pastor who had delivered the address! What was there in Burnett that appealed?

First, he was a fluent speaker and there was some vitality and zeal in the way he delivered his message. To hear him was to hear a man who evidently believed with his whole heart what he was saying. Second, he dealt with human nature in his sermons and tried to meet people's needs with the human touch.

Apart from the occasional printing of notes and sermons in the church magazine, Burnett published only one volume of sermons, *Lord of All Life* (1952). His preface indicates his belief in Paul's guiding principle that, in preaching, "Christ Jesus and Him crucified" was to be proclaimed. This, to him, was the heart of the gospel. "During the past twenty-one years," said the preacher in 1952, "it has been my greatest privilege to preach Christ as the Lord of all life on both sides of the Atlantic. The present volume contains a selection from that preaching." A reading of these indicates how the pastor-preacher sought to bring comfort and courage, hope and peace to men laboring under modern strain. "It is the gospel for prince and statesman, for the senate and the marketplace, for the study and the home. Jesus Christ remains the Lord of all life."

The first group of sermons deals with the theme, "Behold the Man"—an attempt to see Christ as "God with us" and related to our human conditions. As he traces incidents in the life of Jesus from the Christmas tale to ascended glory, we are conscious of a spiritual interpretation of light and beauty. Couched in good running prose and illustrated from hymn, story, and history, Burnett's sermon is never far away from the centrality of the Christ in the midst of life. He touches us at all points. In background the preacher is familiar with the classics and draws freely in quotation. All in all the familiar friend and Savior of men is seen upon the roadway of our common life, and it feels good to be walking on that road with him.

The second group of sermons deals with "Highways of the Heart"—five ways by which the Christian disciple finds the secret of perseverance and growth in the new life. These are based exclusively on the chief events of our Lord's life. Discipline comes out of the Silent Years in Nazareth; Dedication speaks of his Baptism; Decision relates to the Temptation; Consecration is the hour of Transfiguration; and Communion takes us to the Garden of Gethsemane. Here Burnett discloses his theological background and his convictions about the revelation of God in Christ. From that emerges exposition based upon good exegesis of the relevant passages in the Gospels.

The third group of sermons deals with "Common Attitudes toward Christ"—four different ways in which people responded to Christ's call. Familiarity is seen in Nathanael who is invited to come and see the Christ; Prejudice scorns Christ and some do not receive Him; Curiosity is corrupt as when Herod tried to get to Jesus and failed; and Subservience is noted when Jesus submits to John's baptism. These are attitudes which are reflected in our lives, and so we learn from the preacher's insight and skill of application.

The fourth group of sermons deals with "The Power of His Resurrection"—five ways of viewing the fact and the factors of that eternal event in time. As the Risen One, Christ appears to men, overcomes sin, opens the Kingdom to those who believe, and finally reigns in sovereign truth. These sermons move on in ringing words and glowing awareness of the living Christ. The crucified is now with us always. This radiant faith is not of the past but of the present hour. Burnett's preaching is characterized by a singleness of aim, a beauty of expression, and an appeal to rise up and join this Lord of all life. "Can Jesus step out of that picture in which memory and imagination have framed Him and become a living, mighty power in our lives today? Can we know Him as the disciples knew Him, as Master, and Saviour, and ever-loving Friend? That is the incredible miracle which the Gospels proclaim. . . . Jesus meets us face to face."

In that is the essence of the gospel as Burnett saw it from the authoritative Word of God.

The Presbyterian Church had two major educational centers in Knox College, Toronto, and Presbyterian College, McGill, Montreal. These were not affected by the union in 1925 of those who entered the United Church. Preaching continued in the tradition of the mother country, and Canadian-born men began to assume leadership.

A. B. Winchester (1858-1943) had a strong preaching ministry at Knox Church, Toronto, a continuing center of Bible and evangelical teaching. Winchester was one of the founders of Dallas Seminary, Texas, a depository of dispensational hermeneutics.

David Christie ministered throughout Canada, and gave wisdom to others in *The Service of Christ* (1933), where the ministry is scanned for motive, message, and tests. In pithy and epigrammatic prose, he shares forty years of pioneer missionary-pastoral work in the West. No one is likely to forget his treatment of the temptation to recline, to shine, and to whine!

James Whyte Clarke, Scottish born and trained, came to the heights of preaching at Knox Presbyterian Church, Winnipeg, before going to McCormick Theological Seminary, Chicago, to teach. Later years saw him as pastor in the Second Church (U. S. Presbyterian), Richmond, Virginia.

Clarence MacKinnon from Nova Scotia served the Central Church, Winnipeg. His appeal to youth, his evangelical and Biblical preaching, his relevance to his age and his knowledge of books, made him known as an interpreter of the Christian faith. He became the Principal, Presbyterian College, Halifax, N.S.

George G. D. Kilpatrick, Scottish born, son of a distinguished professor, graduate of the University and Knox College, Toronto, served as Chaplain in World War I, and then as pastor, St. Andrew's Church, Ottawa. He resigned to enter the Chalmers United Church, Ottawa. His preaching exposed the easy way of life with its pretensions of the casual. His forceful message stabbed the conscience to recognize the mastery of Christ.

The United Church was composed of three branches of the Presbyterian, Methodist, and Congregational traditions. The Methodist had **Samuel Peter Rose (1853-1936)**, Professor of Practical Theology (1921-31), Wesleyan College, Montreal, whose services of leadership included Chairman of the Committee for editing the Methodist Hymn Book. This vital ally of preaching in worship enriched the larger body, and Rose was the choice to give the sermon at the Communion Service when the historic uniting was celebrated. His message and belief was expressed then as he preached on "The Church, which is His Body" (Eph. 1:22, 23).

William Henry Sedgewick (1876-1945) served well at Hamilton,

Ontario; then in the historic Metropolitan United, Toronto. There his preaching demonstrated a sensitivity of appeal, couched in poetical idealism, and touched with warmth and strength. The sermons have good structure and content, whether judged from manuscript or the oral delivery.

Richard Roberts (1874-1945) came from London and New York to serve the American Presbyterian Church (United), Montreal (1921-26). His lucid English and forceful epigram appealed widely. His preaching influence was given further extension in his written works; his serialized sermons were published as *The Gospel at Corinth* (1924). He had sympathy for people in their struggles and brought faith to hearten and encourage.

Trevor H. Davies (1871-1965) was one of the notable preachers at the Eaton Memorial Church, Toronto (1923-36). An eloquent speaker using words and ideas to stab the conscience of people, he gave in his person and work a message of hope to church and community. He used the Bible as background and sometimes utilized the literary classics to remint the tragedies and triumphs of people. In *Spiritual Voices in Modern Literature* (1919) there is a sampling of his master-touch and insight as the spectrum of color and truth touches life.

John William George Ward (1875-1945) with a background as Congregational pastor, Tollington Park, London (1917-24), where his predecessors were Thomas Manton, Richard Baxter, Ossian Davies, and George Campbell Morgan, came to Emmanuel Church, Montreal (1924-). He enriched Canadian preaching with his ringing voice; he stood as a prophet to a new world, seeing the heart, bringing a persuasive word. Sermons published were *Message from Master Minds* and *The Master and the Twelve*.

Murdoch A. MacKinnon (d. 1942), of Scottish Highland descent from Nova Scotia, served in Halifax, Regina, and came to richer ministry at Runnymede United Church, Toronto, (1928-42). In him was the Celtic fervent emotive power as his sermons spoke the truth in love, fearlessly, vitally, disturbing the complacent and indolent.

James Edwin Hughson (1871-1938), from New Brunswick, Nova Scotia, ministered across the Dominion; at Lethbridge, Edmonton, Winnipeg, and then at the First United Church, Hamilton (1920-34). Possessing a wide experience of pastoral-preaching and an acute understanding of men, he brought to the sermon a discussion of age-long problems and questions. The new age found him ready to wrestle with man's dilemma and teach that the Christian in the world finds in ordinary contexts the place where God can be known and served.

One of those who went to the United States was **Robert James McCracken (1904-1973)**, who came from Scotland after having pastorates and teaching to become Professor of Theology and Philosophy of Religion at McMaster University, Hamilton, Ontario. He served the Baptist Churches of Canada during those years (1938-46), and then was called to Riverside Church, New York, to succeed Harry Emerson Fosdick. **Rabbi Maurice Eisedrath** by his intellectual sermons drew large congregations at Holy Blossom Synagogue, Toronto, before going to New York. **Lloyd C. Douglas,** best known for his best-seller *The Robe,* ministered at Erskine American Church, Montreal, before going to California. **Hugh Thompson Kerr (1871-1950)** was another well-rounded Canadian Presbyterian preacher and author whose major ministry lay at Shadyside Presbyterian Church, Pittsburgh; he shared in the art of the children's sermon, and published lectures on *Preaching in the Early Church* (1942); he was also the first pastor to broadcast weekly in Pittsburgh and the United States. In **James Dick Smart (1906-)**, pastor at Rosedale Presbyterian Church, Toronto, the continuing Presbyterian Church in Canada had a preacher whose exegetical gifts enabled him to continue the tradition of a confessional body and yet bridge over to the new expositions of Scripture discovered in the light of neo-orthodoxy and emerging hermeneutics. In his later teaching post at Union Theological Seminary, New York, as well as his editorship of the Presbyterian Church in the U.S.A. curriculum for Christian education, he adhered to the newer view of Scripture. The 1900s saw many changes including the view of Scripture as the witness to revelation. Many tried out these new interpretations in teaching and preaching. Smart, however, still believed in the efficacy of Biblical preaching, and was disturbed after the 1950s that there was a silence in the pulpit about the revised views then in vogue. His book on *The Interpretation of Scripture* (1961) gives his views on the ideas then affecting the sermon and preaching.

Donald Macleod (1914-), once of the United Church of Canada and now Professor of Homiletics, Princeton Theological Seminary in the United States, has maintained the distinctive Canadian spirit in writing and in preaching. His teaching ministry has given him a unique understanding of what a sermon ought to be. His knowledge of sermons and awareness of outstanding preachers of his day have enriched his own ministry. Always close to the centralities of the Christian faith, he has given guidance and leadership to preaching in the matrix of a generation seeking for certainty while venturing out in experiments.

The United Church of Canada has had many leaders who are represented in **George Stanley Russell (1883-1957)**, Deer Park Church, Toronto (formerly Congregational Church in England); **Frank Crossley Hunter**, Winnipeg; **Aubrey S. Tuttle**; **James S. Thomson**, professor, Dalhousie University, Halifax; **John W. Woodside**; **John Dow (1885-1964)**, professor, Emmanuel College, Toronto; **Ralph Carleton Chalmers (1908-)**, professor, Pine Hill College, Halifax, and Secretary of the Board of Evangelism and Social Service, Toronto; and **Ernest Marshall Howse**, Westminster Presbyterian (United) Church, Winnipeg. Howse succeeded John S. Bonnell at Westminster and has since 1935 used his literary skill to communicate both from the pulpit and through the press in his weekly syndicated articles.

A. Leonard Griffith (1920-) was formerly minister of the City Temple, London, but now is at Deer Park United Church, Toronto. His experience as a preacher has matured him, enabling him to share in lecture and in sermon the convictions which shape his pulpit ideals. "The only great preaching is expository preaching, the faithful interpretation of God's Word in the Bible as it speaks to the needs of the individual and society," is his assessment of preaching. With this standard, Griffith has woven classical illustration, theological emphasis, and well-written prose to proclaim as pastor-teacher the vertebrae of authentic preaching. With the preacher under the compulsion of the Word of God, the need to preach is declared as inherent in the gospel itself.

The new era in Canada saw the ferment of church union and the two world wars with their impact upon the preaching of the various churches. Apart from the tensions and controversy inculcated by ecclesiastical differences and convictions, preaching in this period had in it the personal and social implications of the gospel of Christ. The "good news" was proclaimed from many important pulpits. Samplings of the sermons indicate that a high standard was maintained. The British contribution was decreasing, and more nationals born and trained within Canada began to make their influence felt.

An educated ministry continues to use the sermon, and congregations have not given up the "hearing" attitude in a custom which has not been displaced by other media of communication. Marshall McLuhan spoke and wrote from Toronto that the age of the spoken and printed word was passing, but in the challenge of the visual aid, radio and television, the pulpit still maintains its place.

As a form of expression in public relations, the sermon had not been dismissed as outmoded. Canadians generally welcomed the voice of the pulpiteer.

Much of preaching has related itself to the church year, and the task of relating Christian doctrine to the festivals has not been overlooked. Topics covered in preaching include ecumenicity, ethical tensions, barriers to faith, theological interpretations, moral implications of political practices and social problems, and apologetics in controversies. Attention has also been given to Christian worship, leading congregations to consider properly this sacred task. Through the sermon, the church claims the right to speak to all men that God's sovereignty is over the whole of life. Preachers like **Angus J. MacQueen**, St. George's United Church, Toronto, outline in strong fashion the need and necessity for man's highest act. **Murdo Nicolson**, Grace Presbyterian Church, Calgary, speaks of the Quest, the Answer, and the Implications of that Answer. **Gordon Jones**, First Baptist Church, Vancouver, stresses A Faith to Live By, with Biblical background and historic sweep. **Ernest Marshall Howse**, Bloor Street United Church, Toronto, deals with the moral law with God as the judge of all.

During the century considered, there are representatives from the period of the two World Wars. These were found in the major denominations, and theologically there were those of liberal as well as those of conservative convictions. Pastoral preaching dealt with the adequacy of Christ's salvation, the authority of the Bible, the primacy of spiritual values. To live right with God and then with man was the basis for an optimistic outlook for the future of the Kingdom of God in Canada and throughout the world. Providence and history, personal faith and social-political realism are found in the preaching themes.

The Baptist Church was composed of different conventions and, from coast to coast, vital personalities. **Arthur L. Huddleston**, First Baptist Church, Halifax, N.S., stood for constructive thought in reaching for the future. Within the context of swift changing views, he mediated the eternal assurance of faith.

John MacNeill (1874-1937) lived to preach, the Walmer Road Baptist Church, Toronto, garnering his best years (1906-1930). He also served as Chaplain (1916-18) with the Canadian Expeditionary Force; President of the Baptist World Alliance (1928-34); and finally as Principal of the Faculty of Theology, McMaster University, Hamilton. This author of three books was acclaimed by people as a preacher of rich feeling, a lover of people, a helper of the weak, one who brought the gospel with kindly touch and grace. His preaching showed his gifts of oratory; he seemed naturally to be able to kindle the thoughts of people.

William A. Cameron (1882-1956) had one pastorate, Bloor Street Baptist Church (1908-1928) which became Yorkminster Park Baptist, Toronto (1928-48). Forthright in preaching historic Christianity, dealing with the political, social, and theological ferment of an emerging nation, he spoke to the times in the light of the eternal.

John Gordon Jones (1901-) ministered in Toronto, Hamilton, Calgary, and Vancouver, B.C. The maturity of his pastoral-preaching was noted during the height of his influence at Calgary (1945-56) and thereafter at The First Church, Vancouver. His scholarly and forceful message at the center of each city stressed a faith by which men could live.

Edgar James Bailey (1903-), of Welsh birth and tradition, found Canada to be his door of opportunity in securing a college and a theological education. He served Baptist churches from 1935 on and at the First Church, Edmonton (1948-1956), came to prominence through his leadership in church and community, and during World War II as chaplain. Widely used on radio and television, he was selected by the *Toronto Saturday Night* magazine (1951), as one of Canada's seven outstanding preachers. Men in uniform as well as the members of his congregations liked his down-to-earth, non-academic approach.

The Anglican Church had links with the Church of England and traditionally ministered without much change.

Allan P. Shatford served the Church of St. James the Apostle, Montreal, for twenty-five years. Involved in community life, a Mason and Rotarian of influence, he was honored publically for his services throughout the nation and for his early use of radio. In his preaching he discussed age-long truths in the light of newer views concerning science and religion. He emphasized that in a changing age, "the Word of God was not bound."

William Bertal Heeney (1873-1955), St. Luke's Anglican Church, Winnipeg, brought the pastoral-shepherd plan of the Church of England to a Canadian context. Outstanding in his skill to express in sermon and book the "appeal" of his English Church, he gave to many English immigrants and new Canadians the idea that crossing the Atlantic Ocean did not change worship. Thus Heeney stressed the continuity of liturgical worship, Biblical exposition, doctrinal familiarity, and orderly preaching. The church, in his mission, could bridge gulfs and relate people in diverse ways and cultures to sense their unity in a fellowship of faith. In his use of prayer book, hymns, Scripture readings, and the Church Year for guided preaching, he led the younger Canadian church to establish itself.

Henry John Cody (1868-1951) was outstanding in leadership, with a brilliant mind and an academic record seldom excelled. Canon and Rector of St. Paul's, Toronto, he became the President of the University of Toronto. He and Canon Frederick Hugh Wilkinson (1896-) at the same church (1944-1953) exercised long and influential ministries within the preaching related to the Anglican liturgical tradition. Other Anglicans included Canon Dyson Hague (1857-1935) and William Henry Griffith Thomas (1861-1924), professors at Wycliffe College, Toronto, and notable writers and preachers whose ministries were not limited to the classroom. Ronald Arthur Ward (1908-) also served as Professor of New Testament (1952-63), and later returning from England, as Canon and Rector of St. John's (Stone) Church, Saint John, N.B., giving expository preaching to enrich the whole church.

In Frederick Donald Coggan (1909-), Professor of New Testament, Wycliffe College, Toronto (1937-44), the Anglican Church brought from England one who was destined to influence his generation with scholarly preaching and evangelical spirit. Across Canada his ministry was honored by all groups. His irenic approach, stimulating thought, and pleasing interpretation were outstanding both in his writing and in his speaking. The spiritual life of devotion was foundational. His books teach the principles of preaching as related to both the one who preaches and the whole church as participators in worship and service. He returned to England to be Principal of the London College of Divinity, then Bishop of Bradford, and later the Archbishop of York.

Other leaders included Archbishop Derwyn T. Owen (1878-1947) in Ontario, and Archbishop Philip Carrington (1892-) in the

French section of Quebec. In the West, **Godfrey Philip Gower (1899-)** became Bishop of New Westminster, B.C. These gifted men contributed to the traditional form of address and sermon without much innovation. In their responsibilities to Church and State, the tensions of politics and education, and war and reconstruction, they have dealt with the moral issues of their generation. The continual influx of Anglican leaders from overseas and the interaction with those of Canadian training promises well for the future of preaching through this historic body.

The differences in Canada between the Roman Catholic Church with its strength in the East and the rest of the nation has resulted in a limited amount of preaching which has been recorded. Our knowledge then of the preachers and their work is restricted because of the adopted policy. Meantime, in a poll by *Toronto Saturday Night* (August 31, 1951), out of seven selections of contemporary preachers, only **Francis P. Carroll (1890-1969)**, Bishop of Calgary, was given place alongside one rabbi and five Protestants. Bishop Carroll, a student of the Bible and a graduate of the Biblical Institute of Jerusalem, spent most of his sixty-one years in Canada. A thoughtful speaker, with impeccable diction, he was a good representative of his church and one who was heard with interest in religious gatherings and discussion outside his own communion.

Among the Lutherans there is **Helmet T. Lehmann (1914-)** whose background in Saskatoon, Saskatchewan, gave him identity with his own native land and people. Academic and theological preparation led to his receiving a Ph.D. in Germany. He held pastorates in the years 1939-43, following which he became a teacher and later President, Waterloo College and Seminary, Ontario (1944). His editorial work on parts of *Luther's Works* and other books indicates his influence as preacher-teacher. In *Heralds of the Gospel* (1953), it is clear that he preached what he believed, and that his message showed acute awareness of the needs of people while he sought to show the Word of God as able to meet human problems and perplexities. The divine Book of books was also the most human in relationship. Lutheran preaching has ever been liturgical, based on the pericope of lessons and selections of Scripture, but also has presented the evangelical application of the gospel. Lutherans also are a warm, family-based group in worship.

Representative preachers during the 1900s are inclined to be selected because of their so-called success and influence. However, the ministry has its failures and defections from the Christian faith. No one disputes the meteoric rise of **Charles B. Templeton (1915-)**. In his early years of ministry, he was a foremost evangelist with a public ready to listen. He was compared with Billy Graham in the United States. In the forties he was sought out by crowded gatherings as the ideal between the Billy Sunday and the Billy Graham types of appeal. With strong personality, ringing voice, and moving appeal, especially to men, he was suddenly given widespread endorsement by the public and the church.

From Canada, he later engaged in evangelism on behalf of the National Council of Churches, having in the transition studied at Princeton Theological Seminary, New Jersey, and in turn served the Presbyterian Church in the United States of America as their ordained minister of evangelism throughout the nation. Just as his book, *Evangelism for Tomorrow* (1940s), was published, he suddenly gave up his ministry and returned to Canada to resume other interests as newsman, radio and television commentator, and would-be politician, seeking to enter the Canadian Parliament. The political achievement did not materialize, and here ended for the moment the preacher's calling for this gifted and talented man. Friends and critics have endeavored to weigh up this strange aberration of one who professed the Christian faith and claimed to serve God. In the interests of preaching, there are those who wonder if exposure to theological questions and the climate of his day which cast doubts upon the authority of divine revelation in the Word of God would account for his defection. We do not judge the heart, but record that in the history of preaching the obstacles, tests, and temptations in the ministry are legion and thrice heated for any one standing in the place of the preacher.

Preaching in Canada during this period has been seen as the harvest of the thought, tradition, scholarship, and faith of those whose roots were in Europe, especially Great Britain, Ireland, and France. In the Roman Church in Quebec, preaching was not the essential element of instruction and worship. The sacraments, liturgy, priestly ritual in church, a standard language—these have controlled the congregational and community life. Protestants, on the other hand, with their missionary and evangelical heritage, maintained preaching. Such preaching, when set in the context of the emerging nation, provided a bridge from the old world to the new world. New forms and experiments in preaching and teaching will come, but basically the sermon has been didactic rather than hortatory, theologically based, delivered by educated pastors whose personalities have played a vital role in the appeal to the new Canadian citizen. Two world wars have resulted in changes of attitude within the Dominion, and younger Canadians bring a cross-fertilization of culture, social life, political change, and growing freedom from dependence upon the past. In this context preaching continues to clarify moral and spiritual values for a Canada which seeks to be its own master in its own house. As new and independent groups find freedom for religious expression, new ways of preaching may arise, but for the harvest of the years Biblically-based messages abide.

Chapter IX
Preaching
in Europe
(1900-1950)

The continent of Europe has always had its share of outstanding preachers who have influenced their times. Various countries have produced men for crucial hours of history. Some of these are in this modern period and deserve notice. Two world wars have devastated the land mass of the continent. Millions of people have lost their lives while other millions have been wounded and injured through the ravages of war. In addition to the upheaval caused by bombing and new weapons of destruction, some six million Jews were annihilated under Hitler's policy of extermination of the Hebrew people. Many Christians also suffered similar losses as they stood with and for those who were the suffering minority. Out of that holocaust has emerged certain figures whose preaching cannot be forgotten.

Scandinavian

Before the modern period of history in preaching, Sweden and Norway dominated Lutheran worship and preaching. Not many independent groups had arisen to bring variety of life and expression. The usual pericope regulated the regular exposition of the Word of God for the faithful pastor and this has continued unabated until now. This was characteristic from the Reformation on. The Word of God faithfully preached was in the highest tradition.

Guides and writers of books on preaching included George Norman and Laurentius Petri in the sixteenth century. Rules of composition and formats of sermons were stressed within the theological tradition. The seventeenth century had Petrus Eschilli, Isak Rothovius, and Johannes Rudbeckius with their prophetic and eschatological emphases. Change in style came gradually with Haquin Spegel and Jesper Swedberg with greater stress on exhortation and exuberant appeal. The eighteenth century was noted for its faithful preaching of the Bible. Technical training of pastors was allied to the pietistic spirit. Preaching then was developed against the background of German Lutheranism. Abraham Petterson has left behind a large corpus of notes and sermons illustrative of that period. He used the method of J. J. Rambach of Germany, a synthesis of scholastic style, pietistic appeal, and simplicity of speech for common people.

In the eighteenth century, two men among others of Sweden and Norway should be mentioned. **Anders Nohrborg (1725-1767)** of Sweden in the eighteenth century stood above others in his preaching and influence. He detached the sermon from the pericope and placed it within the relation of the doctrine of salvation from the Bible. The liturgical was replaced by the doctrinal. The atonement loomed large in his preaching and the appeal for Justification by faith was presented with zest and strength. Using the Bible he developed a threefold application, but not primarily as an expositor would. He sought climax in the exordium which dominated the text. Others in Sweden were **Johan Olof Möller (1738-1805)** who wrote *An Essay Concerning the Right Method of Preaching*, stressing that the sermon should not be an academic exercise. Bishop **Magnus Lehnberg (1758-1808)** was outstanding as a pastor and as a pulpit orator, appealing to the intellect as well as to the emotions. The sermons of **Henrik Schartau (1757-1825)** are samples of a heavy type of preaching. Here the message became liturgical in action, yet always was close to Scripture. Orthodox doctrine flowed from this and no doubt the influence of the Moravians is seen in his personal experience.

Norway meantime shared the effective leadership ministry of **Hans Nielsen Hauge (1771-1824)**, a layman of peasant stock who became an evangelist. His conversion to Christ in 1796 transformed him into the fiery apostle of the North. A man of spiritual genius, he shared some of the persecutions then common to those outside the official church structure. He spent ten years in prison because of his preaching. The civil and the religious authorities then did not favor his convictions. However, he wrote thirty-three books, including 'Om Religiose Folelser' *Religious Experiences* (cf. *Autobiographical Writings of Hans Nielsen Hauge*, Eng. trans. by J. M. Njus, Augsburg Press, 1954). Hauge is credited with uniting the Norwegian people and beginning the independent state of that country.

His message was that of salvation. He saw the world submerged in evil. He called men to repentance.

The nineteenth century brought to Sweden men like **J. O. Wallin** **(1779-1839)** who stressed a return in preaching to the authentic Luther of Germany. He tried to be more socially and politically related, thus sin and grace became watered-down concerns. Nevertheless, he brought a return to a poetic affusion of speech with strong overtones from Luther.

Revival movements brought other emphases in preaching. **Peter Wieselgren (1800-1877)** stands out in this era for his original gifts, his oratory, and his extemporaneous preaching. Revivalism and missionary appeal became strong as the English influence pervaded at this time. A new Biblicism appeared with **Peter Fjellstedt (1802-1881)**, and the evangelical revivals then in vogue expressed much of the fervor and emotion of this type of preaching. Outstanding also was the Lutheran professor at Uppsala, **Peter Paul Waldenstroëm (1838-1917)**, who experienced a spiritual transformation and broke with traditional Lutheran theology especially in the doctrine of the atonement. His new and fresh interpretation brought the founding of the Swedish Mission Covenant Church in Sweden. In the United States of America this body became known as the Evangelical Covenant Church. Thus the free church was born as over against the State Lutheran Church.

Characteristically, the preaching in the free churches was noted for its emphasis on the Bible, the need for revival, and a free participation in public worship no longer bound by ritual. Preaching now had in it a directness of appeal, a spirit of freeness of speech, and a sense of the "spiritual" or in some instances a "pentecostal" strain. **Sven Lidman (1882-1960)**, however, revived some liturgical tradition and was able to use the valuable Scriptural pericope but wedded it to the dynamic free spirit. Due to the influence of the English-speaking world the church with its "free spirit" learned to add a strong ethical and social pronouncement in preaching. Because evangelical revivals came to both the free churches and the Lutheran churches in the Scandinavian countries, the differences were lessened and a closer bond united their preaching. In this light we can trace the rise of other personalities whose preaching influenced their people.

In the twentieth century the church and order became important once more. The rise of the ecumenical movement in Europe and the participation of Scandinavian leaders in those councils had a bearing upon the changed emphasis once again. The coming of Biblical criticism also added to the changes especially within the State churches. Passing through the period of uncertainty regarding the text and authority of the Bible, the church found a degree of compromise in that there was a return to the attempt to keep up the confessional and sermonic use of the Scriptures. The text of the Bible is now used and appreciated as the *kerygma* and as part of preaching in the New Testament; therefore, today's preacher may do the same.

In **Johan Alfred Eklund (1863-1945)**, Bishop of Karlstad, this is demonstrated. His sermons revived faith in preaching once more. He struggled for faith and gradually certitude appeared as he endorsed the faith of the church and expounded basic truths of Christianity. Instead of exhortation dominating, he brought back the exposition of the text and passage in clear divisions and order, thus using forcefully the church year with its liturgical appeal, but now in a more relevant way.

In **Nathan Söderblom (1866-1931)**, Archibishop of Sweden, was a personality at once erudite and urbane, yet always the preacher. His brilliant gifts of the mind, his acumen in philosophy, and his acquaintance with the religions of the world as a student and professor combined to make this intriguing personality. He gave the Gifford Lectures at Edinburgh, Scotland, and was an outstanding scholar of his day. His best work lay in his broad association with the leaders of the major denominations. In council and conference he was at home in several languages and had appreciation for all kinds of religious orders and traditions. Above and beyond these traits is what he recorded once in his diary: "Lord, give me humility and wisdom to serve the great cause of the free unity of thy church."

Brought up in Lutheran piety, he found it easy to be a missionary-minded man and never lost this as he rose to the highest post in his Church and State. In time of war he cried for peace but did not receive support to do what he sought. His voice in preaching stressed the function and role of the Christian church as the mediator and peacemaker of that generation. Söderblom's preaching was in the classic tradition of Lutheran piety and ritual, yet there were a few modifications as he moved back from the freer method of those who were in the revival movements. No special method is observable in his sermons and public utterances unless it be the statesmanlike quality of one who has to weigh with care everything he says as he speaks for a whole church and often speaks to the State of which he is a citizen. He was a churchman rather than an evangelist. His analysis of theological and church problems was allied to an exegetical acumen in study so that his unconventional style became pleasing. His books *Humour and Melancholy in Luther* (1904), and the Gifford Lectures at Edinburgh, Scotland, *The Living God* (1931), give the essence of his life-mysticism.

Söderblom's preaching stressed the need to apply Christianity to the whole of life. Politics, economics, and citizenship were within the target of the "wholeness" of his thrust, as he stated "the conviction that the Christian Faith, rightly interpreted and consistently followed, gives the vision and the power essential for solving the problems of today, and that the social ethics of Christianity have been greatly neglected by Christians with disastrous consequences to the individual and to society, and that it is of the first importance that these should be given a clearer and more persistent emphasis." In preaching he also exemplified the pastoral concern, whether as pastor or as the head of the church. His homiletical bent is illustrated in one of the sermons, "The Inner Guest": "the guest within cannot be met in the outer rooms of the soul. Do not neglect the guest in your innermost room! You make ready your house for all kinds of other guests. You are so eager to show them attention and courtesy. But meanwhile the Supreme Guest who awaits you within is forgotten." Language in simple terms and images which brought men to think of the crucified Christ were characteristic of his preaching. Thus the pastor predominated—"the image of the Crucified can help and captivate, if any can. This image can free me from the self. We have the sufferings to bring us consolation. The figure of the Crucified gathers and calms the mind."

As the leader from Sweden, he took his place alongside the distinguished representatives of other lands and different church communions. He stood high in stature intellectually and theologically. The Stockholm Conference (1925) of the denominations was a further advance over the same conference of Edinburgh (1910). Now came contributions from men like Söderblom. "Life and Work" was now equal to "Faith and Order" and the passionate pleas of Söderblom had not a little to do with this achievement.

Norway joyfully recalls the figure of Bishop **Eivind Josef Berg-**

grav (1884-1959) of Oslo who is known for his unflinching stand for truth and righteousness during World War II. Son of a pastor, he was early destined to follow in that same vocation. His experience as journalist prepared the way for the time when he was an educator. As a teacher in high school, he touched the ordinary life of youth and began to see the glory of inculcating truth at the youth level. When as a scholar he continued his studies in theology he never overlooked the value of those early years. His book *The Man Jesus-Christ the Lord* (1941) interprets Jesus as the physician of the soul, and ever after he pleaded in preaching for the pious life of the ordinary man. This was healthy and natural, and abounding in the wholeness of living. When later as Bishop he ordained candidates for the ministry, he asked a standard question concerning the young minister's views on objective redemption. He wished to see that the central point was clearly understood and adhered to.

The heart of Berggrav's preaching is seen in the stand he took when the Quisling worked with the Nazi occupation power to imprison him and many others. Church and State were separate entities under God. Luther said that the Church must not interfere with the State, as the popes did. Now in Norway the problem had changed and the State was threatening the Church. The Lordship of Christ was in jeopardy. Not that the Church should dominate, but that both State and Church should acknowledge God. Thus the preached word maintained the freedom of the Word of God, the unity of the Church, the rights of parents, the education of children by the Church, and the proper relationship between Christians and the Church with respect to the authority of government. In the message "The Foundation of the Church" which he issued to his wife and then to others and which brought his eventual arrest and imprisonment, Berggrav was never more eloquent: "It is Christ I want to write about (and preach?). No one can describe or imagine His being. My belief is that He *is*. And He is *here*. In person. It seems to me that there is a shadow over His face. He is still suffering. Even after entering the Kingdom of God, this chord of pain still vibrates within Him. To me the fact of His resurrection stands forth more clearly than the actual cheers on that occasion. 'It is finished.' The words become the immovable pole of our existence. But it has its cost. The cost of living has not been abolished." His preaching had that quality of deep feeling and emotion. He lived through suffering and tension, but gave strength to others in need. In radio preaching as well as from pulpits Berggrav was effective in dealing with controversial issues and answering people's questions about the Bible, ethics, and destiny.

His preaching was associated with experience so that people sensed he knew what he talked about because he had gone through this before. Subjective in strain and deeply personal, Berggrav's preaching was realistic, true to life. He discussed tangible things and used concrete illustrations. His own word about preaching expressed this truth that the preacher was obligated to reach down into the hearts of people, and to preach the Word of God as it was written. While the first was easy, the second had difficulty. He went through a time of questioning about the Bible, but later an evangelical experience through the Oxford Movement enabled him to know the secret of Biblical preaching. "When God looks at me," he said, "He does not see me—and thank God for that—but He sees Christ in my heart. And then I am just as precious to Him as His own beloved Son." Few of his sermons abide as models; they nevertheless were geared to the times in which he suffered and stood alone.

Others who influenced Scandinavian preaching include Gustaf Aulén, Professor of Theology in the University of Lund, Sweden, and Anders Nygren, Bishop of Lund. These men by their published books more than by their sermons have motivated many others to preach the basic doctrines which they have studied and expounded at length. Connected with this also is Yngve Brilioth, Archbishop of Sweden and for many years Professor at the University of Lund.

Yngve T. Brilioth (1891-1964) not only preached and taught; he also gave us outstanding books on preaching. The first, in Swedish, is *Predikans historia* (1945), a valuable contribution to the subject. Subsequently, an English translation was made by Karl E. Mattson (1965). Brilioth outlines the development of preaching on the continent of Europe; little is said of this in the new world. As a Lutheran he was much indebted to Luther and his ideas of preaching. He gives a good digest of the work of the Reformer as a preacher, who has in a sense no method, and yet his style has been copied and his thoughts on preaching practised by succeeding generations of Lutheran men.

Brilioth followed Luther and in his own preaching there is the hint that only as preaching is part of the ritual of church worship is it effective preaching. Overagainst the Roman Church and its lack of true preaching, this is to be expected. The Word of God must have prominence. This was the genius of the Reformation—to restore the Bible to the people. Thus preaching became the exposition of that Word of God. The pericopes with their outlined format gave substance and direction. All this he emphasizes in his above mentioned book.

He also published *Eucharistic Faith and Practice* (1931). We find here the doctrinal aspect of his thought. He wrestled with the central doctrines of the Christian faith and expressed a profound understanding of the meaning of that which was both evangelical and yet universal or catholic. In this way he proclaimed his message to his people. Both as pastor and then in the bishop's office he stressed the exposition of the gospel. The people heard the good news in the vernacular, a contrast from the days before the Reformation when it came in scant forms in another tongue. At first there was a paraphrase of Scripture, then the reading of parts of the catechism, followed eventually by the homily or exposition. Thus the Swedish sermon directed by Brilioth and others of his school remained within the framework of a liturgical order which has not ceased.

Gustaf Emmanuel Hildebrand Aulén (1879-) is best known for his outstanding work as a theologian. He was perhaps the foremost dogmatic theologian of the Swedish Church. Among his writings this book stands out, for it deals with *The Christian Idea of the Atonement* or, as the English translation has it in more familiar vein, *Christus Victor* (1930). This is a study of the three main types of ideas of the atonement, and stress is laid on the aspect of Christ's victory over sin and death. That "God was in Christ reconciling the world to Himself" is his view, which sets the incarnation in direct connection with the atonement and proclaims that it is God himself who in Christ has delivered mankind from the power of evil. From this background and premise Aulén discusses the historical development of doctrine.

After a survey of patristic teaching, he scans the pre-Reformation period, climaxed by the Reformation and Luther; finally, in the light of the New Testament text, Aulén affirms that this view, the classic view, is the adequate view for the church. The book gives an historical analysis but does not essentially make an *apologia* for the classic idea; yet it appears almost as a vindication of the classic idea. Aulén tells how he wrestled with this doctrine over his early years, especially in preaching. He was not satisfied with the "satisfaction theory" and the "exemplary theory" and thus gave himself to this exacting task of reinterpretation.

Having satisfied himself concerning the truth of the atonement, he sought to spell out in simple and clear language in sermons to congregations what he really believed. Though he dealt with other themes such as our Lord's belief in his Messiahship and the advent of the kingdom of God, the main thrust of his preaching came out of passages in the Gospels on the subject of the atonement. In his sermonic work on Christology, Aulén also endeavored to separate Luther's actual teachings on the atonement from much of later Lutheran theology. The Reformation for Luther and Aulén was more than a protest against abuses. It was an attempt to deliver the church from the slavery of a system which had spoiled the gospel of salvation by a rationalized theology and a moralistic ethic. In this central doctrine of redemption Luther and Aulén were one. And in his preaching he suggested that both Protestants and Catholics needed to return to this idea of the atonement.

The theologian is again heard through the preacher in his statement:

> For my own part, I am persuaded that no form of Christian teaching has any future before it except such as can keep steadily in view the reality of the evil in the world, and go to meet the evil with a battle-song of triumph. Therefore I believe that the classic idea of the Atonement and of Christianity is coming back—that is to say, the genuine, authentic Christian faith. . . . Its revival will show that the fundamental idea of the atonement is, above all, a movement of God to man, not in the first place a movement of man to God. We shall hear again its tremendous paradoxes: that God, the all-ruler, the Infinite, yet accepts the lowliness of the Incarnation; we shall hear again the old realistic message of the conflict of God with the dark, hostile forces of evil, and His victory over them by the divine self-sacrifice; above all, we shall hear again the note of triumph.

Anders Nygren (1890-), another Bishop of Lund, was teacher and preacher. Nygren began as a pastor and then ended as bishop in the high leadership of his church. Throughout his life he remained the faithful servant of the people through the church. Churchly preaching was his general principle, and the familiar liturgical background gave substance to his sermons and exhortations. There was nothing unusual about him as a preacher. He was not distinguished as some others. He used the church year and the church liturgy as a means of faithful and regular exposition. This background became the foundation of his thought and writing when he came to the major work of his life.

He is known in the English-speaking world chiefly by his monumental book *Agape and Eros* (1932), a study of the Christian idea of love and its history. At the time the subject had fallen into neglect and was therefore a clarion call to renewal and hope. When Nygren taught as theologian at Lund, the times were ripe for this theme. Wars and tumult among the nations were part of the European scene. Where was the reality of love now? Had the church any message for the age? Misunderstandings of what love really was were commonplace. Here was an attempt to clarify.

In this volume love is seen as man's love in *eros* and God's love in *agape*. The distinction is vital. In a massive survey of the ideas and the words used, Nygren shows that distorted interpretations have been given. It was his task to expound what he discerned as the true meaning of the words. Overagainst man's love of *eros* is the divine love of *agape*. In the former lies self-love which is a perversion of God's creation. "That which in all things only seeks its own, is thereby closed against God. But when through faith man becomes open to God, the love from on high obtains a free course to and through him. He becomes a 'tube,' which by faith receives everything from God's love and then allows the divine love to stream out over the world. God's love has made a new way for itself down to lost humanity. Once for all, and in a decisive manner, this has come to pass through Christ. He came to us in the form of a servant and in humiliation, yet His majesty has not thereby grown less. He has rather revealed it in still greater glory. His majesty is the sacrificial, self-giving majesty of love." Christian theology and Christian preaching are indebted to his magnificent study and exposition, in which are manifested the accents and overtones of the preacher of love.

While in Norway and Sweden the main stream of preaching lay in the State Church with its Lutheran ritual and theology, there were others who became pietists and independents. Not much is available in print from which to discover the nature and form of their preaching except for their general ideas of Biblical exposition, their evangelistic fervor and appeal, and their practice of forming groups for prayer and fellowship. This warmer and more personal idea of the church has had continual support from many in Scandinavian countries, and not a little of this has carried over to similar groups and denominations in America.

Frank Mangs (1897-), prominent in this connection, is known among Scandinavian peoples for his evangelistic preaching which assisted the work of revival during the early part of this century. Gifted with a warm spirit and a grasp of the Swedish language, he ministered as a Covenant Church pastor before launching out in the wider work of evangelism. Some of his sermons are published in *Spiritual Awakening (Andlig Vackelse)* (1937) and *Launch Out into the Deep* (1937). These reveal the Biblical and textual nature of his preaching. The texts are taken and expounded without any unusual format. They conform to the then Scandinavian method of detailed explanation and exhortation. Strongly evangelistic, they have the appeal for decision and the persuasion of the warm-hearted preacher. To those versed in the knowledge of that culture, his gifts included the colloquial use of a language which could sing for the one familiar with it. Mang's contribution to preaching indicated the place of revivalism through evangelism both in the homeland and also when he ministered on visits to America. Among people of his own culture he stood out in winsome evangelism.

In addition to Mangs are such names as Ole Hallesby and P. P. Walenstroëm. Hallesby is known more through his books on prayer and the cultivation of the Christian life. Walenstroëm led his people out from Lutheranism into a special view of the atonement, a view which is followed, though not slavishly, by the Evangelical Covenant Church in the United States.

The preaching of the Scandinavian countries has left a strong sense of ecumenical relationship with other communions through Söderblom; an emphasis on love through Nygren; and a reemphasis on the atonement as Aulén taught and preached it. Because of these outstanding men these strains have been continued in Scandanavian preaching.

In the Scandinavian culture God honored the life and ministry of others who represent various traditions.

Paavo Henrick Ruotsalainen (1777-1852) of the Finnish Lutheran Church came from a farmer's family with limited education. The piety of that age, the Bible, Luther's Catechism, and the revival spirit set his course. In preaching and teaching he was esteemed as a leader, and without clerical recognition he worked within the national church of Finland. He had balance of judgment and steadied many emotionally-disturbed people. The discipleship he taught was based upon discipline and not fleeting emotion through "the school of the cross." His words in his tract "A Word to the Awakened Peasants" (1847) permeated the mind of the church.

Nikolai Frederik Severin Fruntvig (1783-1872) was one of the Danish preachers whose influence was as profound as that of his fellow countrymen, Hans Christian Anderson, the children's storyteller, and the philosopher-theologian, Søren Aabye Kierkegaard. Fruntvig exposed the religious veneer of modern thought. His gifts included those of the poet, hymnist, statesman, educator, and pastor. He moved in his preaching from romanticism and uncertainty of faith into the heart of Christianity in the doctrine of the atonement. As a Lutheran preacher he awakened the national church in Denmark to the benefits of an evangelical spirit and life.

Carl Olof Rosenius (1816-1868) was a lay preacher in Sweden with unusual acceptance among intellectual leaders. As a lay evangelist, he ministered in revival movements and this countered the excesses of rationalism, secularism, and formalism. Through his preaching vital faith was generated and religious life found warmth, enthusiasm, and moral strength in a time of eroded Christianity.

The dawn of the present century has brought a strong emphasis of Lundensian theology in the teaching and preaching of the churches linked with the State. The independent groups have tended to be freer in forms of worship and given more to evangelistic preaching. The parish minister has been an interpreter of the theology linked with the names of Aulén and Nygren. **Anton Johnson Fridrichsen (1888-1953)**, Norwegian by birth, a Docent in Oslo, became Professor of New Testament Exegesis at Uppsala (1928-53). He shared in the translation of the Bible into Swedish, published 1917, the first new work since the sixteenth century. The influence of Fridrichsen came through his founding of the Uppsala Society of Exegesis (1936), and annual publications with contributions from a circle of men whose sympathies were the same.

Among the emphases influencing preaching has been "the *Messianic* understanding of the works and words of Jesus" by which Fridrichsen interprets almost every narrative and the heart of the Gospels. Behind this is the *Church*—the messianic people of God. The acts of *Baptism* and the *Lord's Supper* are given importance; and the *Ministry*, early and primitive in its origin, is the calling and commissioning of men to proclaim the message of the Messiah.

Thus preaching has been colored by the restudy of the early church, and a revived theology has been proclaimed for the church of today.

The emerging Scandinavian group included Gösta Lindeskog, Krister Stendahl, Harald Sahlin, Harald Riesenfield, and Bo Reicke, teachers in New Testament studies within the orbit of Anton Fridrichsen. The stress upon Biblical Theology was kindled by a typological exegesis certainly different from an earlier somewhat forced allegorical interpretation. The preaching of this first part of the twentieth century had exciting overtones of hope and application in which, as **Gustav Wingren (1910-)** taught, the Word of God and preaching are one in witness.

French

Wilfred Monod (1867-1942) came from a remarkable family of French Protestants who stood for the Reformed faith in its evangelical expression. The distinguished **Adolphe Monod (1802-1856)**, although not related, had already brought luster and fame to the Monod name because of his outstanding services as a pastor in France. He was thought of as the greatest preacher in the Reformed French Church. Pietistic preaching loomed large in his ministry after his earlier years of serious Biblical study.

Wilfred Monod extended the renown accorded the name by his preaching beyond France. His major interest lay in the ecumenical movement which came to birth in his lifetime. He was a pioneer in this. Like his namesake, he served as preacher at the Oratoire du Louvre in Paris, where his influence was far-reaching. Alexander Vinet of Switzerland had given direction to the earlier preachers in the art of homiletics. This was based primarily on the equality of all the Bible although preference was given to the Old Testament and Paul rather than the Synoptic Gospels. Wilfred Monod went beyond that in his maturing life and ministry.

Social passion and a Christian spiritualism were blended into a pattern of noble beauty in his flaming proclamation. These impulses inspired the preacher to go beyond a pietism which was strongly personal to one that was social in its implications. His style was sombre and touching in its tenderness. The language was bold and striking.Vivacity, unction, and simplicity were traits found in Wilfred Monod.

There was an elegance in preaching which the earlier French orator had cultivated; this was the pattern for centuries. However, the ferment of a new era led the preacher to a lessening of oratory and the implication that no suggestion of duty is necessary if what is said is clear. Once the art of preaching was cultivated, but now this had become more direct in seeking a response from listeners. Descriptive power was still there, especially for the Reformed, whereas the Roman Church still counted on logic and declamation.

Marc Boegner (1880-1969) of France can be seen as a Protestant preacher in the tradition of those who had given solidarity to French preaching in the nineteenth century. Boegner arose as the best exponent of the ecumenical ideal in a day when French preaching had declined as a strong force.

First as a parish pastor, then as a national leader, Boegner led the church in France in spite of many splinter groups and disunity of purpose. His chief work was fusing many into an objective outlook in which they could share in a larger and wider fellowship. In the twentieth century this was not an easy task. When in 1948 the representatives of more than a hundred churches came together in Amsterdam, their first task was to decide whether there should be a World Council at all. Then it was that Boegner who represented the French Protestant Church formally proposed "that the first Assembly of the World Council of Churches be declared to be and is hereby constituted . . . and that the formation of the World Council of Churches be declared to be and is hereby completed." There was a long road to unity, but a beginning was made in the direction of union.

The spirit of Boegner is revealed when he was ordered by German authorities to publish a document protesting Allied bombardment of German cities. He refused, saying: "The French Huguenot Church never makes public declarations by order of the temporal power." This brave stand for what he believed was right is indicative of the spiritual quality of his beliefs. His growth as a Christian, as a pastor in the Reformed Church of France, and as a leading figure in church relations on a world scale marks him as a leader.

Through his preaching he was the spiritual leader of his church and although numerically it was not large, its influence has been far reaching in France and beyond. Spiritual crusader, he preached out of a firm belief in Reformed and evangelical theology. His faith was expressed in true churchmanship. His conversion experience transformed his outlook and reshaped his whole life. His larger ministries did not neglect that foundation but were based on the integrity of his fidelity to the Word of God.

Living as he did in a country with greater Roman Catholic than Protestant influence, he was sensitive to the emphases made by that body. He appreciated much of its devotion and yet maintained a critical concern for open relations with people. He was also the missionary and the man of social concern. His work in wartime among refugees, captives, and Jews, gave him a unique opportunity to minister as an evangelical pastor. His association with Christians of all other bodies did not diminish his personal beliefs. For him the prime vocation and calling in a secular age was to be a herald and witness of the saving power of the gospel and the Holy Spirit who makes it possible to live that life.

Boegner was a pastor for most of his life, and for thirty-five years led the Passy Church in Paris. He ministered to a small group of people, a minority of European Protestants. The context of preaching for him was the knowledge that he and his people lived always within that difficult and trying period when world wars raged and when the country they loved was invaded and also occupied by the enemy.

A sampling of his preaching is taken from his Lenten meditations which were also broadcast over the government radio network. This gave the preacher the ear of a vast audience as well as rallying the million-and-a-half Protestants throughout France who looked to him as the symbol and sign of leadership in that generation. Here are choice thoughts and expressive phrases. *The Prayer of the Universal Church* catches the spirit and content of the familiar Lord's Prayer in Matthew 6. To Boegner the happy title he gave for publication was natural as he was one of the few men who could stretch his arms wide and encompass all Christians everywhere. His was the greatheart spirit to share with all and to recognize that all others—whatever their name or sign—were one with him when praying this prayer.

In discussing the opening words of the prayer he dwells on "Our Father" and shows the unity of our praying, not "I" but "our."

> Here we are touching one of the most profound reasons why Christ taught his disciples the Lord's Prayer, and not some other prayer, and especially not such a prayer as those which we offer to God most of the time, in which we speak to him constantly and always

about our personal life, about the intimate circle of our kin and friends, about those whom we love, about our own cares, our own trials, our needs, thereby giving evidence of a Christian life which is hardly even conscious of the place which pride and spiritual egoism hold in it! It is against this tendency that Christ would warn his disciples. It is from this self-seeking carried even into prayer that he would wrest them free. The whole gospel bears witness that he does not permit one to become his disciple for one's own sake alone, or in order selfishly to enjoy the new life which he evokes, to hold oneself apart from those who do not know him or do not believe in him, or, all the more evidently, to stand aloof from other followers. . . . One cannot be Christian through oneself alone and for oneself alone. This is the realization which comes to us every time that we recite the Lord's Prayer, saying these two words: Our Father. However solitary we may be when we pray these words, far from any contact with a church and with church people, isolated in a sickroom or in a prison cell, we cannot pray this prayer alone. . . ."

Boegner brings fresh meaning and spiritual insight into the familiar prayer. There is a clear and simple style in a flow of rich ideas which color the interpretation with deep meaning.

Boegner's preaching was characterized by a tenderness of spirit, a warmth of a pastoral concern, and a genuine feeling of seeking understanding with those who were not in his tradition. The older French classic style of preaching was somewhat stiff and polished. The newer style of the nineteenth century and on promoted a more flexible and popular style. Closer to the latter, Boegner wrote and preached with vigor and freshness. Charm and beauty marked his public utterances. A precision in the use of words was noted. There was a piety in the flavor of his personality and an awareness on the part of his listeners that here stands a man of God. He was a lovable man. His influence on French preaching can be summed up as that of the pastoral office as preeminent. Without the formal title, he lived and led his church as a bishop would, but not with worldly power. His leadership came because all recognized him as the servant who stooped and acted.

Richard Paquier, a minister of the French Reformed Church in Switzerland, is a link with those Reformed pastors of other days, such as the Monods and latterly Boegner. The Reformed Church, in its reaction against Rome at the Reformation, did not have much tradition in the general ways of liturgy except the plain hour of worship. However, not all people of this background wished to continue as Pietists or Independents, but chose to have some appreciation of the Catholic liturgical worship, yet purified and enriched by the Reformed experience. In this situation Paquier sought to contribute his insights for preaching.

As pastor and interpreter within an ecumenical movement, he is no sectarian or nonconformist, but bridges differences within true worship where some unity can be found. In *Dynamics of Worship* (1967) lies a concern in this age for new conversations between Christians. He preaches within a renewal of liturgical worship. The Biblical and historical bases for worship are always in mind. Worship then is the occasion when Word and sacrament unite to share God's sovereignty and the priesthood of believers. Because of the *kerygma* of the gospel, a new *koinonia* results. Preaching centers in the evangel which comes from the Word and which is communicated through the words of the pastor-preacher. It is an "event" in which people reach the climax of their adoration of Almighty God.

Paquier's emphasis in preaching lies in his Christ and congregation centered proclamation, oriented towards the great facts of the faith: the trinity, incarnation, redemption, resurrection, Parousia, church, and sacraments.

Pierre Marcel (1910-) represents the Reformed Church of France, having been born in Paris and educated in theology at Paris and Amsterdam. He has served as pastor of the Reformed Church at Saint-Germain-en-Laye since 1942, and as Professor on the Protestant Faculty of Theology, Paris, since 1951. His theological and academic strength is seen in research and thesis as well as in publications dealing with Calvin, Aquinas, Duns Scotus, and Herman Dooyeweerd. His preaching is in the context of European trial and war. Like others in that vortex of revolution and tension, the message is Biblical and contemporary. Based on a Biblical background or character, such as Abraham, the sermon is applied to the present. The preacher himself and his congregation see him as undergoing Abraham's experience. As expected from one in the heritage of the Reformation, the Word of God is authoritative for all circumstances, and tests and trials become triumphs in Christ.

Dutch

Abraham Kuyper (1837-1920) is the one outstanding figure of Holland, and as a preacher his work had profound influence not only in the congregation but in the society and state of which he was a part. He was a leader of men and his many-sided works indicate how strong he was in the vigor of his life and work. In the church he stood as a preacher and leader. In education, politics, and government he played an important part in constructive leadership. He was a controversial character, but his stature was that of a national figure.

Kuyper was a brilliant student at Leiden University and with his acute mind and stentorian voice he early was marked for leadership. He was a young man of orthodox faith but in the university he imbibed intellectual rationalism so that when he prepared to enter the ministry he had a problem to be solved. For awhile the Reformed Confession of Calvinism seemed outmoded in the light of the newer teaching then in vogue. However, an examination of John Calvin's views with others led Kuyper to a modified position in theology and eventually he became more sympathetic to Calvinism. In later years he was to lead others in forming a new University and Divinity school based upon the principles of the Reformed faith in its orthodox expression.

As a preacher Kuyper at first was usually liberal in doctrine and Jesus was more martyr than Savior and Mediator. His sermons had literary style and good diction, and his voice and gestures cast a spell upon his hearers. In the early years of his pastorate he preached what he honestly knew and believed. Exposed to conservative church members, he discovered that orthodoxy could be without life and religious fervor. He testified that through this experience of dealing with the main issues of faith and life he was led to see that there was a place of reconciliation with God through Christ.

Out of spiritual struggle and soul travail Kuyper grew in grace and in knowledge. He broke with what was then termed "Modernism" and embraced the Reformed theology with all his mind. He now understood Calvin saying that God was our Father and the church our mother. Thus the preacher came alive. He proclaimed the gospel from the Word of God. He taught from that Word. He shepherded from that Word. He governed by that Word. In the orthodox tradition he preached by "opening the Scriptures—the ministry of the Word." This type of discourse was not like other sermons. It savored of an address but one closely held to the actual text of the Bible. From Utrecht to Amsterdam he went as pastor and always with the desire to serve the church and proclaim his beliefs. He turned his thoughts to education—in church and in the state. He was compelled to take a stand politically on issues of the day. In a sermon on "Hold that fast which thou hast" (Rev. 3:11), titled "Conservatism and Orthodoxy," he treated the problem of the church in forceful language and with a dramatic injunction: "Do not bury our glorious orthodoxy in the treacherous pit of a spurious conservatism."

In the consistory Kuyper took leadership at a time of struggle. His sermons at that time were noted for their Biblical basis, their balanced spiritual power, and their pervasive influence. Neither theological lectures nor emotional homilies, they stressed that when the mind, heart, and will were one, action would follow. In his speech were the notes of church reform, life abundant, social action. He was a master of language, his words, phrases, illustrations, and figures of speech coming spontaneously. The classic style was present and his sermon seemed a work of art. The aesthetic pleasure for the hearer was matched with spiritual profit. Also in the custom of that day was the reading of the Scriptures. In the hands of Kuyper, men also found interpretation by the reading.

Analysis of the sermons of this period show that Kuyper preached more topically than with exposition. Nevertheless, what he gave was given after study of the text; and while he dealt with topics he did not fail to present Christ as found in the gospel. This was the time of controversy and Kuyper was blunt and forceful in his denunciation of those who did not follow his orthodox position. Many felt wounded by his attacks from pulpit and addresses, but the church was sifted until the conservatives founded their Free University and developed their own schools and consistories. To the people who followed Kuyper this was a time of progress and stimulus. It was from this background that Kuyper went from the pulpit into Parliament to become a strong force in his nation. From Congressman to Prime Minister is a remarkable achievement. The preacher also became Professor of Theology and correlated disciplines.

As a preacher his influence was nationwide, but in the classroom he taught homiletics as the science and art of preaching. How could he do this—the master to the novices? It is by observation, theory, and most of all practice that one learns. Kuyper endeavored to inculcate in the student that preaching is the laying bare of the

Word of God. The sermon must possess unity. The preacher must himself be stirred with the truth. He must have rapport with the congregation. In those few principles lay Kuyper's philosophy of preaching. He certainly left his impress upon the ministry of the Reformed Church in Holland and especially in the new and freer body then under way. Kuyper was the ten-talented man, outstanding in every way. With encyclopedic mind, he graced all subjects of study with mastery and ease. His preaching stamped the Dutch scene for generations with its virile orthodoxy.

Czech

Josef Lukl Hromadka (1889-1969) will be remembered for his fearless witness as a Christian preacher, scholar, patriot, and pastor in his native land of Czechoslovakia. Born in Moravian country, he had a long ministry which bore fruit beyond his native land in all Europe and the United States. His ministry was unusual in that he lived in the crucial period of World War II when his own country was overrun and he returned from America voluntarily to serve his people and teach in the theological faculty in Charles University, Prague. Throughout, he sought to engage the Communistic leaders in dialog with possible reinterpretation and understanding, without in any way defecting from his Christian position. Thus he became an apologist.

Hromadka's background of Lutheran piety was enriched when the church of his state united with the Reformed Church of Bohemia and Moravia to form the Evangelical Church of the Czech Brethren. He served in pastorates, taught in the Protestant Theological Faculty, came to America for some years, returned to resume teaching and dialog, and was the Dean of the Faculty at retirement. Throughout these years he sought to shape his Christian teaching to appeal to the working classes and the politically minded. Influenced by the historical school in theology, he learned from Ernst Troeltsch, Johannes Weiss, Bernhard Duhm, and David S. Cairns in Aberdeen, Scotland. His European mentors stimulated his thinking in the direction of social and political involvement. Karl Barth also taught him much with the crisis theology of the times. Cairns brought him to see that God was sovereign in history and Christ risen from the dead could transform all areas of man's life and action. In his homeland Hromadka became the evangelist in classroom and in pulpit.

In *Thoughts of a Czech Pastor* as well as in *Doom and Resurrection*, the Czech Protestant spelled out his ideas and convictions. He proclaimed that the disasters of life could be matched by the dynamic thrust of the gospel. By accepting the Communist Revolution as a fact of history, he found tension with his brethren in other lands and through the World Council of Churches he pleaded for deeper understanding with those who were enemies. He stood with Masaryk for the democracy of his country and later shared in the ruin of his country after Munich and World War II. His courage and zeal persisted in spite of opposition, as he tried to be the man of God standing in the crisis hour proclaiming as the prophet to those who derided him and to those who mistrusted him. He knew what it was to stand alone.

His preaching had in it that quality of deep, fervent thought which spilled over like lava in eruption from a volcano. His theological convictions were centered in the historic and apostolic ideals, but he applied them in social-political structures which he saw required change and transformation. When in exile from his native land, he spent four years at Princeton Theological Seminary as Professor of Apologetics and Christian Ethics. He was then viewed as the leading Protestant mind in Central Europe. In his preaching Hromadka exposed sin where it was often hidden—at the highest levels of human nature. When man takes his will and upsets God's will, then tragedy ensues as it did in Europe's wars and convulsions.

His own views on preaching reflect his own eloquent proclamation. "What does it mean to preach?" he asked:

> Before the man in the pulpit lies the Bible, not simply a book, but the everlasting witness of the everspeaking God. The Bible is full of mystery, and before the preacher are seated his hearers, also full of mystery. What now? It is not difficult to be an eloquent speaker, to make impressive talks on various themes, topics, and subjects. It is certainly not depressing; on the contrary it is very pleasant and enviable, especially if one has a pleasant voice and understands how to play the clavichord of the human heart. Preaching, however, becomes *the problem* not only of our thought but of our existence in the moment we realize the meaning of the Word we have to preach. The preacher has to proclaim the presence, the real presence of God in His Word. He is supposed to speak not *about* God or some interesting religious, moral and cultural theme—he has to deliver a personal message from the God of Abraham, Isaac and Jacob, from the Father of Jesus Christ. The preacher is not expected to present his own views and ideas, and to induce his hearers to some lofty and high ideals, to lay down old doctrines, to

comment on contemporary events and movements. He is not expected to lull the people into sleep; he is not expected to entertain them, nor to offer them the best-chosen narcotics. To preach means to take God with agonizing earnestness, and to challenge the very existence of man. His *very existence,* not only his ideas and convictions, his moral or political views, his religious sentiments and habits.

This is the essence of Hromadka when he preached. He spoke as an evangelist. He called on men to act. The times were desperate. This Word of God, he cried, is a terrible word. It is one of indictment, of accusation, of crisis. Even the gospel brings divine judgment. Those are the realities Hromadka spoke about as preacher and testifier against a soft and blind generation. Mankind was on the edge of human existence, so he said. These realities are thus "realities between heaven and earth, eternity and time."

Hungarian

Among the representative preachers of Hungary stands **Béla Vassady (1902-)** whose ministry in the Reformed tradition culminated in Budapest, the capital city, during the horrors of the siege in 1944-45. Several times he had to learn through physical suffering the faith which depended upon divine help, and this is mediated through his preaching. After the holocaust ended, Vassady came to America to lecture at the Reformed Theological Seminary, Lancaster, Pennsylvania, and found pulpits open to his witness and ministry.

Over thirty years, both in Europe and in America, he has been spelling out his "system" of theology. The Word of God has been light and lamp to him, and so his preaching is not artificially illuminated. The light-overcoming-darkness motif has been the guiding principle of his thought. In the volume *Light against Darkness* (1961) this theme is unfolded in didactic sermons.

Systematically, Vassady interprets and expounds his beliefs based on the Bible revelation. "At its heart Christianity," he says, "is an audio-visual religion. It has a message that must be heard and proclaimed, as well as seen and radiated. This message concerns itself with the life of man in the light of God who himself is light." Vassady weaves into his message apt allusions from the poets and from science which now is seen as vindicating the work of the Creator. God as light-nature is revealed in self-disclosure. This act of making himself known to us is the expression of God's creative and redemptive love which never ceases. Thus "the numinous is essentially the luminous."

His preaching brings the fact that God the Creator is the Light behind the universe now being explored. He is known only in the perspective of his other work, which is redemption. Jesus and his church bring more light as reflected in time and through the gospel. He who claimed to be The Light of the World is by the Resurrection (a) way-disclosing light, (b) truth-revealing light, (c) life-breeding light, and last but not least, (d) sight-giving light. Thus the life of the Christian is to walk as "children of light" as they "believe in the light." The end of this experience is not pride, but the glory of God, from whom and through whom and to whom are all things.

Vassady brings a Christian theology of the Old Testament linked with the New Testament as the medium for preaching in the Space Age.

Swiss

Karl Barth (1886-1968) holds a dominant place in the theological spectrum of all time. His modern saga is moving and profound as he was led out of the liberalism of his early years into a revived view of Biblical revelation as the Word of God. His discovery as a young pastor-preacher that the Book of Romans was saying to him and his generation what Paul had said to the first century brought life and quickening to a dead and barren church. Now as he expounded the Epistle he was conscious of life from the dead. Thus the renewal of a European church, and Continental Theology from henceforth was to be known as "Barthian." The publication of his *Commentary on Romans* in 1918 was a bombshell in the religiously complacent world and began a revolution in theological thought. Since then Barth has published his monumental theological corpus *Church Dogmatics* in thirteen volumes, as well as volumes of sermons and other single theological volumes. However, samplings of his preaching abound and these reflect the faith and gospel behind the theology and certainly here is theology preached simply to his fellows.

Deliverance to the Captives (1961), and *Call for God* (1965), are examples of his skill in communicating the Biblical message to people in lowly situations and in unusual environments. Barth had

been a pastor for many years in early life before becoming a
Professor of Theology. However, it is as the latter that he now
brings his mind to share with those in prison. "He hath sent me to
preach . . . deliverance to the captives" (Luke 4:18) is the key to his
motive in preaching. This age might well be called "The Age of
Barth," but he might be known also as the giant theologian who
had time to share with people in prison. This is how his theology
was preached. It is not easy to know what to say to people in
prison, nor how to say it. Yet he simply tells how Jesus Christ is the
way by which God speaks to us.

The sermons are soul-searching and stimulating. They disturb and
stab; they probe and yet comfort; they appeal and bless. God is
transcendent, reason is empty, man is sinful and helpless, and God's
grace is all sufficient. Evangelical preaching is found in his sermon
"Saved by Grace." Man is lost and needs a deliverer. Man cannot do
anything to help himself out of that state: it is God who acts. When
preaching to prisoners Barth preached to himself. There is a personal quality and a simple sense of being sympathetic as one enters
with him into the world of the hopeless and forgotten.

One of his recorded prayers is: "O Lord our God! We give thee
thanks that we may meet in this hour to call on thee, to bring
before thee all that troubles us, to hear together the good news of
the salvation of the world, to give thee honor and glory. . . . Speak
to each one of us in such a way that we may hear that personal
word of help we need. . . . Show thy mercy to all who are gathered
this morning as thy congregation wherever they may be!" As Barth
prayed and then preached to the inmates of the prison, he knew he
talked to some outside of the church and of Christ. Nevertheless, he
spoke to them on their level as one of them in need of mercy and
forgiveness. His opening words are significant: "My dear brothers
and sisters, for you I will try, briefly, to clarify what we have here.
You will see that each word is significant." This Introduction is
characteristic of most of the sermons.

In the body of the sermon there is a reference to the text from
which the theme is taken; for example:

> I now read a passage from Ephesians 2:5: 'By grace have you been
> saved. . . .' This, I think, is brief enough for it to be remembered by
> all, for it to impress itself upon you and, if it be God's will, to be
> understood. . . . How strange to have this message addressed to us!
> Who are we, anyway? Let me tell you quite frankly: we are all
> together great sinners. Please understand me: I include myself. I

stand ready to confess being the greatest sinner among you all; yet
you may then not exclude yourself from the group! Sinners are
people who in the judgment of God, and perhaps of their consciences, missed and lost their way, who are not just a little, but
totally guilty, hopelessly indebted and lost not only in time, but in
eternity. We are such sinners. And we are prisoners. Believe me,
there is a captivity much worse than the captivity in this house.
There are walls much thicker and doors much heavier than those
closed upon you. . . . But now listen. Into the depth of our predicament the word is spoken from on high: 'By grace you have been
saved!' To be saved does not just mean to be a little encouraged, a
little comforted, a little relieved. It means to be pulled out like a
log from a burning fire. You have been saved! We are not told: you
may be saved sometimes, or a little bit. No, you have been saved,
totally and for all times. You? Yes, we! Not just any other people,
more pious and better than we are, no, we, each one of us. . . . This
is so because Jesus Christ is our brother and, through his life and
death, has become our Savior who has wrought our salvation. He is
the word of God for us. And this word is: 'By grace you have been
saved!'

Barth is not unlike Bonhoeffer who dispensed with the Lutheran
pericope in the interests of the confessing church and a more
realistic approach to people outside in the upheaval of war and
revolution. Again and again Barth cuts short the actual text and
gives only the pith of it. For example, he speaks on "Take heart"
from John 16:33—"In the world you face anxiety; but take heart, I
have conquered the world." In a Christmas Communion sermon he
takes the Christmas story of the manger birth and talks simply
about "He stands by us"—which becomes a moving plea for reassurance of God's presence in prison from the one who came in lowly
guise. "He who was born in the stable is he who stands by you,
stands by me and stands by us all." Here is the essence of good
preaching—the proposition easily understood and identified with by
all.

Of course, Barth preached in other ways to his regular congregation as a pastor in earlier years. On "Repentance" he take the
surprising text: "Come unto me, all ye that labor and are heavy
laden" (Matt. 11:28) and by an unusual interpretation catches
attention and makes appeal. The theme is not clearly outlined
except by implication. "Jesus call us . . . " is repeated as divisions of
the sermon. Around these items are woven the call of the Savior
and then the call of the church. Because men are sinners the gospel
call must be proclaimed by the messenger of Christ.

Barth's theory of preaching was linked to his views concerning the Bible. To him the Bible was the Word of God written, the Word of God proclaimed, the Word of God revealed. In that three-fold scheme he reiterated: "The Word of God is God Himself in Holy Scripture. For the God who once spoke as the Lord to Moses and the prophets, the evangelists and the apostles, now speaks through their written word as the same Lord to His church. Scripture is holy and the Word of God as by the Holy Spirit it became and will become to the church the witness of God's revelation." This in substance implies that revelation to Barth is the event in which God makes himself known, the act of self-revelation which issues in an encounter with man. This being so, the Bible is spoken of as the Word of God only in an indirect sense: that it witnesses to Jesus who is the Word of God. There is no actual hearing of that Word by the "book" the Bible: there is the possibility of hearing the Word of God. Barth's message rested upon the truth of reconciliation and his preaching was therefore evangelical in spirit, with good news and joy flooding the message.

The neo-orthodox school of theology which is linked with Barth's name brought encouragement to many to so preach as men rediscovered the value of the Bible. Barth associated himself in preaching with that "proclamation of the word of God . . . expressed in Holy Scripture as the foundation and the final aim of the church." Preaching to him was "in the presence of God and in the context of public worship" when something happened through the sermon. In *The Word of God and the Word of Man* (1928) and *Prayer and Preaching* (1964) Barth enlarged upon this thesis. He stressed that "Preaching is the Word of God which he himself has spoken; but God makes use, according to his good pleasure, of the ministry of a man who speaks to his fellow men, in God's name, by means of a passage from Scripture. Such a man fulfils the vocation to which the church has called him and, through his ministry, the church is obedient to the mission entrusted to her." "Preaching follows from the command given to the church to serve the Word of God by means of a man called to this task. It is this man's duty to proclaim to his fellow men what God himself has to say to them, by explaining, in his own words, a passage from Scripture which concerns them personally." "The reason for making these two statements is that preaching has a dual aspect: the Word of God and human speech." To Barth preaching starts from a fixed point and that fact is that God has revealed himself, and this means that the Word has become flesh.

Heinrich Emil Brunner (1889-1966) represents Switzerland in the honored role of a preacher. He is better known as a theologian whose massive books, *The Mediator, Man in Revolt, The Divine Imperative, Revelation and Reason, The Christian Doctrine of Creation and Redemption ("Dogmatics")*, and *The Christian Doctrine of God ("Dogmatics")*, as well as others, have given him a place in European theological crisis dialog. However, as a preacher he should not be overlooked. In his native land as well as elsewhere he preached consistently and regularly.

The story is told that when he visited Princeton Seminary he was asked to preach in the University Chapel and educators and students crowded to hear him. What would this theological professor of eminence say to that group? He began by saying that as he had come from far to address them, he had tried to prepare what would be most effective and helpful for them. Would this be some rehash of dogmatic theology? Would this be some new and erudite lecture or address to be carefully read and pondered? No! To the surprise of all he simply said that as they were all needy people with himself he had decided to *preach* to them from Romans 1:16, "I am not ashamed of the gospel of Christ: for it is the power of God unto salvation. . . ." That in essence was the heart of Brunner, and when later he ministered regularly in the cathedral in Zurich we catch a glimpse of his spirit and mind at work.

The Great Invitation and Other Sermons (1955), is a sampling of his thought and style. It reflects the method and message to a postwar mood in Europe. In days of war and of reconstruction there are changes. From his own words which indicate his ideals for preaching we glean much: "Printed sermons have always and increasingly seemed to me inadequate. For preaching is essentially a living occurrence which can only very imperfectly be crystallized in writing. For that reason I have up to the present carefully avoided the publication of sermons. But perhaps in this instance the special circumstances will justify a departure from the rule. It is a question here of sermons which without exception were preached in the Fraumunster in recent years."

These were taken from various notes and shorthand manuscripts and they were offered as part of the context of public worship. Here then is part of Brunner's method—to preach either from notes or brief manuscripts so that he would be free in speech and delivery. The man who became Privatdozent at the University of Zurich and later Professor of Systematic and Practical Theology ended his career as the preacher at the Fraumunster Church in Zurich. A reading of these sermons indicates that he must have been a fervent preacher—a man with spirit—who always treated subjects of importance—nothing trivial or catchy. Of course, they are filled with doctrine or theology. Did he brood over the doctrines so that they became afire with meaning and then preach as he felt? Or were the sermons the weekly stint in preparation for a congregation to gather on a Sunday, and did he then draw out of his treasure house things new and old? Certainly Word of God and theology, doctrine and sermon went together.

Pastoral insight and spiritual direction meet in moving passages of prose as the surge of the preacher moves on to climax and application of the truth. Note the familiar way of speaking to a congregation in "The Great Invitation" sermon.

> We Christians to whom the gospel has been preached, and who are ready to believe it, must not confine ourselves to the picture of the future which we can conjure up in our own minds but must look beyond it to the vision of the future which the Lord Jesus Christ proclaims to us with the fullness of divine authority; the great supper, the eternal future, everlasting life in communion with God and all our brothers and sisters in His eternal Kingdom. To this great feast we are all invited; all of us without exception. . . . My friends, I cannot answer for you. What I can do and will do now is simply this: I will draw your attention somewhat to the way in which and the reasons for which so many do not accept the invitation. . . .

At this point Brunner sounds like an evangelist pleading with men about the alternatives because of the awesome nature of man's choice. The wooing note is there and the quiet constrained tones can be heard.

In the sermon "Death and Resurrection" based on I Peter 1:3, Brunner moves swiftly in thought and speech as he is carried along as by a wind of the Spirit to stress the glad hope of the Christian. This was five weeks past Easter Sunday, but on this "ordinary" Sunday he reminds his people that every Sunday is an Easter Day because of the resurrection of Christ from the dead. The celebration must continue to be an anniversary each Lord's Day. On the first day of the week there is no other motif or message! Contrasting life

and death, he pleads with his congregation: "these human treasures—material, cultural, political, social—are destined ultimately to
fall a prey to all-devouring death. Here such human acquisitions are
transitory: they fade away. But here is a testament which death
cannot mock because it does in fact deprive it of something,
namely, of all those who are here made valid heirs."

Brunner's preaching dealt with great themes and the texts chosen
seemed to have chosen him! It is true a preacher's mind inclines to
rove over a wide field of need and within that he cultivates a narrow
patch of Scripture. But Brunner gives the impression that he has
ranged over the entire divine revelation and now can be selective in
preaching as he distills the richness of his mind and knowledge.
Each sermon is not merely a tiny section of a moment's thought.
We feel the heartthrob and the pulse beat of a giant whose aim is to
share the whole in every part given away to hungry people. In
"God, Our Refuge," a sermon from Psalm 90:1-4, we see the man
of God at prayer, and truth spills over in cascading power. "Lord,
Thou," the beginning of the text, brings the preacher to acclaim the
majesty of God as he approaches him in the vestibule of prayer.
"Men are self-enclosed and solitary, alone with their anxieties and
fears, alone on the way—ah! how short!—in which death is ever
drawing nearer to them, nearer and nearer each day with no
possibility of escape. Death is coming to me and I must needs go to
meet it as in a yawning abyss which swallows me up. Such men have
only this one dimension, their journey on this earth, which death
must terminate. They are not aware of the third, the vertical
dimension, as a result of which we can invoke the Lord, *Thou,
Lord, Thou eternal God.*"

Brunner's prose moves swiftly and feelingly, and is at times terse
and stabbing, but always it probes the conscience of his hearers and
demands that they face up to the call of God through the gospel of
Christ. There is beauty in what he says and all of it reads well. Here
is good preaching. It is faithful and true. He believed that "the basic
or primal function of the church is that of preaching: for it is this
which establishes the Church, in every sense of the Word." All this
to Brunner was within the act of worship wherein "the decisive
thing is whether you are offering yourself to God."

Throughout this kind of preaching we discern the quality and
form of Swiss Reformed tradition. The Reformation spirit of keeping to the Word of God and gleaning from the text the source of the

divine message is exemplified in Brunner. Whatever his views on the Bible, there is no hint here of any uncertainty about the inspiration of the Scriptures. He seems to accept them at face value. We are here not in the study or the classroom of the professor weighing the pros and cons of what is decisive for truth. Here is the pastor and the evangelist with commanding voice and pleading utterance asking people to listen to and obey that divine Word of God!

Switzerland was fortunate in having such eminent men as theologians of the first rank in Barth and Brunner. They also were preachers in their own way. Alongside were others who represented the regular pastoral ministry in the writings and utterances, such as **Walter Luthi (1901-1945)** and **Eduard Thurneysen (1888-)**. Luthi served as pastor over most of his life but took time to write books on Biblical studies, which show that his scholarly habits enriched his sermons. Books by Luthi include those on Romans, Acts, Malachi, Amos, etc. Thurneysen published *A Theology of the Care of Souls; Come, Creator Spirit;* and several volumes of sermons, one with Luthi.

Swiss preaching carried on the Reformation impetus in keeping close to the text of Scripture. Pastoral preaching of this kind led a congregation in knowledge and truth with Christian living in view. Character was cultivated in the best sense so that Christian men and women became proponents of evangelical conviction and conduct. During the two World Wars many in Europe were in danger of losing their heritage, but these two pastors are noteworthy examples of many who tried to restore the essence of Protestant affirmation and witness. They stressed the unity found in Christ by all Christians, and their teaching concerning the Lord's Supper enabled the church to renew its vows of allegiance and devotion to the crucified and risen Savior. A confessional church was built up under stress and strain to abide as a strong force of compassion and concern for the world around. Preaching stood at the heart of the life of the ordinals of worship.

Since the Reformation, Protestantism has called itself the "Church of the Word." The sermon assumed the major place of interest in public worship. This was based upon the fact that along with belief in God was the claim that God was pleased to speak or communicate his will to those who were his people. That means of communication was by the written Word, the Bible, and the faithful sound of words through the channel of the preacher. Thus according to the Helvetic Confession (second part) this was true: *"Praedi-catio verbi Dei est verbum Dei"*—"The preaching of the Word *is* the Word of God." By this came authority and the sermon then became a means of grace.

In this context the congregation was part of the interplay when preacher and people listened together and when the pastor-preacher proclaimed that word to them. The people were not only expected to listen; they were also actively to think of what was being said. Such respect for that word of God in the sermon constituted a climate for excellent preaching. The faith and expectancy of the hearer assisted the preacher then to be free and outspoken in the truth conveyed by human words. "The word can do much, even without the voice; the voice is empty without the word"—so Augustine marks this distinction. "The human voice of the preacher is the tool or instrument of which God's divine Word makes use. If the Word of God is not present, there remains nothing but the human voice, which is empty and only a 'mouth speaking great things' (Dan. 7:8)." Luthi called attention to this much-needed condition in preaching. Sowing seed and expecting a harvest was the attitude of the Swiss pastor.

Another quality of preaching lay in the telling of the Good News as the evangelist crying out the victory of Christ. As the word for *evangelium* is the usual word for *gospel*, in German, this thought is a striking factor in Swiss preaching. However, Luthi as well as others saw in the gospel the scandal or offence which it brought in demanding a decision from people. The messenger must not assume that all will welcome the truth; there is the factor of some rejecting it. Luthi saw that preaching was being attacked as an inconsequential and ineffective means of doing things. He and others of his tradition believed that words were mightier than the sword after all! In the didactic element in preaching there was, moreover, the means of increasing faith and developing intelligent Christians who in turn would make an impact upon society. Preaching, however, should not be simply moralistic; it should be "instructive preaching." "The teaching sermon does not consist of lecturing the congregation on dogmatics, important as it is in higher learning. Nevertheless, dogmatics should be imbedded in the sermon like iron rods in reinforced concrete." We have seen in this connection how the dogmatician Emil Brunner preached with this characteristic facility. Swiss preaching stressed Bible reading—the reading of books of the Bible at a sitting—in a day when through war and conflict many were growing up without regular education from the Bible.

Any attempt to be prophetic had to be made in the light of the Bible's words which were uncomfortable and conscience-stabbing. Needs and depths of despair, poverty, homelessness, loss of faith— whatever men experienced in that generation—was to be matched by prophetic preaching, the healing from God's Word. Such prophetic preaching may result in opposition, even suffering and death when the climate around is antagonistic to evangelical truth. The preaching of those who stood to confess the Christian faith against all odds was that which was especially potent within the hours of worship. Then the people of God listened with obedient hearts. It was Thurneysen who claimed that in preaching and worship the congregation must confess its true position before God, namely, not confessing sins to a priest or to one another, but rather making such confession of faith to inspire fellowship with one another and with God. In this preaching was central. Thus the sermon was a cleansing agent and a healing grace.

Luthi in *The Lord's Prayer* deals with the several petitions as he expounds this classic model for prayer step by step. He speaks to the needs and capacities of ordinary people in a congregation. Some of this reveals the tensions all too common in a congregation but heightened during days of war. In talking to a group where there are different nationals present, Luthi does not hesitate to apply the truth of forgiveness as a necessity and reality: "However forgiveness must not be regarded as a universal theory; it must be shown to be a practical reality in every individual case. It is all the more important that there should be a Church with light and salt to offer at a time when not only politics and economics, but all aspects of life, particularly accusation and condemnation, so easily acquire a collective form. It is this mass judgment that the Church has to oppose. Now the Jews are blamed for everything, now the Communists, or the Germans, and they in their turn may be relieved of responsibility by the capitalists. In the face of this kind of wholesale condemnation of humanity the Church must be deeply sincere when it prays, '... as we also have forgiven our debtors. ...' "

As this point comes an illustration of a German who is seated with others in a congregation and some other nationals object to his presence. "It is then," says Luthi, "that one of us must arise and say that this man is in church here, in other words, in the place where forgiveness rules. The lawsuit (pending) concerning our brother in faith is in the hands of the authorities, and will be properly examined by them. But that does not alter the fact that he is our brother in faith. Therefore he must not leave. That is what the church is. The accusers constantly call to us who are in the church: 'That man must leave!' . . . Yet, the accuser even whispers in our own ears: '*You* must leave.' But Christ stands up against the accuser and says, 'For the sake of the blood I have shed you do not have to leave.' You would have to leave if it were not for Christ. Which of us would not have to go if God were to stand up and judge? But the Table is prepared and we are all invited to stay."

In this kind of preaching Luthi exemplified the finest tradition of Reformed theology and faith. Here is first-class pastoral preaching of the shepherd heart. Couched in simple language the pastor-preacher is concerned for people. Light is thrown upon difficult passages. He writes with simplicity and yet with confidence in the power of that living Word which is able to bring healing and health to troubled souls.

Jean Jacques Von Allmen (1917-), Professor of Practical Theology at the University of Neuchatel, has contributed to the preaching ministry of his church and nation. He is a member of the National Reformed Church of Switzerland. During his work he has endeavored to apply the findings of Biblical exegesis, church history and systematic theology to the enrichment of the church. To him Christianity is an incarnational religion, and thus the message of the sermon must bring to human life the word of God for the hour. As a pastor at Lucerne before becoming teacher and author, he has interpreted the miracle of preaching as a continuance of the preaching of Jesus. Preaching is the task of reinterpretation of that life-giving word.

In his books *Vocabulaire Biblique, Worship: Its Theology and Practice*, and *Preaching and Congregation*, Von Allmen sees the sermon as part of worship within the Reformed tradition. The sermon thus given is not only part of the hour of worship—it also becomes worship. It is an offering up to God as much as other acts of worship. Here it completes worship in the actual word spoken by man on behalf of God through his Word.

German

German preaching has within it many strands as we trace it through the beginnings of the century up to and including World War II. The thrust of the higher critical movement in theological study had changed the face of the church. Biblical preaching fell into decline as men became more subjective in theology and followed the influences of Wellhausen, Harnack, Nietzche, Schelling, and Schleiermacher among others. The liberal spirit which they inculcated changed much of the preaching from the earlier Lutheran expository type into a more subjective and topical treatment. If Luther was the greatest influence on preaching for generations, Spener and Schleiermacher were in the nineteenth century. The stress then was on justification by faith and also the life of piety. Later came W. Krummacher whose evangelical expositions won wide hearing.

The cataclysmic changes of the twentieth century affected German thought and religious life. Before and during two world wars, the decline of orthodoxy and the predominance of liberal theological thought ended in a decline in spiritual fervor and a lessening of missionary effort. In part the evangelical portion of the church withstood some of this as pockets within a vast sea of unrest and barrenness. The crisis of the rise of Hitler became the act in history to shake Germany once more and the foundations of religious life were troubled. The resistance movement had taken place and with some success, but eventually it was overpowered by other forces. Roman Catholic, Jew, and Protestant were one in their sufferings in that hour of taking a stand for the right. Among those who resisted were Protestant pastors and leaders whose preaching was outstanding in a day of trouble.

Hanns Lilje (1899-) was a well-known figure in the ecumenical movement, especially at Amsterdam in 1948. There he appeared after surviving the holocaust of war and the imprisonment of Hitler's Nazi concentration camp. What kind of man was he? How did he survive and why? For himself he would say he was a simple Christian man, who, although he was only a preacher of the gospel, fell into the hands of the Gestapo; whom God preserved as He once preserved those three men in the fiery furnace. During his time of trouble he had the same testimony they had: "The angel of the

Lord made . . . the midst of the furnace as it had been moist, whistling wind, so that the fire touched them not . . . ."

As much as any man of his time Lilje could estimate the depths of horror possible in that experience which came to millions—the degradation, the terror, the threats, the sadism, the mockery, the privations, and the sufferings of human beings under devilish tyranny. Nevertheless, he did not allow hatred, revenge or nihilism to spoil his inner faith when he saw evil doing its worst. Banishing despair and bitterness was the way he took courage to make a new beginning in the knowledge that God overruled in history and in human life.

The preaching of this man had its overtones in the belief that the church of Christ was primary in God's design for the world. As a Bishop of his Lutheran Church, he knew what it was to lead and make decisions. He was a yoke-fellow in suffering for the Kingdom of God with others who belonged to the Confessional Church in Germany. When under interrogation by the authorities, he referred to his preaching as somewhat of lecturing to inform people of the issues then before the nation. One of his addresses "Is God Silent?" reveals how he tried to preach the gospel and to explain fundamental Christian convictions. Messages like this became for him part of his resistance to evil powers. The contract between the Christian faith and National Socialism could not be evaded. To Lilje the latter had become a substitute religion in Germany. It was nihilistic in tendency and it ruled out the Christian faith because it would not admit the First Commandment: "Thou shalt not have any other gods before me." In rejecting this, National Socialism rejected all the others as well.

While preaching is the exposition of the Word of God, Lilje found that often he would be discussing the major issues of a social and political nature in the course of a sermon. This also was good preaching when he came to see that he must obey God rather than man. The Word of God was the mightiest weapon to be used in that hour, but as a Christian pastor and witness he did not evade or ignore his citizenship in taking his stand on social and political matters. This principle he shared through his preaching. It was his preaching which caused Hitler to watch him and then imprison him. Such preaching was a great threat to the authorities. Lilje in preaching made it clear that tyrants would ultimately destroy themselves. Usually God destroys them. He said that "the plan of God allows the tyrant to follow his way blindly, to the end, until nothing remains, not even an ambiguous halo of a political martyr's crown."

He testified, "The secular idea of honor knows nothing of that splendid inward independence which faith gives. All through imprisonment I realized with gratitude that the ministry of a preacher of the gospel makes a man independent both of the praise and the blame of the world; hence I have never, at any moment, seriously felt that my honor was impaired by the treatment which was customary in this prison."

Lilje testified that during his period in prison his understanding of the Bible and the words common to the Christian faith took on new meaning. Suffering mellows and hallows accepted truths until they begin to glow with something new. His messages on rare occasions to others within prison walls suggest this. However, when free again he continued his preaching and teaching in more formal ways but enriched by the suffering and hardship.

Meditations on "Abraham, the Father of the Faith," reveal insights of his own confession of faith. He recalls when the Old Testament was attacked in the public opinion of Germany, denying its place in religion, because it was thought of as a Jewish book. Lilje stood for the Christian theology which was based upon the Old Testament and his preaching sought to see parallels for today with its relevant truths. In these Meditations we hear Lilje saying:

> God's revelation is at the beginning of all our knowledge of God and of all our personal piety. Not liturgy and cult, not human pity and the cultic quest of man, not the great achievements and plans which man may harbor, are the beginning of faith, but God's revelation alone . . . . The Word of God must be first in man's life. It was not Abraham's obedience, not his faith, not the genius of his piety, that was first in his life . . . . Temptations are the means by which God forces upon us his greatest gifts. For as a rule he must force us to accept these free gifts. He does this by making it completely plain to us that our lives are fraught with human embarrassment and inner frustration. His main purpose is not to let his chosen people fail or fall. But his purpose is to bind them more securely to himself.

In discussing "The Praise of God," Lilje used meditations on the New Testament songs of praise, such as the Magnificat, the Benedictus, and the Nunc Dimittis. Each of these is viewed as the vestibule or narthex of the cathedral of truth. "It is still dawn," he said. "There is the morning quietness, the stillness of salvation, which like a silver lining on the distant horizons precedes the light of day. The full light of day has not yet appeared. But there is the beautiful light which indicates the first hours of the day. Thus our two chapters (Luke) precede the actual ministry of our Lord. His day has not yet begun, but in the songs of these three pious people (Mary, Zechariah, Simeon) who sing his praises before his birth and during the first few weeks of his earthly life, we see his life's work already reflected." Lilje shows himself a true exegete and interpreter of the text as he discusses the meaning of the language used. He compares ancient language with modern use and allows for the difference. He pleads, however, that in the uniqueness and strangeness of Biblical language from another age we have classic expression which abides without distortion. Actually he claims that in these hymns of praise—used by the church—the words are not empty but full of rich meaning as we have there "the sum total of the experiences of the children of God. What these people have experienced in faith, confession, suffering, love, prayer, and discipline has been expressed in classical clarity and power in these words."

In dealing with our Lord's "Instruction for Life," he does not pass by the hard sayings. His thesis is that to understand the Sermon on the Mount we should not separate the sermon from the person who gave it. In it he found the exposition of our Lord's way of life. It was fron the mount of the sermon that he went to the mount of the cross. "If there is not forgiveness of sins, the sermon will remain utopian . . . . The light from the Hill of Golgotha also shines upon the Mount of the Beatitudes where Christ spoke. And the claim that in this world there is a life without lies, without sexual lusts, without hatred, without vulgar material worries is true only because the resurrection of Christ from the dead has brought about an entirely new reality. Where there is forgiveness of sin, there is also life and salvation. We cannot separate the Sermon on the Mount from the Pauline understanding that the death of Jesus and even more his resurrection have opened up life in his name. The Sermon on the Mount is an instruction for life which springs from an entirely new dimension."

Lilje dealt with the subjects of murder, adultery, and worry as "hard sayings" of Jesus and by clear exposition of the text brought understanding and new light to what has been exploited for selfish ends. "Therefore, it is not religious nonsense but a decisive presupposition if we say that without a thorough and basic change in man himself it is impossible to overcome murderous thoughts. Even organized pacifism is of no help, unless people change. That is a serious but definite condition. The reverse is also true: if people change, then organized movements for peace are no longer necessary. But without a change of heart everything man does may be only of relative value." This from a man who stood against governmental powers and tyranny in high places, knowing the possibility of death! Here was a preacher in Germany faithful to the Word of God and without fear trying to apply it to people living under the shadow of death.

Lilje's book of meditations, *Messages from God's Word* (1961) affords a luminous example of his preaching skill. Here is the traditional Lutheran pastor dealing with Scripture in the ordinary ritual of the church. However, there is a spark, a spirit, a dynamism which can be attributed only to the fact that here is one who has suffered. In that suffering he found the depths of human need and anxiety. Now he meets that need with messages which reflect his faith and courage under testing. This is preaching at white heat—and the unity of thought and balanced outline are not forgotten!

Karl Friedrich Otto Dibelius (1880-1967) as Bishop of the Evangelical Church in Germany, exercised a profound ministry during the struggle against Hitler and the tense situation created by the dominance of Soviet power in East Germany and a divided Berlin. Courage and conviction enabled him to witness against the powers of darkness and proclaim the light of the gospel. When in 1933 he preached an uncompromising sermon before members of the government, in which he said, "the dictatorship of a totalitarian state is irreconcilable with God's will," he was obeying God rather than man. When forbidden to preach, he defied the Nazi regime and defended the rights of the Confessional Church movement. His trial in 1937 was a test case, and his acquittal showed the victory of truth.

Otto Dibelius stands symbolically as the unifier of all Protestant Christians in times of tension and disruption. His leadership over a divided city symbolizes his shepherd-heart's concern for all people. Chairman of the Evangelical Church Council and later one of the Presidents of the World Council of Churches, he had a rare and unusual character which was trusted by people of diverse points of view. He was a reconciler. In theology he was influenced by Friedrich Delitsch, Adolf Harnack, Reinhold Seeberg, and Hermann Gunkel. He learned that preaching and the work of the pastor are the supreme areas of concern in his life's work. Fortunately, he spent two years at Wittenberg in the Preachers' Seminary with its Lutheran tradition.

The pastorates brought joy and discipline to Dibelius, for then he learned that preaching had to be learned outside the classroom and study. He found it hard work. The liturgy was found to be secondary to the effect of the sermon. In the Evangelical Church he came to the realization that the important thing was the sound, average sermon. This required diligence and concentrated spiritual power, but it was the only kind of sermon which would carry conviction.

When liberal ministers thought of the sermon as the way to "discuss religious questions" with the congregation, Dibelius stood for a straightforward presentation of the gospel of Jesus Christ. He believed that everyone needs this for his salvation, old and young alike and people in every walk of life, however exalted and however lowly. He shunned the way of oratory and brilliance, and preferred to speak as the pastor to plain people. He got down to "essentials" and this implied that what people wanted to know in church was not what Dibelius thought about political, religious, or other problems, but what God's eternal Word had to say to them in their need and temptations. Not that Dibelius failed to take his stand on the political and social questions of the hour! However, in preaching to his congregations, he regarded the sermon as a vehicle of pastoral care. When he was arrested and tried, it was because of sermons preached with care from Biblical texts without adornment, but which were understood by congregation and by the Gestapo as having practical application to concrete events and individuals. Thus in his preaching the Word of God was not bound.

In summary, the preaching power of Dibelius can be expressed in what he wrote in looking back: "Lord my God. Through Your Church You kept me true to Your Word, and did not let me lose my way amid the temptations which assailed me from without and from within. Your Word preserved me from skepticism and contempt, those characteristics of an age alienated from God. Your Word sustained me when it was difficult for me to find joy in my ministry. Your word—that is my Lord Jesus Christ. Him I thank that I was able to find my way to You and that I could always be certain of Your pardon. Him I thank that *a theology of the Cross* should have led me to a theology of victory, which is not my victory but Yours." Behind the sermon and preaching was this theology and living faith which was the inner conviction of the preacher. This alone enabled Dibelius to witness and preach.

F. G. E. Martin Niemöller (1892-) is known as the preacher who stood against Hitler and was imprisoned in an attempt to stop his ministry. The attempt failed and soon the whole world learned of the message of this intrepid man. During the Nazi regime, Niemöller was charged with political treason against the State and castigated as an enemy of the people. In the view of Hitler he was guilty, but his courageous stand resulted in his eventual release. He rejected the State religion of the Fuehrer who had cajoled a nation into anti-Christian ways. The preacher said, "We are ready to give unto the world the things of the world. But if the world asks for the things that are God's, then we must manfully resist, lest we give the world the things that are God's; and for the sake of a comfortable life in a strange land lose our home."

Thomas Mann, German writer and world-known thinker, paid tribute to Niemöller. His interpretation of the preacher is apt and relevant to that era. He sees Niemöller as the pastor who expounds the religious message and yet in so doing cannot escape the charge that he is interfering in the decisions of the State. Injustice, cruelty, calloused minds, and the idol of force could not be passed by when the Christian faith was interpreted by the pastor. He who had been a submarine commander was now engaged in a moral and spiritual warfare. At that meeting point he was under surveillance by the secret police, for his sermons were likely to sway the minds of people. His favor with the people in Berlin and his many listeners made him an object of suspicion, and his seizure by the personal order of the Fuehrer of Germany indicated the strength of his religious ministry over against the power of force.

Niemöller stood in the way of Hitler and therefore he was under threat of death. However, his life was spared because Hitler was afraid of the consequences among the population if he carried through the final verdict of condemnation. As a compromise, he was incarcerated as many other likeminded pastors and Christians. He was held in solitary confinement for four years and then sent for another four years to the infamous Dachau camp. "Amidst the horrors of those days," he said, "the Gospel remained alive for us as the power of God. It remains even now our only hope." Selections of his sermons were published, including *God Is My Fuehrer* (1941), and *Dachau Sermons* (1956).

In preaching, the threat of death loomed over his proclamation of the truth. The pressure of tyranny and the intolerable denial of freedom caused the preacher to say with his famous mentor and example, Martin Luther, "Here I stand." From I Corinthians 2:2, "For I determined not to know any thing among you, save Jesus Christ, and him crucified," Niemöller preached a sermon about Martin Luther at Reformation Festival time, October 31, 1936. This preceded his conflict with Hitler, but it shows the thought of the pastor before the onslaught of evil. He calls upon his congregation to see in the past how God came to the aid of Luther and how they learn by looking back. They should move forward in courage and hope knowing only one message—the message of the Crucified—as this would endure in the future.

The titles of his sermons suggest that Niemöller was already living under the shadow of judgment and doom. He thus preached on the eternal themes—Gethsemane, Good Friday, Easter. He used the Church Year for special emphasis and called upon people to face up to the claims of Christ. In the sermon "Christ or Barabbas" (Matt. 27:17), he related the story of Christ's passion and brought himself and his people into that situation of choice. "Dear friends, no man has the right to put this question to other men without giving the answer himself. No man has the right to leave this decision to others without taking a stand personally for this is not a matter of free choice in which anyone who likes can participate and in which anyone who likes can refrain from participating; for bound up with the name *Jesus* there is a claim which even Pilate himself could not pass by, and which no one can pass by who comes into contact with this name. It is the name of Jesus, of Whom it is said that He is Christ." In quiet measured tones, with precision of word, probing the conscience with the alternatives of choice, Niemöller preached as the pastor-evangelist. Divine love over against human mockery was held up in the drama of redemption. All this under the dread shadow of the impending doom of a nation! Preaching then in Germany was apocalyptic and the Word of God had realistic meaning and application.

One of the most loving utterances of Niemöller was given while in

Dachau Prison when on Maundy Thursday he conducted a communion service. The meditation was based on I Corinthians 11:26—"For as often as ye eat this bread, and drink this cup, ye do show the Lord's death till he come." The message is introduced by the retelling of the Biblical story of the Exodus and then the Paschal meal of the Lord and his apostles. Illustrations are not found here, for the hour is late and death is imminent. Every word is freighted with destiny. Interpretations are no longer the subject of argument as in history or by contending groups. The men in that small gathering in a cell are from every kind of home and background. The only meaning of that Supper is suggested as a plain and simple explanation—"this interpretation which Jesus himself gives of his death is plain; but in its wonderfulness incomprehensible and in its depth unfathomable . . . . To this great community of those who proclaim the death of their Lord as a message of joy belong this evening also we, who come here to his table. A small company, everyone of us torn away from his earthly home and from the circle of his dear ones, all of us robbed of freedom and ever uncertain about what the following day or even the following hour will bring. But, despite all this, we are at home."

There is no attempt here to be clever, only the desire to bring the eternal message of hope and salvation to this small group of condemned men. As Richard Baxter of England had said, so Niemöller is preaching "as a dying man to dying men." His words grip and awe—"this is the unparalleled feature of his death, that he dies in our place, the Just for the unjust, the holy one for sinners. And now we stand in his place: freed from all guilt and through him and on his account beloved children of God." This was in 1945, on the eve of release by American forces. But that hour could have been the last hour before execution. Knowing well the horror of that great darkness over all those men who were with him, the preacher lays bare his heart and in moving language portrays the sufferings and death of the Savior. As they look to the Christ in his agony, so they find strength to endure their ordeal. Here is Biblical, evangelical, and soul-searching preaching of a kind unique and unusual. This is the overflow of a mind already saturated with Biblical truth and a heart touched with the feelings and infirmities of others. Truly like the prophet Ezekiel (3:15), Niemöller sat where they sat. As a captive himself, he identified with all prisoners; and in that dread hour the cell became the house of God, the elements of bread and wine became the living Christ, and under the shadow of the cross the presence of God was known. Homeless, lost, doomed men found in that moment "the Cross on Golgotha, the home for the homeless."

Dietrich Bonhoeffer (1906-1945) stands out in Germany as one of the men who defied Hitler and suffered eventual martyrdom because of his Christian faith. As a young man he was unknown and, until his death, practically unnoticed except for the few in America who had known him as a student and friend. The crucial issue of how to "render unto Caesar the things that are Caesar's and to God the things that are God's" could not find better illustration than in his life. The State under Hitler made demands which went beyond the response of conscience, and thus Bonhoeffer stood as a witness in his generation for the eternal verities. The famous Declaration of Barmen (1934), was a confession and creed of the "Confessing Synod" and the "Confessing Church," a body of people gathered together in that tempestuous hour of history.

Young Bonhoeffer had been pastor in Barcelona, Spain; student at Union Theological Seminary, New York; and pastor in London, before returning to his native land. That he did return when he might have sheltered outside of Germany testifies to his devotion to his Lord and his willing service among his own. His imprisonment and his association with those who had tried to get rid of Hitler climaxed with his hanging while attempts were being made to save him. He was not spared by the authorities even at the end of the war. Through his letters and his writings on theological and Biblical subjects a new messenger came to speak to our generation. For him to write was labor and to attempt many books not possible. His *Ethics; Letters and Papers from Prison; Cost of Discipleship;* and other extracts on paper, constitute a sufficient guide to his thought. His preaching lay behind these publications and from them we glean his message and spirit.

Preaching was Bonhoeffer's privilege only for a short time, but it was not casual or careless. What he had to say came out of much thought and suffering. The words *duty, conscience, morals, righteousness, devotion,* and the like found in the common vocabulary of the Christian were not academic or conventional to Bonhoeffer. As he used them in that fiery furnace of persecution and in the light of his choice, they found depth and penetration as never before. He had to wrestle with them before preaching and applying. The rock of his life was Jesus Christ as the supreme authority for life and morals.

"O wondrous change! Those hands once so strong and active, have now been bound. Helpless and forlorn, you see the end of your deed. Yet with a sigh of relief you resign your cause to a stronger hand, and are content to do so. For one brief moment you enjoyed the bliss of freedom, only to give it back to God, that he might perfect it in glory." Thus does he see that a choice is made in preaching and that Jesus Christ is the unchanging reality. In the concentration camp he came to appreciate ordinary individuals outside the organized church, and he ministered to them in what he termed "worldly Christianity." This was an attempt to reach others in the world by living among others where they were. "This is what I mean by worldliness—taking life in one's stride, with all its duties and its problems, its successes and failures, its experiences and helplessness. It is in such a life that we throw ourselves utterly in the arms of God and participate in his sufferings in the world and watch with Christ in Gethsemane. This is faith . . . ." His interpreters have distorted his views somewhat, implying that Christianity has to change to be like the world, but this is not what he meant.

The quality and measure of Bonhoeffer's ministry must be estimated in the light of martyrdom and opportunity. As he was about to be led out to die, Bonhoeffer held a service in prison for his companions and spoke intimately to them. His words touched them deeply and he had the right word to express the spirit of their trials and the resolutions rising within their minds. "This is the end," he said, "for me the beginning of life."

At first in preaching he followed the regular Germanic pattern of the pericope within the Lutheran tradition. Homiletically this was a foundation, but he soon departed from this in the spirit of his searching mind. He was not satisfied with analyzing the present or presenting an accurate and straightforward exegesis of Scripture. He wished to say something important. He believed he had something important to say, and that his hearers should be shaken out of their complacency and won over. In pursuit of this aim he dealt boldly and, taking into account the German homiletical tradition, not over-accurately with his texts. From his theological beliefs he tried to convince his listeners. Not always successful, he was able, however, to create an impression of pastoral warmth and concern.

Bonhoeffer preferred to take brief phrases from the texts and not limit himself to the pericopes. There is a thematic unity as he tended to dramatize what he found and put himself in the situation of the Scripture. His illustrations were not "bookish" but out of life, nature, myth, and story. His early preaching reflects his conviction that religion must be the antithesis of faith, so that faith alone brings justification. The church was the arena of encounter with Christ and the Christian life should be lived in the earthy and concrete situations. Thus his allusions: "We must regain understanding of the meaning of solidarity among mankind . . . . God wants us to see men, not ghosts who shun the world . . . . He made the earth our mother . . . . If you wish for God, hold fast to the world . . . if you want to find eternity, you must serve time . . . . "

Methodologically, he was a quick reader who marked the pages read and followed this with notes. Exegesis was the basis of preaching and lecturing. He sifted what he garnered before passing on to his own reflections. He wrote what he had thought out and had clarified. There was a terseness and tightness in his style. He worked as one under sentence and as if time were short. This intensity of expression marks his writings and sermons. When Bonhoeffer was teaching in the German seminary, he taught homiletics and did this in the context of all other theological disciplines and studies. He insisted that the sermon was to become the voice of Christ as God in Christ spoke through the man of God in the message.

His words were apt: "Do not try to make the Bible relevant. Its relevance is axiomatic . . . . Do not try to defend God's Word, but testify to it . . . . Trust to the Word. It is a ship loaded to the very limits of her capacity." The usual German idea of "application" following the "explanation" in the sermon was treated lightly by Bonhoeffer as "God alone is concrete . . . the concrete situation is the substance within which the Word of God speaks; it is the object, not the subject, of concretion." His knowledge of the sermon was linked to his background of Lutheran Christology, but it also was grounded in the church. He reiterated that "in Christ" there is no room for conditional clauses in preaching. The congregation should be confronted with the heart of the matter at once. Extempore preaching can be done by anyone who really knows his Bible. Thus he pleads: "The Word of the sermon is Christ accepting and bearing human nature. It is not a new incarnation, but the Incarnate One who bears the sins of the world. The Word of the sermon seeks to accept men, no more. The Word of the Bible assumes form as a sermon; thus its goes out to the congregation in order to hear it. The preacher must permit this autonomous outgoing of the Word towards the congregation to take place, he must not hinder it."

In *The Cost of Discipleship* there are allusions to his inner beliefs culled from exegetical preaching: "The Sermon on the Mount is not a Word to be treated cavalierly—this, that or the other is no good, here we find an inconsistency. Its validity depends on its being obeyed. This is not a Word to be freely evaluated, not a Word that you can take or leave. It is a compelling, dominating Word." His conception of faith here was strengthened by his discovery of the social substance of each Christian belief: "It is impossible to become a new man as a solitary individual. The new man means more than the individual believer after he has been justified and sanctified, it means the Church, the Body of Christ, in fact it means Christ himself." This is the summary of his preaching to congregations—to engage in the struggle and the battle for faith. Christianity may seem weakness to others, but in it paradoxically is the strength of God for man to overcome sin and his world. Out of the prison house Bonhoeffer was to ponder and write much more, but preaching in the accepted sense was ended. His notes and writings would henceforth be his means of communicating his message to the world.

Rudolf Karl Bultmann (1884-) came to prominence by his new hermeneutic which he taught as Professor of New Testament at Marburg. His reaction against the older liberalism did not lead him into the Barthian emphasis but into the idea of "demythologizing" the Scriptures. He did not accept Barth's view of revelation in which God had spoken finally to have the Scriptures bear witness to the truth. He tried to unfold Scripture as the depository of revelation but one which had been encrusted over by human agents. Thus the actual text should not be accepted as final and complete. Bultmann believed that there was in it a hard core of truth, but it had been obscured by the faith and teaching of the early church. His task as a teacher then was to uncover that inner core of reality.

To do this was to remove the outer layer of tradition or interpretation and then set forth the essentials. In doing this he took away much that was held as revealed truth by the church. This new hermeneutic or "demythologizing" taught that only the existential word had meaning for us. In his *The Gospel of John: A Commen-*

tary (1971), now in English, his pivotal view is expounded closely. As a commentary it may rank with Barth's *Epistle to the Romans* as a landmark in theological thought. He claims that the author used gnostic sources and other miscellaneous traditions in the incorporation of the final form of "John." The futuristic eschatology has been demythologized and now has become a radically existential and historical eschatology.

Behind these views is Bultmann the preacher. His sermons are based on plain texts of Scripture and his exposition takes the form of straightforward application for the church people. Bultmann's commentary stands alongside his *Theology of the New Testament* (1951), the dogmatics of the theologian. This is based on the same hermeneutic. However, the preaching of the scholar becomes simple, practical, and clear, which characterizes German preaching divorced from the study and classroom.

Helmut Thielicke (1908-) came into prominence in the postwar period after the collapse of the Hitler regime in Germany. Week by week in St. Michael's Lutheran Church, Hamburg, overflowing congregations wait to hear his sermons. All walks of life are represented as his preaching reaches people at the point of need. The first Protestant theologian to serve as Rector of the University of Hamburg, Thielicke has published books of sermons and theological treatises. In *The Waiting Father*, the gospel message of God reaching the prodigals of earth is found; in *Theological Ethics* the moral values of life are discussed in the light of Biblical Theology; and in *The Trouble with the Church* the preacher calls the people of God back to the spiritual foundations of Christianity as life and spirit, rather than institution and form.

He is the theologian turned preacher! He cites his indebtedness to Charles Haddon Spurgeon in the book *Encounter with Spurgeon*. The evangelical pastor-preacher of London was guide and inspiration to Thielicke. The German theologian preaches as if in conversation with his congregation, spelling out the faith. He takes a position and thus exposes himself. He magnifies preaching in a time when in other countries preaching is downgraded. An intellectual demand is made upon him, so that he finds spiritual discipline a necessity in preparation. His speech must be ordered speech, clearly thought out and given good structure for delivery.

When Thielicke wrote *Theological Ethics*, he believed that in this way he could best do the theological background work for preaching. He likes a large canvas and plenty of space. He moves around with big themes. Yet in the sermon he does not always use familiar theological terms, but prefers to speak the words of modern man for reinterpretation. Thus exegetical sermons are best for the purpose. "This is best within the liturgy of the church. [Liturgy to him is the flag-pole.] The sermon is the flag. It must wave in the breeze, risk something. You have to risk something to gain truth."

The nineteenth century has seen Christlieb publish his article on Homiletics (cf. Herzog's *Real Encyclopadie*) which summarized much of the teaching in Germany. Stier also gave counsel on preaching in a small volume, *Keryktik,* to show the proclamation of the gospel as the heart of preaching. Among others who followed was Harnack with his *History and Theory of Preaching* which supplemented Hering on *Instruction on Preaching.* Now with the advent of the twentieth century and the rise of dogmatics and hermeneutics, crying for attention after two world wars, a shift towards homiletics and preaching is obvious.

Heinrich Ott (1925-) once a pastor, now Professor of Dogmatics in the University of Basel, Switzerland, stands in the succession of both Bultmann and Barth to whom he owes much. His *Theology and Preaching* (1965) is a program of work in dogmatics, arranged with reference to Questions 1-11 of the Heidelberg Catechism. Dogmatics is seen to be a guide to preaching. In these is the unfolding of the *kerygma.* Then follows a discussion in which clarification of this program is seen in the light of the doctrine of sin: the Law of God; God's demand and man's failure; the fall of man and original sin; the radical nature of sin and the enslaved will; and finally God's judgment and wrath.

With these factors of teaching, the preacher is to engage in study and preparation of the sermon by homiletical rules, yet with the deep values of theology pervading the sermon. Here he needs the new hermeneutics. The sermon then is born out of the situation in which the preacher faces human need. Human understanding is a prerequisite and then an understanding of the word of *God*. Because God speaks, the preacher must listen and then speak to man. Ott thinks of the return of the church to theology as affecting the sermon. This textbook, rather than being an illustration for the preacher, requires the preacher himself to toil theologically in order to find the message for the sermon.

Ott follows Barth in his insistence that the strength of dogmatic theology is to stand at the service of the preached sermon, to correct and criticize the spoken word of the preacher in the light of the written word of Scripture. Dogmatics deals with the *kerygma*: the bringing together of preaching with an existential situation. Thus the preacher has to face the theological question as to whether the substance of his sermon is true to the gospel, and the theologian, in turn (also a preacher!), has to face the homiletical question as to whether his doctrine can be preached.

In this light, the influence of Bultmann in sifting through to the existential situation, the power of the new hermeneutics to bring tools of interpretation, and the Barthian stress that the Word of God must contain the gospel message together enable Ott to teach that there must come illumination for inspiration and proclamation. In order then to be able to preach well, the preacher must engage in dogmatic reflection, for dogmatics always implies preaching.

From the older orthodoxy through the phase of liberalism with its denial of the supernatural and its emptying out of theological content, the pendulum swings back again to a call for theology and preaching to be in partnership, and for the Scriptures, wherein the Word of God sounds forth for the preacher and his people, to be taken seriously.

Chapter X

Preaching
in Asia, Africa, and Australia
(1900-1950)

The one outstanding fact of the 1900s was the rise of the indigenous church throughout the world. The work of the missionaries sent out from the Anglo-Saxon, European, and American churches had resulted in the establishment of churches in other lands. The nationals of those lands were trained and educated within the life of the church for service and leadership. This took time, but gradually such leadership became an actuality. Japan and Ceylon are luminous examples of this.

The quality and strength of those who have served their own people can be gauged by the fact that these representative men have taken their rightful places in the World Council of Churches. At its beginning the ecumenical movement received leadership from those who were its founders. But after thirty years or so the diversity of leaders was an accomplished fact with contributions of theological insight, worldwide concern, and teaching and preaching ability.

Japan

As an area of evangelism Japan has slowly produced its own national preachers. Among them is **Uemura Masahisa (1857-1925)**. A Shintoist, he accepted Christianity, and through college work was ordained a Presbyterian pastor in 1879. The church and the YMCA engaged his interest. One achievement was his translation of the Old Testament into Japanese. The editorship of *Gospel Newsletter*, a weekly, was also added to his work. He led in the founding of the Japan Theological Seminary, and for thirty years was pastor of Fujimichi Church, one of the largest in Tokyo. As a preacher, he exemplified the pastoral function and laid the foundation of solid church ministry for his followers in office.

Toyohiko Kagawa (1888-1960), a convert to Christianity in his native Japan, was a remarkable man. His story brings before us the romance of missionary work. The message of the crucified and victorious Christ moved this man to conversion and committal. Out of his life came fruitful service and a dynamic thrust in the areas of human need among the teeming millions of his people. He literally "burned out" for his cause. In the history of preaching, Kagawa has a unique place.

Kagawa's ministry was one of diversity and variety. His preaching did not fall into one pattern alone. He was thoroughly evangelical with a social application (as in the best tradition of evangelicalism). He was supremely the evangelist, calling men to repent and accept the gospel of Christ. As a Christian he was devoted to the deepening of spiritual life and faith.

Sermons and addresses of Kagawa have been published in *Meditations on the Cross* (1935), but the major portion of his utterances, of course, are not available. Nevertheless, there is sufficient to form a judgment of his preaching.

The evangelistic messages were obviously preached to his own people with their background of Japanese life and culture. Thus the words, illustrations, and allusions are Japanese with attachment to Biblical truth. Kagawa lived in the slums of the great cities of Japan and was acutely conscious of translating the doctrine of the incarnation by his life and living as well as by his preaching. In his preaching, there is the social consciousness of need, and the work of this social prophet included indentification with people in human need and alleviation of their poverty and suffering. In this the gospel and not humanitarianism was the motive. Here was the missionary who knew firsthand the meaning of what the New Testament recorded, especially in being unjustly arrested, tried, condemned to prison, and persecuted. Like our Lord and also the apostle Paul, Kagawa's life was shot through with these experiences.

Economic and social reconstruction, the cooperative movement, and political influence were all wrapped up in the gospel message which brought hope and healing. In this the cross of Christ was central and foundational. No theology for an ecological wilderness of human need could operate except in terms of the cross. The redemption of the soul led to the emancipation of the whole man in his total environment.

As an introduction to his thought some of the poetry of Kagawa has relevance:

> O Son of Man, bearing the cross upon his exhausted and bruised
> shoulders, climbing the hill of Calvary, I myself have seen him!
> Weighted down by the burden in the road he falls.
> Then Simon the father of Rufus,
> Hurrying up to the spectacle to gaze upon it
> Is pressed into service by the soldiers.
> He, the astonished countryman, grumbles not a little
> As he shoulders and carries forward the unwelcome burden.
> Thus desires our Lord Jesus of us, that we, too,
> Take our turn in bearing his cross.
> For Jesus, after three years of unresting struggle,
> After uncounted nights of prayer, and in particular,
> After the last night of agony in Passion week,
> Jesus, the sturdy manual laborer that he is,
> Has no more strength in him
> To carry the cross alone.

Here is a reference to Jesus in His toil and manhood that Kagawa can relate to the toiling, burdened, enslaved workers in Japan. The theology of the incarnation is foundational to his preaching.

> My heart is grieved within me at human degeneracy
> And at the weak, poor-spirited life of the human race!
> Compared with the lofty figure of Jesus
> I am disgusted with my poor self!
> In this mood Paul longed to have his old self
> Crucified on the cross with Jesus.
> Before asking it of others, I, too, would crucify myself,
> And living henceforth not for my own self,
> Would awaken to the Love of the Universe,
> As it continually dies for others.

Again the overtones of theological conviction—to be identified with Christ in his death, to relate mystically to that historic event as a spiritual factor in his own life—was Kagawa's way to preach. An existential moment is here as faith lays hold of the living, regnant Christ. To meet the needs of degenerate mankind demands another Christly experience. In other sentences we sense the intensity of one who is bathed in this immanent experience:

> As in a single Word, Christ's Love-Movement
> Is summed up in the Cross. The Cross is
> The whole of Christ, the whole of love.

The knowledge of the Love of God comes only
By way of the Bloody Cross; he who fears to bear it
Cannot know the Love of Christ.

Without the Cross there is no victory.
Without the Cross
The real uplifting of humanity is impossible.

Let me go forward!
This day also must my blood flow, following
In that blood-stained pathway.

Thus his sermons center in the cross and its message of sacrifice. He makes much of "The Cross in the Scriptures" and a series of sermons gathers up this theme. He sees Christ making the world's sorrows his own and therefore we must follow in that strain. "That is Christianity. The moment we are saved, we must set ourselves to saving others. The way Christ became the Atoning Lamb was by his hanging on the Cross and dying there. And Christianity for me means to dedicate myself to serve others even unto death." He said, "Tolstoi says the Sermon on the Mount is the great thing, but the actual life of Jesus in which he practised what he preached seems to me greater even than the Sermon on the Mount."

Kagawa uses Japanese illustrations, and in a sermon relates how he published a book in 1919, *Adoration of the Laborer*, and was hauled to court for it, for the first time in his experience. The court records on that occasion read as follows: "Although he appears moderate, temperate and sound, he is really crafty, sly, subtle, insidious, designing, treacherous and double-faced; and through advancing radical theories gives the impression of cherishing revolutionary ideas!" This experience is used to illustrate in Japan how realistic was the life of Jesus the laborer of Nazareth who also went about teaching ideas for which he, too, was tried and sentenced unjustly.

Biblical allusions are generally in the orthodox tradition of language and use, as "the Cross and the Lamb"; "Christ and Moses' serpent"; "the grain of wheat"; "salvation through one man"; "Paul's view of Redemption"; "the clear meaning of Christ's atonement"; the parable of Adoption." Kagawa makes clear his belief in the vicarious substitution of Christ and freely expounds this doctrine. "The blood of Christ" was often on his lips as he preached, an allusion to the New Testament truth of sacrifice. He took this truth and turned it around to see it in the variegated light of divine revelation. In his words: "The scholars of the nineteeth century could not understand how Christ could die as a substitute for man, but for Christ and His disciples the concept of a substitute contained no difficulty. In Matthew 20:28 we find Christ saying, 'The Son of Man came to give his life a ransom for many.' Here the blood of Christ, that is, of one individual, is regarded as the indemnity or reparation which saves many souls."

To Kagawa there was never any doubt concerning the validity of the Scriptural records. Out of his conversion experience and the developing of his doctrine of the cross, he recognized the psychological soundness of the Gospels which brought him to an identification with Christ in his sufferings and death. Thus the sermons of this Japanese preacher and itinerant evangelist to his own people had in them the note of certainty of belief and the persuasive power of a deep love for people. Dealing as he did with the social and moral needs of his nation, he reiterated the truth that only in Christ could men find their way to new life, both personal and social.

Kagawa endeavored to proclaim that Christianity was no mere dogma but a moral power and ideal which brought action through love. Even as the social forces of the first century brought Christ to His cross, so Kagawa saw the social forces in his day forcing him to a similar crisis. In this context he stood to show the relevance of the Christian faith. Referring to prayer in his preaching he would state that "we temporize by praying for things which are inconsequential. We pray for trivial things, regarding which it makes little difference whether we pray or not. . . . There are some who criticize the Kingdom of God Movement, and say scornfully, 'How can a million souls be saved?' But if we were to pray we would be given a million souls. God is ready to give Japan these million souls, but we lack the conscious intention of saving these souls, and of taking up our Cross and bearing it, as we go along our way. . . . In Scotland they claim that if workers are added to the staff of the Salvation Army, the police department can safely decrease its force." In simple and concrete language and with deep emotion and strong assertion, Kagawa brought hope and new life to multitudes.

Throughout all his messages is the cry to get down to social movements for human liberation. Here was the emergence of the message for the working classes and the poor, a cooperative movement motivated by Christian concern, a way of economic and social reconstruction. In this he saw a coming of God's Kingdom.

One of the outstanding preachers of Japan was **David Tsutada (1906-1971)**, whose early years of study brought him to London where he became a Christian and prepared for leadership as pastor in his homeland. He studied at the Biblical Seminary, Tokyo, and then preached and taught in church and seminary. During the Second World War he was imprisoned because of his Christian witness and his affirmation of the coming of Christ as King, a view which was in conflict with State views concerning the Emperor of Japan.

He founded the Immanuel Holiness Church, a body which has one hundred indigenous groups with eight thousand members. During his several years of imprisonment, the name *Immanuel* sustained him in the solitary life he endured. Physically he suffered, but spiritually he became stronger as he meditated on the teaching of the Bible. His preaching and teaching is Biblical in that this is the one text which must be read and studied in the knowledge that there is no final mastery of it in this life.

The doctrine of the Second Coming of Christ was the support of this preacher during prison life. It became the heart of his preaching. He saw the world as a harvest field and taught that the church must evangelize as its prior task. He saw no peace among men until the Prince of Peace returns. In this conviction he preached and taught with urgency a positive message of hope and redemption. Apostolic days were repeated in the church where he ministered.

China

Pastor Hsi (1835-1896) is one of the best evidences of the power of the gospel. Out of oriental culture and civilization, with a background of Confucian training, he gave himself to Jesus Christ. In youth he hated the foreigner and for awhile was the victim of the opium habit, with shattered health and an accusing conscience. His transformation (like Saul-Paul) enabled him to proclaim the eternal gospel to his people.

As a preacher Hsi (pronounced "Shee") had the classical background and training of the Chinese scholar. The scholar was respected in China above all others. Now as a Christian, the scholar turned missionary and preacher was a flaming advocate of the Good News. He had been delivered from the vice of the drug, so his message offered deliverance from the evils of opium. When people were demon-possessed there likewise was power available for their freedom from evil. With grace, wisdom, and ability, Pastor Hsi ministered to groups and congregations, and also reached out to people outside the organized church who came to hear him.

He preached with conviction, and on the streets he was bold and fearless. His style was cultured and interesting. He could speak for long periods of time and hold interest. His use of Chinese illustrations reached all classes, although he rarely referred to the classics. His one weapon was the Word of God. His sermons were chiefly expository, giving new meaning and insight. With this was the pastoral concern for people. He had the shepherd heart, and his preaching had that overtone. Having suffered, he knew how to share the temptations and trials of others.

Pastor Hsi has been associated with the China Inland Mission (J. Hudson Taylor, Founder), under whose auspices Christians of various backgrounds went to China to minister together. In this unity of mission and ecumenical spirit, denominational ideas were limited and the unity of the Spirit prevailed as he worked with all who shared the Christian faith. Here was apostolic ministry and life in Chinese speech and garb.

John Sung (1901-1944) shone as a bright light in oriental preaching. His name will be remembered in China as one of the modern personalities. His background was that of a second generation Christian in a pastor's home. Out of this came his spiritual awakening during revival and the call to service. For awhile he earned a reputation as a boy preacher. Then he determined he would study in the United States. Here he graduated from Ohio Wesleyan University, earned a graduate degree, and finally went on to the study of theology at Union Theological Seminary, New York. At this time he suffered an eclipse of faith, but after a few months he regained his pristine faith and the assurance that God had called him to minister in his own country.

His preaching came out of Bible study and teaching, wherein he ministered to congregations for their spiritual progress. In the Methodist Church he extended this by evangelism and by giving systematic training to local preachers. Thus he became a well-known national figure in the church life of China. He headed a list of six "notable personalities" among leaders of evangelical persuasion published by the National Christian Council. His strength lay in prayer and devotion. He preached that (1) a thorough confession of sin; (2) prayer for the fullness of the Holy Spirit; and (3) public witness for Christ were the required convictions. His preaching was marked by earnestness and passion, as he denounced sin and called people to repentance.

Sung's sermons were partly topical but usually a running commentary on long passages of Scripture, with good illustrations and application. Using a blackboard if necessary, he would illustrate his points. Sung's contribution was that of a scholarly, Bible-centered evangelist, and his ministry finally extended beyond China to Formosa and the Philippines.

In **Watchman Nee (1901-1972)** the newer China begins to speak after the establishment of the church there through missionaries. He was the product of the national body and as such demands a place of his own. His conversion and growth in the Christian faith led him to be a deep student of the Bible. From this vantage point he made a unique place for his life and ministry. The chief characteristic of Nee was his preaching which had the qualities of a profound teacher. His ministry was extended beyond the group by publications in which he speaks not only to his own people but also to the whole church around the world.

From *The Ministry of God's Word* the principles of his stance are outlined. There is the minister and the Word of God; then there is the ministry and the objects of the Word. He sees various ministries in the Bible as he traces God's ways with his people both in the Old and in the New Testaments. The ministry of Christ in the gospels in a high point, followed by Paul's example. In these Nee finds the qualities and standards for Christian ministry.

His style is simple, Biblical, and illustrated from his background. In speaking he advises that "we speak not simply to let the words out but to release the spirit as well. . . . The spirit and the words are both necessary. . . . They must not lose contact. . . . The spirit follows the word and the word follows the anointing. . . . The thought must be under the control of the spirit. . . . Memory must be perfect. . . . The feeling and the word must be one. . . . The word should be clear and high. . . . Preaching to make people understand is the ministry of the word at its lowest level. When it is exhibited at its highest level, people shall see and shall fall."

In essence here is the secret of profound preaching by the Oriental. A Christ-mysticism pervades the thought, and the spoken word has depth and meaning. Out of the turmoil of revolution and resettlement in China, there will come men of stature in preaching who speak of the mind of the people.

Other representatives include **Wang Ming Tao (1900-)** from Red China—independent and itinerant, known as the Elijah of China. Taiwan and Korean preaching had been missionary-minded, and more of national Christian data has yet to be assessed.

India

Among the newer preachers of India we cannot omit **Vedana-yagam Samuel Azariah (1874-1945)** first Bishop of Dornakal and first Indian Bishop of the Anglican Church in India. A man of strong faith in God, he was given gifts as a teacher and a preacher. His vision of the church in India and his courage and eloquent speech were joined with a deep inner spiritual life.

Born and brought up in the south of India, he came from the Nadara, a group not admitted by the Hindu temples. Here, like other converts to Christianity, he pursued an education and reached Madras University. Meanwhile, his study of the Bible and theological training prepared him for his life work. He founded the Indian Missionary Society of Tinnevelly, and among the first work attempted was the field at Dornakal. Azariah had the distinction of attending the World Missionary Conference in 1910 at Edinburgh and was a speaker on behalf of the younger churches.

As Bishop he trained many of his people for witness and annually led processions of witness. He wrote several books of Bible interpretation. His sermons were known for their simplicity of speech and their practical demands. For his preaching and teaching material he would not glean from Indian sources alone—he was familiar with Burma, Korea, Sumatra, Samoa, and Pakistan and from these church areas he drew help and illustrations.

One of his preaching emphases was on Christian marriage. He was concerned with the low level of sexual morality among his people as well as the wrong and non-Christian ideas of marriage. His teaching in this area was based on the Bible and on his own experience of almost forty years of happy, Christian, married life.

Another point he emphasized was Christian giving. He knew that the church in India had the problem of supporting its work. He attacked the problem by saying that Christians lacked spiritual vigor: "Christians do not give their money to God because they have not first given themselves to God. . . . The low ratio of giving is a symptom of this low level of Christian life. The sooner we recognize this the better!" He urged that even the poorest woman in preparing a meal should put aside one handful of grain into a pot for God. At the time the gift would hardly be noticed, but over weeks and months it would amount to quite a sum. Once a month thereafter women would come to the church with their bags or baskets of grain.

Scriptural reasons for giving were also stressed. Biblical texts were woven together in support of adequate giving. Our Lord's teaching about money was at the heart of his message, and a survey of Luke 12, Luke 16, Mark 10, Matthew 13, and John 12, became the basis of exegesis and exposition for the guidance and probing of conscience in this matter. The tithe, the firstfruits, the tenth, the freewill offering—these were terms common in his discourses. The climax of this preaching lay in his demand that Christians should live with simplicity, economy, and self-control. "Abandon all un-Christian ways of raising money in the church. By this we mean not only the giving up of all lotteries, raffles, and all other methods intended merely to make people give in exchange for a little excitement or enjoyment. All assessments should go. . . . Giving must be lifted up to the level of spontaneity and voluntariness, and set free from all ideas of compulsion. . . . God has freely given himself to us; and we should freely give to him ourselves and all we have, asking for no other reward save that of knowing that we are doing his will."

Such preaching carried with it the spirit of a committed Christian, a leader who taught also by his own life and example.

The ministry of Sadhu **Sunder Singh** (1889-1925) took place in the days of Mahatma Gandhi and Rabindranath Tagore, leaders of spiritual thought in that land. In this land of religions it was fitting that the Christian faith should find root and exercise a profound influence. The Sadhu was nurtured in the Sikh religion, a reformed faith which tried to achieve a higher synthesis between Hinduism and Islam. Belief in the forgiving love of God and his revelation of himself in a human being comes very near to the central truths of Christianity. His early training included memorizing the Bhagavadgita by heart, and the constant reading of the Granth, the Upanishads, and the Koran. The peace he sought was found through reading the New Testament, and in Pauline experience and testimony he affirmed his conversion to Christ.

At sixteen years of age he united with the Anglican Church and received instruction, but his studies were limited in that he wished to venture forth as a wandering Sadhu preaching the gospel. In 1909 he was constrained to spend a year in the study of theology at Lahore and there he learned to know the *Imitation of Christ*, which made a lasting impression upon his spiritual life. His simple humility was preserved throughout his life. He traveled in a common robe and sandals, emulating the early aspects of our Lord's own ministry. While he gave himself chiefly to India and penetrated Tibet, he also carried out visits and ministries to the major countries of Europe, Asia, and America. In churches and in colleges, among student conferences and public gatherings, he remained the same winsome preacher and witness to the grace of God. He disclaimed any prowess as a preacher, preferring to be known as "a witness to the saving power of God in Christ."

His preaching did not shrink from outspoken criticism of Western conditions, the unChristian spirit, religious indifference, greed of mammon, and the love of pleasure. Especially in Europe his preaching became a prophetic message of judgment and a call to repentance:

> Because the so-called Christian lands, to such a large extent, are falling away from Christ, He [Christ] is beginning to reveal Himself to heathen peoples, where He is being welcomed and honored. Here, too, the word is fulfilled: "The first shall be last and the last first."

At times his message became a prophecy of judgment in the eschatological sense:

> The people of the West who have received so many blessings from Christianity are losing them now because they put their trust in outward things. . . . Therefore, on that day, non-Christians will receive a lighter sentence because they have not heard of Christ; but the inhabitants of Christian lands will be punished more severely because they have heard His message and they have rejected it. . . . When you see Him in His glory, then you will grieve that you did not believe in Him as your God. But then it will be too late. . . . Now, however, is your opportunity.

As a preacher he was a messenger of the love of God and of his heavenly peace; he also appeared as a herald of severe judgment.

After his last visit to the Western peoples, he returned to India and attempted to enter Tibet with the gospel.

Any estimate of his preaching must not overlook the quality of thought and the heightened spirituality therein. Out of his own religious life of prayer and meditation, he stressed prayer, which he preached "as the heart of true religion, the Alpha and Omega of the Christian life." "Prayer is the greatest necessity of our spiritual life." "When we pray, everything that we need in this life is already granted, so far as the needs of our spiritual life are concerned." The Sadhu often used the symbol of breathing, a figure of speech familiar to him and his people. "In prayer the soul opens up every avenue to the Holy Spirit. God then gently breathes into it that it may become a living soul." "He who has ceased to breathe in prayer is spiritually dead." "Prayer is the breath of the spiritual life . . . prayer means the inhaling of the breath of the Holy Spirit." "Through prayer we become aware of Christ's presence and learn to know Him." "And He will come and give you strength and joy and peace."

His preaching spoke of union with God, the language of the Pauline mystic. By self-revelation (the testimony of the preacher), exhortation (the witness of the truth), and parables (the language of illustration), the Sadhu distilled in his sermons the inward peace he enjoyed, the sense of the ecstatic and the holy, and the power of the cross of Christ. In this last element he knew something of the joy which came through suffering and persecution. Like his Lord and Master, Sadhu Sunder Singh suffered for his Christian witness, but he preached that the paradoxical experience is the way to understand that suffering is the way to communion with God and to blessedness:

> The Cross is like the fruit of the walnut-tree. The outer rind is bitter, but the kernel is refreshing and strengthening . . . . A new-born child has to cry, for only in this way will his lungs expand . . . . Out of my long experience as a Sadhu for Christ's sake, I can say with confidence that the Cross will bear those who bear the Cross, until it bears them up to heaven, into the actual Presence of the glorified Redeemer.

In the preaching of the mystic, Christian "other-worldliness" was not something in the future, but a present gift of grace. In this was no life of dreaming, but of strenuous industry. Tireless work for others characterized him. The preacher who spent days in communion with the Eternal also traveled from land to land with bleeding feet, to bring salvation. He was no recluse, but a man on the roadway of life. He not only preached acts of mercy, he exemplified this in his own life and practice. The message of the Living Christ permeated all his teaching. The theological formulation of his thought is best summed up in the Parable of the Prodigal. When others questioned whether there was any need of mediator or atonement in the well-known parable, the Sadhu took another view:

> One day a pastor came to me and said: "Think about the parable of the Prodigal Son. He needed no mediator, no redeemer. He went direct to the Father." Then I said to him: "You must notice that the Prodigal Son was already in union with his father; it was not so very long since he had gone away from the father. He knew the way back, for he had lived with his father before. Therefore he needed no one to show him the way home. This parable applies to Christians. It is quite possible that some of them become careless in their spiritual life, and for a time are out of touch with the Lord, but they know the way back. The parable does not refer to the heathen, nor to the many nominal Christians, who do not know the way to the Father.

He may miss the main point of the parable and emphasize a detail, but this is Sunder Singh's inimitable way of bringing home the truth to the conscience of his hearer. To him the earthly life of our Lord and the living Christ together give experience.

As a preacher the Sadhu never suffered from a lack of hearing. Crowds thronged him, although he gave himself to the small group and the individual. As an interpreter between the East and the West, and as a mediating preacher of the gospel, his place is assured in the preaching of the Orient. Besides several books extant, there are voluminous notes and excerpts of preaching retained by hearers. In bridging from the Comparative Religions of the East to Christianity, he was a superb translator of truth. Since the light of the Eternal Word to some extent illumines the non-Christian religions, they also are a preparation, a schoolmaster, to lead to Christ. What the Law was to the Jews and Platonist philosophy to the Greeks, the wisdom of the Vedas and of the Sastras is to the people of India. In simple language Sunder Singh has expressed the truth that in Christ is the answer and fulfillment of all that is true in the other religions:

> The Wise Men followed the Star to Bethlehem. But when they
> reached Bethlehem they no longer needed the Star, for they had
> found Christ, the Sun of Righteousness. When the Sun rises the
> stars lose their radiance. In India we have many genuine truth-
> seekers, who faithfully follow their Star; but it is only starlight
> which guides them. But you Christians have the glory of the Sun.
> Hinduism and Buddhism have dug canals, but they have no living
> water to fill them. In this sense I was prepared to receive the Living
> Water from Christ. Christianity is the fulfillment of Hinduism.

In beautiful pictorial language he reached the heart. No one compared to the Sadhu in penetrating the people of India with the
gospel. The Christian mystic proclaimed an eternal message.

Ceylon

One of the rare personalities and gifts of God to a country and to
the world was this dynamic man from Ceylon, **Daniel Thambyrajah
Niles (1907-1970).** Nurtured in the Methodist Church, he worked
with the YMCA and emerged as a leader of the ecumenical movement throughout the world. Early years found him active in the
World Student Christian Federation and out of that came his
concern as an evangelist. He also served as a pastor in his native land
and intimately knew pastoral work and regular preaching.

Niles is a good representative preacher of the Oriental world and
is a luminous example of how God calls men from other backgrounds than those of our Western world. The fact that the church
of Christ is now worldwide brings to focus the contribution of the
younger churches. The leadership is no longer restricted to the
European and American churches. God has raised up others and we
now listen to them with respect and appreciation.

The preaching of Niles can be judged by the sermons and addresses given in many lands and especially to assemblies and ecumenical gatherings in which he was selected as the preacher. We
have many books written by Niles and among these is the Lyman
Beecher Lectures on Preaching, *The Preacher's Task and the Stone
of Stumbling* (1958). Here for the first time the well-known series
moved out from its Western tradition and selection to an Asian. An
heir of missionary work and the pastor of a small church in a
minority group within his native country, what would this man say
to the preaching forces of America? The brilliance of utterance, the
larger vision, the dynamic smiling person, and the exceptional style

which sparkled and shimmered as a light was unusual. Even in lecturing, Niles preached as the evangelist and brought a new dimension of truth to gospel preaching.

In these lectures, there was first the awareness that what he had to say was important. The introduction aroused others to see that the subject matter was important. The title of the lectures would indicate the insight and unusual spirit of Niles. "Behold I am laying in Zion a stone that will make men stumble, a rock that will make them fall; and he who believes in him will not be put to shame" (Rom. 9:33 RSV). "God has acted and men must believe. That is the ground of the preacher's task. But men find in this action of God something they stumble over. That is the heart of the preacher's problem." In a nutshell this opening paragraph contains the lucid and simple style of Niles as a preacher. No one could mistake the clear intent of his proposition in preaching.

In his intriguing way this Asian preacher thought of himself as the missionary-evangelist encountering people from all the world and sought to confront them with the claims of Christ. In this he asked a Hindu, a Buddhist, and a Muslim each to write him a letter, stating why he found it impossible to accept the Christian faith. He stressed that he did not wish an answer discussing the difficult things, but rather that each would state the central affirmation of the Christian faith, as he understood it, which he could not accept because it contradicts a central affirmation of his own faith. Out of these answers, Niles asked himself if their understanding of the Christian faith was his also, and whether that was how he preached it. How then could he change his preaching to avoid the difficulties which others found in it?

Thus his preaching demonstrated first of all the need to see the problems of others and why they stumbled over some unnecessary aspect of the Christian gospel. This began to color all his ministries whether in writing, lecturing, or preaching. He was the apologist for the faith, but he also saw himself as the interpreter of the faith. The only reason and validity in preaching is that men should not stumble.

Three theological and doctrinal affirmations are found in Niles' preaching. Here is the Christ as God Incarnate, as the Crucified One, and as the Risen Lord. According to Niles the claim of Jesus "to be the beginning—the beginning of a new life, the beginning of a new relationship with God, the source of a new birth, the architect of a new house—this claim could never be finally bypassed . . . . The problem of faith is not to receive Jesus into our life but to be received into his: to enter into his death, to enter into his resurrection, to enter into his ministry to save the world, and finally to enter into his glory." He corrected Gandhi in saying that "Christ belongs to the whole world," in the statement, "No, except that Christ belongs to the whole world not as its possession but as its Possessor. He is the Heir of all things (Heb. 1:2). . . . When his light becomes our enlightenment, when his truth becomes our tradition, when his grace becomes our heritage; then we are well on the way to rejecting him. He gives, but we can safely possess what he gives only as we abide in him . . . . There is no Saviour but Jesus and they who are saved are always saved by him (Acts 4:12)."

Basic to his preaching thrust was the belief that sin and depravity are part of man's inheritance. He did not argue how this came to be: he simply recognized the fact. Preaching had to deal with the nature of sin and offer the remedy in Christ. Quoting another, Niles reaffirmed his confession of faith: "I live by faith in the deeds of God, I feel nothing about them, I stand on them . . . . I live by faith in the objective atonement of Christ." He stated, "A person who is unable to begin with the phrase 'I live by faith in' cannot begin to preach . . . . All preaching begins at this point . . . . The temptation to preach religion rather than the Gospel is present." Niles saw that the preacher in this generation must not simply supplant or challenge other religions ouside of Christianity: he must be able to offer a faith which would transform other religions as well as the individual. He saw the world as already redeemed by the mighty acts of God in Christ, but not all men yet saved.

Throughout Niles' messages runs the note of the resurrection— the risen, regnant Christ over this world, readying all people for the day of judgment. Here was the note of hope for human beings living in the context of despair. Here was the note of victory for those who were facing death, the last enemy. Here was the note of love bringing divine activity into life where hatred and evil were rampant. Here was the note of life breaking through to those who were impoverished and lacked the abundant life in Christ. The allusions and illustrations were not from book sources compiled by editors. They sprang out of daily life and his own experience whether in reading or talking or action. No one could be more "alive" than "D. T." when preaching and relating the gospel story as he saw it with such spiritual insight and faith.

Niles' preaching was characterized by a mystical sense of divine power. The gospel as seen overagainst the world, the evangelist and the church, the task and the non-Christian—these categories enabled him to clarify his message and simplify his words. The goal of such preaching was ever that men might find life, life abundant. "To live in a world where Jesus is risen is to live in a world where Jesus is inescapable." The terse, telling, thrustful words form into a sentence and unforgettable statement. These barbs are everywhere in his preaching.

Niles was a man of world vision. The concept that the whole earth is in view (cf. *Upon the Earth: the Mission of God and the Missionary Enterprise of the Church*, 1962) expresses his conviction in preaching. The lectures he gave were the working out of his preaching themes. He criticized the American fashion of "topical" preaching. He said, "My reason for raising this question is not to argue about the relative rightness of 'topical' preaching, or to discuss the different ways in which 'topical' preaching can be done. . . . Suppose someone in a congregation kept a record of the sermons preached to that congregation and at the end of the year wrote a summary of the Christian faith on the basis of those sermons alone, what would that summary be like? Most Christians, among those who attend public worship, live on the basis of the faith they learn on Sunday mornings. The preacher has no right to waste a Sunday morning talking 'tid-bits.' "

The thought-forms and language of this Asian preacher were disciplined for the sole purpose of proclaiming the Christian message in the non-Christian world. Dedicated as evangelist and missionary, Niles never wavered in his life calling from God. He became a voice for God around the world. Men in all nations and in all assemblies of the church heard him gladly. They instinctively recognized the voice of a prophet for his generation. His scholarly studies of the text of the Bible with their expositions for devotional and practical use, his lectures on preaching and kindred topics, and his messages to peoples of all religions enabled him to speak that word in season. He was Pauline in thought, and mystic in belief, standing to proclaim the eternal message to a passing age. To him the various systems had their day; the comparative religions were inadequate; the lights of men's minds in reason were going out; only the Christ, the Light of the world was sufficient. Niles preached to bring light and understanding to men.

Africa

The word *piety* has had its good days and often its bad days in modern times. Originally used to describe the quality and spirit of devoted men in the Middle Ages and during the Puritans' and Reformers' upsurge of preaching, it had full expression in the devotional life of prayer and meditation. Across the centuries God raised up men of this caliber and the list of these "saints" is long. *Sainthood* is not a popular word in this era, but from Biblical times until now it denotes *the man separated unto God.*

The aberrations of interpretation and also of conduct and practice are many. Just as the word *pharisee* lost its pristine meaning of the earlier years and became a synonym for hypocrisy and counterfeit religious life, so the "pious" have been derided as those who spoke one language but in life denied it by their diluted character and conduct. However, in admitting that such has been the case across the years—as all movements have their weaknesses and abuses—we must affirm that piety—devotion to God—is essential to the life and renewal of the whole church of Christ.

Over the centuries the men of piety have been noted more for their prayer and devotion than for their preaching. From Augustine and Bernard of Clairvaux; from Francis of Assissi to Savonarola; from the Huguenots and the Independents to Puritans and Reformers; from George Fox and John Bunyan to Covenanters and Evangelicals; and from the Mystics to the Missionaries of the Cross— the roster is endless. However, those who have also been preachers deserve a place.

In this evangelical succession names stand out such as Samuel Rutherford, Bishop Leighton, Richard Baxter, John Owen, John Bunyan, Thomas Boston, Jonathan Edwards, John Wesley, Alexander Vinet, and Alexander Whyte. These were well-known men in their day and are still recalled as outstanding for their ministries. We turn to one such who ministered in the southern tip of the African continent.

Andrew Murray (1828-1917) was noted for his unusual gift of poetic expression in preaching. His prose flowed in a limpid stream of words delightful to hear and easy to read. Born of Scottish parents in South Africa, he was given a general education in Scotland for seven years, graduating with the M.A. degree from Aberdeen University. Three years of theological study followed in Holland.

During the period in Scotland he was influenced by the scholarly preaching of evangelical Presbyterian ministers, including Thomas Chalmers, Robert Candlish, Robert Murray McCheyne, and the brothers Andrew and Horatius Bonar. The spiritual awakening of 1838-40 was not unlike the revival which stirred parts of America under Charles G. Finney. The man God used in Scotland was William C. Burns, an ordained minister, whose life profoundly influenced Andrew Murray. The bent toward revival and holiness of life was encouraged so that when Murray returned to the land of his boyhood, he engaged in an extraordinary ministry within the Dutch Reformed Church of which he was a pastor.

Though Murray had his base of operations in South Africa, by conferences in America, Canada, and Great Britain, he spread his message. His published works amounted to two hundred fifty books and pamphlets in Dutch and English. He came forth from the presence of God to preach and teach as an evangelist, pastor, missionary, and organizer of educational institutions.

In preaching there is a Biblical mysticism, a Pauline insight, a glow and warmth of spiritual life. His emphases were on prayer, holiness, and power.

Prayer was a subject of paramount importance in Murray's preaching. Here the oratory of the soul and the still hour became priorities of the Christian life. Like a refrain there runs through all his writings and sermons this idea: "Most churches think their members are gathered into one simply to take care of and build up each other. They know not that God rules the world by the prayers of His saints." Again and again he dealt with the subjects of united prayer and persevering prayer. Spelling this out in a hundred ways, he said: "The marks of true united prayer are given us in these words of our Lord (cf. Matt. 18:19, 20—'If two of you shall agree on earth . . . it shall be done for them of my Father. . . .') . . . The first is *agreement* as to the thing asked. The second mark is the *gathering* in, or into, the Name of Jesus. The third mark is the sure *answer*."

Dealing with perseverance, he stressed: "Let it be thus whether you pray for yourself or for others. All labor, bodily or mental, needs time and effort: we must give up *ourselves* to it. Nature discovers her secrets and yields her treasures only to the diligent and through labor. However little we can understand it, in the spiritual husbandry it is the same: the seed we sow in the soil of heaven, the efforts we put forth, and the influence we seek to exert in the world above, need our whole being: we must *give ourselves* to prayer. But let us hold fast the great confidence that in due season we shall reap if we faint not."

The volume, *With Christ in the School of Prayer*, is linked with many others including *The Ministry of Intercession* where the sin of prayerlessness is dealt with by a wise physician of the soul. In a day when pastoral counseling was not known by that term, Murray knew how to probe the inner life through Scriptural patterns and by practical insights. Like his Lord, Paul also was a pattern of prayer for him as he used the many references and incidents throughout the Epistles. These become a thesaurus on prayer as Murray discloses the riches of Paul's praying.

In his works on holiness of life, Murray has a startling and probing way of reaching the conscience. Humility of life, beauty of character, absolute surrender to Christ, obedience to God's will, likeness to Christ, and the growth of interior piety are the dominant notes. Holiness or sanctification led to perfection in the sight of God—this was stressed as an essential for the Christian. Sermons dealing with this theme are found in his books, including *Holy in Christ, The Spirit of Christ, the Full Blessing of Pentecost, The Inner Chamber and the Inner Life,* and *Love Made Perfect*.

"Do all God's children understand this, that holiness is just another name, the true name, that God gives for happiness . . . ?" In this word lies the key to much of Murray's preaching. There was buoyancy and a lilt, an uplift of spirit. "The kingdom of God is joy in the Holy Spirit" (Rom. 14:17).

> The deep significance of joy in the Christian life is hardly understood. It is too often regarded as something secondary, whereas its presence is essential as the proof that God does indeed satisfy us, and that his service is our delight. In our domestic life we do not feel satisfied if all the proprieties of deportment are observed, and each does his duty to the other; true love makes us happy in each other; as love gives out its warmth of affection, gladness is the sunshine that fills the home with its brightness. Even in suffering or poverty, the members of a loving family are a joy to each other. Without this gladness, especially, there is not true obedience on the part of the children. It is not the mere fulfillment of a command, or performance of a service, that a parent looks to; it is the willing, joyful alacrity with which it is done that makes it pleasing.

The blessing of knowing how the Holy Spirit works in the Christian life is set forth by Murray when he says, "First of all, there must be a new discovery and confession and casting away of sin. In this way you come to a new discovery, and reception, and experience of what Christ is and is prepared to do for you. So the soul is prepared to receive the full blessing of the Spirit."

The power of the Spirit in the Christian life is most marked in those sermons which deal with the interior life and its need for divine assurance and strength. The church needs power to witness and work for Christ. The preaching of Murray was not "other-worldly" in any escapism from this world. He raised money for institutions; he built and administered buildings in which people were educated and cared for; he was practical in his ways as a pastor and leader. The teaching of this mystic of common sense living was far-reaching. Thousands across the world were revived and enthused to work for God. Many gave lives for missionary service. Abiding in Christ was not a cliche, rather it was the key to abounding life in the Spirit of God. This was experimental religion at white heat.

Murray's style is terse and simple. The sentences stab and probe. They are aflame with passion and power. Read aloud they bring us close to the center of spiritual faith and devotion. They point to Christ, they guide to richer life, and they impell Bible knowledge and meditation. Murray went to the heart of things. We realize that there is more to the Christian life than yet experienced. Murray lived in the secret place and his writings distilled "the beaten oil of the sanctuary." In his largest work, *The Holiest of All*, Murray has left a commentary, rather an exposition, of the Letter to the Hebrews, in which his sermonic-teaching thrust is handed down as a legacy to later generations. The technicalities of critical study are not here—but a profound, spiritual searchlight upon the text and upon human life is apparent. Timely when published, it is still timeless in its insistence that true Christianity is the life of God in the soul. This piety is the evangelical strain which, if caught, leads on to dynamic deeds in human life.

Albert Schweitzer (1875-1965) of Lambarene, West Africa, was not a national of that continent but no one more than he earned the right in actual demonstration of service to be a fitting representative of that area of preaching, teaching, and healing. This threefold ministry was that of our Lord (Matt. 4:23) and the man from Alsace-Lorraine, Europe, became identified with the people of Africa in this way. He was musician, philosopher, theologian, doctor, and also preacher. His degrees in medicine, music, and theology gave the impression of one apart from preaching, but as missionary he ministered in word as well as in deed. At the height of his influence, Schweitzer was one of the most famous men in the world.

When a young man in Europe, he preached in Strasbourg, France. Preaching to him was a necessity. He spoke, in *Out of My Life and Thought* (1933), as one committed to serious preaching. Unfortunately his European sermons in those days did not reach the public. They were usually only rough drafts in summary and not manuscripts. A friend copied some one hundred fifty of these during World War II. His book *Reverence for Life* (1969) contains the message of all his preaching over the years. In essence, he deals with basic ethical questions. In them there is depth and imagery for rapport with people everywhere. He follows the Christian Year, and the festivals of the church are the occasions of theological emphasis. The missionary emphasis is strong, as would be expected in one dedicated to healing the open sore of human need.

Schweitzer's preaching was drawn chiefly from the New Testament. He was a New Testament scholar in his own right, and he seemed to have regretted that he did not use the Old Testament more. In his sermons more than half of the New Testament messages come from the Synoptic Gospels. Neither moralist nor pharisee, he showed Jesus Christ more than John the Baptist in his interpretation of the gospel as applied to all sorts and conditions of life. The language is simple—no learned phrases; he spoke as a layman, so he said. The illustrations are concrete and not abstract. Without dogmatic terms in seeing the Christ, he possesses a strong mystical strain which pervades the sermon as it reveals heart and spirit in the missionary doctor. If the people at Strasbourg heard the young preacher at the beginning of his work, the people at Lambarene heard the mature and experienced man of God.

The man for all men and for all seasons in that African context took ideas first seen in experiential religion before casting them finally into written form and essay prose. Always contemporary, the sermons bespeak the missionary in the social and moral context of the gospel. He saw creation suffering, hence this call to his mission and life of service. Sermon titles reflect this: "Overcoming Death"; "My Brother's Keeper"; "The Future of Mankind"; "Sacrifice for Others"; "The Ethics of Compassion"; "Fulfill your Destiny"; and "The Peace of God." Personal piety shone through from the character of a preacher whose aim was to follow the steps of the

Master. Schweitzer's theology might show aberrations from orthodoxy, but his life and ministry brought healing and health of body and soul to thousands. Life was made whole again in his reverence for life which prompted sacrifice. As Elton Trueblood has said, "We may long debate his orthodoxy, but we cannot deny his closeness to Christ." The preaching of Schweitzer is expressed not only in sermons and talks but also in the deeds of compassion for others.

The young countries of Africa have slowly emerged in the last century to nationhood and religious leadership. Dependent upon the missionaries from Europe and America, the young churches were not able to assume leadership until trained to bear their own responsibility. Thus the preaching in Africa has not been the product of national aspiration but has leaned heavily upon those who came from without.

Samuel Crowther (1807-1891) deserves mention as one of the earliest sons of Africa whose ability and endowment resulted in education for the ministry. From the Gulf of Guinea in West Africa and its background of slave trading, this youth was rescued and became a Christian. Under the tutelage of the Church Missionary Society, he pursued an education which took in Greek and Latin. Later he went to London for advanced studies and then was ordained in the Church of England. His return to Africa led to college teaching, church pastoring, diocese administration, and the beginnings of the translation of the Bible into the Yoruba language.

As an evangelist and preacher Crowther made his way until he was consecrated the first African Bishop to oversee territory within his native land. His linguistic skills as well as translation work led Oxford University to confer upon him the honorary degree of Doctor of Divinity. Africa witnessed this unique man giving himself later to long journeys to teach and preach the gospel to his people. His message was Biblically based and simple in expression. His spirit of devotion and perseverance gave depth to his preaching. His preaching was not collected in books to indicate his legacy, but the people he reached and the churches built are eloquent testimony that he was heard gladly in his life without reproach.

In **James Emmas Kwedyir Aggrey** (1875-1927) Africa found another leader whose rise to eminence seemed a miracle in his day. From the lowly background of native life on the Gold Coast of West Africa, Aggrey was a convert to the Christian life. He trained in mission schools until ready for teaching and later received a degree from Livingstone College, Salisbury. Becoming a professor, he also was ordained an Elder in the Zion Methodist Church, then went off to the U.S.A. for graduate studies. Columbia University, New York, gave him room for academic advancement until he earned the degree of Ph.D.

Aggrey's life and work read like a romance. The impossible was accomplished in spite of all the handicaps. This African took his place in America with dignity and diligence to be respected by his peers. He became a realistic interpreter of his people and nation to the rest of the world and in like manner interpreted America and the English-speaking world to his own people. The preacher in him gave utterance to many evangelistic and evangelical messages wherever he went. His memorable saying is recalled: "You can play some sort of a tune on the white keys of a piano; you can play some sort of a tune on the black keys; but to produce real harmony you must play both the black and the white keys." This was the ideal for which Aggrey lived, labored, taught, and preached.

In preaching he had the gift of giving a shaft of truth to the conscience, but winging it with laughter. He never denounced even when under provocation. He sought to remove fear and prejudice from warped minds. "Love and work" was his motto to demonstrate by sermon and sweat of brow and of mind that the African could take his place alongside of the European. Thus the parabolic form was his specialty, and the dramatic sense was never absent. He preached and taught that Christianity, education, and agriculture could be combined for his people's progress and advance. Heart, hand, and head were one to Aggrey, and so his emphasis in sermon and lecture was the same.

Australia—New Zealand

Lionel B. Fletcher (1877-1954) was pastor of the Beresford Street Congregational Church, Auckland, New Zealand, before engaging in campaigns of evangelism in his own land, Australia, and Great Britain. Gifted with a strong voice and usually preaching without any microphone aids, he was a voice for God.

In the sermon "Presenting the Good News," based on Acts 24:25 (R.V.), where Paul before Felix "reasoned of righteousness, temperance, and judgment," the preacher showed how this man was "faced by the greatest opportunity of his life. He was listening to the world's greatest preacher, and also because he was being moved by the Holy Spirit . . . Felix was faced by the greatest question of his life. First of all, it was a question concerning his future conduct in this present life. It was the greatest question which had ever faced Felix, because it not only had to do with his future in this life, but it also had to do with his future in eternity. He was faced with the greatest crisis in his life."

Fletcher's style of preaching was pointed, forceful, man-to-man in blunt speech. He stressed the fact of sin and the fact of salvation. His message was related to people and what they thought and felt, not to what they ought to be thinking and feeling. He met his hearers where he found them. His appeal was related to their sociological backgrounds. For example, sailors, he claimed, were more emotional than soldiers, and miners in Wales had to be spoken to in another way than people in other walks of life and in other communities. His sermons exalted the Christ as Savior and Lord. The effects of sin, the challenge to service, the call for decision and personal relationship to God were notes of importance.

Fletcher saw himself as pleading with men—"I am here as God's ambassador to plead with you for my King, and in His Name. I shall come to the Communion Table as we sing the concluding hymn of praise, and you who have not previously acknowledged Christ as your Saviour, but will from this night take upon yourself His Name, and commit your life into His keeping, I invite to come forward and shake hands with me as a token that you accept the gift of Christian love. What better time and what better place could you choose to enlist in His service?"

Over several countries and areas of the English-speaking world, Fletcher did the work of an evangelist with divine approval. Never sensational, not backed by committees or organizations, he went to a church and began his work which would expand in that city from church building to town hall or auditorium, moving from one place to another as warranted by the response. In this he was in the apostolic tradition.

Frank William Boreham (1871-1959) stands supreme as a representative of preaching "down under." The discovery and settlement of that vast continent in the South Pacific has fascinated world travelers and challenged the church in its worldwide ministry. From London where Boreham was born and educated at Spurgeon's College, he became a Baptist pastor in the land of his adoption.

His genius lay in his ability to write well before preaching, but his writing was not the writing of a sermon as such. He specialized in the art of essay writing. These essays were sometimes incorporated into his preaching and the style cultivated affected and influenced his preaching. The substance of most essays appeared in his sermons but this did not detract from his appeal, rather it heightened and matured his sermons.

The discovery that people would be interested in outstanding personalities of the past led him to launch a series of sermons on *Texts that Made History*. From this he steeped himself in biographical, historical, and theological background to catch the character envisaged who had been changed, converted, or motivated by a particular text of the Bible. Out of these studies he dealt with Martin Luther's Text—Romans 1:16; David Livingstone's Text—Matthew 28:19, 20; and others. The interest in this series when first given was so remarkable that it went on for one hundred and twenty-five Sunday nights! After a first preaching, the series was revised and polished in other pastorates before publishing.

His essay-sermon titles are enshrined in books which have as titles *A Bunch of Everlastings; The Luggage of Life; A Nest of Stars; A Casket of Cameos; Mushrooms on the Moor; Arrows of Desire; Mountains in the Mist; Dreams at Sunset; The Tide Comes In; I Forgot to Say* (an attempt to conclude his writing); *My Pilgrimage* (autobiographical); and *The Last Milestone* (before his demise).

His style, cultivated by much writing and the daily discipline of study, was clear and simple. English flowed; even as he spoke he wrote. Illustrations and imagery abound in profusion. He lived in a world of wonder and its sheer beauty and yet tragedy made him write in kinship with Charles Dickens and Mark Rutherford. He also poured himself into his messages with quiet humor and homely philosophy, but always with a charm and grace. His sermons and essays reached a multitude throughout the English-speaking world. Storytelling came naturally and the art of the scribe was no hardship to one who loved to write down the ideas he had found and the riches he had culled from reading in all fields of knowledge. Bring all this to the Bible which was the nerve center of his thought and devotion, and thus a preacher is molded with oratory and verve of speech which touched listeners with light and shades of splendor.

When invited to address the General Assembly of the Church of Scotland in Edinburgh, the Moderator, Professor Daniel Lamont, introduced him as "the man whose name is on all our lips, whose books are on all our shelves, and whose illustrations are in all our sermons." No finer tribute could be given in honor and respect of Australia's best-known preacher of modern days.

Howard W. K. Mowll (1890-1958) represents the finest tradition of evangelical Anglicanism in Australia. Holding the positions of Archbishop of Sydney and Primate of Australia placed this man of God in a responsible ministry. His character, life, and work reveal the early faith which matured throughout his days. Missionary experience in West China also added to his experience in preparation for Australia.

His support of evangelistic campaigns such as those of Torrey and later Graham went far in assuring a hearing on the widest scale for these evangelists. This was part of his own faith and conviction, believing as he did in the simplicity of the gospel to be preached to all men. He was recognized as the leader of all evangelical ministries beyond his own communion. Australia was given direction in the leadership of this Anglican preacher.

He had the advantage of a magnificent presence. His voice matched his figure and he could be heard with ease. Strength and resonance assisted the effect. Gifted by nature to be a leader, he was a man of courtesy and sympathy. In training for preaching, he did early work at Wycliffe College, Toronto, where he worked through the entire Bible in tutoring students. Thus his sermons were full of that quality of spiritual power. To preach the gospel was his delight: to point men to Christ was his privilege in a sermon.

His sermons are not unusual in utterance or substance. Their simplicity reflects the shy, retiring person he was, but they contain the hallmark of genuine faith. Generally he would take the line of the expositor, whether a verse, or passage, or a whole book of the Bible. Drawing out its leading message, he would apply that for practical ends. Although not a theologian, he held to the evangelical position in theology. His personal life with God shone through his preaching as he held to the authority of the Scriptures as supreme, and the absolute necessity of justification by faith. Thus the evangelical Archbishop wrote and preached.

Alan Walker (1911-) has come into worldwide prominence since World War II. His ministry as a Methodist preacher, pastor, and evangelist has caught the imagination of others beyond his own church. Superintendent of the Central Methodist Mission in

Sydney—Australia's oldest Methodist Church—he has led his people and his denomination in many crusades to reach the man outside the church. He is also the founder of Life Line International, a worldwide organization to bring help and healing to those in need. He preaches by television and radio; he lectures in many countries; and several books now bear the imprint of his name as an author.

Walker is in the fine tradition of the older Methodism which believed in the presentation of the gospel of the grace of God but linked it with social redemptive action. Thus in the building of a church in Sydney, as in the major cities of England, he follows a pattern which begins by erecting a Central Hall, much like any hall for concerts and gatherings of all kinds. The purpose is to make it easier for the nonchurchgoer to slip into what looks unlike the traditional church building and when inside to find a large platform and usually individual opera seats as in a theater or cinema building. Here on a Saturday night might be held concerts, musical nights, or lectures by eminent speakers in politics, education, religion, travel, and films. On Sunday the same building is used for public worship and evangelism.

As a preacher, Walker fits in with this well-tested concept of architecture and procedure in religious outreach. He has that personality of a presence, a command of clear, forceful language, and a strong and manly appeal in his Christian witness. His published books and sermons include *A Ringing Call to Mission, A New Mind for a New Age, The Many-sided Cross of Jesus, Jesus Is Enough, How Jesus Helped People,* and *Breakthrough* (rediscovering the Holy Spirit).

In these we hear the preacher proclaiming the eternal message in the accents of modernity. With half of Australia's population under twenty-five years of age, the newness of the continent, the newness of the church, and the new age breaking through demanded a preacher like Alan Walker. He has penetrated deeply into the mentality of his age and speaks the language which appeals. Hear his speech in sermons:

> The Christian Church today shows the sign of inadequate power. Something has overtaken it, which has robbed it of strength. It cannot cross the gulf between itself and millions who live and die beyond its message. Turned in upon itself it seems to have no power to confront the desperate world.

To meet this situation, Walker shares a discovery that:

There is a special baptism of the Holy Spirit available to all who follow Jesus Christ. This is a conviction which slowly, but now irresistibly, has formed in my mind. It is more than the coming of the Spirit in conversion. It goes beyond receiving the Spirit to have power to grow toward maturity. It is a further gift of God offered to all who are surrendering to Jesus Christ for witness and service. It is a baptism which is particularly relevant to the need of the Church and the world today. It is in a very special sense, the baptism of Power.

Thus Walker stands as a preacher of his generation, aware of the clamant needs of men, conscious of divine resources, and ready to proclaim the eternal message.

Preaching in the area of the Southern Cross has not yet been assessed. The settlement of Australia and New Zealand was part of British expansion and thus preaching was the result of colonists inducing "old country" ministers to join them. Those born in the Antipodes came later, by study at home and abroad and by interchange of ministries.

Lionel B. Fletcher, New Zealand, gave service around the world and also in a pastorate in Cardiff, Wales. Philip Carrington, New Zealand, studied at Cambridge, England, and finally became the Archbishop of Quebec, Canada, as leader of the Anglican Church.

Australia nurtured Henry Howard, in Methodism, and then his wider ministry came at Fifth Avenue Presbyterian Church, New York. Howard's scientific background, skill of interpretation, and fervent oratory, gave his sermons a quality well adapted to touch modern minds.

Australia prepared Frederick W. Norwood (1875-1958), whose Baptist experience led him to a chaplaincy with the Armed Forces during World War I. Then came the providential call to become the minister of The City Temple, London (1918-1931), the center of Congregational life and influence. Thereafter, in Canada, he gave the harvest of the years in preaching within the United Church of Canada.

Leyton Richards (1879-1945), from England, gave a period to Australia, then returned to Carrs Lane Congregational Church, Birmingham, in the succession of J. H. Jowett and R. W. Dale.

Frederick C. Spurr, from England, ministered in Melbourne before returning to opportunities at the Baptist Church at Birmingham and national leadership as a distinctive preacher under the National Council of Churches.

Among the interchange of preachers, the Anglicans were strong. Among those worthy of mention are: John S. Moyes, Bishop of Armidale, N.S.W.; Stuart Barton Babbage, Dean, St. Andrew's Cathedral, Sydney; Harrington C. Lees, Archbishop of Sydney; Leon Lamb Morris, pastor, then Vice-Principal, Ridley Hall, Melbourne; Marcus L. Loane, Canon of St. Andrew's Cathedral, Sydney, and Principal, Moore Theological College.

Chapter XI

Preaching
in Great Britain
(1900-1950)

When Dargan ended his notes in Volume II, he had discussed preaching to the end of the previous century. The then British pulpit was viewed in three periods: the First (1801-1833); the Middle (1833-1868); and the Closing Years (1868-1900). There a galaxy of well-known names extends the roster of a large number of men whose impact upon the churches and the public was noteworthy. Names like Joseph Parker, Alexander McLaren, Charles Haddon Spurgeon, James Charles Ryle, William Conner Magee, William Boyd Carpenter, Edward Meyrick Goulbourn, Henry Parry Liddon, Richard W. Church, J. B. Lightfoot, Brooke Foss Westcott, William Stubbs, Henry Scott-Holland, Edward W. Benson, Charles Gore, Arthur B. Stanley, W. J. Knox-Little, Frederic W. Farrar, Frederick Temple, J. E. C. Welldon, Hensley Henson, Alfred Ainger, H. C. G. Moule, H. W. Webb-Peploe, Christopher Newman Hall, Robert W. Dale, Robert F. Horton, Reginald J. Campbell, C. Silvester Horne, George Campbell Morgan, P. T. Forsyth, J. H. Jowett, Hugh Price Hughes, William L. Watkinson, Mark Guy Pearse, John Watson, W. Robertson Nicoll, John Ker, James Stalker, Principal Iverach, Robert Rainy, James Orr, James Denney, George Matheson, Alexander Whyte, William Landels, F. B. Meyer, Archibald Brown, John Clifford, J. T. Forbes, W. Y. Fullerton, Thomas Phillips, and John Wilson, were mentioned.

Of these, attention was given to many, but of those to whom only a reference was made, we must consider a few for larger treatment. Their contribution became greater in influence, in a time of much church-going and steady attendances. This was the age of statesmen of eminence like W. E. Gladstone and Disraeli whose power was great. In Great Britain the Victorian era at its height was unsurpassed, for the idea of the Empire held sway over millions. Brilliant minds and intellects entered the political field. The enlargement of the British Empire coincided with the granting of home rule for Ireland, colonial expansion, better educational facilities, and victory in several wars, including the Boer War in Africa. Social and labor movements within the country increased tensions between classes and parties. Gradually the stage was set for the next century with its far-reaching changes in bringing benefits to all. The major English universities which had been closed to nonconformists were opened to all in 1871. Scotland, Ireland, and Wales differed in this regard as their colleges and universities had no religious tests.

The far-flung changes in Great Britain were aided by the literary output of Carlyle, Ruskin, Arnold, Tennyson, Browning, Trollope, Hardy, Kipling, Stevenson, to mention a few. Scientific and philosophic thought stabbed the conscience as Darwin, Spencer, Huxley, and others challenged dearly-held beliefs. Modern Biblical criticism and historical research disturbed the status quo of conventional belief as scholars in both conservative and liberal schools of thought began to restudy the Bible in the light of its environment and the new knowledge then emerging. Benevolent organizations multiplied as the church tried to meet the clamant needs of poverty and slums, degrading practices, drunkenness, and vice. The church itself was splintered into several parties with labels telling of High, Broad, Low in the Anglican fellowship; and Evangelical over against Liberal. Tradition was strongly held, but newer schools of thought emerged such as the Keswick movement with its pietistic emphasis. It was in this context that preaching was seen with its variegated strength and color. Preachers with followers and a following were commonplace. Centers of preaching dominated. Sermons were published in all communions, and publishing houses prospered from the sale of religious literature.

Among the many events and points of view which affected the preaching of the times, priority might be given to the rise of the *scientific* outlook upon life. Certainly the new attitude was the result of Christian men in earlier periods opening the gates of new knowledge (Francis Bacon, Isaac Newton, Johannes Kepler, Blaise Pascal, Robert Boyle, and others).

The achievements of these explorers of thought and nature opened the gates of new life to multitudes. All was not in contradiction to the revealed word of God within the Bible. The human intellect triumphed at its heights of inventiveness and discovery. Thus natural science arose with the Christian civilization—a fact to be remembered when judgments are made.

The scientific revolution thus begun could not be stopped and within the last sixty years has come to flowering and fullness in the use of atomic fission, television, radio, the airplane, and now the new physics climaxed with a man standing on the moon.

More recently has come the threat to man's survival with the stockpiling of weapons of destruction. The moral implications of this are obvious to the preacher. He is now in a time when he is the one to speak concerning life and death, blessing and cursing, heaven and hell, for has not the scientist but given to his fellow men the means of these ultimates? Thus all human questions have become theological questions and all theological questions are the domain of the preacher.

During September 13-20, 1969, at Stockholm, Sweden, a conference was held on the subject of "Survival." Present were forty people who were Nobel Prize winners. These might be termed the "Superminds" of our age. The Nobel Foundation was host to this intriguing company. Included among them were Arthur Koestler (writer); Konrad Lorenz (animal behaviorist); Linus Pauling (veteran advocate of peace and brotherhood); Margaret Mead (anthropologist); Jaques Monod (biologist); Joshua Lederberg (director of the Laboratory of Molecular Medicine, Stanford); and W. H. Auden (poet). These learned individuals discussed the tragic theme.

Strange to say, the commanding figure at this conference was not, as might have been expected, a scientist but a poet, W. H. Auden. Among wise men, he looked the wisest, with his old-fashioned appearance and ways. In the midst of one discussion that appeared to be taking for granted a mechanistic view of man, Auden suddenly cut in to say: "We have not yet discussed the fact of evil, not just genetic accident, but the fact that people are nasty to one another." No theologian was invited, and Auden, a Christian, was the only man present who was unabashed by religious terminology; the only one, probably, who would attach any precise meaning to the word *evil*.

The significance of this event lies in the context and relation of preaching. If man is to have a new system of values according to these "wise men" and his life must be given a meaning, if he is to survive, then theological ideas reenter man's thought. Here is where preaching takes its central place. The preacher stands in the market place of ideas to present the eternal truth of divine revelation. The nothingness which is all that seems to be left to the present generation cannot satisfy man. In the age in which man feels his "lostness" and the world around him is without "meaning," then he orbits the earth and lands on the moon. This one single step by a man is also spoken of as a "giant leap for mankind." Without detracting from the stupendous scientific achievement, the giant leap needed is one of faith in Almighty God. Thus the preacher stands at the heart of humanity with his message from beyond.

This period was one which moved away from the frontier to the machine age—steel, electricity, national finance, industrial corporations, and the rise of labor organizations to challenge the entrenched capitalism of the old families. Universities were founded to offer education to the multitude, and no longer was the private college the only way of prestige in the new world of thought and invention. The educational emphasis of Dewey brought new ways of self-expression in the schools of America and set the tone of lowered morale when discipline is lost. In the writing of the period is pictured decline and degeneracy of spirit. The old idealism began to wane and the new "realism" of man's nature appeared. The shadow of the muckrake lies athwart this age.

In this era of voices seeking attention, the preacher has had a difficult time. The liberal voices of certain pulpits seemed to capture the popular mind, but the resultant loss of confidence in the Bible has wrought havoc in the churches and in the lowered morale of youth without any anchorage of faith. This period has been characterized by a passion to disbelieve. Men were ready to accept a lie rather than the truth—witness Hitler's record of dinning into the ears of Germany's youth the lie about race. The preaching of this time was disturbed by the breakdown of authority and this was allied to loss of faith in the authority of the Word of God.

Congregational

John Daniel Jones (1865-1942) was known to all as "J.D." Jones. Welsh in birthright, he ministered in England and became the leader of the Congregational Church. His longest pastorate was at Richmond Hill, Bournemouth (1898-1936), and from that pulpit his messages were preached and then published. He refused to give up the pastorate of this pulpit, believing that no greater influence could be his. The history of preaching has no finer example than here in which the vocation and calling of the pastor-preacher is set forth.

Jones was a short, stocky man, with white hair in his prime, and a rich silvery voice of unusual quality and power. He read from a manuscript in preaching and did this superbly. Always Biblical, finding good texts which illumined human life and problems, he was the wise counselor and the undershepherd as he preached to his regular congregation. He influenced more than one generation of people who went out into all walks of life to serve their day and generation by the will of God.

"J. D." stands in the succession of the finest of Welsh preachers who were noted for their imagination and skill in proclamation. Their "catching fire," their musical lilt, and the upsurge of a melodic quality in preaching—all this was his, although not so marked as in the revivalist and the evangelist. The glow of the fire was felt in Jones as he ministered Sunday by Sunday, ever bringing to his people the riches of the gospel.

Hearing a sermon by Jones one could safely anticipate that when it came into print there would be the same text and writing without change. His impeccable writing and thought not only was heard with appreciation, but also the sermons when read, read well—a rare accomplishment. Jones brought comfort or courage based upon a belief in divine providence to thousands. He knew the doubts and trials of life, even suffering and sorrow, hence his profound belief in the resurrection and eternal life brought to light by the gospel. Great preaching by Jones was inspired by this kindling hope.

Associate to Jones was **Thomas Yates (1873-1936)**. His ministry in Belfast, Ireland, prepared him for major maturing. He had a passion and sincerity which touched others. He lived to preach and his preaching could stir a congregation. His style was cultivated by studies of Edmund Burke's speeches. His delivery was that of the youthful "Peter Pan" strain which never left him in the radiance of his personality.

Like Yates to Jones, so later came **Leslie James Tizard (1903-1957)** at Carrs Lane, Birmingham, in the succession of Dale, Jowett, and Berry. An irenic spirit, a sensitivity to people's needs, and his own struggle with a terminal disease gave him a quality of faith and courage which pervaded his preaching. Although he ended his

ministry in the prime of his life, he left a witness to the efficacy of
the gospel he preached by his endurance through suffering.

In the wealth of British preaching, others whose names carry
weight would include those who were known beyond their denominational association. These include **Sidney Malcolm Berry (1881-
1961)** who was a successor of J. H. Jowett at Birmingham and later
became the Secretary and leader of the Congregational denomination. His father had been a leader in the great days of Nonconformity. He inherited something of that fighting spirit for the right
and a persuasive oratory as preacher and speaker. His Warrack
Lectures indicate his convictions on preaching.

The preaching of **George Campbell Morgan (1863-1945)** was
associated with his teaching ability and his unusual facility in
exposition of the Bible. While this method is one of the oldest in
the church universal, it had rebirth during the life of Morgan. His
pastorates included the major years at Westminster Congregational
Chapel, London, where he had two different periods of ministry.
He was known in America, Canada, and Great Britain for the
richness of his expository teaching and preaching. An itinerant
ministry was carried out on both sides of the Atlantic during most
of his life.

Morgan did not come into the Christian ministry in any conventional way. Early in life as a teacher he was asked to consider the
Methodist ministry and was given a trial—at which time he was
embarrassed and failed miserably in the pulpit. Thus he was rejected
as a candidate by the Methodist Church. However, through that
hardship and suffering he was in the process of being matured.
Later, in the independency of Congregationalism he found himself
pastor of a small church. It was then that he began to engage in the
self-study which continued all his life. God made him for one
thing—to be an expositor of the Bible. This was his life passion.

Commanding in appearance, Morgan was well endowed by nature
with a strong face and a sonorous voice. He looked almost gaunt
and ascetic—having been compared with Savonarola of Italy—but in
preaching he was intensely alive and persuasive in appeal. His voice
was well modulated for a large building, and his style of speaking,
after disciplined writing, suggested a clarity of prose merged with
spiritual passion.

Everything Morgan did was submerged in his belief that truth was
final in Jesus Christ, and that this truth was mediated in and

through the Bible. This conviction was the secret of his powerful preaching and teaching. Dogmatic certitude characterized his utterances and his written work. He had wrestled with doubt and had studied the critical questions about the Bible, but had settled these problems in the light of the Christ and the testimony of the whole Bible as God's divine revelation.

In early life he had been a teacher, and his teaching gifts were lavishly used when he entered the ministry. Morgan preached as a teacher, explaining and illustrating the text or the book. His sermon work was the result of systematic Bible teaching. During his ministry in London he taught a Friday night Bible Class, drawing between 1,500 and 2,000 people from all walks of life. Much of this Bible class teaching became the seedbed for sermons and publications.

As a Bible expositor, Morgan early discovered that he had to read and study the entire Bible if he was to be an adequate interpreter of its various parts. With singleness of mind he applied himself to the mastery of the English Bible. He would read and reread book after book of the Bible until he found the scope and message of a book in the light of the whole Bible. Then he would be ready to consult the original languages and scholarly helps and go on to discover the essential meaning of a book or a passage. Sometimes he used a simple outline to sum up an entire book, as he does for Genesis in three words: (1) Generation, (2) Degeneration, and (3) Regeneration. It was after this that he would begin the detailed analysis of the book at hand. He noted its literary structure and was careful to include all references to subject matter which recur, so that there was a building up of material for systematic study and exposition. He did not make a "running comment" as some have done—that would not be exposition to Morgan. He dealt with text, context, background, and style, and labored in word study to elucidate and clarify meanings and application.

As he studied each Bible book in relation to the whole Bible, so he studied each text in relation to the context. Thus he did not prepare sermons in the conventional way of outlining and unfolding a text by itself. He had to see that text in the light of the context, its related theme, and the whole Bible. His exposition was based on a careful exegesis, seen in the light of the whole Bible, resulting in Biblical preaching at its finest. Even his illustrative material was based largely on the Bible. While Morgan had a sense of humor and could use events and incidents from life and literature, he hardly needed these since he found so much in the Bible for illustration. For him, the Bible was its own best commentary.

Morgan could expound as a Turner painted—with fine detail and minute line; he could also expound on a titanic scale as a Rubens painted—with large canvas and broad strokes. In his book *The Gospel According to John* we have a good example of his expository work. The expositions embodied in this book were preached to congregations in different churches and countries. The expositions were stenographically reported, and then edited for publication. Each one is the enlargement of a sermon preached by Morgan as he worked his way through the book. In the first sermon or exposition he deals with "The Writer's Account of the Book." Here he begins with John 20:30, 31, and then discusses the question, Why do we have four Gospels? Following this is a consideration of the meaning and use of "signs" which are viewed as "powers and wonders and signs." Thus the idea of "miracle" is given expression initially before engaging in detailed exposition. Thereafter, comes the declaration of purpose on the part of the writer—"These are written that ye may believe." Here Morgan characteristically takes time to explain what "believing" is. He has done his study of the Greek and now shares with his hearers. He begins with the intellectual process before moving into an obedience to truth and the person of Christ. Now with the person of Christ he explains the deeper meanings of the Suffering Servant of God, divine and human, before setting forth His Sonship and claims of Messiahship. The application of the sermon ends with the distinction between biological life and spiritual life, even as John stressed that there was "life in his name." Here Morgan makes the evangelical appeal to the listener to enter into life eternal through saving faith in Christ.

As a sampling of the Morgan method of exposition, this opening message is characteristic. He states "thus we have considered the writer's account of his book, and so are prepared to study it in harmony with its declared purpose." There is the efficient teacher in the pulpit; and now he is ready for the second sermon-exposition on "The Thesis" (John 1:1, 14, 18). He plunges into the Prologue of John's Gospel. "I am not quarrelling with that word, provided that we do not think that prologue means preface. It is far more than preface. In these eighteen verses we have an explanation of everything that follows. . . . Possibly John wrote these eighteen verses last." At this point of the message Morgan continues to discuss the intricacies of the text and its meaning. He contrasts the King James Version with the American Standard Version of the Bible in the placing of certain words in brackets! For some this would be the end of attention, but in the hands and with the voice of Morgan this became a fascinating vestibule into the house of truth beyond. He led people thus into the inner shrine. In this exposition the stress is largely on the meaning of "The Word was God" and "The Word became flesh." *Logos* in the Greek is explained, and he quotes from *The Aramaic Origin of the Fourth Gospel,* by C. F. Burney, to support the view that the writer of the Gospel is thinking in Hebrew but writing in Greek. "The term would have the Greek significance, qualified by the Hebrew philosophy." If this sounds far away from "popular" sermons, it indicates why Morgan was heard gladly and regularly by throngs of people who were hungry for the message and meaning of the Bible.

Throughout his preaching his theological beliefs emerged. His books of doctrinal themes are an indication of some fundamental beliefs which could not but be expressed in regular preaching. In *The Spirit of God* he laid down the principle:

> Creeds do not ensure orthodoxy, for no individual church holds all the truth of the Church. The great body of truth is the property of the catholic Church, not of any section, nor yet of any individual member thereof. Sometimes one is asked if he holds the truth. Certainly not, for no single person can hold the truth. He may see one side of it—while another person sees another side.

Morgan had fear of being sectarian, and so in his teaching he gloried in the universality of the church and the revelation of God for all Christians. Some of his views at first were strongly dispensational, although modified somewhat later. He taught that the church began at Pentecost and was separate from Israel as a nation. In this new dispensation he saw the work of the Holy Spirit as something unique. He did not believe that in the Old Testament period there was a church of God. He was also premillennialist in eschatology. He saw in Scripture a distinction between the church and the coming Kingdom of God. However, there is evidence that in his later years Morgan had less to say about prophecy than earlier in his ministry. This does not mean that he had given up his belief, but perhaps indicates that he felt the emphasis was needed elsewhere in a period of controversy and division about the subject.

Morgan gradually worked out his beliefs in a systematic way. His published works make this clear. First, there were books related to *The Analyzed Bible* with the attendant books of *The Messages of the Bible*. These represent the foundation which he laid as he sought mastery of the Bible. Second, there were the books of general exposition, such as *The Corinthian Letters, The Acts of the Apostles, Psalms, Hosea, Jeremiah, Hebrews,* and *The Four Gospels*. Here in careful exegesis the exposition is set forth. I recall the publication week of Morgan's book on *The Acts* and taking this to my study to read. Unlike my use of a regular commentary to be consulted from time to time, I found myself reading on and on until the book was read entirely! The sweep and thrill of those hours and that week have remained as an enrichment to my life and ministry. Then, third, there are the books which are more theological in presentation: *The Crises of the Christ, The Teaching of Christ, The Spirit of God, Parables and Metaphors of Our Lord*. Through these we find Morgan clarifying his thought on the major doctrines of the Christian faith. He never wrote a systematic theology, but in these and other books lay the beginnings of such a work.

Morgan's convictions on preaching and homiletics are found in his books, *The Ministry of the Word* (1919), and *Preaching* (1937). The former embodies lectures given to students and pastors. Here again Morgan characteristically begins with the Bible and finds the title and setting of the phrase in Acts 6:4 to distinguish the work of the apostle and the preacher from other ministries in the church. Developing this, he then takes in the passage in Ephesians 4:12 to demonstrate the ministry of the Word as belonging to apostles, prophets, evangelists, and pastors and teachers. The lectures are divided as follows: I. The Fundamental Conceptions, Relating to The Ministry and The Word. II. The Primitive Ideal, Relating to The Word as the Truth of the Apostle; The Word as the Burden of the Prophet; The Word as the Gospel of the Evangelist; and The Word as the Wisdom of the Pastor and Teacher. III. The Modern Application, Relating to The Changed Conditions; The Unchanged Obligation; The Preparation of the Ministry; and The Exercise of the Vocation. IV. Epilogue: The First Responsibility—Prayer. The New Testament ideals for elucidation are obvious. As Morgan said in the Prologue to the book: "During the period . . . I have continued to preach. My work has never been apostolic, as I understand that phase of ministry, and as I shall presently attempt to explain it. It has been upon occasion Prophetic, constantly Evangelistic, and principally Pastoral and Teaching. These then are the facts concerning the experiences which must affect my thinking. I have mentioned them now to dismiss them, having recognized them. I trust they will be as little obvious as possible, and that our consideration may be *wholly conditioned within Biblical light.*" In that last word is the key to Morgan's ideal of the ministry.

In the book *Preaching* which came later chiefly as lectures to students, he sets forth his "methods of preparation in expository preaching." He disavows "rules" and stresses what he calls "principles." In the contents we find: I. The Essentials of a Sermon; II. The Text; III. The Central Message; and IV. The Introduction and Conclusion. These are again the same ruling principles and guide lines as found in all of Morgan's work. This is how he worked all his life. In this volume he has many striking things to say:

> It will be granted that preachers are to preach the Word. You say that means the Bible. Does it? Yes. Is that all? No. Yes, it is all there. But you want more than that, more than all. The Word is truth as expressed or revealed. The Word is never something that I have found out by the activity of my own intellectual life. The Word is something which my intellectual life apprehends, because it has been expressed. If we take the 119th Psalm and study it through—that great Psalm concerning the Word of God—we are not to imagine that it is referring only to the Torah or Law, the Nebiim or Prophets, the Kethubim or Writings. It has in view the truth, the essential truth, and the truth as God makes it known. *All that is focussed in Christ for us as preachers;* and Christ is revealed to us through this literature.
>
> But it may be asked: Is there not an experience of Christ? There is, but the literature tests the experience.
>
> And that is what we have to preach. God's revelation, the truth, as it has been expressed. We must enter upon the Christian ministry on the assumption that God has expressed Himself in His Son, and that the Bible is the literature of that self-expression. The minute we lose our Bible in that regard, we have lost Christ as the final revelation. I don't want to be controversial, but you will find it is always so. Let me speak with profound respect for the men who have suffered this loss. Here is a man who for some reason refuses the authority of the Bible, but says he will stand by Christ. What Christ?
>
> Preaching is not the proclamation of a theory, or the discussion of a doubt. . . . We are never preaching when we are hazarding speculations. . . . Speculation is not preaching. Neither is the decla-

ration of negations preaching. Preaching is the proclamation of the
Word, the truth as the truth has been revealed.

Thus Morgan lets us see himself in his study and background of
prayerful preparation—as he is before he delivers the message. His
convictions about the authority of the Bible as the Word of God
indicate no narrow individual. He is a man of profound thought and
reflection who reads and studies from all points of view and yet
knows his mind and convictions. Out of that background he comes
forth to preach. He concludes with the thought of a sermon
expressing the truth with originality, (to him—"exegesis"), authority, and clarity. Thus the truth is spoken with authority, and
illustrated and applied with clarity.

When we seek to find an explanation for the widespread influence of Campbell Morgan in his generation, there remains one fact
to be noted. He came to his ministry following the waves of
evangelism in Britain and America which climaxed under D. L.
Moody. There were many converts, and people were eager to learn
from the Bible and to strengthen their faith. Morgan came at the
right time with his teaching-evangelism and expository preaching.
The evangelists had done their work for a generation. Now God sent
the teacher to lead His people into the treasury of truth.

In Morgan's preaching there was a grand manner, a spirit of
aliveness, an immediate rapport with people, and a dramatic quality
of speech and appeal. His leonine figure with his white hair and eyes
flashing with emotion while stressing some truth, was something to
have seen and experienced. Because he was intrigued with big
themes, he always attempted to preach accordingly. Everything he
did was done well. "System," "method," was everywhere in Morgan. Whether writing, preaching, lecturing, or sharing his life with
his family and friends, he was the man dedicated to one end—that
of the preacher-teacher of the Word of God. We may never see his
like again. The times have changed and the mood is different.
Nevertheless, wherever men attempt the Morgan method of preparation and preaching, they will not want for an audience or congregation to listen. Morgan gloried in his work and only a last illness at
eighty years of age slowed him and finally stopped him. Genius
does not explain him, nor force of personality or even a keen
intellect. Only the baptism of the Spirit of God upon a dedicated
mind and a sanctified imagination begins to point to the secret of

the disciplined workmanship of this man whose legacy of preaching is found in the ten volumes of *The Westminster Pulpit.*

John Henry Jowett (1864-1923) was one of the band of Englishmen who found his ministry on both sides of the Atlantic and was always appreciated. He was the pastoral-expository preacher serving in Newcastle-on-Tyne and Birmingham, England, before seven years at Fifth Avenue Presbyterian Church, New York, from which he returned to Westminster Chapel, London. He was successor to Dale at Carrs Lane Congregational Church, Birmingham, and there became widely known for his remarkable sermon power. He was meticulous in preparation, writing out carefully and working over sermons for several weeks in advance of delivery. He was one of the few men who could read a sermon manuscript in the pulpit and read well, holding the interest of the people, and preaching as he read.

Jowett was evangelical in conviction and never disturbed by the controversies concerning Biblical literature. He gave himself to the proclamation of the evangel; and with the wooing note of comfort or strength, the word *grace* was his outstanding message throughout his life. His Biblical and expository style of preaching wore well, and he never lacked large congregations. In the Yale Lectures, *The Preacher: His Life and Work* (1911), we find the heart and substance of all that Jowett was and did as a preacher. Here are his faith, his practical piety, his disciplined writing, and the high ideals he set for his goals. The pulpit to Jowett was like a throne and at one time he was estimated to be the leading preacher in England. He loved his calling and lived for it. Nothing detracted him from its demands. He said he had but one passion and he lived for it—"the absorbingly arduous yet glorious work of proclaiming the grace and love of our Lord and Saviour Jesus Christ." He felt, like Paul, "separated unto the gospel of God" and this makes the preacher. He believed that as he ministered "something always happens"— deep and gracious and beautiful.

The changing theology of **Reginald John Campbell (1867-1956)** whose ministry was at the City Temple, London, the historic center of nonconformity since the Puritan Thomas Goodwin, shattered the complacency of many. While all churches were then disturbed by the ferment of theological liberalism and the application to Scripture of the higher criticism, Campbell preached his new ideas and interpretations, shocking the conservatives of his church. Forced to be honest in a theological dilemma, he published his views in *A Spiritual Pilgrimage* (1916), and then resigned. He later entered the ministry of the Church of England. Campbell's lucid, pulsating style of writing and preaching won a wide hearing.

Associated with the City Temple after Campbell, was an assistant pastor and preacher, **Agnes Maude Royden (1876-1956)**, who was one of the first women to engage in this type of ministry. She came with a rich background of social, educational, and cultural strength. She was a speaker and writer of ability. A woman as pastor-preacher was a rare experience at that time. Maude Royden stands as a representative and pioneer of those still to follow. The universal church has not yet accepted ordination of women to the pastorate although women find many avenues of ministry open to them in other walks of life. The door opens ever wider in this regard, but Maude Royden's work marked a breakthrough of tradition.

Her books included: *Sex and Commonsense, Prayer as a Force, Friendship of God,* as well as published sermons. One of her characteristics in preaching was simplicity, the clarity from depth of thought and awareness of human need. She was introduced by **Joseph Fort Newton** as his colleague and during World War I she made a significant contribution in meeting people at their crucial hour of strain and stress. She dealt with the issues of faith and hope, teaching a sanctified commonsense able to face life with courage. Without affectation the woman preacher pioneered a way of conversational preaching fitted to heal and bring spiritual health.

D. Martyn Lloyd-Jones (1899-) has been the natural successor to G. Campbell Morgan at Westminster Congregational Chapel, London, where from 1938 to 1968 he upheld the tradition of that pulpit with its expository ministry. People came on Friday nights to hear the Bible Lectures which covered the books of the Bible. Sundays brought not only his regular congregation but also visitors to hear the evangelical message based on a belief in the authority and veracity of Scripture.

Lloyd-Jones belongs to the Welsh school of preachers. His native skill with language, his literary polish, and his medical training gave him more than the ordinary preparation for preaching. As a Harley Street Specialist for the Heart he knew the physical needs of people. As a preacher he diagnosed their spiritual and moral maladies and prescribed for the whole man. Preaching to him lay not in preparing a sermon for each service, but simply continuing where he was in the ongoing exposition of a book of the Bible. He was in the succession of the earlier giants, such as Joseph Parker and Alexander McLaren.

As preaching to him was the exegesis of a passage and then setting it forth with its meaning and application, so he believed in the primacy of this kind of preaching. Behind this lay careful scrutiny of text, relevance of theology in which he favored the Puritans, and a common sense application to life. In his lectures *Preachers and Preaching* (1971) he shares his views and convictions based on thirty years at Westminster Chapel. "The highest and the greatest and the most glorious calling to which anyone can ever be called, preaching is the greatest work in the world, the most thrilling, the most exciting, the most rewarding, and the most wonderful."

Such preaching was not the conventional sermon type, but a regular, steady, and persistent unfolding of the text of Scripture. His *Studies in the Sermon on the Mount* or on *Romans 5—8* express the typical style of preaching which appeals to many.

The Congregational Church has had a galaxy of men with preaching gifts. In the 1900s we find Leyton Richards, Birmingham; Fred W. Norwood, London and Canada; J. Morgan Gibbon, London; Ernest James, London; John Bevan, London; G. Stanley Russell, London and Canada; Nathanael Micklem, Principal of Mansfield College, Oxford; H. Cunliffe-Jones; Leslie Cooke; and Charles S. Duthie, Principal, New College, London.

Methodist

In **Dinsdale Thomas Young (1861-1938)** the Methodist Church in England had an unusual exponent of apostolic faith. Victorian in dress and manner, he ministered at the Methodist Central Hall, London, like a king upon his throne. Of the old school in the Victorian era then ending, he did not apologize for his theology and preaching. He knew nothing of a generation gap as young people thronged to hear him. "Preaching as an ordinance," he said, "is part of 'God's good pleasure.' It is *the* Sacrament. The churches grieve God's Spirit when they ignore or depreciate preaching."

His preaching style owed much to an organlike voice. Rich, full, and resonant in its tones, he used it with all the skill of a master speaker. His theology was linked to the Puritans and his Wesleyan convictions were proclaimed with assurance and confidence. He lectured and preached, using the *Unfamiliar Texts* of the Bible and also espoused *Popular Preaching* (book titles). He used the Bible as a mine to find riches, and by "popular" he meant the Good News told in simple speech and ardent spirit to the popular mind.

In contrast to Dr. Young, there was **Alfred Edward Whitham (1879-1938)**, whose long ministry at Bournemouth is recalled for its winsome and poetic beauty. In *The Pastures of His Presence* some of his messages are recorded where the catholicity of his mind overflows in making faith a radiant reality. Something of the troubadour bubbled up in his preaching style. He preached goodness and gaiety as the blend of our Lord's life and so for the disciple's life.

There was a sacramental touch in his preaching as if he already had entered within the veil of the unseen. The vision of God was the supreme experience in worship and this was mediated through preaching. He stressed the art of keeping the festivals of the church and preached the Biblical message as something present. He taught the value of the devotional life as implicit in the life of churchmanship. His preaching moved like music, beginning low, rising in gradual crescendo, then finishing on a quiet stretch, leaving the hearers at rest.

Samuel Chadwick (1860-1932) was one of the distinguished preachers in a long roster of eminent men. Amid the excellently trained men of scholastic ability, no one would discredit the fact that Chadwick with his limited education reached heights of influence through his self-discipline and dedication in the ministry. Pastor, preacher, evangelist, editor, author and principal of Cliff College, he had an incomparable record.

His books, *The Call to Perfection, The Path of Prayer, The Way to Pentecost,* and *The Gospel of the Cross* among many, constitute a confessional of spiritual pilgrimage. One volume of sermons, *Humanity and God,* has the idea of his own love for people within the love of God. At the heart of his preaching was the cross of Christ. Out of his own conversion grew compassion for others. For twenty-five years he edited the weekly journal *Joyful News,* in which his editorials manifested spiritual depth in communicating the rich things of God.

Chadwick was saturated in the Authorized King James Version of the Bible, the devotional classics, and the English dictionary. His writing was unmatched by the majority. Pellucid English poured from his pen, and in preaching his speech was a rugged Anglo-Saxon of beauty and light. He was easy to follow and simple to understand because of this. He said himself, "a sharp spear needs no polish"; and the fact that his sermons were blessed of God was his reward.

In his sermons there was the short sentence, the clear allusion, the lighted illustration from literature or life, and the appeal for commitment. His homiletics grew out of private study and experience. He taught a generation to preach with fidelity, unity, order, substance, aim, and natural, reverent, earnest delivery. Methodist evangelical preaching reached new heights in Chadwick's ministry and by his influence.

Leslie Dixon Weatherhead (1893-) was another of the soulful Methodists whose work in the pulpit and whose books touched the lives of thousands. Both at Leeds and in London where he became minister of the City Temple (Congregational), he was one of a few who held the crowds in a day of decline. His distinction lay not in expository preaching, but rather in the ability with which he used the new psychology to commend the Christian message. In London from 1936 to 1960 he maintained an unusual ministry. He dealt with the fears, frustrations, anxieties, hopes, and complexes of people. His method was not that of exposition, but of problem-solution discussion.

The Yale Lectures *Psychology, Religion and Healing* (1949) charted a new course for that series. He did not deal with sermon preparation as such, but pointed a new way of reaching the minds of people by using psychology as an ally. A well-modulated voice, fluency in speech, and a freedom from manuscript enabled him to have rapport with his hearers. A criticism made of him was that he had little theology and too much psychology. However, this was the trend of the times and Weatherhead capitalized on it. Like Norman Vincent Peale in New York, he had a clinic for counseling in private as an adjunct to his preaching.

Part of his strength lay in his stress upon prayer and forgiveness, themes always at the heart of his message. His method was to emphasize the positive rather than the negative. For example, in discussing public worship, he entitled a sermon "Why People Do Go to Church" rather than why some neglect this. Religious psychology gave to him a new power as a physician of souls. Sermons were therapeutic in theme and treatment. His Christology made much of Jesus as Friend, Healer, Savior, for he saw people lonely, lost, fearful, and frustrated. He represents a large group of preachers who at that period began to use the insights and help of psychology in the service of the soul.

William Edwin Sangster (1900-1960) was in the long tradition of Methodism from the evangelical witness of the Wesleys. After several pastorates, he came to Westminster Central Hall, London (1939-1945), the period of World War II. There he sustained a preaching and pastoral ministry to his congregation and also the homeless of central London. War and air raids drove people to the air raid shelters and there Sangster worked with people in distress. He also found time to study and take the Ph.D. degree from London University with the thesis "The Path to Perfection" 1943.

As a preacher Sangster combined the intellectual with the spiritual. He proclaimed the doctrine of perfection, the maturity of a love which flowed from God through the Christian to others. John Wesley's teaching was reinterpreted for moderns by a true disciple of Wesley. His sermons focused upon the need for man to be reborn and then for the Christian to live the abundant life. Thus holiness or sanctification came alive in the homespun ways of a modern preacher whose words and work gave evidence of unusual power.

Sangster was able to share with others the methods and habits he had cultivated in learning to preach. *The Craft of Sermon Construction* and *The Approach to Preaching* are worthwhile texts which have inspired others. In another book, *Power in Preaching,* he reiterated that "doctrines must be preached practically and duties doctrinally." He was a link with the Victorian age and in pulpit garb seemed formal and austere, yet when proclaiming the gospel he seemed another Wesley come alive. Preaching to him did things, the most important things. Nothing could take the place of preaching to this evangelical greatheart.

His final basis of preaching was found in his thesis that no one could preach without preparing his own inner life. His greatest sermon was most moving as he for many months was slowly dying of an incurable disease. In that experience he touched more preachers and people "by the amassing of a great soul so as to have something worthwhile to give."

Donald Oliver Soper (1903-) came from a religious, educated, cultured background, and is a man endowed with gifts of strength and religious convictions. In the John Wesley tradition, he retained his scholarly aptitudes, plunged into pastoral and mission work in London, and identified himself with the social and political aspirations of the masses who were frustrated in the '30s—'40s of this era.

The British scene after the depression and the first World War brought disillusionment to millions, especially the working class of England, Scotland, Wales, and Ireland. Soper was a young Methodist preacher when he began his major task of life at the Kingsway Hall in London's West End. There he carried on a multiple ministry of preaching, teaching, pastoral oversight, evangelism, social work, political involvement, and open air dialog with men. The last is in the Wesley tradition as the founder of Methodism did most of his work in the open air. Soper's preaching on Sundays was tested out in the heckling and close discussion with people who gathered to hear him each week at Tower Hill and later wherever opportunity came in other places where crowds were gathered.

His style of preaching was affected by this means so that he developed a conversational manner. The declamatory style of the Victorian era was passing in England, the pulpit giants were fewer and people did not throng to hear a pulpit orator as formerly. However, Soper was one who appealed to people in his discussions of present-day problems and issues, but always with a presentation of the Christian view of God and the world. His apologetic talks and sermons brought a frontal attack on Communism and at the same time expounded the vast superiority of a committal to Jesus Christ for this life as well as for the future.

Soper studied Communism as well as the social and political needs of his time. Thus he was able to stand his ground and in controversy engage other sharp minds with ability. His Biblical preaching for the church was in the context of a worship which was liturgical. He aimed at the conversion of the individual and also sought by social service to heal the hurts of the poor, the outcast, the rejected, and the hopeless, found at the heart of London. Politically he was a pacifist, but while he argued for his conviction at this point, he did not preach a pacifist gospel as such, but a full-orbed gospel of personal and social redemption. His sermons spelled out clearly that to be a Christian meant personal committal to Christ and the challenge to Christianize the environment. In his sermons was "the insight of the Bible as a whole and the life and teaching of Jesus Christ in particular, in the light of the week's headlines and the relationship between the two which came up week by week, freshly minted, vital, topical, to earn acceptance in the minds of people."

When Soper preached at Kingsway, Weatherhead was at the City Temple, and Sangster at Westminster—three outstanding Methodist preachers, yet each different. Weatherhead's preaching was psychological and brought healing to the mind. Sangster brought the eternal gospel to moderns with the classic tradition of Bible and prayer in evangelism. Soper complemented these with his social and political involvement to identify the Christian with people in social-redemptive ministries. Each would claim they believed the same in orthodox faith, but each expressed his message in a different manner as only different personalities can. Unlike his friends, Soper found time to share in the counsels of the London City Council with its oversight of Metropolitan London. He believed that there he could stand as a Christian to guide others in dealing with the causes of much of London's ills. Then in the House of Lords in the British Parliament (to which he was elected) he also spoke to his peers of faith in Jesus Christ and the need for legislation to implement Christian ideals because of the moral problems involved.

In his preaching he often said: "Christianity is the real focus-point of all our questioning and in it can be found the answer to every problem that vexes human kind." "I believe that what is morally wrong can never be politically right." These sayings were proclaimed in sermons, but also in the open air to the restless, frustrated, and disillusioned men with no employment. Then again, he used similar words in the highest governmental level of influence in politics in the House of Lords. There he spoke with conviction and pointed speech to those who had the destiny of millions in their hands politically and socially. He stood as Christ's representative and bore witness before rulers.

Donald Soper will be remembered for his fiery speech, the compelling idea, the repetitive sentence which broke through over the years to thousands who heard him in solemn assemblies of his church or in the ranks of the members of the Labor Party of Great Britain. When critics have asked, What does the church do for people?—the answer has been incarnate in this preacher. He has brought identification of the church with people in their need. He has fought their battles in the political arena. He has stood for the social rights of all men. He has not hesitated to make clear that all these spring from a faith which finds in Jesus Christ the salvation of the whole man. This was the hallmark of his preaching. He stands as the representative of a generation thus involved at all levels of life and destiny.

John Ernest Rattenbury (1870-1963) had a life of ministry (1893-1963), as a Methodist preacher, writer, author, and interpreter of Wesleyana. His books on the passion and the death of our Lord saw him living at the heart of things. In *The Adoration of the Lamb, The Conversion of the Wesleys,* and *Vital Elements of Public Worship* (1936), the versatility of this devout mind and spirit is seen. Alongside of preaching, Rattenbury believed that John Wesley owed much to his brother Charles. The Evangelical Revival of the Eighteenth Century needed preaching and singing. Thus the gospel was spread abroad. In his studies and ministrations, Rattenbury expounded the relationship of the Biblical message as expressed in sermon and in song. In the praise and hymns of the Methodist movement—and since—pastors and leaders saw the evangelical nature as well as the eucharistic spirit of the hymns.

The Methodist Church could claim such men as L. Maldwyn Edwards, historian and preacher; William Russell Maltby (1866-1951); and J. Scott Lidgett (1854-1953), Wesleyan leader in Church and State affairs.

English Methodism was blessed by the riches of many personalities whose preaching reached the people through the central halls built in the major cities. Among the distinctive preachers was **Frederick Luke Wiseman (1858-1944).** His unusual gifts included musical ability which he used to advantage. He served as President of the Methodist Conference, gave lectures in many colleges, and was not only a pastor but, when historic churches were vacant, also served as interim pastor. His final tenure of office was at Wesley's Chapel, London.

As preacher he had a dramatic force of utterance which swept everything before him. Eloquence and oratory fused in sound gospel preaching. He would break into his sermon by suddenly singing to illustrate a point, or he would leave the pulpit to play on a piano or an organ. This was not acting; in proclaiming the gospel he was carried away and it was natural for him in his versatility of gifts to do these things. He had a comprehensive knowledge of hymnology and he could conduct a choir as easily as sing and preach. His voice was rich and deep in quality and, whether lecturing or preaching, he could use it naturally without strain, playing upon it as an organ produces various tones. To hear Wiseman was an unforgettable experience. He stood as a representative of Wesley's preachers at their best and finest hours.

George Jackson (1864-1945) is recalled as a strong Methodist pastor who penetrated the citadel of Presbyterianism. His preaching in Edinburgh drew large congregations, and his fervent and contemporary preaching was such as to appeal to the discriminating hearer. Psychology and modern writings were used to communicate the eternal truth. In *The Preacher and the Modern Mind* (1912) there is the heart of his lectures on the theme which was paramount in that day.

Wilfred Hannam (1881-1952), Central Hall, Edinburgh, followed him to sustain a rich and abiding ministry of strength and beauty. He, too, used the insights of psychology in his exposition of the gospels and the presentation of the figure of the Christ. Winsome and with feeling, these men brought interest to truth in a period of strong dogmatism.

Baptist

John MacBeath (1881-1967) was one of Scotland's preachers of eminence. Hearing him was an experience of sheer captivity to the winsomeness of delivery in prose read from a manuscript, but which sang as it came through like poetry. The pleasing quality of his style added luster to his preaching. His literary bent was unmistakable and all the riches of his literary knowledge shone through in allusion, quotation, and interpretation of themes expounded. What he wrote was preached and then later was reproduced in books which continue to carry his message. *The Hills of God, The Great Unities, The Life of a Christian,* are titles which redeem the ordinary and seek the stimulus of majestic ideas for daily living. Scholarly exposition and beauty of thought and expression helped the worshiper to soar to heights.

One of his gifts was preaching to children. This related him to a few special men who did this regularly. Out of his background of wide reading he could weave, in simple language, stories and events for youthful minds at worship with their elders. *Roadmakers and*

Roadmenders, Lamps and Lamplighters, A Number of Things, are titles of books enshrining the best of these children's talks.

William Graham Scroggie (1877-1958), of Scottish ancestry, was nurtured in England, and was in business before entering theological study at Spurgeon's College, London. From his early pastorate he found tension and frustration which ended when he set himself aside to master the English Bible. Like his distinguished predecessor G. Campbell Morgan, he laid the foundation of a ministry which became worldwide as well as Biblical in depth. From Sunderland to Charlotte Chapel, Edinburgh, he made his way to the zenith of his pastoral-preaching ministry. At the close he became the pastor of Spurgeon's Tabernacle, London, and this temporary assignment lasted for seven years.

During his active life Scroggie specialized in having a midweek School of the Bible which drew young and old to hear his Bible lectures over the years. This enabled him to work his way through the books of the Bible and was a valuable supplement to his expository preaching on Sundays. In addition, he gave Bible Readings, especially at the Keswick Convention, Keswick, England, held annually in July. Travels and writings widened his teaching ministry and among the almost forty books published, *A Study of the Gospels* (a monumental detailed examination of all facets of the Life and Work of Christ) and in three volumes *The Unfolding Drama of Redemption* (a survey of the Bible, synthetically, analytically, and Christologically), continue to be issued.

Scroggie was the Bible expositor above all others after Morgan ended his ministry. He had the gifts of a teacher and toiled strenuously in preparing subjects and manuscripts. He was a tall and gaunt man, with white hair and pleading voice, for whom preaching was a passion. Although not an evangelist, he did the work of an evangelist in a teaching evangelism. He liked a large canvas in preaching. A few titles of sermons illustrate this: "What the Gospel Means to Me"; "The Adequacy of Christ"; "The Invincibility of Christian Certitude"; "What are the Fundamental Realties?"

In preaching there was the blend of careful exegesis, wise illustration, a subtle humor on rare occasions, skillful use of alliteration, and above all a message steeped in Biblical allusion. Everything, whether from a passage or from a text, was expository in the strictest sense. He said:

Jesus Christ is the world's only hope. It is not surprising that the world does not believe this, but it is a tragedy and a crime that the organized Christian Church only half believes it. I do not suppose that Christendom will ever frame a formula of belief which all can accept, but if this means that the Church has no theology by which she is prepared to live, then it were better that there should be no Church, for to be creedless is only to cumber the ground. Let it be frankly admitted that the truths of divine revelation are too great to be crushed into a formula, and admitted also that interpretation can never become static and final, yet if the Church is not to perish there are some things which she must believe with all her soul, and of these, the deity of Christ, and His redeeming and saving death and resurrection must stand at the center, for these truths are witnessed to alike by revelation, history and experience.

Logical, acute, systematic, balanced, reasonable—these are some of the qualities of his preaching. He appealed to the whole man for a verdict in the light of the claims of Christ. Scroggie worked by expounding the thesis in the sermon, carefully building it to the climax when he would appeal, with passion and persuasion, largely to the mind of the hearer. Such intellectual preaching based upon the Bible alone had its own authority and power.

Harry Tydeman Chilvers (1872-1963) reached the zenith of his pastoral work when he assumed the leadership of Metropolitan Tabernacle, London, made famous by the long ministry of Charles Haddon Spurgeon. Modernity seeks change and progress into the new, but here was one who was a Strict Baptist and after twenty-five years at Bethesda Church, Ipswich, a center in East Anglia of the strictest sort, he proceeded to continue the same preaching in London. Certainly he was a modern Puritan!

Chilvers was himself and no copy of his distinguished predecessor. His preaching was Calvinistic and divine sovereignty the bulwark of his faith. He liked to use short texts, for example the phrase "To the uttermost." He had a natural gift of expression; his gestures were few, usually effective, especially the movements of the hands. Illustrations were simple incidents. Forthright in preaching, he proclaimed the doctrines of grace. He believed that Calvinism put iron into the blood. He stood in the tradition of Spurgeon in this.

Tydeman Chilvers lived to preach and was sensitive to the divine leading of the Holy Spirit in everything. His message was positive and not negative in days of controversy. That he maintained this ministry over fifty-four years in four pastorates is a testimony to the strength of his pastoral preaching. At the center of his sermons was the cross of Christ, either by actual mention or certainly by inference. The gospel of the grace of God held him like a magnet and when he preached there was a magnetism of power in one who dwelt within the divine presence.

Fred Townley Lord (1893-1962) serves as an exponent of contempory Baptist preaching. His scholarship and literary skill combined with an evangelical spirit enabled him to serve acceptably in a changing age. The *apologia* of the gospel and the Christian faith was central. Successive pastorates came to a climax at Bloomsbury Baptist Church, London. He also served as editor of *The Baptist Weekly*. Religious journalism was wedded to the sermonic art, and vigorous speech proclaimed a reasonable faith.

Frederick Chambers Spurr (1862-1942) could look back with thanksgiving to "Sixty Years as a Preacher." His early conversion and subsequent zest for knowledge and education beyond the opportunity of formal schooling gave him a dedication early in life. His goal was sure and his fervor and zeal for the Christian faith encouraged him in his self-discipline. Lacking many of the opportunities of culture, he became a self-taught young man. After maturity he spent five years as a Baptist minister in Melbourne, Australia (1909-1914), preaching to the largest congregations. He returned to England to become F. B. Meyer's successor at Regent's Park Chapel, London, and thereafter gave a rich ministry at Hampstead Road, Birmingham, until retirement in 1936.

Spurr's legacy of preaching lay in his adherance to the substance of the message, unchanging in changing times. In form the sermon was structured by outline, analysis, exposition, and illustration. His sermon substance advocated the facts of faith. War and its aftermath of doubt found him the apologetic preacher, ever ready to revise form and find new applications of eternal truth in newly minted speech and relevant spirit. To him the sermon must be prepared with care and detail in a written outline and manuscript before delivery. In this he followed the French master from whom he owed much as a student of speech and preaching, Abbe H. Coudry, *L'Eloquence de la Chaire*. In precise terms Spurr pointed to standards which demanded concentration and consecration.

The Baptist Church was represented also by the preaching of Samuel W. Hughes who followed Charles Brown, London; John

Pitts, Liverpool and Montreal, Canada; H. Wheeler Robinson, Old Testament scholar; Ernest A. Payne, Regent College, Oxford; Melbourne E. Aubrey, Secretary of The Baptist Union; R. Guy Ramsay, Hillhead, Glasgow; Henry Cook, London; John O. Barrett, Newcastle; and Howard H. Williams, Bloomsbury.

Anglican

The period of World Wars I and II gave rise to several preachers in the Church of England whose power was widespread. Because of the times and the background, their ministries bore a definite relationship to each other. Among these are Geoffrey Anketell Studdert Kennedy, Dick Sheppard, and Canon William H. Elliott. Their distinctive work lay in London at its heart. The manner and habit of these pastors was to cultivate the colloquial and conversational speech in the pulpit. They were known for their "man-to-man" speech which somehow reached out over the radio then being used increasingly.

Geoffrey Anketell Studdert Kennedy (1883-1929), better known as "Woodbine Willie" for his chaplaincy work among the troops in France and Flanders during World War I, came of Irish stock. He exuded that native wit and pungent talk which appealed to the "man in the street." An intensely lovable man, generous to a fault, he could reach men in the services of their country quicker than any other chaplain. If men shied away from the church and religion, it was Kennedy who lured them back with an ease of speech and a winsome personality lit up with wit and wisdom.

The messages of Woodbine Willie were not the conventional type, for he sprinkled his speech with barbs common to the earthiness of the soldier's vocabulary. In slang and joke, his language was unrestrained and his shock tactics repaid him in the ready hearing and response of the crowd from outside the church. He could out-think anti-Christian speakers in debate, and he learned from open-air preaching the easy flow of speech to men. He had the gift of poetry and turned many themes into rhyme so that his poetry, still being read, has in it that pungency and punch characteristic of the gifted Irish chaplain.

His message was that God suffered in Christ—

> God, the God I love and worship,
> Reigns in sorrow on the Tree,

> Broken, bleeding, but unconquered,
> Very God of God to me.

Out of that incarnate love came his own identification with the poor and the suffering which issued in the cry for social redemption. Unconventional preacher as he was, he translated the eternal gospel into the speech of the street and so reached forgotten men.

In contrast to "Woodbine Willie" was "Dick" Sheppard (1880-1937) whose full name was Hugh Richard Lawrie Sheppard. He, too, was unconventional, but not another "Woodbine Willie." He was the pastor of St. Martin-in-the-Fields, the parish church at the heart of London. Like Kennedy, Sheppard had been brought up in a minister's home and knew the hardships of poor people in sordid surroundings in other cities. The book, *The Impatience of a Parson,* tells of hopes and fears common to Sheppard's ministry. It is said that he was not as impatient as Kennedy.

At the church in London, Dick Sheppard exercised a unique ministry, popular, down-to-earth, using an unconventional manner of speech and approach. He showed the relevance of the church to everyday life when the Episcopal Church was in critical straits, losing contact with the masses. He dusted off the image of a sober-minded institution and made it unbend to think of every man. He wished the church to be open day and night with light to guide the fallen and the lost. In the crypt under the main building, beds were provided and meals were given where the prodigals from the street might come and find shelter.

The messages of Sheppard radiated the love of God and an understanding of people as persons. Never profound or too intellectual, they evinced the throb of a sympathetic heart. This kindly and courteous man deliberately upset the conventional ways of the church in order to get a hearing from those without. Utilizing the radio, he would begin with a joke to catch attention, and then he held people by the winsome and sincere word he spoke. The difficulties of speaking over the broadcast system, not knowing and not seeing anyone, were overcome by Sheppard as people listened eagerly to him in the knowledge that he was talking to them personally.

Like Kennedy the use of a nickname was a token of the reception given by the people who were helped by him. His preaching was sprayed with the words "love" and "home," but always the love from God and the invitation for prodigal man to come home.

Canon **William Henry Hatchard Elliott (1883-1962)** was the third of this group who ministered at the heart of London and made the Church of England a new order of divine ministry. He came to St. Michael's Church, London, in 1930, and his work was sustained throughout the Great Depression. A new radio broadcast service late on Thursday evenings was begun in the hope that by a simple service of Scripture readings, prayers, well-known hymns, and a short talk people would be helped in that time of depression. Based on the awareness that many were dispirited and lonely as well as losing hope, this broadcast service became the means of reaching millions of listeners during eight years. Similar broadcast services have been given in the English-speaking world since and with success. Nevertheless, this particular one stands out for its pioneering quality and its achievements.

Elliott was not a prominent preacher, but for this special service he was admirably suited. He spoke in an intimate manner, just talking to individuals as if they were there with him in the room. A slight informality broke away from the more studied form of the Anglican service. The "orders" were still there, but did not intrude. His messages were based on Scripture and were freely illustrated with stories of those who had struggled and overcome. He learned that the secret of religious broadcasting was to think of one person and talk to that one. This was something new in preaching; the new ally of the mechanical device could be a handicap, but he made it a means of grace. More than fifty volumes of these radio messages were published, an indication of the widespread interest.

His was a gospel of assurance in time of despair, of comfort in a time of challenge. If he did not cover the greater theological doctrines of the faith, he did bring support to people that was desperately needed in a time of crisis and upheaval.

The Anglican Church has not lacked for its mighty men in theology and in philosophy as well as in all forms of Biblical scholarship. However, in preaching there are also giants who stand out above their fellows. One of these was **William Temple (1881-1944)** who climaxed a full life as the Archbishop of Canterbury. Born into affluence, intellectual endowment, and natural gifts of personality and speech, he early became a leader and preacher of distinction. Temple had an urbanity about him, a bigness (not just in stature), an amplitude of thought, and a stature which men respected. Theologian, philosopher, worldwide religious statesman, social and educational reformer, Temple stood at a juncture of history as a defender of the Christian faith. His preaching came out of his theological and philosophical strength. His theological books dealt with Apologetics, *Christus Veritas* (1924) is a sampling. The Gifford Lectures, *Nature, Man, and God* (1934), is his philosophical treatise. For spiritual light and devotion one work lives on, *Readings in St. John's Gospel* (1939).

Utilizing the insights of his books, one can easily find the secret of his preaching skill. He brought a rich mind to bear upon the theological and philosophical problems of his day. Having satisfied himself that Christ was the answer, he went on to take from the Scriptures the simple things of the Christian life. In his devotional life and personal faith, he found joy in the mystical yet practical Fourth Gospel, the epitome of spiritual life. His sermons were not noted for anything unusual in their composition, but they did possess that rare quality of devotional conviction.

One such sermon on faith (Heb. 11:1) was given with such simple words and glowing illustrations that young people present understood him with ease and appreciation. His profundity had become an incarnation of humility and simple speech. Here was the bishop of souls, the shepherd of the flock, the wise teacher and the sure guide to the heart of the Eternal.

Herbert Hensley Henson (1863-1947) represented the Anglican Church at its strength during the ecumenical age. In writing and sermon he was strong in faith and courageous in utterance. He was best known in his later years as Bishop of Durham. His long pastorates gave him an opportunity to perfect his prose of which he was a master. His was the stainless steel of perfect English prose. Sermons from his pen always had in them that clarity of expression which made for understanding for reader or listener.

He lived in a time of conflict when theological views were in ferment. His aim, therefore, was to bring certainty where there was doubt, and hope where there was fear. The apologetic nature of his preaching was a strong feature of his age. Henson based his message on Biblical revelation and found in the text sufficient matter to speak to his generation. He scanned the times in which he was set and then let the light of divine truth illuminate the will of God for moral standards and demands upon the church and also the nation. Many of his best sermons are those which speak to a national crisis or remind the nation of its heritage.

The Yale Lectures on Preaching were given by him in 1909 with the title, *The Liberty of Prophesying*. As an independent spirit and a mind untrammeled by either man or fear, Henson found that preaching based on the Greek New Testament and then translated into modern English life was potent. He did not speak comfortable words and was never free from the ferment of people being aroused pro and con by what he said. In the revolutionary age through which he ministered, Henson preached to eternity and yet to the times with their political, social, and intellectual unrest. Henson's sermons came incisively to the hearer. There was pungent wit, terse epigram, and prophetic demand. That he gave offense to men on the left hand and on the right hand is obvious, but his fearless conviction in standing for Christ and the church in his day enabled him to proclaim the message with feeling.

One of the marks of his strong preaching lay in his discrimination between essentials and nonessentials so that in "speaking the truth in love" he kept close to the heart of the gospel in its redeeming facts. He was sure that preaching was the principal function of the minister, whatever else he did. His claim was that he had "the right to think freely, and to speak freely, within the limits prescribed by personal discipleship and pastoral duty." In the sermon on "Divine Vocation" based on Isaiah 6, where Isaiah receives God's call to minister, Henson discusses the springs of character and the original endowment of one who became great in the sight of the Lord. He saw in the prophet's crisis the elements which must also indicate the "same cycle of spiritual experiences which must be traversed by the man who would face his fellows with the tremendous message. First, the vision which creates personal conviction and then the crushing sense of personal sin, followed by the absolving touch of divine forgiveness, and in that God's call, clear, audible, coercive. Then the answer of obedient faith; finally, the divine commission. Isaiah tells the secret history of every true ministry while the world stands."

In dealing with the authority of God in life and in religion (Mark 11:28) or in speaking of Christian teaching (Matt. 7:6), Henson's sermons are down-to-earth, spiritually poised, and aesthetically

written for delivery. In the stern teacher of righteousness seen in
John the Baptist or the discriminating teacher of truth seen in the
Lord Jesus Christ was brought to him the necessary thrust and
application. The cross of Christ was still a stumbling stone and a
rock of offense to the unbelieving and disobedient, and Henson did
not hesitate to announce this, almost with bluntness. In his autobiography, *Retrospect of an Unimportant Life* (3 vols.), he distills
the wisdom of an important preacher whose impact upon life and a
national church was profound.

John Robert Walmsley Stott (1921-) represents in this era
another wing of evangelical preaching which has its roots in the
strong Anglican tradition. Like Charles E. Simeon (1759-1836) and
W. H. Griffith Thomas (1861-1924), he sustains one of the strongest ministries at the heart of London by expository preaching. He is
the scholar touched by pastoral concern and motivated by gospel
thrust. At All Souls', Langham Place, he proves that there is need for
this kind of preaching when people require instruction in the
Christian faith in a time of ignorance.

To Stott the Bible is the textbook for the pulpit, and in the
context of liturgical worship such expository preaching comple-
ments and endorses what the worshiper confesses in creedal statement. This is where authority is found and made articulate in
modern dress, for the preacher has no other source of power.

Out of such preaching have come books distilling the same
message of the pulpit. In *Basic Christianity* is the preaching of the
crucial doctrines of the Christian faith. In *Preacher's Portrait* his
ideas and ideals for the ministry are spelled out in a series of New
Testament studies of the various terms used for the man of God. In
Christ The Controversialist (1970) the exposition of basic truths in
Christology are formulated and given concrete expression for the
modern day. Other publications are primarily expository studies of
Biblical sections, such as the Lord's Discourse in the Upper Room,
John 14—17, the Galatian Letter, or the Letters to Timothy. Thus
the printed page widens the ministry of the sermon from the pulpit.

Stott in preaching has emerged as one of the strong evangelical
voices within the Anglican Church, unashamed and fully committed
to the apostolic faith. He stands for the Protestant and Reformed
basis of The Thirty-Nine Articles. He proclaims that "evangelical"
Christianity is authentic Christianity, true, original and pure. Thus

he preaches from the Bible as the Word of God. Historic Christianity is essentially dogmatic, because it purports to be a revealed faith. On that basis he is the preacher.

The Anglican Church has had leaders who have given strength by preaching, including Bishops Arthur Foley Winnington-Ingram, London; Edwards Woods, Litchfield; Kenneth Ernest Kirk, Oxford; Emery Waller Barnes, Birmingham; George Kennedy Allen Bell, Chichester; Leslie Hunter, Sheffield; F. R. Barry, Southwark; Archbishops Cosmo Gordon Lang, York and Canterbury; Randall Davidson, Canterbury; Cyril Foster Garbett, York; Geoffrey Francis Fisher, Canterbury; and Canon Peter Green, Manchester.

David Richard Davies (1899-1960), like R. J. Campbell, left the Congregational Church to become a preacher of power in Brighton, having moved from faith to unbelief combined with Socialism; then returned to orthodoxy and proclamation.

Walter Robert Matthews (1881-1973), Dean of St. Paul's Cathedral, London, was noted for his press articles as well as his constructive theology in preaching and teaching.

Any selection of representative preachers is bound to omit men who have served well and who because of the limits of space in this work must await another day for recognition. Those who have not only preached with distinction, but have also lectured under different foundations find mention accordingly (see Bibliography and Lectureships on Preaching).

Anglican **Douglas William Cleverley Ford (1914-)**, is a graduate of the London College of Divinity and pastor and lecturer; his experience of preaching and then assisting to equip preachers has given him a unique place in the Church of England in the period of the '30s to '50s. Having lectured to the College of Preachers, London, he has since become the Director. During these years he has stimulated many of his communion to restore preaching to its rightful place within the liturgy of the church. He and F. Donald Coggan, formerly Principal of the London College of Divinity and later Bishop of Bradford and Archbishop of York, have revived the preaching emphasis throughout the Church of England. Ford has shared his own style and goal in stressing expository preaching as well as the sermon themes linked to the Church Year. To him, such preaching is opening the Scriptures to speak for themselves. Thus it "keys into worship." Ford taught within the homiletics of construction and was the example of preaching sermons as part of the pastoral oversight. His books which have since been published indicate the quality and ideals of such goals, as in *An Expository Preacher's Notebook* (1960).

Bryan Stuart Green (1901-) is the leading Anglican evangelist who has conducted preaching missions in Great Britain, Canada, the United States of America, and in Africa, India, and New Zealand. At the Cathedral of St. John the Divine, New York, in 1948 his congregations averaged six thousand per night. Unlike Billy Graham, he works best within the atmosphere of the church building; and without organization by a team, he conducts evangelistic services himself. Theologically conservative, he ministers within the historic tradition of the church he has served as Rector and Canon of Birmingham Cathedral, England, since 1948. He speaks without any gimmicks, and his message is given simply as in any other service at home. As a pastor he engages in the outreach for others using a Biblical sermon with a context of public worship. No appeal is made for outward response, but at the end of the service he asks those who wish to remain to come to another smaller gathering place where he will meet with them and share with them the ways of the Christian life to be lived.

The preaching of Bryan Green is simple, vivid, dynamic in appeal. Doctrines of the Christian faith are explained, the gospel call is given, and the Christian life within the fellowship of the church is demanded. Analogy, illustration, and conversational style of sermon make him effective as a public speaker. He always preaches with a sense of the urgency for decision and the supernatural work of God in the life of man. His book on evangelism is significant and although some of his sermons have been published, he is better to listen to than to read.

Lay

Especially in Great Britain has the work of the layman been recognized. The Methodist Church since the days of the Wesleys leaned heavily on the preaching of these often forgotten men. Following their regular daily toil during the week, they were found on the road and in travel on the weekend to fill the many pulpits of the land. This reminds us that at the first the Christian faith was a lay movement, for the apostles themselves were ordinary working men associated with Christ in His ministry. After the establishment of the church, they gave leadership to the missionary movement as Christians everywhere witnessed throughout the world of that day. Later periods of history saw the rise of the clergy as a group separated from the laity. The centuries witness to many unfortunate results because of an overemphasis on this distinction and the consequent impoverishment of the whole church. However, since the Reformation and the Evangelical Revival, the lay person has found outlets for his witness and opportunity for a ministry where gifts and endowment have allowed.

Methodism and other nonconformist groups, such as Baptist and Congregational, and occasionally Presbyterian, were not slow to utilize this pool of manpower. In the nineteenth century the Church of England lost many irreplaceable men when the Brethren movement began. At first it was not unlike the Wesleyan spirit of an earlier period, but this was among laymen and not clergy. Lord Radstock, John N. Darby, Benjamin Newton, are typical.

Among those who have special mention is the name of the Congregational preacher-layman, **Bernard Lord Manning (1892-1941)**. His like has not been equalled. Erudition in his chosen field of knowledge and scholarship gave him a unique place of leadership and influence. He was Senior Tutor of Jesus College, Cambridge, but was widely known in the churches of his connection for his preaching. Well informed in Biblical foundations of faith, he was skillful in the impartation of truth. His brilliant theological insights revealed the consummate artist of words and ideas. His fine literary skill shone through all he wrote and preached. Before C. S. Lewis appeared on the scene as a modern apologist for Christianity in writing and teaching as a man of letters, Manning was the man with the flaming torch going from congregation to congregation with the glad tidings.

Most of the sermons of Manning are found in *A Layman in the Ministry* (1942), which captures and distills the essence of his preaching. Many were delivered in small chapels across the lesser populated stretches of England, but his personalized sermons were meant for people of all kinds as well as for the more sophisticated. When the premonition of his own death startled him, he preached a sermon at Cheshunt College, Cambridge, in which he defended "the once familiar office for the Burial of the Dead in The Book of Common Prayer." It illustrates his liturgical instinct as well as his knowledge of the human heart. He did not like that lesser lessons should be substituted for the grandeur of Scripture and especially to take the place of I Corinthians 15, of which he said:

> The merit of 1 Corinthians XV is that it does deal with the matter in hand in the simplest and the most direct manner. . . .
> To replace this proclamation of the Resurrection of Christ by some general hope of immortality culled from The Wisdom of Solomon or by the allegory of "the golden city pictured in the legends old"—this is to offer the broken-hearted only half, or less than half, of the good words and comfortable words that we have.

The titles of some of his sermons suggest his interest in people: "Jabez and His Sorrow"; "Achan and Achor"; "Jeroboam and His Sin"; "Jehu and His Zeal"; "Ezekiel and God's Glory"; "Ezra and Being Ashamed"; "Pilate and His Cowardice"; "Three Men and St. Paul." Above all else Manning sounded the note of the gospel as he faced people in the struggles of life.

The doctrines were always there. This is well illustrated as he wrestled with them in a sermon: "Does This Generation Need the Gospel?"

> We Christians commend the Gospel of our Redeemer to other men, and to ourselves, too often for reasons that are less than the true reasons; and then we wonder that neither we nor other men respond. The modern world has almost forgotten the great reasons for receiving the Gospel. Christ's religion is confused with good causes, with psychological healing, with philosophic doctrine. Many people do not want any of these things, and they have not understood what freedom from the law of death means, nor how confident is the Christian in his escape from it. There is so often a note of doubt and wistfulness, even when we Christians dare to contemplate this corruption that has eaten into the very stuff of our lives. The glorious Gospel is before us. . . . Now is Christ risen from the dead, and become the first-fruits of them that slept. For as in Adam all die, even so in Christ shall all be made alive. . . . That, brethren, is true; and Christianity is nothing less than the truth of it. We have precisely what this present age requires.

There was always the thrill of confident assertion and the splendor of a radiant witness of a person wholly committed to truth in Christ. When asked to address students for the ministry, no one could do this better than Manning as he talked out of experience and wide knowledge. In "Effectual Preaching: The Reflections of One Hearer" he gives what has become one of the finest definitions or descriptions of preaching. It stands in that highest of all relationships with the famous statement of Phillips Brooks. In the course of his address he deplored the tendency to set preaching overagainst worship in order to belittle preaching. He said:

> The sacrament of the preached Word is part of our inheritance from the Reformers. If preaching were for us the mere expression of an individual's opinions about things in general or a personal exhortation to good manners and pure life, it would deserve this depreciation when contrasted with the other acts of worship. But to preach the Gospel, as we have received that means of grace from our fathers, is not to express the opinion of an individual, is not personal exhortation or instruction; it is *a manifestation of the Incarnate Word, from the Written Word, by the spoken word;* it is a most solemn act of worhsip, in which the thing given—the Gospel of the Son of God—overshadows and even transfigures the preacher by whom it is declared. In the preached word Christ Himself is set forth before us as He is set forth in the Bread and Wine of the holy Supper, as we often remind ourselves, is administered from the Lord's table; from His table, not ours. But His Gospel is preached from His Word, not ours; and the pulpit is no more the minister's than the communion table is his. . . .

This central statement about preaching will serve to remind those who denigrate preaching or who have defected from the high office of the preacher in the vain assumption that it is no longer of influence in society. Throughout Manning's ministry he was capable of meeting any opponents of Christianity on their own intellectual level. He championed the faith in season and out of season, in speech and in writing. He did this with full knowledge and deliberate commitment. His life and words were one in unison of witness. His publications were in seven volumes dealing with historical subjects in connection with his professorial work, but including sermons and addresses in "Essays in Orthodox Dissent"; "Why Not Abandon the Church?"; "The Hymns of Wesley and Watts"; and "The Making of Modern English Religion." In all these is the heartbeat of the preacher, even as he writes as well as preaches.

Manning's preaching has been attested by many as that of the scholar turned evangelist. In this he was not unlike John Wesley, although he did not engage in an itinerant ministry, preferring to serve the many vacant pulpits of the Congregational order. In his sermons there is a freshness of exposition, as texts are taken and seen in new ways. There is a deep spirituality with faithful application to moral needs. Free from conventional cliches, shot through with occasional glimpses of humor, the written word in its literary

grace is matched with an incisive style. The scholar-preacher did not
stoop to careless utterance. Everything was the product of a lively
mind, and a finer witness to Christian truth would be hard to find.
As a layman in the ministry, Manning stands in the footsteps of the
tent-maker, the apostle Paul.

Terrot Reaveley Glover (1869-1943) was one of that choice
group of men who were the product of nonconformity when in
Great Britain the "nonconformist conscience" was something to be
reckoned with. He was a faithful deacon in the Baptist Church and
like certain New Testament men of the same office he was a witness
to the Christian faith. His scholastic career was spent partly in
Queen's University, Kingston, Canada, and after five years there his
major work was at Cambridge University. There as a classical
scholar, teacher, and Public Orator he served well when presenting
famous people for honorary degrees.

The Orator's duty was "to select what can be said with truth and
to be reticent where he cannot praise sincerely." Glover carried
through his duties in excellent vein and for twenty years gave his
Latin orations in the grand tradition. Over the years he also
preached in outstanding pulpits and regularly gave his sermons in
village churches. He was not the best of speakers, by no means a
finished speaker; yet with all the limitations of his elocution his
preaching was strong and inviting. He commanded attention by the
challenge of his thoughts. He seemed to wrestle with the subject
and the congregation joined in so that both were thinking things
out together. For this an "easy conversational pulpit style of a
somewhat staccato kind" was his mode of address. He usually spoke
from notes, brief notes in a small pocket book and, as a rule, not
more than two pages to a sermon. In preaching he seldom, if ever,
used a written-out sermon.

Glover would not claim to be a preacher of standing, yet his
contemporaries reckoned him high in the scale. The pastoral ministry was not his field, but the preacher-lecturer of the classroom
found outlet in the pulpit in a "conference" style. There was a
freshness of wonder with which he faced Christ and the expansive-
ness of the gospel which he acknowledged. He spoke as one thrilled.
That wonder was expressed in the simplest, most colloquial, and
practical language; but the thrill was there nonetheless, in all its
self-communicating and propagating power. Glover's "talk" had a
dynamic quality, a glow, the talk of a man who saw the gospel in its

glory and greatness. Nothing dull was there. He was the layman, the Baptist deacon, the college tutor and lecturer, the university Public Orator bearing witness to his faith and his Lord.

A sermon to Glover was like a poem—simple and passionate, appealing to the imagination in order to stir the affections. Vivid concrete illustrations, drawn from his knowledge of history and his experience, colored his speech. It was said of Glover that he had many sermons but only one theme. Whatever the text, beginning from that Scripture, he preached Jesus. He knew he was not called to be a pastor-preacher, and felt he did right to remain a lay preacher.

His contribution lay not only in the spoken word but also in his many writings, including religious articles in the secular press. His best-known books were *The Jesus of History* and *Jesus in the Experience of Men.* Coming not from the professional theologian or preacher, they made a significant impact upon the thought of his generation. Glover mediated in a controversial time when older forms of speech were being replaced by more relevant ideas. He claimed to keep true to the fundamentals of Christianity, even as he spelled out the eternal ideas in fresh and vital terms. In the former book he poured in his spiritual fervor and passion with illumination of history and life seen in the first century. In the latter book he enlarged his theological perspective in an attempt to explain. His views were not yet finalized and he had his critics, but he claimed to be the evangelical in spite of all. At heart these books were the reflection of his thought in which vital faith and fearless thinking were wedded.

Clive Staples Lewis (1898-1963) was one of God's gifts to a period when in England the Christian faith needed a voice to command attention, not from the pulpit but from the classroom and in books to appeal to the outsider. The apologetic role of Lewis has never been questioned. His own conversion to Christ and his literary strength gave him added powers of contact with a generation of skeptical people. Because he was not a clergyman, perhaps his appeal to the student world was doubly acute. In his own special field of study and teaching he was accepted as an expert. Thus in coming to share his faith in Christ, he was the scholar speaking as a disciple and sharing his experience.

Lewis preached occasionally and these sermons were given rapt attention. A volume titled *The Weight of Glory* (1949) includes some of these messages. Instead of popular common sense for students there was careful argument and relevant illustration in unfolding the historic doctrines of Christianity. In *The Screwtape Letters* there is the confrontation with the devil as a reality and as a spirit of evil. He wrestled with the ideas of heaven and hell to bring to moderns the thought of destiny. In broadcast messages, *Mere Christianity,* there is a dynamic survey of orthodox Christianity, relating to belief and behavior. In a day when permissive ethics emerged, Lewis stood for the age-long virtues, and for chastity at a time when morals were being eroded.

Behind the preaching and witness of Lewis lay deep convictions concerning God and the Scriptures. "Common Christianity is for all who believe that there is one God and that Jesus Christ is His only Son." This is the heart of that positive faith he proclaimed. Lewis was loyal to his Anglican tradition, but he spoke for Christians of all backgrounds. In style he writes and speaks with humor, irony, epigram, and some satire. When he tells of how he became a Christian almost against his will in *Surprised by Joy* he has a quality of thought and utterance not unlike Augustine.

The rich contribution made by Lewis to the preaching of the times was that of the devout layman whose intelligence matched his spirituality. The rapier thrust of truth in his hand was a weapon not to be forgotten.

Henry Drummond (1851-1897) will be remembered for his association with Dwight L. Moody, the American evangelist, and also for his beliefs in the emerging science of his day which often seemed in contradiction to the basic beliefs of the church. During Moody's mass meetings (1873-75) Drummond helped as a personal worker and was given leadership among young men. Moody trusted him and used him extensively. Gradually it became evident that Drummond was a choice young man destined for greatness. His evangelical beliefs and his devotion were unquestioned. Moody invited him to America where he took part in other meetings and also preached at the Northfield Conference.

Drummond's continuing education was theological as well as scientific. Later he was made Professor at New College, Edinburgh, where he lectured on the relation of science and religion. Thousands of students waited on his ministry in pulpits and at conferences in the English-speaking world. His voice was the dominant one in a day of tension and widespread confusion. On the one hand was the orthodox belief in the Bible. On the other hand was the new teaching about science and evolution. For many these were irreconcilable. For others there had to be a meeting place. Thus Drummond tried to be a mediator and also a reconciler. However, he could not please everyone and with his early death at forty-six years of age, his influence quickly ended.

His book *Natural Law in the Spiritual World* (1883) was widely read for its attempted balanced views. Drummond would preach as an evangelist of orthodoxy from the pulpit and then lecture as a scientist who believed the new views then emerging. At that time, the tension was deep. Churchmen were divided and many thought that Drummond was blind to his position in the light of the facts. However, his book *The Greatest Thing in the World* remains as the richest and choicest exposition of I Corinthians 13. Delivered at the invitation of Moody, this became a classic of the devotional life and still abides so. By this we know the heart of this unusual man as a preacher.

Salvation Army

From the days of the founder, General William Booth, through William Bramwell Booth and Commissioner Jeffries to General Edward J. Higgins and George L. Carpenter the emphasis was the same. When **Albert William Thomas Orsborn (1886-1967)** assumed leadership, the work of the Salvation Army had become worldwide and had expanded into far-flung social work in addition to its soul-saving thrust. One thing this arm of the church had and never relinquished was its witness to the saving grace of God, and its proclamation of the gospel of Christ.

The leadership changed across the years, but whether at the beginning or in the more recent years, we find the strong demand that men should find the Savior. God raised up William Booth and his successors to do a special work. This was the work of reaching the underprivileged, the outcast, and the poor and unfortunate in the submerged areas of society. The Army did not set out to cultivate a group of preachers, but to make soul-winners. This was not to downgrade preaching, using the word in its best sense. The history of the Salvation Army has demonstrated that an officer can be a good witness and personal worker and an indifferent preacher.

However, there always was a place for the officer who preached with power and sought the salvation and sanctification of people.

Since William Booth as founder and example, its preaching has been noted for its sense of authority found in the oracles of God. Emphatic, dogmatic, it has attacked specific wrongs and evil. Preaching specialized in evangelism on the streets and in halls where people gathered. Complementing this was the preaching for instruction in holiness of life given to their own trainees and officers.

Unitarian

Laurence Pearsall Jacks (1860-1955) was destined to assume leadership within his church group and early became an assistant to the well-known Stopford Brooke who was a literary critic as well as preacher. At Manchester College he served his denomination well and then was transferred to Oxford. Jacks became the best known of the Principals because of his versatile ministry of preaching, teaching, and writing. In the latter capacity he was editor of *The Hibbert Journal* as well as its founder. The journal expressed the liberal thought and the philosophical theology of the times. A generation that knew its value accepted it beyond the confines of the denomination which brought it into being.

Jack's preaching was like his writing—clear, simple, almost informal. In "The Right to Be Happy," a sermon given to boys at school, he ends with: "To the young people who hear me today I would say this—'When the time comes for choosing your vocation, choose one that challenges your skill; choose one that will put your mind, your whole personality, on its mettle: the happiness best worth having on those lines. Beware of soft jobs. Don't listen to the people who tell you that man was made for happiness. He wasn't. He was made for doing difficult, beautiful, heroic work, and the only happiness he is entitled to is the happiness that comes from doing it.' "

Jacks, like James Martineau, his distinguished predecessor, beautified worship, enriched prayers, and proclaimed a gospel of transcendence and nature for the natural man. In his autobiography, *Confessions of an Octogenarian,* his distilled wisdom is unveiled. Here is theological belief and faith revised from earlier years to become a confident affirmation in his personal acceptance of the Resurrection of Jesus Christ, a modifying of earlier Unitarian belief!

Roman Catholic

William Edwin Orchard (1877-1955) was one of a group of men who in the heyday of theological liberalism moved from one position to another. Several men were in that category, including R. J. Campbell and D. R. Davies. Campbell was a strong influence when as a Congregationalist at the City Temple he taught views expounded in his work, *The New Theology,* and later became an Anglican, an event set forth in *A Spiritual Pilgrimage* (1916). Davies as a Congregationalist finally left the ministry to become active in the Labor Party of Great Britain, but was disillusioned and finally entered the Anglican ministry, taking the pulpit made famous by the late F. W. Robertson of Brighton. At the same time Orchard made his odyssey of faith.

From Faith to Faith is an attempt to explain the life-movements of this intrepid spirit. In the Anglican Church and then the Presbyterian Church in England, he found nurture. Then came an evangelical conversion associated with the Moody-Sankey influence, followed by this young man's earnest witness to his faith. The ministry beckoned and after training he came to a pastorate in the Presbyterian Church. His experience deepened as he prepared a book of prayers, *The Temple.* Then he came to be the pastor of The King's Weigh House in London, a Congregational Church.

Orchard's preaching gradually changed from the freer context of worship to that of ritual. He took what he found and increased the ritual so that it became a manifestation of what was Catholic. Like Cardinal John Henry Newman, Orchard finally stood with the Roman order. Here was a Free Church of nonconformity expressing in association the heritage of Rome. Although poor in voice, he preached long sermons mixed with much heavy theology. Nevertheless, his appeal was striking with its blend of evangelical fervor and ritualistic practice. Orchard was known as a preacher of what he believed with intensity. He was convinced that Catholic doctrine—dogmatic, ascetic, and mystical—was a true guide. He preached that this doctrine made for a healthy mind, overcoming temptation, fear, and loneliness.

His preaching aimed to reach the ordinary man who found

difficulty with more profound preachers. He testified that he had a love for souls spurred on by his evangelical faith. His sermon preparation consisted of choosing a text and having his secretary find relevant material. The original outline was drawn up first at the time of the Sacrament of the Lord's Supper, the whole sermon dictated, a précis of this taken out, from which he then preached. Certainly he did this out of a vast reservoir of reading and study, a devout spirit, and his own commitment to the truth. In preaching there was "the welcome opportunity of testifying to others what Christ had been to his own soul." From this strange admixture of Roman and sacramental practice joined with nonconformist and evangelical belief was a ministry touching many seeking and discriminating people.

Ronald Arbuthknott Knox (1888-1957) exemplified the best tradition of Catholic preaching not unlike that of Newman of an earlier generation. He, too, came from an Anglican background so that he had breadth of outlook and experience. His "solitary" life was given to an incredible amount of work. With this was his bubbling nature with gaiety and wit cascading forth from a fertile and clever mind. Whether in writing or in speech, Knox represented a joy and gladness based on deep faith and hope.

Knox moved from an evangelical Anglicanism to the Roman communion and with his scholarship and gifts proved to be one of the brilliant preachers of that church. Whether in writing, broadcasting, addressing young people, or preaching, he had the gift of arresting words and ideas. *A Spiritual Aeneid* gives his spiritual pilgrimage, not only a "confession" but a banner of truth for him.

In preaching there was the Biblical passage, an interpretation based on his translation (he left a translation of the Bible, both Old and New Testament), and this was used for apologetic or pastoral application. He served his church well and was faithful in the exposition of her doctrines. Like many Protestants he exercised a similar preaching method, but preaching within the context of worship. Mind and heart were thus touched. Liturgical preaching may be an ideal of following the Church Year with its changing emphases. This brings steady and repeated educational thrusts. In *The Mass in Slow Motion* the sermons typify the best of Knox in explaining his faith; also *The Creed in Slow Motion* and *The Gospel in Slow Motion* have the same devotional and instructional elements.

As a preacher Knox brought to the English scene a sanity and balanced interpretation of those elements of Catholicism often rejected by those outside his communion. He tried to bridge that gap. If he did, it brought understanding, but not always converts. Mind and imagination, wit and epigram served him well; and the Biblical nature of the discourses brought power for sermon themes. A conversational tone added to the quiet dignity of this preacher.

In **Cyril Charles Martindale (1879-1963)** and **Martin D'Arcy (1859-1938)** the Roman Church had two preachers whose message resounded throughout Great Britain, especially by sermon, publications, and broadcasting. Priests, professors, and Jesuits, they gained a hearing in their day and broke down the barrier of prejudice which had been a restriction against their church's acceptance. From the Farm Street Church and also Westminster Cathedral, London, the preaching was usually in sermon series which later became books. Martindale's *Christ the King* (1927); *The Kingdom and the World* (1928); and *What Think Ye of Christ?* (1931) are samples of the pastoral stress and spirit. The doctrines of the Roman church were expounded clearly and the apologetic stress was marked.

Preaching opened the door to testify on subjects about which the ministers were convinced. Personal faith, dedication to a vocation, and persuasive speech characterized the preachers. They were prodigious workers, unsparing of self, known for deep and abiding sympathy for their fellowmen in suffering and need. Spiritual welfare was the chief concern in such preaching.

Jewish

The freedom of a persecuted people came to fruition when Jewish leaders gave their gifts of mind and heart to the nation which was blessed by this new homeland for many. Whether as statesman, scientist, economic executive, or financial leader, the Jewish life paid tribute to the religious strength which gave it character. Among the teachers and preachers in synagogue and temple, no name has a higher place than that of Rabbi **Joseph Herman Hertz (1872-1946)** whose influence as the Chief Rabbi (1912-1937) gave him open doors of service for his people and also for the nation in a time of war and cataclysmic change. By radio, public addresses, lectures, sermons, and published works, Hertz gave evidence of a mind and spirit devoted to God. In whatever he did in the communication of faith by preaching-teaching, we trace the man of letters, Hebrew scholar, Bible believer convinced of the spirit and essence of faith in the one true and living God. He brought understanding and good will to all men, and among the Christian church was read for the spiritual essence of knowing the truth. His commentary and notes on the *Pentateuch & Haftorahs* (5 vols., 1929-36) will abide as a monument of scholarship to show the preacher the value of exegesis and exposition as the basis of the sermon to be preached. His sermons reveal the economy of style which is the careful task of the teacher who does not pass shoddy work.

As representative of Jewish preaching, Hertz will be remembered as a mind at once liberal in sweep as he thinks and lives in our modern world, but not finding it necessary to lose that reasoned faith of his fathers which bridges the gaps and enriches our Hebrew-Christian tradition of the Anglo-Saxon world. The depth and quality of his preaching has brought a communion for many in the Messiah. The Covenant of God for those chosen by God, election for service, man's freedom in truth, the absolutes of the moral law, and a vision of God's kingdom upon the earth—these themes are taught and proclaimed in the light of the symbol of the burning bush. Heritage is a sacred stewardship for destiny.

The Scholar as Preacher

The new century in Great Britain brought into prominence scholarly pastors who also became professors and teachers to share with others the findings of research and study. Special gifts of mind and knowledge gave them aptitudes of communication through lecture, articles, and books. Some continued as preachers without pastoral responsibility. Others were committed to teach in colleges, theological and academic schools and universities, and a few assumed editorial work for the wider proclamation of the Christian faith.

Representative names leap to mind in John Baillie, Donald Macpherson Baillie, William Manson, Daniel Lamont, Hugh Watt, William P. Paterson, George D. Henderson, David S. Cairns, Archibald M. Hunter, William M. Macgregor, J. G. Riddell, Ian Henderson, Edgar P. Dickie, and others mentioned in this book. The Presbyterian tradition in Scotland loomed large in this. Others like

David M. McIntyre and Francis Davidson brought Presbyterian and Original Secession Church teachers together as they shared scholarship and spiritual depth as Principals of The Bible Training Institute, Glasgow, on behalf of men and women training for missionary service.

In England, the Anglicans had Charles Gore, Walter Robert Matthews, Alexander C. Vidler, F. Donald Coggan, as well as many of the leaders of the Church of England mentioned elsewhere.

Ireland had Charles Frederick D'Arcy, Archbishop of Armagh, whose coordination of religion and science met a need. His idealism in philosophy colored his theological thought.

British scholars as preachers include Andrew M. Fairbairn, Thomas G. Selby, Nathaniel Micklem, Albert Peel (whose editorial work and historical research stimulated preaching), H. Cunliffe-Jones, Daniel T. Jenkins, and Thomas Hyll Hughes, who gave richly in preaching as Congregationalists. Methodists could point to Robert Newton Flew, who dealt with Christian perfection; L. Maldwyn Edwards, Wesleyana historical studies; and Norman H. Snaith, pointing to the wise use of the Old Testament for the preacher. The Baptist fellowship had Hugh Martin, editor and author, S. C. M. Press; H. Wheeler Robinson, interpreting the cross in the Hebrew background; Principal Underwood, studies in conversion.

To mention also James Moffatt, John Oman, Carnegie Simpson, C. Anderson Scott, and Alexander Fleming as Presbyterian teachers and preachers in England is to sample further veins of exploration. That the Quakers at Selly Oak, Birmingham, had J. Rendal Harris and then Herbert Wood, is to indicate that Christian groups were not in competition but their findings were the complement of all the others.

In selecting some for special mention, we must understand that these are solely representative names and do not exhaust other, less prejudiced, lists.

Of the men who stood gallantly in the center of the changing currents of theology and philosophy none was greater than **Peter Taylor Forsyth (1848-1921)**. A Scot, he became a Congregational minister and later gave his best years as Principal of New College, London. There he trained men for the ministry and by his sermons and writings brought stability and poise in a shifting age. At the time he was not always appreciated, but after sixty years he is now seen for what he was—a champion of the truth. His mind could roam over philosophy, science, and theology in days of ferment, but he refused to be pushed off the rock foundation upon which he stood in the belief that the Bible was still the revelation of God. At the heart of his expository preaching and writing he affirmed the centrality of the atonement. Standing by the cross he dared to affirm that nothing could change that eternal event of God's act in time.

Among his books is the trilogy, *The Cruciality of the Cross* (1909); *The Person and Place of Jesus Christ* (1909); and *The Work of Christ* (1910). Characteristically, these followed rapidly one after the other. The flow of his pen and the volcanic outburst of his thought are felt in these works. Some of these were lectures given extempore to groups of pastors and people in conferences, while others represent the substance of sermon effort. A popular method of conversational speech was used to bring theological convictions to the minds of others. To Forsyth doctrine was at the base of all belief and witness. Spiritual life to him was nothing unless it derived its strength from creedal affirmation of truth. Nothing undogmatic could live, according to Forsyth. He was concerned to stress that God's love was holy and therefore spiritual life must be holy.

Forsyth had discovered the melancholy Dane and Christian man, Kierkegaard, long before the moderns of a later era. The encounter and existential nature of truth by the individual intrigued him and led him to stress the value of theology engaging the mind at the point of commitment and personal experience. Forsyth was aware of the critical school then emerging in British theological discussion. He was not unfamiliar with the principles of study as applied to the Bible. However, he saw its possible excesses and dangers. He stood for a balanced, spiritual criticism and the right to criticize the criticism of his contemporaries. He stood at the center and that center was the cross in all its wonder and power. In the three volumes mentioned he spelled out his views.

The emphasis of his lectures and sermons lay in the centrality of the sacrifice of Christ for man's redemption. Here lay the principle of reconciliation as the work of God. Forsyth exulted in the victory of Christ over evil, the finality of his satisfaction or atonement presented to God, and the compelling power and influence of that work in the lives of people. In dealing with the person and work of Christ, he called attention to the preexistence of Christ, the *kenosis* or self-emptying; and the *pleroma* or the self-fulfillment of Christ. Hear him speak with conviction:

> The closeness of the Church's bond with Christ will always go hand in hand with its belief in His deity. And the more it realises his salvation the more it will know the roots of it to be in the great act of a Christ before the worlds. The whole faith of the Church has turned upon a conception of Christ which sees in him the act of God, and worships in him God's immediate revelation, God's personal guarantee of His holy saving love, and the eternal mediator of our communion with Him *(The Person and Place of Jesus Christ,* p. 323).

Or ponder this utterance:

> Christianity as a religion stands upon salvation. Religion which does not grow out of salvation is not Christian religion; it may be spiritual, poetic, mystic; but the essence of Christianity is not just to be spiritual; it is to answer God's manner of spirituality, which you find in Jesus Christ and in Him crucified. Reconciliation is salvation before it is religion. And it is religion before it is theology. All our salvation in this matter rests upon the certain experience of the fact of God's salvation. It is salvation upon divine principles. It is salvation by a holy God *(The Work of Christ,* p. 45).

Forsyth's Yale Lectures on Preaching, *Positive Preaching and the Modern Mind* (1907), have never gone out of date. There is a perennial freshness about his words and ideas which time has not eroded. While each age becomes "modern," there is a quality about Forsyth which defies age. He calls for a positive utterance from the pulpit, one that is backed by "authority" which is based upon Christ and is an inward spirit, and that is an objective message which demands ethical results because it is centered in the cross of Christ. The theologian-preacher proclaimed his theology in speech. He stressed that "with its preaching Christianity stands or falls. . . . Wherever the Bible has the primacy which is given it in Protestantism, there preaching is the most distinctive feature of worship. . . . Preaching is a feature of worship. It is the most distinctive institution in Christianity. It is quite different from oratory. The pulpit is another kind of place from the platform. The Christian preacher is not the successor of the Greek orator, but of the Hebrew prophet." "The note of the preacher is the Gospel of a Saviour. With preaching Christianity stands or falls because it is the declaration of a Gospel—it is the Gospel prolonging and declaring itself" (pp. 3-5).

Forsyth revealed his inner life when he testified that for the years he preached before becoming a professor he was interested in purely scientific criticism. This, however, did not satisfy him when he faced the practical demands of people. Thus he was led to the central truths of the gospel. "And so, whereas I first thought that what the churches needed was enlightened instruction and liberal theology, I came to be sure that what they needed was evangelization, in something more than the conventional sense of that word" (pp. 282, 283).

In paradox and antithesis of speech, the scholar-preacher pierced the armor of unbelief and disbelief. In a day of shifting standards and nebulous meanderings, his voice sounded as a trumpet blast to recall men to the eternal verities of faith in the gospel. His summing up is striking. "Preaching to the Church must recognize more fully the element of judgment, and preaching to the world the element of love. . . . There is nothing the Church needs more profoundly than an ethical conversion in regard to its great doctrines. . . . The more ethically we construe the Gospel the more are we driven upon the holiness of God. And the deeper we enter that sacred ground the more we are seized by the necessity of a real and objective atonement offered by a holy God by the equal and satisfying holiness of Christ under the conditions of sin and judgment" (pp. 372, 373). Ever after, Forsyth has been guide and mentor to many who have engaged in positive preaching with minds loving God.

One of the shattering denouements of New Testament scholarship came in the reaction against certain liberal assumptions when **Charles Harold Dodd (1884-1973)**, professor at Manchester, Oxford, and Cambridge Universities, published his epoch-making book *The Apostolic Preaching and its Development* (1944). The fruit of a lifetime study of the documents of Christianity, Dodd's work expounds the thesis that the historic records showed that preaching was *kerygma* as distinguished from *didache*. Tracing all the occasions in the New Testament in the light of its background, he came to the conclusion that *kerygma* was the key to apostolic preaching and the heart of the good news in Christ. Preaching then was proclamation, and teaching was a separate emphasis for those within the church.

Dodd may have overstated the case in the light of further study by others. Nevertheless, his book had a distinctive and profound bearing on preaching thereafter. Leaving behind the undogmatic "teaching" of morality and ethics which passed as a gospel sermon, he called preachers back to the essentials of the gospel. Here the facts of the death and resurrection of Jesus Christ constituted the *kerygma*. Proclamation was then in order for true preaching, which brought again the doctrines of the Christian faith to light. A revived interest in preaching and the sermon at the heart of worship resulted.

Another scholar who influenced preaching was **John Seldon Whale (1896-)** whose *Christian Doctrine* (1941) shaped the thinking of many in a richer odyssey of sermon content. A Congregationalist, Whale was President of Cheshunt College, Cambridge, then Headmaster of a private boy's school in London. Broadcasts, lectures, and occasional preaching enabled him to mold the minds of many in search of doctrinal stability. He was an able preacher and his books continue in the Forsyth tradition of lucid and exciting challenge.

In the same period was **John Wood Oman (1860-1939)**, a Presbyterian pastor at Alnwick, Northumberland, whose parish experience brought to fruition books of theology and philosophy. Then as Principal of Westminster College, Cambridge, he came to the height of his powers in teaching theological students. From his significant service came a smaller book not to be overlooked alongside of his massive philosophical thinking, *Concerning the Ministry* (1937). Its erudition, its prodding nature, its subtle style, and its acute observation, make this an enduring volume which has influenced the lives of preachers to be the kind of men whose message is enduring.

Other scholars who have held the attention of the preacher of that era include **Arthur Samuel Peake (1865-1929)**, Methodist layman; **William Thomas Manson (1893-1958)**, Presbyterian pastor; and since then **Fred Fyvie Bruce (1910-)**, Plymouth Brethren leader and teacher. These professors have held the Chair of Biblical Literature, History, and Language at Manchester University, England. From a more liberal theology through a mediating theology, there is now in F. F. Bruce a conservative and evangelical emphasis. Peake's *Commentary,* Manson's *Synoptic Studies,* and Bruce's many commentaries of the New Testament are lasting influences upon generations of preachers. These men in different religious traditions stood for scholarship of the highest order and through their spoken and written word stimulated the whole church of God.

James Stalker (1848-1927) was known for the singleness of purpose which dominated his ministry. Pastor in Kirkcaldy and Glasgow, Scotland, he took the Chair of Church History at Aberdeen College. He was thought of as a better preacher than teacher. However, his books over the years have brought much more to a wider audience than even the classroom. As an author he gave the church two Bible Class Handbooks which are outstanding and never out of date, *The Life of Jesus Christ,* and *The Life of St. Paul.* The Yale Lectures, *The Preacher and His Models,* are also noteworthy.

Stalker brought to preaching through his sermons and books the sense of proportion and balance. We discover that here is one secret of effective preaching—a man who has steeped himself in the English Bible and in William Shakespeare's works, read each year. From those wells of English came the pellucid style and the clear, running prose of this scholar-preacher.

His models whom he sought to emulate were Isaiah the prophet and Paul the apostle. To him, the Old and New Testaments are not separate entities, but one book in a unity which brings the divine revelation. The evangelical prophet Isaiah and the evangelical preacher Paul bring challenge and goals to the modern preacher. Man of God, Patriot, Man of the Word, False Prophet, Man, Christian, Apostle, and Thinker, are the categories in which Stalker saw the preacher.

In a simple rhyme he offers a method of sermon preparation and delivery: "Begin low; Proceed slow; Rise higher; Take fire; When most impressed be self-possessed; To spirit wed form; Sit down in a storm." Instruction, illustration, impression are the key words of sermon structure. In this order the preacher appeals to the public.

James Denney (1856-1917) has an abiding influence both as preacher and scholar. From pastorates where he gave his people the fruits of scholarly exegesis in Biblical exposition, he was called to be Professor of New Testament at Glasgow Trinity College of the Presbyterian Church. There, for the rest of his life, he lectured and wrote. No other name means more to the evangelical world of scholarship than his.

As a preacher he was the master of a telling phrase and was noted for his simplicity and clarity of utterance. After years of teaching he remained the preacher—in classroom and in many pulpits. He had a well-stored mind from wide reading, and with retentive memory was able to recall much so that he was known for his skill in delivering an impromptu speech with rich meaning. Denney lived in the day of the newer criticism of the Bible and studied and clarified what was in that for his own use. However, he remained orthodox at the center of the Christian faith and avowed his belief in the doctrines held by the church.

In his books we have the unfolding of his study and preaching. *Studies in Theology* probes the questions of that day with insight and skill. *Jesus and the Gospel* takes the heart of the Creed and interprets. Commentaries in *The Expositor's Bible* and in the *Expositor's Greek New Testament* reveal the rich mind and the devout spirit whose unfolding of Scripture is unmatched. To read him on Corinthians or Romans is to dwell deep. These studies were based on careful exegesis of the text and also indicate the basis of his rich preaching. *The Way Everlasting* and *The Christian Doctrine of Reconciliation* are samplings of sermonic work now printed for reading as studies. In *The Death of Christ* and *The Atonement and the Modern Mind* Denney stands at the cross and the infinite sacrifice of God for man's sin. *The Death of Christ* is a classic and has been reprinted again and again. Never out of date, it expounds the heart of the gospel with warmth and devotion.

George Adam Smith (1856-1942) had a varied ministry within the Presbyterian Church. One of the prominent pastors of his day, he also was Professor of Hebrew and Old Testament at Glasgow, archaeologist and geographer of the Bible, and Principal of Aberdeen University.

During his first pastorate he preached through books of the Bible and laid the foundation for his full commentaries on the Old Testament prophets, especially Isaiah (2 vols.), The Twelve Prophets (2 vols.) and Jeremiah. These were primarily based on the exegesis of the text and are models of expository preaching. It is true that he had been influenced by the German higher critics but in clinging to the faith of his fathers, Smith tried to hold both extremes without loss. He brought some of the newer views to the pulpit and the classroom but only as an interpreter of faith.

As a preacher he delivered sermons with insight and poetic force. The scholar with his technical skill did not intrude. He had a popular mode of speech to reach people. His erudition was concealed. One of the best things from Smith was *Historical Geography of the Holy Land* (1894) still in print. Here the land and the book are intertwined as he leads the Christian to see the background of Christianity. Texts of the Bible are quickly and easily illumined under his skilled guidance.

The Yale Lectures on Preaching, *Modern Criticism and Preaching of the Old Testament* (1901), were an attempt to clarify an evangelical liberal position in a time of theological ferment concerning the authority of Scripture. He had worked with D. L. Moody in evangelism and was known for his evangelical faith. Here he justifies the right of criticism as a literary task. Proceeding from that premise, he sought to unfold the basic ideas of progressive revelation as associated with the methods of God toward man. He believed that the Old Testament lay "not *under*, but *behind* the New"—a wise distinction. Preaching to him demanded the use of the Old Testament with the New Testament to know the full message of God in Christ.

Arthur John Gossip (1873-1954) will be remembered for the sheer verve of his preaching artistry. Pastor in Liverpool, England, then in Forfar and Aberdeen, Scotland, he became Professor of Christian Ethics and Practical Theology at Trinity Theological College, Glasgow. There, in the last period of his life, he shared with students his ways of preaching. Several volumes of sermons were published, including *The Galilean Accent, The Hero in Thy Soul,* and *From the Edge of the Crowd.* At once we see the mind of Gossip ever reaching out to the man beyond the church pew. His book on prayer, *In the Secret Place of the Most High,* is enriching.

Gossip preached without notes, using only an outline; he began quietly and slowly until he caught fire and then he was off! Then followed a torrent of rapid speech and cascading quotations and allusions in exposition of the text or theme. The sermon would be written out on the Monday after being preached. His Warrack Lectures, *In Christ's Stead* (1925), embodies his views about preaching. A fertile mind stored with what is read, a humble spirit, a keen awareness of man's plight today, and then the convincing note that the preacher is Christ's ambassador or he is nothing, and thus stands to plead with men—that is preaching.

When all else has been forgotten, the Christian world is not likely to forget the sermon he preached on the Sunday following his wife's death, "When Life Tumbles In, What Then?" Unforgotten and unforgettable is the tumult of soul in the preacher. The sense of a man's sorrow and heartache and the sharing with his people what he had taught them but which now had become his own experience made the sermon one of the world's great ones. In the flood of sorrow he had found the promises of God sure, and his feet found the bottom upon which to walk by faith. When tested and tried the preacher could stand and testify to the grace of God—that is the heart of great preaching!

Alfred Ernest Garvie (1861-1945) began as a pastor in the Congregational Church in Scotland but his chief work was done in England as the Principal of New College, London, and as a theologian whose books were widely read. He gave an excellent book as a legacy on preaching: *The Christian Preacher* (1920). In this book Garvie expounds his views concerning the art of preaching and gives a survey of history as a foundation for the preacher. Then he deals with the preparation and delivery of the sermon.

Garvie stood in his day for an enlightened liberal evangelicalism and the use of modern knowledge to assist the preacher. His own preaching was solid, theological, and philosophical. Nothing here of the popular preacher. Narration and description abound in his sermons and the sweep of thought, the profound knowledge, and an intellectual application served to overcome any lack of emotional stress. His chief influence lay with students who followed him into their own preaching vocations.

In literary style his sermons are well written and read with clarity. "Glorying in the Cross" (Gal. 6:14) is a sampling of this. Here Garvie develops this profound subject by (1) Historical Fact; (2) Theological Truth; (3) Individual Experience; so that no one is in any doubt about the theme as applied. "It is in the experience that the fact becomes truth; because for Paul, more than for any other Christian thinker, his personality was the channel of his theology; he could think as he did because he had become what he was. Since he had been crucified and been raised again with Christ experientially, he could interpret, as no other has done, the crucifixion and the resurrection doctrinally. It is in this way, and this way alone, that theology can be made vital; and that in preaching, truth may come through personally."

Herbert Henry Farmer (1892-) has an eminent place as a preacher, ranking with Niebuhr and Tillich in America and Temple and Mackintosh in Great Britain. The philosopher is thought of as a man of erudition and rarified thought above the ordinary, but in preaching Farmer is clear and plain. His Presbyterian background in

England fitted him as a mediator of truth. Among many honors he had the distinction of being the lecturer for the Yale Lectures, *God and Men* (1946); the Warrack Lectures, *The Servant of the Word* (1940); and the Gifford Lectures in Natural Theology at Glasgow (1950).

Farmer's preaching held to the Bible as the foundation of God's message. He saw himself as "the servant of the Word" and thus he was a theological preacher. He wrestled with the deep problems of life, setting forth the eternal solution by spelling out a clear Christology attuned to that day. He trafficked in words, and tried for concrete speech to arrest attention and demand a hearing. He endeavored to proclaim the Christian view of life in an age which was skeptical of dogma. Naturalism, positivism, and other views deluged thought with new ideas which robbed life of its divine origin and destiny.

The apologetic strain was ever present as the theologian-philosopher confronted people with the reasonableness of the Christian faith. He had spiritual discernment, and in preaching his epigrammatic speech awakened the lethargic mind. In the sermons published as *The Healing Cross,* there are samples of this style— "Suffering must be a vocation before it can be a victory." In *Things Not Seen* are these statements: "A dumb God spells a dead faith." "Without religion morals easily become mere manners." "The Cross was a parable in flesh and blood."

In style there is a concise manner and a briskness of pace, the preacher hurrying on to the climax and not wasting time in much summary or repetition. Here is the teacher-preacher making the most of the allotted time in worship. His cosmic sense seeks that the Christian message should bring healing to a troubled world, and in this it comes to persons.

In **Hugh Ross Mackintosh (1870-1936)** Scotland had for a long time one of the finest exponents of Christian theology and a rare preacher. He is remembered most as the Professor of Theology, New College, Edinburgh University, but he has a niche in the proclamation of truth through preaching. During his lifetime he was marked early for scholarship by that rare and intuitive facility of winning academic success in school and university, so that it was no surprise when he was called to grace a chair in theology and teach and train others for the ministry.

His ministries were as a pastor in Tayport, Fife, and Beechgrove,

Aberdeen, where his preaching was marked by a study and sharing of foundational truths. When relieved from pastoral responsibility, he still knew how to preach with distinction and devotion. His major works in theology are *Types of Modern Theology, The Christian Experience of Forgiveness,* and *The Doctrine of the Person of Jesus Christ.* These volumes unfold his theological insights and convictions. As an interpreter of the leading theological movements then in vogue, he had no peer. All he wrote and taught came from a richly stored mind and a facile pen. His was the art which concealed art. His lectures on homiletics and preaching were given alongside of deep and dogmatic theology. In this he imparted the wisdom of sharing with others what a man believes. This was the essence of his preaching. He preached his theology. Thus he came from study and classroom to the pulpit with a fully charged mind and a sermon which was easy to understand and grasp. He knew how to speak with simplicity and in truth.

In the developing of sermons Mackintosh on one occasion let it be known that he owed much to a little devotional book called *Daily Light.* In that daily devotional reading the page correlated texts of Scripture under a common heading and subject. Many a seed thought and sermon starter came from this for the theologian. Not that he dispensed with serious study in sermon preparation, but he did not despise the initial beginning of a subject or idea for his own development later.

Some of his sermons expressed the Christology of his major work on the person of Christ; and the book he said he most enjoyed writing, on the doctrine of forgiveness, also pervaded his preaching of the full-orbed truth of divine revelation. In the volume *Life on God's Plan* we trace profound thought and simple exposition. Bible readers will find that he kept close to Bible subjects. Sermon volumes include *The Highway of God* and *Sermons (with Memoir).*

The sermon "Life Hid with Christ" was given before Communion. In Scotland there is a tradition of holding a preparatory service during the week preceding the actual Sunday celebration. The text, "Ye are dead, and your life is hid with Christ in God" (Col. 3:3) reveals how Mackintosh dwelt deeply in a devout spiritual life. There is the touch of the mystic and the life of God in the soul of man. We note how easily he introduces the theme:

> Words like these, it is obvious, are not addressed indiscriminately to the world at large. They describe a class of people, and demand

an audience, which, if fit, is also few. Not that the text is in any sense obscure, although it belongs to an age far from our own. Not that it raises needless barriers. Only, it takes for granted that we have undergone a great peculiar experience, which has brought us into a new world. In short, as very few sayings even in the New Testament do, it touches the centre and focus of personal Christianity. It tells the open secret of discipleship.

Here Mackintosh stands in the pulpit aware of the special occasion and sensitive to the needs of his congregation. In quiet measured tones he speaks as in a conversation. His preaching here is not declamatory. He is not attempting to convert and convince the skeptic. His aim is simply to remind Christians of their heritage and to help them enter into their spiritual possessions. Thus the professor of theology converses with men and women who have come out of the work and toil of the week to see if God has some word for them. He does not disappoint as he unfolds the profound truth in simple and moving language. He stands as an interpreter.

Having spent time and care in preparation, Mackintosh wrote out his sermons with the listener in view. He was not unlike the well-known Alexander McLaren, of Manchester, England, who was renowned as an expositor of the Bible. In substance and form his preaching was influenced by McLaren. He tried to be the expositor and there was a practical note in his sermons. Shot through was the evangelistic note as he would plead for a verdict. The scholar and professor is not always thought of as an evangelist or even as a good preacher. Mackintosh was a joyful exception and did not live in the ivory tower of study without coming out to engage in the marketplace of human need. His own thought about this is given as he taught a weekly class on the preparation of sermons alongside of his regular classes in theology:

> Sometimes, you and I, as preachers, are led to ask ourselves whether what we are preaching is really the Gospel. Do our sermons bring home to our people the immensity of the difference between good advice—which the moralist too can give—and good news, which only the evangelist can bring? If the message we are laying before the people has nothing marvellous about it, then it may be philosophy, science, ethics, the wisdom of life, or what you will; but the Gospel of God it cannot be. If there is nothing in what we say to make a sinner catch his breath and feel his heart leap up with joy and peace in believing, then we have somehow lost our way. But if we are telling those who listen such things about God's mighty works in Christ that, in Wesley's famous phrase, they "feel

their heart strangely warmed" and see the glory of Redeemership round Christ's head, then we are in line with those whose message in the past has arrested conscience, and evoked faith, and changed lives. Men know, in their secret mind, that if there *is* a Gospel, it must be astonishing. This is a tragic world, and nothing but a tragic and amazing Gospel will cope with its bitter need.

The preaching of Mackintosh was the overflow of a well-stored mind which speculated about the deep things of God. He was more than a scholar: he was also a man of God. In that combination a dedicated will worked without ceasing to unveil the divine revelation and make it clear and plain to others. His theology was what he often declared—the test of theology is whether it will preach well. Thus theology to him prepared for the proclamation of the gospel. He never could get over the wonder of the majesty of God and the wonder of the gospel.

His sermons then were capsules of this distillation and principle. What he taught others he did himself. That attitude of his is well expressed in one of his characteristic utterances:

To part with the glory and wonder of this faith [he had been speaking of the preexistence of our Lord] is in a grave measure to part with the native joy of the Christian religion; and to remove the scene of sacrifice from heaven to earth will inevitably stimulate the less worthy impulse felt at some time by all to preach about man instead of God.

Any aspect of preaching which had departed from the sense of wonder was to him inadequate preaching. In one of his sermons, "Wonder and Religion," he recalls how the note of wonder is often struck in Scripture revealing "the astonished mind of the believer and giving a note of exhilaration to his voice." Wonder touches the whole of life, as Mackintosh illustrated, but its supreme worth lies in the personal relationship to God. Worship comes from wonder. This sermon is typical in structure and follows a simple line as he deals with the facts which awaken wonder: (1) The Holiness of God; (2) The Wonder of the Cross; and (3) The Wonder of Immortality.

To Mackintosh preaching dealt with the divine initiative above all else. We are asked not to believe like Jesus but to believe in Him. It is personal commitment to him in love and trust that is demanded of us. He also stressed the mystical union of the believer with his Lord. "God in Christ for us, we in Christ for God" was a typical saying. To him the most wonderful thing of all was that God has forgiven our sins through the atoning work of Christ. Thus his book *The Christian Experience of Forgiveness* which came out of preaching, and his preaching out of his brooding on that subject.

For estimating the value of the scholar as preacher, no better example could be found than Professor Mackintosh. He was committed to preaching as well as teaching. His point of view was obvious—the reason why the gospel should be studied by the scholar was that it might be more effectively proclaimed by the evangelist. His theological position was orthodox with a liberal mind of inquiry and scrutiny. Such a position is one that has maintained the character of Christianity as being a gospel, the announcement of good tidings about God. It is as a gospel that Christianity claims to be the religion for all mankind, and he was confident that it could sustain such a claim. In preaching he never ceased to advocate the claims of missions and the carrying out of the Great Commission. In addition to his sermons there is also a book on this theme, *The Originality of the Christian Message* (1920) which summarizes much of his thought at this point.

As a preacher Mackintosh was a convinced and committed Christian whose personal experience of God shone through all he proclaimed. He stood at the center of the Christian faith and advocated the finality of Christ and the gospel. He was a man persuaded in mind, and with loving heart he ministered the doctrines of the faith with persuasion and grace. Thus theology was translated into preaching the good news of God. His day was swept by the currents of change and liberal thought in theology, but he never shifted his position although he was familiar with all schools of thought. Schleiermacher, Hegel, Ritschl, Troeltsch, Kierkegaard, and Barth— names of different theological positions—were all known to Mackintosh. He could take the best of their insights and then in his own way relate the divine revelation in Christ for his own interpretation in teaching and in preaching.

Among the preachers of this era **James Stuart Stewart (1896-)** stands out. His expository preaching, wedded to practical needs, was heard with profound respect. He wielded a spiritual influence far beyond many. His pastorates in Scotland and his professorship at New College, Edinburgh (New Testament department) provided him with that rare opportunity to mold other preachers-to-be. His stream of influence continues, and through his writings there is an unending flow of dynamic inspiration.

To Stewart preaching was the vocation of the herald. Proclamation is the key word for preaching in the New Testament. Whatever else lies in the gospel, this is the heart of it in preaching. The trumpet sounded with no uncertain sound when this man stood to exalt Christ and the gospel. He was not one of those who denigrated preaching in a period when the cry was to downgrade preaching and magnify other trivial activity in the minister's life and work. The Yale Lectures on Preaching, entitled *A Faith to Proclaim* (1953), and the Warrack Lectures, entitled *Heralds of God* (1946), indicate his thinking about preaching. What is there is demonstrated in the pulpit utterances. The clarity of thought, the contemporary allusions, the classical quotations, the Biblical exposition, and the forthright utterance make his sermons alive and powerful. *The Gates of New Life* (1937), *The Strong Name* (1941), and *The Wind of the Spirit* (1969), are volumes of sermons now in print which distill the best of Stewart's thought and spirit. In them is the lilt of the gospel, the sense of urgency about salvation, and the dynamic glow of a spirit surcharged with divine unction.

Stewart's sermons and messages have that timeless quality about them. They are not merely limited to the time in which he ministered. They transcend the moment for the eternities. Apart from a few casual allusions to contemporary events, they have in them a quality which relates them to any time and age. Basic to these sermons is the student of the Bible, the scholar as preacher, the man of God who dwells deep in meditation. Having been a pastor for most of his life, Stewart knew people and the deep-seated demands of life.

Throughout his preaching is the thrust of the evangel and the evangelistic appeal for commitment and decision. Take this closing paragraph from the sermon "The Lord God Omnipotent Reigneth" based upon the text, "Alleluia: for the Lord God omnipotent reigneth" (Rev. 19:6). This is the quiet ending which was most effective in his sermons:

> This is the Lord God who has come again to the gate of your life and mine to-day. This is the Lord God who claims the right to reign, and from whose patient, haunting pursuit we can never in this world get free. Behold, He stands at the door, and knocks. While the sands of time are running out, and the hurrying days

mould our destiny, He stands at the door and knocks. Tenderer than the kiss of a little child, mightier than the flashing lightnings of Heaven, He stands at the door and knocks. What will your answer be? "You, out there at the door, you who have been haunting and troubling me all these years—begone, and leave me in peace!" Is that it? Or is it not rather this? "Blessed and glorious Lord Almighty, dear loving Christ of God—come! Come now. My life is yours. See, here is the throne. Oh, Christ, take your power— and reign!"

Stewart is the strong evangelical in the historic and best sense. Everything in his preaching is related to the living Christ. Notice in these excerpts the weaving in, as many strands of gold, of references out of a background of reading and culture—Browning's "gate of new life"; Thompson's "haunting pursuit"; Hunt's "He stands at the door and knocks"; Rutherford's "the sands of time"; the gospel hymn "What will your answer be?"; and the New Testament affirmation "Whose right it is to reign."

Such preaching reveals a rich culture and a well-stored mind. Out of a background of education and garnered knowledge, ripe with the wisdom of the years, and inspired by the Holy Spirit, he has in his sermons a richness and fullness not found anywhere else. Stewart in his day was the outstanding preacher of Scotland and followed in the succession of Alexander Whyte and other notable men.

In the evangelical succession there is always the awareness of the eternal Christ who is risen from the dead. In another book, *A Man in Christ* (1935), Stewart has interpreted the thought and theology of the apostle Paul. While written as lectures and as theological conviction, the work still gives the sense of a man preaching and evangelizing. Imaginative reason is aflame with the burning zeal of the evangelist. The passionate pleader with men is heard. These lectures are not for the museum but for the study and the pulpit.

In the history of preaching no one has a better right to be discussed and heard than James Stewart. His name will live on for others to catch the spirit of a dedicated man of God. His voice was never silent; it was tempered by the compassion and concern of a gallant Christian mind suffused with the love of Christ.

John T. Forbes (1857-1936) was not a normal type of Scottish Baptist preacher, moving from the earlier pietistic and revivalistic stress to a more cultured and intellectual view. His chief distinction

lay in his scholarly preaching which culminated in the pastorate at
Hillhead Church, Glasgow. At the same time he became the Principal of the Baptist Theological College, Glasgow. If seemingly austere, he brought stimulus and challenge to questing minds and his
preaching bore the mark of solid work. He liked to stretch the
minds of his congregation and students.

William Robertson Nicoll (1851-1923), a young and promising
preacher, had his pastorate terminated through illness. At Kelso,
Scotland, he laid the foundation of a wider ministry, using sermon
and essay as well as book and Bible. As editor of *The British
Weekly*, he was the preacher to preachers. He also discovered men
and women who could write. Thus began a ministry through editing
theological works and the correlation of writers. In *The Expositor's
Greek Testament, The Expositor's Bible, The Expositor*, and a host
of other works, Nicoll used his preaching and teaching talent to the
full.

During this period of the 1900s and since, the conventional
homily and sermon has been dynamically permeated by the thought
of **Charles Gore (1853-1932)** whose reconstruction of belief, in his
wrestling with tradition and criticism, evoked a development of.
Liberal Catholicism. Thereafter came William Temple, stressing the
incarnation as the key to theology and preaching. Scripture, tradition, and reason were the watchwords of an established church
seeking to be a "bridge" among other right and left emphases.
However, a new approach was imminent in the teaching and preaching of **Edwyn Clement Hoskyns (1884-1937)**.

As Hoskyns wrestled with the new ideas coming from Barth and
his *Commentary on Romans* (1933) and the reaction against a
liberalism which tended to obscure the heart of the gospel, he
reaffirmed that Jesus and not Paul was the founder of the Christian
faith. In his book *The Riddle of the New Testament* (1931),
embodying his struggle for certitude of belief, and then later his
monumental theological commentary on *The Fourth Gospel*
(1940), Hoskyns spelled out his convictions that here was history
and behind the Greek language and age there was also the Hebrew
tradition and ideas.

At first the teacher himself preached to students in a Cambridge
chapel, and in *Cambridge Sermons* (1940) he presents his view that
soundings should be taken and interpretations offered so that
preaching is geared to life. A generation of ministers were given

guidance on what to preach. "The Church has a language: it possesses words and phrases—and in sermons are, World, Neighbor, Now-Then, Here-There, Tribulation-Comfort, Flesh-Blood, Spirit, Weak-Strong." As Hoskyns taught, "The Church does not require of us that we should master a new vocabulary, but that we should apprehend the meaning of the commonest words in our language; it demands that we should not, at the critical moment, turn away from the meaning of words, but that we should wrestle with them and refuse to let them go." The era of Kittell's *Theological Dictionary of the New Testament* (8 vols.), has spurred word study and influenced much exegesis and sermon making.

Pietistic

In pietistic preaching there is the strength of strong conviction and resolute faith. Critics of the piety of other ages have tended to dismiss such as weak, effeminate, impractical, and out of touch with earthly things. Such an attitude is devoid of up-to-date knowledge of what a pietist is. He is no hypocrite, no counterfeit Christian, no pharisaical person. He is the man of God linked with the saints of all the ages who comes in modern guise and homespun clothes. Such a man was **Oswald Chambers (1874-1913)**.

This extraordinary man has been hailed as an evangelical prophet, a master of the spiritual life, a Christian aesthetician, a disciplined teacher, and a missionary to men. His books and writings are voluminous, yet they were not the plan of an author but the result of his preaching-teaching ministry as he gathered the fruits of his study and notes. Born in Scotland, he had an exceptional ministry not from any one church pulpit, but from service during the First World War to men who served their country in battle, especially in Egypt. This brief life, short and full, exercised a profound influence on tens of thousands in all parts of the world—and still does through the continued issuance of his writings.

People in all schools of thought paid tribute to the ministry of Chambers. An Anglican Franciscan in Egypt told of finding Chamber's book, *My Utmost for His Highest,* and meditating on it constantly to the end of his days. Others of Episcopal and varied denominational attachments testify how Chamber's words brought to mind the authors of the great classics of the soul's quest like Lancelot Andrewes, John Bunyan, Von Hugel, Blaise Pascal, Henry

Martyn, and Robert Murray McCheyne. These all have a reputation of "saintliness" or "piety" which breathes the atmosphere of the Holy Place in the inner shrine of devotion.

To be bracketed with the so-called "great" of the past is no mean distinction. Not that Chambers would have believed this. However, following his demise this has been the estimate made of him and his message. The rare qualities of his mind, the clarity of his thought and the forceful expression of his words left an abiding impact on those who heard him. His words came from a heart aflame with faith and out of a mind which had been polished and furbished from years of preparation. As a student at Edinburgh University he imbibed the riches of the Arts Course which gave him familiarity with literature, psychology, philosophy, and classical archaeology. The poets especially attracted him and his ease of expression owed much to the wealth of illustration which leaped from that well of inspiration.

The spiritual experience of "new birth" and inward renewal which came to Oswald Chambers was a foundation for ministry and mission. The fiery baptism of the divine affluence never left him but abode to the end. He was also to be "baptized into the condition of all men." He knew the human heart and was skilled in moral and spiritual diagnosis of sin. He was led to found a Bible Training College in London to offer to men a disciplined life of study and development of the spiritual life. From this came a stream of men ready to engage in missionary work of all kinds. He, himself, later went to Egypt to serve the soldiers then in that center of warfare. Through the YMCA he gave servant-service of all kinds to the men and gradually enlisted their interest in Bible study, worship, and other avenues of service to their fellowmen.

Chambers owed much to other theological teachers and believed that he was a better preacher and teacher because he had sat at the feet of some of the "great" through their books. He preached that Christians should fill their minds with the thoughts and ideas of the best writers and ask God to set their minds on fire! He believed that Christians, especially the preacher, should be thinkers. His own example was that of acting as a Christian and thinking as a Christian, so he advocated wide reading as a basis of thought and action. Although a man of one book and that the Bible, Chambers was not narrow but broad and catholic in taste in his reading.

His preaching and teaching reflected his beliefs and theological convictions. In dealing with the atonement he could speak on the text John 17:4, "I have finished the work which thou gavest me to do" in part as follows:

> The Death of Jesus Christ is the performance in history of the very Mind of God. There is no room for looking on Jesus Christ as a martyr; His death was not something that happened to Him which might have been prevented: His death was the very reason why He came. . . . Never build your preaching of forgiveness on the fact that God is our Father and He will forgive us because He loves us. It is untrue to Jesus Christ's revelation of God; it makes the Cross unnecessary, and the Redemption "much ado about nothing." If God does forgive sin, it is because of the Death of Christ. God could forgive men in no other way than by the death of His Son, and Jesus is exalted to be the Savior because of His death. We see Jesus . . . because of the suffering of death, crowned with glory and honor. The greatest note of triumph that ever sounded in the ears of a startled universe was that sounded on the Cross of Christ—"It is finished." That is the last word in the Redemption of man.

In dealing with the subject of "The Key to the Master's Orders" based on the text, "Pray ye therefore the Lord of the harvest, that he will send forth laborers into his harvest" (Matt. 9:38), he says:

> The key to the missionary problem is in the hand of God, and that key is prayer not work, that is, not work as the word is popularly understood today because that may mean the evasion of concentration on God. The key to the missionary problem is not the key of common sense, nor the medical key, nor the key of civilization or education or even evangelization. The key is prayer. Naturally, prayer is not practical, it is absurd; we have to realize that prayer is stupid from the ordinary common-sense point of view. . . . There are no nations in Jesus Christ's outlook, but *the world*. How many of us pray without respect of persons, and respect to only one Person, Jesus Christ? He owns the harvest that is produced by distress and conviction of sin, and this is the harvest we have to pray that laborers may be thrust out to reap. . . .

On the theme of "Sanctification" which colored all his sermons and teaching, he said:

> There is *the Death Side*—"This is the will of God, even your sanctification" (I Thess. 4:3). In this God has to deal with us on the death side as well as on the life side. The Spirit of God will strip me until I am nothing but "myself." That is the place of death. To be ready for death—that is the condition of sanctification. Then there is *the Life Side*—"Of him are ye in Christ Jesus, who of God is made unto us . . . sanctification" (I Cor. 1:30). The mystery of sanctification is that the perfections of Jesus Christ are imparted to me, not gradually, but instantly when by faith I enter into the

realization that Jesus Christ is made unto me sanctification. This does not mean anything less than the holiness of Jesus being made mine manifestly. The one secret of a holy life lies not in imitating Jesus, but in letting the perfections of Jesus manifest themselves in my mortal flesh. It is "Christ in you." Am I willing for God to make sanctification as real in me as it is in His word? It means the impartation of the holy qualities of Jesus Christ. It is His patience, His love, His holiness, His purity, His godliness, that is manifested. Sanctification is an impartation, not an imitation. Imitation is on a different line. In Jesus Christ is the perfection of everything, and the mystery of sanctification is that all the perfections of Jesus are at my disposal, and slowly and surely I begin to live a life of ineffable order and sanity and holiness: "Kept by the power of God."

Chambers knew the function of alliteration and his outlined messages are full of this quality. There was no idea of forcing this, but his keen mind saw the value of this as a device to implant the outline in others' minds. By means of repeated words and ideas his teaching was compelling, and those who knew him testified to this trait in his presentation of truth. Titles and outlines had to be clear and plain. His mastery of the sacred page was evident. His imagination was charged with clarity of appeal. On the subject of "Prayer" he used the following outline: (1) Prayer the Work—John 14:12-14; (2) Prayer the Fruit—John 15:16; (3) Prayer the Battle—Eph. 6:11-20. Utilizing words and repetition, he says: "Am I stubborn or substituted? Petted or perfect in my relationship to God? Sulky or spiritual?" "Discernment is God's call to intercession, never to fault-finding."

His preaching was noted for its stab and thrust. The mind was quickened and the will challenged. No one could hear him without feeling the stern demand of surrender to the will of God. Conscience was probed as Chambers was not content to deal with the surface life of man but its depths. Quietly and with irenic didacticism, he plumbed the depths of the inner life.

Keswick

By Keswick is meant the stress and emphasis made in preaching by those who have been the leaders and expositors at the Keswick Convention. This began in 1875 and was the outcome of the heart-searching of several Anglican clergymen for a deeper experience of God and power to overcome sin and temptation. In this they were in line with others around the English-speaking world who sought for a perfection in keeping with Biblical holiness or sanctification of life.

For almost seventy years an annual convention has been held for a week in July in tents at the town of Keswick which nestles in the beauty of the Lake District of Northwest England. There amid the lakes and mountains, famous also for the outstanding English poets of the romantic and Victorian era who lived there, thousands of Christian people have gathered to hear the messages of men of God who not only preached but who "witnessed" to the experience of the Holy Spirit in their lives.

Spontaneity was never allowed to degenerate into diffusiveness. The convention had a specific purpose, and kept to this. Without deliberate premeditation, a progression of teaching began to emerge beginning with the exceeding sinfulness of sin, especially sin in the believer; moving to the consequent defeat and powerlessness in life and witness; and finally reaching God's provision for the rehabilitation of the sinner in Christ—sanctification, consecration, and the Spirit-filled life. This sequence of teaching has never been followed in any mechanical way. It is just the underlying pattern, Spirit-given, and developed year by year in the liberty of the Spirit.

A sampling of the preaching indicates how men of every denomination have contributed to the richness of the total ministry of Keswick. Hundreds of young people have dedicated their lives for missionary service throughout the world. A depth of Christian living has penetrated the church life of Great Britain. The message of Keswick has not been that of "sinless perfection" but rather that the Christian being tempted and tested will be enabled to overcome and live a victorious life in the presence and power of the indwelling Spirit of God. Samplings of the teaching and preaching reveal that the Bible was accepted without reservation as the divine Word. In this the Old Testament was used as well as the New Testament to throw light upon the principles and practices of holy living. Typology and analogy were used without stint to show how in the Old Testament God spoke to the believer then, and also spoke in these "latter days" to the believer by the same word. Following are examples of Keswick preaching.

I. *Sin in the Believer*

In order to promote Scriptural holiness preaching began by the diagnosis of the ills of the Christian life. Because "the heart is deceitful above all things and desperately wicked," sin must be dealt with in the believer. H. W. Webb-Peploe (1837-1916, Anglican); Arthur T. Pierson (1837-1911, Presbyterian, USA); Bishop Handley C. G. Moule (1841-1920, of Durham); F. B. Meyer (1847-1929, Baptist); Charles Inwood (1851-1928, Irish Methodist); and Archbishop Harrington C. Lees (an Australian)—from such a group we have emphases in sermons like these:

> I wish to put before you what I believe to be the mind of God on the subject of sin, in order that we may realize as believers in Christ what a marvelous blessedness it is for us to have the propitiation that God has given us in his own dear Son; for there seem to be many who do not quite understand what the Lord Jesus Christ has intended to do, or what it is that they really need Him for. . . . A friend said to me, "I thought you preached absolute deliverance from the principle of sin, eradication of the root of sin." I said, "God forbid." "Then," she said, "what is the difference?" My answer was, "You preach a perfect sinner; I preach a perfect Savior." I thank God for a perfect Christ (Webb-Peploe).

> We have designedly left to the last the sin, folly, and crime of unbelief, partly because this great sin lies at the basis of every other; partly because it is the one sin that damns the soul; and partly because its removal means the relief of all other forms of spiritual difficulty. . . . Turn to Hebrews 3—4. This review is a parable of that desert journey treated in Psalm 78. Never study that story in Exodus, Leviticus, Numbers, and Deuteronomy, without putting over alongside of it this remarkable passage in Hebrews. God has given us here an inspired explanation, interpretation, and application of the whole story of the Israelites in the desert . . . (A.T. Pierson).

> Go thy way; first be reconciled to thy brother, and then come— Matthew 5:24. GO . . . THEN COME. I am almost certain that there are hundreds of people in this tent tonight who are children of God by faith, who want to come to the act of consecration, but there is something previous. He says, "Go . . . then come." It seems to me as if at this moment the Lord is going to send us back to our homes, that in some letter we shall write, or some word we shall speak, there shall be the first necessary preparation for the work of consecration which shall follow presently (F. B. Meyer).

> One is more and more impressed with the fact that our fathers in the work of this Convention were guided by the Holy Spirit when, from year to year, Tuesday was given up to heart-searching in the presence of God; and, guided by that same Spirit, I trust, I want, as He may speak through me, to search and possibly wound, hearts

that need it this morning. The theme of this morning's study will be "The Unveiling of the Carnal," and I want to turn your thoughts to the first *Epistle to the Corinthians.* In this Epistle we have a solemn unveiling that the carnal is the deadliest foe of the spiritual. Satan and the world assail us from outside, but the carnal is the traitor within. Now, what do we mean by this. By the carnal I mean the human, as divorced from the divine; just as by the spiritual I mean the human, possessed, indwelt, controlled, and transfigured by the divine (C. Inwood).

II. *God's Remedy for Sin*

Grace abounding to the chief of sinners—Bunyan's well-known phrase might well be adopted as the motto of the second phase of Keswick teaching. Christians need this as well as sinners according to such men as Evan H. Hopkins (1837-1918, Anglican); Pastor Otto Stockmayer (German-Swiss); George H. C. Macgregor (1864-1900, Scottish Presbyterian); Alexander Smellie (1857-1923, Reformed Presbyterian); and Bishop John Taylor Smith (1860-1938, Chaplain General). From them we glean these extracts.

> There are very many who find great difficulty in the seventh chapter of Romans, not because that chapter does not echo their own inner experience, but because they find it impossible to reconcile that experience with a life of victory over sin. A key, therefore, is needed to explain that difficulty. . . . Too often this chapter has been used by those who are leading an inconsistent life, and expecting defeat. . . . Some have looked at this as describing the experience of an unconverted man. . . . The passage is descriptive of the Christian man (Evan Hopkins).

Hopkins was the outstanding exponent of Keswick teaching for forty years. He speaks of "Threefold Deliverance"—(1) Deliverance from sin as a defilement, (2) Deliverance from sin as a habit, and (3) Deliverance from sin as a tendency, sin as a law. Three texts of the New Testament are woven together to stress these truths.

"God can—God will!" is a message from Mark 5:21-29, the healing of the woman with the issue of blood. This is used to illustrate how Christ works in a miracle to teach a parabolic truth. The life of disease, of disappointment, of shame, and of loss prepares for the woman's definiteness of purpose and the conscious cure, complete, and confessed by her (George Macgregor).

"The God of Bethel" and "Go to Bethel, and dwell there" tell how the sinful saint can enter into an overcoming life by the grace of God. Here C. G. Moore and F. B. Meyer witness. In "The Blessed

Life" the Chaplain General of the British Forces, Bishop Taylor Smith, opens up the depths and wonders of such a life as a practical issue for the Christian. Alexander Smellie in literary beauty and winsome speech appeals in "A Summons to Newness of Life" based upon the prophet's invitation—"Come and let us return unto the Lord; for he hath torn, and he will heal us; he hath smitten, and he will bind us up" (Hos. 6:1). The Scottish preacher-writer spoke of evangelical repentance and God's grace in the gracious manner characteristic of his life and ministry.

III. *Consecration*

The next step appeals to thought and will for reflection and decisive response. Here is the heart of the preaching of Keswick. The teaching of holiness centers in the Lordship of Christ. Dedication and consecration are allied. Pastor Theodore Monod (French Reformed); Andrew Murray (1828-1917, South Africa Reformed); W. H. Griffith-Thomas (1861-1924, Anglican); J. Stuart Holden (1874-1934, Anglican); and W. Graham Scroggie (1877-1958, Scottish Baptist) among others, spell out the message here.

"With the whole heart"—(Jer. 32:41) is used as text and theme to press home the claims of Christ to all that is the Christian's. God wishes not a part of human life, but the whole. Monod's French thought is turned into English speech with many an unusual turn of phrase. "Being, then, accepted of Him, boldly claim and take all that belongs to Him, and call it yours. Just as a young bride, who has left her father's humble home for her husband's stately mansion, has to learn that all that belongs to him, now belongs also to her. She has but to call it all her own, and use it as such. Let us simply do the same. Make yourself at home with God. In Christ all that He has is yours" (Theo. Monod).

"The Pathway to the Higher Life" is shown as the way of consecration, and this implies nearness to Jesus, likeness to Jesus, and power for Jesus. Only once did Andrew Murray speak at Keswick, yet his influence was phenomenal. Later, by the publication of his message through many books, he not only was claimed by South Africa as their leading preacher, but the universal Church is indebted to him, then and up to this day.

Keswick's message did not come in casual dress. There have been scholars whose mind and spirit brought blessing to thousands gathered. One has been the Principal of Wycliffe Hall, Oxford, and later

Principal of Wycliffe College, Toronto, Canada. In Griffith-Thomas was combined the skill of an expert homiletician and exeᵧ̮ete with the theologian's knowledge and the humility of the devout heart. In "Knowing and Showing" and in "Abiding and Abounding" he brought the congregation face to face with the enlargement of the Christian life when the will is devoted to Christ. "Who art Thou, Lord?" and "What wilt Thou, Lord?" (Acts 22:14) bring the heart of the Keswick message. "It was in the life-long willingness of Paul to know and to do what Jesus would reveal to him that he found the secret of peace and power, of sanctification and service." The divine purpose, the divine plan, and the divine project are then skillfully outlined and expounded.

The crisis and the process of the way of holiness are related to identification with Christ in His death and resurrection. Union and communion are related here. The transfigured life follows. In Stuart Holden, leader of Keswick for almost thirty years, a notable ministry was exercised. A man of engaging personality and persuasive manner, and Vicar of St. Paul's Church, Portman Square, London, he was known on both sides of the Atlantic for his convention ministries. Skilled as a diagnostician of the spiritual life, he had discernment between spurious and genuine faith.

In "The Faith Christ Seeks," based on "Jesus did not commit himself unto them, because he knew all men, and needed not that any should testify of man; for he knew what was in man" (John 2:23-25), Holden sees (1) the discrimination which our Lord exercised; (2) the disqualification which He found in these professed believers; and (3) the distinction by which He ever seeks to seal and assure our relationships with Him. "The test which I propose to myself and to you tonight is just this one—Have I an unsleeping zeal for His glory? Have I in my life a dominating passion for holiness? Have I an increasing impulse to soul-saving service? If not, is it because Jesus has never committed Himself to me? If He has not committed Himself to me, is it because my faith is of the wrong order? Oh, search your hearts! And may there be effected at the very commencement of these convention days that reciprocal committal which shall mean to you the life more abundant in all its unspoken and unspeakable implicates, for His name's sake."

To W. Graham Scroggie belongs the distinction of having delivered the Bible Readings at Keswick more frequently than any other man in the Convention's history. Unlike others whose fervor and emotion carried them away in appeal, his teaching and preaching was quiet, logical, and forceful. Tall and slim, with a didactic manner and Scots' dry humor, this eminent preacher excelled in the exposition of "the Word." Sometimes the born preacher in him took command, however, and he spoke with compelling fervor—as he did on a memorable occasion at the close of a convention, using the text of II Samuel 3:17, 18, "And Abner had communication with the elders of Israel, saying, Ye sought for David in times past to be king over you. Now, then, do it." "Now, then, do it!" is the subject and with passionate spirit and word came this appeal:

> After the exposition comes the action. All such gatherings as these must be productive, if they are to be of any use at all. We must come to what is practical, intensely practical, and personal. There are some blessings that are collective; there are some that are intensely individual. . . . Whatever is done, must be done intelligently. . . . We must think clearly if we are to act soundly. There were saints in the Church at Corinth that thought the less they had of intelligence, the more they were likely to have of the Spirit; and they have a large posterity. But that is a fallacy. I am not asked to close down my intelligence in order to exercise faith. Faith is not credulity; faith is not ignorance: faith is intelligent; faith is open-eyed; faith has a reason as well as an emotion, and that man is in grave peril who is resting on emotion rather than upon intelligent understanding. What we do must be done intelligently. . . . We must distinguish between the work of Christ *for* us and the work of Christ *in* us; between cleansing and holiness; our standing and our state; union and communion. Now, then, do it—make Christ King—do it intelligently. Do it deliberately.

IV. *The Spirit-filled Life*

The climax came with the aspiration of earnest Christians seeking this deeper experience of the grace of God. Whatever terminology is used concerning further tokens of God's presence and power in life beyond the initial committal of faith, the witness of thousands is that here God takes control of our daily lives. The fulness of the Holy Spirit is variously interpreted, but primarily it is for witness and for the harvest of the fruit of the Spirit (Gal. 5). Men of all denominations and from diverse backgrounds testified to this as they ministered in the persons of A. T. Pierson (American Presbyterian); William Young Fullerton (1857-1932, Irish Baptist); Amzi Clarence Dixon (1854-1925, American Baptist); and Joseph Rus-

sell Howden (1872-1959 Anglican). During the Welsh Revival
(1905) a wave of emotionalism was always a danger for church life.
The Convention speakers were sensitive to this and characteristically A. T. Pierson, more than any other, was a stabilizing influence.

Speaking on "The Inbreathed Spirit" Pierson conveyed spiritual
power with emotion, yet without emotionalism. "Receive ye the
Holy Spirit" said Christ (John 20). Pierson pointed out that the
Greek word is not "breathed on them," but "breathed *into* them."
The clarity of this teacher was apparent as he developed the theme.
As this was the first message to the assembled disciples after the
Resurrection, nothing according to him was more wonderful in the
New Testament than this message, when taken in all the surround-
ings of its utterance. Here was the risen Christ, who speaks three
things to the apostles: first, "peace be unto you"; second, "As my
Father hath sent me, even so send I you"; third, "receive ye the
Holy Spirit." The first is a message of peace, the last is a message of
power, and the middle one is a commission. "Peace founded upon
the blood of the cross, a testimony founded upon the salvation that
comes by the blood, and power for the testimony to be given. It
might be said that, beyond this, in the New Testament, there is not
a new idea: it is all here. And everything that this means may come
to you in this tent tonight."

In "Christian Life and Christian Living" W. Y. Fullerton gave a
Bible Reading based upon Romans 5–8, using one chapter at a
time. The intent was not expository, but to show the Christian
experience behind the doctrine of these chapters. Thereby he
sought also to prove that the distinctive Keswick message was
basically Pauline. With Irish wit and telling story Fullerton brought
out the heart of the fifth chapter. In Chapter 5 is the doctrine of
justification, while sanctification does not begin until Chapter 6.
"Always remember," he said, "that behind every experience; that
behind every great word of the New Testament there lies an
experience. These words are not a mere philosophical term: they
are chosen by the apostle, under the guidance of the Spirit, to
express something that he, in the deepest recesses of his nature, had
experienced." Thus he outlined the life of God's grace—a life of
faith, a life which demonstrates the living of a new way.

In "Glorying in the Cross" A. C. Dixon emphasized the unique
place of the death of Christ, not only for man's redemption, but

also for the Christian's life and power. There was sacrificial love, sacrificial light, sacrificial truth, sacrificial power, sacrificial holiness, sacrificial mercy, and sacrificial life and beauty. Around this outline and analysis was woven the tapestry of apt allusion in life and in literature and the Biblical exposition of "God forbid that I should glory, save in the cross of our Lord Jesus Christ" (Gal. 6:14). The magnetism of the cross is the central affirmation of faith by which Christians find strength to live godly lives.

The question of "How is this life to be realised?" was discussed by J. Russell Howden. "Remember that all life begins as a gift. Natural life is a gift. You do not make yourself live; you live because you had to; you had no option in the matter. And in similar fashion your Christian life, the new life that is in Christ, is a gift. . . . Then if you have been born again, remember that is only the beginning, not the ending. After birth comes growth, and growth is just as much a gift as birth. You cannot make yourself grow. . . . Growth depends upon factors you cannot command, and cannot even fully understand. And so in spiritual things. Growth also is a gift of God."

Howden discussed the laws for growth from that one sentence, "Be filled with the Spirit" (Eph. 5:18).

> Notice that the verb is *passive*—"be filled." It is nothing you have to do; it is rather something you have to let God do. Then the verb is *imperative*—"be filled with the Spirit." It is a command. We have no option in the matter. Then the verb is also in the *present tense*. This implies a definite beginning, and leads to a course of action, of experience and of happening. You are to be filled with the Spirit this morning. Here is the Gospel to announce, the Good News for the Christian as well as the unsaved, the Good News for the saint as for the sinner. . . . And it is God who gives you His Spirit, and He will fill you now. And it is God who Himself will enable you to fulfil the conditions upon which alone He can fill your life with the Holy Spirit.

In those words Howden stood as a representative preacher of Keswick. Life and life abounding was stressed at this Convention for the deepening of the spiritual life. Sainthood and holiness were taken seriously in modern dress. The pious were urged to be practical, the godly to be gracious, the separated to be sent. As W. Graham Scroggie summed it up in talking about the distinctive message of this movement: "Conference has a subject, but a convention has an object." As applied to Keswick, that is not a mere epigram, but a great truth. The object is the life more abundant.

Welsh

No study of British preaching would be complete without the inclusion of the most imaginative sermons from the Principality of Wales. From that small land which historically and economically has been allied to the rest of Great Britain, a steady stream of preachers has come forth to enrich and bless the world. Preaching, like poetry and song, is in the blood. For a century and more the people of Wales have thrilled to the bard and the master musician and choirs, but the eloquence of the pulpit has held a nation enthralled in mind and has moved and motivated in conscience as nothing else.

During the nineteenth and twentieth centuries the contribution to preaching is most marked. Christmas Evans (1766-1838); John Elias (1774-1841); William Williams (1717-1791, Wern); Edward Matthews (1813-1892, Ewenni); John Jones (1796-1857, Talsarn); Robert Roberts (1762-1802, Clynnog); Evan Herber Evans (1836-1896); Elvet Lewis; John Daniel Jones (referred to elsewhere as "J. D." Jones, Congregationalist); and the revivalist Evan Roberts (1878-1950). By heritage these men were nurtured within the home and the church to accept and translate a faith based upon a Bible at once true and acceptable for life. The waves of revival which swept the valleys and towns of Wales reminded the people that God's revelation was something unchanging from Biblical times. Like Israel of old the nation of Wales knew the mighty hand of God in chastisement, judgment, renewal, healing, and revival. It was in this setting that much of the moving preaching was felt.

During the period when more critical views of the Bible were being circulated, Herber Evans preached against the new tendency to find fault with the Bible on the ground that its history was poor, its influence failing, its theology full of holes and its meaning in places very doubtful.

To illustrate his story Herber Evans described an old preacher who had come a long way to address his congregation, and who had to return home that night along a dark road beset with dangers and difficult to follow. As he was leaving, a woman in the congregation put a small lantern into his hands with the words: "It is only a little lantern, Mr. Evans, and it is full of holes and very old; but it will light you home, Mr. Evans, it will light you home." And lifting up the great Bible from the pulpit, the preacher held it aloft, and cried: "Thy word is a lantern unto my feet, and a light unto my paths."

The art of illustration and story-telling is characteristic of the Welsh preacher and many are the stories told concerning their use in moving a congregation. David Lloyd George, Prime Minister of Great Britain, loved to tell of the sermon of "The Lost Sheep" as preached by Edward Matthews (Ewenni). The speaker, as he told the familiar parable over again, held his congregation, mostly farmers and their families, spellbound, as he took them over hill and dale, across torrents and through thickets in the search for the missing animal.

"Is she there?" he called. "No, she is not there." "But she must have come this way: here is wool from her coat on the brambles" (holding up an imaginary strand). And again, "Is she there?" The search continues, till the congregation itself seems to be joining in it, and its excitement rises. At last, with a great cry, and with the movement of hoisting the animal onto his shoulders, "She is found," he shouts. "Glory be to God," shouts the congregation with him.

Another was the sermon on "The Feast of Belshazzar and The Writing on the Wall," preached by John Elias. This was more than a sermon, it was a studied performance, and the stage had to be set for it. John Elias, visiting the chapel before the service, directed that the candles should be so arranged that his outstretched hand while preaching, should cast a shadow on the whitewashed wall of the chapel. "Place that one there, and this one here—no, a little farther back." The arrangements were completed with the greatest care, and then the preacher embarked upon his famous sermon "The Writing on the Wall," in relation to the sins of the present generation. Imagine the terror of the people when, at the psychological moment, the awful message was actually written on the wall. And no matter how often the sermon was repeated, and it was repeated often, and by request, John Elias was able to produce the same effect upon his audience.

It was the same dramatic gift that enabled another preacher to describe the crucifixion with such power and vividness that the congregation implored him to cease, that they might not have to witness the last agonizing scene.

These men had the power of bringing the Bible to life for their congregations, by reproducing Biblical events almost as it were in modern dress, and recounting imaginary conversations between the characters to illustrate the theme in question. Christmas Evans, for instance, whose message was always the infinite mercy of Jesus, took for his text Christ's command: "Go ye into all the world, and preach the gospel to every creature." He described the disciples questioning Jesus. "In *Jerusalem,* Lord?" "Yes." "But, Lord, it was there that Thou wast crucified! Surely we are not to preach *there.*" "Yes, you must preach to all." "To the man who plaited the crown of thorns and placed it on Thy head?" "Yes, and tell him he can obtain a crown of glory out of that shame." "What if we come across the man who nailed Thy sacred hands and feet to the Cross? And the man who stabbed Thy side? . . . and he who spat on Thy face?" "Preach the gospel to all of them; tell them there is a welcome for all to partake of the blessings of my salvation; that I am the Lord, and generous to all who seek me."

Thus in these and similar ways did the Welsh preachers hold their congregations spellbound, playing upon their emotions and their imagination. The quality and vibration of voice, the eloquence, no eye flashing more passionately, no gesture more dramatic or com-pelling—these thrilled congregations more than some actors on the stage of a theater.

In style, the preacher often did not start off with a flourish. It was more like a ship getting out of harbor. The sermon had difficulty in getting away—there would be an occasional bump—one could hear the chain creaking; but soon it came sailing out easily and smoothly on the fairway. Then a speeding up and a slight heaving roll and the listener knew he was being carried along into the open sea, the breeze filling the sails as the ship drove through the hurricane.

Sometimes it was reported that the preacher would make a false start, occasionally more than one! Then the congregation might begin to weary, and then, suddenly, the sermon would "break," and they were lifted along in ecstasy by a master hand. The uncle of David Lloyd George, Richard Lloyd, would sometimes preach in this fashion (so it was reported), ending on an inspired note and with his congregation transported with joy and ecstasy. The preachers held the listeners without any modern resources at their disposal, but with a spiritual message.

The sermons were carefully prepared in every detail—intonation, gesture, even to the timing of the "breaking" of the performance, when the congregation would sometimes lose its control. The preacher then could mold them in his hands. When John Elias, for instance, hurled his message at the congregation in the form of an imaginary arrow, those in the line of the arrow moved aside in order not to interrupt it!

The Welsh preachers of that generation were more than preachers; they were poets, dramatists, prophets, and accomplished orators. They were remarkable not only for their spiritual intensity but also for their intellectual power. They aroused and awakened the intellectual interest of the people. They informed their people as well as inspired them. The sermon was the way of educating the masses of the people. Thus for a period of 150 years they succeeded in enriching Welsh life. Many men of public life have studied them and acknowledged a debt to that impassioned oratory and imagination. The testimony of Britain's Prime Minister, David Lloyd George, is striking: "One of the things," he said, "that I should like to enjoy when I enter Paradise is a Preaching Festival, with John Elias, Christmas Evans, William of Wern and others occupying the pulpit. That is how these Fathers of Nonconformity appeal to me."

Of all the Welsh preachers the name of **Evan Roberts (1878-1950)** was prominent during the first decade of the twentieth century. The church of God universally knew his name and thought much upon his work during the Welsh Revival. His name became synonymous with revival. He was in the tradition of the prophets. Coming out of obscurity, he did a work for God for a short season and then returned to obscurity. He was a man molded by God and then broken by God for a task so unusual that no explanation of this is to be found except that the divine Spirit selected him and used him, and no human equipment can explain the influence and power of this preacher.

His ministry was short by the judgment of time, but its abiding influence is still spoken of by those who were caught in its spell. He lacked everything supposed to be required for a successful religious leader. He left school before he was twelve years of age; his intellectual gifts were limited; he came of common stock and labored as a miner and blacksmith before starting his spiritual work.

He was not noted as a great preacher. His theology he felt rather than learned, and his doctrines were few and simple. Though he was not a fluent speaker, there was about his utterances the unmistakable sound of inspiration. When he spoke he told of things he had experienced.

Any explanation of his life and power must accept the fact that he was anointed by the Holy Spirit. "I have to say strange things," he said, "I have to open my mouth and speak out. And, thank Heaven, those things are very effectual. The Spirit convicts powerfully." He believed in and spoke of the baptism of the Holy Spirit. "It is one thing for a man to be converted," he said, "and quite another for him to receive the baptism of the Spirit." Whatever the discussion pro and con about this doctrine which finds differences of interpretation among church people, the fact remains that here was a man who evidently lived by the power of the Spirit.

His preaching was simple and followed a marked pattern of appeal: (1) confess to God every sin in your past life; (2) put away anything doubtful out of your life; (3) surrender yourself completely to the obedience of the Spirit; (4) confess Christ publicly. For Christians he had one word: open your heart wide to the incoming of the Spirit; ask God to fill you with the Holy Spirit and believe he does it. After that it is just a matter of obedience. And all this worked powerfully among people of every age and class wherever the flaming preacher-evangelist went.

During the movement of revival which swept Wales in 1904-1905, Evan Roberts was God's instrument and his preaching was used to awaken a generation. The purifying effects were seen in the moral purity of people, the filled churches for worship, and the influence of Welsh Christians everywhere. His prayers alone were at floodtide, and multitudes were found in the valley of decision. There is no explanation for this preacher arising when he did—only that God girded him for a special task, for a short time, and then left him in obscurity thereafter. Nevertheless, those who heard him preach knew that an Elijah and the fire of God had visited Wales.

Most of the outstanding preachers in Wales were men of nonconformist persuasion. However, in this period **Charles J. Vaughan (1816-1897)** stood out as a notable example of Anglican preaching at its best. Within the liturgical service of Episcopacy there was room for his Christian witness through the sermon. As the Bishop of Llandaff Cathedral, Glamorganshire, he came to the zenith of his influence through the pulpit. His sermons were typical of the Welsh in their felicity of language, descriptive power, and forceful application. Men of letters waited upon his ministry when they might not have gone to hear others of more limited endowment. The quality of the preaching lay not in its literary style but rather in the spiritual fervor which brought instruction and hope to those who waited on his ministry. Fortunately, the sermons and many other studies were published. This was not so with many of the best-known Welsh preachers whose work is recalled by oral tradition and not writing. Vaughan can still be read and studied. His *Commentary on The Epistle to the Hebrews* (1890) is a distillation not only of exegetical study but also of expository preaching, and the two volumes on the *Book of the Revelation* are among the finest interpretations extant.

Of the more modern preachers the name of **Howell Elvet Lewis (1860-1953)** is prominent. In his later years he suffered the loss of his sight, but this did not deter him from preaching magnificent sermons. His gifts were manifold in that he was also hymn writer and poet (winning the bardic crown at the National Eisteddfod) and archdruid of Wales. His prolific output of some two hundred hymns and many books of sermons and biography testify to the richness of his mind and spirit. How was such a man prepared for preaching? Perhaps the secret lay not in the college or seminary studies but in the environment of his early years. The Welsh people are patriotic; they love their native land with its hills and valleys. Freedom is in the blood. Most of all they are a people given to song and sermon. Each village or town has had its choirs, its singers, its preachers, and its congregations of people who found satisfaction in sharing and in listening to their own selected youth in competition and in service. The atmosphere as such was charged with an emotion of joy and an inspiration to share in the overall delight of being one in that community of people dedicated to the end of making melody and listening for the voice of God.

In that background we find the secret of Elvet Lewis and the preparation he was privileged to have. Lewis competed at many a gathering and over the years was helped to polish his voice and sharpen his mind for the ministry. He learned that there was a fire in the Welsh tongue not found in the English. The Celtic tradition brought something to those who claimed to be called of God in preaching. The voice of Lewis was melodious and clear. Diction was concise and pointed. The pleading and wooing note was ever present. The preacher wrote prose but preached as if it were poetry. The cadences of the words and syllables brought music to the listeners. The young man of that day who desired to preach was given ample opportunity. Weekdays as well as Sundays were occasions for people to gather to hear the preacher. When the quiet conversational tones ended, then the animated feeling mounted to reach the climax of the *hwyl*. The preacher had gone up the scale of varied tones and come to the pinnacle of a shout or a note of music which would then descend to the other varied notes of the voice range. Such emotion came naturally and the language incited it.

Presbyterian

The Scottish pulpit was graced by many men of ability and dedication during this period. Their names are household words to those who came under their spell. They lived for the pulpit and of many a man it was said that "the pulpit was his throne." Of these men the name of **Alexander Whyte (1836-1921)** towers high in an unforgettable ministry among his own people in his native land. His biography is one to be read and studied by the theological student. Written by G. F. Barbour, *The Life of Alexander Whyte* (1923), it is one of the most entrancing biographies to be read by men in the ministry or those who aspire to the work of the ministry. Voluminous and scholarly, this book has in it the spirit of its subject. Reflected upon the pages is the light of a personality whose chief merit lay in his industry and toil. Out of that background of dedication Whyte emerged as the preacher above all others in his generation.

Alexander Whyte was known as a shy man with a certain aloofness and tenderness of heart. His outward appearance and rugged strength brought a stern aspect to his life and work. His background and intimate life were, no doubt, the cause of that stern front. His mother did not marry his father, and this was a shadow across his life. His inner circle of friends knew him in the warmth of his affection; but when he was preaching, there was always this overtone of the dreadful nature of sin. The preparation for pastoral ministry came largely through years of disciplined study and reading. Next to the Bible came the Puritans and the Covenanters. Thomas Goodwin was his favorite, and he told how his Goodwin "fell out of his boards, and I bound him in morocco." John Bunyan, Jonathan Edwards, Fraser of Brea, and Thomas Shepard were others who fed the inner resources of faith and devotion.

Something new was introduced by Whyte when he created the modern Scottish type of Bible class, which replaced the old Catechism class. In this he lectured on Bunyan characters, Bible characters, appreciations of outstanding men and women who lived for God. Poets, philosophers, writers, saints—any choice personality whose utterances held a message for the Christian—were laid under tribute. Whyte's literary taste led him to toil prodigously, and his love of word study gave him a catholicity of expression, whether in prayer or in preaching.

The foremost quality in his preaching was his Puritan spirit. He was a Puritan risen from the dead as far as Scotland was concerned. There was this sense of the greatness of the pulpit for he was a man of passionate speech and testimony. Truth through his personality did not come as stale or cold truth. To him the Word of God glowed and was alive when the Spirit of God moved upon him. The characters he spoke of were not alone from the Bible or Bunyan; they also walked the streets of Edinburgh! His sense of sin was overwhelming. The depths of the heart in its intricacies made him probe and prod the conscience when he himself felt the searing flame of judgment.

In one of his sermons he told of a man who had sinned and who was now the victim of remorse. God set his hellhounds on him, and the listener could see the man shivering under his blankets as he hears the baying while he tries to sleep in his bed at night, and on and on until the ghastly chase ends in death. Then it was that Whyte shouted, "You may be saved, but they will follow you up to the very gates of heaven, and leave their marks on the golden bars." Thus he scourged the good people of his day, not with smooth words but with the bite and sting of a man in travail.

The sermon to Whyte was the means of reaching people with the divine message. He wrote out his sermons in full, and evidence is not wanting that he did this many times before a sermon was ready. He was convinced that ministers generally could accomplish far more than they did because their aim was not high enough. His ministry was notable for its intensity of conviction and feeling which became contagious because of his character and faith. The theme of his preaching is best explained in something he said. He had received a message when walking in the Highlands that urged him to go on in the evangelical strain:

> What seemed to me to be a divine voice spoke with all-commanding power in my conscience, and said to me as clear as clear could be, "No, Go on, and flinch not! Go back and finish the work that has been given you to do. Speak out and fear not. Make them, at any cost, to see themselves in God's holy law as in a glass. Do you that, for no one else will do it. No one else will so risk his life and his reputation as to do it. And you have not much of either left to risk. Go home and spend what is left of your life in your appointed task of showing My people their sin and their need of My Salvation." I shall never forget the exact spot where that clear command came to me, and where I got fresh authority and fresh encouragement to finish this part of my work. I know quite well that some of you think me little short of a monomaniac about sin. But I am not the first that has been so thought of and so spoken about. I am in good company, and I am content to be in it. Yes, you are quite right in that. For I most profoundly feel that I have been separated first to the personal experience of sin and then to the experimental preaching of sin above and beyond all my contemporaries in the pulpit of our day. And I think I know why that is so.

That intense sense of sin never left him, but grew stronger and stronger. These words of Whyte's give the clue to his preaching. His emphasis was on "the personal experience of sin and the experimental preaching of sin." In the sermon "The Blood of God" (Acts 20:28) his sense of sin was so overwhelming that he saw the "unspeakable evil sin must be! We would not have been altogether ignorant of the awful evil of sin, even if it had not gone the length of the blood of God. . . . But all the sickbeds, and all the deathbeds, and all the battlefields, and all the broken hearts, from the fall of man to the day of judgment, would not have proclaimed the unspeakable malice and wickedness of sin. God's own blood, shed by sin, and shed for sin—that alone, in all the universe, is the full measure of the infinite evil of sin. 'Whatever your thoughts about sin may be; whatever your experience and estimate of sin may be, *that* is my experience and estimate of sin,' says Almighty God, pointing us to Gethsemane and Calvary." There are four points to the sermon—(1) The unspeakable evil of sin; (2) The seal to the holiness of God's law; (3) The sinner's guilty conscience is silenced; and (4) The blood of God brings reconciliation and love.

Any analysis of the sermon senses the imaginative way of the preacher whose own life is part of the background of the message.

The love of God seen in atonement and daring figure of speech reminding of the infinite, eternal sacrifice are used effectively. His conclusion and appeal are typical: "My brethren, I can recommend this great Scripture to every guilty conscience and corrupt heart. For, times and occasions without number, when every other Scripture has threatened to fail myself, this Scripture has been a rock and a refuge to me. The very awfulness of the word used has again and again silenced the almost as awful accusation of my conscience and the almost as awful despair of my heart. I know all that has been said against the above reading in this glorious passage; but once read by me I shall never let it go, though I have to hold it against all the world. The *Blood of God* has an inward, and an experimental, and an all-satisfying evidence to me, and I recommend it to you with all my heart."

If Whyte was unsurpassed in the experimental note in preaching, he was also a master of the inner life of devotion. The sermons in *Lord, Teach Us to Pray* illustrate the depth of his piety, for here he sees prayer as conversation with God and in all relationships of life. One sermon entitled "Imagination in Prayer" (and who else would have such a title?) shows how much Whyte read and lived with other masters of the interior life. He refers to some of his favorites—Butler, Pascal, Edwards—and these have fed his mind and imagination. He, himself, was not lacking in that quality and spirit. His insights into divine truth and his uncanny unravelling of Scripture are still the profoundest writing in preaching. If, occasionally, Whyte seems to wander off from the main subject when he quotes from these men, it is only to show what imagination meant to them, and then to stress in contrast his own powerful view of Christian imagination as it pertained to the sermon in hand.

"If, then, you would pray to perfection, that is to say, to pray with all that is within you, never fail, never neglect, to do this. Never once shut your bodily eyes and bow your knees to begin to pray, without, at the same moment, opening the eyes of your imagination. . . . Open the eyes of your inner man. . . . Imagination, as God in his goodness gave it at first to man—imagination is nothing less than the noblest intellectual attribute of the human mind. And his imagination is far more to every spiritually minded man than a merely intellectual attribute of his mind."

This sermon does not stand out for its outline or points, as it surges onward from start to finish in one sweeping torrent of words and ideas. It moves thematically to the climax and on the way gathers in references to Old and New Testaments where prayer is mentioned. The penetrating power of this sermon is sensed when Whyte asks his hearers to put themselves in the place of these Bible characters and most of all Jesus himself. Then, he cries, you will indeed know what imagination in prayer is like, for then you will experience the agony of the cross and the cry of dereliction. "Did you ever imagine yourself to be crucified? Paul did. And the imagination made him the matchless apostle of the Cross that he was. And then imagine yourself Christ risen, and in glory. . . ."

To those who heard Whyte preach, the word was always the same. These have testified that in him the spirit of the Covenanters had been reborn and for others the last of the Puritans was speaking to his generation. The sermon volumes include also *The Nature of Angels, With Mercy and With Judgment.* In addition, there are the *Appreciations* of certain spiritual giants, with the well-known expositions of *Bible Characters* and also the *Bunyan Characters.* After many studies he wrote *The Apostle Paul,* which tells of the evangelical mystic in Whyte's unforgettable way.

In a sermon on "David and His Vices" is this word: "Preaching is magnificent work if only we could get preachers like Nathan, if our preachers had only something like Nathan's skill, serpentlike wisdom and evangelical instancy. But even Nathan would be helpless with some of you. . . . We ministers must far more study Nathan's method. Nathan's sword was within an inch of the king's conscience before David knew that Nathan had a sword. One sudden thrust, and the king was at Nathan's feet." Among the greatest sermons preached, according to W. Robertson Nicoll, was that of "The Ransom" (Matt. 20:28). At the Communion Service that day Whyte was so moved and carried away out of himself in utterance and imagination that the congregation was caught up in the mood and spirit of solemn majesty into the presence of God.

The last sermon Whyte preached in Free St. George's, Edinburgh, was memorable. In "The Swelling of the Jordan" (Jer. 12:5) is the personal note as Whyte speaks of his own struggles and yet finds God's strength sufficient. Nearing the end of his own pilgrimage, he sees Jesus in the Gethsemane agony, hears the prayer on the cross, watches others who have suffered and endured, such as Stephen,

Paul, Augustine, Luther and Butler—the latter two favorites of Whyte. Near the end is the quotation of a hymn, "Just as I am . . . ," which occurs many times in Whyte's preaching. The use of a well-known poem or hymn was a common ending to seal the message.

Whyte's secret as a preacher lay in his hard work and consecrated fidelity. The words *conscience* and *character* were often in his speech. He knew the gospel of God's grace and applied it with ethical and moral power. He had a catholicity of mind and breadth of intellectual affinity. He drew from the Puritans, Goodwin, and Bunyan; from the Roman Church in Newman and Teresa; from the Anglican Church in Law and Butler. He walked with the truly great and was at home with the penitent and prodigal hearts of men who had sinned.

His preaching was characterized by a sanctified imagination and he was a scathing prophet against sin in his generation. The dark line in God's face came afresh in him, but it was illumined by the soft glow of an inner radiance of holy love and tenderness for the sinner. He was a master of experimental preaching. In one of his *Bunyan Character* studies he said:

> Peter examined Dante in heaven on faith, James examined him on hope, and John took him through his catechism on love, and the seer came out of the tent with a laurel crown on his brow. I do not know who the examiner on sin will be, but, speaking for myself on the matter, I would rather take my degree in that subject than in all the other subjects set for a sinner's examination on earth or in heaven.

That was Alexander Whyte—an interpreter of the intricacies of the heart.

Whyte's style was intimate and personal as he leaned over the pulpit, Bible in hand; and his reading was impressive. Some of his impromptu asides were effective as he lifted his head and in sudden emotion would speak dramatically and arrestingly. The sermons are glowingly direct and penetrating, at white heat. An omnivorous reader and note taker, Whyte never ceased to urge his congregation to "discover and select some great author or authors in divinity" to be read and lived with. He, himself, stands in that apostolic succession.

Alexander Whyte of Free St. George's Church, Edinburgh, had colleagues of stature in preaching. **Hugh Black (1868-1953)** and

John Kelman (1864-1929) exercised diversity of gift. Hugh Black, brother to James Black, was more liberal in theology than Whyte and marked the changing period then emerging. At Union Seminary, New York, he shared with the new world the discipline and culture of a Professor of Practical Theology in teaching the art of preaching and conducting public worship. John Kelman had a rich store of mind, and unusual literary gifts and powers of expression. He was able to be Biblical in foundation while utilizing the works of Robert Louis Stevenson and John Bunyan in catching the ear of a new generation. After a few years at Fifth Avenue Presbyterian Church, New York, he returned to the last phase of ministry at St. Andrew's Presbyterian Church, Hampstead, London.

George Herbert Morrison (1866-1928) was known familiarly as "Morrison of Wellington." After the formative years at Thurso and Dundee, he came to the zenith of his ministry at Wellington United Free (Presbyterian) Church, Glasgow, where for twenty-six years he poured out his life in gracious preaching and teaching.

Morrison spent the mornings in the study, the afternoons in pastoral visitation, and a lifetime in writing. He did not serve on committees, preferring to give himself to what he deemed was his chief responsibility in the church. To read any of his sermon volumes is to be aware of a style, quiet and gentle, never turgid but always flowing freely. Here was "the beaten oil of the sanctuary," the toil of a man who lived for his vocation.

When Morrison was preparing himself at the University and in theology, he took time off to spend two years as an assistant on the staff of the Oxford New English Dictionary then in preparation. This must have assisted him in the selection of words, their allusions and meanings. He had a sense of a word's fitness in his mastery of the English language. All his writings reveal the limpid prose of a masterhand and a spirit rich and strong in thought. From Scripture he drew the insights for sermons of power which were then expressed with sincerity and simplicity. The human touch was never absent as Morrison knew his congregation and was touched by a feeling of their struggles and needs.

When Moderator of the General Assembly of his church, he spoke on "Revival" and drew from history and his own life the desire to see this again in his own time. His evangelical spirit was so molded by this. His counsel to young preachers was: "I can think of nothing, except that young preachers will do well to guard against the tendency to rush, which is the bane of modern life. The habit of unprofitable bustle and rush, the present-day preoccupation with small affairs and engagements, is withholding many good things from us. For myself it is essential that I have leisure to brood and meditate." That was the secret for him.

John White (1867-1951) has a special niche in Presbyterian memories as the architect of the reunion of the United Free Church with the then Church of Scotland by acting as the Moderator of that Union Assembly (1929). Pastor of South Leith Church and then for forty years at the Barony, Glasgow, he labored in church administration and pastoral oversight. Throughout the strenuous years of working toward the goal of a united Presbyterianism, he was ever the preacher.

His preaching was fresh and virile as he probed the conscience by his sermons. From his first pastorate to the climax of his life's work, he took seriously this part of his vocation. He was embroiled in patronage, abolition, government, endowment, law, acts, covenants, buildings—these words denoting the manifold areas of legal procedures to be revised and authorized for a new day in the midst of the church's spiritual ministries. Amid the demands of his leadership nationally, White did not neglect the proclamation of the Word of God. Kindness, zeal, hard work, initiative are words to describe his active life.

A sermon during Holy Week tells the story of that week which ended in the resurrection. Simply, vividly, imaginatively, he recasts the events, dwelling chiefly on "Is it nothing to you, all ye that pass by? behold, and see if there be any sorrow like unto my sorrow, which is done unto me" (Lam. 1:12). This is his key to know and understand that week of weeks for the Savior. His words of application find relation to everyday life as he includes the people listening as part of that first small group who witnessed the sufferings, death, and the resurrection. In style there is a swift and pleasing transition from history to experience. "With one quick cry of joy, Mary sprang towards Jesus. 'Rabboni,' she exclaimed, and in that one passionate cry she uttered all her heart, all her love, and all her wonder; her whole soul was revealed in the word. . . . Death is dead. Christ is risen and is alive for evermore. He is living in our midst, making all things new and alive." Here is White's spirit in preaching as he calls for response and committal. Other sermons reveal the church statesman dealing with national issues.

John Alexander Hutton (1868-1947) was marked by a deep intensity of feeling and a prodigality of expression in speech. Presbyterian pastor in Newcastle-on-Tyne, then Glasgow, followed by a ministry at Westminster Chapel, London, he was also famed for his editorship of *The British Weekly,* for many years the leading nonconformist religious journal. Founded by William Robertson Nicoll, this weekly exercised a profound influence on the religious, theological, social, and even the political life of the nation.

Hutton was a short, stocky figure, "Friar Tuckish" in appearance, with a robust expression and vitality. To have heard him when he delivered the sermon in connection with the annual service for the British Association of Science was an unforgettable experience. He had lost one of his sons in the War shortly before that. Following the reading of Psalm 90, he engaged in its exposition. His identification of the soul with God in the travail of suffering and loss, of death and eternity, came out of his own heart-rending crisis. The whole Psalm was the text; his own inner sorrow was the context; and the exposition was like a volcano in eruption, with the molten lava pouring out.

Steeped in Robert Browning and Russian literature, Hutton paid tribute to these in his preaching. He learned from them the secrets of soul surgery, the spiritual analysis necessary for acute and deep preaching. Sin and grace were never far away. His eloquence came out of having written much, brooded constantly, and being moved in spirit when he preached. Forgetting the manuscript he would pour out his heart in vivid, exciting utterance. Sentence after sentence would cascade down upon his congregation who listened with awe and respect.

Hutton was not given to short sentences. His writings used the long, intertwined sentence. His editorials and articles in *The British Weekly* and his thirty books reveal the quality of his mind and heart. Later in life he delved more and more into Pauline material and wrote *The Weapons of our Warfare* and *Finally, with Paul to the End.* He did not give the Yale Lectures on Preaching, but he was honored by being the first in Scotland to give the Warrack Lectures. His theme was *That the Ministry Be Not Blamed.* Here the New Testament text and ideal was expounded and related to his own life and work in sharing with others. This was not a straightforward exposition of the orderly processes usually presented by lecturers. His inimitable way lay in the *obiter dicta,* the asides, the many facets of truth pertaining to the ministry. He scintillated and his lectures were provocative and displayed the kind of preacher he was.

Archibald Campbell Craig (1888-) made his contribution in a time when technology and science came to their zenith in the midst of two World Wars. He was a pastor, chaplain to Glasgow University students, soldier in France, Lecturer in Biblical Studies in the University, and Moderator of the Church of Scotland. His acceptance of God's call to the ministry was not of a profession but of a vocation.

His preaching has in it an intensity of thought. Preaching of such compelling depth and power as his comes only from the mind and heart of one who has made his way through hard intellectual striving to the conviction that here, in the Word which he proclaims, is the redemptive truth which illumines all the mystery of human life. Compassionate by reason of searching experiences in war and human tragedy, he knows where he stands as a preacher with gay and buoyant spirit. His Warrack Lectures, *Preaching in a Scientific Age* (1952), indicate the bent of his mind. This approach to preaching will remain a classic of its kind in which science is seen not to be omniscient and in which man's intelligence is seen to be a limited instrument in the presence of the eternal and a world which is a storehouse of wonders. From science and miracle in the resurrection of Christ, he proclaims the last things with the assurance that time and eternity must be at the heart of the gospel.

James MacDougall Black (1879-1949) was one of three brothers who became Presbyterian ministers. Hugh, his elder brother, was the associate to Alexander Whyte before leaving for America and a professorship at Union Seminary, New York. Singularly, James, after fourteen years at Broughton Place Church, Edinburgh, went to Free St. George's where Whyte had been and maintained a strong ministry until he retired. America tried to secure him but he preferred to stay in Edinburgh.

Black's ability as a preacher lay in the endowment of a vivid imagination, a well-modulated voice, and a skilled use of religious psychology in relating Biblical truth to modern man. His sermons followed the conventional Church Year, but he would also branch out in dealing with themes found in his book titles, *The Foes of the Faith,* and *An Apology for Rogues,* and other more startling themes. In the former he treats the cults and new forms of religion in the light of the orthodox faith. In the latter he depicts Bible characters, such as Pilate, Judas, Cain, Esau, and others who had been blackened in judgment, but who in Black's estimate had some good points and qualities worth noting. This shows the skill of an analyst in spiritual detail as well as in psychological thrust.

Among his lectures were those given as the Sprunt series, Richmond, Virginia, and the well-known Warrack Lectures. These were a combination of the same subject and were published as *The Mystery of Preaching*. Here are choice unfoldings of the man and his ministry, the preparation and delivery of the sermon, and the standards and ideals necessary to accomplish the best work. Black pioneered his own way of speaking and sharing his own ideas but always in the light of a Biblical background. Imaginative and incisive, these lectures abide among the best ever given. The *mystery* was sensed in why God would call a man to stand and proclaim the eternal message; why week by week people would listen to the preacher; and amazingly so, why God should continue to use this means to extend the Kingdom of God.

Hubert Louis Simpson (1880-1953) was overshadowed by the worldwide influence of his predecessor G. Campbell Morgan; but after filling Scottish pastorates, he filled the pastorate of Westminster Congregational Chapel, London, with incisive preaching and appeal to the untheologically minded outsider.

Simpson was nurtured in the grand Scottish tradition of serious worship and exacting sermon preparation. In London his ministry expanded slowly and was cut short by a serious illness and retirement. However, the samplings of his sermons and the series he gave indicate the skills and insight of a cultured and spiritual preacher.

The sermon, "The Burning Question"—"What Think Ye of Christ" (Matt. 22:42), is an example of Simpson's method. He was no professional evangelist, but as pastor-preacher he spoke directly to affluent, well educated, socially acceptable people. In a day when there was a reaction against certain types of evangelists, Simpson was not deterred from the evangelistic sermon. "The best way to redeem the idea of evangelism, and to save his own way-soiled and routine-hardened soul, is for the preacher as part of his regular business to do the work of an evangelist, and thus, in making full proof of his ministry, to find and reveal ever-changing lights and fresh sheen in 'the many-colored grace of God.' "

The sermon indicates the well-read, cultured apostle of grace.

The structure is strong, with four divisions ably developed and aptly illustrated. The question is "the burning question." Other questions do not burn long. Some produce only sparks or clouds of smoke; some heat, but give little light. His outline was: (1) Jesus taught men to think for themselves; (2) We are awed by the question; (3) A day is coming when we shall not hear this question asked; (4) This question judges you. His conclusion was: "There is, after all, a burning question, and this is only one: What will Christ, the Judge of all, think of *me*?"

Simpson's literary work was superb with the finest prose. Among volumes of sermons was *Put Forth by the Moon*. In his works he stressed that the messages were for "the untheologically minded." The doctrines and the theological truths were reminted into the thought forms and idiom of his generation as he tried to reinterpret the orthodox dogmas into the speech of the people.

Scotland has from time to time known its own evangelists, born and nurtured in the midst of Presbyterianism. **John McNeill (1854-1933)** was reckoned as one of the best of many preachers of that period. He had a sense of poetry and drama, of nimble wit and humor; and although he was world renowned, he had a humility of no ordinary kind. Biblical characters and historical incidents from the Bible were given lavish treatment and applied with skill to the soul. It was this man who in preaching once in Glasgow made an indelible impression upon a Highland lad, **Alexander Frazier (1870-1964)**, who notes that experience as the hour of conversion and God's call for him.

Frazier of Tain, as he became known, held charges in Aberdeen and Edinburgh, but his ministry reached the smaller kirks and also the wider congregations through Conventions. His rugged frame and yet gracious manner, his human touch with the common people, his powers of persuasive speech shot through with the lilt of humor which bubbled up regularly—all these were turned to good account in his preaching.

He was the evangelist and whether in the open air, the YMCA, the tent meeting, the convention, or the regular churches, he was filled with the spirit of compassion and spoke to win others to his Lord. The Christian faith was to him an exhilarating thing and with his Calvinism there went a gaiety and zest which told of the depths of his inner life "hid with Christ in God."

Such preaching was characterized by the wonder of God's holiness, the clear belief in the doctrines of the Biblical faith, the awe awakened by the mystery of Christ's death, and the wooing note seeking a verdict in the souls of men. Evangelistic preaching of this type was welcomed in the churches of Scotland. Frazier lived in a devotional atmosphere in all he did. Highland piety poured itself through him as he preached with intensity, passion, fervor, and grace. Style was linked with almost the histrionic, and his own dramatic gifts were used naturally and effectively. Central in his mind was the Word of God and its binding spell.

David Patrick Thompson (1896-1974) was known throughout Scotland as a Presbyterian evangelist in modern dress. He engaged in this work during the past fifty years and in the course of that time probably had a greater variety of experience in this field than any other minister in Scotland. In 1915 he began with a small team of men in uniform who were serving in the Army in World War I, and after his discharge from the Army he led student campaigns of evangelism. In 1934 the Church of Scotland set him apart for this full-time ministry.

Along with Tom Allan and Charles Duthie, he brought stimulus to the churches of Scotland to engage in this work before and since the crusades of Billy Graham. Part of his task was to train others in this service for the church. He has written some twenty books on evangelism and biography. His preaching has been known for its evangelistic insight and incisiveness.

Evangelistic preaching in Scotland has always been a decisive factor in the life and work of the churches, especially the predominantly Presbyterian. Allied to a rich tradition of theology there have been times of revival and awakening. During the 1900s and on, the spirit of the evangelical has continued in outstanding men. Thompson's contribution is characteristically expressed in a sermon "The Threshold of the Kingdom"—"Thou art not far from the Kingdom of God" (Mark 12:34). The spoken word is still heard when this message is read. The rough, literary style is there, but the preacher knows that the actual audience addressed invariably creates its own atmosphere. Many times he spoke in open air gatherings. In this sermon Thompson defines the nature of that Kingdom as the fact that some are in and some not far from it. The reasons why are these: (1) the young man had been brought up in a good home and had lived a straightforward life; (2) he had given religion a place in his life; (3) he had begun to think seriously about the biggest things in life; (4) he was convinced in his own mind that Christ was right and he had the courage to say so; (5) he was deeply moved by the appeal of Jesus.

This was the type of message preached by the evangelist and it had results, especially among students and men.

Scotland has not lacked for men in the tradition of strong, scholarly, pastoral preaching. Those who have given the Warrack Lectures have made their contribution in service, sermon, writing, and influence upon preaching.

James Reid (1877-1963) at Paisley, Scotland, and then at Eastbourne, England, stood high with appreciative congregations. His pen also reproduced the sermonic content in literature. Following J. H. Jowett and George H. Morrison, Reid provided the devotional article each week for *The British Weekly*. His pellucid style was a joy to read. The courage of this pastor-preacher is exemplified in *The Victory of God* (1933), sermons which revealed his own victory. He was blind for the major time of his ministry, a condition which denied him the activity of reading for himself. His preaching had that rare sensitivity to suffering and handicap, a "caring" identity in message and prayer. Those who heard and those who read knew that Reid spoke of what he knew, had tested it out for himself, and now shared with others from a mind and heart aflame.

Andrew Nevile Davidson (1899-), Minister of Glasgow Cathedral (1935-), Chaplain to the Armed Forces and also the Royal Household, has been a preacher in touch with the national life. He has been an interpreter of the essentials of the Christian faith by restatement for his day. He stands as a Scottish Churchman of the highest devotion in life and work.

George Baillie Duncan (1912-), also from Episcopal Church, emerged at St. George's Church, Glasgow, with an evangelical witness in succession to Tom Allan. His Biblical and expository preaching stressed the Keswick note of the deepening of the spiritual life.

Ernest David Jarvis (1888-) continued the strong pastoral preaching at Wellington Church, Glasgow, in the manner of George M. Morrison. During this period, he preached with naturalness and spontanaeity.

Adam Wilson Burnet (1883-) maintained the strong preaching characteristic of St. Cuthbert's Church, Edinburgh, during a pastorate from 1938-55. A memorizer of the sermon, he is helped by a retentive memory. A gracious and sympathetic approach is noted.

Looking into the next decade we find **Robert Leonard Small**, the leader at St. Cuthbert's from 1956 to the present. He speaks without notes, extemporaneously. Stressing the historic doctrines of Christianity, he gives series of sermons, expecting both the mature and the young to understand. He is not afraid to invite his listeners to ask questions and discuss the themes afterwards.

Andrew Wallace Williamson (1856-1926) arose with unusual gifts of personal maturity at St. Cuthbert's and then to historic St. Giles' Cathedral, Edinburgh. There from 1910-26 he ministered as a preacher to the conscience of a nation in the place redolent with memories of John Knox. Williamson's delivery was that of the orator who had caught fire in a rhetoric which had melody and power.

Charles Laing Warr (1892-) came to St. Giles' pulpit in 1926 where his cultured and polished sermons were attractive to a wide circle of discriminating hearers. The beauty of holiness characterized his ministry with the sermon at the heart of worship. Beyond him lies the explosive ministry of **Henry C. Whitley (1907-)** whose preparation had been in social, political, and industrial problems. With him began a new era of criticizing the status quo of the Kirk.

Roderick Bethune (1902-) has been true to his God-given endowments of character and sense of dedication. Any one who has the unusual distinction of following in the succession of Hugh R. Mackintosh, Arthur J. Gossip, and James S. Stewart at the Beechgrove Church, Aberdeen, and then afterwards repeating by being called to North Morningside Church, Edinburgh, again succeeding James S. Stewart, is also distinguished in his own right. Pastor-preacher, Bethune has given himself to the regular discipline of sermon preparation by brooding, writing, reflecting, and cultivating his own spiritual life. This is representative of the best in Scottish preaching.

George Finuary Macleod (1895-) brought to the ministry a challenging spirit, ever probing the traditional ways of the church of his fathers. In the line of many distinguished forebears in the national Presbyterian heritage, he finally rejected war as the way to achieve peace as a result of his World War I experience as a soldier. Then, as a minister at St. Cuthbert's Church, Edinburgh, and at Govan, Glasgow, he espoused an interpretation of the gospel as that of the pacifist for the Christian. The founding of the Iona Community on the little island where Christianity was cradled in Scotland gave him opportunity to work and worship, train others for Christian witness, and demonstrate that in the Second World War men needed to learn to use hand and head in the greater work of Christ. His Warrack Lectures, *Speaking the Truth in Love* (1937), stress the spirit of his message. Like his counterpart in England, Donald Soper, the Methodist, who was given the title, Lord Soper of Kingsway, so Lord Macleod of Finuary, also sits in the House of Lords in the British Parliament. Thus alongside the Episcopal Bishops of England, they exercise their right to speak on the affairs of the nation—as well as preach from the pulpit. Such preaching has had in it the essence of Amos stabbing the conscience of both churchmen and politician, in the belief in God's sovereignty over the whole of life.

Others who matured in pastorates and then became teachers include **William McCallum Clow (1853-1930)** who is remembered at the Barclay Church, Edinburgh, before being called as Professor of Practical Theology and Ethics at Trinity College, Glasgow. There in class and in his many books he stressed that the ministry should live at the heart of the sufferings and sacrifice of the Savior. *The Cross in Christian Experience* (1908); *The Evangel of the Strait Gate* (1916); and other books indicate his skill as an exegete and his strength in homiletical structure. At the heart of the message, the death and victory of our Lord shone through. He interpreted, like diamonds of many facets, the sayings of Scripture which related to the death on the cross in its variegated colors and glory. The atonement was the primary message for Clow.

William Malcolm Macgregor (1861-1944) of Highland culture, slow in speech, serious, not given to lilt of the Gael in fiery rush and speech, gave sermons of quality before assuming the post of Professor of New Testament and then Principal of Trinity College, Glasgow. He taught the discipline of the polished manuscript, and his addresses and sermons read well in print. *For Christ and the Kingdom* (1932) gathers up his wise counsel and teaching ideals for younger men to learn that preaching is not of the sophists, "the lying art" of the counterfeit, but the serious business of a man standing before the judgment seat of Christ.

In **W. Macintosh Mackay** of Sherbrooke Church, Glasgow and **Lauchlan Maclean Watt** of St. Stephen's Church, Edinburgh, and the Cathedral, Glasgow, are men who held patient and steady pastorates. These men represented Presbyterian life at its best. Sermons in series, relevant dealing with crucial issues of the day, and their books of doctrine and sermon gather up their maturity of thought. *The Disease and Remedy of Sin* (1918) is one of Mackay's best. Watt has left volumes of value, demonstrating the Highlander's gift of poetic insight and expression.

Another preacher of note was **Norman Maclean (1869-1952)** whose climax of service came at St. Cuthbert's, Edinburgh (1915-37). Recognized as an outstanding religious journalist whose prose and power was taken from the pulpit to the press, he had a national congregation beyond the church pew. Nurtured in the Gaelic and the Highland background, he had gifts of expression in preaching which touched the springs of life with emotive power. His was the distinction to preach the opening sermon of the League of Nations at Geneva in 1930.

Hamish Currie MacKenzie (1903-), pastor of the Orchardhill Presbyterian Church, Giffnock, Glasgow, since 1937, moved from a liberal to a conservative theology. The evangelical spirit, the irenic approach, and a Biblically-based message has enriched his ministry in pastoral preaching. Seeing life as a whole, he has given the invitation to others to take up the cross of his Master and Lord. Careful studying and preparation of heart for a spiritual ministry has been distilled in the Warrack Lectures (1961) with the reminder in the title that *Preaching the Eternities* is the preacher's business.

Beyond this period stands **William Barclay (1907-),** formerly pastor and lecturer, and since 1947 Professor of Divinity and Biblical Criticism at the University of Glasgow. To youth or the man in the street, to church member or minister, his gifts of interpretation over radio and television have given him worldwide publicity outside of the classroom. Over one million copies of his commentaries and books have been sold. His knowledge of the Greek text and the background of the ancient world has given him the means of elucidating the terms of the first century into the common speech of our day. His method in preaching as in teaching is to make clear to contemporary minds the exposition and application of the Scriptures about which many moderns are ignorant. Interpretation is reminting and restating the eternal doctrines in the thought forms of today.

Ireland also had its religious leaders in men like Henry Montgomery, Wylie Blue, and David Smith in the Presbyterian Church;

Charles Inwood in the Methodist Church; with Baptist and Anglican men sharing the Protestant influence in the North. Part of the British ethos, preachers went and returned while a few native born brought their fervor and gifts to enrich the manifold life in Britain. Inevitably the type of preaching in Ireland was an extension of what was common to the rest of the British Isles.

The period of the 1900s had brought many changes in the ways of preachers. The rise of science, technology, and the new psychology gave to the church the insights of men like James Stalker, F. Scott-Fletcher, Thomas H. Hughes, Leslie D. Weatherhead, W. L. Northridge, and others who utilized the best they gleaned in the new disciplines which affected preaching. Sermons began to be more person-centered, dealing with the inner life as well as the place of man in the creation and in the universe.

Scottish Free, Reformed, Covenanting

Scottish preaching has been predominantly in the Presbyterian tradition. However, this has had its own selectivity. Not all of it has been found within the larger and national bodies of the Church of Scotland and the United Free Church. Smaller bodies linked with the Covenanters and the Original Secession have much in common with the Free Church. In the intricacies of church history, these groups have played a vital part in the spiritual life of the nation, and their special types of preaching deserve mention.

Alexander Smellie (1857-1923) at the Original Secession Church, Carluke, spent his life in pastoring a small congregation yet touched the world. Out of the beaten oil of the sanctuary his preaching was captured in publications of a high literary standard. His *Daily Bible Notes* were issued regularly and his monumental *Men of the Covenant* (2 vols., 1908) abides as a treasury of information concerning the Covenanters whose work and sacrifices can never be forgotten.

A preacher of rare persuasiveness and quiet power, had he been willing, he might have been the successor to Alexander Whyte. Smellie won a worldwide reputation through the brilliance of his pen. Of broad and sound scholarship, displaying a wizardry with words, he dwelt deeply in the things of the Spirit and carried in him the convictions of the Covenanters.

His style is clear. "The discipline of life is God's instrument for the unfolding of His Word. In weakness and sorrow many a text grows plain. In difficult duty many a promise glows with new light. In temptation many a precept shines out as they never did formerly." "God's wounding is my healing, His sorrow my rest."

John Paterson Struthers (1855-1915) was of the smallest body of that group which continued to uphold the doctrines of their forefathers as Covenanter and Cameronian, knowing that martyrdom was their lot. His ministry at Greenock was redolent with scholarship, painstaking preparation, diligent pastoral preaching, and compassionate service. A Reformed Presbyterian of that time, James Denney, was knotted in heart with him and found him to be a man who, though he had declined the position of Professor of Greek in a University, preferring to be the pastor of a small congregation, was the only genius he knew. No one in that time had greater respect of character and value of ministry.

For twenty-seven years Struthers edited, rather, wrote *The Morning Watch*, a monthly magazine for church people. Denney said of him that he was the most gifted preacher in the West of Scotland in that day, being very reserved, very shy, very humble, and very lovable. Humorist and melancholian, he possessed a modesty which enabled him to decline the honorary degree of Doctor of Divinity offered by the University of Glasgow. From a ministry based upon the Psalms, the Catechisms, and the Confession of Faith, Struthers was an able interpreter of the Bible. His sanctified imagination could have him preach the striking thought concerning Enoch: "God took him to be with Himself, because heaven itself was not quite heaven till a living human being was there. It was not quite heaven till Christ should see before His face that human nature which He was to save by His death on the Cross." Struthers, like many of his people, would be termed a "character" in his own way.

Linked in modern days with those men of the Spirit are those whose heritage is the Free Church of Scotland. With sacrifice and sanctification, standing for their convictions as a minority group, these preachers of influence have included men who held the Reformed Faith and, in the Disruption of the Presbyterians of the 1800's, firm commitments were made by several groups. Among the leaders of the Free Church are preachers whose emphasis is the historic faith and the fundamentals of a Christian witness.

Donald Maclean (1869-1943), John Macleod (1872-1948), Roderick Alexander Finlayson (1895-), and Alexander Ross (1888-1965) are fine samples of the preachers whose enduring influence was strong both upon students in training and congregations. The first two were Principals of the Free Church College, Edinburgh, in addition to maintaining earlier pastorates. The second pair were professors in the same college of theology.

The preaching was Reformed and orthodox in the finest tradition, Biblical in exegesis and exposition. Theology and doctrine were at the heart of the sermon. The Gaelic language of parts of Scotland, the Celtic inheritance, the people of the Highlands, and the resolute Protestant affirmation—these were part and parcel of preaching. "Strong meat" came from the Word of God combined with scholarship and piety for an informed and educated people within the church.

Maclean was a thorough-going Calvinist but his irenic and loving spirit could not fail to appeal. Pastor of Free St. Columba's Church, Edinburgh (1905-18), he published *The Literature of the Gael: Aspects of Scottish Church History* and *The Counter-Reformation in Scotland, 1560-1930.* In addition he was joint founder and first editor of *The Evangelical Quarterly.* Macleod, like Maclean, had a writing as well as preaching ministry. His book based on lectures, entitled *Scottish Theology in Relation to Church History Since the Reformation* (1943), was his *magnum opus* and fills a niche in the history and theology of Scotland as he gathered material not always known or available. The book is a salutory contribution to the history of theology. The apologetic strain was prominent as these men were the survivors of years of conflict theologically.

The later scholars and teachers also preached with regularity. Finlayson stressed the providence of God in history. His preaching demonstrated that the God of Israel was also the God of the Christian and that history held meaning with that divine presence. In a Free Church service there was a heightened sense of awe and reverence, almost fear in the Old Testament sense. Ross, with his New Testament emphasis, never got away from surprise when meeting with the Christ of God. Free Church preaching used Psalms for the singing, rather than hymns. From that vantage ground the way was made clear toward the cross and the preaching of the gospel.

Others in the Free Church orbit have been **Alexander Stewart**, a strong pastoral preacher, proclaiming the glory of the spiritual life in modern context; and **George N. M. Collins**, pastor, author, editor, Professor of Church History at the Free Church College, Edinburgh, where the heritage of the church is continued in teaching and preaching. The Bible is accepted as the Word of God and the final authority. The Westminster Confession of Faith continues to be the subordinate standard containing the system of doctrine most surely believed, taught, and preached.

Chaplains, Interdenominational

The two World Wars brought into focus the work of the chaplain in the armed forces. The Christian church not only gave full-time men, but also provided pastors who left their congregations to serve during periods of war. Thus the church ministered to the men and women away from home and facing the dangers and tests of war experience.

Representative chaplains are recalled in the person of **Charles W. Gordon** ("Ralph Connor"), Presbyterian pastor who was Senior Chaplain of the Canadian armed forces during World War I. Bishop **Taylor Smith**, Episcopalian, was the Head of the British Chaplains during World War I and beyond. His terse, pithy words and evangelical faith touched many and set standards for other chaplains. In World War II **Studdert Kennedy** was best known. **Edgar Primrose Dickie** served as Presbyterian Chaplain in World War II. He became Professor of Theology, St. Andrew's University, Scotland, while still continuing his preaching ministry to ex-service men and to children, a rare and unique gift.

Of the preaching of these men (and their larger number throughout the world), no study has yet been made. Little has been recorded as the ministry of this kind had unusual demands. The sermon was shorter, for the moment, and given in all sorts of buildings, and often in the open air during the dangers of war. A hint of what might be preached can be gleaned from the lives of these representative men and from books since issued by them.

"Greater Love Hath No Man"; "One of the Few"; "Rise Up Ye Dead"; "A Book of Remembrance Was Written," are texts used by Dickie. Memorial Days, Armistice Days, National Anniversaries—these are occasions for the chaplain to see God in history and to recall sacrifices made for freedom. Here the chaplain has been the medium of inspiration and strength, especially bringing comfort to the sorrowing and hope to those whose lives stand in jeopardy. Thus the preaching has been a call to courage and faith, to cleanse self of hatred, and to dedicate life to a nobler order.

Conclusion

The Space Age demands new rapport with truth as it impinges upon a generation brought up in an age of expanding worlds, acceleration of speed, and social and religious movements in tension and ferment. This new century has in it the seeds of disruption and revolution. The church and the preacher cannot disregard the times in which we live.

Each decade has its meaning and message. The 1930s and subsequent periods brought the nations through two world wars with their impact upon religious life. Days of reconstruction demanded from the pulpit an understanding message for those in disillusionment and despair. A new wave of enthusiasm came by the 1950s with membership in the churches at its highest. The 1960s brought a reaction with a guilt complex concerning national decisions and actions around the world. At home the race question and city riots made the headlines, and religious matters receded but only for a short time. Then came resurgent youth turning away from moral aberrations to seek again and ask questions about the Christian faith. While the "death of God" theological movement wanes, there has come a revival of simple and direct evangelism on the part of youth.

At this juncture there are those who denigrate preaching, seeing its end in the eclipse of the sermon and the demise of the institutional church. Others, seeing the rise of new eschatological hopes in the threat of doom by nuclear holocaust, population explosion, and a polluted ecology, cry out for a revival of historic Christianity. Elmer G. Homrighausen, Dean of Princeton Theological Seminary, evaluates the times as showing "a decided eclipse of liberalism and a resurgence of evangelicalism. The latter indicates a new wave of

531

conservatism, evangelism, and Biblical realism, and this is seen in two trends: (1) orthodoxy in a rigid form, or (2) a neo-orthodoxy with a Christian humanism of its own. Some believe that this evangelicalism has within it the secret of survival for all the churches."

If this is so, what then is the role of the preacher? Once again the nature of the church is under review. Evangelism has become a top priority for many denominations, and theological study points to new and exciting interpretations and formulations of truth. All this is for the best and there is hope that the decades ahead will witness new forms of ministry to a confused and frustrated world. At the heart of it will be the preacher in one form or another. The "marching orders" of the Risen Lord and Master have never been revised or cancelled. The church moves in obedience to the Great Commission. Truth must have its advocates. Christ must have His witnesses. Therefore the place of the preacher is secure. Preaching has exciting days before it. The sermon or Christian message will continue to sway the hearts and minds of new generations. There will always be those in every nation who ask if there is any word from the Lord? Man does not live by bread alone.

> For whosoever shall call upon the name of the Lord shall be saved. How then shall they call on him in whom they have not believed? and how shall they believe in him of whom they have not heard? and how shall they hear without a preacher? And how shall they preach, except they be sent? as it is written, How beautiful are the feet of them that preach the gospel of peace, and bring glad tidings of good things!　　　　　　　—Rom. 10:13-15

Bibliography

In order to bring up to date the titles of Lectures on Preaching, this list of the *Yale Lectures* (Lyman Beecher Lectures on Preaching), the *Sprunt Lectures* (Union Theological Seminary, Richmond, Va.), and the *Warrack Lectures* (Preachers' Lectureship, Scotland), is given.

YALE LECTURES:

Baxter, Batsell B. *The Heart of the Yale Lectures* (1950)—a digest of the lecturers' statements on the preacher, the delivery and the content of the sermon.

Jones, Edgar DeWitt. *The Royalty of the Pulpit* (1951)—Summaries of published and unpublished lectures, with biographies of the lecturers.

1872 (1) Beecher, Henry Ward. Yale Lectures on Preaching, 1st Series.
1873 (2) ————. Yale Lectures on Preaching, 2nd Series.
1874 (3) ————. Yale Lectures on Preaching, 3rd Series.
1875 (4) Hall, John. *God's Word through Preaching.*
1876 (5) Taylor, William M. *The Ministry of the Word.*
1877 (6) Brooks, Phillips. *Lectures on Preaching.*
1878 (7) Dale, Robert W. *Nine Lectures on Preaching.*
1879 (8) Simpson, Matthew. *Lectures on Preaching.*
1880 (9) Crosby, Howard. *The Christian Preacher.*
1881 (10) Dyrea, J. T.; G. Harris; S. E. Herrick; N. J. Burton; and L. D. Bevan. (Lectures not published)
1882 (11) Robinson, Ezekiel G. *Lectures on Preaching.*

1883   (No Lectures)

1884 (12) Burton, Nathaniel J. *In Pulpit and Parish.*

1885 (13) Storr, Henry M. *The American Preacher.* (Not published)

1886 (14) Taylor, William M. *The Scottish Pulpit.*

1887 (15) Gladden, Washington. *Tools and the Man.*

1888 (16) Trumbull, Henry C. *The Sunday School.*

1889 (17) Broadus, John A. *On the Preparation and Delivery of Sermons.*

1890 (18) Behrends, Adol. J. F. *The Philosophy of Preaching.*

1891 (19) Stalker, James. *The Preacher and His Models.*

1892 (20) Fairbairn, Andrew M. *The Place of Christ in Modern Theology.*

1893 (21) Horton, Robert F. *Verbum Dei.*

1894   (No Lectures)

1895 (22) Greer, David H. *The Preacher and His Place.*

1896 (23) Van Dyke, Henry. *The Gospel for an Age of Doubt.*

1897 (24) Watson, John. *The Cure of Souls.*

1898 (25) Tucker, William J. *The Making and the Unmaking of the Preacher.*

1899 (26) Smith, George Adam. *Modern Criticism and the Preaching of the Old Testament.*

1900 (27) Brown, John. *Puritan Preaching in England.*

1901   (No Lectures)

1902 (28) Gladden, Washington. *Social Salvation.*

1903 (29) Gordon, George A. *Ultimate Conceptions of Faith.*

1904 (30) Abbott, Lyman. *The Christian Ministry.*

1905 (31) Peabody, Francis G. *Jesus Christ and the Christian Character.*

1906 (32) Brown, Charles R. *The Social Message of the Modern Pulpit.*

1907 (33) Forsyth, Peter T. *Positive Preaching and the Modern Mind.*

1908 (34) Faunce, William H. P. *The Educational Ideal of the Ministry.*

1909 (35) Henson, Herbert H. *The Liberty of Prophesying.*

1910 (36) Jefferson, Charles E. *The Building of the Church.*

1911 (37) Gunsaulus, Frank W. *The Minister and the Spiritual Life.*

1912 (38) Jowett, John H. *The Preacher: His Life and Work.*

1913 (39) Parkhurst, Charles H. *The Pulpit and the Pew.*

1914 (40) Horne, Charles S. *The Romance of the Ministry.*

1915 (41) Pepper, George W. *A Voice from the Crowd.*
1916 (42) Hyde, William DeWitt. *The Gospel of Good Will.*
1917 (43) McDowell, William F. *Good Ministers of Jesus Christ.*
1918 (44) Coffin, Henry S. *In a Day of Social Rebuilding.*
1919 (45) Kelman, John. *The War and Preaching.*
1920 (46) Fitch, Albert P. *Preaching and Paganism.*
1921 (47) Williams, Charles D. *The Prophetic Ministry for Today.*
1922 (48) Merrill, William P. *The Freedom of the Preacher.*
1923 (49) Brown, Charles R. *The Art of Preaching.*
1924 (50) Fosdick, Harry E. *The Modern Use of the Bible.*
1925 (51) Inge, William R. *The Preaching of the Kingdom of God in History.* (Not published)
1926 (52) Calkins, Raymond. *The Eloquence of Christian Experience.*
1927 (53) Sclater, John R. P. *The Public Worship of God.*
1928 (54) Freeman, James E. *The Ambassador.*
1929 (55) Mouzon, Edwin D. *Preaching with Authority.*
1930 (56) McConnell, Francis J. *The Prophetic Ministry.*
1931 (57) Buttrick, George A. *Jesus Came Preaching.*
1932 (58) Tittle, Ernest F. *Jesus after Nineteen Centuries.*
1933 (59) Jacks, Lawrence P. *Elemental Religion.*
1934 (60) Day, Albert E. *Jesus and Human Personality.*
1935 (61) Bowie, Walter R. *The Renewing Gospel.*
1936 (62) Park, John E. *The Miracle of Preaching.*
1937   (No Lectures)
1938 (63) Sperry, Willard L. *We Prophesy in Part.*
1939 (64) Morrison, Charles C. *What Is Christianity?*
1940 (65) Buttrick, G. A.; E. M. Poteat; A. H. Bradford; E. M. McKee; W. A. Smart; and E. F. Tittle. *Preaching in These Times.*
1941 (66) Sockman, Ralph W. *The Highway of God.*
1942 (67) Noyes, Morgan P. *Preaching the Word of God.*
1943 (68) Scherer, Paul E. *For We Have This Treasure.*
1944 (69) Oxnam, G. Bromley. *Preaching in a Revolutionary Age.*
1945 (70) Niebuhr, Reinhold. *Faith and History.*
1946 (71) Farmer, Herbert H. *God and Men.*
1947 (72) Phillips, Harold C. *Bearing Witness to the Truth.*
1948 (73) Sherrill, Henry K. *The Church's Ministry in Our Time.*
1949 (74) Weatherhead, Leslie D. *The Minister's Relation to the Community.*

1950 (75) Auden, W. H., A. Flemming, C. P. Taft, H. M. Wriston, Helen Kenyon, Edmund W. Sinnott. *"The Church and Its Ministry"* (not published, except "Science and Religion" by E. W. Sinnott).
1951 (76) Douglas, Truman B. *Preaching the New Reformation.*
1952 (77) Stewart, James S. *A Faith to Proclaim.*
1953 (78) Luccock, Halford E. *Communicating the Gospel.*
1954 (79) Kennedy, Gerald H. *God's Good News.*
1955 (80) Robinson, James H. *Adventurous Preaching.*
1956 (81) Dun, Angus. *The Saving Person.*
1957 (82) Niles, Daniel T. *The Preacher's Task and the Stone of Stumbling.*
1958 (83) Horton, Douglas. *The Meaning of Worship.*
1959 (84) Sittler, Joseph. *The Ecology of Faith.*
1960 (85) Soper, Donald O. *The Advocacy of the Gospel.*
1961 (86) Bartlett, Gene E. *The Audacity of Preaching.*
1962 (87) Miller, Samuel H. *The Dilemma of Modern Belief.*
1963 (88) Barr, Browne. *Parish Back Talk.*
1964 (89) Jenkins, Daniel. "The Man of Few Words" (not published).
1965 (90) Burns, Jackson. "Preaching to the Divided House" (not published).
1966 (91) Newbigin, J. E. Lesslie. *The Finality of Christ.*
1967 (92) Mead, Sidney. "Aspects of Lyman Beecher's Theology" (not published).
1968 (93) Pruyser, Paul W. *A Dynamic Psychology of Religion.*
1969 (94) Ramsey, Paul. *The Patient as Person.*
1970 (95) Illich, Ivan. *Strategy for Education* (not published).
1971 (96) Cook, John W. *Multi-Media Presentation* (not published).
1972 (No Lectures)
1973 (97) Read, David H. C. *Sent from God: The Enduring Power and Mystery of Preaching.*
1974 (98) Mitchell, Henry H. *The Genius of the Black Pulpit.*

SPRUNT LECTURES:

1913 Burrell, David J. *The Sermon, Its Construction and Delivery.*
1914 Morgan, G. Campbell. *The Ministry of the Word.*
1923 Vance, James I. *Being a Preacher: A Study of the Claims of the Christian Ministry.*

1924   Black, James. *The Mystery of Preaching.*
1926   Alexander, Maitland. *The Minister in Action.*
1951   McCracken, Robert J. *The Place of Theology in Preaching.*
1970   Hall, Thor. *The Future Shape of Preaching.*

WARRACK LECTURES:

1921 (1) Hutton, John A. *That the Ministry Be Not Blamed.*
1922 (2) Sclater, John R. P. *The Public Worship of God.*
1923 (3) Black, James M. *The Mystery of Preaching.*
1924 (4) Reid, James. *In Quest of Reality.*
1925 (5) Gossip, Arthur J. *In Christ's Stead.*
1926 (6) Coffin, Henry S. *What to Preach.*
1927 (7)
1928 (8) Scott, A. Boyd. *Preaching Week by Week.*
1929 (9) Jones, John D. (Not published)
1930 (10) Philip, Adam. *Thoughts on Worship and Preaching.*
1931 (11) Watt, Lauchlan Maclean. *The Preacher's Life and Work.*
1932 (12) Anderson, R. Sangster. "A Preacher at Work" (not published).
1933 (13) Fleming, Archibald. (Not published)
1934 (14) Cairns, Frank. *The Prophet of the Heart.*
1935 (15) Burnet, Adam W. *Pleading with Men.*
1936 (16) Berry, Sidney M. *Vital Preaching.*
1937 (17) Macleod, George F. *Speaking the Truth in Love.*
1938 (18) Gauld, William W. (Not published)
1939 (19) Black, Hugh. (Not published)
1940 (20) Milligan, Oswald B. *The Ministry of Worship.*
1941 (21) Farmer, Herbert H. *The Servant of the Word.*
1942 (22) Macgregor, William M. *The Making of a Preacher.*
1943 (23) Stewart, James S. *Heralds of God.*
1944 (24) Whale, John S. *Baptism and Eucharist* (Victor and Victim).
1945 (25) Cockburn, J. Hutchison. "The Church's Message for an Age of Turmoil" (not published).
1946   (No appointment)
1947 (26) Niebuhr, Reinhold. *Faith and History.*
1948 (27) Jeffrey, G. Johnstone. *This Grace Wherein We Stand.*
1949 (28) McIntyre, Robert E. *The Ministry of the Word.*

1950 (29) Jarvis, Ernest D. *If Any Man Minister.*
1951 (30) Read, David H. C. *The Communication of the Gospel.*
1952 (31) Craig, Archibald C. *Preaching in a Scientific Age.*
1953 (32) Menzies, Robert. *Preaching and Pastoral Evangelism.*
1954 (33) Cowan, Arthur A. *The Primacy of Preaching Today.*
1955 (34) MacLennan, David A. *Entrusted with the Gospel.*
1956 (35) Wright, James. *A Preacher's Questionnaire.*
1957 (36) Niles, Daniel T. *The Preacher's Calling to be Servant.*
1958 (37) Boyd, Alexander J. *Christian Encounter.*
1959 (38) Small, R. Leonard. *With Ardour and Accuracy.*
1960 (39) Keir, Thomas H. *The Word in Worship: Preaching and Its Setting in Common Worship.*
1961 (40) MacKenzie, Hamish C. *Preaching the Eternities.*
1962   (No appointment)
1963   (No appointment)
1964 (41) Cleland, James T. *Preaching to be Understood.*
1965   (No appointment)
1966   (No appointment)
1967   (No appointment)
1968 (42) McWilliam, Stuart W. *Called to Preach.*
1969   (No appointment)
1970   (No appointment)
1971   (No appointment)
1972 (43) Pitt-Watson, Ian. *Theology Is for Preaching.*
1973   (No appointment)

In Dargan's two volumes no mention is made of the numerous works of general reference of which constant or occasional use has been made in the preparation of his *A History of Preaching.* Histories of nations; histories of the church; of doctrine; of philosophy and of literature; encyclopaedias, general, ecclesiastical and biographical; as well as miscellaneous works were consulted. The lives and sermons of individual preachers were also omitted, except in footnotes and references in the text. The Index gives names in abundance. Only a few literary or critical studies, where they bear on preaching, were included. The selective bibliography, therefore, was given under the captions of "American Authors"; "British Authors"; "Dutch Authors"; "French Authors"; "German Authors"; and "Italian Authors."

The present volume has its boundaries of subject matter with selected periods and representative preachers mentioned within their respective areas of influence and countries. The bibliography thus offers a selected list of volumes which are outstanding in the field of investigation. Each period and emphasis is thus within the purview of the larger emphasis upon the history of preaching.

CHAPTER I

Addison, D. D. *The Clergy in American Life and Letters.* New York: Macmillan, 1900.

Albro, J. A. (ed.) *The Works of Thomas Shepard.* 3 vols., 1638, New York and Hildesheim: George Olms Verlag (repr.), 1853.

Ames, W. *The Marrow of Sacred Divinity.* London: 1638.

Bernard, R. *The Faithful Shepherd.* London: 1607.

Boorstin, D. J. *The Americans: The Colonial Experience.* London: Penguin, 1965.

Bradford, W. *Of Plymouth Plantation.* New York: Capricon, 1962.

Bulkeley, P. *The Gospel Covenant: Preached in Concord in New England.* London: 1651.

Calvin, J. *Institutes of the Christian Religion.* 3 vols., Edinburgh: Calvin Translation Society, 1845.

Chappell, W. *The Preacher and the Art and Method of Preaching, (Methodus Concionandi).* London: 1651. New York: Russell and Russell, 1962 (repr.).

Cotton, J. Works and manuscript sermons. London and Boston: "A Brief Exposition Upon Ecclesiastes," Nichol's series of Commentaries. Edinburgh: 1868.

Covey, C. *The American Pilgrimage: the Roots of American History, Religion and Culture.* New York: Collier, 1961.

Gaer, J. and S. Siegel. *The Puritan Heritage: America's Roots.* New York: New American Library, 1964.

Hall, D. D. *The Antinomian Controversy, 1636-1638.* A Documentary History (ed. with Intro. and Notes). Middleton, Conn: Wesleyan University, 1968.

————. *The Faithful Shepherd.* A History of the New England Ministry in the Seventeenth Century. Chapel Hill: University of North Carolina Press, 1972.

Haller, W. *The Rise of Puritanism.* New York: Columbia University, 1938.

————. *Liberty and Reformation in the Puritan Revolution.* New York: Columbia University, 1955.

Hooker, T. *The Soules Preparation.* London: 1632.

Levy, B. M. *Preaching in the First-half Century of New England History*. Hartford: The American Society of Church History, 1945.

Miller, P. *Orthodoxy in Massachusetts, 1630-1650*. Boston: Beacon, 1933.

————. *Roger Williams*. New York: Bobbs Merrill, 1953.

————. *The New England Mind: The Seventeenth Century*. New York: Macmillan, 1939.

Parrington, V. L. *The Colonial Mind, 1620-1800: Main Currents in American Thought*. London: Rupert Hart-Davis, 1954.

Perkins, W. *Works*. 3 vols. (1592-1605), *The Art of Prophesying*. Vol. II., Cambridge, England: John Legatt, printer to the University of Cambridge, 1612-13.

Savelle, M. *Seeds of Liberty: The Genesis of the American Mind*. Seattle: University of Washington, 1965.

Shepard, T. *The Parable of the Ten Virgins Opened and Applied*. London: Rothwell and Thomson, 1660.

Singer, C. G. *A Theological Interpretation of American History*. Philadelphia: Presbyterian and Reformed Pub. Co., 1964.

Sweet, W. W. *Religion in Colonial America*. New York: Scribner, 1942.

————. *The American Churches*. Nashville: Abingdon-Cokesbury, 1948.

Smith, J. W. and A. L. Jamison, (eds). *Religion in American Life*. 4 vols. *The Shaping of American Religion*. Vol. I., Princeton: Princeton University, 1961.

Smith, H. S., R. T. Handy, and L. A. Loetscher, (eds). *American Christianity: An Historical Interpretation with Representative Documents*. Vol. I. 1607-1820; Vol. II. 1820-1960. New York: Scribner, 1960, 1963.

Trinterud, L. J. "The Origin of Puritanism," *Church History*. XXI. Chicago: American Society of Church History, 1952.

Turnbull, R. G. "Puritan Preaching," *Baker's Dictionary of Practical Theology*. Grand Rapids: Baker, 1967.

Walzer, M. *The Revolution of the Saints: A Study in the Origins of Radical Politics*. Cambridge: Harvard University, 1965.

Williams, R. *The Bloudy Tenet of Persecution*. London: 1644.

Winslow, O. E. *Meeting House Hill, 1630-1783*. New York: Macmillan, 1952.

————. *Master Roger Williams, A Biography*. New York: Macmillan, 1957.

Winthrop, J. *Winthrop's Journal.* "History of New England," 1630-1649, J. K. Hosmer (ed). 2 vols. New York: 1908.

CHAPTER II

Carroll, P. N. *Puritanism and the Wilderness.* The Intellectual Significance of the New England Frontier, 1629-1700. New York: Columbia University, 1969.

Danforth, S. *A Brief Recognition of New-England's Errand into the Wilderness.* Cambridge: 1671.

Davies, H. *The Worship of the English Puritans.* London: Dacre, 1948.

Fitch, J. *An Holy Connection.* Cambridge: 1674.

Hubbard, W. *A General History of New England from the Discovery to 1680.* Cambridge: Hillard & Metcalf, as reprinted entire. Boston: Little & Brown, 1843.

Mather, Cotton. *Magnalia Christi Americana.* Of The Ecclesiastical History of New England from its First Planting in the years 1620, unto the year of our Lord. 1698. 2 vols., London: Printed for Thomas Parkhurst, 1702.

——————. *Manductio ad Ministerium.* Directions for a Candidate for the Ministry. Reproduced from the Original Edition, Boston, 1726, with a Bibliographical Note by T. J. Holmes and K. B. Murdock. Published by the Facsimile Society, New York: Columbia University, 1938.

Mather, Increase. "The First Principles of New England, Concerning the subject of Baptisme and Communion of Churches." Cambridge: 1675.

Mather, Richard and John Davenport. Church-Government and Church-Covenant discussed in an answer of the elders of the several churches in New England to two and thirty questions. London: 1643.

Miller, P. *The New England Mind.* From Colony to Province, Cambridge: Harvard University, 1953.

——————. *Errand into the Wilderness.* Cambridge: Harvard University, 1956.

Miller, P. and T. H. Johnson. *The Puritans.* 2 vols. (rev. ed.), New York: Harper & Row, 1963.

Morrison, S. E. *The Intellectual Life of Colonial New England.* (formerly *The Puritan Pronaos*), Ithaca, N. Y: Cornell University, 1960.

Oakes, U. New England Pleaded with, And pressed to consider things which concern her Peace, at least in this her Day. Cambridge: 1673.

Turnbull, R. G. *The Preacher's Heritage, Task, and Resources.* Grand Rapids: Baker, 1968.

Van Dyken, S. *Samuel Willard: Preacher of Orthodoxy in an Age of Change.* Grand Rapids: Eerdmans, 1972.

Wendell, B. *Cotton Mather: The Puritan Priest.* New York: Harcourt, Brace & World, 1963.

Willard, S. *Brief Directions to a Young Scholar Designing the Ministry for the Study of Divinity.* Boston: 1735.

CHAPTER III

Allen, A. V. G. "The Place of Edwards in History," *Jonathan Edwards: A Retrospect.* Boston: Houghton, Mifflin, 1901.

Bainton, R. H. *Yale and the Ministry.* A History of education for the Christian Ministry at Yale from the founding in 1701. New York: Harper & Brothers, 1957.

Baldwin, M. *The New England Clergy and the American Revolution.* Durham, N. C: Duke University, 1928.

Chauncey, C. *The New Creature Describ'd and Consider'd.* Boston: 1741.

————. *God's Mercy.* Shewed to his people in giving them a faithful Ministry and schooles of Learning for the continual supplys thereof. Cambridge: 1755.

Edwards, Jonathan. *Works.* S. Austin (ed.), Worcester, 1806, 4 vols. Reprinted with additions and indexes, 1843.

————. *Works.* S. E. Dwight (ed.), 10 vols., New York: 1829-30.

————. *Works.* P. Miller & J. E. Smith (eds.), 10 vols. (I-IV pub. to date) New Haven: Yale University, 1957.

————. *The Edwards Manuscripts* at Yale University Library (Rare Book Room) and at Andover-Newton Library.

Gambrell, M. L. *Ministerial Training in Eighteenth-Century New England.* New York: AMS Pr., 1937.

Gausted, E. S. *The Great Awakening in New England.* New York: Harper & Brothers, 1957.

Heimert, A. *Religion and the American Mind from the Great Awakening to the Revolution.* Cambridge: Harvard University, 1966.

Heimert, A. and Perry Miller (eds.) *The Great Awakening: Documents Illustrating the Crisis and Its Consequences.* New York: Bobbs-Merrill, 1967.

Hitt, R. T. (ed.) *Heroic Colonial Christians: Edwards, G. Tennent, Brainerd, Witherspoon.* New York: Lippincott, 1966.

Howell, W. S. *Eighteenth-Century British Logic and Rhetoric.* Princeton: Princeton University, 1971.

Lovejoy, D. S. *Religious Enthusiasm and the Great Awakening.* Englewood, N. J: Prentice-Hall, 1969.

McGraw, J. *Great Evangelical Preachers of Yesterday.* Nashville: Abingdon, 1961.

Miller, P. *Jonathan Edwards.* New York: Sloane Associates, 1949.

Stoddard, S. *A Treatise Concerning Conversion.* Boston: 1719.

Turnbull, R. G. *Jonathan Edwards the Preacher.* Grand Rapids: Baker, 1954.

————. "Jonathan Edwards: Bible Interpreter." *Interpretation.* Vol. VI., No 4., Oct., 1952, Richmond: Union Seminary.

Winslow, O. A. *Jonathan Edwards.* New York: Macmillan, 1940.

CHAPTER IV

Asbury, F. *The Journal and Letters of Francis Asbury.* 3 vols., London: Epworth, 1958 and Nashville: Abingdon, 1958.

Barton, F. (ed.). *Pulpit Power and Eloquence or One Hundred Sermons of the Nineteenth Century.* Cleveland: Barton, 1901.

Collins, V. L. *President Witherspoon.* 2 vols., Princeton: Princeton University, 1925.

Cunningham, C. E. *Timothy Dwight.* New York: Macmillan, 1942.

Dallimore, A. *George Whitefield: The Life and Labours of.* Vol. I., London: Banner of Truth Trust, 1970.

Dwight, T. *Sermons.* 2 vols. New Haven: Yale University, 1828.

Goen, C. C. *Revivalism and Separatism in New England, 1740-1800.* New Haven: Yale University, 1962.

Hawley, T. O. B. *The American Revolution and Religion: Maryland, 1795-1850.* Washington, D. C: Catholic University, 1971.

Macartney, C. E. *Sons of Thunder.* New York: Revell, 1929.

————. *Six Kings of the American Pulpit.* Philadelphia: Westminster, 1942.

Miller, P. *The Life of the Mind in America: from the Revolution to the Civil War.* New York: Harcourt, Brace and World, 1965.

Mol, J. J. *The Breaking of Traditions: Theological Convictions in Colonial America.* Berkeley: Glendessary, 1968.

Moulton, P. P. (ed.). *The Journal and Major Essays of John Woolman.* New York: Oxford University, 1971.

Pilcher, G. W. *Samuel Davies: Apostle of Dissent in Colonial Virginia.* Knoxville: University of Tennessee, 1971.

Ryle, J. C. (ed.). *Select Sermons of George Whitefield.* London: Banner of Truth Trust, 1958.

Smith, E. A. *The Presbyterian Ministry in American Culture, A Study in Changing Concepts, 1700-1900.* Philadelphia: Westminster, 1962.

Steiner, B. E. *Samuel Seabury, 1729-1796. A Study in the High Church Tradition.* Columbus: Ohio University, 1972.

Tanis, J. *Dutch Calvinistic Pietism in the Middle Colonies.* A Study in the Life and Theology of Theodore Jacobus Frelinghuysen, The Hague: Martinus Nijhof, 1967.

Tappert, T. G. and J. W. Doberstein (eds.). *The Journals of Henry Melchior Muhlenberg.* 3 vols., Philadelphia: Muhlenberg, 1942-58.

Trinterud, L. J. *The Forming of an American Tradition: A Re-Examination of Colonial Presbyterianism.* Philadelphia: Westminster, 1949.

Tyler, M. C. *A History of American Literature, 1607-1765.* New York: Crowell-Collier, 1962.

Wagenknecht, E. *Ambassadors for Christ.* Seven American Preachers. New York: Oxford University Press, 1972.

Whitefield, G. *Journals.* (The Seven Journals, 1738-1741) and a new edition with additional materials. London: Banner of Truth Trust, 1960.

Witherspoon, J. *Works.* 4 vols., Philadelphia: 1801.

CHAPTER V

Adger, J. B. and J. L. Girdeau (eds.). *The Collected Writings of James Henry Thornwell.* 4 vols., Richmond: Presbyterian Publications, 1873.

Albright, R. W. *A History of the Evangelical Church.* Harrisburg: Evangelical, 1942.

—————. *Focus on Infinity: A Life of Phillips Brooks.* New York: Macmillan, 1961.

Allen, A. V. G. *The Life and Letters of Phillips Brooks.* 2 vols., New York: Dutton, 1900.

Alexander, A. *The Log College.* London: Banner of Truth Trust, 1968.

Alexander, J. W. *The Life of Archibald Alexander.* Philadelphia: Presbyterian, 1856.

Barnes, A. *The Church and Slavery.* Philadelphia: Parry and Mc-Millan, 1857.

Broadus, J. A. *Sermons and Addresses.* Baltimore: Wharton, 1886.

Brooks, P. *Sermons.* 10 vols., New York: Dutton, 1878-1904.

Cartwright, P. *Autobiography of Peter Cartwright.* Nashville: Abingdon, 1956.

Clark, R. S. *The Life of Matthew Simpson.* New York: Macmillan, 1956.

Drury, R. W. *History of the Church of the United Brethren in Christ.* Dayton: Otterbein, 1924.

Dunn, D. and J. Wagner. *A History of the Evangelical and Reformed Church.* Philadelphia: Christian Education Press, 1961.

Findlay, J. F. *Dwight L. Moody, American Evangelist, 1837-1899.* Chicago: University of Chicago, 1969.

Finney, C. G. *Autobiography of Rev. Charles G. Finney.* New York: Revell, 1876.

———. *Revival Lectures.* New York: Revell, 1868.

Foster, C. L. *An Errand of Mercy, The Evangelical Front, 1790-1837.* Chapel Hill: University of North Carolina, 1960.

Garrison, W. E. and A. T. DeGroot. *The Disciples of Christ: A History.* St. Louis: Bethany, 1958.

Gordon, A. J. *Sermons.* Great Pulpit Masters, Vol. VIII, New York: Revell, 1951.

Gordon, E. B. *A. J. Gordon, D.D.* A Biography by his son. London: Hodder & Stoughton, 1896.

Hodge, A. A. *The Life of Charles Hodge.* New York: 1880.

Hodge, Charles. *Princeton Sermons.* London: Banner of Truth Trust, 1958.

Jones, Sam. *Sermons.* Great Pulpit Masters, Vol. IV, New York: Revell, 1950.

Nevin, J. W. *The Anxious Bench, and The Mystical Presence.* Philadelphia: United Church, 1844, 1946.

Nichols, J. H. (ed.). *The Mercersburg Theology.* New York: Oxford, 1966.

Robertson, A. T. *Life and Letters of John Albert Broadus.* Philadelphia: American Baptist, 1901.

Schaff, D. S. *The Life of Philip Schaff.* New York: Scribner, 1897.

Schaff, P. *Historical Writings.* Philadelphia: United Church, 1964.

Smith, T. L. *Revivalism and Social Reform in Mid-Nineteenth Century America.* New York: Abingdon, 1969.

Steffens, D. H. *Dr. C. F. W. Walther.* Philadelphia: Lutheran, 1917.

Talmage, M. (ed.). *The Treasury of T. DeWitt Talmage.* Grand Rapids: Baker, 1968.

Thornwell, J. H. "The Rights and Duties of Masters" (sermon) Charleston: Walker and James, 1850.

Turnbull, R. G. (ed.). *A Treasury of Dwight L. Moody.* Grand Rapids: Baker, 1971.

Walker, G. T. *Preaching in the Thought of Alexander Campbell.* St. Louis: Bethany, 1954.

Walther, C. F. W. *The Proper Distinction between Law and Gospel.* St. Louis: Concordia, 1929.

CHAPTER VI

Abbott, L. *Henry Ward Beecher.* Boston: Houghton, Mifflin, 1903.

Beecher, Lyman. *Beecher's Works.* Cleveland: Jewett, 1861.

Bushnell, H. *The New Life.* New York: Scribner, 1858.

Brown, J. W. *The Rise of Biblical Criticism in America, 1800-1870.* Middleton, Conn: Wesleyan University, 1969.

Cauthen, K. *The Impact of Religious Liberalism.* New York: Harper, 1962.

Channing, W. E. *The Works of William E. Channing.* Boston: American Unitarian, 1895.

Commanger, H. S. *Theodore Parker.* Boston: Beacon, 1947.

Cross, B. *Horace Bushnell: Minister to a Changing America.* Chicago: University of Chicago, 1958.

———. *Autobiography of Lyman Beecher.* Cambridge: Harvard University, 1961.

Currie, A. H. *Nine Great Preachers.* Boston: Pilgrim, 1912.

Dorn, J. H. *Washington Gladden: Prophet of the Social Gospel.* Columbus: Ohio State University, 1967.

Gladden, W. *The Christian Pastor and the Working Church.* New York: Scribner, 1903.

Handy, R. T. *The Social Gospel in America: Gladden, Ely and Rauschenbusch.* New York: Oxford Univeristy, 1966.

Higgens, P. L. *Preachers of Power* (Beecher, Brooks, Rauschenbusch), New York: Vantage, 1950.

Hopkins, C. H. *The Rise of the Social Gospel in American Protestantism, 1865-1915.* New Haven: Yale University, 1940.

Hudson, W. S. *American Protestantism.* Chicago: University of Chicago, 1961.

————. *Religion in America.* New York: Scribner, 1965.

Marsden, G. M. *The Evangelical Mind and the New School Presbyterian Experience.* A Case Study of Thought and Theology in Nineteenth Century America. New Haven: Yale University, 1970.

Munger, T. T. *Horace Bushnell: Theologian and Preacher.* Boston: Houghton, Mifflin, 1899.

Parker, T. *Speeches, Addresses, and Occasional Sermons.* Boston: Crosby & Nichols, 1852.

Peabody, F. G. *Jesus Christ and the Social Question.* New York: Scribner, 1900.

Rauschenbusch, W. *Christianity and the Social Crisis.* New York: Macmillan, 1920.

Thompson, E. T. *Changing Emphases in American Preaching.* Philadelphia: Westminster, 1948.

CHAPTER VII

Bayne, S. F., Jr. *Enter with Joy.* Greenwich: Seabury, 1961.

Bowie, W. R. *Learning to Live.* An Autobiography, Nashville: Abingdon, 1969.

Barnhouse, D. G. *Romans.* Expositions, 10 vols., Grand Rapids: Eerdmans, 1952-64.

Blackwood, A. W. *This Year of Our Lord.* Philadelphia: Westminster, 1943.

————. *The Preparation of Sermons.* Nashville: Abingdon, 1948.

————. (ed.). *Evangelical Sermons of Our Day.* Great Neck, N.Y.: Channel, 1959.

————. (ed.). *Special-Day Sermons for Evangelicals.* Great Neck: Channel, 1961.

————. J. R. Blackwood, ¿d. *College Talks: Howard F. Lowry.* New York: Oxford University, 1968.

Bonnell, J. S. *What Are You Living For?* Nashville: Abingdon, 1950.

Brown, C. E. *A History of the Church of God, Reformation Movement.* Anderson, Ind.: Warner, 1951.

Brown, C. R. *Finding Ourselves*. New York: Harper, 1935.

Brown, H. C. (ed.). *More Southern Baptist Preaching*. Nashville: Broadman, 1964.

Bryan, W. J. *Orthodox Christianity versus Modernism*. New York: Revell, 1924.

Bryan, W. J. and M. B. Bryan. *The Memories of William Jennings Bryan*. Chicago: Winston, 1925.

Burr, A. R. *Russell H. Conwell and His Work*. Philadelphia: Winston, 1923.

Buttrick, G. A. *Prayer*. New York: Abingdon, 1942.

Cadman, S. P. *Adventure for Happiness*. New York: Macmillan, 1935.

Chapman, J. W. *Revival Sermons*. New York: Revell, 1911.

Chappell, C. G. *Sermons on The Lord's Prayer and Other Prayers of Jesus*. Nashville: Abingdon, 1934.

————. *Anointed to Preach*. Nashville: Abingdon, 1951.

Chrisman, L. H. *The Message of the American Pulpit*. New York: Richard R. Smith, 1930.

Coffin, H. S. *God's Turn*. New York: Harper, 1934.

Crocker, L. (ed.). *Harry Emerson Fosdick's Art of Preaching*. An Anthology. Springfield, Ill.: Charles C. Thomas, Publisher, 1971.

Crowe, C. M. (ed.). *Great Southern Preaching*. Sermons. New York: Macmillan, 1926.

Dallman, W., W. H. T. Dau, and T. H. Engelder (eds.). *Walther and the Church*. St. Louis: Concordia, 1938.

Eldersveld, P. H. *The Word of the Cross*. Grand Rapids: Eerdmans, 1959.

Elson, E. L. R. *America's Spiritual Recovery*. Westwood, N.J.: Revell, 1954.

English, E. S. *H. A. Ironside: Ordained of the Lord*. Grand Rapids: Zondervan, 1946.

Evans, L. H. *Youth Seeks a Master*. New York: Revell, 1941.

Fant, D. J., Jr. *A. W. Tozer: A Twentieth Century Prophet*. Harrisburg: Christian Publications, 1964.

Ferris, T. P. *This Is the Day*. A Collection of Sermons. Chicago: Wilcox and Follett, 1951.

Fosdick, H. E. "Shall the Fundamentalists Win?" A sermon printed privately, May 21, 1922.

————. The Farewell Sermon of Dr. Harry Emerson Fosdick to the

First Presbyterian Church of New York, Sunday, March 1, 1925: privately published.

————. *The Living of These Days.* An Autobiography. New York: Harper, 1956.

————. *Living under Tension.* New York: Harper, 1941.

Freehof, S. *Modern Jewish Preaching.* New York: Bloch, 1941.

Gaebelein, F. E. *A Varied Harvest: Out of a Teacher's Life and Thought.* Grand Rapids: Eerdmans, 1967.

Giboney, E. P. and A. M. Potter. *The Life of Mark A. Matthews.* Grand Rapids: Eerdmans, 1948.

Gordon, A. *Norman Vincent Peale: Minister to Millions.* Englewood Cliffs, N.J.: Prentice-Hall, 1958.

Graham, W. F. ("Billy") *World Aflame.* New York: McGraw-Hill, 1965.

————. *Decision* Magazine: Monthly Messages, Minneapolis: Graham Association.

Gunsaulus, F. W. *Paths to Power.* New York: Revell, 1905.

Hamilton, C. V. *The Black Preacher in America.* New York: Morrow, 1972.

Hamilton, J. W. *Ride the Wild Horses.* Westwood, N.J.: Revell, 1952.

Hamlin, F. *S. Parkes Cadman: Pioneer Radio Minister.* New York: Harper, 1930.

Hargis, B. J. *The Real Extremists: The Far Left.* Tulsa: Christian Crusade, 1962.

Hatcher, W. E. *John Jasper.* New York: Revell, 1908.

Henry, J. C. (ed.). *The Making of a Minister.* Autobiography of Clarence Edward Macartney. Great Neck, N.Y.: Channel, 1961.

Heschel, A. J. *Man's Quest for God.* Studies in Prayer and Symbolism. New York: Scribner, 1954.

Hollenwegers, W. J. *The Pentecostals.* London: S.C.M., 1972.

Huss, J. E. *Robert G. Lee.* The Authorized Biography. Grand Rapids: Zondervan, 1967.

Ironside, H. A. *Except Ye Repent.* New York: American Tract Society, 1936.

James, P. W. *George W. Truett.* A Biography. Nashville: Broadman, 1953.

Jones, E. DeWitt. *American Preachers of Today.* Indianapolis: Bobbs-Merrill, 1933.

Jones, E. S. *A Song of Ascents.* A spiritual autobiography. Nashville: Abingdon, 1968.

——. *The Christ of the Indian Road.* Nashville: Abingdon, 1925.

Jones, Rufus M. *Finding the Trail of Life.* New York: Macmillan, 1926.

Kemp, C. F. *Life Situation Preaching.* St. Louis: Bethany, 1956.

Kennedy, G. H. *Who Speaks for God?* Nashville: Abingdon, 1954.

Kerr, H. T. *Preaching in the Early Church.* Westwood, N.J.: Revell, 1942.

King, M. L., Jr. *Strength to Love.* New York: Harper, 1963.

Kraus, C. N. *Dispensationalism in America: Its Rise and Development.* Richmond: Knox, 1958.

Kromminga, J. H. *The Christian Reformed Church: A Study in Orthodoxy.* Grand Rapids: Baker, 1949.

Krumbine, M. *American Lutheran Preaching.* New York: Harper, 1928.

Laubach, F. C. *Prayer the Mightiest Force in the World.* New York: Revell.

Lee, R. G. *The Top Ten of Robert G. Lee.* Grand Rapids: Baker, 1971.

Lewis, D. L. *Martin Luther King.* A Critical Biography. New York: Praeger, 1970.

Lewis, E. *The Faith We Declare.* Nashville: Cokesbury, 1939.

Lindsell, H. *Park Street Prophet: The Story of Harold Ockenga.* Wheaton, Ill.: Van Kampen, 1951.

Lippmann, W. *A Preface to Morals.* New York: Macmillan, 1929.

Luccock, H. E. *Preaching Values in New Translations.* Nashville: Abingdon, 1928.

——. *Marching Off the Map and Other Sermons.* New York: Harper, 1952.

McCracken, R. J. *Questions People Ask.* New York: Harper, 1951.

McIntyre, C. *Biblical Christian Unity.* Collingwood, N.J.: Twentieth Century Hour, 1965.

McLoughlin, W. G., Jr. *Billy Sunday Was His Real Name.* Chicago: University of Chicago, 1955.

——. *Billy Graham: Revivalist in a Secular Age.* New York: Peter Smith, 1960.

McPheeters, J. C. *I-II Corinthians.* "Proclaiming the New Testament," Vol. VII, Grand Rapids: Baker, 1961.

McNeil, J. J. *The Preacher-Prophet in Mass Society.* Grand Rapids: Eerdmans, 1961.

Macartney, C. E. *Things Most Surely Believed.* Nashville: Cokesbury, 1930.

————. *Preaching without Notes.* Nashville: Abingdon, 1946.

Machen, J. G. *Christianity and Liberalism.* New York: Macmillan, 1923.

————. *The Virgin Birth of Christ.* New York: Harper, 1950.

Maier, P. L. *A Man Spoke: A World Listened.* New York: McGraw-Hill, 1963.

Maier, W. A. *The Airwaves Proclaim Christ.* St. Louis: Concordia, 1948.

Marshall, C. *A Man Called Peter.* The Story of Peter Marshall. New York: McGraw-Hill, 1951.

Marshall, P. *Mr. Jones, Meet the Master.* New York: Revell, 1949.

Matthews, M. A. *In the Beginning—God.* Chicago: Bible Institute Colportage, 1924.

Mead, F. S. (ed.). *The Pulpit in the South: Sermons for Today.* New York: Revell, 1950.

Meyer, C. S. (ed.). *Letters of C. F. W. Walther.* A Selection. Philadelphia: Fortress, 1969.

Miller, D. G., *Fire in Thy Mouth.* Nashville: Abingdon, 1954.

Miller, R. M. *How Shall They Hear without a Preacher?* The Life of Ernest Fremont Tittle. Chapel Hill: University of North Carolina, 1971.

Mitchell, H. M. *Black Preaching.* Philadelphia: Lippincott, 1970.

Morris, F. M. *Preach the Word of God.* New York: Morehouse-Gorhan, 1954.

Morrison, C. C. (ed.). *The American Pulpit.* New York: Macmillan, 1925.

Newton, J. F. (ed.). *If I Had Only One Sermon to Prepare.* New York: Harper, 1932.

————. *River of Years.* An autobiography. New York: Lippincott, 1946.

Nichol, J. T. *Pentecostalism.* New York: Harper, 1966.

Niebuhr, H. Richard. *Christ and Culture.* New York: Harper, 1951.

————. *The Kingdom of God in America.* New York: Harper, 1959.

Niebuhr, Reinhold. *The Nature and Destiny of Man.* 2 vols., New York: Scribner, 1943.

————. *Leaves from the Notebook of a Tamed Cynic.* Chicago: Willett, 1929.

————. *Discerning the Signs of the Times: Sermons for Today and Tomorrow.* New York: Scribner, 1946.

Ockenga, H. J. *I-II Thessalonians.* "Proclaiming the New Testament," Vol. X, Grand Rapids: Baker, 1961.

Olson, Adolf. *A Centenary History.* As Related to the Baptist General Conference of America, "A Century of God's Grace," 1852-1952. Chicago: Baptist Conference, 1952.

Olson, Arnold T. *The Background and Exposition of the Doctrinal Statement of The Evangelical Free Church of America.* Minneapolis: Free Church Publications, 1961.

————. *Believers Only.* An Outline of the History and Principles of the Free Evangelical Movement in Europe and North America affiliated with the International Federation of Free Evangelical Churches. Minneapolis: Free Church Publications, 1964.

Olsson, Karl A. *A History of The Evangelical Covenant Church of America.* Chicago: Covenant, 1962.

Oxnam, G. B. *Preaching and the Social Crisis.* New York: Abingdon, 1930.

Peale, N. V. *The Power of Positive Thinking.* New York: Prentice-Hall, 1952.

Phelps, M. P. *Henry Sloane Coffin: The Man and His Ministry.* New York: Scribner, 1964.

Pollock, J. C. *Billy Graham.* The Authorized Biography. New York: McGraw-Hill, 1966.

Rees, P. S. *Philippians, Colossians, Philemon.* "Proclaiming the New Testament," Vol. IX, Grand Rapids: Baker, 1961.

Riley, M. A. *The Dynamic of a Dream.* Life Story of Dr. William B. Riley. Grand Rapids: Eerdmans, 1938.

Riley, W. B. *The Menace of Modernism.* New York: Christian Alliance, 1917.

Robertson, A. T. *The Glory of the Ministry.* Paul's Exultation in Preaching (II Cor.), Grand Rapids: Baker, 1967 (repr.).

Sandeen, E. R. *The Roots of Fundamentalism, British and American Millennarianism, 1800-1930.* Chicago: University of Chicago, 1970.

Scherer, P. E. *Facts That Undergird Life.* New York: Harper, 1938.

Scofield, C. I. *In Many Pulpits.* Grand Rapids: Baker, 1966 (repr.).

Sheen, F. J. *God Loves You.* The Best of Fulton Sheen. New York: Macs Magazine, 1955.

Shoemaker, H. S. *I Stand by the Door.* The Life of Sam Shoemaker. New York: Harper, 1967.

Shoemaker, S. M. *Twice-Born Ministers.* New York: Revell, 1929.
————. *The Gospel According to You.* New York: Revell, 1934.

Shroeder, F. W. *Preaching the Word with Authority.* Philadelphia: Westminster, 1954.

Simpson, A. B. *The Christ Life.* Harrisburg: Christian Publications, n.d.

Sizoo, J. R. *Preaching Unashamed.* Nashville: Abingdon, 1949.

Smith, G. G. (ed.). *The Tozer Pulpit.* Selections from his Sermons. Harrisburg: Christian Publications, 1967.

Smith, R. ("Gipsy"). *His Life and Work.* New York: Doran, 1902.

Smith, W. M. *A Voice for God.* A Life of Charles E. Fuller. Boston: Wilde, 1948.

Snowden, J. H. *The Psychology of Religion and Its Application in Preaching and Teaching.* New York: Revell, 1916.

Sockman, R. W. *How to Live.* New York: Abingdon, 1946.

Speer, R. E. *The Finality of Jesus Christ.* New York: Revell, 1933.

Stamm, F. K. *So You Want to Preach.* Nashville: Abingdon, 1958.
————. (ed.). *The Best of Charles E. Jefferson.* New York: Crowell, 1960.

Stevenson, D. E. *Disciple Preaching in the First Generation.* An Ecological Study. Nashville: Disciples of Christ Historical Society, 1969.

Stonehouse, N. B. *J. Gresham Machen.* A Biographical Memoir. Grand Rapids: Eerdmans, 1954.

Sullivan, W. L. *Under Order.* The Autobiography of William Laurence Sullivan. New York: Richard R. Smith, 1945.

Sunday, W. A. ("Billy"). *Wonderful: and Other Sermons.* Grand Rapids: Zondervan, n.d.

Tillich, P. *The Courage to Be.* New York: Harper, 1952.
————. *On the Boundary.* An Autobiographical Sketch. New York: Scribner, 1966.

Tittle, E. F. *The Religion of the Spirit.* New York: Abingdon, 1928.

Torrey, R. A. *The Fundamental Doctrines of the Christian Faith.* New York: Revell, 1918.

Torrey, R. A., et. al. (eds.). *The Fundamentals.* A Testimony to the Truth, 4 vols., Grand Rapids: Baker, 1970 (repr.).

Tozer, A. W. *Wingspread: A. B. Simpson, A Study in Spiritual Altitude.* Harrisburg: Christian Publications, 1943.

Trueblood, D. E. *The People Called Quakers.* New York: Harper, 1966.

Truett, G. W. *We Would See Jesus and Other Sermons.* Grand Rapids: Baker, 1969 (repr.).

Vining, E. G. *Friend of Life.* The Biography of Rufus M. Jones. Philadelphia: Lippincott, 1958.

Volbeda, S. *The Pastoral Genius of Preaching.* Grand Rapids: Zondervan, 1960.

Voss, C. H. (ed.). *Stephen S. Wise: Servant of the People.* Selected Letters. Philadelphia: Jewish Publications, 1969.

Ward, C. M. *Revivaltime Sermons.* Grand Rapids: Baker, 1966.

Wheeler, W. R. *A Man Sent from God.* The Biography of Robert E. Speer. New York: Revell, 1956.

Wilson, J. C. *Apostle to Islam.* A Biography of Samuel M. Zwemer. Grand Rapids: Baker, 1952.

Wirt, S. E. and V. Blake (eds.). *Great Preaching.* Evangelical Messages by Contemporary Christians. Waco: Word Books, 1970.

Zwemer, S. M. *The Solitary Throne.* Glasgow: Pickering and Inglis, 1937.

CHAPTER VIII

Bonnell, J. S. *Pastoral Psychiatry and Psychology for Pastor and People.* New York: Harper & Row.

Burnett, A. I. *Lord of All Life.* New York: Rinehart, 1952.

Carrington, P. *The Anglican Church in Canada.* Toronto: Collins, 1963.

Christie, D. *The Service of Christ.* London: Hodder and Stoughton, 1933.

Clark, S. D. *Church and Sect in Canada.* Toronto: University of Toronto, 1948.

Coggan, F. D. *The Ministry of the Word.* London: Canterbury, 1945.

Gordon, C. W. *The Life of James Robertson.* Toronto: Westminster, 1908.

Gordon, J. K. *Postscript to Adventure.* The Autobiography of

Ralph Connor (Charles W. Gordon). London: Hodder and Stoughton, 1938.

Grant, J. W. *The Canadian Experience of Church Union*. Richmond, Va.: John Knox, 1967.

————. *George Pidgeon*. A Biography. Toronto: Ryerson, 1962.

Griffith, A. L. *The Eternal Legacy From an Upper Room*. New York: Harper, 1963.

Heeney, W. B. *Leaders of the Canadian Church*. Toronto: Mussons, 1918.

Lehmann, H. T. *Heralds of the Gospel*. Philadelphia: Muhlenburg, 1953.

McNeill, J. T. *The Presbyterian Church in Canada, 1875-1925*. Toronto: Presbyterian Board, 1925.

Machray, R. *Life of Archbishop Machray, Primate of All Canada*. Toronto: Macmillan, 1909.

MacLennan, D. A. *Resources for Sermon Preparation*. Philadelphia: Westminster, 1957.

Morrow, E. L. *Church Union in Canada*. Toronto: Allen, 1923.

Mutchmor, J. R. *Mutchmor*. The Memoirs of James Ralph Mutchmor. Toronto: Ryerson, 1965.

Norwood, F. W. *Indiscretions of a Preacher*. London: Hodder & Stoughton, 1932.

Pidgeon, G. C. *The Indwelling Christ*. Toronto: Clarke, Irwin, 1948.

Shields, T. T. *The Gospel Witness*. Toronto: 1922.

Short, J. *All Things Are Yours*. London: Hodder & Stoughton, 1939.

Silcox, J. E. *Church Union in Canada*. New York: Institute of Social and Religious Research, 1933.

Smart, J. D. *The Interpretation of the Scripture*. Philadelphia: Westminster, 1961.

Smith, O. J. *The Revival We Need*. London: Marshall, Morgan & Scott, 1938.

Tarr, L. K. *Shields of Canada: T. T. Shields*. Grand Rapids: Baker, 1967.

Thomas, W. H. Griffith. *Let Us Go On: Epistle to the Hebrews*. London: Marshall, Morgan & Scott, 1954.

Walsh, H. A. *The Christian Church in Canada*. Toronto: Ryerson, 1956.

Young, W. H. (ed.) *Great Canadian Preaching*. Edited with Introduction and Biographical Notes. New York: Doran, 1932.

CHAPTER IX

Arden, G. E. *Four Northern Lights*. Men who shaped Scandinavian Churches. Minneapolis: Augsburg, 1964.

Barth, K. *God's Search for Man*. New York: Round Table, 1935.

———. *Deliverance to the Captives*. New York: Harper, 1961.

Bethge, E. *Dietrich Bonhoeffer*. A Biography. London: Collins, 1970.

Boegner, M. *The Long Road to Unity: Memories and Anticipations*. London: Collins, 1970.

Bonhoeffer, D. *The Cost of Discipleship*. London: S.C.M., 1959.

Brilioth, Y. *Predikans Historia*. Lund, Sweden: Gleerup, 1945.

———. *Landmarks in the History of Preaching*. London: S.P.C.K., 1950.

———. *A Brief History of Preaching*. Philadelphia: Muhlenberg, 1965.

Brunner, E. *Truth as Encounter*. (The Divine-Human Encounter). London: S.C.M., 1964.

Bultmann, R. K. *Theology of the New Testament*. London: S.C.M., 1955

Cairns, D. *A Gospel Without Myth? Bultmann's Challenge to the Preacher*. London: S.C.M., 1960.

Come, A. B. *An Introduction to Barth's Dogmatics for Preachers*. Philadelphia: Westminster, 1963.

Dibelius, R. F. O. *In the Service of the Lord*. The Autobiography. New York: Holt, Rinehart, Winston, 1964.

Ebeling, G. *Word and Faith*. Philadelphia: Fortress, 1963.

Fridrichsen, A. J. *The Root and the Vine: Essays in Biblical Theology*. New York: Philosophical Library, 1953.

Haug, N. N. *Om Religiøse Følelser*. (Religious Experiences: translated by Joel M. Njus, published as Autobiographical Writings of Hans Nielseb Hauge). Minneapolis: Augsburg, 1954.

Heim, K. *The Power of God*. Sermons. London: R.T.S., 1937.

———. *Christian Faith and Natural Science*. New York: Harper, 1957.

Hromádka, J. L. *Doom and Resurrection*. Richmond: Madrus House, 1945.

———. *Thoughts of a Czech Pastor*. London: S.C.M., 1968.

Johnson, A. *Eivind Berggrav: God's Man of Suspense*. Minneapolis: Augsburg, 1960.

Lilje, H. *The Valley of the Shadow.* London: S.C.M., 1947.

Luthi, W. and E. Thurneysen. *Preaching, Confession, The Lord's Supper.* Richmond: John Knox, 1960.

Mangs, F. *Andlig Vackelse.* (Spiritual Awakening). Stockholm: Harrison Bokforbeg, A. B., 1937.

Niemöller, M. *From U-Boat to Pulpit.* New York: Willett, Clark, 1937.

——. *The Challenge to the Church.* Philadelphia: Westminster, 1965.

Nygren, A. *The Gospel of God.* London: S.C.M., 1951.

O'Mahoney, D. *Great French Sermons.* London: Sand, 1919.

Ott, H. *Theology and Preaching.* London: Lutterworth, 1965.

Paquier, R. *Dynamics of Worship* (trans. by Donald Macleod). Philadelphia: Fortress, 1967.

Shaw, J. M. *Pulpit under the Sky.* A Life of Hans Nielsen Hauge. Minneapolis: Augsburg, 1955.

Skarstedt, C. W. *Predikoverksamhetens Och den Andliga vältightens Historie.* i Sverige Till Omkring. Lund, Sweden: C.W.K. Gleerups, 1850.

Sundkler, B. *Nathan Söderblom: His Life and Work.* Lund, Sweden: Gleerups, 1968.

Thielicke, H. *The Waiting Father.* New York: Harper, 1959.

——. *Encounter with Spurgeon.* Philadelphia: Fortress, 1963.

Vassady, B. *Light Against Darkness.* Philadelphia: Christian Education, 1961.

Von Allmen, J. J. *Preaching and Congregation.* London: Lutterworth, 1962.

Waldenstroëm, P. P. *The Christian Doctrine of the Atonement.* Chicago: Covenant, 1937.

Wingren, G. *The Living Word, A Theological Study of Preaching and the Church.* Philadelphia: Fortress, 1960.

——. "Swedish Theology since 1900," Svensk ted ogi efter 1900: trans. by Ross Mackenzie, *Scottish Journal of Theology,* Edinburgh, June, 1956.

CHAPTER X

Azariah, V. S. *Christian Giving.* New York: Association, 1955.

Boreham, F. W. *A Casket of Cameos.* London: Epworth, 1924.

——. *My Pilgrimage.* London: Epworth, 1950.

Davey, C. J. *Kagawa of Japan.* Nashville: Abingdon, 1961.

Douglas, W. M. *Andrew Murray and His Message.* London: Oliphants, 1934.

Fletcher, L. B. *After Conversion—What?* London: Oliphants, 1923.

Heiler, F. *The Gospel of Sadhu Sunder Singh.* New York: Oxford University, 1927.

Howard, H. *The Peril of Power; and Other Sermons.* New York: Doran, 1925.

Loane, M. L. *Archbishop Mowll.* The Biography of the Archbishop of Sydney and Primate of Australia. London: Hodder & Stoughton, 1960.

Lyall, L. T. *John Sung.* A Biography. London: Lutterworth, 1954.

Nee, W. *The Ministry of God's Word.* New York: Christian Fellowship, 1971.

Neill, S. *A History of Christian Missions.* Grand Rapids: Eerdmans, 1965.

Niles, D. T. *The Power at Work among Us.* London: Epworth, 1968.

Schweitzer, A. *Out of My Life and Thought.* An Autobiography. London: Black, 1949.

Seamond, J. T. *Pioneers of the Younger Churches.* Nashville: Abingdon, 1967.

Smith, E. W. *Aggrey of Africa: A Study in Black and White.* London: Lutterworth, 1934.

Taylor, H. *Pastor Hsi: Confucian Scholar and Christian.* London: Marshall, Morgan & Scott, 1919.

Turnbull, R. G. (intro.). *The Treasury of Andrew Murray.* Grand Rapids: Baker, 1969 (repr.).

Walker, A. *The Whole Gospel for the Whole World.* London: Epworth, 1957.

CHAPTER XI

Baillie, D. M. *To Whom Shall We Go?* Edinburgh: St. Andrews, 1955.

Baillie, J. *The Sense of the Presence of God.* London: Oxford University, 1962.

Barabas, S. *So Great Salvation.* Westwood, N.J.: Revell, 1950.

Barbour, G. F. *The Life of Alexander Whyte.* London: Hodder and Stoughton, 1924.

Barry, F. R. *Period of My Life*. London: Hodder & Stoughton, 1970.

Beaton, D. *Noted Ministers of the Northern Highlands*. Iverness: Northern Counties Publications, 1929.

Bell, G. K. A. *Randall Davidson: Archbishop of Canterbury*. London: Oxford University, 1935.

Black, J. M. *Days of My Autumn*. London: Hodder and Stoughton, 1950.

Brittain, F. *Bernard Lord Manning: A Memoir*. Cambridge: Heffers, 1942.

Bull, P. B. *Lectures on Preaching and Sermon Construction*. London: S.P.C.K., 1922.

Campbell, R. J. *A Spiritual Pilgrimage*. New York: Appleton, 1917.

Carman, P. *C. C. Martindale*. A Biography. London: Longmans, 1967.

Carpenter, S. C. *The Biography of A. F. Winnington-Ingram, Bishop of London, 1901-1939*. London: Hodder & Stoughton, 1949.

Carson, J. T. *Frazier of Tain*. (The Rev. Alexander Frazier). Glasgow: United Committee, 1966.

Cassels, T. *Men of the Knotted Heart*. Greenock: McKelvie, 1915.

Chadwick, S. *Humanity and God*. London: Hodder & Stoughton, 1904.

Chambers, O. *My Utmost for His Highest*. London: Simpkin Marshall, 1933.

Chilvers, H. T. *Christ's Replies to Vital Questions*. London: Martin, 1923.

Clow, W. M. *The Cross in Christian Experience*. London: Hodder & Stoughton, 1908.

Collins, G. N. M. *Donald Maclean*. Edinburgh: Lindseys, 1944.

————. *John Macleod*. Edinburgh: Free Church, 1951.

Corkey, W. *Glad Did I Live: Memoirs of a Long Life*. Belfast: News-Letter, 1963.

Cumming, J. E. *Through the Eternal Spirit*. Stirling, Scotland: Drummond, 1937.

Darlow, T. H. *William Robertson Nicoll: Life and Letters*. London: Hodder & Stoughton, 1925.

Davidson, N. *Reflections of a Scottish Churchman*. London: Hodder & Stoughton, 1965.

Davies, D. R. *In Search of Myself*. London: Bles, 1961.

Davies, G. C. B. *Men for the Ministry*. The History of the London College of Divinity. London: Hodder & Stoughton, 1963.

Davies, H. *Varieties of English Preaching, 1900-1960*. London: S.C.M., 1963.

Denney, J. *The Death of Christ: including The Atonement and the Modern Mind*. London: Hodder & Stoughton, 1903.

———. *The Way Everlasting; Sermons*. London: Hodder & Stoughton, 1911.

———. "Preaching Christ," Hasting's *Dictionary of Christ and the Gospels*, 2 vols., New York: Charles Scribner's Sons, 1906 (repr. Baker Book House, Grand Rapids, in *The Dictionary of the New Testament*, 4 vols., 1973).

Dixon, H. C. A. *A. C. Dixon: A Romance of Preaching*. London: Putnam, 1931.

Docherty, G. M. *The Greatest Sermons of George H. Morrison*. New York: Harper, 1959.

Dodd, C. H. *The Apostolic Preaching and Its Development*. London: Hodder & Stoughton, 1944.

Drummond, H. *The Greatest Thing in the World*. New York: Revell, 1968.

Dunning, N. G. *Samuel Chadwick*. London: Hodder & Stoughton, 1933.

Duthie, C. S. *God in the World*. Nashville: Abingdon, 1960.

Edwards, D. L. *Leaders of the Church of England, 1824-1944*. London: Oxford University, 1971.

Edwards, J. *Nineteenth Century Preachers and Their Methods*. London: 1902.

Elliott, W. H. *Undiscovered Ends*. The Autobiography. London: Peter Davies, 1951.

Farmer, H. H. *The Healing Cross*. London: Hodder & Stoughton, 1941.

Finlayson, R. A. *God's Light on Man's Destiny*. Edinburgh: Knox, 1959.

Ford, D. W. C. *An Expositor's Notebook*. London: Hodder & Stoughton, 1960.

Forsyth, P. T. *Positive Preaching and the Modern Mind*. London: Hodder & Stoughton, 1909.

———. *The Person and Place of Jesus Christ*. London: Independent, 1909.

Fullerton, W. Y. *The Christly Life*. New York: Revell, 1931.

Fullerton, W. Y. *F. B. Meyer: A Biography.* London: Marshall, Morgan & Scott, 1931.

Gammie, A. *Dr. George H. Morrison: The Man and His Work.* London: Clarke, 1928.

————. *Rev. John McNeill: His Life and Work.* Glasgow: Pickering and Inglis, 1935.

————. *Archibald Fleming of St. Columba's.* London: Clarke, 1932.

Garvie, A. E. *The Christian Preacher.* Edinburgh: T. & T. Clark, 1920.

Glover, T. R. *The Jesus of History.* London: S.C.M., 1917.

Goodykoontz, H. G. *The Minister in the Reformed Tradition.* Richmond, Va.: Knox, 1963.

Gossip, A. J. *The Galilean Accent.* Edinburgh: T. & T. Clark, 1926.

Grant, J. (ed.). *History of Free Presbyterian Church of Scotland (1893-1933).* Dingwall: Ross-shire, 1965.

Grant, W. (ed.). *Free Presbyterian Pulpit.* Selected Sermons. Inverness: Carruthers, 1961.

Green, B. S. *The Practice of Evangelism.* London: Hodder & Stoughton, 1951.

Guntrip, H. (ed.). *Facing Life and Death.* A Volume in Commemoration of Leslie T. Tizard. London: Allen and Unwin, 1959.

Hall, C. W. *Samuel Logan Brengle: Portrait of a Prophet.* New York: Salvation Army, 1933, 1974.

Hay, A. M. *Charles Inwood: His Ministry and Its Secret.* London: Marshall, Morgan and Scott, 1929.

Henson, H. H. *Retrospect of an Unimportant Life.* 3 vols., London: Oxford University, 1942-50.

Hertz, J. H. *The Pentateuch and Haftorahs.* 5 vols., London: Oxford University, 1829-36.

————. *Sermons, Addresses, and Studies.* 3 vols., London: The Socino Press, 1938.

Holden, J. S. *A Voice For God.* London: Hodder & Stoughton, 1932.

Hopkins, E. H. *The Law of Liberty in the Spiritual Life.* London: Marshall, Morgan & Scott, 1884.

Howden, J. R. *Victory in Life.* Convention Addresses. London: Marshall, Morgan & Scott, 1916.

Hughes, T. H. *The Psychology of Preaching and Pastoral Work.* London: Allen & Unwin, 1939.

Hurst, D. Frazer. *"Wylie Blue": The Life of A. Wylie Blue.* London: James Clarke, 1957.

Hutton, J. A. *The Proposal of Jesus.* London: Hodder & Stoughton, 1920.

Huxtable, J. *The Preacher's Integrity.* London: Epworth, 1966.

Inge, W. R. *Diary of a Dean, St. Paul's 1911-1934.* London: Macmillan, 1950.

Iremonger, F. A. *William Temple: Archbishop of Canterbury.* Life and Letters. London: Oxford University, 1949.

Jacks, L. P. *The Confession of an Octogenarian.* London: Allen and Unwin, 1942.

Jasper, R. *Arthur Cayley Headlam.* Life and Letters of a Bishop. London: Faith Press, 1960.

―――. *George Bell: Bishop of Chichester.* London: Oxford University, 1967.

Jones, J. D. *A Plea for Preaching.* London: Congregational Union, 1925.

―――. *The Lord of Life and Death.* Grand Rapids: Baker, 1972 (repr.).

Jones, O. *Some of the Great Preachers of Wales.* London: Pasmore, 1885.

Jowett, J. H. *Life in the Heights.* Grand Rapids: Baker, 1972 (repr.).

Kemp, E. W. *The Life and Letters of Kenneth Escott Kirk, Bishop of Oxford, 1937-1954.* London: Hodder & Stoughton, 1959.

Kennedy, G. A. S. *The Word and the Work.* London: Hodder & Stoughton, 1925.

Knox, R. A. *The Gospel in Slow Motion.* New York: Sheed and Ward, 1950.

Langston, E. L. *Bishop Taylor Smith.* A Biography. London: Marshall, Morgan & Scott, 1939.

Lees, H. C. *The Sunshine of the Good News.* London: Robert Scott, 1912.

Lewis, C. S. *Surprised by Joy; The Shape of My Early Life.* London: Geofrey Bles, 1955.

―――. *Reflections on the Psalms.* London: Geofrey Bles, 1958.

Lloyd-Jones, D. M. *Preachers and Preaching.* London: Hodder & Stoughton, 1971.

―――. *Exposition of Romans Chapter 5.* London: Banner of Truth, 1971.

Lockhart, J. G. *Cosmos Gordon Lang.* London: Hodder & Stoughton, 1949.

Lord, F. T. *The Unity of Body and Soul.* London: S.C.M., 1929.

Macaulay, A. B. *H. R. Mackintosh.* Sermons and Memoir. Edinburgh: T. & T. Clark, 1938.

MacBeath, J. *The Life of the Christian.* London: Marshall, Morgan and Scott, 1932.

Macgregor, D. C. *George H. C. Macgregor.* A Biography. London: Hodder & Stoughton, 1900.

Macgregor, G. H. C. *A Holy Life and How to Live It.* London: Marshall, Morgan and Scott, 1946.

Macinnes, J. *The Evangelical Movement in the Highlands, 1688-1800.* Aberdeen: University Press, 1951.

Mackay, J. *The Church in the Highlands.* Or The Progress of Evangelical Religion in Gaelic Scotland, 563-1843. London: Hodder & Stoughton, 1914.

Mackintosh, H. R. *Life on God's Plan.* London: Hodder & Stoughton, 1909.

Maclean, A. *The Quiet Heart and High Country.* London: Allenson, 1939.

Maclean, N. *The Former Days; Set Free; The Years of Fulfilment.* Autobiography, 3 vols., London: Hodder & Stoughton, 1943-53.

Macleod, J. *Scottish Theology in Relation to Church History since The Reformation.* Edinburgh: Free Church, 1943.

McNeill, J. *John McNeill's Sermons.* 3 vols., New York: Revell, 1890.

Manning, B. L. *A Layman in the Ministry.* London: Independent, 1942.

Marchant, J. (ed.). *British Preachers.* 3 vols., London: Putnam, 1925-27.

Martindale, C. C. *What Think Ye of Christ?* London: Longmans, 1931.

Matthews, W. R. *Memories and Meanings.* London: Hodder & Stoughton, 1969.

Meyer, F. B. *Great Pulpit Masters.* Vol. VI, Westwood, N.J.: Revell, 1950.

Micklem, N. *My Cherry-Tree.* London: Geoffrey Bles, 1966.

Micklem, N. (ed.). *Christian Worship: Studies in Its History and Meaning by Members of Mansfield College.* Oxford: University, 1936.

Monod, Th. *The Gift of God.* London: Morgan & Scott, 1876.

Morgan, G. C. *Westminster Pulpit.* Sermons. 10 vols. Westwood, N.J.: Revell, 1944.

Morgan, J. *A Man of the Word.* Grand Rapids: Baker, 1972.

Morgan, J. V. *Welsh Religious Leaders in the Victorian Age.* London: Nisbet, 1905.

Morrison, G. H. *Morrison's Sermons.* 6 vols., Grand Rapids: Baker, 1971.

Moule, H. C. G. *Christ and the Christian: Keswick.* London: Marshall, 1919.

Muir, A. *John White.* London: Hodder & Stoughton, 1958.

Murray, A. *The Full Blessing of Pentecost.* New York: Revell, 1908.

Nicoll, W. R. *The Return to the Cross.* London: Hodder & Stoughton, 1910.

Oman, J. *The Paradox of the World.* Sermons. Cambridge: University, 1921.

————. *Concerning the Ministry.* London: Harper, 1937.

Orchard, W. E. *From Faith to Faith.* An Autobiography of Religious Development. London: Putnam, 1933.

Orsborn, A. W. T. *The House of My Pilgrimage.* London: Salvation Army, 1958.

Pierson, A. T. *The Keswick Movement in Precept and Practice.* New York: Funk and Wagnall, 1903.

Pierson, D. L. *Arthur T. Pierson.* A Biography. London: Nisbet, 1921.

Porritt, A. *John Henry Jowett.* London: Hodder & Stoughton, 1924.

————. *J. D. Jones of Bournemouth.* London: Independent, 1942.

Prestige, G. L. *The Life of Charles Gore.* London: Heinemann, 1935.

Purcell, W. *Woodbine Willie.* The Biography of G. A. Studdert Kennedy. London: Hodder & Stoughton, 1962.

————. *Fisher of Lambeth.* A Portrait From Life. London: Hodder & Stoughton, 1969.

————. *Portrait of Soper.* The Definitive Biography. London: Mowbrays, 1972.

Rattenbury, J. E. *The Evangelical Doctrines of Charles Wesley's Hymns.* London: Epworth, 1941.

Reid, J. *The Victory of God.* London: Hodder & Stoughton, 1933.

Roberts, R. E. *H. R. L. Sheppard: Life and Letters.* London: John Murray, 1942.

Sands, Lord. *Life of Andrew Wallace Williamson.* Edinburgh: Blackwood, 1929.

Sangster, P. *Doctor Sangster.* London: Epworth, 1962.

Sangster, W. E. *The Craft of Sermon Construction.* Grand Rapids: Baker, 1972.

————. Westminster Sermons, 2 vols., London: Epworth, 1960-1961.

Scroggie, W. G. *Facets of the Faith.* Glasgow: Pickering and Inglis, 1933.

Selby, T. G. *Present-Day Preachers,* London: Marshall, 1904.

Selby, W. B. *The Life of Andrew Martin Fairbairn.* London: Hodder & Stoughton, 1914.

Sheen, H. E. *Canon Peter Green.* A Biography. London: Hodder & Stoughton, 1965.

Sheppard, H. R. L. D. *The Impatience of a Parson.* London: Hodder & Stoughton, 1927.

Simpson, H. L. *Put Forth By The Moon.* More Essays for the Untheologically Minded. London: Hodder & Stoughton, 1923.

Simpson, J. B. *The Hundredth Archbishop of Canterbury.* New York: Harper, 1962.

Smellie, A. *Evan Henry Hopkins.* A Memoir. London: Marshall, 1920.

————. *Lift Up Your Hearts.* Four Addresses on Sanctification. London: Melrose, 1915.

Smith, G. A. *The Life of Henry Drummond.* London: Hodder & Stoughton, 1898.

————. "Isaiah," 2 vols., *Expositor's Bible,* London: Hodder & Stoughton, 1888.

Smith, L. A. *George Adam Smith.* A personal memoir and family chronicle. London: Hodder & Stoughton, 1943.

Smith, L. P. *Unforgotten Years.* Boston: Little, Brown, 1939.

Smyth, C. *Cyril Forster Garbett: Archbishop of York.* London: Hodder & Stoughton, 1959.

Spurr, F. C. *A Preacher's Legacy.* London: Epworth, 1945.

Stalker, J. *Imago Christi: The Example of Jesus Christ.* London: Hodder & Stoughton, 1889.

Stevenson, H. F. *Keswick's Authentic Voice, 1875-1957.* London: Marshall, Morgan & Scott, 1959.

Stewart, J. S. *The Gates of New Life.* Edinburgh: T. & T. Clark, 1940.

Stockmayer, O. *The Glory of the Lamb.* New York: Y.W.C.L., 1915.

Struthers, J. P. *Life and Letters of John Paterson Struthers*. London: Hodder & Stoughton, 1908.

Temple, W. *Fellowship with God*. London: Macmillan, 1920.

Thomas, W. H. Griffith. *The Work of the Ministry*. London: Hodder & Stoughton, 1910.

Thompson, D. *Donald Soper*. A Biography. Nutfield: Denholm House, 1971.

Thomson, D. P. (ed.). *The Professor as Preacher*. London: James Clarke, n.d.

————. (ed.). *Sermons by Leaders of the Scottish Pulpit*. London: James Clarke, n.d.

Tizzard, L. J. *Preaching: The Art of Communication*. London: Allen & Unwin, 1958.

Tomkins, O. *The Life of Edward Woods*. London: S.C.M., 1957.

Turnbull, R. G. (ed.). *The Treasury of Alexander Whyte*. Grand Rapids: Baker, 1968.

————. (ed.). *A Treasury of G. Campbell Morgan*. Grand Rapids: Baker, 1972.

Warfield, B. B. *Perfectionism*. 2 vols., New York: Oxford University, 1931.

Watt, H. *New College Edinburgh*. A Centenary History. Edinburgh: Oliver and Boyd, 1946.

Waugh, E. *The Life of Ronald Knox*. London: Chapman and Hall, 1959.

Weatherhead, L. D. *The Significance of Silence and Other Sermons*. Nashville: Abingdon, 1945.

Webb-Peploe, W. H. *Calls to Holiness*. London: Marshall Brothers, 1900.

Whale, J. S. *Christian Doctrine*. Cambridge: University, 1941.

Whitham, A. E. *The Pastures of His Presence*. London: Hodder & Stoughton, 1939.

Whyte, A. *Lord, Teach Us to Pray*. London: Hodder & Stoughton, 1922.

Wood, H. G. *Terrot Reavley Glover*. A Biography. Cambridge: University, 1953.

Young, D. T. *Sermons on Unfamiliar Texts*. Grand Rapids: Baker, 1970.

GENERAL WORKS OF REFERENCE

Histories of Preaching

Blaikie, W. G. *The Preachers of Scotland: From the Sixth to the Nineteenth Century.* Edinburgh: T. & T. Clark, 1888.

Brastow, L. O. *Representative Modern Preachers.* New York: Doran, 1904.

————. *The Modern Pulpit; A Study of Homiletic Sources and Characteristics.* New York: Doran, 1906.

Brilioth, Yngve. *Predikans Historia.* Lund, Sweden: Gleerups, 1945.

————. *A Brief History of Preaching.* (trans. K. E. Mattson). Philadelphia: Fortress, 1965.

Broadus, J. A. *Lectures on the History of Preaching.* New York: Armstrong, 1893.

Dargan, E. C. *A History of Preaching: From the Apostolic Fathers to the Great Reformers, A.D. 70-1572.* New York: Armstrong, 1906.

————. *A History of Preaching: From the Close of the Reformation Period to the End of the Nineteenth Century, 1572-1900.* (The above two volumes now in reprint, Grand Rapids: Baker, 1970.)

————. *The Art of Preaching in the Light of Its History.* New York: Doran, 1922.

Gammie, A. *Preachers I Have Heard.* Glasgow: Pickering and Inglis, 1946.

Garvie, A. E. *The Christian Preacher.* Edinburgh: T. & T. Clark, 1920.

————. *The Preachers of the Church.* London: James Clarke, 1926.

Holland, DeWitte (ed.). *Preaching in American History: Selected Issues in the American Pulpit, 1630-1967.* Nashville: Abingdon, 1969.

Howard, H. C. *Princes of the Christian Pulpit and Pastorate.* 2 vols., Nashville: Cokesbury, 1928.

Jeffs, E. H. *Princes of the Modern Pulpit.* London: James Clarke, 1931.

Ker, J. *Lectures on the History of Preaching.* London: Hodder & Stoughton, 1888.

Macleod, D. "Preaching." *Christianity Today,* Aug. 10, 1973, Washington, D.C.

Nicoll, W. R. *Princes of the Church.* London: Hodder & Stoughton, 1921.

Pattison, T. H. *The History of Christian Preaching.* Philadelphia: American Baptist, 1912.

Porritt, A. *The Best I Remember.* London: Hodder & Stoughton, 1918.

Sinclair, H. *Voices of To-Day; Studies of Representative Modern Preachers.* London: James Clarke, 1912.

Smyth, C. *The Art of Preaching.* A Practical Survey of Preaching in the Church of England, 747-1939. London: S.P.C.K., 1940.

Sprague, W. B. *Annals of the American Pulpit.* 9 vols., New York: Carter and Brothers, 1857-69.

Telford, J. *A History of Lay Preaching in the Christian Church.* London: Kelly, 1897.

Webber, F. R. *A History of Preaching in Britain and America.* Including the Biographies of Many Princes of the Pulpit and the Men who Influenced Them, 3 vols., Milwaukee: Northwestern, 1952-57.

Selections of Sermons and Other Background Publications

Bayne, S. F., Jr. (ed.). *Space-Age Christianity.* New York: Morehouse-Barlow, 1963.

Butler, P. (ed.). *Best Sermons of the Year.* (annually), New York: Trident, 1950-.

Caemmerer, R. R. (ed.). *Toward a More Excellent Ministry.* St. Louis: Concordia, 1964.

Cunliffe-Jones, H. *Christian Theology Since 1600.* London: Duckworth, 1970.

Davies, H. *Worship and Theology in England, 1534-1965.* 5 vols., Princeton: Princeton University, 1961-74.

Fant, C. E. and W. M. Pinson (eds.). *Twenty Centuries of Great Preaching.* An Encyclopedia of Preaching, 13 vols., Waco: Word Books, 1971.

Gifford, F. D. (ed.). *The Anglican Pulpit To-Day.* Representative Sermons by Leading Preachers of the Anglican Communion. London: Mowbray, 1953.

Hastings, J. and E. Hastings (eds.). *The Speaker's Bible.* 18 vols., Aberdeen, Scotland and Grand Rapids: Baker, 1973.

Holland, DeWitte (ed.). *Sermons in American History.* Nashville: Abingdon, 1971.

Jeffrey, G. J. (ed.). *The Sacramental Table.* A Series of Addresses by Representative Scots Preachers. London: Clarke, 1954.

Kleiser, G. (ed.). *The World's Great Sermons.* 10 vols., New York: Funk and Wagnall, 1908.

Kuiper, H. J. *Sermons on the Heidelberg Catechism.* 5 vols., Grand Rapids: Zondervan, 1937.

Loetscher, L. A. *The Broadening Church.* A Study of Theological Issues in the Presbyterian Church since 1869. Philadelphia: University of Pennsylvania, 1954.

Lutheran Preaching (ed.). *The Concordia Pulpit.* (annually). St. Louis: Concordia, 1935-1954.

Macartney, C. E. (ed.). *Great Sermons of the World.* Grand Rapids: Baker, 1958.

McNeill, J. T. *A History of the Cure of Souls.* New York: Harper, 1951.

Mozley, J. K. *Some Tendencies in British Theology.* London: S.P.C.K., 1952.

Neill, S. *The Interpretation of the New Testament.* (1861-1961) London: Oxford, 1966.

Niebuhr, H. R. *The Purpose of the Church and Its Ministry.* New York: Harper, 1956.

Niebuhr, H. R. and D. E. Williams (eds.). *The Ministry in Historical Perspective.* New York: Harper, 1956.

Niebuhr, H. R., D. E. Williams, and J. M. Gustafson. *The Advancement of Theological Education.* New York: Harper, 1957.

Ramsey, A. M. *From Gore to Temple.* The Development of Anglican Theology between *Lux Mundi* and the Second World War, 1889-1939. London: Longmans, 1960.

Revell, F. H. *Great Gospel Sermons: Classic and Contemporary.* 2 vols., New York: Revell, 1949.

Sadler, W. A. (ed.). *Master Sermons Through the Ages.* New York: Harper, 1963.

Scott, C. and W. C. Stiles (eds.). *Modern Sermons by World Scholars.* 10 vols., New York: Funk and Wagnall, 1908.

Toohey, W. and W. Thomson (eds.). *Recent Homiletical Thought.* A Bibliography 1935-1965. Nashville: Abingdon, 1967.

————. (ed.). *The American Pulpit Series.* 7 vols., Nashville: Abingdon, 1945.

Encyclopedias, Dictionaries, Histories

Addison, J. T. *The Episcopal Church in the United States, 1789-1931.* New York: Scribner, 1951.

Ahlstrom, S. E. *A Religious History of the American People.* New Haven: Yale, 1972.

Albright, R. W. *A History of the Protestant Episcopal Church.* New York: Macmillan, 1964.

Brigance, W. N. (ed.). *A History and Criticism of American Public Address.* Vols. I and II, New York: Russell and Russell, 1943.

Catholic Encyclopedia. New York: McGraw Hill, 1965.

Dargan, E. C. "Preaching," *The New Schaff-Herzog Encyclopedia of Religious Knowledge.* 15 vols., Grand Rapids: Baker, 1959.

Encyclopedia of Southern Baptists. 2 vols., Nashville: Broadman, 1958.

The Encyclopedia of Religion and Ethics. 13 vols., Edinburgh: T & T Clark, 1908-.

Furnas, J. C. *The Americans: A Social History of the United States, 1587-1914.* New York: Putnam, 1969.

Hockmuth, M. (ed.). *A History and Criticism of American Public Address.* Vol. III, New York: Longmans, 1955.

Hudson, W. S. *Religion in America.* An Historical Account of the development of American Religious Life. New York: Scribner, 1965.

Johnson, A. and D. Malone (eds.). *A Dictionary of American Biography.* 21 vols., New York: Scribner, 1928-1940.

Jones, I. T. "The Literature of Preaching" and "The Literature of Homiletics," *Baker's Dictionary of Practical Theology.* Grand Rapids: Baker, 1967.

Lutheran Cyclopedia. St. Louis: Concordia, 1954.

Marcus, J. R. (ed.). *Essays in American Jewish History.* Cincinnati: American Jewish Archives, 1958.

The Mennonite Encyclopedia. 4 vols., Hillsboro, Kansas: Mennonite Publ., 1955-59.

Morrison, S. E. *The Oxford History of the American People.* New York: Putnam, 1969.

Moyer, E. S. *Who Was Who in Church History.* Chicago: Moody, 1962.

Orr, J. E. *The Second Evangelical Awakening in Britain.* London: Marshall, Morgan & Scott, 1949.

————. *The Second Evangelical Awakening in America.* London: Marshall, Morgan & Scott, 1952.

————. *The Flaming Tongue.* The Impact of 20th Century Revivals. Chicago: Moody Press, 1973.

Reid, L. (ed.). *American Public Address: Studies in Honor of Albert Craig Baird.* Columbia: University of Missouri, 1961.

Roth, C. and G. Wigoder (eds.). *Encyclopedia Judica.* 16 vols., Jerusalem: Keter, 1971.

Scharpff, P. *History of Evangelism.* Grand Rapids: Eerdmans, 1966.

Smith, J. W. and A. L. Jamison (eds.). *Religion in American Life.* 4 vols., Princeton: Princeton University, 1961.

Spiller, R. E., W. Thorp, T. H. Johnson, H. S. Canby, and R. M. Ludwig (eds.). *Literary History of the United States.* 3rd ed., rev., New York: Macmillan, 1968.

The Standard Jewish Encyclopedia. New York: Doubleday, 1958-59.

Stephens, L. and S. Lee (eds.). *Dictionary of National Biography.* 21 vols., London: Smith, Elder, 1882-1959.

Thompson, E. T. *History of the Presbyterian Church* [Southern] *in the United States.* 3 vols., Richmond: John Knox, 1963-73.

Turnbull, R. G. (ed.). *Baker's Dictionary of Practical Theology.* Grand Rapids: Baker, 1967.

List
of
Sermons

Index

Abbott, L., 291
African preaching, 416-422
Aggrey, J. E. K., 421f.
Adams, T. F., 311
Adler, F., 282f.
Alexander, A., 72, 90
Allan, T., 521, 522
Allen, R., 202
American Bible Society, 85, 312
American Board of Commissioners for Foreign Missions, 85, 312
American Preaching, 315-318
American Sunday School Union, 85, 312
American Tract Society, 85, 215, 312
Andrewes, L., 491
Anglican (Episcopal) preaching, 454-461
Antinomianism, 211
Antinomian controversy, 25, 34
Apologetic preaching, 181, 190
Arminianism, 137
Arnold, S., 37
Asian, Australian, African preaching, 399-428
Asbury, F., 79, 91, 276
Aubrey, M. E., 454
Augsburger, D., 281
Augsburger, M. D., 281f.
Augustine, 210, 379, 467
Aulen, G. E. H., 355ff.
Australian preaching, 422-428
Authority—
　Barth's idea of, 182ff.
　of the preacher, 26, 459, 476

　of the Word of God, 26, 43, 115, 379, 384, 440, 459
　shift in, 155f, 430, 431
Awakening, Great, 56, 59, 73, 83
Awakening, Second, 71, 86, 97, 135
Azariah, V. S., 407f.

Bailey, E. J., 344
Baillie, D. M., 473
Baillie, J., 473
Bancroft, A., 157
Baptist World Alliance, 216, 344
Barclay, R., 18, 228
Barclay, W., 525
Barnes, A., 97-99
Barnes, E. W., 460
Barnhouse, D. G., 247
Barrett, J. O., 454
Barry, F. R., 460
Barth, K., 12, 179, 182, 183, 371-375
Bast, H., 269f.
Baughman, H. F., 306
Baxter, B. B., 271f., 533
Baxter, R., 34, 416
Bayne, S. F., Jr., 304
Beecher, H. W., 102, 110, 113, 135, 138, 140-145
Beecher, L., 72, 97, 98, 135, 137-140, 157
Bell, G. K. A., 460
Bellamy, J., 61
Bennett, R. A., 209
Bethune, R., 523
Berggrav, E. J., 353-355
Berry, S. M., 434

577